MW01253151

PERSONALITY ASSESSMENT: NEW RESEARCH

PERSONALITY ASSESSMENT: NEW RESEARCH

LAUREN B. PALCROFT
AND
MELISSA V. LOPEZ
EDITORS

Nova Science Publishers, Inc.
New York

For permission to use material from this book please contact us:
Telephone 631-231-7269; Fax 631-231-8175
Web Site: http://www.novapublishers.com

Library of Congress Cataloging-in-Publication Data

Available upon request.

ISBN: 978-1-60692-796-0

Published by Nova Science Publishers, Inc. ✝ New York

CONTENTS

PREFACE

Personality assessment is the determination and evaluation of personality attributes by interviews, observations, tests, or scales.

What, then, are the common properties of assessment, regardless of which area is examined? It is proposed that there are three common denominators: (a) Decisions, (b) Procedures, and (c) Data acquisition. In general, assessment may be defined as a procedure whereby data is collected for decision making purposes. Specifically, then, psychological assessment is a procedure whereby data is collected for making decisions about people. Such a definition. although short and simple, has a major advantage in emphasizing the role of decision making in assessment. This new book presents the latest research developments in the field.

Chapter 1 - This review approaches child and adolescent personality assessment from a developmental psychopathology perspective. Essential to understanding personality assessment in children is understanding how individual personality development occurs in children and adolescents. An overview of emotional and personality development will be presented, including discussion of temperament, emotional expression and understanding, and emotion regulation and coping. Temperament and personality are discussed and differentiated. Relational influences on personality development such as parent-child relationships, marital relationships, family processes, and sibling relations are considered. Preliminary results from our new study on the bi-directional effects of marital relations and infant emotionality are highlighted. Multi-method procedures, including observational data assessing parents' conflict behaviors and emotions and infants' emotional and behavioral regulation in the context of parents' conflict are presented. The role of infants' temperament in these relations is considered. Extra-familial influences on personality, such as culture and religion are also presented. Finally, normal and abnormal personality development and assessment in children and adolescents are discussed from a developmental psychopathology approach, which emphasizes that both the assessment and development of personality in children are fluid processes to be considered over time, rather than static constructs observed at a single point in time. Borderline personality disorder is used as an example to describe how the developmental psychopathology approach can elucidate understanding of the abnormal development of personality over time. Recommendations for assessment approaches are made based on these overviews, including a discussion of specific methods' strengths and weaknesses. An objective, multi-method, multi-source, multi-setting approach for assessment is offered. Age-specific approaches to assessment and age-related issues to consider in assessment are integrated into the recommendations. Future directions for research are discussed.

Chapter 2 - Child maltreatment is associated with detrimental developmental effects. In view of the fact that child maltreatment typically occurs within the context of a caretaking relationship, attachment-guided treatments have been found effective in addressing developmental problems in abused children. This chapter describes the dissemination of a trauma-focused cognitive behavioral treatment model (TF-CBT) into a Theraplay-guided therapeutic preschool for maltreated children. At the end of the study all of the children in the program displayed significant developmental gains. The study did not support the expectation that children receiving the integrated treatment model would show greater gain. There was a small difference in outcome, particularly the adaptive domain. Although the differences were not significant, the authors believe they are in accordance with theoretically guided expectations. These results are discussed as are both the Theraplay-guided and TF-CBT models.

Chapter 3 - Teams and teamwork have become very popular areas of organizational strategy, but selecting competent employees for teamwork remains difficult to do, let alone do well. This chapter addresses the requisites we consider important for the team "worthiness" of an individual. These fundamental team "worthiness" elements are factors of the Big Five Personality model, organizational citizenship behavior (OCB) contextualized as dispositions, and cognitive aptitude specific to teamwork. We review briefly the history of each of these constructs, illustrate assessments of the constructs, and then describe an original research study in which the unique and shared variance of these constructs was examined with confirmatory factor analysis. The results indicated the Big Five personality and organizational citizenship behavior constructs were comparably related to the teamwork aptitude construct. The most surprising result was the strong relationship of the sportsmanship variable to the Big Five construct. This result supports our conjecture that organizational citizenship represents a lower level factor of personality.

Chapter 4 - Previous research has shown that personality traits and emotional states are associated with variations in blood pressure. The major aim of this chapter is to examine the relationship between personality traits and diary reports of moods on a work and an off-work day. Secondary aims are to compare mood reports in men and women as a function of the day of recording. A healthy sample of 110 women and 110 men rated their moods in a diary three times an hour on a work and a nonwork day. Personality scales were administered. Significant effects of mood intensity were obtained for work vs. off days and in interaction with scores on personality tests of anxiety, anger out, cynical hostility, and depression. Given the health significance of emotion in mental and physical health, these findings in healthy individuals suggest that personality traits may affect the regulation of blood pressure via their effects on emotional responses to daily life events and thereby serve as risk factors for hypertension.

Chapter 5 - Importance weighting is a common practice in Quality of Life (QOL) research. The basic idea is that items for specific life domains contained in a QOL measurement have different importance for different individuals; therefore, in capturing participants' perceptions, feelings, or evaluations in these domains, information on domain importance should be incorporated into the scoring procedure and reflected in the final score. Accordingly, importance weighting is proposed to serve this purpose, and the common procedure is to weight the satisfaction score by the importance score for each domain. This idea is so common that many instruments adopted this weighting procedure in their scoring system without examining its necessity and appropriateness. To date, there is extensive evidence to draw the conclusion of the (in)appropriateness of using importance weighting of satisfaction scores. Hence, the purpose of this article is to provide a systematic review of the literature on the issue of importance weighting. In the following sections, I first introduce the notion of importance weighting. Then, the empirical utility of importance weighting is reviewed to see if importance weighting contributes to predicting criterion variables. In the third section, the literature on the appropriateness of importance weighting based on a psychological perspective is reviewed. Finally, a conclusion on importance weighting and the implications for QOL are provided.

Chapter 6 - In daily life, adjectives as "sympathetic" "aggressive" are used to speak about people. But what do we mean when we say that Mary is sympathetic? What kind of knowledge do we communicate about Mary? This chapter aims at analyzing the different meanings of those adjectives within trait psychology and social psychology frameworks. In trait psychology, they are called "personality traits" and are defined as "generalized and personalized determining tendencies - consistent and stable modes of an individual's adjustment to his environment" (Allport & Odbert, 1936, p. 26). Sympathetic is considered as a descriptive psychological property of Mary. This definition is convenient in personality assessment tradition, because it enables the measure of individual differences based on correlational design. Nevertheless, this definition of traits is subordinate to the study of personality and individual differences and does not enable to analyse the meaning and the function of traits-labels. In social psychology, two complementary perspectives share the idea that trait labels are polysemous entities and that their meaning is directly linked to their social function. The perspective of the theory of traits as generalized affordances (Beauvois & Dubois, 2000) enables to distinguish evaluative knowledge- how others act toward targets who possess these traits (behavioral affordances)-, from descriptive knowledge- how targets who possess theses traits act (descriptive behavior)-, deemed to be of limited importance in trait common usage. Sympathetic is used to communicate the social value of Mary, her social affordance which guides my own behavior towards Mary (I invite Mary to my birthday) rather than her psychological property. The other perspective stipulates that traits refer to both the descriptive behaviors and the descriptive states (Mollaret & Mignon, 2007). Sympathetic is also a descriptive knowledge of Mary's states Mary's state (e.g. Mary feels happy). This description implying a state verb directs a perception of Mary as acted by the situation (Brown and Fish, 1983). We will report new research, based on experimental design, showing that person perception depends on the function of personality traits which is determined by social practices. Implications of different meanings of traits, both for individual differences and also for other kind of judgments (e.g. judgment of responsibility) will be presented.

Chapter 7 - This study used the mean and covariance structures analysis approach to examine if there is measurement and construct invariance across the common items of the abbreviated (JEPQRA) and short (JEPQRS) versions of the Junior Eysenck Personality Questionnaire Revised (JEPQR). Participants were adolescents, between 15 and 17 years of age. One group of 439 participants completed the JEPQRA, while another groups of 466 participants completed the JEPQRS. The findings showed equivalency for factor structure, loadings, variances, covariances, and mean scores. Most of the item intercepts and error variances were also invariant. The implications of these results for the development of shorter questionnaires from their longer counterparts are discussed in relation to the JEPQR, and for questionnaires in general.

Chapter 8 - As traditionally conceptualized, psychopathy comprises a constellation of interpersonal, affective, and behavioral traits, including glib charm, shallow affect, deceit, lack of insight, and poor impulse control. Most psychopaths display a peculiar mix of being superficially likeable and engaging yet interpersonally destructive.

Chapter 9 - Score reliability is a central feature of measurement. Both researchers and practitioners are under ethical obligation to ensure that any assessment devise utilized have strong psychometric qualities. This is true when the instrument is needed to conduct research or used to derive therapeutic goals. However, a simple knowledge of the reliability coefficient is not sufficient. A true understanding of reliability theory is necessary to fulfill this obligation. Helms, Henze, Sass, and Mifsud (2006) rightly note the reliability data are often treated as "mystical forces that supercede validity rather than as data that should be analyzed and interpreted in a manner analogous to validity data" (p. 631). Hence, the primary ambition of this chapter is to inform the reader of reliability theories and estimation procedures, including the assumptions underlying such estimates, and provide researchers and practitioners with accessible information for the interpretation and reporting of reliability data. Before this goal may be pursued, however, it is necessary to briefly mention the theoretical nature of personality measurement.

Personality measurement is a reflection of personality theory. Specifically, there are two major theoretical models of personality measurement. One is appropriate for the types of psychometric analyses discussed in this chapter; the other is not. Researchers must examine the theoretical basis for personality measurement and not blindly follow a given set of procedures. The two models have been given various names. Hershberger (1999) used the terms *taxonomic* and *dimensional* to describe these models of personality. Speaking in broader terms, but reflecting the same theoretical foundation, Bollen and Lennox (1991) used the terms *causal indicators* and *effect indicators*, and more recently, Edwards and Bagozzi (2000) used the terms *formative* and *reflective* constructs.

Chapter 10 - Personality is a matter of assessment, not an objective natural science; at least for the near future, that alternative is not in sight. Consequently, students of personality might as well try to optimize their assessment methods as such. One obstacle to optimal personality assessment is reliance on self-report, and the subjective definition of personality that it implies. To enhance the reliability and validity of assessments, knowledgeable others should be enlisted to report on the characteristic behavior of the target person. This intersubjective approach to personality appears to have consequences for the content of personality questionnaires: A shift from experiential to behavioral item content is appropriate. Another obstacle to faithful assessment is the reliance on relative scales in reporting about personality. The implied model, based on classical applied statistics, ignores the bipolar nature (e.g., introverted vs. extraverted) of personality assessments; its range of application is limited to approaches in which individuals are compared with one another. I explore the consequences of an alternative psychometric-statistical model based on proportional scores on a bipolar scale. Its side-effect is to challenge current ideas about personality structure.

Chapter 11 - This Chapter introduces theoretical and empirical comprehensive models that combine three well-established theories and relate to the underlying cultural contexts of individuals completing Likert-type questionnaires. The theoretical model incorporates the stages of responding to Likert-type questionnaires, the effects of response sets and cross cultural effects measured by collectivist and individualist attributes. This theoretical model, named the ImpExp, is empirically tested by measuring the effects of a range of response biases (social desirability, extreme/mid point response set, 'don't know' response, acquiescence, and context) and collectivist and individualist attributes. This results in a second model, the Collectivist-Individualist Model of Response Bias (CIMReB), which suggests an explanation for the way in which collectivist and individualist attributes affect how people respond to Likert-type questionnaires. The CIMReB relates to the five stages of the cognitive process of responding to questions and partially supports the ImpExp model.

These two models together provide a comprehensive framework for the design and implementation of psychological scales within cross cultural contexts. The main findings indicate that collectivist and individualist attributes interact with other response sets and mostly affect the magnitude of the answers (i.e. the extent to which extreme responses are used). The actual content of the answers is affected to a lesser extent. Some examples are provided to demonstrate the usefulness of the models in interpreting answers to Likert-type questionnaires within cross cultural and cross national environment. The Chapter concludes with some practical recommendations relating to the design and analysis of such questionnaires.

Chapter 12 - Graphic rating scales are frequently used in the collection of self-report data. Although the specification of these response scales is common, they have been identified as being particularly susceptible to several response biases – most notably acquiescence, central tendency, and extremity. The possibility that these response styles may be more or less prominent in individuals of different *trait* standing has been acknowledged, but has resulted in conflicting conclusions and recommendations. The current chapter posits that response biases are particularly problematic in the assessment of personality, because they may be characterized as sources of true construct variance (i.e., extreme option endorsement or avoidance, central tendency, and yeah/nay-saying are facet dimensions of some FFM constructs). Unfortunately, the source of true construct variance is scattered across different traits. This is problematic for establishing trait orthogonality – if "other" construct variance is introduced into FFM measurement because of response bias, scale correlations would be expected not solely because of construct association, but also because of measurement method/response bias shared across trait specifications. We used a large archival dataset to estimate relationships between FFM trait (and subfacet) standing and response styles along a 5-point graphic rating scale (ranging from response options of Very Inaccurate to Very Accurate). In addition to identifying personological content associated with acquiescence and extremity, implications of this investigation: 1) point toward some of the observed FFM trait correlations potentially being attributable to response style confounds, and 2) suggest adjective checklists or forced-choice formats may be preferable to graphic rating scale specification in personality assessment.

Chapter 13 - Procrastination is a complex psychological behavior that affects everyone to some degree or another. This study examined academic procrastination (AP) and procrastination in everyday life (EP) and their relations to the Five-Factor Model (FFM) of personality among 267 male and female Israeli students, who filled in a demographic questionnaire, the shortened version of Costa and McCrae's (1992) NEO-FFI, Milgram, Srolof, and Rosenbaum's (1988) everyday life procrastination scale, and Toubiana and Milgram's (1992) academic procrastination scale. The two types of procrastination were strongly and positively associated with one another, AP was positively related to neuroticism

(N) and extraversion (E) and negatively related to conscientiousness (C); and EP was also positively related to N but not to E and negatively related to C. Stepwise regression analyses indicated that when EP is the dependent variable, only AP, A, and E are included in the regression equation, whereas when AP is the independent variable, EP and all the FFM variables are included in the equation. Men scored significantly higher than women on AP but not on EP. In light of these findings, we discuss a personality typology of procrastinators, based on the FFM.

Chapter 14 - Dream research focuses mainly on the formal characteristics of dreams (e.g., mood, realism, coloring, dream recall frequency) and dream content but little research has been conducted to date on the functional aspects of dreams. Dreams have always been the focus of human enquiry and have always played a significant part in human life. Every society has developed its own theories of dreams. Therefore, the functional aspects of dreams such as affective response to dreams and dreaming (liking/disliking, fear, curiosity etc.), subjectively perceived role of dreams, private concepts of dreams and dreaming, or different kinds of behavior influenced by dreams (trying to interpret one's own dreams, believing they have special meaning, behaving according to the clues offered by the dream, sharing dreams with other people, etc.) all seem to be equally important in the investigation of dreams. In studies on the functional aspects of dreams, the term *attitude toward dreams* is commonly used. No clear definition of attitude toward dreams has been provided, however. Furthermore, different studies take different components of attitude into account — some measure only the affective response to dreams, others also consider beliefs about dreams or the influence of dreams on waking life. Because of this ambiguity, the present authors propose their own definition of attitude toward dreams based on the classical, three-component definition of attitude. Some of the previous research has shown that attitude toward dreams correlates substantially with personality traits, particularly with the openness to experience factor of the Five Factor model of personality. Some results also suggest a relationship between attitude toward dreams and neuroticism. The present study was designed to explore the relationship between attitude toward dreams and the Big Five personality factors. The sample consisted of 108 participants aged 19-33, 62 women and 46 men. Attitude toward dreams was measured with a 56-item self-report scale (Attitude toward Dreams Scale – ADS) specifically developed for the present study and psychometrically verified. Participants also completed the Polish version of the NEO-PI-R.

Chapter 15 - Abortion continues to be one of the most hotly debated issues in American politics. Despite its prominence in the public discourse, little social psychological work has been done to understand the ideological bases of individuals' attitudes toward abortion. The current chapter seeks to address this oversight by using social dominance theory (Sidanius and Pratto, 1999) and the theory of ambivalent sexism (Glick and Fiske, 1996) to explain attitudes toward abortion. Specifically, we argue that individuals with a preference for group-based hierarchy – a variable referred to as social dominance orientation (SDO) – use beliefs about gender roles in order to justify their attitudes toward abortion. We tested this hypothesis by having 242 participants complete the SDO scale (Pratto, Sidanius, Stallworth, and Malle, 1994) and the Ambivalent Sexism Inventory (ASI; Glick and Fiske, 1996) – a measure that divides gender role attitudes into two components: 1) hostile sexism (HS) and 2) benevolent sexism (BS). After controlling for religiosity and previous abortion experience, multiple regression analyses indicated that SDO was significantly associated with attitudes toward both elective abortion (e.g., the woman wants an abortion, regardless of the reason) and traumatic abortion (e.g., the woman is pregnant as a result of rape or incest). The relationships between SDO and attitudes toward the two types of abortion were, however, mediated by the ASI. Specifically, HS and BS mediated the relationship between SDO and opposition to elective abortion, while only BS mediated the relationship between SDO and opposition to traumatic abortion. The implications of these findings are discussed within the context of intergroup relations.

Chapter 16 - The Junior Eysenck Personality Questionnaire Revised-Abbreviated (JEPQR-A) provides scales for measuring extraversion, neuroticism, psychoticism, and lie. This study used the multiple-indicators multiple-causes model procedure, with robust estimation, to examine simultaneously the factor structure of the JEPQR-A, the differential item functioning (DIF) of the JEPQR-A items as a function of sex, and the effects of sex on the JEPQR-A factors, controlling for DIF. Male (N =218) and female (N = 220) adolescent participants, between 15 and 17 years of age completed the JEPQR-A. The results provided support for the 4-factor structure of the JEPQR-A. Although an extraversion item and a psychoticism item showed DIF, their magnitudes were small. Controlling for DIF, females scored higher than males for the extraversion and neuroticism factors, while males scored higher for the psychoticism factor.

Short Communication A - Desktop videoconferencing and project-based online collaborative learning can create new directions in higher education. However, the transition from the "safe space" of a conventional classroom course to a new learning environment often represents a major change for both faculty and students. Faculty need to know what kind of support can help students cope with the challenges of an unfamiliar learning environment in order to make this transition less difficult. In this paper we describe how we create conditions for an effective online collaborative learning environment within the framework of a course module. During the course, the students acquire judgment and decision making abilities for integrating technological systems into their field of expertise. We discuss the difficulties of evaluating outcomes in learning environments that are essentially different from conventional university courses. We conclude by sharing the lessons learned and identify critical factors that helped our students move from the familiar "chalk and talk" model to the relatively uncharted territory of project-based online collaborative learning and show that provision of "safe places" represents one of the most important contributions of online collaborative learning environments.

Short Communication B - **Introduction**

Patients with schizophrenia exhibit a broad range of cognitive, emotional and behavioral symptoms that affect their psychosocial functioning. Research findings that link symptom dimensions to functioning in schizophrenia are inconsistent. This suggests that other variables may contribute to patients' functioning. It has been documented that personality differences are detectable among patients with schizophrenia and are stable after illness onset. Thus, personality seems to be a particularly promising form of individual difference that may be related to functioning in schizophrenia.

Objective

To determine the influence of personality features and symptom severity in the level of functioning of patients with schizophrenia.

Method

One-hundred patients with schizophrenia were recruited. Diagnoses were based on the SCID-I. Symptom severity was assessed with the Scales for the Assessment of Positive and

Negative Symptoms (SAPS and SANS) while personality was assessed using the Temperament and Character Inventory (TCI). The Global Assessment of Functioning (GAF) was employed to estimate global psychosocial functioning. Sample was divided in groups, based in a cutoff point of 60 of the GAF score, forming groups of high and low functioning.

Results

More than half of the patients were classified in the low functioning group (61%). Significant differences were found between groups in terms of symptom severity and temperament and character dimensions. The temperament dimension "Persistence" and the character dimension "Self-directedness" were significant predictors of low functioning as well as the negative symptom "Apathy."

Conclusions

Motivation and goal directed behaviors are important factors that promote an adequate functioning in patients with schizophrenia. Patients with a combination of low "Persistence" and low "Self-directedness" might be an especially vulnerable group for which efforts should be made to provide supportive and reinforcing treatment interventions.

Short Communication C - This paper presents a recently developed method for the indirect assessment of emotional traits and states, the Implicit Positive and Negative Affect Test (IPANAT). In the IPANAT individuals make judgments about the degree to which artificial words sound like mood adjectives (e.g., happy or helpless). It is proposed that cognitive representations of emotions as being dominant in individuals with high sensitivity to these emotions instantaneously bring the judgments into their line. Recent findings are summarized that speak for appropriate reliability and validity of the IPANAT. As a paper-pencil test, the IPANAT is easy in application and takes no longer than 2 minutes. These properties may render this measure attractive for both basic and applied psychology.

Short Communication D - Contemporary structured psychotherapies are often designed for manualized, short-term (usually 12-16 sessions) delivery with observable and focused targets of therapeutic change. The time-limited nature of many contemporary psychotherapies limits therapists to a focus on a small number of treatment targets and objectives. The role of traditional psychometric testing in structured therapies has been difficult to discern from the literature. Reliance on broad trait based symptom inventories has been largely replaced by functional applied behavior analysis with an emphasis on observables. An additional shortcoming of traditional psychometric evaluation has been the absence of a systematic approach to identifying treatment targets from findings and providing clients digestible feedback about their results. The present article explores some of these theoretical and pragmatic limitations in the use of broad symptom inventories such as the Minnesota Multiphasic Personality Inventory (MMPI-2) in the course of assessment for short-term structured interventions. A method described previously in the literature (McCray & King, 2003) for providing systematic test feedback and identifying supplemental treatment goals was modified in this chapter for use with the MMPI-2. While unreasonable to expect full remission of broader maladaptive response tendencies through short term interventions, the recognition and partial attenuation of disruptive behavioral, attitudinal and emotional reactions to stressors could prove exceedingly helpful in a subset of clinical cases. Randomized controlled trials of structured therapies with and without reliance on traditional testing would provide a new and interesting line of research with potential promise for enhancing the efficacy and effectiveness of treatment.

Short Communication E - Although the five factor model (FFM) has served as an important catalyst for personality-related organizational research, we agree with the suggestions of previous researchers that personality research should expand beyond this basic framework (Block, 1995; Lee & Ashton, 2004). This is especially true for researchers seeking to understand and predict counterproductive or deviant behaviors. The basic thesis of this commentary is that optimal, dispositionally-based prediction of counterproductive organizational criteria will be achieved when researchers begin assessing counterproductive personality traits. In short, we believe prediction may be enhanced by increasing the nomological convergence between our predictor and criterion spaces.

Although a number of aberrant personality traits may be relevant to predicting counterproductive and deviant behaviors, we briefly introduce three of the most promising traits labeled by some as the "Dark Triad" (Paulhus & Williams, 2002): Machiavellianism, narcissism, and psychopathy. Below we 1) define each of these traits, 2) describe how they are related to (but not redundant with) the global traits comprising the FFM, and 3) illustrate how these constructs may be mapped into the nomological space of organizational criteria (especially counterproductive and deviant work behaviors).

Short Communication F - The Autobiographical Memory Test (AMT; Williams & Broadbent, 1986) is frequently used by researchers to assess specificity of memory retrieval. This test asks respondents to describe a specific autobiographical memory in response to cue words. In contrast to the AMT's frequent use, however, little is known about its reliability. The present paper examined the test-retest reliability of the AMT. In five studies, undergraduates completed the Autobiographical Memory Test (AMT; Williams & Broadbent, 1986) twice, with mean time interval between test an retest varying over studies from 1 to 5 months. Each time, an alternate AMT was used at retesting. In a sixth study, depressed patients completed the AMT twice: once at admission to a hospital, and again 3 months later. Results document relatively satifactory test-retest reliability of the AMT in assessing people's level of memory specificity.

RESEARCH AND REVIEW STUDIES

In: Personality Assessment: New Research
Editor: Lauren B. Palcroft & Melissa V. Lopez
ISBN 978-1-60692-796-0

Chapter 1

CHILD AND ADOLESCENT PERSONALITY DEVELOPMENT AND ASSESSMENT: A DEVELOPMENTAL PSYCHOPATHOLOGY APPROACH

Tina D. Du Rocher Schudlich, Ryan C. Erps, Britnee Davenport and Alyssa Hertel
Western Washington University, Bellingham, Washington USA

ABSTRACT

This review approaches child and adolescent personality assessment from a developmental psychopathology perspective. Essential to understanding personality assessment in children is understanding how individual personality development occurs in children and adolescents. An overview of emotional and personality development will be presented, including discussion of temperament, emotional expression and understanding, and emotion regulation and coping. Temperament and personality are discussed and differentiated. Relational influences on personality development such as parent-child relationships, marital relationships, family processes, and sibling relations are considered. Preliminary results from our new study on the bi-directional effects of marital relations and infant emotionality are highlighted. Multi-method procedures, including observational data assessing parents' conflict behaviors and emotions and infants' emotional and behavioral regulation in the context of parents' conflict are presented. The role of infants' temperament in these relations is considered. Extra-familial influences on personality, such as culture and religion are also presented. Finally, normal and abnormal personality development and assessment in children and adolescents are discussed from a developmental psychopathology approach, which emphasizes that both the assessment and development of personality in children are fluid processes to be considered over time, rather than static constructs observed at a single point in time. Borderline personality disorder is used as an example to describe how the developmental psychopathology approach can elucidate understanding of the abnormal development of personality over time. Recommendations for assessment approaches are made based on these overviews, including a discussion of specific methods' strengths and weaknesses. An objective, multi-method, multi-source, multi-setting approach for assessment is offered. Age-specific approaches to assessment and age-related issues to consider in assessment are integrated into the recommendations. Future directions for research are discussed.

The field of developmental psychopathology has garnered new interest in the role of emotions and personality in normal development in recent years. New findings about the effects of both internal (e.g. temperament) and external (e.g. family environment) stimuli on the development of emotional understanding, and subsequently personality, have reenergized this field of study. Developmental psychopathologists have taken new interest in and offer a comprehensive approach to child and adolescent personality assessment. This chapter reviews the developmental literature surrounding personality – its origins, antecedents, and assessment in childhood – and offers suggestions for future assessment approaches.

As an understanding of emotional and personality development is key to understanding personality assessment, and overview of these topics are presented, including up-to-date findings on relational influences on personality development. Consequently, influences such as parent-child relationships, marital relationships, family processes, and sibling relationships are examined and the effect of each of these relationships on the personality development of a child is discussed. Temperament, the early development of emotional response patterns, and the development of emotional regulation also have key influences on normal personality and social development and are addressed as well. Additionally, preliminary findings from a new study on bi-directional effects of marital relations and infant emotionality are highlighted as exemplar of the new directions in this field. In this study, multi-method procedures, including observational data of both parents' conflict behaviors and infants' emotional and behavioral regulation in the parental conflict context, were used.

Lastly, the developmental psychopathology approach is discussed in its application to personality development and assessment. There is a focus on normal and abnormal personality development and assessment in children and adolescents. Emphasis on the fluidity of these processes is highlighted, as each should be considered over time, rather than assessed as a single point in time. Based on these overviews, recommendations for assessment approaches are made, including a discussion of specific method's strengths and weaknesses. A multi-method, multi-source, multi-setting assessment approach is proffered. Integrated into these recommendations is a consideration of age-specific issues in assessment and approaches.

As dramatic new findings about personality and emotional development are once again becoming the focus of an evolving developmental literature, this chapter serves to highlight the importance of relational considerations and adequate multi-modal assessment of personality in children and adolescents.

I. Emotional and Personality Development

Emotional Expression and Understanding

Basic and Secondary Emotions

The development of emotions is thought to occur primarily in two stages: with early development of basic emotions and the later development of more complex, secondary emotions (Draghi-Lorenz, Reddy, & Costall, 2001). While there is some contention about the distinct classifications of the basic emotions, emotions typically included in this category are interest, anger, distress, joy, fear, and sadness. These emotions are commonly thought to develop within the first six to eight months as a result of cognitive differentiation, but some theorists suggest that some or all of the basic emotions may be innate (e.g. Carroll Izard). However, a majority of research supports the idea that expressions in the first months of life cannot be considered true emotions because they are undifferentiated and are not event-related. That is, they are simple reactions based purely on the dimensions of contentment--distress and interest--disinterest and are not reactionary to specific events (Lewis, 1993). As Sroufe suggests, a subject-object relationship must be present (i.e. there must be awareness of and reaction to another person or object) for a reaction to be considered as truly emotional (1996).

The most widely-held theoretical explanation of emotional development posits that after the basic emotions develop within the first year, the secondary emotions are based on these primary emotional building blocks. For example, joy in self-efficacy becomes pride in the outcome of that efficacy. The secondary, non-basic emotions are generally thought to appear during the second year of development and require the distinct senses of objective self and self-evaluation (Draghi-Lorenz et al., 2001). For example, the widely studied development of empathy suggests that empathy requires first that the child can distinguish between self and other. Self-evaluation abilities become visible as emotions such as shame, guilt, pride and embarrassment develop near the end of the second year. While some researchers hold that these emotions may indeed develop earlier, all agree that the some sort of interpersonal awareness is necessary for the development of these secondary emotions and that the development of this awareness should be viewed as a continuum and in the context of the individual child's development (Draghi-Lorenz et al., 2001).

Development of Emotional Understanding

Emotional understanding also undergoes significant development during the first two years. During the development of the primary emotions, memory plays a large role in the production of emotional signals. Around the age of nine months, children begin to develop emotional expectancy and anticipation, feeling an emotion before an event occurs (Bretherton, Fritz, Zahn-Waxler, & Ridgeway, 1986). For example, babies at this age begin to exhibit sadness before a parent is to leave and cringe before an immunization shot is given. At twelve months, babies' growing cognitive abilities allow them to begin to speak in meaningful one-word utterances, requiring them to have an understanding of others as comprehenders of emotional messages. This cognitive ability is the same that allows the development of empathy, as discussed above. By the age of one and a half years, toddlers are beginning to understand that they and others communicate emotion (Bretherton et al., 1986).

By the toddler years, children begin to use emotion words to discuss past and future events, emotional antecedents and consequences of actions, and play emotion-based games. To do so, toddlers must understand that one person's emotions can motivate another's behavior and vise-versa; this new understanding is reflected in the types of commands or statements made by children this age (e.g. a toddler throwing a tantrum in a store may cry and scream "I want it!" or a toddler offering a teddy bear to an upset friend).

The later years of childhood and adolescence are characterized by the development of emotional control and the understanding that emotions experienced are not always the same as emotions exhibited. This knowledge moves from an understanding of only direct correlations between emotional display and actual feelings to an understanding that one can deceive and be deceived about emotions to the adolescent understanding that unconscious motivations may drive emotions (Bretherton et al., 1986). The control over the display and experience of emotions is acquired in similar stages (Selman, Schorin, Stone, & Phelps, 1983).

Theories of Emotional Function

There are multiple theories about why emotional development is important. For example, Izzard asserts that affective cognitive structures are developed through learning patterns of secondary emotions and cognitive skills (1992). In this regard, emotions are thought to help infants begin to form a sense of self by tying interpersonal awareness into the cognitive development schedule (Draghi-Lorenz et al., 2001).

The functionalist theory of emotion holds that emotions are adaptive, survival-promoting behaviors. That is, emotions and emotional understanding are crucial for finding meaning in ambiguous events. For example, understanding that an emotion on a sibling's face is fear alerts a child to possible danger. Emotions and emotional communication allow us to interpret ambiguous situations as safe or unsafe, positive or negative (Bretherton et al., 1986). Emotions, from a functionalist perspective, have an interpersonal function as well. In this way, emotions help people to appraise others' motivations and emotional states. For example, staying out of the way of an angry relative will keep a child safer than approaching this person would. Thus, when children learn how to read and manipulate others' emotions, they are gaining functional skills which will help them physically and socially thrive. The functionalist theory of emotions surmises that development of emotional language and understanding serve the functional purpose of helping children better adapt to and control their environment.

Influences on Emotional Understanding and Child Functioning

There is a great emphasis in the developmental literature on the importance of emotional understanding in social functioning and personality development. Children's level of adaptive functioning is greatly influenced by their appropriate emotional understanding and regulation (Cummings, Braungart-Rieker, Du Rocher Schudlich, 2003). A child's very sense of self is affected by how she understands her own emotional processes and those of others (Izzard, 1992). In addition, peer acceptance is affected by a child's ability to identify and discuss causes and consequences of emotion, with children who struggle with these skills being less accepted by peer groups (Cummings et al., 2003).

Similar to much of the literature on developmental gender differences, the literature on emotional development indicates that there are differences in the ways boys and girls learn and use emotion. For example, girls aged 36 months were more likely than boys to have more coherent emotional narratives and generally exhibited higher levels of verbal ability, which are predictive of later early success in emotional understanding (Laible & Thompson, 2002). In a study on emotional response patterns, Wintre, Polivy, and Murray (1990) predicted that, like adults, children would differentially respond to emotional experiences based on their sex, and that these differences would grow more distinct with age. Indeed, they found no sex differences in the self-predicted responses of the youngest subjects (age seven), with progressively more differences in the pre-teen and again in the adolescent group. Clearly, children learn what emotional responses are appropriate for their gender early on, with lifetime emotional responses patterns beginning to form by the age of five (Wintre et al., 1990). With this early creation of response patterns, the environment that the child is in is obviously highly influential on the child's later emotional functioning.

In one recent study, Labile and Thompson (2002) found that mothering style was highly influential on toddlers' emotional understanding. Mothers who used high levels of justification in rule making and discipline with their children tended to have children with a more developed sense of emotional understanding, whereas the opposite was true for children of mothers who made frequent references to needs, desires, and wants during this conversations. This study supports that idea that children acquire emotional understanding skills through modeling in their primary environment.

Emotional Regulation and Coping

Coping is the use of psychological resources to manage taxing environmental and intrapersonal stressors (Weiten &Lloyd, 2006). While children are not born with innate coping strategies, they quickly start to develop their precursors – the ability to regulate their own emotions. Emotional regulation refers to the strategies used maintain control over emotional states (e.g. feelings of anger), emotional behaviors (e.g. facial reactions), emotional cognitions (e.g. reactive thoughts), and emotion-related physiological processes, such as heart rate.

Development of Emotional Regulation and Coping Strategies

Cognitive and emotional development shape every aspect of how children cope with stress. Children learn to regulate their emotions gradually through their constitutional structure and through social interactions with both parents and peers (Skinner & Zimmer-Gemback, 2007). Multiple accomplishments in emotional regulation are thought to occur during the first year of life alone, leading to the ability to respond to and understand meaningful emotional expressions of others (e.g. empathy). At twelve months of age, children begin to learn to regulate their own emotions as well (Bretherton et al., 1986). For example, at this age a child will turn away from or move away from something that is alarming or upsetting.

As children leave the infant stage and enter the toddler and preschool years, they begin to recognize that emotions shown are not always the same as the emotions that are being felt (e.g. "mom's smiling at my older brother, but she's really upset at him"). Between ages three and five children begin to express awareness that emotional experiences can be controlled in this way. They are also learning at this age that emotions may carry over from one situation to another (e.g. mom's in a good mood and therefore may be generous and buy me an extra toy) and become adept at interpreting the emotional overview of a situation (Bretherton et al., 1986).

By the time the children reach primary school, they have learned some active conflict resolution skills as a way of dealing with frustration (e.g. share, take back, etc.). These skills are supplemented by cognitive coping skills during middle childhood (e.g. counting to ten, deep breaths, etc.) and become meta-cognitive coping skills by adolescence (e.g. thinking "it's not that big of a deal that you don't want to eat salad for dinner, just calm down"; Skinner & Zimmer-Gembeck, 2007).

The conflict resolution and coping styles that develop early during the elementary school years tend to remain relatively stable over situation and time through adult life. Interestingly, we again see the influence of parent attachment here, with mutually-focused conflict styles (e.g. integration and compromise) being associated with secure attachment while insecure attachments were associated with avoidance of mutual engagement tactics (Corcoran & Mallinckrodt, 2000). Similarly, Creasey and Hesson-McInnis (2001) found a correlation between adolescents' parental attachment and confidence in emotional regulation and positivity during conflict with romantic partners. That is, insecurely attached adolescents reported more negative emotions and less confidence in emotional and behavioral regulation during conflict. As these differences were found as a function of attachment security, the patterns created in the early environment of a child clearly have vital long-term outcomes on emotional adjustment.

Coping styles have also been compared using a variety of personality measures, such as the five-factor model of personality. In one study, the factors of conscientiousness and neuroticism were found to be the most strongly related to coping styles, with high neurotic scores being broadly associated with passive and ineffective forms of coping (e.g. giving up, distraction, ignoring, and denial). Highly conscientious people, on the other hand, generally used more active, problem-focused response strategies, such as persistence and planning (Watson & Hubbard, 1996).

Clearly, both the structure and function of lifelong coping mechanisms are greatly influenced by the development of new capacities through childhood (e.g. attachment, language, voluntary behavior, and meta-cognition). More research needs to be done to fully understand how development in other areas affects emotional regulation and coping (Skinner & Zimmer-Gemback, 2007).

Role of the Caregiver

A child's home environment also has a strong influence on his ability to recognize and regulate his own emotions, in addition to the influence it exerts on the ability to recognize and understand the emotions of others. Just as families are the first place where a child learns how to express emotion, they are also the first place a child learns how to control her own emotions. For example, Volling and Belsky (1992) found that over-controlling and intrusive mothering set the example for later aggressive and conflicted sibling relationships. In another study, it was found that parental negativity was significantly correlated with sibling conflict and general unrest in the home environment (Lemery & Goldsmith, 2001). Other studies support these findings as well. For example, Saarni and Buckley (2002) suggest that children easily learn the social scripts from their parents about appropriate behavior, all of which have potential implications for their long-term emotional regulation.

In fact, Saarni and Buckley (2002) suggest that a secure attachment to at least one parent figure is the very basis for the development of normal emotional regulation; without the opportunities to learn from a secure relationship, a child may develop significant deficits in emotional understanding and regulation. For example, if a parent is emotionally unavailable, a child will develop coercive methods for gaining attention and getting needs met, potentially leading to a lifelong pattern of negative interpersonal interactions.

Other parenting factors may also affect the child's normal emotional development. For example, high levels of marital conflict are correlated with higher levels of both externalizing and internalizing emotional problems in the children of these families (see El-Sheikh, Keller,

& Erath, 2007 for a review of this literature). Parent stressors, such as depression, are another potential threat to normal childhood emotional development. In fact, parent depression is linked with child emotional and regulation problems and more impaired child-parent emotional communication (Jacob & Johnson, 1997). Clearly, parenting is a major factor in children's development of emotional regulation mechanisms.

Temperament and Personality

Dimensions of Temperament

Each child is born with a distinctive pattern of dispositions and sensitivities, referred to as temperament. Temperament is inborn and can be defined as a set of inherited behavioral traits which guide behavior when confronting new environmental challenges (Goldsmith, Buss, Plomin, Rothbart, Thomas, et al., 1987). That is, temperament is characterized by stylistic behavioral tendencies, as opposed to discrete behaviors, whose expression is affected by context. Although there is some contention across different research groups about which specific traits should be assessed and are elemental to temperament, the following dimensions have been fruitful in empirically differentiating temperament types: rhythmicity regarding biological functions, activity level, autonomic reactivity when faced with novel situations, sensory alertness, adaptability to change, characteristic moods and intensity of responses, distractability, and persistence (Thomas & Chess, 1977).

In their pioneering work, Thomas and Chess (1977) pooled various combinations of these dimensions to distinguish among three types of infants: easy, slow to warm-up, and difficult. Easy infants react positively to novel situations and stimuli, are well-regulated and rhythmic, and are easily soothed. Slow-to-warm-up infants are more shy, have a low activity level, require some experience and familiarity in situations before reacting positively, take time to create rhythmic patterns, and prefer to stick to interact with a smaller number of people. Difficult infants tend to be fussy, demonstrate a greater preponderance of negative mood, react negatively to novel situations, and are low in soothability and rhythymicity. Current research suggests that temperament characteristics in babies significantly predict scores on behavioral scales at the age of five (Komsi, Raikkonen, Personen, Heinonen, Keskivaara, et al., 2006). In the New York Longitudinal Study (which followed infants through adulthood), Thomas & Chess (1977) found that although no specific dimensions of temperament predicted adult adjustment, difficult temperament at age three was negatively associated with emotional adjustment in adulthood. In addition, difficult temperaments were more commonly found in children who developed psychiatric problems.

There has been a recent interest by researchers in exploring biological markers of temperament. There are numerous psychophysiological measurement approaches, including behavioral genetics, heart rate and its variability, skin conductance, cortisol, and electroencephalograms (EEGs). Emerging evidence across each of these various approaches suggests that there is a biological basis, at least in part, to temperament characteristics (for a fuller review see Cummings et al., 2003). For example, from behavioral genetics it has been determined that the degree of heritability for temperamental characteristics is approximately 40%. Cortisol levels have a complex relationship with temperamental characteristics. Some evidence has linked higher levels with both behavioral inhibition and more aggressive behavior, but additionally indicates that cortisol levels may also reflect the context in which the child is examined (deHaan, Gunnar, Tout, Stansbury, 1998). Inhibited children also tend to show higher resting heart rates and less variability in their heart rate (Kagan et al., 1997). EEG studies have shown additional support for the biological basis of temperament. For example, right frontal asymmetry has been found in infants who demonstrated greater fear and inhibition (e.g. Fox, Calkins, & Bell, 1994). Finally, skin conductance is inversely associated with prosocial behaviors and positively related to internal dysregulation (Fabes et al., 1994). Thus, findings across methodologies consistently coalesce to suggest that there is a strong biological basis to children's temperament.

Temperament (and biological maturation, more generally) does not operate in isolation, however; it is thought to interact developmentally with other attributes like cognition, arousal, emotionality, and motivation over time, leading to individualized reactions to novel situations. For this reason, the reactive characteristics in infancy may be somewhat discontinuous, but the style of reaction will hold steady over time (Goldsmith et al., 1987). Furthermore, the environmental context in which temperament is expressed is instrumental to understanding continuities and discontinuities in temperamental course over time.

It is important to consider the interactive, agentic nature of children in their environment and how their biological predisopositions strengthen the probability that certain traits may become more established (Millon & Davis, 1995). On the other hand, consideration of the environment, its expectations, demands, opportunities, and how compatible those are with the child's temperament and ability to effectively master such challenges is essential in understanding developmental outcomes. Chess and Thomas (1990) referred to the match or mismatch between the child's environment and his/her temperament as "Goodness of Fit." When demands and challenges are consistent with the child's capabilities for mastery, there will be constructive consequences. Parents play the largest role in the goodness of fit interaction early in a child's life. How effectively the parents manage this and adapt their own parenting and interactions accordingly will determine in great part how successfully the child navigates their own environmental demands.

Temperament vs. Personality

Whereas temperament conveys basic inborn traits and behaviors, personality conveys much more. Beyond one's basic biological traits, personality also encompasses perceptions of self, relation of self to others and to events, habits, skills, and values (Cummings et al., 2003). As discussed above, to fully understand developmental continuities and discontinuities in temperament over time, one must consider the transactions between the individual child and the environment. It is these transactions with the environment over time that help contribute to what will ultimately be described as an individual's personality. For example, children with temperaments prone to anger are more likely to develop aggressive personalities, whereas children with temperaments prone to be fearful may be likely to demonstrate a shy personality (Goldsmith et al., 1987; Komsi et al., 2006). Although temperament increases the likelihood of a child developing a certain type of personality, the child is in no way completely constrained to follow down a particular pathway of personality given their temperament. Taking into account the goodness of fit with the environment, a child who early on would be characterized as slow-to-warm-up, may later become quite sociable and extraverted if raised by sensitive, responsive, and encouraging parents who provided manageable social interactions for the child early on and throughout childhood. In this way, people with different personalities may be very similar in temperament, and those with similar personalities may be quite different temperamentally. In other words, temperament is merely a building block for the more encompassing construct of personality.

II. Relational Influences on Emotion and Personality Development

Given the significance of family environment on the emotional development of children from infancy through adolescence, an examination of the interpersonal influences on emotional development is warranted. Due to the focus of previous research, the majority of information collected on interpersonal influences on child personality revolves around the mother-infant relationship in an attachment-oriented perspective. While findings from these studies are discussed, and are certainly important, a look beyond the mother-child dyadic relationship is also necessary. More recent research of environmental influences on child emotionality and regulation have focused on specific parenting traits, family processes, and cultural contexts. These studies have revealed the wide array of developmental contributors and added considerable knowledge to the understanding of child personality development and expression. To begin with the clearest contributor, we turn first to the parent-child relationship.

Parent-Child Relationship

Many influences have been targeted as the primary source of infant emotion regulation development. Two broad classes are the intrapersonal, physiological underpinnings of behavior and the environmental, interpersonal influence. While both significant, ongoing research has continually found the interconnectedness between these factors, making hard and fast distinctions less apparent, and quite possibly, less relevant. Likewise, specific elements of parenting qualities (attachment, acceptance, parenting styles) may be referenced separately but are of course intimately connected. Previous developmental work highlighting multifinality and equifinality (e.g. Sroufe, Egeland, Carlson, & Collins, 2005) give reason to examine these qualities apart from each other, however. Not every child will be impacted by the same background in the same way. Briefly, multifinality describes the process by which similar etiological factors can lead to diverse developmental outcomes, whereas equifinality points toward the occasion in which similar developmental outcomes result from disparate histories of experience. Consequently, conceptualizing in more than one way the interpersonal parenting qualities that contribute to child outcome warrants more flexibility within assessment and understanding of etiological courses.

Also of significance are the complementary roles that parent-child relationships serve. Functional relationships on the parent-child level are not ones of equality, given that children are mostly the recipients of emotional regulation and development assistance from their parents, not vice-versa. For this reason, the parent's support, greater emotional experience, emotional expression, and emotional communication are key components by which parents contribute to their child's affective functioning (von Salisch, 2001). This is opposed to peer or friend relationships in which children give and take emotional support and/or advice on equal levels.

Acceptance and Warmth

Parent acceptance and warmth are often referenced as key parenting qualities contributing uniquely to child emotional development and regulation. Namely, more positive child outcomes have been linked to parenting styles that are more accepting and warm in nature. Such parenting qualities are synonymous with the emotional support, responsiveness, and positive expression of affect that help children regulate their own emotions and understanding of them (Denham, 2007). At the earliest stages, these parenting behaviors have been cited as crucial for the proper neural development for infants' future emotional regulating abilities (Gerhardt, 2004). The substrates of infant behavior are still underdeveloped in the first year, making infants' emotional regulation very much a dependent and transactional phenomenon with their caregiver(s). Mother's tone of voice, facial expressions, and touch have all been shown to be key features involved in aiding infant emotional regulation (Gerhardt,2004). Consequently, the close connection between infant regulation and parenting interactions is further supported by the findings that infant heart rate, growth hormones, gene expression, and neurotransmitter production have all been linked to the quality of parenting practices (Gerhardt, 2004). In general, positive affective stimuli from parents has been noted as the most vital element to infant emotional and social development.

To be certain, child sociability, self-regulation, prosocial behavior, self-esteem, and constructive play have all been positively predicted from the quality of parenting practices (Cummings, Braungart-Rieker, & Du Rocher Schudlich, 2003). The importance of these parenting qualities has been demonstrated beyond infancy and into mid-childhood, as well (Colman, Hardy, Albert, Raffaelli, & Crockett, 2006). In their four year longitudinal study, Colman et al. (2006) found that warm parenting, low in use of punitive methods, promoted children's self-regulation capacities at 8-9 years old. These findings held true after controlling for children's earlier regulation abilities, gender, and ethnicity. The absence and/or antithesis of acceptance and warmth in parenting behaviors have conversely been linked to poor outcomes for children. Internalizing and externalizing behaviors, social withdrawal, aggression, and attention deficit disorder have all been noted to result (Calkins & Fox, 2002; Darling & Steinberg, 1993; Hastings, Sullivan, McShane, Coplan, Utendale, & Vyncke, 2008; Maccoby & Martin, 1983; van Leeuwen, Mervielde, de Clercq, & de Fruyt, 2007).

Child functioning in relation to parenting quality has been measured on physiological levels as well. For example, vagal regulation was observed to serve as a moderator between parenting behaviors (e.g. over-protective and supportive) and child characteristics (e.g. internalizing problems, inhibited temperament, and social wariness) (Hastings et al., 2008). In this study, maternal support was negatively associated with internalizing behavior in children. Greater child social wariness was an outcome, however, only when highly protective mothers had children either with lower vagal tone baseline readings or more vagal suppression, pointing once again to the intimate links between child physiology and interpersonal influences. Taken together, these studies point toward the dimensions of effective parenting characteristics. Similarly, the outcome of children subject to distinct parenting styles has also been a noteworthy investigation.

Parenting Styles

Another approach linking parent influences to child personality has been drawn through Baumrind's (1967, 1971) work classifying parenting styles. Along with Maccoby & Martin's (1983) elaboration on Baumrind's work has come the four parenting styles recognized widely in psychology today. The four parenting styles are determined by the presence or absence of two continuous parenting characteristics: demandingness and responsiveness. The four styles will briefly be covered due to their extensive coverage throughout the field.

Authoritative parents are high on both demandingness and responsiveness. As such, they set clear expectations for their children's behavior, promote autonomy, and engage in give-and-take discussions on certain decisions regarding child roles. As such, some negotiation and compromise is permitted in the parent-child relationship. Authoritative parents are adept in responding to the needs of their children in warm and loving ways. Children from these environments have been noted to display greater levels of independence, creativity, and social skills (Baumrind, 1991, Steinberg, 2000); as such, these children express opportune levels of agency and interpersonal harmony.

Authoritarian parents are highly demanding while not very responsive. These parents are noted to use strict enforcement of rules and expect children's compliance without much flexibility for alternative behavior. Authoritarian parents show little warmth in relationships with their children, and consequently, dependent, passive, and conforming personalities have been noted as outcomes in adolescents from these environments (Baumrind, 1991; Lamborn, Mounts, Steinberg, & Dornbusch, 1991; Steinberg, 1996). More internalizing symptoms, self-devaluation, social submissiveness, and low self-efficacy are also noted in these children (Baumrind, 1967, 1971, 1991).

Permissive parents remain highly responsive to their children's needs, focusing on providing a loving environment to the exclusion of creating structure or guidelines for child behavior. As such they are low on demandingness, and even though children from these homes may have high levels of self-worth and self-esteem, it remains that irresponsible, conforming, immature, and impulsive child outcomes have all been found to result from permissive parenting.

Indifferent/Disengaged parenting styles account for the fourth group that is low on both demandingness and responsiveness. These parents are removed from their children emotionally and have little investment in childcare. Parenting strategies are often oriented to minimize the effort required to handle their children. As such, the most detrimental outcomes have been noted to result from disengaged parenting, including impulsiveness, low social and academic ability, delinquency, and involvement with early sexual activity and substance use (Baumrind, 1991; Patterson, DeBaryshe, & Ramsey, 1989; Steinberg, 1996; Steinberg, 2000).

Attachment

The hallmark of parent-child relationship contributors to child outcomes has certainly been the attachment classification system developed by Bowlby and Ainsworth (Ainsworth, Blehar, Waters, & Wall, 1978; Bowlby, 1969). Resulting from the interactions of infant reactivity, parent responsiveness, and relationship history, attachment classifications have continually been found to serve as unique predictors for many child characteristics and even the well-being and relationship approaches taken by adults. To date, four distinct attachment classifications have been identified through assessments using the Strange Situation (Ainsworth, et al., 1978).

A *secure* attachment classification is most often related to healthy child outcomes. Secure attachments are often achieved in parent-child relationships that embody much of the same characteristics leading to good child outcomes identified above (i.e. warm, responsive parenting of an authoritative nature). Securely attached children are hypothesized to develop healthy and stable internal working models of what they can expect from their caregivers and of the ways in which close interpersonal relationships function (Bowlby, 1969). Parents of securely attached children are available to help regulate their infant's or child's emotions, thereby dually serving as effective guides for how to deal with arousal. Simultaneously, close, nurturing connections are fostered between these children and their caregivers. Children have been noted to benefit from secure attachments by developing healthy relationships later in life, developing fewer internalizing and externalizing behaviors, and maintaining proper emotional regulation abilities (Kerns, Ambraha, Schlegelmilch, & Morgan, 2007).

Three other classifications are included within the *insecure* category of attachments. These attachment formations often develop from less responsive /adept parenting practices, namely those which are neglectful or intrusive. Neglectful parents are limited in their quality responses and interactions with infants and children. As such, their children miss out on the supportive role that parents play in fostering emotional development. Intrusive parenting, on the other hand, refers to parenting that fails to appropriately read and respond to children's behavioral cues and needs. Interactions with children are more forced and perhaps hostile when they occur. At the same time, parents may prolong interaction with their children beyond what is needed or signaled by their behavior. As a result, the soothing and regulating parenting roles are overshot as the child is subjected to greater, rather than attenuated, arousal in the hands of their parent. Unfortunately, additional arousal may actually prove harmful for the well-being of children and their future outcomes.

When parents are less accepting and warm to children and their needs, insecure attachments often result. For example, parents with little tolerance for emotional expression in their children, especially negative emotion, may step into intrusive roles. Distressing situations lead parents to snap or yell at their children to enforce a termination of such behavior. Such messages fail to validate and elaborate on proper emotional expressions that children are usually luck enough to receive from responsive parents. Instead, children learn that emotions should be hidden and/or disregarded. As a result, a*voidant* attachment patterns often develop from parenting practices that discredit or punish behaviors related to child emotional regulation (Gerhardt, 2004).

Resistant attachments are likely to result from neglectful and inconsistent parenting. In contrast to avoidant children, resistant children often display dysregulated behavior, likely due to the failure of consistent support and emotional guidance from parents. As a result, children remain overly expressive to bid for parent's attention among its unpredictable availability (Gerhardt, 2004).

Disorganized/Unclassified attachment patterns are less straightforward and were later added after further research advancement. This pattern may signal a history of abuse either for the caregiver or child. The turmoil surrounding disorganized classifications does not offer children a consistent method for reacting to the environment. These circumstances result in confused behavior and the display of more negative moods (Kerns et al, 2007)

Recent studies have revealed more about the developmental pathways in early childhood for children with various attachment patterns. Kochanska (2001) has conducted a longitudinal study over the first three years of 112 children to explain the development of fear, anger, and joy in early childhood. Attachment classifications made at 14 months uniquely predicted later child emotional expressions. Resistant children were found to be more fearful and less joyful at the beginning of the study compared to other attachment groups. Across the next two years, these children became even less joyful. Avoidant children showed a developmental trend of becoming more fearful between 14 and 33 months. Disorganized/ unclassified children increased in anger across the time span. Those who were securely attached at 14 months became less fearful and angry. Initial attachment assessment remained a significant predictor of child behavior, especially for the trajectory of negative emotions, after conservative tests controlling for earlier behavior were conducted. As this study show, attachment patterns are clearly related to the emotional development of children. However, the pathways for such developmental mechanisms may be many.

Pathways to Personality Influence

Beginning in infancy, parent-child interactions can exert an influence on many levels of emotional regulation. One attempt to conceptualize these domains of emotional development identified three areas impacting one's emotions: cognitive appraisals, subjective experiences, and emotional expressions (von Salisch, 2001). As a result, several areas exist by which parents can contribute to their infant's emotional regulation and development.

On the immediate level, parents are the primary source of support for children experiencing negative emotions, especially at young ages. When rocked or soothed in the arms of a parent, infants are the benefactors of powerful physical communicating. A calm, relaxed parent provides a mirroring system for infants to find comfort in. Remarkably, infants' heart rate has been found to match that of their support providing parent (Gerhardt, 2004). Cassidy (1994) discusses how parents' responsiveness to child distress and frustration is important for both calming their children and for helping them develop the ability to regulate themselves in future instances of distress. Parent reactions and assistance with helping their child understand emotional expression can also be noted for teaching children the meaning and appropriateness of specific emotional displays.

Parents also serve to help children understand the antecedents and consequences of actions by placing their child's emotions in context. By increasing the understanding of emotions and comfort in predicting the emotional course of events, parents can further children's regulation abilities. Parents' increased vocabulary also aids in distinguishing the nuances of emotion as they start to become apparent to children. As children age and experience a greater range and complexity of emotion, not being able to express or comprehend the experience can add to child frustration and hamper regulation abilities.

Along the same lines, parents help develop their children's narrative building skills for life events. Especially when related to negative life events or circumstances, children are better able to make sense of and find meaning in the experiences they are having. Parents foster narrative skills by asking open ended and elaborative questions when discussing past events, creating a scaffolded environment for child emotional maturity. As such, it is evident that by 8 years of age, children with elaborative parents have better coping skills, fewer internalizing and externalizing problems, and fewer problem behaviors (Fivush review).

Also noteworthy is the finding that more secure parent-child dyads engage in more emotionally expressive dialogue around emotional events that are appropriately matched to each other (Oppenheim, Koren-Karie, & Sagi-Schwartz, 2007). These findings offer support for the shared importance of parents' contribution to their children's emotional development when they are in tune and responsive to their child's needs. Parent reactions and discussions in the face of child emotionality also serve as a coaching agent by providing feedback on appropriate and inappropriate ways to express feelings (Denham, 2007).

Marital Relationship

The nature of the martial relationship also provides an important source of information for children's developing emotional maturity and functioning. Within the context of emotional security (Davies & Cummings, 1994) there are three ways in which the disruption caused by conflict can impact children: a) its effects on emotional regulation, disruption, and physiological arousal, b) by providing a motivating factor to regulate their own behavior and feelings, and that of their parents', and c) influences on internal representations of family relationships. Davies and Cummings (1994) theory is a family wide system extension of attachment theory, and has implications for children's personality development over time.

Lewis, Siegel and Lewis (1984) previously identified the potential harm to children who witness parent conflict. Populations of fifth and sixth grade children were used to create and validate a measure of childhood life stressors. Results from this measure indicated that observing parent arguments was among the greatest childhood stressors. These findings have been widely confirmed through various methods. Self report measures of affective response to an audio recorded conflict analog found that greater conflict elicited more negative emotional reactions in children, such as feeling mad, sad, helpless, and ashamed (Grych & Fincham, 1993). Physiological measures have also been used to reveal distressed reactions by children to background parent anger (El-Sheikh, Cummings, & Goetsch, 1989). In response to adult's angry behavior, increases in heart rate and blood pressure have been observed (El-Sheikh & Cummings, 1992). Studies using vagal tone and skin conductance have also proved successful in measuring distressed reactions to conflict (as cited in Cummings, 1994; Porter, Wouden-Miller, Silva, & Porter, 2003). Porter et al. (2003) found an increased history of conflict was related to lower vagal tone and emotional regulation in a six-month-old population. All of the above findings point towards the negative arousal resulting from witnessing conflict.

Child adjustment problems have been linked to marital discord across many studies and assessment methods (Brook, Zheng, Whiteman, & Brook, 2001; Cummings & Davies, 1994; Cummings, Goeke-Morey, & Papp, 2003; Davies & Cummings, 1998; Emery, 1989; Grych, & Fincham, 1990;; Harold et al., 2004; Howes & Markman, 1989; Katz & Gottman, 1993; Peterson & Zill, 1986), including externalizing disorders (e.g. aggression), internalizing difficulties (anxiety, withdrawal), and academic problems. Marital discord has been shown to carry over into parenting practices, as well (Holden, & Ritchie, 1991; Stoneman, Brody, & Burke, 1989; Belsky, Youngblade, Rovine, & Volling, 1991; Cox, Owen, Lewis, & Henderson, 1989), including inconsistency in child rearing practices, disciplinary problems, increased parental negativity, intrusive control, and low levels of parental warmth and responsiveness. Prenatal and early parent conflict even predicts the formation of insecure child attachments (Cox, & Owen, 1993; Howes, & Markman, 1989; Isabella, & Belsky1985).

Clearly displays of disruptive conflict are harmful, but it is also not the case that the best child outcomes result from homes that refrain from emotional expression. Parental displays of positive emotions and constructive management of negative emotion where parents reach a resolution are educational opportunities and have even resulted in greater child social competence and emotional understanding (Cummings, 1994; Denham & Gout, 1992; Garner, Jones, & Miner, 1994). At the other end of the spectrum, emotionally unexpressive parents impart little learning opportunities to their children. However, environments of parent conflict remain most harmful because child emotional development is challenged by the over-arousing impact of domestic disputes. Indeed, the interpersonal influences on child personality development may make matters worse if all that children are learning is how to express emotions negatively (Denham, 1998). Furthermore, a history of exposure to conflict leads to an increased sensitivity to future events of it (Cummings & Davies, 1994, Cummings, Zahn-Waxler, & Radke-Yarrow, 1981). The impacts of conflict may begin fairly early, as well, given that distressed reactions to adults' conflict have been measured in infants as young as 6 months of age. Additionally, for toddlers who experience high levels of maternal negativity, paths from aggressiveness to externalizing problems between years 2 and 4 have been documented (Rubin, Burgess, Dwyer, & Hastings, 2003).

Children's internal representations of parent relationships can also regulate the impact of conflict, such that more insecure representations are linked to greater internalizing problems in children from hostile environments (Davies & Cummings, 1998). Children's differences in support-seeking, distancing from the conflict, positive reappraisal of conflict, or attempts to problem solve the situation also lend themselves to individual levels of resiliency (Cummings & Davies, 2002). Taken together, parental conflict presents a double blow to children by serving to disrupt child emotional security and, if severe enough, establish poor internal representations resulting in poorer coping. Furthermore, the effect of conflict can be seen on children in that both their physical health and peer relations suffer when they are surrounded by marital discord (Gottman & Katz, 1989).

Current Study

A current study being conducted to examine the earliest connections between live parent problem-solving discussions and infant reactions has found continued support for these pathways to problems (Du Rocher Schudlich, et al., 2008). In infants 6-12 months old, parent displays of anger in their discussion challenged infant emotional security the most by eliciting distressed reactions. Infants also appeared to attend more to parental discussions when sadness was displayed. Furthermore, another pathway to conflict's impact on children may be present, as it was found that parents with a history or currently display of conflict drew their infants into the discussion more by keeping them within closer proximity and using them as sources of distraction from the current conflict. As such, clearer links between parent conflict and it earliest pathways to developmental disruption are being uncovered. As more families continue to participate, we expect to begin outlining unique family system contributors to infant emotional and personality development.

Sibling Relationships and Birth Order

Working from a family systems approach (Cox & Paley, 1997), the influence of other relationships within the family is also important to consider in terms of effects on the personality development. In depth investigations into the effects of sibling relationship influences on child and adolescent personality development are only recently emerging.

Overall, support has been found for the role of sibling relationships providing unique contributions to several aspects of child outcomes, including internalizing (e.g. depressive symptoms), externalizing (e.g. aggression) symptoms, self-esteem, and peer competence.

Tucker, McHale, and Crouter (2008) provide evidence for several pathways by which siblings influence each other's personality development. Four such contributing factors were amount of time together, type of activities shared, birth order, and gender composition. Their two year longitudinal investigation of mid-adolescents and their younger siblings showed that even though mixed genders appeared to spend less time together their influence on each other's development was just as significant as same-sexed dyads influence. Their findings were unique by showing that both old and younger siblings can influence each other's outcomes through hypothesized pathways of modeling. For example, younger sisters developed the highest self-esteem at time 2 if they spent more constructive time (sports, hobbies) with their low self-esteem older sister. In another instance, younger brothers' self-esteem at T1 predicted older brothers' self-esteem at T2 based on the amount of unstructured shared time. In this case, the greatest self-esteem was developed by older brothers who spent the most time with their younger low-self-esteem brother. Looking at cross-gender sibling dyads, less time with well adjusted older sisters led to better outcomes for boys. In contrast to pathways improving child outcomes, other research has focused on detrimental effects of sibling relationships.

Dunn, Slomkowski, Beardsall, and Rende's (1994) seven year investigation beginning with three and five year old siblings discovered that lack of friendly behavior to siblings in earlier time points was linked to internalizing and externalizing behavior for older siblings. Younger siblings who were not friendly with their sibling had greater internalizing behavior two years later, as well. It is noteworthy that sibling relationships that mimic harmful parenting styles (e.g. lack of warmth) are also associated with detrimental outcomes. In addition, associations between sibling relationships and later outcomes were clearer for older siblings. An additional study of older siblings (Kim, McHale, Crouter, & Osgood, 2007) found that increased sibling conflict was associated with greater depressive symptoms and increased sibling intimacy was associated with greater peer competence regardless of birth order. Gender differences existed for depressive outcomes, however, being that greater sibling intimacy was linked to reduced depressive symptoms only for girls. Social learning and modeling pathways were hypothesized for these links.

Additional work, controlling for economic hardship and parenting influences, found further support for the significance sibling relationships. In this case, the developmental trajectory of aggression in adolescence was examined as a function of younger sibling gender and level of aggression (Williams, Conger, & Blozis, 2007). The developmental course of aggression was predicted more strongly by sibling gender than the individual's gender. Those having a male sibling (older or younger) as opposed to female sibling developed higher aggression (for both girls and boys). In one case (having a younger girl sibling) aggression was actually found to decrease aggression for older siblings.

As such, the literature is clear on the developmental impact siblings can have on each other. These studies point to the importance of examining gender, age, and birth order when considering the influence of sibling relationship due to their unique contribution to the sibling relationship. Furthermore, while the impact of immediate relationships (e.g. siblings) may be intuitive, influences from the surrounding environment can be just as significant and are worth investigating.

Extra-Familial Relationships

Culture

Cultural contexts are easily the most overlooked area of personality development influence. Certainly, influences on the broadest level may go unnoticed until they are made obvious, such as by visiting another nation. Given that the majority of psychological literature and research has taken place in predominately Western, industrialized countries, a far more diverse body of literature addressing the remaining global cultures awaits authorship. In Bronfenbrenner's (1979) ecological perspective, exosystem and macrosystem levels point directly towards the overarching cultural beliefs, values, customs, traditions, and institutions that influence one's development on the broadest scale. Additionally, the current trend to treat culture as a transactional process between person and environment over time (Keller & Greenfield, 2000; Cummings, Davies, & Campbell, 2000), rather than an independent variable, captures the importance of Bronfenbrenner's chronosystem. To neglect the impact of these forces would be to assume that the models formulated from one culture equally apply to all others.

Looking at the big picture, Aldwin (2007) expresses the ways which culture has an impact on the daily stress and coping process of one's daily life. She notes that the types of stressors, the appraisal of them, the preferred coping strategies, and the cultural institutions available to aid in coping all vary by culture. Culture also defines what stressors are normative (e.g. puberty rituals, arranged marriages) which can influence the appraisal process of stressful events, thereby leading to different outcomes from similar stimuli. Examples of this may even be found within certain subcultures. For example, physical punishment has been repeatedly linked to externalizing problem in Caucasian samples. However, in African American samples physical punishment has not been found to result in more aggressive child or adolescent outcomes, and may actually *decrease* externalizing behavior (Lansford, Deater-Deckard, Dodge, Bates, & Pettit, 2004). Indeed, it appears that cultural discipline norms moderate the effect of parenting practices to some degree (Lansford, Chang, Dodge, Malone, Oburu, Palmerus, et al., 2005). Given the difference of discipline norms between cultural groups, physical punishment may even be seen by some children as having caring and involved parents, thus contributing to the various outcomes that have been observed.

Cultures are also in charge of resource allocations and stress appraisals that influence how one acts in a given life context (Aldwin, 2007). For example, Arsenian and Arsenian (1948) proposed the existence of both tough cultures (where few life goals are seen as valuable and access to them is restricted) and easy cultures (where many life goals are valued and equal opportunity exists to reach them). For example, the value of obtaining material wealth in American society is representative of a tough culture due to the challenging and uneven pathways that exist to obtain it. American versus Japanese school systems is another example. The rigorous and mandatory exams required to advance in some Asian school systems is a way of life for students in those cultures. While certainly a stressful experience for any person having to endure them, students accustomed to them would likely have a very different appraisals and reactions to the process than students foreign to such a process.

The interactions of culture and personality are rarely simple, as well. To assume that individuals from collectivistic cultures may be naturally inclined to access greater social support in times of need may be deceiving. In Aldwin and Greenberger's (1987) study of Korean American versus European American students in universities, it was found that

Korean American students were actually more reluctant to seek social support in difficult times so as not to "lose face" – an important Korean cultural value. Such examples point toward the need to further study the impact and ways in which culture shapes emotional and personality development to better understand its contribution more accurately.

Even with recent developments in the understanding of sibling relationships and personality development, cultural differences remain significant factors of influence given that the meaning of social relationships also vary by culture. For example, sibling relationships may be even larger developmental influences when family time and relationships are valued more, such as in collectivistic cultures (Coon & Kemmelmeier, 2001). Likewise, the significance of birth order and gender varies widely by culture. Cultural customs that favor firstborn male children represent inherent influences on the way children are viewed and treated (Herrera, Zajonc, Wieczorkowska, Cichomski, 2003). Even more so, countries with laws placing limits on offspring production may create or intensify parent attitudes toward their children, ultimately decide if and how a child will live. As it has already been discussed that how children are raised (e.g. maternal characteristics, parenting styles) impacts their personality, and such cultural mechanisms should be clear indicators of personality influence.

Even parenting styles vary in meaning by culture. The tradition of filial piety (honoring and obeying one's parents through life), and respect in Latino cultures, can lead to parenting style classifications that do not fit well or are not appropriate. In fact, African America, Latino, and Asian American parents are more likely to be classified as authoritarian than European Americans (Steinberg, Dornbusch, & Brown, 1992; Steinberg, Lamborn, Darling, Mounts, & Dornbusch, 1994). Yet, the collectivistic customs and values of these cultures hardly fits parents who are low on responsiveness, and at the same time better child outcomes are predicted from these parenting styles that are not necessarily classified as authoritative. As a result, Baumrind has included the *traditional parenting style* to account for these types of parenting patterns. These differences signal either the need for further recognition and understanding of what quality parenting practices are universal or specific to regions in order to advance understanding in the field.

Finally, a recent study (Bornstein, Putnick, Heslington, Gini, Suwalsky, Venuti, et al., 2008) examined how such ecological influence exists on maternal emotional availability between country (Argentina, Italy, America), region (rural or urban), and child gender. Italian mothers were found to be more sensitive and structuring, and likewise their infants were more responsive and involving. Regional differences were also found with rural mothers being more intrusive, and complementarily, urban sons were more responsive than boys from rural areas. Finally, the mother-daughter dyad also seemed to reciprocate higher maternal sensitivity with more responsive and involving daughters compared to the mother-son dyad. These connections seem to point toward the universal aspects of quality parenting rather than unique cultural differences in optimal parenting styles. Likewise, Ainsworth's attachment theory was been validated across many cultures (Cummings, Braungart-Rieker, 2003).

As such, culture is a pervasive influence on personality development that should not be overlooked. Research in this area has continued to confirm both the importance of culture and its universal impact. Further work is needed to both identify what constitutes optimal parenting, and especially, the distinct ways these practices are represented within various cultures.

III. NORMAL AND ABNORMAL PERSONALITY DEVELOPMENT: A DEVELOPMENTAL PSYCHOPATHOLOGY APPROACH

Viewing personality development and assessment through the lenses of a developmental psychopathology perspective offers a broadened view and unique approach to conceptualizing personality. Historically, approaches to understanding personality development focused on describing personality traits in childhood, which were considered to be stable, primarily biologically based traits, and documenting links between these early traits and later adult personality. More recently, however there has been an increasing emphasis on understanding the underlying dynamic processes that contribute to the normal and abnormal development of personality over time (Cummings, Davies, & Campbell, 2000; Cicchetti & Cohen, 1995). Although there is certainly a strong genetic component to personality, developing research in the past decade has begun to focus on and show strong support for the role of interpersonal experiences and interactions between children and their environments in the development of both normal and abnormal personality traits (Caspi et al, 2002; Costello, Foley, & Angold, 2006; Foley et al., 2004). The developmental psychopathology approach lends itself particularly well to guiding future directions for studying personality development and offering guidance on how to approach assessing personality comprehensively in children. This section will review emerging directions for research in personality development and assessment in children from a developmental psychopathology perspective. Both normal and abnormal personality development will be discussed.

Personality as an Evolving Process Over Time

Normal and Abnormal Personality as Developmental Processes

Historically, psychopathology in childhood has been considered from a traditional medical model approach in which disorders were viewed as distinct, discrete, and enduring pathologies (typically biological in nature) residing within the individual child (Sroufe, 1997). Disorders were considered to follow inevitable trajectories in terms of causes and outcomes and the focus of disorders was primarily on description or categorization and identifying correlates (Rutter, 1986), rather than on dynamic etiological processes. Psychopathological outcomes were viewed as being qualitatively different from normal outcomes and the emphasis was primarily on pathology.

The field of developmental psychopathology has facilitated a broadening of our conceptualization of psychopathology. The developmental psychopathology perspective focuses on elucidating the interplay between biological, psychological, familial, individual, social and cultural processes that influence both normal and abnormal development (Cicchetti, 2006). Thus, rather than assuming pathology resides within the child, it assumes a transactional model of development, in which psychopathology (and development in general) arises from ongoing interactions between active, changing agents and their dynamic, changing contexts (Cummings, Davies & Campbell, 2000; Sroufe, 1997). It emphasizes delineation of the pathways through which normality or abnormality can be achieved (Cicchetti & Sroufe, 2000), with a focus on an in-depth understanding of the developmental processes and pathways that precede and account for the development of disorders. A pivotal element of the developmental psychopathology approach is its emphasis on both normality and abnormality, and risk and resilience, which provides the most comprehensive understanding of how psychopathology may emerge in children. Furthermore, unlike previous perspectives, it follows the assumption that normality and abnormality lie on a continuous spectrum, suggesting that psychopathology is more quantitatively different than normality, rather than qualitatively different.

Whereas previous considerations of psychopathology in children focused on categorizing and describing psychopathology and identifying its correlates, the goal of the developmental psychopathology approach is to discover the dynamic processes over time that explain psychopathology. Thus, it aims to uncover the mediators and moderators of child outcomes (Ciccehtti, 2006). For example, it has been well established that parental depression serves as a risk factor for child maladjustment (for reviews see Downey & Coyne, 1990; Gotlib & Goodman, 2002). The developmental psychopathology approach extends researchers' line of questions to include examination of questions such as how, why, and for whom is parental depression a risk. Recent research in this area has indicated that it is not as simple of a correlation as previous work identified. In recent years, researchers have identified numerous mediating factors that help explain how and why parental depression may affect children, including factors such as specific negative forms of marital conflict (Du Rocher Schudlich & Cummings, 2003), maternal and paternal parenting styles (Du Rocher Schudlich & Cummings, 2007), family conflict (Du Rocher Schudlich, Youngstrom, Calabrese, and Findling, in press), and parental rejection (Sturge-Apple, Davies & Cummings, 2006).

Developmental psychopathologists underscore the fact that children with disorders may move between both pathological and normal functioning (Cicchetti, 2006). Unlike traditional medical model approaches, it does not assume that once children have a disorder they will inevitably have that disorder for their lifetime. There may be times in which they function better and do not display pathology, only to move back to pathology during other more stress points in their lives. Thus, psychopathology is considered from a probabilistic perspective in which change is possible at any point, but is constrained by prior adaptation. Development extends throughout the lifespan and at each new stage it is important to take into account not only the different pertinent agendas, but also how each stage prior has contributed to the current development and how each prior stage will affect future adaptation. Key life turning points may be times when protective mechanisms may help individuals redirect themselves toward more adaptive pathways of development (Rutter, 1988). Furthermore, children may display adaptive functioning even in the midst of psychopathology (Cicchetti, 2006). What may be dysfunctional in one context may be adaptive in another and therefore the contexts in which children are in remains highly significant. For example, a highly aggressive child with conduct disorder may find himself repeatedly in trouble at school for acting out and causing fights, whereas he is revered in his neighborhood for his toughness and as a result safe from the neighborhood gang violence. Thus, both the transition points in a child's life, their current developmental level, and their context must all be taken into account.

It is apparent that the developmental psychopathology approach provides a powerful framework for guiding future directions for studying normal and abnormal personality development in children. It allows for the consideration that many dynamic processes of maladjustment will not fit neatly into a nosological category (Cicchetti, 2006) and as such moves researchers beyond merely describing disorders to delineating the processes, histories and contexts which contribute to children's outcomes. As such, it becomes less useful to focus on describing and identifying specific disorders and more important to take into account the processes over time that have contributed to children's current and future personality functioning.

Defining and Assessing Personality in Children

Although there is an extensive history of work conceptualizing definitions of personality in adults, the literature on personality in children is more recent and fragmented (Tackett & Krueger, 2005). In infancy and toddlerhood personality has been conceptualized as being primarily a factor of temperament, whereas starting in early to middle childhood temperament is considered merely a foundation for the development of more complex and differentiated personality traits (Rothbart & Ahadi, 1994). Although assessment methods and classification categories vary by research group, methods for assessing personality/temperament in infancy and toddlerhood are well established (Thomas & Chess, 1984; Rothbart and Bates, 1998; Kagan, 1994). Methods for assessing adolescents have typically relied on adult measures of personality. A significant gap exists in our understanding of personality development and assessment in the early to middle childhood years, however. Researchers have been mixed in their approaches to defining and understanding personality in this age group, with some researchers extending temperament models upward to cover this age span, while others have applied adult personality models downward (Tackett & Krueger, 2005).

Two emerging approaches offer converging and promising results for understanding personality in the early to middle child hood range. Work by Haverson and colleagues (2003) and Shiner and Caspi (2003) indicates that a personality taxonomy incorporating the personality factors of Extraversion, Agreeableness, Conscientiousness and Neuroticism connects notions of early temperament with later personality in adulthood and is a useful tool to communicate about personality across the lifespan (Tackett & Krueger, 2005). In general, it has been established that temperament is broadly continuous with adult personality (Caspi, Harrington, et al., 2003). However, temperament characteristics are often not stable until toddlerhood or preschool ages and there have been few studies examining different temperament characteristics from infancy through adulthood (Paris, 2007). Whether temperament is associated with specific vulnerabilities to psychopathology remains to be established (Kagan & Zentner, 1996; Paris, 2007).

Considering personality structure assessment from a developmental psychopathology perspective raises additional questions. Integration of personality variables across the various lines of research is essential to developing a cohesive model of personality development across the lifespan. Further work is needed to delineate the continuities and discontinuities in these new taxonomic models over time. For example, how do conceptualizations of temperament traits such as rhythmicity, mood, intensity, persistence or behavioral inhibition map onto the personality factors in early to middle childhood identified by Haverson et al (2003) and Shiner and Caspi (2003)? How stable or predictive are these identified traits assessed in early to middle childhood of personality traits later in adulthood? Recent research by DeFruyt and colleagues (2006) is beginning to support the notion of personality continuity from childhood to adolescence. Additional future directions include examining whether specific identified traits from early to middle childhood using this approach lead to increased risk for psychopathology. Finally, does the risk imposed by certain traits from childhood result from similar underlying processes identified both earlier and later in life?

Models for Conceptualizing links between Personality and Psychopathology

There is a vast amount of literature documenting links between personality traits and psychopathology. Previous work in this area has been primarily correlational and has attempted to document the strength of such associations. Much less research, however, has focused on understanding how and why these associations come to exist, which are questions central to a developmental psychopathology perspective. There are several models for conceptualizing links between personality and the development of psychopathology, however two models stand out as potentially being the most consistent with a developmental psychopathology approach: the spectrum model and the vulnerability-predisposition model. Each model addresses slightly different facets of the link between personality and psychopathology.

The spectrum model postulates that disorders are not discrete, qualitatively different taxon, but rather represent the extreme endpoints of continuously distributed personality dimensions (Widiger & Clark, 2000). Recent research on the links between normal personality dimensions and abnormal personality disorders supports this model (Costa & Widiger, 2002). A study by Van Leeuwen and colleagues (2007) further extended support for the spectrum model with their findings that suggested that personality, parenting, and personality-parenting interactions all predicted child behavior problems in both clinic referred and non-referred samples, showing differences in the *strength* of the relationships for referred and no-referred groups, but not in the *kind* of relationships. Consistent with the developmental psychopathology approach, these results clearly indicate that a dimensional model of psychopathology may be most appropriate when conceptualizing childhood psychopathology.

The vulnerability-predisposition model purports that certain personality traits may predispose an individual to developing certain types of psychopathology (Tackett & Kreuger, 2005). Ample evidence supports this model as well. For example, individuals with life-course persistent delinquency demonstrate personality traits such as greater negativity in childhood and greater disinhibition in adolescence (Moffitt, Caspi, Dickson, Silva & Stanton, 1996). The vulnerability-predisposition model does not, however, encompass the role of stress and the environment, nor how individuals shape and interact with their own environments, which may place them at further risk for (or protect them from) psychopathology. From a transactional developmental psychopathology perspective, it would be necessary to consider how children's early personality traits may predispose them to more stressful life events or more negative interpersonal interactions, compared to children without such traits and how these events and interactions in turn affect children's development. Thus, a key determinant of whether a particular trait or temperament will lead to psychopathology may be parental acceptance of the child's individuality (Millon & Davis, 1995). Parents who can accept their child's temperament and adapt their own parenting accordingly can mitigate potentially negative consequences, whereas parents who experience repeated frustration in interactions with their child and his or her disposition are likely to create a worsening of the child's adjustment.

In all likelihood, more than one model may explain a given individual with psychopathology (Millon & Davis, 1996). Considered together, both models can be used in conjunction with a developmental psychopathology perspective to aid our understanding of links between personality and psychopathology to comprehensively conceptualize psychopathology. A presentation of more specific examples how personality traits may serve as risk or protective factors for psychopathology follows in section below.

Personality Traits as Risk Factors for Psychopathology

Determining which personality traits serve as risk factors for psychopathology is an important first step in the research. One of the most prevalent areas of study within the personality trait-psychopathology link has focused on antisocial and aggressive behaviors. Several dimensions of temperament have been examined as vulnerabilities for the emergence of behavioral disorders, including negative emotionality (or neuroticism), prosociality (or agreeableness), impulsivity, and “difficult” or “resistant” temperament patterns. Negative emotionality, which is defined as frequently experiencing intense, negative emotions with little provocation, is positively correlated with a wide range of antisocial behaviors in adults (e.g. Moffitt et al., 2001). It is associated with many child conduct problems as well (see Hankin, Abela, Auerbach, McWhinnie & Skitch, 2005 for a review). Prosociality, defined as demonstrating empathy and concern for others, also has links with psychopathology. Children who exhibit behavioral problems tend to be lower in prosocialty and low levels of this trait can predict criminal behavior well into adulthood (Hankin et al., 2005). Impulsivity, defined as a lowered ability to inhibit ones behaviors and emotions, predicts increased antisocial behavior in childhood and adolescence, even when assessed at only 3 years of age (for a review see Tacket & Krueger, 2005). Levels of impulsivity and negative emotionality can even differentially predict adolescent-limited versus life-course persistent delinquency; individuals on the life-course persistent pathway have higher levels of disinhibition and negative emotionality in childhood than do children on the adolescent only pathway (Moffitt, Caspi, Dickson, Silva, & Stanto, 1996). Chess and Thomas (1984) assessed temperament in infants who were followed longitudinally into adulthood and found that of all the temperament types studied (easy, normal, slow-to-warm-up and difficult) only *"difficult"* infants had an increased risk for psychopathology in adulthood (Chess & Thomas, 1990). Furthermore, these early temperamental traits are much more likely to elicit negative reactions from caregivers and parent frustration from these negative daily interactions further solidify the child’s inborn tendencies.

Temperament and personality traits are also predictive of anxiety and mood disorders through out development as well, albeit somewhat different traits are implicated for internalizing disorders than for antisocial and aggressive disorders. Dimensions of temperament most important for the prediction of internalizing disorders include behavioral inhibition and negative emotionality. Behavioral inhibition, defined as shy-withdrawn and fearful behavior, (Kagan, 1998) is particularly implicated in the etiology of anxiety disorders. Behavioral inhibition is best conceptualized as a combination of low extraversion and high neuroticism (Tackett and Kreuger, 2005) and has biological markers such as an abnormally high heart rate (Kagan & Snidman, 1995). Measured as early as toddlerhood and early childhood, behavioral inhibition is predictive of anxiety disorders through childhood (e.g. Caspi et al., 1995) and adolescence (Schwartz, Snidman & Kagan, 1999). Negative emotionality is linked with both anxiety and depression throughout childhood and adolescence; children and adolescents who are depressed are significantly more likely to have negative emotionality (Anthony, Lonigan, Hooe, & Phillips, 2002; Clark, Watson & Mineka,

1994; Watson, Gamez, & Simms). A recent prospective study embodying the developmental psychopathology transactional nature of disorders found that initial levels of neuroticism predicted the occurrence of stressors in the future, and these stressors helped to explain the prospective link between earlier neuroticism and depressive symptoms (Lakdawalla & Hankin, 2003).

Personality Disorders

Personality disorders are an area within psychopathology that may especially benefit from the application of developmental psychopathology to their understanding. Although the Diagnostic and Statistical Manual of Mental Disorders, fourth edition, text revision (DSM-IV-TR; American Psychiatric Association, 2000) considers personality disorders to be discrete entities that are distinctly different from each other and from normal personality functioning, there is a clear continuum and hierarchy from temperament to personality traits to personality disorders (Rutter, 1987). As described earlier, temperament consists of inborn predispositions which affect cognition, affect, and behavior. Personality traits are enduring dispositions reflecting a combination of temperament and experience, and their interactions over time. Personality disorders refer to pervasive, rigid and dysfunctional personality trait profiles (Paris, 2007). Thus, temperament provides the foundation for normal and abnormal (i.e. personality disorders) personality development, indicating they may share common underlying personality traits.

Although there may be certain temperament traits that may predispose children to later developing psychopathology, most children even with such traits do not develop disorders (for reviews see Clarke & Clarke, 2003; Merviede, De Clercq, De Fruyt, & Van Leeuwen, 2005). Similarly, many children with personality traits falling more within the normal range may also display disordered personality as they face highly adverse circumstances, such as trauma or abuse, throughout their life. Therefore, the importance of considering the person-environment interactions in the development of personality disorders is essential. Borderline personality disorder offers an excellent example for applying such an approach to personality disorders.

Borderline personality disorder (BPD) is a persistent and enduring condition involving a pervasive pattern of dysfunctional cognitive, emotional and behavioral functioning. DSM-IV criteria requires that individuals demonstrate five out of the following nine criteria to be diagnosed with BPD: affective instability; inappropriate, intense anger; chronic feelings of emptiness; recurrent suicidal thoughts or behavior; impulsivity; intense or instable interpersonal relationships; efforts to avoid real or imagined abandonment; identity disturbance; and paranoia or dissociative symptoms (American Psychiatric Association, 2000). Both constitutional and social factors have been identified in the etiology of BPD. Because the DSM-IV-TR discourages diagnosing children and adolescents with personality disorders (which is consistent with notions that stable personality does not emerge until adulthood), much of the research on BPD focuses on adulthood. We will discuss what is known about BPD in adulthood and then discuss how it can be used in conjunction with developmental psychopathology to better understand the development of BPD in children and adolescents.

A number of biological factors are believed to contribute to the emergence of BPD in adulthood. First, there are some genetic underpinnings to BPD, with moderate heritability demonstrated in twin studies (Torgersen et al., 2000). The corollary question is, what exactly is it that is inherited that results in greater risk for BPD? Given that there are also high rates of mood disorders in families of persons diagnosed with BPD (Kendler, Neale, Kessler, Heath, & Eaves, 1993), it is possible there is more of a general risk for mood lability that is inherited. It is also probable that the inherited traits associated with BPD place children at risk for psychopathology in general, rather than at risk for the development of BPD more specifically. Consistent with this possibility is evidence suggesting that impulsivity (Siever, Torgersenn, Gunderson, Livesley, & Kendler, 2002) and affective instability (Torgersen et al., 2000) are two facets of personality that are moderately heritable and may contribute to BPD. Additional work has pointed to disruptions in serotonergic activity and links with BPD (Hansenne et al., 2002). This too is a non-specific risk factor since levels of serotonin are associated with impulsivity in general and as such, links are also found between low serotonin levels and antisocial personality disorder, as well. Finally, Functional magnetic resonance imagery (fMRI) studies demonstrate that people with BPD display greater activation of the amygdala in response to pictures of emotional faces, compared to individuals with mood or anxiety disorders, which may contribute to difficulty in regulating their emotional states (Donegan et al., 2003). It is not clear however, whether these differences found in serotonergic activity and the amygdala are contributors to or consequences of BPD. Furthermore, as previously emphasized, simply inheriting risk factors for BPD does not necessarily connote the development of BPD; the context in which the child develops and interacts with contributes significantly to long-term outcomes.

A number of environmental factors are also believed to place children at greater risk for later developing BPD. Broad risk factors include childhood maltreatment as well as maladaptive parenting as risks for the development of BPD (for review see Johnson, McGeoch, Caskey, Abhary, Sneed, & Bornstein, 2005). Reviews of the literature suggest that individuals who develop BPD are more likely to have a history of childhood physical and or sexual abuse, emotional neglect, physical neglect, supervision neglect, and any form of neglect in general (Johnson et al, 2005). These adverse experiences are non-specific risk factors though, and may contribute to a range of psychopathology in children and adults. Research examining risk factors more specific to BPD has focused primarily on specific forms of impaired parenting and parent-child interactions. Numerous studies have linked problematic parenting and parental bonding with BPD (for an overview see Bradley & Westen, 2005) For example, low parental affection (Johnson et al., 2005); disturbed mother-infant communication, including frightening maternal behavior, asynchrony in maternal emotional responding, and mother-child role reversal (Lyons-Ruth, Yelin, Melnick, & Atwood, 2005); as well as inappropriate maternal withdrawal from the infant (Lyons-Ruth et al., 2005) have all been documented as increasing risk for the development of BPD. Studies assessing theory based parent-child interactions associated with BPD, including object relations and attachment theory have also provided support for the role of the family in BPD. Disturbed object relations may be contributing to the pattern of problematic relationships adults with BPD have, such as difficulty forming well-bounded differentiated representations of other and relationships (Diguer et al., 2004; Leichsenring, 2004). Disturbed parent-child attachment, particularly the disorganized pattern, yields very similar results to studies of object relations. Parents of offspring with BPD are often described as unavailable, frightening or frightened during Adult Attachment Interviews (Solomon, George, & De Jong, 1995).

It is apparent that both biological and environmental contributions need to be considered in the development of BPD. A leading hypothesis, proposed by Linehan (1993), on how these interactions lead to BPD suggests that there is an interaction between biological vulnerability to emotion dysregulation, as demonstrated by high sensitivity and reactivity to painful affect, in addition to a diminished ability to return to a normal emotional baseline after arousal, and a highly invalidation environment. Linehan (1993) characterizes invalidating environments as those with caregivers who: (a) are erratic or inappropriate in response to private emotional experiences; (b) are insensitive to other's emotions; (c) tend to overreact or underreact to emotional events; (d) prefer rigid control over negative emotions; and (e) trivialize emotional pain. Thus, these children may be born with an impaired biological ability to regulate their own emotions and impulsivity – the very behaviors which may elicit harsh treatment by their caregivers. This emotional instability then interacts with a highly negative environment. Being continually exposed to harsh, inappropriate parenting, combined with not being taught to regulate their emotions and behavior, and experiencing abnormal bonding with their caregivers may be the elements that coalesce into BPD in adulthood. Ultimately it results in inability to label and modulate emotions, tolerate or manage emotional distress and trust one's own emotional experiences as valid.

An obvious gap in the literature is direct examinations of the interaction between genetic and environmental risk factors in the etiology of BPD. No studies examining this exist to date. Studies in areas related to BPD suggest that early life stress modifies brain circuits implicated in stress regulation, resulting in a priming effect that interacts with genetic vulnerabilities to increase risk for later psychological disturbance (Heim, Meinlschmidt, & Nemeroff, 2003). Considering BPD from a developmental psychopathology approach, yields other important directions for future research. Examining high risk infants with different profiles of biological vulnerabilities through adulthood to see which pathways of development emerge for which children under which environmental circumstances will help elucidate how factors converge to create different personality disorders or other psychopathology. Additionally, specifically delineating how children can overcome these inherited vulnerabilities and adverse circumstances to develop along a more normal pathway is essential.

Resilience

The developmental psychopathology approach emphasizes the need to understand both normal and abnormal behavior together, and risk and resilience. The previous sections of this paper focused primarily on the abnormal and risk end of the spectrum. We will now turn to a discussion of resilience and how this construct informs and is informed by risk, normal and abnormal behavior. Definitions and operationalization of resilience have varied greatly across theorists and researchers. Resilience has typically referred to the ability of children to function well in the face of adversity.

Cutting edge conceptualizations for resilience refer to the dynamic processes of psychological functioning that foster increased positive and diminished negative outcomes in the face of adversity, both presently and in the future (Cummings, Davies & Campbell, 2000). Resilience subsumes both risk, which is a condition carrying high odds for maladjustment, and positive adaptation, which is adaptation which is substantially better than what would be expected give the adverse high risk circumstances one is exposed to (Luthar, 2006). Positive adaptation is often manifested as social competence or competence/success in meeting other developmentally salient tasks (Masten, Burt & Coatsworth, 2006).

Previously, resilience was assumed to be homogenous and either present or absent. More recent conceptualizations have acknowledged that risk and resilience are not all-or-none phenomena and are heterogeneous. Whereas assessing risk may involve one or more adverse circumstances, competence necessarily must be defined across multiple domains and contexts to avoid constricted and misleading pictures of success in the context of adversity. For example, children may demonstrate strong behavioral resilience (e.g. demonstrating appropriate conduct or low aggressiveness), but low cognitive resilience (e.g. low intelligence) or vice versa (Kim-Cohen, Moffitt, Caspi, & Taylor, 2004). Additionally, children may display competence in some contexts or time points, but not others. For example, studies on at-risk inner city children found that children experiencing high stress who demonstrated behavioral competence at one point in development were highly vulnerable to emotional distress over time (Luthar, Doernberger, & Zigler, 1993). It is important to emphasize that resilience does not necessarily imply competence at a level achieved by those not facing adversity, but rather in some situations may be better conceptualized as functioning that is "better than expected" (Luthar, 2006, p. 743).

Central to understanding resilience in child development, is identifying vulnerability and protective factors that may moderate or mediate associations with psychopathology or normality (Masten, 2001). Risk and resilience or vulnerability and protective factors are mutually defining and informing in charting processes affecting children's development. For example, examining how and why protective factors buffer risk for resilient children from families with a depressed parent is just as informative as looking at risk factors leading to psychopathology. Vulnerability factors exacerbate the negative risk conditions to which one is exposed. For example, children with low intelligence are more vulnerable to negative community influences compared with those with higher intelligence (Masten, 2001). Whereas protective factors, on the other hand, are factors that modify effects of risk in a positive direction. For example, having a positive relationship with at least one adult helps to enhance positive adaptation for those children exposed to significant adversity (Masten, 2006).

Protective factors are not restricted to positive, pleasant factors; they may, in fact, actually be stressful or adverse. Challenge models purport that small amounts of adversity may have "Steeling effects" – similar to immunizations – that over time enhance coping and help to inoculate children against future adversity. For example, children of divorce (Hetherington & Kelly, 2002) may learn particularly adaptive interpersonal skills (e.g. empathy, sensitivity) and gain increased maturity as a result of their exposure to adverse divorce processes and the extra responsibilities placed on them.

A review of research on resilience over the past 25 years has identified remarkably consistent results pointing to qualities of the child and context that are associated with better psychological functioning following adversity (Masten & Coatsworth, 1998). Results of the review indicated a protective triad of child, family and extrafamilial characteristics that contribute to resilience. Child characteristics associated with resilient functioning were high intelligence, having an easygoing disposition, self-efficacy and confidence, high self esteem, talent, and faith. Family characteristics associated with resilience included having a close caregiver-child relationship, authoritative parenting style, socioeconomic advantages, and connections to extended family members. Finally, characteristics of extrafamilial contexts associated with resilience were having bonds and receiving support from prosocial adults outside of the family, being connected to prosocial organizations, and attending effective schools.

Thus, it is equally important to examine not just the risk factors and their underlying processes that contribute to children's abnormal development over time, but to also consider the underlying protective processes that contribute to resilience over time, rather than merely documenting a factor's positive association with adaptation.

FUTURE DIRECTIONS

The developmental psychopathology approach provides many promising avenues for future research in both normal and abnormal development of personality. Much of previous work in the field has focused on identifying risk and protective factors and the processes underlying them. Application of the knowledge of these processes to empirically testable interventions for children in specific adverse conditions is an important next step. Luthar (2006, p. 782) has put forth broad guidelines for future applied research in the field. She has recommended that researchers focus most intensively on risk factors with high "promotive potential," defined as having the following characteristics:

1. Conceptually highly *salient* in the context of that particular high-risk setting;
2. Relatively *malleable*, or responsive to environmental interventions;
3. *proximal* to the individual rather than distal;
4. *enduring* for long periods in the individual's life; and
5. *generative* of the assets, catalyzing or setting into motion other strengths, and mitigating vulnerability.

The developmental psychopathology perspective is a complex, comprehensive model of development which can provide a more accurate representation of children's personality development. Given its complex nature, this approach necessarily prescribes microscopic analysis of multiple levels of functioning, in multiple domains, in multiple contexts over time. Integrating these microanalyses of functioning into more macroscopic models that reveal the broader picture of functioning remains an important future goal (Cummings, Braungart-Rieker, & Du Rocher Schudlich, 2003). Although the field of developmental psychopathology has well embraced and empirically tested ways in which normal development can inform understanding of abnormal development, much less research has been done examining how abnormal development can inform our understanding of normal development.

IV. RECOMMENDATIONS FOR ASSESSMENT: A MULTIDIMENSIONAL, MULTICONTEXTUAL, MULTIMETHOD, DEVELOPMENTAL PSYCHOPATHOLOGY APPROACH

From a developmental pathology perspective, it is recognized that the extension of adult psychopathology testing methods and theories are not accurate in assessing children and adolescents. As such, assessment practices have been able to step away from such exploratory testing methods that mimic the current trend of prescribing adult psychotropics to children for "off label" use. Recently, more accurate models of human and personality development processes are being recognized. The changing and developing child is seen as just one part of a transactional counterpart within his or her environment. Therefore, not only are multiple levels of child characteristics of interest, but also assessment of the various environmental contexts and interpersonal influences need to be considered as key components for diagnosis and treatment planning (Carter, Marakovitz, & Sparrow, 2006). There are few existing guidelines in clinical settings that can be used for systematically integrating information that spans multiple domains of functioning, multiple informants and multiple methods. Using a developmental psychopathology approach to guide comprehensive assessments of emotional and personality development in children is a natural step given its interdisciplinary nature, integrating, biological, psychological, social, and cultural processes over time. Carter and colleagues (2006) present guidelines and recommendations for such an approach. Using a developmental psychopathology approach offers a three-dimensional perspective to comprehensive assessments: breadth, by examining multiple individual and contextual domains; depth, by highlighting greater in-depth focus on stage-salient domains and contextual influences, including both adaptive and maladaptive features of each; and time, by recognizing developmental continuities and discontinuities over time and the need for continued prospective assessment. As such, the recommendations for assessment from this perspective will incorporate a multidimensional, multilevel, dynamic approach.

A multidimensional assessment approach is essential because no single score in a single area can comprehensively provide the full picture of a child's functioning. As discussed previously, children may function well in some domains, but not others, and to not address some domains may provide and inaccurate picture. For example, a child who intervenes in her parents' conflict by offering to help, may appear behaviorally to be well adjusted and mature, but broader exploration of her reactions may reveal that emotionally and cognitively she is distressed and physically she is over-aroused; her mediating behavior is a maladaptive attempt to regulate herself and her family's problem. Pertinent domains recommended by Carter and colleagues (2006) include cognitive, language, academic skills and achievements, physical skills, social development, emotional development, biological functioning, genetics, and neurobioogical processes. Historically these domains have been considered individually, but it is important to keep in mind that these domains are all in fact dynamic and interdependent, influencing each other concurrently and over time. Furthermore, assessing both strengths and weaknesses and adaptive and maladaptive functioning is essential within each of these areas.

Consideration of child functioning in multiple contexts entails assessing children in the multiple nested contexts with which they interact (Bronfrenbrenner, 1986). Generally, multiple nested contexts are viewed as a series of concentric circles, with the child in the innermost circle, and proximal influences such as immediate family, placed in the circles immediately surrounding the child, with more distal influences, such as culture and institutions placed in the outermost circles. Contexts in which to assess children should include immediate family, extended family, peer and friend contexts, school settings, daycare or other caregiving contexts, parents' work and social environments, the family's neighborhood, and political and cultural contexts. Similar to the multidimensional components, the multiple domains also need to be considered as dynamic, in terms of their interplay and influences on one other. For example, excessive stress in the parent's work environment, combined with a lack of community resources in the neighborhood may lead to poor parenting practices, which combined with a poor school environment may multiply the negative effects on the child. Furthermore, a child may display different patterns of behaviors in different contexts, thus requiring multiple informants from each context to ensure accurate description. Culture plays an important role in terms of how a child with given difficulties is viewed and supported or not, and is directly relevant to the appropriateness of chose assessment measures for the child.

Methods for Assessment

Next we present a discussion of specific methods for assessment of child emotional and personality functioning. Once the appropriate dimensions and contexts for assessment have been chosen, selecting appropriate methods for assessing functioning is necessary. Following a developmental psychopathology approach, a multi-method approach is preferred since no one method or measure offers the ultimate truth of a child's functioning. Each methodology has its own strengths, limitations and biases and it is only with the combination of methods that a comprehensive picture arises. Furthermore employing a multi-reporter approach is necessary as different informants may have different access to different samples of behavior. Use of multiple reporters also helps alleviate single-reporter bias. The contributions, strengths, and weaknesses of different assessment methods are briefly discussed below.

Questionnaires

Questionnaires offer an easy, quick, and relatively inexpensive option for assessment. They have the benefit of being standardized, most are reliable, and scores resulting from them can be compared to norms of various populations. There remains the concern of potential reporter bias with the use of questionnaires, thus requiring the use of multiple reporters to detect and response style biases that may be present. In particular, when assessing children through the use of questionnaires, it is important to gather information from the children themselves, their primary caregivers, teachers, and other important people in their lives.

Child Report

Until recently, it was believed that children lacked the reading comprehension needed to accurately report their feelings and behaviors through self-report measures (Kamphaus & Frick, 1996). The use of these measures has only just begun to be accepted and used. Using child self reports can be a bit paradoxical. While children are themselves in an advantaged position to report their experiences, feelings, and appraisals, a complete understanding from self-reports can be limited due to children's cognitive, emotional, and language abilities. Consequently, when child self reports are being used, it is crucial to consider both the child's intellectual functioning and developmental level (Peery & Reynolds, 1993). Specifically with reference to behavior related to various developmental levels, a constellation of stress reactions for toddlers may signal normal functioning, yet be signs of poor development or behavior problems in older children. Continuous and stepwise theoretical models (e.g. Piagetian vs. Eriksonian models) also need to be considered in properly structuring and interpreting test results, as the framework within a model will influence the final outcomes and meaning of assessment results. As the use of child self-reporting has grown, a number of omnibus personality inventories have been created and are now available.

While child self-report personality assessment may not yet be up to par with IQ and achievement testing, these measures have improved over the last decade (Kamphaus & Frick, 1996). However, reliability of assessment subscales can often be low and the challenge creating clear assessment norms can be limiting in the use in making diagnosis decisions. Child personality self-report measures can pose a problem for clinicians because they cannot assume that they provide reliable information in determining their conclusions about the child's behavior. Consequently, confirmation through parents and teacher reports are generally favored due to their greater accuracy.

Parent Reports

Parent reports are popular in part due to the various problems with child self-reports measures. They cover a wide range of problems that are valuable to assessing the specific areas of child functioning. Wide scale implementation of child reporting measures began with the Personality Inventory for Children (PIC; Wirt, et al., 1984), which has a similar development to the MMPI. Parent reports have the advantage of being concise and cost and time efficient. When conceptualizing child behavior, parents' perspectives are extremely valuable due to the considerable experience and perspectives they have. Additionally, understanding parents' perceptions of their children's behavior is invaluable if one is to address the ways in which parental influence is contributing to the developmental context (Kamphaus & Frick, 1996). Using parents to collect information on child functioning also promotes objectivity and clarity by taking previously vague behavioral reports from parents and converting them into operationally defined characteristics (Witt, Heffer, & Pfeiffer, 1990). The breadth of parent reports can help to ensure a global picture of the child's functioning is captured that interview sessions may miss. Finally, the span of parent rating scales is considerable, including multidomain/multisyndrome/omnibus measures, single-domain/syndrome measures, and specialized trait scales.

Regardless, challenges using parent reports still exist. As with any self-reporting, bias on behalf of the rater is always a concern. However, in certain cases reporter bias may used to its advantage when they may be problematic for child functioning (Kamphaus & Frick, 1996). By examining differences between reporters (observer, mother, father, teacher), parent bias can aid in developing an understanding of a child's family environment and functioning, and the ways parenting perspectives may be contributing to pertinent behavior problems. When choosing questionnaires it is important to select ones which have established reliability and validity and questionnaires designed for multiple cross informants, such as the Achenbach's Child Behavior Checklist (CBCL) or the Behavior Assessment System for Children (BASC), are ideal.

Teacher Report

The amount of time children spend in the school setting gives teacher rating scales considerable significance. Additionally, separate influences from home versus school environments makes teachers the primary informant for child behavior in response to a wider range of environments. Specific demands are placed upon children in school that may not be present in the home (e.g. following instructions and staying seated) (Kamphaus & Frick,

1996). Understanding children's problematic behavior within the school context and grade level demands provides valuable information for assessing problems in their overall adaptation and functioning. Ultimately, teacher reports are essential to comprehensive assessment practices because of the impact child adjustment within the school setting can have on other domains of their life and psychological functioning.

Teacher reports share the same advantages as other self-report measures, being cost efficient, time efficient, clear, and concise. The structured nature of the classroom also makes teach reports useful for collecting information on attention problems and overactivity. As previously mentioned, being a third party reporter adds the advantage of being able to compare for similarities and differences with other reporters for meaningful patterns. While bias may still be present, teachers can offer a more objective perspective through less emotional investment compared to parents.

Some disadvantages may be a limited use in assessing antisocial behaviors or internalizing problems because these behaviors have a chance to be less frequently observed in school settings (Loeber, Green, Lahey, & Stouthamer-Loeber, 1991). Teachers are also unique in that they have experience with a wide range and large number of children. As a result, when teachers assess child functioning they have a broad range of norms to compare with. However, in certain situations these social references may be less than beneficial, for example, when one's frame of reference is guided by working with special populations (Kamphaus & Frick, 1996). Finally, depending on grade level, teacher knowledge and insight into child functioning also varies. When middle and high school teachers only teach children for one class period they are more limited in providing information compared to elementary school teachers.

Projective Assessments

Although projective techniques have a long history of use, their effectiveness is highly disputed. Controversy remains as to whether they offer valuable insight into a child's functioning, or if they should be thrown out for not meeting psychometric standards (e.g. reliability, validity). Some projective tests that are known within assessment include inkblot tests (e.g. Rorschach), thematic storytelling techniques (e.g. Thematic Apperception Test), sentence completion techniques, and drawing techniques (e.g. draw a person). In addition, play interview techniques can also be employed with younger children. For example, the MacArthur Story Stem Battery (Emde, Wolf, & Oppenheim, 2003) uses story stems organized around particular themes, which children complete to reveal functioning in a range of domains (e.g. attachment, family functioning, marital and family conflict, misbehavior, parenting, etc.).

Advantages include their unstructured style, which minimizes demand characteristics and creates flexibility in interpretation. They can be useful for assessing internalized processes such as drives, motivations, and desires which are lacking from observations and rating scales (Kamphaus & Frick, 1996). Such assessment techniques may also be non-threatening to children and help in building rapport.

On the other side, projective tests have questionable reliability and/or validity. These assessments are based heavily on clinician's interpretation and likewise are extremely subjective. Thus, results from these methods need to be considered in conjunction with a wide battery of tests and methods, to see if results are consistent with the broader pattern of functioning. In spite of their significant psychometric limitations, projective techniques continue to be employed as a primary means of assessing children's emotional and personality functioning.

Behavioral Observations

Behavioral observations are highly respected as a source of assessment. That the validity of other forms of assessment is often measured by how well they match up to behavioral observations is evidence for this. Behavior assessments have the advantage of not being influenced by informant perceptions (e.g. teacher or parent). Also, direct observation is more accurate and eliminates much of the bias and interpretive problems associated with rating scales. By directly observing a child's behavior the observer is able to accurately place it within the specific environmental context that may be contributing to the behavior.

At the same time, these methods may be considerably more expensive and time consuming, especially when assessments are done by professionals or involve specialized training. Often gathering information by observation is not as brief as self-reports since short observations are not always effective in capturing the required information. Behavioral observations can also lack normative sample comparisons, and obtaining a sufficient sample of behaviors is challenging (Kamphaus & Frick, 1996).

Observational techniques also fail to capture information about internal cognitions and emotions, and it cannot be taken for granted that children act the same in the presence of observers or observational situations. Observations may become even more challenging as children grow older due to the increased reactivity they show compared to young children (Keller, 1986). Also, while observers can make note of the environmental context surrounding child behavior, assessments may be limited in their generalization to other settings/conditions. For example, when child behavior is influenced by internal influences (child may be having a really good day or a really bad day). Finally, standardized observational assessments are not as readily available compared to rating scales making interpretation a challenge.

Interviews

Structured and Unstructured

Interviews are historically a commonly used procedure in assessment. Due to concern over unreliability of unstructured interviews, more structured forms have recently become more popular. Before this, they were primarily used for research on adult populations rather than assessment.

In structured interviews, answers are systematically scored and there are specific follow-up questions for each answer to preliminary questions. Most structured interviews for assessments are based upon DSM criteria, but the degree of structure varies from interview to interview Less structure allows for more flexibility in adjusting to the specific child, but at the same time, also requires more clinician experience to guide the assessment in the necessary direction, potentially causing reliability to suffer (Hodges & Zeman, 1993). Some interviews focus mainly on the *present* symptomology while others take a more longitudinal perspective by probing into the child's history. Depending on the interviews, responses are coded into categories while others use Likert scales to avoid creating dichotomous classifications in symptoms that exist across a continuum (Kamphaus & Frick, 1996).

Advantages of structured interviews include their approach toward detailed information on behaviors and emotions. Structured interviews provide parameters of the behavior not assessed in rating scales, and provide more detailed information on quantity/duration/onset of behaviors by use of follow up questions. Many take a developmental perspective and seek to determine a timeline of symptoms or behaviors to pinpoint specific diagnosis. Details can further be gleaned through the use of questions assessing the level of impairment caused by specific aspects of a child's functioning.

Like behavior observation, structured interviews can be time consuming and require flexibility in administration time do to differences in the amount of follow up questioning required. The format of many interviews also remains dependent on DSM criteria, thereby losing sensitivity to less severe syndromes/disorders. Additionally, the focus on symptomology in structured interviews can result in overlooked child norms. Reporter bias is again a concern, and obtaining an accurate history of events from children can be a challenging task. While additional interview formats exist for some scales to cross reference child and parent answers, there are few teacher formats to provide additional cross-referencing. This prohibits the use of rater comparison described above in self-reports. Child age differences can also add a challenge, given that test reliability is often lower for children below the age of 9 (Hodges & Zeham, 1993).

Due to the systematic nature of structured interviews, unstructured interviews are often better at building rapport and maintaining the flexibility to address additional issues unforeseen in the structured process. This is certainly related to the fact that unstructured interviews are often considered *relationship-oriented interviews* whereas structured interviews are referred to as *information-oriented interviews*. Indeed, unstructured interviews may leave room to highlight topics that the child feels is most relevant. While the unstructured nature may produce a smaller breadth of information about a child's functioning, the payoff may be in the form of better identifying key issues of relevance. The difference in interview methods may of course be an over simplification, given that many counselors or psychologists may choose an eclectic approach that suits their specific needs for gathering information while simultaneously building rapport to strengthen the counseling relationship.

Family Assessment

As previously described, a multidomain assessment approach is essential, and given the significant impact of the family on children, we will provide a further elaboration of assessing the family context. Parents' own level of adjustment and mental health can be important indicators of potential heritability of disorder and the family climate. For example, depressed or disturbed parents have an extra challenge facing them when providing optimal styles of parenting that require attention, focus, warmth, and responsiveness (Downey & Coyne, 1990). As such, obtaining a complete picture of parent adjustment offers further advantage to understanding the course of children's behavior patterns. Given the strong parent-child psychopathology link, obtaining a comprehensive family history of psychopathology is very useful in diagnosing children and predicting outcomes, especially for affective disorders such as depression and bipolar disorder. For example, a child having one parent diagnosed with bipolar has a fivefold risk of developing bipolar disorder (Hodgins, Faucher, Zarac, & Ellenbogen, 2002) and knowing this background may help to more definitely clarify fuzzy symptom presentations. Potential for child abuse is also a critical family context to assess. Overall, assessing family context helps the clinician to determine the best course of intervention.

Parenting and Parent-Child Relationships

The ways in which family members interact with the child and with each other can be very enlightening regarding the general climate of the family environment. Regarding parenting and parent-child interactions, there are numerous self- and child-report measures that may be appropriate, as well as measures assessing parents' level of stress and satisfaction in their parenting role. Given the importance of a child's attachment security, assessing a child's attachment type and security level may be useful for understanding areas of treatment to target. Furthermore, assessing the nature and quality of parent-child interactions through structured or unstructured behavioral observations can reveal level of parental warmth, support, hostility, disciplinary techniques and appropriateness, problems solving strategies and effectiveness and conflict levels.

Marital Conflict

The links between marital conflict and children developing behavior and emotional problems has been very clear. Conceptualization of the source of marital influences has made much headway and has increased in usefulness for assessment purposes. Marital dissatisfaction and conflict are currently identified as the main sources of child problems. The display of aggression and dysfunctional behavior models problematic display patterns for children. Furthermore, while child problem behaviors are elevated in children from divorced or separated homes, research has pointed towards the history and/or presence of disruptive conflict as the actual source contributing to child adjustment problems (e.g. Emery, 1982). As such, details beyond simple categorizations such as parental marital status are necessary to address the source of harmful influences in the child's home environment. Assessment methods of marital conflict can be a problem. While self report measures are the most widespread method, they are fraught with reporter bias, social desirability biases, and recall problems. Behavioral observations and coding of marital interactions and discussions has also been successful in identifying relationships exhibiting higher or lower ranges of conflict, but has the same limitations as other observational techniques.

In sum, uncovering the pertinent information causing, supporting, or likely to lead to dysfunctional child behavior is a fine art. As a more complete, albeit complex, understanding of troubling etiologies has been formed, it has become clear that the best diagnosis or intervention plans will be pieced together by a tapestry of assessment types, methods, and dimensions. By understanding the advantage to this approach, practitioners can ensure they are working towards the most complete solution to those events causing hardship for both children and their parents. Likewise, with this goal in mind, efforts in the pursuit of treatment can focus on the strength of using these measures together, rather than the possible weakness of using them apart.

Conclusion

This chapter highlights the multitude of emerging directions in research concerning the effects of both internal (e.g. child characteristics) and external (e.g. family environment) influences on the development of emotions and personality in children and adolescents. It is evident from our review that the comprehensive approach that the developmental psychopathology perspective offers to research and assessment on personality development in children is crucial to further our understanding of these complex processes. We highlighted promising avenues for future research in both normal and abnormal development of personality, including further examination of how abnormal emotional and personality development can inform our understanding of normal development in these domains. Application of our knowledge to empirically testable interventions for children in specific adverse conditions is another important next step. Prospects for future process-oriented approaches to research in emotional and personality development and assessment hold significant promise in further elucidating our understanding of the complex interactive processes underlying children's development.

References

Ainsworth, M. D. S., Blehar, M., Waters, E., & Wall, S. (1978). *Patterns of attachment.* Hillsdale, NJ: Erlbaum.

Aldwin, C. M. (2007). *Stress, Coping, and Development: An Integrative Perspective* (2nd ed.). New York: Guilford, 2007.

Aldwin, C. M., Greenberger, E. (1987). Cultural differences in the predictors of depression. *American Journal of Community Psychology, 15,*789-813.

Allen, J. P., Porter, M., McFarland, C., McElhaney, K. B., & Marsh, P. (2007). The relation of attachment security to adolescents' paternal and peer relationships, depression, and externalizing behavior. *Child Development, 78,* 1222-1239.

American Psychiatric Association (2000). *Diagnostic and statistical manual of mental disorders DSM-IV-TR (Text Revision).* Washington, D.C.: Author.

Anthony, J.L., Lonigan, C.J., Hooe, E.S., & Phillips, B.M. (2002). An affect-based, hierarchical model of temperament and its relations with internalizing symptomatology. *Journal of Clinical Child and Adolescent Psychology, 31,* 480-490.

Arsenian, J. & Arsenian, J. M. (1948). Tough and easy cultures: A conceptual analysis. *Psychiatry, 11,* 377-385.

Baumrind, D. (1967). Child care practices anteceding three patterns of preschool behavior. *Genetic Psychology Monographs, 75,* 43-88.

Baumrind, D. (1971). Current patterns of parental authority. *Developmental Psychology Monograph, 41,* (1, Pt.2), 101-103.

Baumrind, D. (1991). The influence of parenting style on adolescent competence and substance use. *Journal of Early Adolescence, 11, 56-95.*

Belsky, J., Youngblade, L., Rovine, M., & Volling, B. (1991). Patterns of marital change and parent-child interaction. *Journal of Marriage and the Family, 53,* 487-498.

Bornstein, M. H., Putnick, D. L., Heslington, M., Gini, M., Suwalsky, J. T. D., Venuti, P., et al. (2008). Mother-child emotional availability in ecological perspective: three countries, two regions, two genders. *Developmental Psychology, 44,* 666-680.

Bowlby, J. (1969). *Attachment and loss: Vol. 1. Attachment.* New York: Basic Books.

Brofenbrenner, U. (1979). *The ecology of human development: Experiments by nature and design.* Cambridge, MA: Harvard University Press.

Bronfrenbrenner, U. (1986). Ecology of the family as a context for human development: Research perspectives. *Developmental Psychology, 22,* 723-742.

Bradley, R. & Westen, D. (2005). The psychodynamics of borderline personality disorder: A view from developmental psychopathology. *Development and Psychopathology, 17*(4), 927-957.

Bretherton, I., Fritz, J., Zahn-Waxler, C., & Ridgeway, D. (1986). Learning to talk about emotions: A functionalist perspective. *Child Development, 57,* 529-548.

Brody, G. H., Stoneman, Z. & Burke, M. (1987). Child temperaments, maternal differential behavior.

Brook, J. S., Zheng, L., Whiteman, M., & Brook, D. W. (2001). Aggression in toddlers: Associations with parenting and martial relations. *The Journal of Genetic Psychology, 162,* 228-241.

Calkins, S. D. & Fox, N. A. (2002). Self-regulatory processes in early personality development: A multilevel approach to the study of childhood social withdrawal and aggression. *Development and Psychopathology, 14,* 477-498.

Carter, A.S., Marakovitz, S.E. & Sparrow, S.S. (2006). Comprehensive psychological assessment: A developmental psychopathology approach for clinical and applied research. In D. Cicchetti & D.J. Cohen (Eds.), *Developmental psychopathology, Vol 1: Theory and Method (2nd ed.).* (pp. 181-210). Hoboken, NJ, US: John Wiley & Sons Inc.

Caspi, A., Harrington,H., Milne, B., Amell, J.W., Theodore, R.F., & Moffitt, T.E. (2003). Children's behavioral styles at age 3 are linked to their adult personality taits at age 26. *Journal of Personality, 71,* 595-513.

Caspi, A., Henry, B., McGee, R.O., Moffitt, T.E., & Silva, P.A. (1995). Temperamental origins of child and adolescent behavior problems: From age three to fifteen. *Child Development, 66,* 55-68.

Caspi, A., McClay, J., Moffitt, T.E., Mill, J., Martin, J., Craig, I.W. et al. (2002). Role of genotype in the cycle of violence in maltreated children. *Science, 297,* 851-854.

Caspi, A., Roberts, B. W. & Shiner, R. L. (2005) Personality development: Stability and change. *Annual Review of Psychology, 56,* 453-484.

Cassidy, J. (1994). Emotion regulation: Influences of attachment relationships. In N. Fox (Ed.), The development of emotion regulation: Biological and behavioral considerations. *Monographs of the Society for Research in Child Development, 59,* 228-249.

Chess, S. & Thomas, A. (1984). *Origins and evolution of behavior disorders: From Infancy to adult life.* New York: Brunner/Mazel.

Chess, S. & Thomas, A. (1990). The New York Longitudinal Study: The young adult periods. *Canadian Journal of Psychiatry, 35,* 557-561.

Cicchetti, D. (2006). Developmental psychopathology, Vol 1: Theory and method (2nd ed.). (pp. 1-23). Hoboken, NJ, US: John Wiley & Sons Inc. xvii, 1084 pp.

Cicchetti , D., & Cohen, D.J. (1995). Perspectives on developmental psychopathology. In D. Cicchetti & D.J. Cohn (Eds.), *Developmental psychopathology: Vol 1. Theory and methods* (pp. 3-22). New York: Wiley

Cicchetti, D., & Sroufe, L.A. (2000). The past as a prologue to the future: The times, they've been a changin'. *Development and Psychopathology, 12*, 255-264.

Clark, L.A., Watson, D. & Mineka, S. (1994). Temperament, personality, and the mood and anxiety disorders. *Journal of Abnormal Psychology. Special Issue: Personality and psychopathology, 103*, (1), 103-116.

Clarke, A. & Clarke, A. (2003). Human Resilience: A fifty year quest. Philadelphia: Jessica Kingsley.

Colman, R. A., Hardy. S. A., Albert, M., Raffaelli, M., & Crockett, L. (2006). Early predictors of self-regulation in middle childhood. *Infant and Child Development, 15,* 421-437.

Coon, H. M. & Kemmelmeier, M. (2001). Cultural orientations in the United States: (Re)examining differences among ethnic groups. *Journal of Cross-Cultural Psychology, 32,* 348-364.

Corcoran, K. O. & Mallinckrodt, B. (2000). Adult attachment, self-efficacy, perspective taking, and conflict resolution. *Journal of Counseling and Development, 78,* 473-483.

Costa, P.T. & Widiger, T.A. (2002). Personality disorders and the five-factor model of personality (2nd ed.). (pp. 3-14). Washington, DC, US: American Psychological Association.

Costello, E.J., Foley, D.L. & Angold, A. (2006). 10-year research update review: The epidemiology of child and adolescent psychiatric disorders: II. developmental epidemiology. *Journal of the American Academy of Child & Adolescent Psychiatry, 4,* 8-25.

Cox, M. J. & Owen, M. T. (1993). *Marital conflict and conflict negotiation: Effects on infant-mother and infant-father relationships.* In M. Cox & J. Brooks-Gunn (Chairs), *Conflict in families: Causes and consequences.* Symposium conducted at the meeting of the Society for Research in Child Development, New Orleans, LA.

Cox, M. J., Owen, M. T., Lewis, J. M., & Henderson, V. K. (1989). Marriage, adult adjustment, and early parenting. *Child Development, 60,* 1015-1024.

Creasey, G. & Hesson-McInnis, M. (2001). Affective responses, cognitive appraisals, and conflict tactics in late adolescent romantic relationships: Associations with attachment orientations. *Journal of Counseling Psychology, 48,* 85-96.

Cummings, E. M. (1994). Marital conflict and children's functioning. *Social Development, 3,* 16-36.

Cummings, E.M., Braungart-Rieker, J., & Du Rocher Schudlich, T. (2003). Emotion and personality development in childhood. In R.M. Lerner, M.A. Easterbrooks, & J. Mistry (Eds.), *Comprehensive Handbook of Psychology: Volume 6: Developmental Psychology,* (pp. 211-239). New York: John Wiley & Sons, Inc.

Cummings, E. M. & Davies, P. T. (2002). Effects of marital conflict on children: Recent advances and emerging themes in process-oriented research. *Journal of Child Psychology and Psychiatry, 43,* 31-63.

Cummings, E. M. & Davies, P. T. (1994). *Children and marital conflict: The impact of family dispute and resolution.* New York: Guilford Press.

Cummings, E. M., Davies, P. T., & Campbell, S. B. (2000). *Developmental psychopathology and family processes: Theory, research, and clinical implications.* New York: Guilford Press.

Cummings, E. M., Goeke-Morey, M. C. & Papp, L. M. (2003). Children's responses to everyday marital conflict tactics in the home. *Child Development, 74,* 1918-1929.

Cummings, E. M., Zahn-Waxler, C., & Radke-Yarrow, M. (1981). Young children's response to expressions of anger and affections by others in the family. *Child Development, 52,* 1274-1282.

Darling, N. & Steinberg, L. (1993). Parenting style as context: An integrative model. *Psychological Bulletin, 113,* 487-496.

Davies, P. T. & Cummings, E. M. (1994). Marital conflict and child adjustment: An emotional security hypothesis. (*Psychological Bulletin, 116,* 387-411.

Davies, P. T. & Cummings, E. M. (1998). Exploring children's emotional security as a mediator of the link between marital relations and child adjustment. *Child Development, 69,* 124-139.

De Fruyt, F., Bartels, M., Van Leeuwen, K.G., De Clercq, B, Decuyper, M., & Mervielde, I. (2006). Five types of personality continuity in childhood and adolescence. *Journal of Personality and Social Psychology, 91*, 538-552.

DeHaan, M., Gunnar, M.R., Tout, K., Hart, J., & Stansbury, K. (1998). Familiar and novel context yield different associations between cortisol and behavior among 2-year old children.

Denham, S. A. (1998). *Emotional development in young children*. New York. NY: Guilford.

Denham, S. A. (2007). Dealing with feelings: How children negotiate the worlds of emotions and social relationships. *Cognition, Brain, Behavior, 11,* 1-48.

Denham, S. A. & Grout, L. (1992). Mothers' emotional expressiveness and coping: Topography and relations with preschoolers' social-emotional competence. *Genetic,Social, and General Psychology Monographs, 118*, 75-101.

Diguer, L., Pelletier, S., Herbert, E., Descoteaux, J., Rousseau, J.P., & Daoust, J.P. (2004). Personality organizations, psychiatric severity, and self and object representations. *Psychoanalytic Psychology, 21*, 259-275.

Donegan, N.H., Sanislow, S.A., Blumberg, H.P., Fulbright, R.K., Lacadie, C., Skudlarski, P., Gore, J.C., Olson, I.R., McGlashan, T.H., & Wexler, B.E. (2003). Amygdala hyperreactivity in borderline personaliy disorder: Implications for emotional dysregulation. *Biological Psychiatry, 54,* 1284-2393.

Downey, G., & Coyne, J.C. (1990). Children of depressed parents: An integrative review. *Psychological Bulletin, 108*, 50-76.

Draghi-Lorenz, R., Reddy, V. & Costall, A. (2001). Rethinking the development of "nonbasic" emotions: A critical review of existing theories. *Developmental Review, 21,* 263-304.

Du Rocher Schudlich, T.D. & Cummings, E.M. (2003). Parental Dysphoria and Children's Internalizing Symptoms: Marital Conflict Styles as Mediators of Risk. *Child Development, 74,* 1663–1681.

Du Rocher Schudlich, T.D., & Cummings, E.M. (2007). Parental Dysphoria, Marital Conflict, and Parenting: Relations with Children's Emotional Security and Adjustment. *Journal of Child Abnormal Psychology*, *35*, 627-639.

Du Rocher Schudlich, T.D., Youngstrom, E.A., Calabrese , J.R., & Findling, R. (in press). The Role of Family Functioning in Bipolar Disorder in Families. *Journal of Child Abnormal Psychology*.

Dunn, J., Slomkowski, C., Beardsall, L., & Rende, R. (1994). Adjustment in middle childhood and early adolescence: Links with earlier and contemporary sibling relationships. *Journal of Child Psychology and Psychiatry, 35,* 491-504.

El-Shiekh, M, Cummings, E. M., & Goetsch, V. L. (1989). Coping with adults' angry behavior: Behavioral, physiological, and verbal responses in preschoolers. *Developmental Psychology, 25,* 490-498.

El-Shiekh, M., & Cummings, E. M. (1992). Perceived control and preschoolers' responses to interadult anger. *International Journal of Behavioral Development, 15,* 207-226.

El-Sheikh, M., Keller, P. S. & Erath, S. A. (2007). Marital conflict and risk for child maladjustment over time: Skin conductance level reactivity as a vulnerability factor. *Journal of Abnormal Child Psychology, 35,* 715-727.

Emde, R.N., Wolf, D.P., & Oppenheim, D. (2003). *Revealing the inner worlds of young children: The MacArthur Story Stem Battery and Parent-Child Narratives.* New York: Oxford University Press.

Emery, R. E. (1982). Interparental conflict and the children of discord and divorce. *Psychological Bulletin, 92,* 310-300.

Emery, R. E. (1989). Family violence. American Psychologist, 44, 321-328.

Fabes, R.A. Eisenberg, N., Karbon, M., & Troyer, D. (1994). The relations of children's emotion regulation to their vicarious emotional responses and comforting behavior.

Foley, D.L. Eaves, Lindon, J. Wormley, B., Silberg, J., Maes, H.H., Kuhn, J., & Riley, B. (2004). Childhood Adversity, Monoamine Oxidase A Genotype, and Risk for Conduct Disorder. *Archives of General Psychiatry, 61,* Jul, 738-744.

Fox, N.A., Calkins, S.D. & Bell, M.A. (1994). Neural plasticity and development in the first two years of life: Evidence from cognitive and socioemotional domains of research. *Development and Psychopathology, 6,* 677-696.

Garner, P. W., Jones, D. C. & Miner, J. L. (1994). Social competence among low-income preschoolers: Emotion socialization practices and social cognitive correlates. *Child Development, 65*, 622-637.

Gerhardt, S. (2004). *Why love matters: How affection shapes a baby's brain.* New York: Routledge.

Goldsmith, H. H., Buss, A. H. & Lemery, K.S. (1997). Toddler and childhood temperament: Expanded content, stronger genetic evidence, new evidence for the importance of environment. *Developmental Psychology, 33,* 891-905.

Goldsmith, H. H., Buss, A. H., Plomin, R., Rothbart, M. K., Thomas, A., Chess, S., et al. (1987). Roundtable: What is temperament? Four approaches. *Child Development, 58,* 505-529.

Gotlib, I.H., & Goodman, S.H. (2002). Children of depressed parents: Mechanisms of risk and implications for treatment. (pp. 3-9). Washington, DC, US: American Psychological Association.

Gottman, J. M. & Katz, L. F. (1989). Effects of marital discord on young children's peer interaction and health. *Developmental Psychology, 18,* 287-293.

Grych, J. H. & Fincham, F. (1990). Marital conflict and children's adjustment: A cognitive-contextual framework. *Psychological Bulletin, 108,* 267-290.

Grych, J. H. & Fincham, F. D. (1993). Children's appraisals of marital conflict: Initial investigations of the cognitive-contextual framework. *Child Development, 64,* 215-230.

Hankin, B.L., Abela, J.R., Auerbach, R.P., McWhinnie, C.M., & Skitch, S.A. (2005). Development of behavioral problems over the life course: A vulnerability and stress perspective. (pp. 385-416). Thousand Oaks, CA, US: Sage Publications, Inc.

Hansenne, M., Pitchot, W., Pinto, E., Reggers, J., Scatamburio, G., Fuchs, S, et al, (2002). 5-HT dysfunction in borderline personality disorder. *Psychological Medicine, 32,* 935-941.

Harold, G. T., Shelton, K. H., Goeke-Morey, M. C., & Cummings, E. M. (2004). Marital conflict, child emotional security about family relationships and child adjustment. *Social Development, 13,* 350-376.

Hastings, P. D., Rubin, K. H. & DeRose, L. (2005). Links among gender, inhibition, and parental socialization in the development of prosocial behavior. *Merrill-Palmer Quarterly, 51,* 467-493.

Hastings, P. D., Sullivan, C., McShane, K. E., Coplan, R. J., Utendale, W. T., & Vyncke, J. D. (2008). Parental socialization, vagal regulation, and preschooler's anxious difficulties: Direct mothers and moderated fathers. *Child Development, 79,* 45-64.

Heim, C., Meinlschmidt, G., & Nemeroff, C.B. (2003). Neurobiology of early-life stress. *Psychiatric Annuals, 33,* 18-26.

Herrera, N. C., Zajonc, R. B., Wieczorkowska, G., & Cichomski, B. (2003). Beliefs about birth rank and their reflection in reality. *Journal of Personality and Social Psychology, 85,* 142-150.

Hetherington, E.M. & Kelly, J. (2002). For better or for worse: Divorce reconsidered. New York: W.W. Norton & Company.

Hodges, K. & Zeman, J. (1993). Interviewing. In T. H. Ollendick & M. Hersen (Eds.), *Handbook of child and adolescent assessment* (pp. 65-81). Needham Heights, MA: Allyn and Bacon.

Hodgins, S., Faucher, B., Zarac, A., & Ellenbogen, M. (2002). Children of parents with bipolar disorder. A population at high risk for major affective disorders. *Child & Adolescent Psychiatric Clinics of North America, 11,* 533-553.

Holden, G. W. & Ritchie, K. L. (1991). Linking extreme marital discord, child rearing, and child behavior problems: Evidence from battered women. *Child Development, 62,* 311-327.

Howes, P. & Markman, J. J. (1989). Marital quality and child functioning: A longitudinal investigation. *Child Development, 60,* 1044-1051.

Isabella, R. & Belsky, J. (1985). Marital change across the transition to parenthood and the security of infant-parent attachment. *Journal of Family Issues, 6,* 505-522.

Izard, C. E. (1992). Basic emotions, relations among emotions, and emotion-cognition relations. *Psychological Review,* 99, 3, 561-565.

Jacob, T. & Johnson, S. L. (1997). Parent-child interaction among depressed fathers and mothers.

Johnson, J.G., McGeoch, P.G., Caskey, V., Abhary, S.G., Sneed, J.R., & Bornstein, R.F. (2005). Development of psychopathology: A vulnerability-stress perspective. (pp. 417-464). Thousand Oaks, CA, US: Sage Publications, Inc. x, 510 pp.

Kagan, J. (1994). Prevention and early intervention: Individual differences as risk factors for the mental health of children: A festschrift for Stella Chess and Alexander Thomas. (pp. 35-41). Philadelphia, PA, US: Brunner/Mazel.

Kagan, J. (1998). *Galen's prophecy.* Boulder, CO: Westview Press.

Kagan, J., Reznick, J.S. & Gibbons, J. (1989). The physiology and psychology of behavioral inhibition. *Child Development, 58,* 1459-1473.

Kagan, J. & Zentner, M. (1996). Early childhood predictors of adult psychopathology. *Harvard Review of Psychiatry, 3,* 341-350.

Kagan, J. & Snidman, N. (1995). *The long shadow of temperament.* Cambridge, MA: Belknap Press/Harvard University Press.

Kamphaus, R. W. & Frick, P. J. (1996). *Clinical assessment of child and adolescent personality and behavior.* Boston: Allyn and Bacon.

Katz, L. F. & Gottman, J. M. (1993). Patterns of marital conflict predict children's internalizing and eternalizing behaviors. *Developmental Psychology, 29,* 940-950.

Keller, H. & Greenfield, P. M. (2000). History & future of development in cross-cultural psychology. *Journal of Cross-Cultural Psychology, 31,* 52-62.

Keller, H. R. (1986). Behavioral observation approaches to personality assessement. In H. M. Knoff (Ed.), *The assessment of child and adolescent personality* (pp. 353-390). New York: Guilford Press.

Kendler, K.S., Neale, M.C., Kessler, R.C., Heath, A.C., & Eaves, L.J. (1993). A test of the equal-environment assumption I twin studies of psychiatric illness. *Behavioral Genetics, 23,* 21-28.

Kennedy, A. E., Rubin, K. H., Hastings, P. D., & Maisel, B. (2004). Longitudinal relations between child vagal tone and parenting behavior: 2 to 4 years. *Developmental Psychobiology, 45,* 10-21.

Kerestes, G. (2006). Birth order and maternal ratings of infant temperament. *Studia Psychologica, 48,* 95-105.

Kerns, K. A., Ambraha, M. M., Schlegelmilch, A., & Morgan, T. A. (2007). Mother-child attachment in later middle childhood: Assessment approaches and associations with mood and emotion regulation. *Attachment & Human Development, 9,* 33-53.

Kim, J.Y., McHale, S. M., Crouter, A. C., & Osgood, D. W. (2007). Longitudinal linkages between sibling relationships and adjustment from middle childhood through adolescence. *Developmental Psychology, 43,* 960-973.

Kim-Cohen, J., Moffitt, T.E., Caspi, A., & Tayor, A. (2004). Genetic and environmental processed in youn children's resilience and vulnerability to socio-economic deprivation. *Child Development, 75,* 651-668.

Kochanska, G. (2001). Emotional development in children with different attachment histories: The first three years. *Child Development, 72,* 474-490.

Komsi, N., Raikkonen, K., Pesonen, A. K., Heinonen, K., Keskivaara, P., Jarvenpaa, A. L., et al. (2006). Continuity of temperament from infancy to middle childhood. *Infant Behavior and Development, 29,* 494-508.

Laible, D. J. & Thompson, R. A. (2002). Mother-child conflict in the toddler years: Lessons in emotion, morality, and relationships. *Child Development, 73,* 1187-1203.

Lakdawalla, Z. & Hankin, B.L. (2003, November). *Personality as a prospective vulnerability to depression: Proposed mechanisms.* Paper presented at the 37th Annual Meeting of the Association for the advancement of Behavior Therapy, Boston.

Lamborn, S. D., Mounts, N. S., Steinberg, L., & Dornbusch, S. M. (1991). Patterns of competence and adjustment among adolescents from authoritative, authoritarian, indulgent, and neglectful families. *Child Development, 62,* 1049-1065.

Lansford, J. E., Deater-Deckard, K., Dodge, K. A., Bates, J. E., & Pettit, G. S. (2004). Ethnic differences in the link between physical discipline and later adolescent externalizing behaviors. *Journal of Child Psychology and Psychiatry, 45,* 801-812.

Lansford, J. E., Chang, L., Dodge, K. A., Malone, P. S., Oburu. P., Palmerus, K., et al. (2005). Physical discipline and children's adjustment: Cultural normativeness as a moderator. *Child Development, 76,* 1234-1246.

Leichsenring, F. (2004). Quality of depressive experiences in borderline personality disorders: Differences between patients with higher levels of personality organization. Bulletin of the *Menninger Clinic, 68*, 9-22.

Lemery, K.S. & Goldsmith, H.H. (2001). Genetic and environmental influences on preschool sibling cooperation and conflict: Associations with difficult temperament and parenting style. *Marriage and Family Review, 33,* 77-99.

Lewis, M. (1993). The emergence of human emotions. In M. Lewis & J. M. Haviland (Eds.), Handbook of emotions (pp. 223-235). New York: Guildford Press.

Lewis, C. E., Siegel, J. M. & Lewis, M. A. (1984). Feeling bad: Exploring sources of distress among pre-adolescent children. *American Journal of Public Health, 74,* 117-122.

Linehan, M.M. (1993). *Cognitive behavioral treatment of borderline personality disorder.* New York: Guilford Press.

Loeber, R., Green, S. M., Lahey, B. B., & Stouthamer-Loeber, M. (1991). Differences and similarities between children, mothers, and teachers as informants on disruptive child behavior. *Journal of Abnormal Child Psychology, 19,* 75-95.

Luthar, S. (2006). Resilience in development: A synthesis of research across five decades, In D. Cicchetti, and D. J. Cohen (Eds.), *Developmental psychopathology: Vol 3. Risk, disorder, and adaptation (2nd ed.)*, (pp. 739-795). Hoboken, NJ, US: John Wiley & Sons Inc.

Luthar, S.S., Doernberger, C.H. & Zigler, E. (1993). Resilience is not a unidimensional construct: Insights from a prospective study of inner-city adolescents. *Development and Psychopathology, 5*, 703-717.

Lyons-Ruth, K., Yellin, C., Melnick, S., & Atwood, G. (2005). Expanding the concept of unresolved mental sates" Hostile/helpless states of mind on the Adult Attachment interview are associated with disrupted mother-infant communication and infant disorganization. *Development and Psychopathology, 17,* 1-23.

Maccoby, E. & Martin, J. (1983). Socialization in contexts of the family: Parent-child interaction. In E. M. Hetherington (ed.), *Handbook of child psychology, Vol, 4. Socialization, personality, and social development*, (4th ed. pp. 1-10). New York, Wiley.

Masten, A. (2001). Ordinary magic: Resilience processes in development. *American Psychologist, 56,* 227-238.

Masten, A.S. (2006). Developmental psychopathology: Pathways to the future. *International Journal of Behavior Development, 30*(1), 47-54.

Masten, A.S., Burt, K.B. & Coatsworth, J.D. (2006). Competence and psychopathology in development, In D. Cicchetti, and D. J. Cohen (Eds.), *Developmental psychopathology: Vol 3. Risk, disorder, and adaptation (2nd ed.)*, (pp. 696-738). Hoboken, NJ, US.: John Wiley & Sons Inc.

Masten, A.S. & Coatsworth, J.D. (1998). The development of competence in favorable and unfavorable environments: Lessons from research on successful children. *American Psychologist, 53,* 205-220.

Mervielde, I., De Clercq, B., De Fruyt, F., & Van Leeuwen, K. (2005). Temperament and personality as broad-spectrum antecedents of psychopathology in childhood and adolescence. *Journal of Personality Disorders, 19*(2), 171-201.

Millon, T., & Davis, R.D. (1995). The development of personality disorders. In D. Cicchetti and D.J. Cohen (Eds.), *Developmental Psychopathology: Vol 2. Risk, Disorder, and Adaptation*. New York: John Wiley & Sons.

Millon, T. & Davis, R.D (1996). *Disorders of personality: DSM-IV and beyond (2nd ed.).* Oxford, England: John Wiley & Sons.

Moffitt, T.E., Caspi, A., Dickson, N., Silva, P., & Stanto, W. (1996). Childhood-onset versus adolescent-onset antisocial conduct problems in males: Natural history from ages 3 to 18 years. *Development and Psychopathology, 8,* 399-424.

Moffitt, T.E, Caspi, A., Rutter, M., & Silva, P., (2001). *Sex differences in antisocial behaviour: Conduct disorder, delinquency, and violence in the Dunedin Longitudinal Study*. Cambridge: Cambridge University Press.

Oppenheim, D., Koren-Karie, N. & Sagi-Schwartz, A. (2007). Emotion dialogues between mothers and children at 4.5 and 7.5 years: Relations with children's attachment at 1 year. *Child Development, 78,* 38-52.

Patterson, G. R., DeBaryshe, B., & Ramsey, E. (1989). A developmental perspective on antisocial behavior. *American Psychologist, 44,* 329-335.

Peterson, J. L., & Zill, N. (1986). Marital disruption, parent-child relationships, and behavior problems in children. *Journal of Marriage and the Family, 48,* 295-307.

Porter, C. L., Wouden-Miller, M., Silva, S. S., & Porter, A. E. (2003). Marital harmony and conflict: Links to infants' emotional regulation and cardiac vagal tone. *Infancy, 4,* 297-307.

Peery, M. L. & Reynolds, C. R. (1993). Developmental theory and concerns in personality and social assessment of young children. In J. L. Culbertson & D. J. Willis (Eds.), *Testing young children: A reference guide for developmental, psychoeducational, and psychosocial assessments* (pp. 12-12). Austin: Pro-ed.

Rice, M. S. & Gaines, S. K. (1992). Measurement of child temperament: Implications for researchers, clinicians, and caregivers. *Children's Health Care, 21,* 177-183.

Rothbart, M.K., & Ahadi, S.A. (1994). Temperament and the development of personality. *Journal of Abnormal Psychology, 103*, 55-66.

Rothbart, M.K., & Bates, J.E. (1998). Temperament. In W. Damo (Series Ed.) & N. Eisenberg (Vol. Ed.), *Handbook of child psychology: Vol.3. Social, emotional and personality development* (5th ed., pp. 105-176). New York: Wiley.

Rubin, K. H., Burgess, K. B., Dwyer, K. M., & Hastings, P. (2003). Predicting preschoolers' externalizing behaviors from toddler temperament, conflict, and maternal negativity. *Developmental Psychology, 39*(1), 164-176.

Rutter, M. (1986). Child psychiatry: Looking thirty years ahead. *Journal of Child Psychology, Psychiatry, and Allied Disciplines, 27,* 803-840.

Rutter, M. (1987). Temperament, personality, and personality disorder. *British Journal of Psychiatry, 150,* 443-458.

Rutter, M. (1990). Psychosocial resilience and protective mechanisms. In J. Rolf, A. Masten, D. Cicchetti, K. Nuechterlein, & S. Weintraub (Eds.), *Risk and protective factors in the development of psychopathology* (pp. 181-214). New York: Cambridge University Press.

Saarni, C. & Buckley, M. (2002). Children's understanding of emotion communication in families. *Marriage & Family Review, 34,* 213-242.

Schwartz, C.E., Snidman, N. & Kagan, J. (1999). Adolescent social anxiety as an outcome of inhibited temperament in childhood. *Journal of the American Academy of Child and Adolescent Psychiatry, 38,* 1008-1015

Selman, R. L., Schorin, M. Z., Stone, C. R., Phelps, E. (1983). A naturalistic study of children's social understanding. *Developmental Psychology, 19,* 82-102.

Shiner, R. & Caspi, A. (2003). Personality differences in childhood and adolescence: Measurement, development, and consequences. *Journal of Child Psychology and Psychiatry, 44*, 2-32.

Siever, L.J., Torgersen, S., Gunderson, J.G., Livesley, W.J., & Kendler, K.S. (2002). The borderline diagnosis: Pt. III. Identifying endophenotypes for genetic studies. *Biological Psychiatry, 51,* 964-968.

Skinner, E. A., & Zimmer-Gemback, M. J. (2007). The development of coping. *The Annual Review of Psychology, 58,* 119-144.

Solomon, J., George, C. & De Jong, A. (1995). Children classified as controlling at age six: Evidence of disorganized representational strategies and aggression at home and at school. *Development and Psychopathology, 7*, 447-463.

Sroufe, L. A. (1996). Emotional development. Cambridge, UK: Cambridge Univ. Press

Sroufe, L.A. (1997). Psychopathology as an outcome of development. *Development and Psychopathology, 9*, 215-268.

Sroufe, L. A., Egeland, B., Carlson, E., & Collins, W. A. (2005) *The Development of the Person: The Minnesota Study of Risk and Adaptation from Birth to Adulthood.* New York: Guilford Publications.

Steinberg, L. (2000, April). *We know some things: Parent-adolescent relations in retrospect and prospect.* Presidential Address, presented at the biennial meeting of the Society for Research on Adolescence, Chicago, IL.

Steinberg, L. (1996). *Beyond the classroom: Why school reform has failed and what parents need to do.* New York: Simon & Schuster.

Steinberg, L., Dornbusch, S. M. & Brown, B. B. (1992). Ethnic differences in adolescent achievement: An ecological perspective. *American Psychologist, 47,* 723-729.

Steinberg, L., Lamborn, S., Darling, N., Mounts, N., & Dornbusch, S. (1994). Over-time changes in adjustment and competence among adolescents from authoritative, authoritarian, indulgent, and neglectful families. *Child Development, 65,* 754-770.

Stoneman, A., Brody, G. H. & Burke, M. (1989). Marital quality, depression, and inconsistent parenting, Relationship with observed mother-child conflict. *American Journal of Orthopsychiatry, 59,* 105-117.

Sturge-Apple, M.L., Davies, P.T. & Cummings, E.M. (2006). Hostility and withdrawal in marital conflict: Effects on parental emotional unavailability and inconsistent discipline. *Journal of Family Psychology, 20,* 227-238.

Tackett, J.L. & Krueger, R.F.(2005). Development of psychopathology: A vulnerability-stress perspective. (pp. 199-214). Thousand Oaks, CA, US: Sage Publications, Inc. x, 510 pp.

Thomas, A. & Chess, S. (1985). The behavioral study of temperament. (pp. 213-225). New York, NY, US: Hemisphere Publishing Corp./Harper & Row Publishers. xiv, 259 pp.

Torgersen, S., lygren, S, Oien, P.A., Skre, I., Onstad, S., Edvardsen, J. et al. (2000). A twin study of personality disorders. *Comprehensive Psychiatry, 41,* 416-425.

Tucker, C. J., McHale, S. M. & Crouter, A. C. (2008). Links between older and younger adolescent siblings' adjustment: The moderating role of shared activities. *International Journal of Behavioral Development, 32*, 152-160.

Van Leeuwen, K.G., Mervielde, I., De Clerco, B.J., & DeFruyt, F. (2007). Extending the spectrum idea: Child personality, parenting and psychopathology. *European Journal of Personality, 21*(1), 63-89.

von Salisch, M. (2001). Children's emotional development: Challenges in their relationships to parents, peers, and friends. *International Journal of Behavioral Development, 25,* 310-319.

Volling, B. L. & Belsky, J. (1992). The contribution of mother-child and father-child relationships to the quality of sibling interaction: A longitudinal study. *Child Development, 63,* 1209-1222.

Watson, D., Gamez, W. & Simms, L.J. (2005), Basic dimensions of temperament and their relation to anxiety and depression: A symptom-based perspective. *Journal of Research in Personality, 39,* 46-66.

Watson, D., & Hubbard, B. (1996). Adaptational style and dispositional structure: Coping in the context on the five-factor model. *Journal of Personality, 64,* 737-774.

Weiten, Wayne & Lloyd, Margaret A. (2006) *Psychology Applied to Modern Life*. Thomson Wadsworth; Belmont California.

Widiger, T.A. & Clark, L.A. (2000). Toward *DSM-V* and the classification of psychopathology. *Psychological Bulletin, 126,* 946-963.

Williams, S. T., Conger, K. J., & Blozis, S. A. (2007). The development of interpersonal aggression during adolescence: The importance of parents, siblings, and family economics. *Child Development, 78,* 1526-1542.

Witt, J. C., Heffer, R. W. & Pfeiffer, J. (1990). Structured rating scales: A review of self-report and informant rating processes, procedures, and issues. In C. R. Reynolds & R. W. Kamphaus (Eds.), *Handbook of psychological and educational assessment of children: Personality, behaviors and context.* New York: Guilford Press.

Wintre, M. G., Polivy, J. & Murray, M. A. (1990). Self-predictions of emotional response patterns: Age, sex, and situational determinants. *Child Development, 61,* 1124-1133.

In: Personality Assessment: New Research
Editor: Lauren B. Palcroft & Melissa V. Lopez
ISBN 978-1-60692-796-0

Chapter 2

INTEGRATING EVIDENCE-BASED TREATMENT INTO AN ATTACHMENT GUIDED CURRICULUM IN A THERAPEUTIC PRESCHOOL: INITIAL FINDINGS

Karen Stubenbort*, Veronica Trybalski, and Krista Zaccagni
Family Resources of Pennsylvania
141 S. Highland Avenue, Stevenson Building
Pittsburgh, PA 15206 USA

ABSTRACT

Child maltreatment is associated with detrimental developmental effects. In view of the fact that child maltreatment typically occurs within the context of a caretaking relationship, attachment-guided treatments have been found effective in addressing developmental problems in abused children. This chapter describes the dissemination of a trauma-focused cognitive behavioral treatment model (TF-CBT) into a Theraplay-guided therapeutic preschool for maltreated children. At the end of the study all of the children in the program displayed significant developmental gains. The study did not support the expectation that children receiving the integrated treatment model would show greater gain. There was a small difference in outcome, particularly the adaptive domain. Although the differences were not significant, the authors believe they are in accordance with theoretically guided expectations. These results are discussed as are both the Theraplay-guided and TF-CBT models.

Keywords: child maltreatment; child abuse; attachment theory; therapeutic preschool; trauma-focused CBT.

* Corresponding author: Karen Stubenbort, Ph.D.
Family Resources of PA.
141 S. Highland Avenue,
Pittsburgh, PA 15206.
Phone: 724.355.5075, Kstubenbort@zoominternet.net

Introduction

Each year in the United States hundreds of thousands of children suffer some form of maltreatment. In 2005, an estimated 899,000 children in the US and Puerto Rico were victims of child abuse or neglect (NCANDS, 2007). Very young children have the highest rates of victimization (NCCAN, 2005; NCANDS, 2007) and are more likely than their older maltreated peers to experience harmful effects on development (e.g., Alessandri, 1991; Beeghly and Cicchetti,1994; Cicchetti & Toth, 1995; Lyons-Ruth, 1996). Thus, the experience of child maltreatment must be considered with regard to its impact on the normal progress of development. Specifically, socio-emotional, cognitive, and representational competencies, which emerge in the early years and build upon each other over the course of the life span, are impacted by neglectful or negative interactions with primary caregivers, (Ayoub, O'Connor, Rappolt-Schllichtmann, et al., 2006; Cicchetti & Sroufe, 1978; Sroufe & Waters, 1976; Toth, Maughan, Manly, et al., 2002). The following chapter describes the dissemination of an evidence-based trauma focused cognitive behavioral treatment model into a Theraplay-guided model at therapeutic preschool for maltreated children. The study sought to determine the efficacy of the integrated treatment model in comparison with the Theraplay-guided only treatment used in prior years at the preschool.

Literature Support

Young maltreated children present a number of challenges across developmental lines including insecure attachment relationships with caregivers (Crittenden, 1992; Crittenden & Ainsworth, 1989), disturbances in the development of self (Cicchetti & Barnett, 1991), ineffective peer relationships (Cicchetti, Lynch, Shonk, & Manly, 1992) and disturbance in the organizational structure of the brain (DeBellis, 2005; DeBellis, Keshavan, Clark, et al, 1999; Siegel, 2003; Schore, 2003). Victims of child maltreatment may experience developmental interference or persistent symptoms throughout their lives (Lyons-Ruth & Jocobvitz, 1999). Attachment theory and cognitive theory both recognize the impact of past and current experiences on the developmental course (Sroufe, 1988; Sroufe, Egeland, & Kreutzer, 1990; Vygotsky, 1977). Thus, both theories are important in addressing the problem of child maltreatment.

Child Maltreatment and Attachment Theory

According to Bowlby, attachment is a "lasting psychological connectedness between human beings" (1969, p 4) that begins in infancy and lays a crucial developmental and psychosocial foundation that endures throughout the lifespan. Children seek proximity with attachment figures so as to experience comfort, safety, and pleasure. Through repeated interactions with caregivers, children develop strategies of behavior (working models) that serve the function of maintaining a sense of connectedness in the attachment relationship (Ainsworth, Blehar, Waters, & Wall, 1973; Crittenden, 1994). When relationships with caregivers are problematic, children will create behavioral strategies that reflect their conflicted need for proximity and safety (Ainsworth, et al., 1973; Crittenden, 1994; Main & Solomon, 1990

Particular experiences in the parent-child relationship influence both attachment security and development. According to Stern (1985) empathic caregiving is critical in the regulation of infant emotional states. When primary caregivers respond in an emotionally attuned/organized manner to their children's emotional states, their presence is comforting. Furthermore, when caregivers enhance their infants' positive emotional experiences and alleviate negative emotional experiences, their infants learn trust and emotional regulation. Children experiencing trust and pleasure in the caregiving relationship feel free to explore and play (Hesse, Main, Abrams, & Rifkin, 2001). In contrast, when parents respond in an incongruous/disorganized manner to their children's emotional states, their presence is distressing or alarming. These children are left in a state of anxiety will respond to their environment in maladaptive ways (Main & Hesse, 1990).

Affective regulation is central to secure attachment, but becomes distorted in the maltreating parent-child relationship. Rather than emotional regulation, maltreated children are presented a paradoxical situation that creates unease (Main & Hesse 1990). Specifically, maltreated children experience fear of the caregiver. Fear arouses the attachment system which gives rise to attachment-related behavioral phenomenon; behaviors that obtain the attention and proximity of caregivers and relieve stress (Ainsworth, 1967),. In a state of fear, children are compelled to seek the safety and comfort that typically comes with proximity to the caregiver, yet proximity to the maltreating caregiver increases fear. Caregivers are viewed as both "the source of and the solution to its alarm" (Main & Hesse, 1990, pg 163). There is no resolution and the outcome is a breakdown in the behavioral system and a disorganized affective state (Hesse & Main, 1999; Schuengal, Bakersmans-Kranenburg & van Ijzendoorn, 1999).

In summary, in situations of child maltreatment, caregivers are a source of emotional and physiological disorganization rather than comfort. Young children do not have the capacity to process the distressful information from their external (maltreating caregivers) or internal environment (stress and bodily chaos). These children, who are unable to organize their behavior in the presence of their caregivers, are likely to have attachment styles that are described as disorganized/disoriented (Main & Solomon, 1986; 1990).

Child Maltreatment and Cognitive Theory

According to cognitive theory, mental representations are constructed from information received over time (Miller, 1956). Simply put, individuals hold aspects of their world in their thinking and language. This information exists in "chunks" or constructs, which allows for more efficiency in memory. Experiences are organized according to their significance and meaning. As meaning is assigned to an event, emotional response evolves (Kelly, 1955). Attributions applied to an event add to the emotional response (Weiner, 1986). Attributions, expectations, and perceived control over life events are considered motivation for behavior; the higher perceived expectations, the greater the task performance and persistence (Beck, 1976; Brewin, 1988). Attributions, expectations, and behaviors are closely tied to culture which, in the case of young age, primarily involves the home environment.

Culture influences memory processes through language and other social exchange. In very young children, memory processes are immature. Through repeated interactions, children construct their understanding, build their expectations and attributions, and develop behaviors. They become particular kinds of thinkers based upon the world in which they live. Given their limited life experience, children who experience maltreatment are at an increased risk for developing a number of cognitive distortions. For example, abused children are more likely to hold a negative world view (Ayoub, et al., 2006), harbor representations that distort self image (Cohen, Mannarin, & Deblinger, 2006), and normalize harmful parental behavior (Toth, et al., 2002).

Distortions in maltreated children's mental representations are observed in their social and solitary play (Alessandri, 1991; George & Main, 1979; Howes & Eldrege, 1985; Lyons-Ruth, 1996; Lyons-Ruth, Alpern, & Repacholi, 1993), in interpersonal relationships (Cicchetti & Toth, 1995; Lyons-Ruth, 1996), and in the manner in which they approach social tasks and generally cope (Kobak, 1999). It is likely that negative representational models of the self, of the self in relation to others, and of expectations from the culture in general, arise from child maltreatment which impacts both attachment insecurity and thinking more generally. In addition, child maltreatment may hinder inner resources for support seeking, coping, and adapting, thus setting a trajectory leading to long term developmental and psychological difficulties. Treatment models for abused children should address both attachment security and cognitive representations that arise in the context of the abusive parent-child relationship. The major purpose of this study was to examine the effectiveness of a treatment model combining both attachment-guided and trauma-focused cognitive behavioral treatment interventions in a population of maltreated preschool children being served at a therapeutic preschool.

Study

The present study examines the effectiveness of a group treatment model based in Theraplay (Jernberg, 1979; Jernberg & Booth, 1999) and Trauma-Focused Cognitive Behavioral Therapy (TF-CBT) (Cohen, Mannarino, 1993; Cohen, Mannarino, & Deblinger, 2006) at a therapeutic preschool (TPS) for maltreated children. The overarching goal of the Theraplay-guided treatment (TGT) model in the TPS is to provide a corrective relational experience within a structured environment. The goals of the TF-CBT model include increasing affective awareness, decreasing general arousal, correcting cognitive distortions, enhancing coping, and interrupting trauma-repetitive behaviors. Specific goals of the group setting include building social skills, increasing environmental trust, and preparing children for the demands of the future school environment.

Agency Setting

The study agency is a large child abuse prevention and treatment agency in the greater Pittsburgh area. There are a variety of both prevention and treatment services offered at the agency. The TPS is the only one in the area offers such service specifically to maltreated children, ages two through six years, who evidence developmental and psychosocial delay. The TPS operates 6 hours per day, 4 days per week, from September through mid-July, with the exception of a winter holiday and spring break.

Agency Model

The TPS uses attachment-based interventions having their foundation in the Theraplay model (Jernberg, 1979; Jernberg & Booth, 1999) and TF-CBT (Cohen, Mannarino, 1993; Cohen, Mannarino, Deblinger, 2006), along with a variety of more general preschool activities designed to facilitate developmental gain. Theraplay is a child-focused treatment model designed to increase healthy attachment and build self-esteem and trust in children. TF-CBT is a psychotherapeutic intervention designed to help children and their parents overcome the negative effects of traumatic life events such as child sexual or physical abuse or other emotional trauma.

Theraplay activities are designed to facilitate attachment security, enhance affective attunement, build an internal locus of control, and advance social, motor, and communication skills to developmentally appropriate levels (Jernberg, 1979). The TPS curriculum uses Theraplay activities to provide corrective early childhood interactions and increase healthy, more secure relationships with primary caregivers and peers. The activities stress emotional involvement and physical proximity as important aspects of engaging with children. The therapists are closely involved with the children through the course of the day. The program includes a great deal of physical contact (safe touches) and interpersonal connectedness (e.g., proximity, eye contact, feeding, and general playfulness) in the classroom.

Theraplay-guided activities (Jernberg & Booth, 1999; Rubin,& Tregay, 1989) are structured into the classroom, used at home visits, and monthly family nights. Theraplay activities are gently introduced in the classroom since the purpose of the activities is to elicit attachment-related behavioral phenomena and mimic the parent-child relationship. The intensity of the activities is gradually increased as children are more familiar with the environment and children are encouraged to increasingly engage in safe eye contact, increased proximity, and affective touch with therapists and peers. The number one rule of the classroom is "no hurts." This rule is repeated daily, but it takes time for the children to trust the environment.

An example of a TPS Theraplay-guided activity that is meant to elicit attachment-related phenomena is called "Rock-a-By." During "Rock-a-By" the two therapists hold opposing ends of a blanket. One at time, each child lies in the blanket and the blanket and child are gently swung in back and forth, cradle-like, while the group sings "Rock-a-By-Baby." The ending of the song is changed to say, "…and we will catch (child's name), baby and all." This activity mimics the rocking and singing that might take place in a typical early parent-child relationship, but may be missing in the life of maltreated children. It takes place in a safe, predictable manner, thus helping to promote trust, self-regulation, and self-awareness. "Rock-a-by" reinforces that the classroom is a safe place where the therapists will continually assure empathy, consistency, security, and safety. All of the children are engaged in singing for each individual child, therefore, the activity also increases trust and engagement with peers.

Trauma-focused cognitive behavioral therapy is an empirically-supported treatment model designed to assist children and their caregivers deal with the symptoms following traumatic experiences, such as child maltreatment (e.g., Cohen & Mannarino, 1993; Deblinger, Lippmann, & Steer, 1986; Kolko, 1996). Children experiencing trauma exhibit a variety of symptoms, dependent on the extent of the trauma, inherent resiliency, the nature of coping mechanisms, and the emotional and social support surrounding the children (Bolger & Patterson, 2003: Cohen & Mannarino, 1996a). Trauma symptoms can be divided into three categories: affective, behavioral, and cognitive (APA, 2000). Affective symptoms include trauma specific fear and anger, along with and more general emotional dysregulation. Behavioral symptoms may include avoidance of thoughts, people, places, and/or things that could remind children of the traumatic experiences. Children who live in abusive homes may develop modeling behaviors. For example, maltreated children may believe that hitting, shouting, or oppositional acts are acceptable ways of managing upsetting feelings. Cognitive symptoms are evident in the manner in which traumatized children reveal distorted thoughts about themselves, the people in their lives, or their world view. Children who are abused seem particularly vulnerable to cognitions that include self blame (Cohen, Mannarino, & Deblinger, 2008) possibly because the acts of abuse are directed towards them by the people in their lives who are meant to care for them.

TF-CBT helps children identify their feelings, manage emotional arousal, control their behaviors, and talk about their traumatic experiences. Conducted in a supportive environment, TF-CBT addresses the important aspects of the children's relationships with the abuse perpetrators, the attributions applied to the abuse, and more general issues surrounding interpersonal trust. Furthermore, TF-CBT emphasizes the relationship between thoughts, feelings, and behaviors. Children begin to learn that they can take control of upsetting and disturbing thoughts and begin to take charge of their behavior.

TF-CBT provides children with a number of important tools for future safety and symptom reduction. For example, the children at the TPS are taught to recognize safe and unsafe touches using story telling procedures. The children hear short stories about touching situations involving children with children or children with adults. They are asked to identify whether each situation is an "ok touch" an "ouch touch" (physical hurt) or an "uh-oh touch" (sexual situation). Children are also coached to take charge of their thoughts. This is done through the use of story telling, game playing, and crafts. Taking charge of one's thoughts includes thinking about one's dreams. One activity that the children engage in is making dream catchers. The dream catchers are hung on the wall over their resting mats in the classroom. This helps remind the children that they can take charge of their thoughts. Dream catchers are also made during a family night activity. In this manner, caretakers and other members of the children's families learn about taking charge of thoughts. Caregivers use these tools to help remind children to stay in charge of their thoughts outside of the school environment.

METHOD

Sample

The present study includes a sample of 35 children enrolled in the TPS during the years 1998-2000 (Group 1) and 2006-2008 (Group 2). The children in Group one (N= 18) received the Theraplay-Guided Treatment interventions that had been in practice in the TPS for over 10 years. In 2004, the TPS began incorporating TF-CBT interventions into the program. Group two consists of 17 children receiving an integration of Theraplay-Guided and TF-CBT interventions. The purpose of this study is to examine the efficacy of Theraplay-guided (TGT) only treatment in relation to the integrated treatment (InT) services for maltreated preschool children receiving services at the TPS. All of the children were determined to have experienced maltreatment by Child Protective Services (CPS), law enforcement, or an independent child abuse expert. For inclusion in the study, the children had to attend the TPS for at least 6 months of the program year, which runs from September through July.

The mean age of the children at the start of treatment was 48 months. The ethnic distribution includes 13 (37%) Caucasians, 18 (51%) African-Americans, 3 (8%) Biracial and one (3%) Native American. There were 20 female and 15 male children. With respect to maltreatment, six (17%) children experienced physical abuse, 8 (22%) children experienced sexual abuse, 5 (14%) children experienced neglect, and 14 (40%) children experienced multiple forms of maltreatment. Along with maltreatment, 4 children also witnessed domestic violence.

Measurement

The Battelle Developmental Inventory [Battelle] (Newborg, Stock, Wnek, Guidubaldi, & Svinicki, 1984) has been is used to inform treatment planning and assess the efficacy of the TPS for the past 15 years. The Battelle is a 341 item, nationally standardized, individually administered, assessment battery designed to estimate a child's developmental age in months. The Battelle assesses growth and developmental progress of children from birth to eight years of age. It was normed using a sample of 800 subjects representing a 75% urban and 25% suburban population. Subjects were selected based on data taken from the US Bureau of Census Statistical Abstract using a stratified quota sampling procedure (Harrington, 1985). Validity of the Battelle was investigated using a random sample of 124 kindergarten-aged children.. Concurrent and predictive testing, using widely recognized developmental tests such as the Peabody Picture Vocabulary Test (Dunn & Dunn, 1959) and the Bender Visual Motor Gestalt Test (Koppitz, 1975), along with the verification of test items by content experts, helped to assure both content and predictive validity. Test-retest and inter-rater coefficients are generally in the .90 range (Harrington, 1985). Thus, the Battelle appears to be a valid measure of overall early and middle childhood development.

The items contained in the full scale Battelle are organized into five developmental domains: personal-social, motor, communication, cognitive, and adaptive. Scores are available for each domain and are summed across domains to yield a total score. An increase in developmental age indicates the degree of developmental gain. Given the disturbances in self, emotional regulation, and peer relationships, following maltreatment, the personal-social and adaptive domain scores are of particular interest in the study of the children treated at the TPS.

Procedure

All of the children who attend the TPS experience developmental delay in at least one domain, as measured by the Battelle. At the TPS the therapists complete the Battelle by observing each child on the required tasks within the first month of attendance to establish pre-treatment developmental age, reported in months. The children are again observed within one month prior to the end of the school year to establish post-treatment age. At the time of intake, the difference between the chronological age in months and developmental age, as per the Battelle, was calculated. This generated a pre-treatment score in terms of developmental delay in months. The same was done at the time of discharge, generating a post-treatment score. Outcome was determined by subtracting the pre-treatment from the post-treatment score, thus arriving at a score representing overall developmental gain. Success in treatment was defined in developmental gain such that an individual child was experiencing a smaller discrepancy between developmental age and chronological age than was identified at the onset of treatment, as defined by the Battelle. The purpose of this study was to generally examine the effectiveness of the integrated treatment model and, more specifically, to look at the efficacy of TGT only in relation to the InT services for maltreated preschool children receiving services at the TPS.

RESULTS

Paired samples t-tests were performed to examine overall program effectiveness. These tests looked at the entire population (N=35) in regard to developmental gain over time. Paired samples t-tests were used to examine the effectiveness of treatment on general developmental delay as well as the personal-social and adaptive domains of development (see Table 1). These tests show a significant gain in overall developmental outcome and in the domains of interest.

Table 1. Paired Samples T-tests Examining Developmental Outcome

Independent Variable	N	Pre-tx Delay	Post-tx Delay	Standard Deviation	*t*
Total Outcome	35	11.03	5.65	3.98	- 7.97*
Personal-Social Domain	35	17.31	10.44	8.1	- 5.07*
Adaptive Domain	35	14.25	6.63	7.34	- 6.14*

df=34
p.<.000

Independent samples t-tests were used to determine the efficacy of TGT only in relation to the InT. These test show there is no significant difference between the two groups in overall developmental gain or in the domains of interest. Overall developmental gain between the two groups is almost equal (mean developmental gain of 5.2 months in the TGT group and 5.4 months in the InT group). In the case of the personal social domain, the TGT group had a mean developmental gain of 6.3 and the InT group had a mean gain of 7.4. The adaptive domain was more impressive, but still not significant (p = .33). In the TGT group had a mean developmental gain of 6.5 months and the InT group had a mean gain of 9 months.

Table 2. Independent Samples T-tests Examining Developmental Outcome

Independent Variable	N	Mean tx gain	Standard Deviation	*t*	*p*
Total Outcome	35			-0.141	0.889
TGT	18	5.27	3.64		
InT	17	5.47	4.43		
Personal-Social Domain	35			-0.368	0.715
TGT	18	6.38	7.72		
InT	17	7.41	8.72		
Adaptive Domain	35			-0.977	0.336
TGT	18	6.5	7.96		
InT	17	9	7.11		

df=33

CONCLUSION

Attachment theory helps us understand developmental and psychosocial functioning in the context of primary relationships (Cicchetti & Barnett, 1991; Cicchetti & Toth, 1995). Given that internal and external working models are derived from early attachment relationships (Bowlby, 1969/1982) one would expect maltreated children to perceive and respond to relationships and events through the lens of a disordered primary attachment Previous research has shown that an attachment driven program has a positive impact on the developmental delay of young children attending the TPS (Stubenbort, 2003; Stubenbort, Cohen, & Trybalski, in press).

TF-CBT provides a systematic, evidence-based, approach for responding to abuse specific symptoms that may have a long lasting negative impact on functioning. Previous research has consistently indicated that TF-CBT is effective in ameliorating these symptoms (e.g., Cohen & Mannarino, 1993; Deblinger, Lippmann, & Steer, 1996; Kolko, 1996). In addition, it is recognized as a Model Program by the Substance Abuse and Mental Health Services Administration (SAMHSA, 2008). It is believed that the dissemination of abuse-specific TF-CBT into the TPS would serve to augment an already valuable program.

All of the children enrolled at the TPS evidence developmental delays; that is, when they enter the program they score lower than expected for their chronological age on at least one developmental domain on the Battelle. When examined as a group, the program is continuing to significantly impact the developmental delay of the children being served. The mean developmental delay for children treated during the study years was just over 11 months of age. Delays in the personal-social and adaptive domains of development were even greater. The mean delay in the personal-social domain was 17.3 months and the delay in the adaptive domain was 14.25 months. At the end of treatment, the children being served by the program had made significant overall gains as well as significant gains in the personal-social and adaptive domains of development. The average developmental delay at the time of discharge had gone from 11.2 to 5.6 months, with three children reaching developmental points beyond their chronological age. In the personal-social domain, the delay went form 17.3 to 10.3 months delay and in the adaptive domain, the average delay went from 14.25 to 6.6 months.

It is the adaptive domain that of considerable interest in the InT group. This group had a nine month mean gain in treatment outcome in this domain. Given the importance of emotional dysregulation in maladaptive behaviors along with the understanding that abused preschool children face extreme risks in adaptive outcomes (Allesandri, 1991; Troy & Srouf, 1987), this change is in accordance with theoretically derived expectations. Although the change is not significant, it leads the authors to continue to consider the importance of disseminating the TF-CBT model.

It was believed that the addition of the TF-CBT model to the existing attachment guided program would augment treatment and that this might be evident in the developmental outcome scores of the children being served. The present study did not support this expectation. Although there was some difference in outcome, particularly in the adaptive domain, the differences were not significant. There are several issues to consider in this regard. First and foremost is the fact that the Battelle does not measure trauma specific symptoms, but TF-CBT is targeting trauma-specific symptomatology. Using a trauma-specific measure for preschool children, such as the Weekly Behavior Report (Cohen & Mannarino, 1996b) may give us greater insight into abuse-specific change in this population and the efficacy of the integrated treatment model. Another consideration is the small population of the study. There were only 18 children in group one and 17 children in group two. It is important to note that even with such small groups, the children in group two did show somewhat greater developmental gain the personal social and adaptive domains. It is possible that with a larger population, the InT model will evidence a significant difference in treatment outcome.

One must also consider that the TF-CBT model is not significantly different from the TGT or is not as effective on a group level with very young children as it has been shown to be with preschoolers in individual treatment (Cohen & Mannarino, 1993; 1996a). TF-CBT targets the affective dysregulation and behavioral disruption secondary to maltreatment. The TGT model addresses these issues, but in a different manner. The greatest difference in models lies in the psychoeducation and cognitive components. In the psychoeducation component, the children are educated about body parts, body safety, and child maltreatment. In the cognitive component the children are educated about the relationship between thoughts, feelings, and behaviors. They are also encouraged to tell their maltreatment story; to create a trauma narrative. One must keep in mind that in very young children memory processes are immature, and given their limited language, capturing these memories may be difficult. Furthermore, some of these children were removed from the care of their parents prior to age two and prior to the development of much language. The memories they have available through language may be tied to secure relationships with adoptive parents. Thus, a trauma narrative component of the treatment may not be possible, or even in the best interest, with some of the children.

There are a number of weaknesses that must be acknowledged in this study. One weakness is the presence of a convenience sample. With the use of a convenience sample, the findings cannot be generalized beyond the agency population. Furthermore, the study and comparison group were both convenience samples taken from the agency. In the absence of a true control group one cannot say with certainty that treatment was the distinct factor promoting developmental gain. Nevertheless, the authors believe that the developmental gains shown are an aspect of treatment at the TPS as the center has consistently evidenced treatment gains for the children enrolled in the program (Stubenbort, 2003; Stubenbort, Cohen, & Trybalski, in press). The authors also believe that the addition of the TF-CBT to the attachment-guided model has enhanced treatment and the small changes evident thus far are indicative of such. The authors will continue to disseminate the TF-CBT model into the TPS program. We have begun manualized the curriculum in order to more rigorously measure its effectiveness over the next several years.

REFERENCES

Ainsworth, M.D.S., (1967). Infancy in Uganda. Baltimore: Johns Hopkins University Press.

Ainsworth, M.D.S., Blehar, M.C., Waters, E. & Wall, S. (1973). Patterns of attachment: A psychological study of the Strange Situation. Hillsdale, NJ: Erlbaum.

Alessandri, S.M. (1991). Play and social behaviors in maltreated preschoolers. *Developmental Psychology*, 4, 257-270

American Psychiatric Association (2000). Diagnostic and statistical manual of mental disorders (4th ed., text rev.). Washington, DC: Author.

Ayoub, C.C., O'Connor, E., Rappolt-Schlichtmann, G., Fischer, K.W., Rogosch, F.A., Toth, S.L., & Cicchetti, D. (2006). Cognitive and emotional differences in young maltreated children: A translational application of dynamic skill theory, *Development and psychopathology*, 18, 679-706.

Beck, A.T. (1976). Cognitive therapy and the emotional disorders. New York: International Universities Press.

Bolger, K.E. & Patterson, C.J. (2001). Developmental pathways from child maltreatment to peer rejection. *Child Development*, 72, 549- 549.

Bolger, K.E. & Patterson, C.J. (2003). Sequelae of child maltreatment: Vulnerability and resilience. In, S.S. Luthar, (Ed.), *Resilience and vulnerability*: Adaptation in the context of childhood adversities (pp. 156-181). Cambridge University Press.

Bowlby, J. (1969/1982). Attachment and loss: Vol. 1, *Attachment*. New York: Basic Books.

Brewin, C.R. (1988). Cognitive foundations of clinical psychology. Hillsdale: Lawrence Earlbaum Associates.

Cicchetti, D. & Barnett, D. (1991). Attachment organization in preschool aged maltreated children. *Development and Psychopathology*, 3, 397-411.

Cicchetti, D., Lynch, M., Shonk, S., & Manly, J.T. (1992). An organizational perspective on peer relations in maltreated children. In, R.D. Park & G.W. Ladd (Eds.), *Family-peer relationships*: Modes of linkage (pp. 345-383). Hillsdale, NJ: Earlbaum.

Cicchetti, D., Rogosh, F.A., Lynch, M., & Holt, K.D. (1993). Resilience in maltreated children: Processes leading to adaptive outcome. *Development and Psychopathology*, 5, 629-647.

Cicchetti, D. & Sroufe, L.A. (1978). An organizational view of affect: Illustration from the study of Down's syndrome infants. In M. Lewis & L. Rosenblum (Eds.), *The development of affect* (pp. 309-350). New York: Plenum Press.

Cicchetti, D. & Toth, S.L. (1995). Developmental psychopathology perspective on child abuse and neglect. *Journal of the American Academy of Child and Adolescent Psychiatry*, 34, 541-565.

Cohen, J.A. & Mannarino, A.P. (1993). A treatment model for sexually abused preschoolers. *Journal of Interpersonal Violence*, 8, 115-131.

Cohen, J.A. & Mannarino, A.P. (1996a). Factors that mediate treatment outcome of sexually abused preschool children. *Journal of the American Academy of Child and Adolescent Academy,* 35(10), 1402-1410.

Cohen, J.A. & Mannarino, A.P. (1996b). The weekly behavior report: A parent report instrument for sexually abused preschoolers. *Child Maltreatment,* 1(4), 353-360.

Cohen, J.A., Mannarino, A.P., & Deblinger, E. (2006). Treating trauma and traumatic grief. New York, Guilford.

Crittenden, P.M. (1992). Children's strategies for coping with adverse home environments: An interpretation using attachment theory. *Child Abuse and Neglect*, 6, 329-343.

Crittenden, P.M. (May, 1994). The preschool assessment of attachment. Unpublished coding manual. *Family Research Laboratory*, University of New Hampshire.

Crittenden, P.M. & Ainsworth, M.D.S. (1989). Child maltreatment and attachment theory. In, D. Cicchetti & V. Carlson, (Eds.), *Child maltreatment*: Theory and research on the causes and consequences of child abuse and neglect (pp. 432-463). New York: Cambridge University Press.

Cummings, E.M., Hennessy, K., Rabideau, G., & Cicchetti, D., (1994). Responses of physically abused boys to interadult anger involving their mothers. *Developmental Psychopathology*, 6, 31-42.

DeBellis, M.D. (2005). The psychobiology of neglect. *Child Maltreatment*, 10, 150-172.

DeBellis, M.D., Keshavan, M.S., Clark, D.B., Casey, B.J., Giedd, J.N., Boring, A.M., et al. (1999). Developmental traumatology: Part II. Brain development. *Biological Psychiatry*, 45, 1271-1284.

Deblinger, E., Lippmann, J., & Steer, R. (1996). Sexually abused children suffering from posttraumatic stress symptoms: Initial treatment outcome findings. *Child Maltreatment,* 1, 310-321.

Dunn, L.M, & Dunn, L.N. (1959). Peabody Picture Vocabulary Test._Circle Pines, MN: *American Guidance Service*.

George, C. & Main, M. (1979). Social interactions of young abused children: Approach, avoidance, and aggression. *Child Development*, 50, 306-318.

Harrington, R. (1985). Battelle Developmental Inventory. In D.J. Keyser, & R.C. Sweetland (Eds.), *Test critiques,* (Vol. II). Kansas City, MO: Test Corporation of America.

Hesse, E. & Main, M.M. (1999). Second generation effects of unresolved trauma in non-maltreating parent: Dissociated, frightened, and threatening parental behavior. *Psychoanalytic Inquiry*, 19, 481-540.

Hesse, E., Main, M., Abrams, K.Y., & Rifkin, A (2001). Unresolved states regarding loss or abuse can have "second-generation" effects: Disorganization, role inversion, and frightening ideation in the offspring of traumatized non-maltreating parents. In, M.F. Solomon & D.J. Siegel (Eds.), Healing Trauma: Attachment, mind, body, and brain (pp 57-107), New York: W.W. Norton.

Howes, C. & Eldrege, R. (1985). Responses of abused, neglected, and nonmaltreated children to the behaviors of their peers. *Journal of Applied Psychology*, 6, 261-270.

Jernberg, A.M. (1979). Theraplay: A new treatment using structured play for problem children and their families. San Francisco: Jossey-Bass Publishers.

Jernberg, A.M. & Booth, P.B. (1999). Theraplay: Helping parents and children build better relationships through attachment-based play. (2nd Ed.) San Francisco: Jossey-Bass Publishers.

Kelly, G.A. (1955). The psychology of personal constructs. Vols 1 & 2, New York: W.W. Norton.

Kobak, R. (1999). The emotional dynamics of disruptions in attachment relationships: Implications for theory, research, and clinical intervention. In, In, J. Cassidy & P.R. Shaver, (Eds.), *Handbook of attachment*: Theory, research, and clinical applications (21-43). New York: Guilford Press.

Kolko, D.J. (1996). Individual cognitive behavioral treatment and family therapy for physically abused children and their offending parents: A comparison of clinical outcomes. *Child Maltreatment*, 1, 322-342.

Koppitz, E. (1975). The Bender Gestalt Test for young children. New York: Grune and Stratton.

Lyons-Ruth, K. (1996). Attachment relationships among children with aggressive behavior problems: The role of disorganized early attachment patterns. *Journal of Consulting and Clinical Psychology*, 64, 64-73.

Lyons-Ruth, K, Alpern, L. & Repacholi, B. (1993 Howes, C. & Eldrege, R. (1985). Responses of abused, neglected, and nonmaltreated children to the behaviors of their peers. *Journal of Applied Psychology*, 6, 261-270.

Howes, C. & Eldrege, R. (1985). Responses of abused, neglected, and nonmaltreated children to the behaviors of their peers. *Journal of Applied Psychology*, 6, 261-270.

Lyons-Ruth, K, Alpern, L. & Repacholi, B. (1994). Disorganized infant attachment classification and maternal psychosocial problems as predictors of hostile-aggressive behavior in the preschool classroom. *Child Development*, 64, 572-585.

Lyons-Ruth, K.& Jocobvitz, D. (1999). Attachment disorganization: Unresolved loss, relational violence, and lapses in behavioral and attentional strategies. In, J. Cassidy & P.R. Shaver, (Eds.), *Handbook of attachment:* Theory, research, and clinical applications (520-554). New York: Guilford Press.

Main, M. & Hesse, E. (1990). Parents' unresolved traumatic experiences are related to infant disorganized attachment status: Is frightened and/or frightening parental behavior the linking mechanism? In, M.T. Greenberg, D. Cicchetti, & E.M. Cummings (Eds.), Attachment in the preschool years: Theory, research, and intervention (pp. 161-182), Chicago: University of Chicago Press.

Main, M. & Solomon, J. (1986). Discovery of a new insecure-disorganized/disoriented attachment pattern. In T.B. Brazelton & M.W. Yogman (Eds.), Affective development in infancy (pp. 95-124). Norwood, NJ: Ablex.

Main, M. & Solomon, J. (1990). Procedures for identifying infants as disorganized/disoriented during the Ainsworth Strange situation. In, M.T. Greenberg, D. Cicchetti, & E.M. Cummings (Eds.), Attachment in the preschool years: Theory, research, and intervention (pp121-160), Chicago: University of Chicago Press.

Miller, G.A. (1956). Human memory and the storage of information. *IRE Transactions of Information Theory,* 2(3), 128-137.

National Clearinghouse on Child Abuse and Neglect Information (2005). National child abuse and neglect data system (NCANDS): Summary of key findings from calendar year 2003. DHHS Publication [On-line] Available: www.calib.com/nccanch/factsheetsstat.cfm.

National Child Abuse and Neglect Data System (2007). Child Maltreatment 2005. DHHS Publication [On-Line] Available: http://www.acf.hhs.gov/programs/cb/stats_research/ index.htm#can.

Newborg, J., Stock, J., Wnek, L., Guidubaldi, J., & Svinicki, J., (1984). The Battelle Developmental Inventory: Examiner's manual. Dallas TX: *DLM Teaching Resources*.

Rubin, P. & Tregay, J. (1989). Play with them: Theraplay groups in the classroom. Springfield, IL: Charles C. Thomas.

Substance Abuse and Mental Health Services Administration (2008). SAMHSA Model Programs. Trauma-Focused Cognitive Behavioral Therapy. [On-line] Available: http://modelprograms http://modelprograms.samhsa.gov/pdfs/model/TFCBT.pdf).

Schore, A.N. (2003). Early relational trauma, disorganized attachment, and the development of a predisposition to violence. In, M.F. Solomon & D.J. Siegel (Eds.), *Healing Trauma: Attachment, mind, body, and brain* (pp107-167), New York: W.W. Norton.

Schuengal, C., Bakersmans-Kranenburg, M.J., & van Ijzendoorn, M.H. (1999). Frightening maternal behavior linking unresolved loss and disorganized infant attachment. *Journal of Consulting and Clinical Psychology*, 67, 65-63.

Siegel, D.J. (2003). An interpersonal neurobiology of psychotherapy: The developing mind and the resolution of trauma. In, M.F. Solomon & D.J. Siegel (Eds.), *Healing trauma: attachment, mind, body, and brain* (pp 1-56), New York: W.W. Norton.

Sroufe, L.A. (1988). The role of infant-caregiver attachment in development. In J. Belsky & T. Nezworski (Eds.), *Clinical implications of attachment* (pp. 18-40). Hillsdale, NJ: Erlbaum.

Sroufe, L.A., Egeland, B., & Kreutzer, T. (1990). The fate of early experience following developmental change: Longitudinal approaches to individual adaptation in childhood. *Child Development*, 61, 1363-1373.

Sroufe, L.A. & Waters, E. (1976). The ontogenesis of smiling and laughter: A perspective on the organization of development in infancy. *Psychological Review, 83,* 173-189.

Stern, D.N. (1985). *The interpersonal world of the infant.* New York: Basic Books.

Stubenbort, K. (2003). The effectiveness of intervention for maltreated preschoolers: An attachment theory perspective. (Doctoral Dissertation, University of Pittsburgh, 2003). *Dissertation Abstracts International,* 3104768.

Stubenbort, K, Cohen, M, & Trybalski, V (in press, available on-line). A study of the effectiveness of an attachment-focused treatment model in a therapeutic preschool for abused children. *Clinical Social Work Journal.*

Toth, S.L., Maughan, A., Manly, J.T., Spagnola, M., & Cicchetti, D. (2002). The relative efficacy of two interventions in altering maltreated preschool children's representational models: Implications for attachment theory. *Developmental Psychopathology*, 14, 877-908.

Troy, M. & Srouf, L.A. (1987). Victimization among preschoolers: The role of attachment relationship theory. *Journal of the American Academy of Child and Adolescent Academy,* 26, 166-172.

Vygotsky, L.S, (1977). Play in its role in the mental development of the child. In M. Cole (Ed.), *Soviet Developmental Psychology* (pp. 76-99). White Plains, NY: M.E. Sharpe. (Original work published in 1966).

Weiner, B. (1912). An introduction to psychology (R.Pintner, Trans.). London: George Allen, Reprinted by Arno Press, New York, 1973.

In: Personality Assessment: New Research
Editor: Lauren B. Palcroft & Melissa V. Lopez

ISBN 978-1-60692-796-0

Chapter 3

ASSESSING INDIVIDUALS FOR TEAM "WORTHINESS": INVESTIGATING THE INTERSECTION OF THE BIG FIVE PERSONALITY FACTORS, ORGANIZATIONAL CITIZENSHIP BEHAVIOR, AND TEAMWORK APTITUDE

Janet L. Kottke and Shinko Kimura
California State University, San Bernardino, California USA

ABSTRACT

Teams and teamwork have become very popular areas of organizational strategy, but selecting competent employees for teamwork remains difficult to do, let alone do well. This chapter addresses the requisites we consider important for the team "worthiness" of an individual. These fundamental team "worthiness" elements are factors of the Big Five Personality model, organizational citizenship behavior (OCB) contextualized as dispositions, and cognitive aptitude specific to teamwork. We review briefly the history of each of these constructs, illustrate assessments of the constructs, and then describe an original research study in which the unique and shared variance of these constructs was examined with confirmatory factor analysis. The results indicated the Big Five personality and organizational citizenship behavior constructs were comparably related to the teamwork aptitude construct. The most surprising result was the strong relationship of the sportsmanship variable to the Big Five construct. This result supports our conjecture that organizational citizenship represents a lower level factor of personality.

INTRODUCTION

Imagine you are responsible for selecting employees to form a team that is to solve a recurring customer service problem. You have 15 employees who work for you; they vary in job skill, general ability, and dispositions. How would you select, from among these people, a team that will gel and succeed at the task? After job knowledge, which set of characteristics would be most important to consider? Intelligence? Personality? Attitudes? This chapter addresses the building blocks of this key question, one that is faced often by managers. Although meta-analytic research has demonstrated that cognitive ability (i.e., intelligence) is one of the best single predictors of *individual* job performance (Schmidt & Hunter, 1998), many of us can testify personally to the value of dispositions in working with others. After all, a group of intelligent, disagreeable introverts is unlikely to coalesce into a dynamic problem-solving group. It is easy to see why attention (e.g., Morgeson, Campion, Dipboye, Hollenbeck, Murphy, & Schmitt, 2007a, 2007b; Ones, Dilchert, Viswesvaran, & Judge, 2007) has been placed on assessing personality in the personnel selection process, especially of those who will work extensively with others.

Personality Assessment in Personnel Selection: A Little History

Personality and its assessment has a long history within industrial psychology, dating in the modern era to Wadsworth's Personal Data Sheet (1917; Wadsworth, 1920), an early psychoneurotic assessment of World War I draftees' suitability for foxhole duty. After WWI, industrial psychology blossomed, in part because of its application of psychological assessments to business (Koppes, 2003). Throughout this lengthy history of personality testing, the results have been rather disappointing. More than 50 years ago, Ghiselli and Barthol (1953) surveyed the use of established personality inventories for selection across a broad spectrum of occupations and found a wide range of validity coefficients (.14 to .36). Of specific concern, they noted "personality inventories have proved to be effective for some occupations in which personality factors would appear to be of minimal importance (e.g., clerks and trades and crafts), and ineffective for other occupations in which these factors could reasonably be expected to be of paramount importance (e.g., supervisors and foremen)" (Ghiselli & Barthol, 1953, pp. 19-20). Guion and Gottier (1965) took up the review of personality tests a decade later and reported that there was not yet much reason for optimism in the use of personality tests to select employees. More troubling, as with the Ghiselli and Barthol review, the pattern of results did not clarify occupations for which personality testing might be feasible. The Guion and Gottier review did not eliminate interest in personality testing (i.e., the executive personality testing program continued at Sears, Roebuck; Bentz, 1962; 1983) but their review did seem to herald a slowing of personality testing for personnel selection during the next 20 years.

Interest was rekindled in the 1980s because meta-analyses had begun to demonstrate the considerable value of ability testing (Schmidt & Hunter, 1998). Ability testing, like personality testing, had been continued only very cautiously because of the mistaken belief that the United States Supreme Court's rulings in early Civil Rights Act cases (e.g., Griggs v. Duke Power) had indicted all ability testing. In addition to the chilling effect of these early court cases, the pattern of empirical data from cognitive ability tests was a checkerboard of significant and nonsignificant correlations, not unlike the results of the Guion and Gottier review of personality testing. However, Schmidt and Hunter (1998) were able to demonstrate thorough meta-analytic re-reviews of ability test studies that the previously uninterpretable pattern of results could be attributed largely to sampling error and, that in fact, cognitive ability tests were valid predictors of individual job performance across many jobs. With high expectations, several meta-analytic reviews (Barrick & Mount, 1991; Barrick, Mount, & Judge, 2001; Hurz & Donovan, 2000; Judge, Bono, Ilies, & Gerhardt, 2002) were undertaken to uncover the population validities of personality tests for personnel selection. These meta-analyses, which relied on more focused definitions of personality (i.e., the Big Five framework), revealed correlations between measures of personality and job performance considerably smaller (ρs in the teens and .20s) than those found with ability tests. Conscientiousness, the most consistent predictor of individual job performance, was correlated across all jobs investigated (ρ = .22). Despite the low correlations, these meta-analytic results generally demonstrated a more meaningful pattern of results than had been found by Guion and Gottier (1965). For instance, Barrick and Mount (1991) found that the Big Five factors of extraversion and agreeableness were predictive of performance in sales and managerial jobs, as might be expected; both sales and managerial occupations require the characteristics of being social, friendly, outgoing and assertive. The other Big Five factors have been less reliably predictive of job performance, but more recent analyses have suggested that level of analysis and framing of the job outcome measure may be important (Rothstein & Goffin, 2006). For example, conscientiousness can be considered to have several facets, which when unwrapped, yield better predictions of specific elements of job performance (Roberts, Chernyshenko, Stark, & Goldberg, 2005). Later in this chapter, we will return to this theme of more detailed facets of personality.

While industrial psychologists were grappling with the value of ability and personality tests for personnel selection, personality researchers were parsing the large amount of research conducted to identify personality dimensions. Much effort was directed at identifying a workable taxonomy to help manage the enormous amount of research being conducted and the large number of personality traits being proffered. Emerging from these efforts was the overarching taxonomy of the Five Factor Model of Personality and the Big Five Personality Factors (Goldberg, 1990; McCrae & Costa, 1987, 1997).

The Big Five Personality Factors and the Five-Factor Model of Personality[1]

The number of terms identified by researchers that could be used to describe personality during the modern era has been astonishing (Goldberg, 1993). Among the first, Allport and Odbert (1936) selected 4504 terms from Webster's Unabridged Dictionary that could be used to describe features of personality. Choosing adjectives in the fashion of Allport and Odbert characterizes the lexical tradition that has been taken up by several personality researchers who use factor and cluster analyses to reveal commonalities among the variable sets. Raymond Cattell can be credited as one of the most thorough and systematic in attempting to uncover fundamental personality characteristics through factor analytic techniques. Starting with Allport and Odbert's extensive list, he created 35 bipolar variable sets, which he

[1] The Five Factor Model (FFM) and the Big Five, though identical in appearance, are not synonymous in meaning. The FFM is presumed to have links to underlying biological markers whereas the Big Five is typically portrayed as being descriptive of personality (Saucier & Goldberg, 1996).

subjected to extensive factor analyses and proposed 11 or 12 primary personality factors (Cattell, 1945, 1947). Attempts by other researchers to replicate Cattell's factor structure, however, characteristically yielded far fewer factors. We describe a few of these prominent early attempts next.

Fiske (1949) asked supervisors to rate their clinical psychologist trainees on 21 of Cattell's scales; he found a five factor solution best represented these ratings. Tupes (1957) conducted a study of US Air Force cadets using 30 of Cattell's scales. He found, like Fiske, a five factor solution. Later, Tupes and Christal (1961) reanalyzed some of Cattell's earlier data and Fiske's data and arrived at a five factor solution with labels similar to the current Big Five: Surgency, Agreeableness, Dependability, Emotional Stability, and Culture. Others (Borgatta, 1964; Norman, 1963; Smith, 1967) in these early years confirmed a five factor solution in empirical analyses of data, regardless of whether ratings were derived from self report or supervisor and peer ratings (Digman, 2000). Unfortunately for trait personality researchers, the next decade ushered in an era in which several well-known personality theorists (e.g., Cattell, Eysenck) theorized factor structures other than a five factor model and the situationalists (e.g., Mischel, 1968) held sway and this early work demonstrating a five factor solution waited to be rediscovered and reconfirmed later.

Much of the credit for this rediscovery can be attributed to Goldberg who himself initially did not subscribe to a five factor structure (Goldberg, 1993). After collecting and analyzing voluminous data (e.g., Peabody & Goldberg, 1989), Goldberg became convinced of a five factor structure of personality. Independently, McCrae and Costa (1987, 1997), who began with a three factor model (i.e., the NEO of the NEO-PI; Costa & McCrae, 1992), also settled on a five factor structure.

Stimulated by the work of Goldberg, McCrae, and Costa, many of the leading personality inventories were subjected to factor analyses and the resulting, distilled factors scrutinized. Dissimilar inventories such as the Personality Research Form (Jackson, 1984), the Edwards Personal Preference Schedule (Edwards, 1959), and the Myers-Briggs Type Indicator (Myers, Briggs, & McCaulley, 1985), when factor analyzed, demonstrated an underlying, definable five-factor structure (cf., McCrae & Costa, 1987). When these results are combined with cross-cultural research (e.g., Salgado, Moscoso, & Lado, 2003), the support for a five-factor taxonomy[2] is powerful (McCrae & Costa, 1997; Pytlik Zillig, Hemenover, & Dienstbier, 2002).

The Big Five Factors

The widely-used five-factor model consists of neuroticism (emotional stability), extraversion, openness to experience, agreeableness, and conscientiousness. Each personality factor can be clarified by a description of the polar opposites of each dimension[3]. People high

[2] To be fair, there has been vigorous debate regarding the number of broad factors that are best suited to serve as a framework for personality, with the number of factors proposed as few as two (Wiggins, 1968) and three (Eysenck, 1991) to as many as nine (Hough, 1992).

[3] There remains some debate about the explicit meanings of the five factors. Goldberg (1993) noted that "warmth" is a descriptor of Agreeableness in the Goldberg lexical model but a facet of Extraversion in the McCrae and Costa FFM. Openness to Experience has been difficult to label accurately. The terms "Intellect" and "Imagination" have also been proposed (Goldberg, 1993; Saucier, 1994b). Despite these differences in labels,

in *neuroticism* are prone to negative emotions such as anxiety, depression, and anger. Those who score low in neuroticism (i.e., high in emotional stability) are calm and less likely to become upset. *Extraversion* is characterized by assertiveness, activity, excitement seeking, and positive emotions. Extraverts seek out people and stimulation. Introverts are deliberate, quiet and reserved; they prefer time alone. *Openness* to experience includes openness to adventure, feelings, actions, ideas, and values. Those high on this factor are typically intellectually curious and imaginative. Individuals low in this factor are likely to be described as straightforward and conventional. The facets of *agreeableness* include altruism, compliance, modesty, tender-mindedness, and trust. Agreeable people value social harmony and are friendly; those with a disagreeable personality value their interests above others and are thus less likely to be cooperative. *Conscientiousness* includes achievement striving, competence, order, and self-discipline. Those low on conscientiousness tend toward spontaneous action and a lack of planning.

As noted earlier, conscientiousness is a Big Five factor that emerges as the most reliable predictor of job performance across occupations (Salgado, 2003; Salgado, & deFruyt, 2005), yet has relatively small zero order correlations. One possibility for these results may lie in the "broadness" of the Big Five factors. Conscientiousness as a broad factor probably has multiple facets (or lower order factors) that are related, but not too highly (cf., DeYoung, Quilty, & Peterson, 2007). Hough (1992), a notable critic of the broad Big Five, insists that conscientiousness consists of at least two factors, dependability and achievement, each of which may not be relevant in equal proportion, depending on the context. Dependability refers to the ordered and planned aspect of conscientiousness and achievement refers to the propensity to strive for high standards, work hard, and persist to complete a task. This possibility is made evident by Roberts, et al. (2005) who showed that lower order factors of the Big Five, specifically Conscientiousness, might be differentially related to outcomes. Their findings are consistent with the idea that narrow bandwidths (Jenkins & Griffith, 2004) or lower level factors (DeYoung, et al., 2007) of the Big Five may be important to identify and more useful to predict job outcomes effectively. From our perspective, both the higher order and lower order factors of the Big Five may be important for predicting the contribution of an individual to a team.

Personality Assessment

The primary self-report approaches to measuring the Big Five correspond to the two key developers of the five factor structure. One approach uses statements (e.g., Costa & McCrae, 1992) and the other, lists of adjectives (e.g., Goldberg, 1992; Saucier, 1994a). Costa and McCrae's Neo Five Factor Inventory (NEO-FFI) is an illustration of a statement-based measure. The NEO-FFI is a briefer version of the parent NEO-PI inventory developed by Costa and McCrae. It is composed of 60 items with 12 measuring each of the Big Five factors. Respondents read a statement such as "I'm pretty good about pacing myself so as to get things done on time" and use a five-point scale anchored with "strongly disagree" to

which probably stem largely from the difference in the starting points of Goldberg and McCrea and Costa, the overall factor structure is widely accepted.

"strongly agree." The NEO-FFI has excellent internal consistency and correlates highly with the much longer 240-item NEO-PI-R measure (Costa & McCrae, 1992).

The other approach follows Goldberg's lexical hypothesis that the most important human attributes are those that can be captured using everyday language. From an initial list of 1431 adjectives and several validating studies, Goldberg (1992) settled on 100 Adjective Markers (also called Adjective Trait Descriptors, Pytlik Zillig et al., 2002) in which respondents use a 9-point Likert scale anchored with "extremely inaccurate" and "extremely accurate" to describe themselves in reference to people of their gender and age. The psychometric properties of the Adjective Markers have held up well in subsequent studies (cf., Pytlik Zilling et al., 2002). With an eye toward creating a shorter inventory, Saucier (1994a) began with Goldberg's 100 Adjective Markers and reduced the list to 40 adjectives that captured the essence of Goldberg's longer set. Besides seeking a shorter measure, Saucier also wanted to create an inventory that would minimize correlations among the subscales and have fewer difficult words. The data presented by Saucier (1994a) indicate that he succeeded in creating a short, yet fairly robust, Big Five marker set.

There is emerging evidence that the adjectival method may be a superior method for measuring personality (Gill & Hodgkinson, 2007). First, the purity of the factors extracted appears more pronounced for the adjectival approach (Dunbar, Ford, Hunt, & Der, 2000). Further, brief items tend to provide more reliability and validity (Holden, Fekken & Jackson, 1985). Taken together with the administrative efficiency of adjective lists, there is much to recommend the use of adjectival measures.

Personality Assessment for Teams

Personality characteristics have been identified as a potentially useful selection variable in the determination of optimal team composition (Kichuk & Wiesner, 1998; Peeters, VanTuijl, Rutte, & Reymen, 2006). Only a handful of studies have examined the relationships between the big five personality factors and objective team performance (Kichuk & Wiesner, 1998; Neuman & Wright, 1999). Kichuk and Wiesner (1998) found that successful teams were characterized by higher levels of extraversion and agreeableness and lower levels of neuroticism than unsuccessful teams. The precise means by which individual personality drives team performance, however, appears to depend on whether the method of personality measurement is an average within a team or taken as variances across team members' personalities (Neuman, Wagner, & Christiansen, 1999). Neuman et al. (1999), for example, found that high performing teams were collectively high in conscientiousness, agreeableness, and had the greatest differences in extraversion and emotional stability. That is, the teams that performed best were composed of individuals who were high in conscientiousness and agreeableness, but included both extroverts and introverts as well as a range of emotional stability. These results indicated that as with individual performance, conscientiousness—planning, attention to detail—pays off in teams. Also, agreeable people are better at cooperating, another plus for working in a team setting. Further, for teams to succeed, both extroverts and introverts are needed to enact and accommodate the different roles within a team. Finally, the unexpected finding for emotional stability suggests that perhaps having a combination of calm and excitable people stimulates team process. These results reinforce the importance of personality characteristics for team member selection.

ORGANIZATIONAL CITIZENSHIP BEHAVIORS

The historical roots of organizational citizenship behavior (OCB) appear to lie in Chester Barnard's concept of "informal organization," which for Barnard (1938) represented the personal interactions and informal groupings of people at work. Bernard proposed that the informal organization complemented the formal structure of the organization. Katz (1964) further argued that assigned roles were insufficient for organizational success. For Katz, employee "spontaneous behavior" that goes beyond role specifications is critical for organizational effectiveness. Among the elements of spontaneous behavior Katz suggested were cooperating with and helping fellow employees, protecting the organization from damage, and providing suggestions to improve the organization's functioning. These behaviors can be recognized readily within the definitions by later developers of the organizational citizenship behavior construct (Smith, Organ, & Near, 1983; Borman & Motowidlo, 1993).

Organ (1988) originally defined OCB as "individual behavior that is discretionary, not directly or explicitly recognized by the formal reward system and that in the aggregate promotes the effective functioning of the organization" (p. 4). Borman and Motowidlo (1993), working from the direction of defining the job performance construct, defined contextual performance as "behaviors [that] do not support the technical core itself so much as they support the broader organization, social, and psychological environment in which the technical core must function" (p.73).

Several researchers (e.g., Morrison, 1994; Van Dyne, Cummings, & Parks, 1995) disagreed with Organ about the discretionary aspect of OCB. For some jobs, what Organ labeled OCBs fall within the role expectations (Conway, 1996). For example, the fulfillment of some jobs (e.g., nursing) may require helpfulness and cooperativeness although the job description may not explicitly include the terms "helpful" and "cooperative." Further, because these behaviors are implicitly expected by the supervisor and thus incorporated into their evaluations of subordinates, OCBs may be rewarded by the organization[4] (Werner, 2000). In light of these criticisms, Organ (1997) later redefined the construct to be more consistent with Borman and Motowidlo's (1993) contextual performance definition, as activities that contribute "to the maintenance and enhancement of the social and psychological context that supports task performance" (Organ, 1997, p. 91).

There has been continued debate about the dimensionality of OCB with several attempts to assimilate and categorize the divergent views (cf., Coleman & Borman, 2000; LePine, Erez, & Johnson, 2002; Podsakoff, MacKenzie, Paine, & Bachrach, 2000). Williams and Anderson (1991) suggested OCB could be categorized simply into two dimensions: OCB-I and OCB-O that represent behaviors directed toward other people within the organization (OCB-I) and behavior directed toward supporting the organization (OCB-O). Borman, Penner, Allen and Motowidlo (2001) have proposed three basic clusters of citizenship behavior: *personal support*, which is helpfulness directed toward others, *organizational support* which consists of defending the organization and complying with its rules (i.e., organizational compliance), and *conscientious initiative* which is persisting in the face of

[4] Research by Vey and Campbell (2004) revealed that most items tapping OCBs were considered by independent observers to represent in-role, as opposed to extra role, behavior. Vey and Campbell found, however, that altruism and civic virtue were seen as reliably extra-role.

difficult conditions and finding and completing work not part of one's duties, including self improvement efforts. Organ (1994) proposed five categories of OCB: altruism, conscientiousness, sportsmanship, courtesy, and civic virtue. The first, *altruism*, represents behaviors that have the effect of helping a specific other person with an organizationally relevant task or problem. *Conscientiousness* involves behaviors on the part of the employee that go beyond the minimum role requirements of the organization, in the areas of attendance, obeying rules and regulations, taking breaks, and so forth. The third, *sportsmanship,* is the willingness of the employee to tolerate less than ideal circumstances without complaining. *Courtesy* includes behaviors that are aimed at preventing work-related problems with others from occurring. Finally, *civic virtue* is characterized by behaviors on the part of an individual that indicates he or she participates in, is involved in, or is concerned about the life of the company (Podsakoff, MacKenzie, Moorman, & Fetter, 1990).

The commonalities of the different definitions suggest the different facets emanate from a core construct. Although there has been some discussion in the literature that OCB is an aggregate construct (cf., LePine et al., 2002), we support the idea that OCB is a latent construct and agree with LePine et al.'s proposition that the underlying factor is that of a willingness to help and cooperate in organizational contexts.

Measuring OCBs

Measuring OCBs has been done by creating instruments specific to the investigation (cf., LePine et al., 2002). These instruments typically are written to align items with one of the several prevailing structures of the construct (e.g., Borman & Motowidlo, 1993; Smith et al., 1983). The most common of these instruments in use appear to be those developed by Smith, et al. (1983) or Podsakoff, MacKenzie, Moorman, and Fetter (1990). Smith et al. (1983) created a 16-item measure of two dimensions: altruism and generalized compliance—both constitute helping behaviors with the former directed toward coworkers and the latter behaviors that are helpful for the organization (e.g., not being tardy or wasting company time). This scale has often been adapted for use by others (e.g., Wayne, Shore, & Liden, 1997) with the resulting alphas for both dimensions usually in the high .80s. The other scale that often has been used is that developed by Podsakoff et al. (1990). Using Organ's five facet OCB construct, Podsakoff et al. developed through factor analysis a 24-item measure that displayed good psychometric properties. Reported coefficient alphas have ranged from .67 to .91 for specific subscales with the overall scale typically in the .90s.

Big Five Personality Factors and OCB

There is an emerging consensus that elements of personality are related to OCB (Borman, et al., 2001; Organ, 1994; Organ & Ryan, 1995) although the proportions of variance accounted for are modest (*r*s in the .10s and .20s). Of the Big Five, the two personality factors that have most consistently correlated with OCB are conscientiousness and agreeableness (Organ, 1994; Organ & Ryan, 1995; Borman, Penner, Allen & Motowidlo, 2001). The Big Five factor of conscientiousness correlates most highly with organizational compliance (similar to Organ's conscientiousness variable) and with altruism. Conscientious people are more likely to accept responsibility and be thorough in their approach to life's tasks; these characteristics translate well into an organizational setting such as following rules and helping others with their work.

Given the types of items that appear on Big Five Personality inventories and those that measure OCBs, we are surprised that scores on the Big Five do not correlate more highly with OCB. For instance, if we compare items from the typical OCB measure for the conscientiousness facet (e.g.," I believe in giving an honest day's work for an honest day's pay") with an item from a statement based inventory for the Big Five factor of the same name (e.g., "I do just enough work to get by" [reversed scored]), there is considerable similarity in concept. As another example, compare an item tapping Organ's OCB facet of courtesy (e.g., "does not abuse the rights of others") with these items from a statement based Big Five inventory (e.g., "I respect others", "I am concerned about others") measuring agreeableness. (Big Five statements taken from the International Personality Item Pool (2008) for illustration.) These items appear to have considerable conceptual overlap so we wonder why the correlations are not greater.

In addition, based on the review of the *types* of items found on both types of measures, we believe that the measure of the OCB construct could be construed as narrow bandwidth (or lower order) personality factors. We realize the low correlations of OCB with conscientiousness (and other Big five factors) revealed in meta-analyses would appear to contradict this assertion. However, if we consider the possibility that conscientious might have multiple facets that are not necessarily highly correlated, it would make sense that OCBs might correlate at a fairly low level with the broad factor of conscientious, but at a moderate level with more narrowly defined facets of conscientiousness.

OCB and Teams

All of these elements of OCB could be valuable for harmonious team functioning (Ehrhart & Naumann, 2004; Van der Vegt, Van de Vliert, & Oosterhof, 2003). The behaviors that constitute OCBs would be expected to generalize to the team setting. Interestingly, relatively few researchers have investigated OCBs in teams (cf., Van der Vegt et al., 2003). In part, this lack of interest is probably a function of the level of analysis typically undertaken in team research where the unit of analysis is the team, not the individual. However, we would argue that the type of behaviors that constitute OCBs (i.e., altruism, courtesy) would be extremely useful in the team setting. Returning to the question we posed at the beginning of the chapter about how to form an effective team to solve a problem, it would seem that employees who are predisposed to be cooperative and helpful would be more prepared to listen to other team members and promote a constructive group process.

Cognitive Ability and Teams: Teamwork Knowledge, Skills, and Abilities (KSAs)

The utility of ability testing has already been briefly noted previously in this review for its role in predicting job success for individuals. Given the importance of cognitive ability to job performance (Schmidt & Hunter, 1998), it would seem that analogous aptitudes would be necessary to becoming good team members. The use of teams has become a popular strategy for organizations to accomplish complex tasks and projects requiring multiple perspectives. When individuals work in group or team environments, certain abilities and skills are likely to be important to maintain smooth functioning and effectiveness of a team (Stevens & Campion, 1994). Stevens and Campion (1994) reviewed the existing research relating individual teamwork competencies with team process. Based on this review, they developed a conceptual model that specified two primary drivers—interpersonal and self-management skills—that facilitate teamwork.

Teamwork Interpersonal KSAs

First, we will address the components that constitute interpersonal skills. For teams to become effective, the individual members of the group must effectively manage the interpersonal relationships with each other. A team-based setting requires team members to communicate effectively, to collaborate, and to resolve conflict.

Conflict Resolution KSAs

Team conflict occurs when "the actions of one or more members of the group are incompatible with, and resisted by, one or more of the other group members" (Forsyth, 1990, p. 79). When people work together, conflict is inevitable, but optimal team performance requires constructive conflict. How well a team manages those conflicts is an important indicator of success for the group. Individuals in teams need to recognize and encourage productive, and discourage unproductive, team conflict. When conflict arises, team members need to resolve it with appropriate strategies. To apply an appropriate strategy, team members must first recognize the type and source of conflict confronting the team and then implement an appropriate resolution for that conflict. In team contexts, the best resolution will focus on a win-win negotiation strategy rather than a win-lose. Not only does an integrative negotiation strategy help the team members resolve a problem efficiently, it also lays the foundation for solving future problems effectively (Gersick & Davis-Sacks, 1990).

Collaborative Problem Solving KSAs

In work teams, the problem solving demands are greater than the demands placed upon individuals. Teams need to understand how to manage the degree of group participation. The best group decision will usually result from the collective ideas and information shared by the group members. Teams, however, are not always better than individuals in decision making or problem solving. For example, groupthink (Janis, 1982), group polarization, or conformity could inhibit group dynamics and divergent thinking. To avoid these kinds of difficulties, groups must use different techniques to avoid such obstacles and achieve positive group process and actions. Therefore, team members need the ability to recognize the obstacles to collaborative group problem solving and the skills to implement appropriate corrective actions (Forsyth, 1990).

Communication KSAs

Effective communication has long been established as a strong influence on important team processes and outcomes (Leavitt, 1951). Without understanding how communications flow in a group setting, members might create a structure that prevents some members from sharing their information. For example, the decentralization of information channels is one technique to avoid communication obstacles. Members need to understand communication networks, and to use decentralized networks where possible. Members should openly exchange their information and also support others to do so. Members must understand one another in a complex interactive process. Listening becomes an important component of communication to smooth information exchange. Because communication does not always take place in a verbal form, members must also understand other forms of communication. Members should understand how daily conversations, small talk, or greetings “grease” team interactions. Therefore, knowledge of and ability to use small talk and ritualistic greetings is also important to team functioning.

Teamwork Self-Management KSAs

The second major dimension of Teamwork KSAs is Self-Management. One of the benefits attributed to teams is that they can function without direct supervision. Teams are often permitted considerable autonomy to engage in their work. This autonomy means that the team must have the ability to govern its direction. The ability to govern itself by setting appropriate goals, planning and coordinating the efforts of the team members toward those goals, and evaluating the outcomes, are key elements in the KSAs of a team to self-manage.

Goal Setting and Performance Management KSAs

These KSAs involve the understanding of establishing specific and challenging goals that are accepted by the team. Groups as well as individuals need to set appropriate goals that are challenging but attainable. Groups consist of members who need to reach an agreement in goal setting to enhance clarity and support among themselves. Self-managed groups evaluate continuously their progress and provide feedback to modify their plans if necessary. They also need to monitor individual performance to prevent social loafing or “free riding” from occurring. In addition, the KSA to provide feedback on both overall team performance and individual team member performance becomes especially important in self-managed groups (Stevens & Campion, 1994).

Planning and Task Coordination KSAs

This set of KSAs represents the capability to plan and coordinate activities, information, and task interdependencies among team members. Coordination and synchronization of team activities are necessary and they are central to self-management. As interdependency among team activities increases, the amount of required coordination increases and becomes more difficult. In an effective group, members specify what is expected for their tasks and roles and also share work by distributing a fair amount of workload assignments among the team members (Stevens & Campion, 1994). When team members understand the tasks to be done, their roles in accomplishing those tasks, and feel that the workload has been shared equitably, the group will be effective in guiding itself toward its objectives.

Assessing Teamwork KSAs

Using their model of teamwork skills as a guide (Stevens & Campion, 1994), Stevens and Campion developed the Teamwork-KSA Test (Stevens & Campion, 1997). The Teamwork-KSA Test focuses on the individual behaviors that are expected to contribute to group level performance. The TKSA consists of 35 multiple choice items based on the model of teamwork proposed by Stevens and Campion (1994). One point is given for each correct answer. Although the test contains five subscales, the authors suggest using a single composite score. Here is an example item tapping goal setting knowledge:

Suppose you are presented with the following types of goals. You are asked to pick one for your team to work on. Which would you choose? The four response options for this question are:

A. An easy goal to ensure that the team reaches it, thus creating a feeling of success;
B. A goal of average difficulty so the team will be somewhat challenged, but successful without too much trouble;
C. A difficult and challenging goal that will stretch the team to perform at a high level, but attainable so that effort will not be futile;
D. A very difficult task, or even impossible goal, so that even if the team falls short, it will at least have a very high target to aim for.

Stevens and Campion (1999) validated the TKSA test in two samples of employees. The TKSA was predictive of supervisory ratings of teamwork and peer evaluations with *r*s ranging from .21 to .52. They reported internal consistency at .80. McClough and Rogelberg (2003) administered the TKSA to student teams and found that the TKSA was predictive of individual team members' performance within their teams as rated by peers (.34) and independent raters (.31). In a manufacturing setting, Morgeson, Reider, and Campion (2005) found that the TKSA correlated .32 and .36 with job performance (contextual and task). Taken together, these four studies are supportive of the TKSA Test (as well as of cognitive ability in general; Stevens & Campion, 1999) in predicting individual success in teams. Now we move to a combination of variables we believe would be relevant for determining the "team worthiness" of an individual.

TEAM WORTHINESS?

As the TKSA studies to date show, ability testing is a valuable predictor of an individual's competence and behavior within a team setting. Also as noted, personality is a relevant element for individuals' contributions to a team[5]. Here, we propose that OCB would

[5] The context cannot be ignored. Different task demands on the team may call upon different resources of the team (Bond & Ng, 2004; LePine, 2003). Le Pine found, for example, that when teams experienced unexpected

complement TKSA aptitude and has already been demonstrated to be related to some components of the Big Five. In addition, if we conceptualize the measurement of the OCBs as dispositional and representative of lower order personality factors, we would expect OCBs to correlate more highly with the Big Five than has been found in previous studies. When we consider the question posed at the beginning of the chapter, our answer to what makes a team "worthy" individual is one who has an aptitude for team process, is conscientious, agreeable, cooperative, helpful, and courteous to team members.

PURPOSE OF STUDY

The purpose of this study was to assess the construct overlap of the aptitudes of TKSA, the personality factors of the Big Five, and the dispositions represented by OCBs. Because components of the Big Five (e.g., conscientiousness and agreeableness) have displayed small correlations with OCBs, we expected a significant relationship between the composite constructs of the Big Five and a typical measure of OCB. What previous research has not explicitly addressed, however, is the relationship of specific aptitudes such as the TKSA to OCB or Big Five. More specifically, we expect that the three constructs, (Big Five, TKSA, and OCB) would correlate significantly with each other and that the measured variables for each would load on their respective constructs.

METHOD

Procedure

Participants were recruited from upper-level undergraduate psychology and business school classes offered at a mid-sized university in southern California. Three instruments measuring teamwork KSAs, OCBs, and the Big Five personality factors were combined into a single survey packet. Instructors of classes were approached and if they approved, students were invited to participate in a survey. The survey was offered in both an online and paper version[6]. Twenty six percent of the resulting sample was administered paper copies; the majority (73%) of the surveys were completed online. If instructors permitted, students received participation credit toward their course grades.

Participants

Participants were 593 students enrolled in undergraduate and graduate psychology courses at a mid-sized university in southern California who voluntarily agreed to complete

changes to their tasks, those teams composed of members high in cognitive ability, achievement (one facet of conscientiousness), and openness but low in dependability (another facet of conscientiousness) performed best.

the survey. Nearly half (46%) of the students were seniors and another 31 percent were juniors. Of the sample, 10% of the sample was African-American, 6% were Asian, 42% White, 36% Hispanic, and 6% reported "other". The average age for the participants was 24.8 (SD = 7.2, range 18 to 57) years and women constituted 82% of the sample. Ninety-three percent of the sample had work experience. The average number of months working was 77.0 (6.4 years, SD=6.2). Of these, 16% had supervisory or managerial experience, 16% were full time non management employees, 38% were part time non management employees, 7% were not currently employed and 23% identified as full time students.

Measures

The Big Five Personality Mini-marker Scale (Saucier, 1994a). As noted earlier, this instrument is based on the five-factor model of personality. The factors measured are: 1) extraversion; 2) agreeableness; 3) conscientiousness; 4) emotional stability and 5) openness. The response scale is a Likert-type with anchors of 1, "extremely inaccurate" to 9, "extremely accurate." The items consist of 40 single adjectives (e.g., "Systematic"). Alphas for the five subscales for this study were as follows: extraversion .81, agreeableness, .80, conscientiousness, .78, emotional stability, .79, and openness, .78.

Organizational Citizenship Behavior Scale (Podsakoff, et al., 1990)

The scale is a 24-item Likert-type scale anchored with 1, "strongly agree" and 7 "strongly disagree". This measure assesses the extent to which a person reports engaging in organizational citizenship behaviors[7]. Four or five items are used to assess each of these subscales. An example item from the Altruism sub scale is, "I help others who have heavy workloads." To facilitate interpretation, the items were reverse coded so that higher scores represent more of the OCB. The alphas obtained in this study for each of the five subscales were as follows: Conscientiousness, .72, Sportsmanship, .71, Civic Virtue, .72, Courtesy, .65, and Altruism, .75.

Teamwork-KSA Test (Stevens & Campion, 1995)

This test is used to assess the aptitude to work successfully in teams. It is a 35-item multiple-choice test that is dichotomously scored. The test is based on the conceptual framework described earlier: interpersonal KSAs (knowledge, skill, and ability and conflict resolution and communication KSAs) and self-management KSAs (goal setting and performance management and planning and task coordination KSAs). It is used to identify those with the knowledge and skills necessary to work cooperatively in teams with the expectation that they would display those qualities in a work situation. Alpha has been reported at .80 (Stevens & Campion, 1999). For this sample, Cronbach's alpha was .74.

---

[6] [6]Though there have been concerns about measurement comparability with online testing relative to paper and pencil testing, the empirical evidence indicate little to no difference in scores (means, variances) or emergent factor structures (Meade, Michels, Lautenschalter, 2007; Potosky & Bobko, 2004).

[7] This scale was originally designed and used by peers to rate others. We revised the scale for use as a self-report. Others have used this (and other instruments initially developed for use by peers and supervisors) as self report (cf., Podsakoff et al., 2000).

RESULTS

A confirmatory factor analysis (CFA) was performed using EQS (Bentler, 1995). Each of the primary constructs (latent variables) of interest--OCB, Teamwork KSA, and Big Five PF--had five indicators. The three latent variables, OCB, Big Five Personality, and Teamwork KSAs were hypothesized to covary with each other.

Before conducting the CFA analysis, the data were examined for univariate and multivariate normality[8]. Eighteen cases were deleted from further analyses because of nonormality and 47 cases were dropped because of missing data. After deleting cases with missing data or outliers, 546 cases remained for the CFA.

Factorability of the matrix was also assessed prior to the CFA. The Kaiser-Meyer-Olkin measure of sampling adequacy was .83 and Bartlett's Test for Sphericity was 2075.48, $p<.001$, indicating the data set was suitable for factoring (Bentler & Dudgeon, 1996).

Means and standard deviations of the measured variables can be found in Table 1. Zero order correlations of the measured variables are in Table 2.

Model Fit

To identify relationships among factors and measured variables, structural equation modeling was conducted using EQS. Figure 1 shows the model and factor loadings (standardized coefficients) and correlations between the latent constructs. The independence chi-square that the variables were unrelated was easily rejected, χ^2 (df=105, N = 546) = 1981.41, $p < .001$. Because Mardia's test for multivariate kurtosis was significant (z=4.42), the Satorra-Bentler scaled χ^2 test was used. The Satorra-Bentler scaled χ^2 indicated significant differences between the estimated population covariance matrix and the sample covariance matrix, χ^2 (df=87, N = 546) = 328.59, $p < .001$. The comparative fit index (CFI) indicated an initially poor fitting model, CFI = .87, based on recommendations by Bentler (1990) and Marsh & Han (1996). The RMSEA, .07, was within the acceptable maximum (.08) suggested by Browne and Cudeck (1998). The Lagrange multiplier (LM) test and Wald test were inspected to assess for paths to add or remove. On the basis of the LM test, paths for 9 correlated errors were added to the model[9]. No paths were deleted. A chi-square difference test indicated a significant improvement to the model, $\Delta\chi^2$ (df=9) = 164.55, $p < .001$, with the addition of these paths. The Satorra-Bentler scaled χ^2 test and the comparative fit index

[8] Several variables were significantly skewed. For the OCB measure, these variables were conscientiousness, courtesy, and altruism. The Big Five variables agreeableness and conscientiousness were skewed. None of the variables were significantly kurtotic. With 15 measured variables in the analysis an examination of linearity through all pairwise scatter plots was impractical; therefore, a spot check of a few scatter plots including the smallest pairwise correlation revealed linear relationships only and no curvilinear relationships. The determinant of the matrix was larger than zero, suggesting no singularity. Evaluation of the residuals by examining the distribution of standardized residuals in EQS showed that the residuals were small, centered around zero and fairly symmetrical.

[9] The nine correlated errors were for 1)the communication and collaboration subscales of the TKSA, 2)the extraversion and conscientiousness subscales, 3)openness and extraversion subscales, and 4)emotional stability and openness subscales of the Big Five, and 5)conscientiousness subscale of the Big Five and the OCB subscale conscientiousness, 6)the Big Five subscale of emotional stability and OCB sportsmanship subscale and 7)the Big Five subscale of agreeableness and OCB civic virtue, 8)Big Five subscale openness and TKSA subscale of planning, and 9) Big Five subscale openness and TKSA subscale of collaboration.

demonstrated a good model fit [χ^2 (78, N = 546) = 175.59, p < .001, CFI = .95, RMSEA = .06] based on Hu and Bentler (1999) who suggest a CFI of .95.

Table 1. Means and Standard Deviations of the Measured Variables

Construct	Measured Variable (subscale)	Mean	SD
Teamwork KSAs[a]			
	Conflict resolution	2.57	1.05
	Collaborative problem solving	3.73	1.75
	Communication	6.25	2.14
	Goal setting	2.89	1.30
	Planning	3.00	1.35
Organizational Citizenship Behavior[b]			
	Altruism	4.83	.80
	Civic virtue	3.97	1.17
	Conscientiousness	4.47	.96
	Courtesy	4.86	.79
	Sportsmanship	3.62	.99
Big Five Personality Factors[c]			
	Agreeableness	7.25	1.15
	Conscientiousness	6.89	1.08
	Emotional stability	5.71	1.39
	Extraversion	5.82	1.38
	Openness to experience	6.59	1.22

Notes. N = 593
[a]Subcale total is average number correct
[b]Mean of item endorsement, 7-point scale
[c]Mean of item endorsement, 9-point scale

Each measured variable had a significant relationship with its latent variable. All three latent variables were significantly correlated, OCB with Teamwork KSA (.38), Teamwork KSA and the Big Five (.40), and OCB with the Big Five (.69).

Another inspection of the LM post hoc test indicated that adding another path would contribute to a better fit of model to data. The measured variable of sportsmanship (OCB) was permitted to cross load on both the Big Five latent factor and the OCB factor. Adding this path improved the CFI to .98 and RMSEA to .04 [Satorra Bentler χ^2 (77, N = 546) = 119.31, p = .001; the chi-square difference, $\Delta\chi^2$ (df=1) = 23.00, p < .001]. (See Figure 2 for the revised model.) The standardized loadings remained nearly the same for all measured variables with the exception of the OCB measured variable sportsmanship, which when permitted to cross load, loaded significantly on the Big Five composite construct and became nonsignificant on the OCB composite construct.

Table 2. Intercorrelations of Measured Variables

Variable	1	2	3	4	5	6	7	8	9	10	11	12	13	14	15
1. TKSA-Conflict resolution															
2. TKSA-Collaborative problem solving	.29														
3. TKSA-Communication	.35	.44													
4. TKSA-Goal Setting	.27	.29	.25												
5. TKSA-Planning	.35	.40	.39	.32											
6. OCB-Altruism	.15	.12	.08	.09	.13										
7. OCB-Civic Virtue	.10	.14	.06	.15	.21	.43									
8. OCB-Conscientiousness	.10	.10	.09	.10	.15	.51	.43								
9. OCB-Courtesy	.21	.18	.15	.16	.27	.60	.47	.50							
10. OCB-Sportsmanship	.14	.20	.17	.10	.23	.23	.16	.19	.28						
11. Big Five-Agreeableness	.22	.14	.17	.11	.25	.39	.26	.37	.47	.41					
12. Big Five-Conscientiousness	.21	.15	.17	.11	.20	.27	.19	.34	.28	.34	.54				
13. Big Five-Emotional Stability	.00	.04	.00	.04	.04	.20	.19	.21	.23	.40	.33	.23			
14. Big Five-Extraversion	.08	.06	.05	.02	.05	.17	.15	.10	.07	.14	.13	.25	.16		
15. Big Five-Openness to Experience	.20	.22	.12	.07	.28	.26	.22	.21	.28	.21	.38	.33	.07	.37	

Notes. N= 546. Correlations greater than .14 are statistically significant at p< .01.

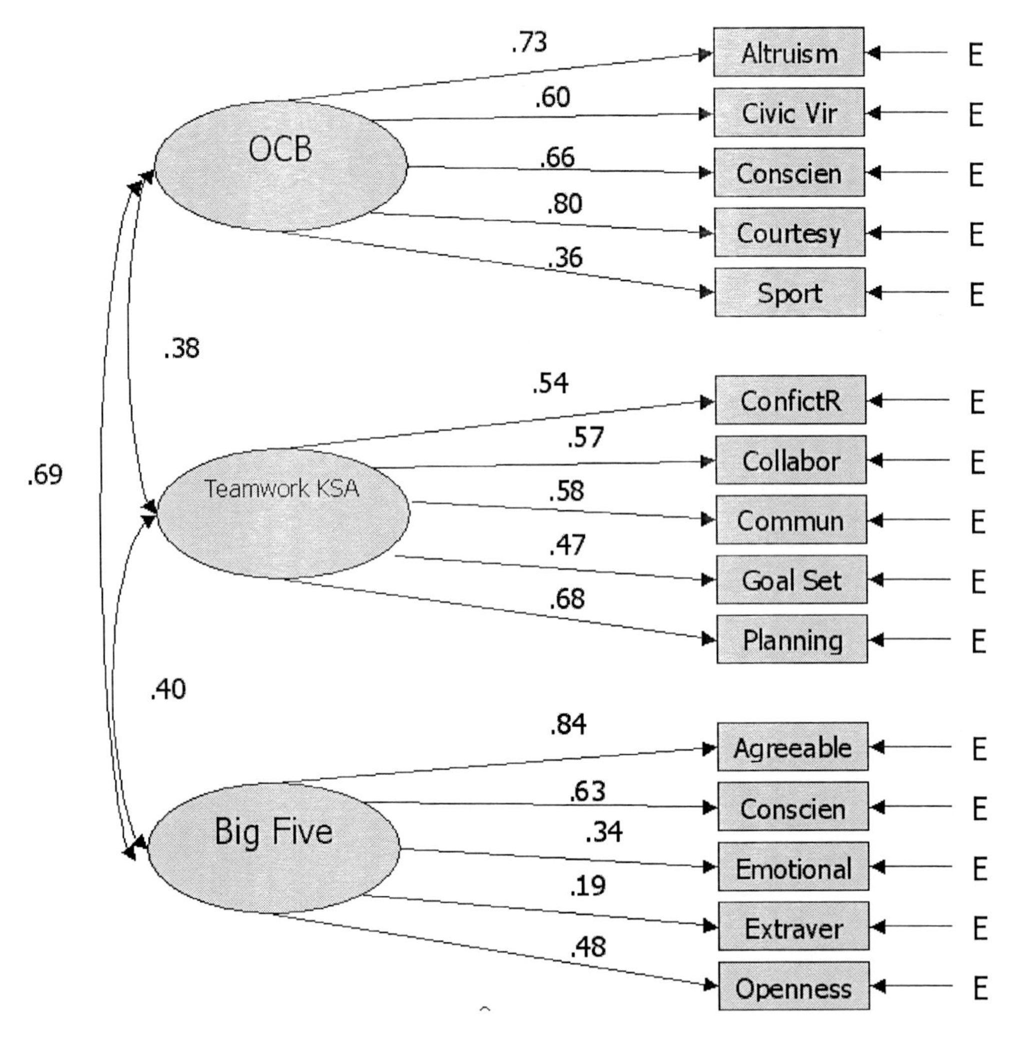

Figure 1. Model 1: Structural model of organizational citizenship behavior, the Big Five personality factors, and Teamwork Knowledge, Skills, and Abilities.

Discussion

The model as predicted (Figure 1) fit the data well, within the range of the fit indices most frequently employed, and the model was in line with our expectations and previous research and theory. However, one of the post hoc fit indices suggested a significantly better fitting model with the addition of the OCB measured variable sportsmanship to the Big Five composite construct. While we are in no way suggesting a change to the Big Five structure, this additional path, based on the data, provides some support for our contention that OCBs, as typically measured, may contain narrow bandwidths of personality traits. We discuss, in turn, a description of each construct as defined in Model 1 (Figure 1), starting with the Teamwork KSA construct, and then turn to a discussion of the intersections of the three constructs.

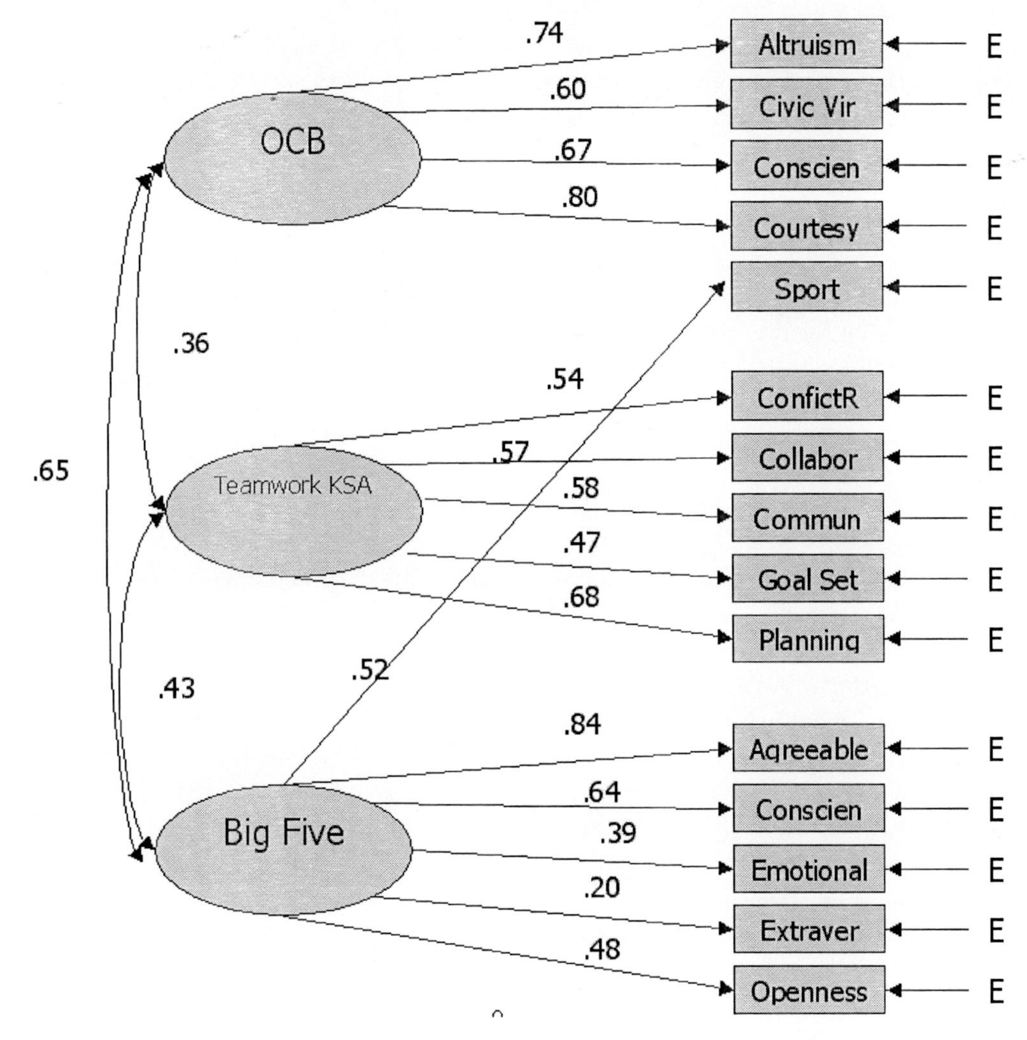

Figure 2. Model 2: Structural model of organizational citizenship behavior, the Big Five personality factors, and Teamwork Knowledge, Skills, and Abilities with sportsmanship path to Big Five added.

Teamwork Knowledge, Skill and Ability Factor Structure

All measured variables loaded highly and relatively consistently on the TKSA latent construct, with a difference of .21 separating the lowest loading from the highest. The subscale, planning and task coordination was the highest loading measured variable on the latent variable with the measured variables, conflict resolution, collaboration, and communication, nearly equally loading at slightly lower loadings. Goal setting is not as well represented as the previous four measures, but is still a significant subfactor.

The intercorrelations indicate that the scales are moderately, not highly, correlated with each other (see Table 2) and the pattern for intercorrelations define meaningful relationships. For example, the highest intercorrelation (.44) is between collaborative problem solving and communication: knowledge of how to collaborate with others would require some knowledge of how to communicate with team members. The lowest intercorrelation (.27) is between goal setting and communication. Knowledge of goal setting would not necessarily require one to have skill in using communication; clearly, knowledge and skill in communication would be necessary for conveying the goals to team members.

Although the test's authors (Stevens & Campion, 1997) recommend using the TKSA as a composite score, the factor structure[1], loadings, and the moderate intercorrelations of the subtests suggest that using subtests independently may be feasible in circumstances where time constraints might be critical and two or three of the concepts tapped by the subscales are the most relevant for the type of team to be composed. (Our primary reservation would be that the reliabilities of the relatively short subtests are likely to be below or at the low end of the acceptable range).

Big Five Personality Factor Structure

If we consider the measured variables that loaded most highly on the latent construct as central to the composite, we find that agreeableness (loading of .84) best describes the collective personality construct, with conscientiousness (.63) also heavily weighted. Agreeable people are easy going, tolerant, friendly, and value social harmony. Those high in conscientiousness are achievement driven, dependable and prefer to operate from a plan. Openness and emotional stability loaded at a moderate level. Most notably, extraversion loaded rather low, though significantly, on this composite construct. Musek (2007) has suggested that a composite Big One factor subsumes all of the Big Five into a combination of all personality characteristics that are personally valued[2]. If so, then this composite describes the most valued personality as a very agreeable, conscientious, moderately open and emotionally stable person with little surgency.

The low loading of Extraversion is the most surprising result as extraversion has been a commonly extracted factor of the Big Five from the earliest work (Tupes & Christal, 1961). Hough's (1992) work may serve to provide some insight. She has suggested that extraversion has two primary facets: Affiliation and potency. A person high in affiliation is social, outgoing, and likes to be with people; in contrast, those low in the facet are shy, reserved, and uncomfortable in social situations. Potency can be conceptualized as energy with high scorers being active and forceful, and low scorers, lethargic. An inspection of the adjectives in the

[1] Two CFAs in which a one factor solution was contrasted with a two-factor solution (interpersonal KSAs and self management KSAs) yielded identical CFIs (.99), nearly identical factor loadings on factors in both solutions, very similar chi square probabilities and RMSEA values. The correlation between the two latent constructs in the two-factor solution was .95, indicating that a single factor was adequate for defining the structure of the five subtests.

[2] We conducted a principal axis factor analysis on the Big Five measured variables and found two possible higher order factors in which agreeableness, conscientiousness and emotional stability loaded on a first factor and extraversion and openness loaded on a second (and much smaller) factor. These results replicate Digman's (1997) meta-analysis findings of two higher order factors he labeled Superfactors Alpha and Beta. Superfactor Alpha consisted of Agreeableness, Conscientiousness and Emotional Stability while Superfactor Beta consisted of Extraversion and Openness. Though investigating higher order factors was not our intention with this study, our findings provide evidence that Digman was correct in proposing higher order meta-traits. Therefore, this finding of meta-traits has limited applicability to our premise that personality is related to the selection of team "worthy" individuals; that is, we are more concerned with more thinly sliced facets of the

Mini-marker Big Five measure used (Saucier, 1994a) shows that the measured variable extraversion contains both affiliation and potency facets. To explore the possibility that the low loading of extraversion may be a result of a complex factor, we conducted an exploratory principal axis factor analysis (PAF) with varimax rotation of the extraversion items. This PAF resulted in two factors. The solution tended to mirror Hough's two factors of affiliation (i.e., shy, bashful, and quiet) and potency (i.e., energetic, talkative, extroverted, bold, and withdrawn), but the solution is confounded by the fact that three of the four reverse scored items loaded on one factor.

A complex construct, however, could explain the relatively strong zero order correlation of extraversion with openness (.37) and yet low correlations (.13, .16) with agreeableness and emotional stability. We might expect a potency facet to correlate with openness but not with agreeableness or emotional stability. Energetic and outgoing individuals would seem to have more curiosity and potential for adventure; however, energy levels and preference for affiliation could be related differentially to agreeableness or emotional stability. The implication of this finding for teams is that the two facets of extraversion may operate differentially in team settings. For example, an affiliative disposition would be an important foundation for cooperation among team members, but potency might interfere with team process if there were too much or too little among the team members.

OCB Factor Structure

A review of the factor loadings for the OCB construct indicated that the measured variable courtesy (.80) was the highest loading variable with the measured variable altruism also loading highly (.73). This structure compares favorably with previous research that indicates helpfulness is a consistent theme in the meta-analyses as well as the conceptual review of OCBs. Civic virtue and conscientiousness also load highly; both of these measured variables address intentions that can be seen as helpful to the organization[3], i.e., not taking extra breaks, keeping up to date with changes in the organization. In the team context, civic virtue might take the form of making sure that team members know about any organizational policy changes that might affect the functioning of the team; conscientious team members would be sure to attend all team meetings and prepared to participate.

In the first model (Figure 1), the lowest loading measured variable was sportsmanship (.36). Permitting this variable (sportsmanship) to load on the Big Five composite led to a significantly better fit of the model to the data. When sportsmanship was permitted to cross load, it loaded significantly on the Big Five composite and became a nonsignificant loading on the OCB composite. Though this modification was not consistent with our initial proposed model, this result supports our conjecture that OCBs as typically measured are more a disposition than a pure sample of behavior. The significant loading of sportsmanship on the

Big Five that predict team behavior. However, that we found the same factor structure as Digman (1997) in a data set collected for a different purpose provides support for the existence of meta-traits.

[3] CFAs of a single and two-factor solution of the OCB subscales were conducted. In the two-factor solution, we placed altruism and courtesy on an OCB-I factor, and conscientiousness, civic virtue and sportsmanship on an OCB-O factor. The CFIs were identical (.99) for both the single and two factor solutions. In the case of the two-factor solution, the correlation between the two latent constructs was .97, suggesting a single underlying factor. Sportsmanship was the lowest loading factor in both factor solutions as it was in Model 1's SEM.

Big Five supports the idea that aspects of OCBs as usually measured are a narrow bandwidth of personality and would reasonably emerge from a foundation of a broad base of personality traits such as the Big Five framework.

Relationship of the Latent Constructs

The Big Five and TKSA

At a factor level of analysis, Teamwork KSA and Big Five personality were significantly and positively correlated. This suggests, not surprisingly, that individuals' personalities may significantly affect their ability to work and interact with others. At the measured variable level of analysis, Big Five's conscientiousness, agreeableness, and openness were correlated with the measured TKSA variables of conflict resolution and planning and coordination, a result consistent with other research linking ability and personality (Busato, Prins, Elshout, & Hamaker, 2000). Openness was also related to collaborative problem solving.

Duff, Boyle, Dunleavy, and Ferguson (2004) found that personality influenced individuals' learning style and academic performance. Individuals high in conscientiousness tended to take deep and strategic learning approaches. Individuals who use a "deep" learning style relate new material to already learned information and personal experience, thus processing the information more deeply. If this result is also true for learning Teamwork KSAs, individuals high in conscientiousness will learn the KSAs, utilize them practically, and be efficient team members. As a result, they may perform better in an environment where collaboration is necessary.

An individual who is conscientiousness would be more likely to pay attention to his or her environment. Therefore, a conscientious person may be more likely to notice objectives that need to be achieved and emerging problems within a team. Reasonably, an individual noticing these issues would be likely to exhibit Teamwork KSA planning, coordination, and conflict resolution in an effort to perform well in a teamwork setting. Therefore, it makes sense that individuals who are high in Teamwork KSAs are also likely to be conscientious. Agreeable people may be more sensitive to noticing disagreements or may have had more psychological experience in how cooperation lubricates team process and thus would be better able to comprehend the best means to coordinate and to resolve conflict.

The correlation of the measured variable, openness, with the three TKSA subscales (planning and coordination, collaborative problem solving, and conflict resolution) suggests that the personality variable openness may represent intellect as well as openness to experience, something that has been proposed by several personality researchers (Digman & Takemoto-Choeck, 1981; Peabody & Goldberg, 1989). There has been debate about the meaning of this Big Five factor (Saucier, 1992, 1994b). This factor has creative, reflective, and intellectual facets. Any of these concepts might graft well into the aptitudes for planning and coordination (r=.28), collaborative problem solving (.22) and conflict resolution (.20). Although openness has not been shown to relate reliably to team outcomes, these correlations of teamwork aptitude with openness suggests that this variable cannot be dismissed as a factor of team "worthiness."

The Big Five and OCBs

If we accept that the "Big One" (Musek, 2007) of the Big Five in this sample was heavily weighted by Agreeableness, that the measured variable OCB sportsmanship would load also on the Big Five is a logical outcome. Sportsmanship is defined as not complaining about small inconveniences or finding fault with the organization. Sportsmanship in the team context is wholly consistent with the idea of being tolerant and adaptive such as we are likely to see in people with the trait of agreeableness. To be a "good sport" means not complaining when a team meeting is running long or when team plans need to be changed to accommodate changes in the situation.

Taken together, sportsmanship and agreeableness are two individual characteristics that should lay the groundwork for good team cohesion. These characteristics are not sufficient but may be considered necessary ingredients to develop camaraderie among team members. Previous research (Kichuk & Wiesner, 1998) has shown that both conscientiousness and agreeableness was useful for teams. We suggest that sportsmanship as conceptualized could be considered a more finely sliced facet of the Big Five agreeableness factor. Further, sportsmanship can be very useful for pleasant working relationships within a team. A "squeaky wheel" makes for a disagreeable team member and just one disagreeable team member can disrupt team cohesion (Barrick, Stewart, Neubert, & Mount, 1998).

OCBs and TKSAs

Our hypothesis was that OCB and Teamwork KSA would share variance due to their ability to assess the skills and personality necessary for individuals to interact and work together effectively. Results indicated a moderate correlation between OCB and Teamwork KSAs, r = .38. The correlation between the OCB and Teamwork KSAs latent constructs was moderate, signifying that individuals presenting altruistic behaviors, such as helping other coworkers, may also demonstrate Teamwork KSAs (i.e., conflict resolution, planning and coordination). Helping other team members complete tasks may resolve conflicts that arise within a team. This type of behavior may be demonstrating both altruistic behaviors and conflict resolution skills. Other OCBs such as courtesy may also relate to conflict resolution. An individual who avoids problems with other team members may be resolving conflict by preventing it from happening in the first place. Behaviors that demonstrate sportsmanship, such as not complaining, may also enhance an individual's ability to resolve conflict within a team environment. Demonstrating a positive attitude by not complaining could be a contributing factor to a team member's conflict resolution skills.

We argue that although OCBs have typically been conceptualized as desired outcomes (i.e., part of job performance, Borman & Motowidlo, 1993), they could also be treated as predictors, especially if conceptualized as facets of personality. We believe this because the kinds of behaviors described by Organ and others are likely to be more specific representations of personality, especially in how they are measured. There is some evidence for this idea in the work of Penner, Fritzsche, Craiger, and Freifeld (1995) who have proposed and developed a personality measurement of a prosocial personality construct. Their prosocial personality construct consists of two facets: other-oriented empathy and helpfulness. These two factors can function independently of each other and differentially predict helping behavior. The helpfulness factor better predicts helping behaviors while the other-oriented empathy factor correlates more consistently with personality factors such as agreeableness and nurturance (Penner et al., 1995). Interestingly, these two facets resemble the two factors

Williams and Anderson (1991) proposed for OCB: OCB-I and OCB-O. Both prosocial facets would seem to be important for teamwork. OCB-I and OCB-O factors, when conceptualized as directed toward the team instead of the organization (cf., Janssen, & Huang, 2008), would also be important for predicting team members' propensities to work well with others on a team toward a common objective.

Limitations

All measures were collected at one time and analyzed using correlational statistics. Because all data were collected via survey, common method variance could have inflated the correlations (Podsakoff, MacKenzie, Lee, & Podsakoff, 2003). Spector (1987, 2006) has strongly argued that common, systematic method variance is not as problematic as originally imagined in survey research. Furthermore, the use of a SEM approach also mitigates this concern somewhat (Kline, Sulsky, & Rever-Moriyama, 2000). Although the problem of common method variance is not resolved with SEM techniques, the effects related to measurement error are diminished and permit a better potential for identifying the existence of common method variance.

The use of self report measures of personality has also received criticism from several industrial psychologists (cf., Morgeson, et al., 2007a) for use within applicant populations. The concern is that applicants will use self-enhancement (e.g., faking) strategies and thus not reveal their true personalities. We recognize this concern but argue that in this data set these participants had little to gain by altering their responses to the personality measure. In the case of the TKSA, a cognitive ability test, faking is not an issue. Even allowing for self-enhancement, the strength of the relationship of the two self reported (personality, OCB) constructs with a cognitive ability test (TKSA) suggest that not all variance can be attributed to either spurious self report or common method variance. That TKSA correlated moderately with OCB and Big Five supports the idea that certain cognitive abilities and dispositions are related. Those with more intellectual insight into how groups function are also more likely to see themselves as good organization citizens and as possessing favorable personality dispositions—more agreeable, more conscientious, and more open.

Conclusion

In this chapter, we examined the factorial structure and interrelationships of three individual characteristics that demonstrate team worthiness: Personality as defined by the Big Five, organizational citizenship behavior which we argue are usually measured at the level of narrow bandwidths of personality, and aptitude for teamwork. We found support for our conjecture that OCBs are dispositions similar to personality traits in that the latent constructs correlated highly and the OCB measure variable sportsmanship loaded on the Big Five composite construct more highly than on the OCB construct. We propose that these three constructs are meaningful fundamentals for team success.

Author's Notes

A paper based on an earlier analysis of a portion of these data was presented at the American Psychological Society (now Association for Psychological Science) in Los Angeles, California, May 28, 2005.

The authors thank Hikari Moreno, Toshio Murase, Jeremy Holforty, and Will Wyatt, who collected and entered data for this project. We also thank Kathie Pelletier who provided helpful suggestions on an earlier draft.

Please address correspondence to jkottke@csusb.edu.

References

Allport, G. W, & Odbert, H. S. (1936). Trait-names: A psycho-lexical study. *Psychological Monographs, 47*, (1, Whole No. 211).

Barnard, C.I. (1938) *The functions of the executive*. Cambridge, MA: Harvard University Press.

Barrick, M. R., & Mount, M. K. (1991). The Big Five personality dimensions and job performance: A meta-analysis. *Personnel Psychology, 44*, 1-26.

Barrick, M. R., Mount, M. K., & Judge, T. A. (2001). Personality and performance at the beginning of the new millennium: What do we know and where do we go next? *International Journal of Selection and Assessment, 9*(1/2), 9-30.

Barrick, M.R., Stewart, G.L., Neubert, M.J., & Mount, M.K. (1998). Relating member ability and personality to work-team processes and team effectiveness. *Journal of Applied Psychology, 83*, 43-51.

Bentler, P.M. (1990). Comparative fit indexes in structural models. *Psychological Bulletin, 107*, 238–246.

Bentler, P.M. (1995). *EQS structural equations program manual*. Encino, CA: Multivariate Software, Inc.

Bentler, P.M., & Dudgeon, P. (1996). Covariance structure analysis: Statistical practice, theory, and directions. *Annual Review of Psychology, 47*, 563–592.

Bentz, V. J. (1962). *The Sears Experience in the Investigation, Description, and Prediction of Executive Behavior*. Chicago: Sears, Roebuck and Co.

Bentz, V. J. (1983, August). *Executive selection at Sears: An update.* Paper presented at the Fourth Annual Conference on Frontiers of Industrial Psychology, Virginia Polytechnic Institute, Blacksburg.

Bond, M.H. & Ng, I.W.-C. (2004). The depth of a group's personality resources: Impacts on group process and group performance. *Asian Journal of Social Psychology, 7*, 285-300.

Borgatta, E. F. (1964). The structure of personality characteristics. *Behavioral Science, 9*, 8-17.

Borman, W.C. & Motowidlo, S.J. (1993). Expanding the criterion domain to include elements of contextual performance. In F. Schmidt & W. C. Borman (Eds.). *Personnel selection in organizations.* San Francisco: Jossey-Bass.

Borman, W.C., Penner, L.A., Allen, T.D., & Motowidlo, S.J. (2001). Personality predictors of citizenship performance. *International Journal of Selection and Assessment, 9*, 52-69.

Browne, M.W., & Cudeck, R. (1993). Alternative ways of assessing model fit. In Bollen, K.A., Long, J.S. (Eds.), *Testing structural equation models* (pp. 445–455). Newbury Park, CA: Sage.

Busato, V.V., Prins, F.J., Elshout, J.J., & Hamaker, C. (2000). Intellectual ability, learning style, personality, achievement motivation and academic success of psychology students in higher education. *Personality and Individual Differences, 29*, 1057-1068.

Cattell, R. B. (1945). The description of personality: Principles and findings in a factor analysis. *American Journal of Psychology, 58*, 69–90.

Cattell, R. B. (1947). Confirmation and clarification of primary personality factors. *Psychometrika, 12*, 197-220.

Coleman, V.I. & Borman, W.C. (2000). Investigating the underlying structure of the citizenship performance domain. *Human Resource Management Review, 10*, 25-44.

Conway, J.M. (1996). Additional construct validity evidence for the task/contextual performance distinction. *Human Performance, 9*, 309-329.

Costa, P. T. Jr., & McCrae, R. R. (1992). *Revised NEO Personality Inventory (NEO-PI-R) and NEO Five-Factor (NEO-FFI) Professional Manual.* Odessa, FL: Psychological Assessment Resources.

DeYoung, C.G., Quilty, L.C., & Peterson, J.B. (2007). Between facets and domains: 10 aspects of the Big Five. *Journal of Applied Psychology, 93*, 880-896.

Digman, J.M. (1997). Higher-order factors of the Big Five. *Journal of Personality and Social Psychology, 73*, 1246–1256.

Digman, J.M. (2000). Personality structure: Emergence of the five-factor model. *Annual Review of Psychology, 4*, 417-440.

Digman, J. M., & Takemoto-Choek, N. K. (1981). Factors in the natural language of personality: Re-analysis, comparison, and interpretation of six major studies. *Multivariate Behavioral Research, 16,* 149-170.

Duff, A., Boyle, E., Dunleavy, K., & Ferguson, J. (2004). The relationship between personality, approach to learning and academic performance. *Personality and Individual Differences, 36*, 1907-1920.

Dunbar, M., Ford, G., Hunt, K., & Der, G. (2000). Question wording effects in the assessment of global self-esteem. *European Journal of Psychological Assessment, 16*(1), 13-19.

Edwards, A.L. (1959). *The Edwards Personal Preference Schedule*. New York: Psychological Corporation.

Ehrhart, M.G. & Naumann, S.E. (2004). Organizational citizenship behavior in work groups: A group norms approach. *Journal of Applied Psychology, 89*, 960-974.

Eysenck, H. J. (1991). Dimensions of personality: 16, 5, or 3?—Criteria for a taxonomic paradigm. *Personality and Individual Differences, 12,* 773-790.

Fiske, D. W. (1949). Consistency of the factorial structures of personality ratings from different sources. *Journal of Abnormal and Social Psychology, 44*, 329-344.

Forsyth, D.R., (1990). *Group dynamics,* 2nd ed. Pacific Grove, CA: Brooks/Cole.

Gersick, C.J.G. & Davis-Sacks, M.D. (1990). Summary: Task forces. In J.R. Hackman (Ed.), *Groups that work (and those that don't): Creating conditions for effective teamwork* (pp. 146-153). San Francisco: Jossey-Bass.

Ghiselli, E. E. & Barthol, R. P. (1953). The validity of personality inventories in the selection of employees. *Journal of Applied Psychology, 38*,18-20.

Gill, C.M. & Hodgkinson, G.P. (2007). Development and validation of the Five-Factor Model Questionnaire (FFMQ): An adjectival-based personality inventory for use in occupational settings. *Personnel Psychology, 60*, 731-766.

Goldberg, L. R. (1990). An alternative "Description of personality": The Big-Five factor structure. *Journal of Personality and Social Psychology, 59,* 1216-1229.

Goldberg, L.R. (1992). The development of markers for the Big-Five factor structure. *Psychological Assessment, 4*(1), 26-42.

Goldberg, L.R. (1993). The structure of phenotypic personality traits. *American Psychologist, 48*, 26–34.

Griggs v. Duke Power Co., 401 U.S. 424 (1971).

Guion, R.M. & Gottier, R.F. (1965). Validity of personality measures in personnel selection. *Personnel Psychology, 18*, 135-164.

Holden, R. R., Fekken, G.C., & Jackson, D. N. (1985). Structured personality test item characteristics and validity. *Journal of Research in Personality, 19*(4), 386-394.

Hough, L.M. (1992). The "Big Five" personality variables–construct confusion: Description versus prediction. *Human Performance, 5*, 139–155.

Hu, L.-T., & Bentler, P.M. (1999). Cutoff criteria for fit indexes in covariance structure analysis: Conventional criteria versus new alternatives. Structural Equation Modeling: *A Multidisciplinary Journal, 6*, 1–55.

Hurtz, G.M. & Donovan, J.J. (2000). Personality and job performance: The Big Five revisited. *Journal of Applied Psychology, 85*, 869-879.

International Personality Item Pool, *A Scientific Collaboratory for the Development of Advanced Measures of Personality and Other Individual Differences*, http://ipip.ori.org//. Retrieved July 15, 2008.

Jackson, D.N. (1984). *Personality research form manual.* Port Huron, MI: Research Psychologists Press.

Janis, I.L. (1982). *Victims of groupthink*, 2nd ed. Boston: Houghton Mifflin.

Janssen, O., & Huang, X. (2008). Us and me: Team identification and individual differentiation as complementary drivers of team members' citizenship and creative behaviors. *Journal of Management, 34*, 69-88.

Jenkins, M., & Griffith, R. (2004). Using personality constructs to predict performance: Narrow or broad bandwidth. *Journal of Business and Psychology, 19*, 255-269.

Judge, T.A., Bono, J. E., Ilies, R., & Gerhardt, M.W. (2002). Personality and leadership: A qualitative and quantitative review. *Journal of Applied Psychology, 87,* 765-780.

Kamdar, D., & Van Dyne, L. (2007). The joint effects of personality and workplace social exchange relationships in predicting task performance and citizenship performance. *Journal of Applied Psychology, 92*, 1286-1298.

Katz, D. (1964) The motivational basis of organizational behavior. *Behavioral Science, 9*, 131-146.

Kline, T.J.B., Sulsky, L.M., & Rever-Moriyama, S.D. (2000). Common method variance and specification errors: A practical approach to detection. *Journal of Psychology, 134*, 401-421.

Kichuk, S.L., & Wiesner, W.H. (1998). The Big Five personality factors and team performance: implications for selecting successful product design teams. *Journal of Engineering and Technology Management, 14*, 195-221.

Koppes, L.L. (2003). Industrial-Organizational Psychology. In I.B. Weiner (Series Ed.) & D.K. Freedheim (Vol. Ed.), *Handbook of Psychology: Volume I, History of Psychology*, pp.367-389. Hoboken, NJ: John Wiley & Sons.

Leavitt, H.J. (1951). Some effects of certain communication patterns on group performance. *Journal of Abnormal Social Psychology, 46*, 38-50.

LePine, J.A. (2003). Team adaptation and post change performance: Effects of team composition in terms of members' cognitive ability and personality. *Journal of Applied Psychology, 88*, 27-39.

LePine, J.A., Erez, A., & Johnson, D.E. (2002). The nature and dimensionality of organizational citizenship behavior: A critical review and meta-analysis. *Journal of Applied Psychology, 87,* 52-65.

Marsh , H.W., & Han, K.T. (1996). Assessing goodness of fit: Is parsimony always desirable? *The Journal of Experimental Education, 64*, 364–390.

Meade, A.W., Michels, L.C., & Lautenschlager, G.J. (2007). Are internet and paper-and-pencil personality tests truly comparable ? An experimental design measurement invariance study. *Organizational Research Methods, 10*, 322-345.

McClough, A.C. & Rogelberg, S.G. (2003). Selection in teams: An exploration of the Teamwork Knowledge, Skills, and Ability Test. *International Journal of Selection and Assessment, 11*, 56-66.

McCrae, R.R., & Costa, P.T. Jr. (1987). Validation of the five-factor model of personality across instruments and observers. *Journal of Personality and Social Psychology, 52*, 81-90.

McCrae, R.R., & Costa, P.T., Jr. (1997). Personality trait structure as a human universal. *American Psychologist, 52*, 509-516.

Mischel, W. (1968). *Personality and assessment.* New York: Wiley.

Morgeson, F.P., Campion, M.A., Dipboye, R.L., Hollenbeck, J.R., Murphy, K., & Schmitt, N. (2007a). Are we getting fooled again? Coming to terms with limitations in the use of personality tests for personnel selection. *Personnel Psychology, 60*, 1029-1049.

Morgeson, F.P., Campion, M.A., Dipboye, R.L., Hollenbeck, J.R., Murphy, K., & Schmitt, N. (2007b). Reconsidering the use of personality tests in personnel selection contexts. *Personnel Psychology, 60*, 683-729.

Morgeson, F.P., Reider, M.H., & Campion, M.A. (2005). Selecting individuals in team settings: The importance of social skills, personality characteristics, and teamwork knowledge. *Personnel Psychology, 58*, 583-611.

Morrison, E.W. (1994). Role definitions and organizational citizenship behavior: The importance of the employee's perspective. *Academy of Management Journal, 37*, 1543-1567.

Musek, J. (2007). A general factor of personality: Evidence for the Big One in the five-factor model. *Journal of Research in Personality, 41*, 1213-1233.

Myers-Briggs, I., & McCaulley, M. (1985). *A guide to the development and use of the Myers-Briggs Type Indicator.* Palo Alto, CA: Consulting Psychologists Press.

Neuman, G.A. & Wright, J. (1999). Team effectiveness: Beyond skills and cognitive ability. *Journal of Applied Psychology, 84*, 376-389.

Neuman, G.A., Wagner, S.H., & Christiansen, N.D. (1999). The relationship between work-team personality composition and the job performance of teams. *Group & Organization Management,* 24, 28-45.

Norman, W. X. (1963). Toward an adequate taxonomy of personality attributes: Replicated factor structure in peer nomination personality ratings. *Journal of Abnormal and Social Psychology, 66,* 574-583.

Ones, D.S., Dilchert, S., Viswesvaran, C., & Judge, T.A. (2007). In support of personality assessment in organizational settings. *Personnel Psychology, 60*, 995-1027.

Organ, D.W. (1988). *Organizational citizenship behavior: The good soldier syndrome.* Lexington MA: Lexington Books.

Organ, D. W. (1994). Personality and organizational citizenship behavior. *Journal of Management*, 20(2), 465-478.

Organ, D.W. (1997). Organizational citizenship behavior: It's construct clean-up time. *Human Performance, 10*, 85-97.

Organ, D.W. & Ryan, K. (1995). A meta-analytic review of attitudinal and dispositional predictors of organizational citizenship behavior. *Personnel Psychology, 48*, 775-802.

Peabody, D., & Goldberg, L. R. (1989). Some determinants of factor structures from personality-trait descriptors. *Journal of Personality and Social Psychology, 57*, 552-567.

Peeters, M.S.G., VanTuijl, H.F.J.M., Rutte, C.G., & Reymen, I.M.M.J. (2006). Personality and team performance: A meta-analysis. *European Journal of Personality, 20*, 377-396.

Penner, L.A., Fritzsche, B.A., Craiger, J.P. & Freifeld, T.R. (1995) Measuring the prosocial personality. In J. Butcher and C. D. Spielberger (Eds.) *Advances in personality assessment.* (Vol. 10). Hillsdale, NJ: LEA

Podsakoff, P.M., MacKenzie, S.B., Moorman, R.H., & Fetter, R. (1990). Transformational leader behaviors and their effects on followers' trust in their leader, satisfaction, and organizational citizenship behaviors. *Leadership Quarterly,* 1(2), 107-142.

Podsakoff, P.M., MacKenzie, S.B., Paine, J.B., & Bachrach, D.G. (2000). Organizational citizenship behaviors: A critical review of the theoretical and empirical literature and suggestions for future research. *Journal of Management, 26*, 513-563.

Potosky, D., & Bobko, P. (2004). Selection testing via the Internet: Practical considerations and exploratory empirical findings. *Personnel Psychology, 57*, 1003-1034.

Pytlik Zillig, L. M., Hemenover, S. H., & Dienstbier, R. A. (2002). What do we assess when we assess a Big Five trait? A content analysis of the affective, behavioral, and cognitive processes represented in Big Five personality inventories. *Personality and Social Psychology Bulletin, 28*, 847–858.

Roberts, B.W., Chernyshenko, O.S., Stark, S., & Goldberg, L.R. (2005). The structure of conscientiousness: An empirical investigation based on seven major personality questionnaires. *Personnel Psychology, 58*(1), 103–139.

Rothstein, M.G., & Goffin, R.D. (2006). The use of personality measures in personnel selection: What does current research support? *Human Resource Management Review, 16*, 155-180.

Salgado, J. F., Moscoso, S., & Lado, M. (2003). Evidence of cross-cultural invariance of the Big Five personality dimensions in work settings. *European Journal of Personality, 17*, 567-576.

Salgado, J.F. (2003). Predicting job performance using FFM and non-FFM personality measures. *Journal of Occupational and Organizational Psychology, 76*(3), 323-346.

Salgado, J.F., & deFruyt, F. (2005). Personality in personnel selection. In A. Evers, N. Anderson, and O. Smit-Voskuijl (Eds.), *Handbook of Personnel Selection* (pp. 174-198).Oxford, UK: Blackwell.

Saucier, G. (1992). Openness versus intellect: Much ado about nothing? *European Journal of Personality, 6*, 381-386.

Saucier, G. (1994a). Mini-Markers: A mini-version of Goldberg's unipolar Big-Five Markers. *Journal of Personality Assessment, 63*, 506-516.

Saucier, G. (1994b). Trapnell versus the lexical factor: More ado about nothing? *European Journal of Personality, 8*, 291-298.

Saucier, G., & Goldberg, L.R. (1996). The language of personality: Lexical perspectives on the five-factor model. InWiggins JS (Ed.), *The five-factor model of personality*. London: Guilford.

Schmidt, F.L., & Hunter, J.E. (1998). The validity and utility of selection methods in personnel psychology: Practical and theoretical implications of 85 years of research findings. *Psychological Bulletin, 124*, 262-272.

Smith, G. M. (1967). Usefulness of peer ratings of personality in educational research. *Educational and Psychological Measurement, 27*, 967-984.

Smith, C.A., Organ, D.W., & Near, J.P. (1983). Organizational citizenship behavior: Its nature and antecedents. *Journal of Applied Psychology, 68*, 653-663.

Stevens, M. J. & Campion, M. A. (1994). The knowledge, skill, and ability requirements for teamwork: Implications for human resource management. *Journal of Management*, 20 (2), 503-530.

Stevens, M.J. & Campion, M.A. (1997). *Teamwork-KSA test: Examiners manual*. Rosemont, IL: McGraw-Hill/London House.

Stevens, M. J. & Campion, M. A. (1999). Staffing work teams: Development and validation of a selection test for teamwork settings. *Journal of Management*, 25(2), 207-228.

Tupes, E.C. (1957). Personality trait related to effectiveness of junior and senior Air Force officers. *USAF Personnel Training Research Center Research Report* No. 57-125.

Tupes, E. C. & Christal, R. E. (1961). Recurrent personality factors based on trait ratings. Technical Report ASD-TR-61-97. Lackland Air Force Base, TX: U.S. Air Force; also published in *Journal of Personality, 60*: 225-25 1.

Van der Vegt, G.S., Van de Vliert, E. & Oosterhof, A. (2003). Informational dissimilarity and organizational citizenship behavior: The role of intrateam interdependence and team identification. *Academy of Management Journal, 46*, 715-727.

Van Dyne, L., Cummings. L.L. & Parks, J.J. (1995). Extra role behaviors: Inn pursuit of construct and definitional clarity (a bridge over muddled waters). In L.L. Cummings & B.M. Staw (Eds.), *Research in organizational behavior* (Vol. 17, pp. 215-285). Greenwich, CT: JAI.

Vey, M.A. & Campbell, J.P. (2004). In-role or extra-role organizational citizenship behavior: Which are we measuring? *Human Performance, 17*, 119-135.

Wadsworth, R.S. (1920). *Personal Data Sheet*. Chicago: Stoelting.

Wayne, S.J., Shore, L.J. & Liden, R.C. (1997). Perceived organizational support and leader-member exchange: A social exchange perspective. *Academy of Management Journal, 40*, 82-111.

Werner, J.M. (2000). Implications of OCB and contextual performance for human resource management. *Human Resource Management Review, 10*, 3-24.

Wiggins, J.S. (1968). Personality structure. *Annual Review of Psychology, 19*, 293–350.

Williams, I. J. & Anderson, S.E. (1991). Job satisfaction and organizational commitment as predictors of organizational citizenship and in-role behaviors. *Journal of Management, 17*, 601-617.

In: Personality Assessment: New Research
Editors: Lauren B. Palcroft and Melissa V. Lopez
ISBN: 978-1-60692-796-0

Chapter 4

PERSONALITY TRAITS AND DAILY MOODS

***Cristina Ottaviani*[a], *David Shapiro*[*b], *Iris Goldstein*[b] and *Valerie Gofman*[b]**
[a]Department of Psychology, University of Bologna, Italy
[b]Department of Psychiatry, University of California, Los Angeles, USA

ABSTRACT

Previous research has shown that personality traits and emotional states are associated with variations in blood pressure. The major aim of this chapter is to examine the relationship between personality traits and diary reports of moods on a work and an off-work day. Secondary aims are to compare mood reports in men and women as a function of the day of recording. A healthy sample of 110 women and 110 men rated their moods in a diary three times an hour on a work and a nonwork day. Personality scales were administered. Significant effects of mood intensity were obtained for work vs. off days and in interaction with scores on personality tests of anxiety, anger out, cynical hostility, and depression. Given the health significance of emotion in mental and physical health, these findings in healthy individuals suggest that personality traits may affect the regulation of blood pressure via their effects on emotional responses to daily life events and thereby serve as risk factors for hypertension.

INTRODUCTION

In the diagnosis and treatment of behavioral, mental, and physical disorders, we largely depend on verbal reports of pain and discomfort, physical and mental dysfunctions, and emotional states and distress. In medicine, such reports are usually followed up by objective tests, the results of which vary in their diagnostic value. A good example is the relation between ambulatory blood pressure and coincidental emotional reactions and states, as noted in a diary. In one of the first studies of this kind, negative affect states during the day were found to be associated with a rise in blood pressure (Sokolow, Werdegar, Perloff, Cowan, &

Brenenstuhl, 1970), and research since then has documented the association between various reported mood states and concurrent blood pressure and heart rate (e.g., Shapiro, Jamner, Goldstein, & Delfino, 2001). Besides the thoroughly documented association between negative moods and health outcomes, positive affective states have also been demonstrated to be protective and directly related to health-relevant biological processes. Specifically, Steptoe and colleagues showed an association between greater happiness and lower salivary cortisol both on working and nonworking days, reduced fibrinogen stress responses, and lower ambulatory heart rate in men. The effects were independent of age, socioeconomic status, smoking, body mass, and psychological distress and were stable at a 3-year follow-up (Steptoe, Wardle, & Marmot, 2005). The authors further demonstrated that positive affect is associated with reduced levels of inflammatory markers in women (Steptoe, O'Donnell, Badrick, Kumari, & Marmot, 2008). Furthermore, in the Shapiro et al. (2001) study, although the intensity of positive mood diary reports was not directly related to the concurrent level of blood pressure, the simultaneous occurrence of positive mood countered the effects of negative mood on blood pressure.

These observations provided the impetus for the adoption and promulgation of diary methods in psychological research, now dubbed "ecological momentary assessment," as an alternative to laboratory and questionnaire methods (for review, see Shiffman, Stone, & Hufford, 2008). Moods are affected by the activities and circumstances in which the individual is engaged during the day (Stone, Neale, & Shiffman, 1993). Aside from their ecological validity as compared with retrospective reports or moods obtained under special and limited circumstances in the laboratory, the large number of mood ratings provides reliable estimates of individual differences in mood. For example, Mitsutake and colleagues (2001) found a noteworthy positive association between the circadian amplitude of negative affect and the rhythm of both systolic and diastolic blood pressure, suggesting that blood pressure is raised in the presence of large swings in negative affect.

Diary methods of obtaining mood data have been applied in everyday settings in comparing emotional expression and reactivity in different patient groups (Ebner-Priemer, Kuo, Kleindienst, Welch, Reisch, Reinhard, Lieb, Linehan, & Bohus, 2007; Hallas, Thornton, Fabri, Fox, & Jackson, 2003), in examining the effects of environmental stimuli and substances on emotional states (Aan Het Rot, Moskowitz, & Young, 2008; Macht & Dettmer, 2006), in field studies of cardiovascular, hormonal, and other biological correlates of emotional states (Adam, 2006; Davydov, Shapiro, & Goldstein, 2004; Davydov, Shapiro, Goldstein, & Chicz-DeMet, 2005; Steptoe, Gibson, Hamer, & Wardle, 2007), in research on aging (Carstensen, Pasupathi, Mayr, & Nesselroade, 2000), and in basic studies of everyday mood in different conditions (Kashdan & Steger, 2006; Shapiro, Jamner, & Goldstein, 1997). This research has advanced our knowledge of the role of emotion and mood in mental and physical well-being, a fundamental topic in health psychology and psychosomatic medicine.

In this paper, we present mood data obtained in a large sample of healthy adults who participated in an ambulatory study in which blood pressure was recorded three times an hour on a work day and on a day off work. The participants were asked to rate their moods in a diary at each of these times. The participants also filled out personality tests on anger out, anxiety, cynical hostility, and depression. The importance of these characteristics for cardiovascular disease was thoroughly reviewed by Rozanski, Blumenthal, and Kaplan (1999)

* Department of Psychiatry, 760 Westwood Plaza, Los Angeles, CA 90095, USA (e-mail: dshapiro@ucla.edu).

with many studies cited of clinical samples, such as individuals with major depression or anxiety disorder, as well as normal populations with these behavioral dispositions. The review discussed pathophysiological mechanisms that appear to link these dispositions with cardiovascular disease. These individual characteristics have been extensively investigated in epidemiologic studies and their role in health well documented. Such factors have also been investigated in other mental and physical disorders — for example, see reviews for cancer (Baltrusch, Stangel, & Titze, 1991), irritable bowel disease (Talal & Drossman, 1995), diabetes (Cox & Gonder-Frederick, 1992), and asthma (Wright, Rodriguez, & Cohen, 1998).

In previous studies in our laboratory of various samples of healthy individuals, diary mood ratings and the personality traits of hostility, anger out, and anxiety were found related to ambulatory blood pressure, in some cases as a function of day of recording as well as individual differences in ethnicity, family history of hypertension, and menstrual cycle (Davydov et al., 2004; Goldstein & Shapiro, 2000; Jamner, Shapiro, Goldstein, & Hug, 1991; Shapiro, Goldstein, & Jamner, 1996; Shapiro et al., 1997). The primary objective of this paper is to examine the link between personality and mood reports to test the hypothesis that the personality traits of anger, anxiety, hostility, and depression are associated with the intensity of positive and negative moods. The relation between these traits and mood reports provides a psychological mechanism for the link between personality and blood pressure and risk for hypertension. It also examines differences in mood between genders and between a work day and an off-work day, which are assumed to differ in degree of challenge and stress for the individual.

The relationship between personality and moods has been deeply studied in adolescents with the aim of developing targeted preventive interventions. For example, Whalen, Jamner, Henker, & Delfino (2002) found that girls high in depression and aggression also reported more anxiety, stress, and fatigue, less happiness and well-being than did their peers. The authors successively tested one hundred fifty-five teenagers every 30 minutes for two 4-day intervals, and found that high-anxiety teenagers, compared with low-anxiety teenagers, expressed higher levels not only of anxiety and stress but also of anger, sadness, and fatigue, along with lower levels of happiness and well-being (Henker, Whalen, Jamner, & Delfino, 2002). Moreover, Robbins & Tanck (1997) found a relationship between dispositional depression and diary-rated angry feelings in undergraduate students. Underwood, Froming, & Moore (2006) investigated the influence of a mood manipulation on personality measures and found that mood manipulation did not affect any of the personality measures suggesting a plausible direction of the relationship between these two variables. One study specifically addressed the relationship between personality factors and mood dimensions in a sample of two hundred subjects (Aitken Harris, & Lucia, 2003) and suggested that personality and moods are related constructs. However, these results were obtained from the correlations between a personality inventory and a standardized mood scale, thus ignoring the mood variability that accompanies daily events. The same approach was taken by Kokkonen & Pulkkinen (2001) in a study of gender differences in mood but relied on a single measure of moods. Our goal in this chapter was to overcome the limitations of previous studies by examining the link between personality and moods in a large healthy sample using ecological assessment, considering gender differences and the impact of real life stress on moods by comparing a work and an off-work day.

METHOD

Participants

The participants were 110 men and 110 women, 22 to 50 years of age (mean 32.5, SD 7.2), mean years of education 17.1 (SD 2.8), 82% of whom were employed in full-time day shifts in a variety of jobs at the University of California, Los Angeles. The remainder held full-time jobs in the surrounding Los Angeles area. Exclusionary factors were significant health problems (coronary heart disease, diabetes, use of antihypertensive drugs, and prior diagnosis of hypertension) and moderate obesity (body mass index > 32 kg/m^2). Also excluded were women who were post-menopausal or had been pregnant or lactating the 12 previous months. The ethnic distribution was 41 % Caucasian-, 31 % Asian-, 16 % African-, and 12 % Latino-American. Men and women did not differ in age, education, or ethnicity. All participants gave informed consent, approved by the UCLA Institutional Review Board.

Procedures

The study consisted of three sessions. In the first session, the participants provided information on demographics and filled out scales on personality traits, social support, and job stress. During sessions 2 and 3, ambulatory blood pressure was recorded for 24 hours on a work day and an off work day, counterbalanced. The interval between the two sessions was a few days to a week. During the work day, the ambulatory session began approximately ½ hour before the person's work shift, with a comparable time on the off day. The ambulatory recorder operated on a variable schedule three times per hour during waking hours and once per hour during sleep. On each inflation of the cuff during waking hours, participants were asked to fill out a paper-and-pencil diary, indicating time, location, activity, and ratings of moods. This paper is focused on the mood reports.

Moods

Participants used a 5-point numerical scale from "none" to "extreme amount" to rate the following moods: alert, angry, anxious, happy, sad, sleepy, stressed, and tired. Factor analysis of average mood ratings per person or of all mood reports pooled indicates that moods fall into three independent dimensions: positive (alert, happy); negative (angry, anxious, sad, stressed); energy/fatigue (sleepy, tired) (see Shapiro et al., 2001).

Personality Measures

The following personality scales were administered. Cook-Medley Hostility Inventory (CM) reflects a cynical and mistrusting attitude toward others (Cook & Medley, 1954). Spielberger Anger Expression Scale (Spielberger, 1988) provides scores on two dimensions of anger expression, Anger In and Anger Out. As previous research in our laboratory has shown few findings for Anger In, only the data for Anger Out (ANGOUT) are presented in this paper. Spielberger State-Trait Anxiety Inventory (STAI) measures the general disposition to experience anxiety frequently (Spielberger, Gorsuch, Lushene, Vagg, & Jacobs, 1979). Center for Epidemiologic Scale of Depression (CESD) is designed to measure depressive symptoms in the general population (Radloff, 1977).

Data Analysis

The mean (sd) of diaries completed was 46.1 (7.7), range 18-72, on the work day and 43.9 (7.4), range 21-61, on the off day. For each day, to control for individual differences in the total number of mood reports per day, we calculated the percentage of the total number of ratings at each of the five levels of intensity, per day, per participant. As observed in our previous studies of diary data, mood ratings are not evenly distributed across level of intensity. They can be highly skewed and clustered in a few levels. In using percentages, we provide exact information on the relative frequency of mood reports at each level of intensity. For each of the 8 moods, General Linear Models were used with the two sets of five repeated percentages (intensity 1 to 5) for each day as the dependent variables and gender as an independent variable. In these analyses, the within-subject dependent variables were DAY (work day, off day) and INTENSITY (5 levels) and the independent variable was GENDER (men, women). These analyses assessed the effects of DAY, GENDER, and DAY X GENDER. Then, the analyses were repeated with each personality test score entered in singly as an additional independent variable. These models included the following within-subject dependent variables, DAY (work day, off day) and INTENSITY (5 levels) and the following between-subject independent variables, GENDER (women, men) and a personality test score, such as ANGOUT, entered one at a time in each model. The models included all interactions. As the total percentage across the 5 levels of intensity summed to 100, only findings pertaining to INTENSITY are presented. For ease of presentation, the personality measures were dichotomized. To reduce the amount of detail and make the paper more readable, we restricted the latter analyses to one mood in each of the three dimensions, stressed, happy, and tired, the same moods we reported on previously in a study of mood and blood pressure based on data from a large sample of women nurses (Shapiro et al., 2001). Multivariate tests (Wilks' Lambda) were used to test the statistical significance of all within-subject effects. The .05 level was regarded statistically significant.

RESULTS

We first present the basic mood data, followed by the effects for personality.

Day and Gender

Table 1 shows the percentage of ratings at each level of intensity for the work day and the off day for men and women. For the negative moods (angry, anxious, sad, and stressed), the ratings were mainly made at level 1 (none). Of these moods, the ratings for stressed and anxious were distributed more evenly. For the positive moods (alert and happy), most ratings were made at levels 2, 3, and 4. The energy/arousal moods (sleepy, tired) were rated mainly at levels 1, 2, and 3. For all moods, the main effect for INTENSITY was significant at $p < .001$, reflecting the uneven distributions of the percentages. Men and women did not differ in the distribution of mood ratings as a function of level of intensity.

Table 1. Mood rating frequency (%) by intensity, day, and gender

MOOD	GENDER	WORK					OFF WORK				
		INTENSITY					INTENSITY				
		1	2	3	4	5	1	2	3	4	5
ALERT	Men	10.9	17.9	34.4	26.8	10.0	12.8	17.2	37.0	24.6	8.1
	Women	8.7	16.9	28.9	26.3	19.0	9.8	15.2	30.4	27.2	17.2
ANGRY	Men	90.8	6.1	2.3	0.5	0.2	92.6	4.9	1.5	0.7	0.2
	Women	92.9	5.0	1.4	0.6	0.2	94.0	4.3	0.9	0.1	0.1
ANXIOUS	Men	71.9	16.8	6.4	2.2	0.5	75.0	17.3	5.5	1.4	0.6
	Women	74.8	18.1	5..3	1.3	0.3	79.8	14.5	4.6	0.6	0.2
HAPPY	Men	5.8	16.0	44.7	29.1	4.3	4.9	13.9	42.8	31.4	6.8
	Women	7.7	15.0	41.3	28.1	7.7	6.0	12.5	37.7	33.1	10.6
SAD	Men	92.6	4.6	1.4	0.9	0.3	93.0	4.7	1.4	0.9	0.3
	Women	92.9	5.1	1.7	0.1	0.1	93.2	5.2	1.0	0.1	0.1
SLEEPY	Men	62.1	21.0	10.0	4.8	2.0	63.4	21.2	8.1	4.8	2.2
	Women	63.5	20.7	10.3	4.0	1.3	63.5	19.6	9.5	4.8	2.4
STRESSED	Men	65.7	24.0	7.2	2.1	0.7	75.3	17.2	4.7	1.7	0.7
	Women	67.9	21.7	7.8	1.8	0.5	77.5	16.2	4.6	1.1	0.4
TIRED	Men	44.5	32.7	15.1	5.6	1.9	49.6	31.8	11.6	4.4	2.4
	Women	42.9	33.3	16.7	5.6	1.3	45.8	31.7	14.7	5.8	1.7

The interaction of DAY and INTENSITY was significant for anxious ($p < .02$), happy ($p = .001$), and stressed ($p < .001$). For anxious and for stressed, fewer ratings of "none" were made on the work day. The ratings for happy were more positive on the off day than the work day (see Table 1).

Personality Traits

STAI: INTENSITY X STAI effects were significant for happy ($p = .05$) and stressed ($p = .004$). See Figure 1. Participants scoring low on STAI rated themselves as happier and less stressed than high STAI participants.

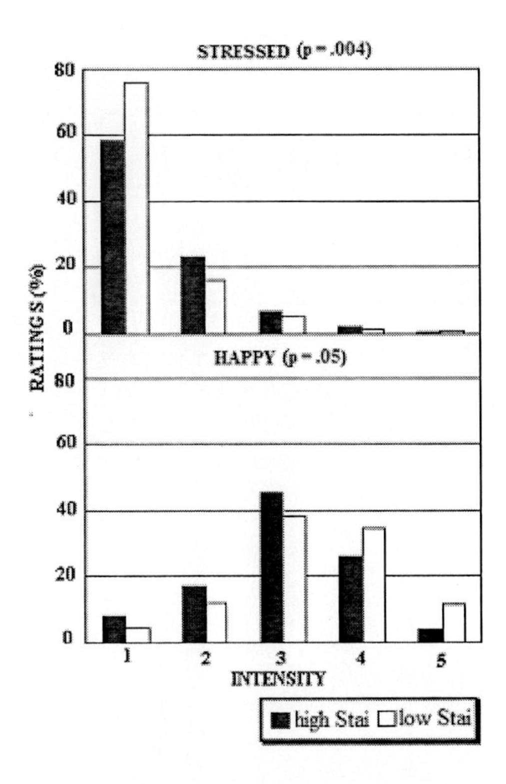

Figure 1. The effect of anxiety (STAI) on ratings of stressed and happy.

ANGOUT: The effect for GENDER X INTENSITY X ANGOUT was significant for stressed ($p = .02$), and the effect for DAY X INTENSITY X ANGOUT was significant for tired ($p = .04$). See Figure 2. High scores on ANGOUT were associated with relatively higher intensity of ratings of stressed in men than in women. Low ANGOUT participants reported being less tired on both days, the effect being more pronounced on the work day.

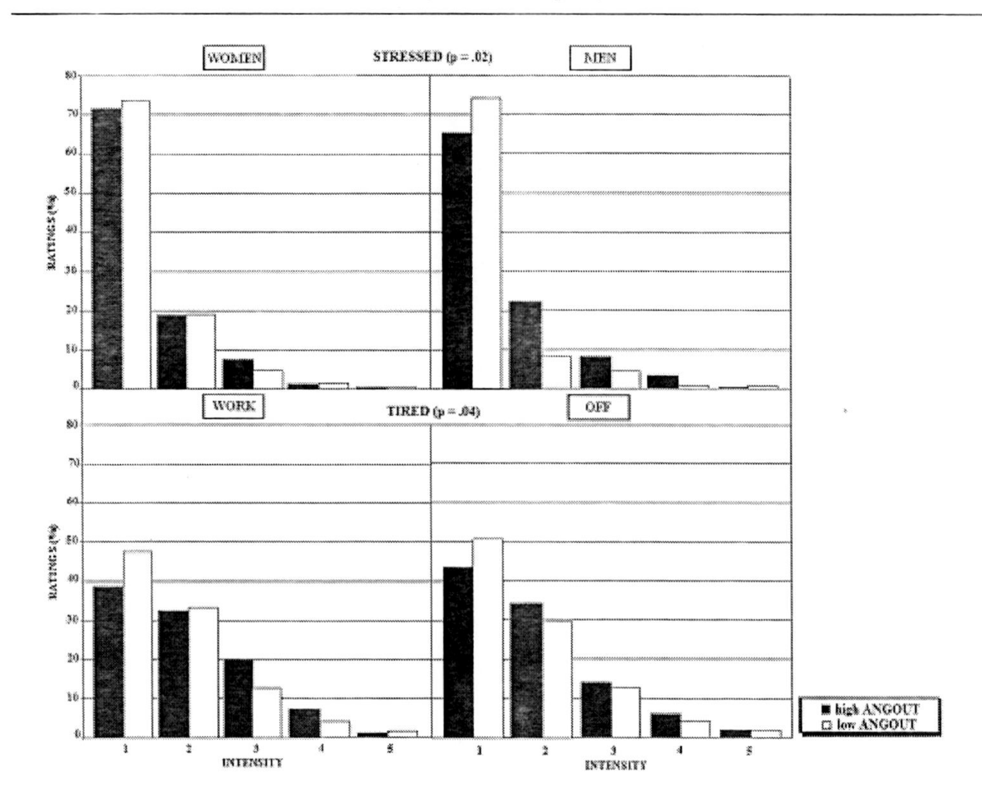

Figure 2. The effect of gender and anger out on ratings of stressed.

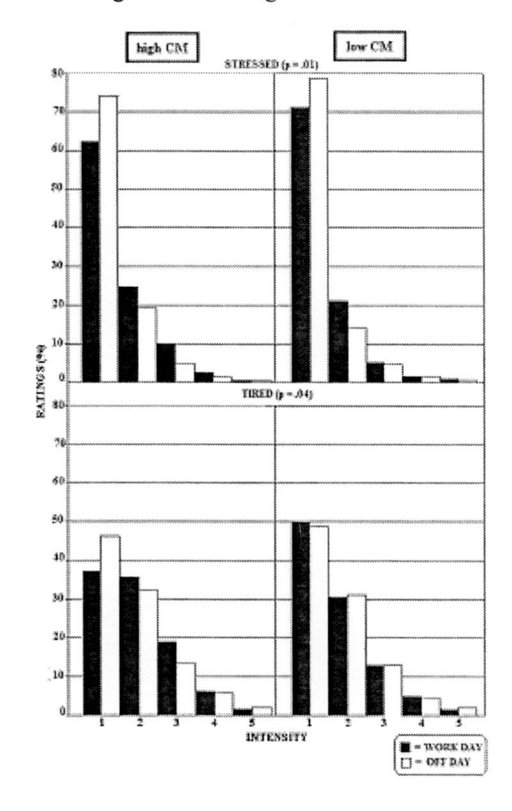

Figure 3. The effect of day and hostility on ratings of tired.

CM: DAY X INTENSITY X CM effects were significant for stressed (p = .01) and tired (p = .04). See Figure 3. High CM participants reported being more stressed and tired on the work day than the off day. Low CM showed little difference between the two days.

CESD: The INTENSITY X CESD interaction was significant for happy (p = .008), stressed (p = .02), and tired (p = .01), and the 4-way interaction was significant for tired (p =.04). See Figure 4. High CESD participants reported being more stressed and tired and less happy than low CESD participants (bottom panel). For the 4-way effect for tired (top panel), the CESD effect was greater in men than women, especially in the work-off day comparison.

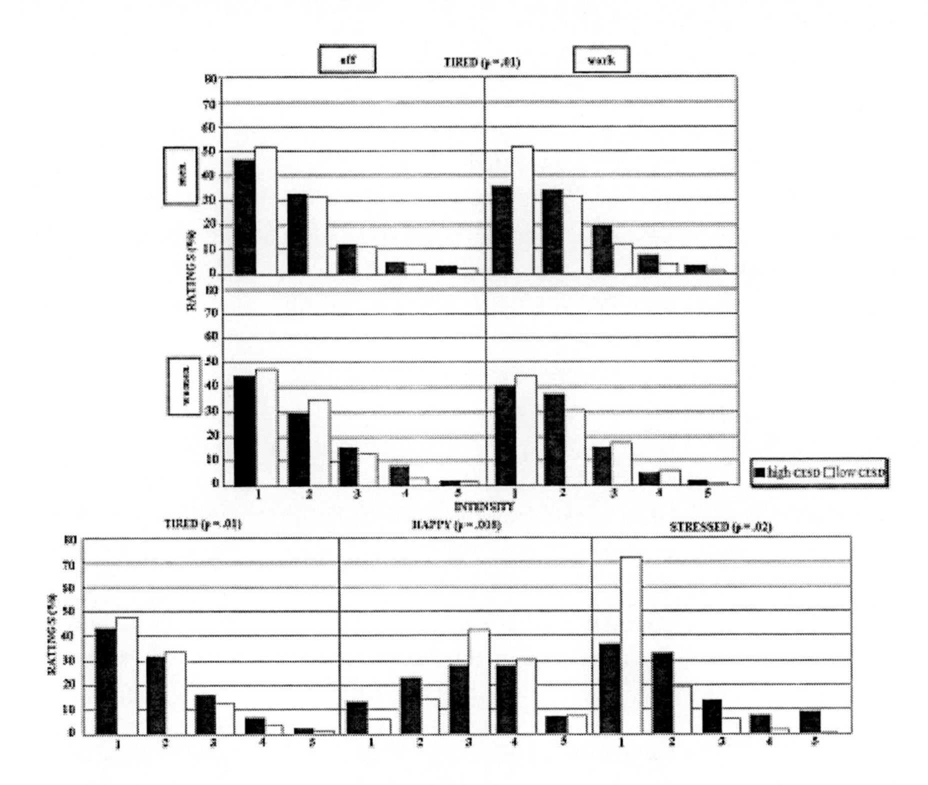

Figure 4. The effect of depression on ratings of tired, happy, and stressed (bottom panel). The effect of depression and gender on ratings of tired (top panel).

Conclusion

This large sample of healthy, employed, and relatively well educated adults rated their moods an average of 46 times on a work day and 44 times on an off-work day. Negative moods, particularly the moods angry and sad, were seldom reported at an intensity level greater than 1 (none). The moods anxious and stressed tended to be reported somewhat more frequently, but mainly at intensity levels 1 and 2. Ratings of the negative moods at the more extreme levels of intensity (levels 4 and 5) were very rarely reported (about 1% of the time for angry and sad and about 2-3% for anxious and stressed). In general, negative mood states were not experienced often during the day in this sample. We assume that an angry reaction is likely to be elicited in special circumstances involving relatively intense interpersonal interactions. Apparently, these circumstances did not occur during the two days of the study. The conditions for feeling sad did not occur often during the day. The other two negative moods, anxious and stressed, seem more likely to be associated with a variety of eliciting conditions, which may account for their more frequent report. In large measure, the data for negative as well as positive and energy-arousal moods are comparable for women and men and similar to the findings for the same moods in our study of women nurses (Davydov et al., 2004) using the same diary methods. That study reported mean ratings close to 1 (the lowest intensity possible) for angry and sad and slightly higher mean ratings for anxious and stressed.

Ratings of the two positive moods (alert and happy) were distributed throughout the scale of intensity, tending to occur most often at levels 2 to 4, again comparable to the mean rating of about 3 for happy in the Davydov et al. (2004) study. Unlike the few instances of high intensity negative mood, the participants rated themselves as not happy or not alert somewhat more often, about 7% of the time. It may be easier to acknowledge not feeling happy than feeling highly stressed or anxious. In general, the data suggest that these healthy subjects were in a more or less good mood during the day. As to the energy/arousal mood dimension (sleepy and tired), these ratings tended to show some variability, clustered in intensity levels 1 to 3, again comparable to the data from the Davydov et al. (2004) study of women.

Men and women did not differ in their mood ratings except in a few instances in interaction with other measures of individual differences, as discussed below. Although there are common cultural beliefs about gender differences in emotional expression and recognition, in these two ordinary days of self observation, men and women did not differ in their mood reports, and the data of the present study for both men and women are consistent with the data obtained from women nurses. The lifetime prevalence for having a psychiatric disorder is about equal in women and men, although women have consistently higher rates than men for depression and generalized anxiety and affective disorders (Brown, 2001). The present data in healthy women, however, do not indicate any trend in greater emotional response in moods related to these disorders, independently of their traits or other factors.

As in the study of nurses, as expected, the participants, both women and men, reported higher levels of the moods stressed and anxious and lower levels of happy on the work day than on the off day, although the day effect for tired was not significant in the present study. This suggests that the particular energy-related demands of a high stress occupation, such as nursing, are greater than for the varied occupations in the present sample.

Higher scores on the scales of anxiety, anger out, hostility, and depression were associated with higher intensity ratings of stressed and tired and lower ratings of happy. For both anxiety and depression, these effects were independent of day or gender, suggesting that these personality dispositions are linked closely with mood and tied to highly specific emotional reactions. Even the non-clinical level of higher depression scores on the CESD showed up in daily mood. The effects of anger out and depression on mood were somewhat greater in men than women, a finding that is inconsistent with the higher prevalence of depression in women (Brown, 2001).

The presumed higher level of stress on the work day also had an influence on how traits affected mood. Low anger out participants reported being less tired than high anger out subjects, with the difference being greater on the work day than the off day. A possible explanation comes from Marci, Glick, Loh, and Dougherty (2007) who found the expression of anger to be the only emotion to show a significant increase in sympathetic activity, accompanied by a significant decrease in vagal activity. The effect of the day on whether one felt stressed or tired was greater for high hostile subjects on the work day. These effects are consistent with the findings of a stronger association between daily stress and negative affect for persons high in neuroticism as compared to those low on the trait (Mroczek & Almeida, 2004). In addition, the effects for anxiety are consistent with the findings of Henker et al. (2002), who studied a younger sample. In that study, sharper differentiations among anxiety subgroups emerged when stratification was based on diary reports rather than on questionnaire scores. Moreover, consistent with the present study, there were few gender differences.

In conclusion, this chapter provides information about the experience of moods in everyday life in a large sample of healthy individuals and can serve as a basis for comparison to other healthy samples and to individuals with varying mental and physical health conditions. The interactive effects of daily stress and personality disposition make intuitive sense. The fact that men and women did not differ very much in their emotional experiences during the day challenges commonly held views. Although researchers have tended not to trust or rely on verbal reports of psychological states, the self reports of moods in this chapter and the interrelationships between mood and individual characteristics agree in the main with psychological viewpoints on emotion and personality. Given the health significance of emotional states and the central role of emotion in psychology and mental health, the development and application of these methods in further basic and clinical research is warranted. Mood diaries, used in combination with paper-and-pencil psychosocial measures, have great potential utility in the diagnosis and treatment of physical and mental disorders. The findings support the hypothesis of a link between personality and mood changes in response to daily life events and suggest that personality traits may affect the regulation of blood pressure via these mood changes. That these effects were observed in a healthy, non-clinical sample suggests that personality traits may serve as potential risk factors for hypertension

REFERENCES

Aan Het Rot, M., Moskowitz, D. S., & Young, S. N. (2008). Exposure to bright light is associated with positive social interaction and good mood over short time periods: A naturalistic study in mildly seasonal people. *Journal of Psychiatric Research*, *42*, 311-319.

Adam, E. K. (2006). Transactions among adolescent trait and state emotion and diurnal and momentary cortisol activity in naturalistic settings. *Psychoneuroendocrinology*, *31*, 664–679.

Aitken Harris, J., & Lucia, A. (2003). The relationship between self-report mood and personality. *Personality and Individual Differences*, *35*, 1903-1909.

Baltrusch, H. J., Stangel, W., & Titze, I. (1991). Stress, cancer and immunity. New developments in biopsychosocial and psychoneuroimmunologic research. *Acta Neurologica* (*Napoli*), *13*, 315–327.

Brown, C. S. (2001). Depression and anxiety disorders. *Obstetrics and Gynecology Clinics of North America*, *28*, 241-268.

Carstensen, L. L., Pasupathi, M., Mayr, U., & Nesselroade, J. R. (2000). Emotional experience in everyday life across the adult life span. *Journal of Personality and Social Psychology*, *79*, 644–655.

Cook, W., & Medley, D. (1954). Proposed hostility and pharasiac-virtue scale for the MMPI. *Journal of Applied Psychology*, *38*, 414–418.

Cox, D. J., & Gonder-Frederick, L. (1992). Major developments in behavioral diabetes research. *Journal of Consulting and Clinical Psychology*, *60*, 628–638.

Davydov, D. M., Shapiro, D., & Goldstein, I. B. (2004). Moods in everyday situations: Effects of menstrual cycle, work and personality. *Journal of Psychosomatic Research*, *56*, 27–33.

Davydov, D. M., Shapiro, D., Goldstein, I. B., & Chicz-DeMet, A. (2005). Moods in everyday situations: effects of menstrual cycle, work, and stress hormones. *Journal of Psychosomatic Research*, *58*, 343–349.

Ebner-Priemer, U. W., Kuo, J., Kleindienst, N., Welch, S. S., Reisch, T., Reinhard, I., Lieb, K., Linehan, M. M., & Bohus, M. (2007). State affective instability in borderline personality disorder assessed by ambulatory monitoring. *Psychological Medicine*, *7*, 961–970.

Goldstein, I. B., & Shapiro, D. (2000). Ambulatory blood pressure in women: family history of hypertension and personality. *Psychology, Health & Medicine*, *5*, 227-240.

Hallas, C. N., Thornton, E. W., Fabri, B. M., Fox, M. A., & Jackson, M. (2003). Predicting blood pressure reactivity and heart rate variability from mood state following coronary artery bypass surgery. *International Journal of Psychophysiology*, *47*, 43-55.

Henker, B., Whalen, C. K., Jamner, L. D., & Delfino, R. J. (2002). Anxiety, affect, and activity in teenagers: monitoring daily life with electronic diaries. *Journal of American Academy of Child and Adolescent Psychiatry*, *41*, 660–670.

Jamner, L. D., Shapiro, D., Goldstein, I. B., & Hug, R. (1991). Ambulatory blood pressure and heart rate in paramedics: Effects of cynical hostility and defensiveness. *Psychosomatic Medicine*, *53*, 393-406.

Kashdan, T. B., & Steger, M. F. (2006). Expanding the topography of social anxiety. An experience-sampling assessment of positive emotions, positive events, and emotion suppression. *Psychological Science*, *17*, 120–128.

Kokkonen, M., & Pulkkinen, L. (2001). Examination of the paths between personality, current mood, its evaluation, and emotion regulation. *European Journal of Personality*, *15*, 83-104.

Macht, M., & Dettmer, D. (2006). Everyday mood and emotions after eating a chocolate bar or an apple. *Appetite*, *46*, 332-336.

Marci, C. D., Glick, D. M., Loh, R., & Dougherty, D. D. (2007). Autonomic and prefrontal cortex responses to autobiographical recall of emotions. *Cognitive, Affective, & Behavioral Neuroscience*, *7*, 243–250.

Mitsutake, G., Otsuka, K., Cornélissen, G., Herold, M., Günther, R., Dawes, C., Burch, J. B., Watson, D., & Halberg, F. (2001). Circadian and infradian rhythms in mood. *Biomedicine & Pharmacotherapy*, *55*, 94s-100s.

Mroczek, D. K., & Almeida, D. M. (2004). The effects of daily stress, personality, and age on daily negative affect. *Journal of Personality*, *72*, 355–378.

Radloff, L. S. (1977). The CES-D Scale: a self report depression scale for the general population. *Applied Psychological Measurement, 1*, 355–401.

Robbins, P. R., & Tanck, R. H. (1997). Anger and depressed affect: interindividual and intraindividual perspectives. *Journal of Psychology, 131*, 489-500.

Rozanski, A., Blumenthal, J. A., & Kaplan, J. (1999). Impact of psychological factors on the pathogenesis of cardiovascular disease and implications for therapy. *Circulation, 99*, 2192-2217.

Shapiro, D., Goldstein, I. B., & Jamner, L. D. (1996). Effects of cynical hostility, anger out, anxiety, and defensiveness on ambulatory blood pressure in Black and White college students. *Psychosomatic Medicine, 58*, 354-364.

Shapiro, D., Jamner, L. D., & Goldstein, I. B. (1997). Daily mood states and ambulatory blood pressure. *Psychophysiology, 34*, 399–405.

Shapiro, D., Jamner, L. D., Goldstein, I. B., & Delfino, R. J. (2001). Striking a chord: moods, blood pressure, and heart rate in everyday life. *Psychophysiology, 38*, 197–204.

Shiffman, S., Stone, A. A., & Hufford, M. R. (2008). Ecological momentary assessment. *Annual Review of Clinical Psychology, 4*, 1–32.

Sokolow, M., Werdegar, D., Perloff, D. B., Cowan, R. M., & Brenenstuhl, H. (1970). Preliminary studies relating portably recorded blood pressures to daily life events in patients with essential hypertension. *Bibliotheca Psychiatrica, 144*, 164–189.

Spielberger, C. D. (1988). *State trait anger expression inventory*. Psychological Assessment Resources, Odessa, Florida.

Spielberger, C. D., Gorsuch, R. L., Lushene, R., Vagg, P. R., & Jacobs, G. A. (1979). *Manual for the State-Trait Anxiety Inventory. STAI (Form Y)*. Palo Alto, CA: Consulting Psychologists Press.

Steptoe, A., O'Donnell, K., Badrick, E., Kumari, M., & Marmot, M. (2008). Neuroendocrine and inflammatory factors associated with positive affect in healthy men and women: the Whitehall II study. *American Journal of Epidemiology, 167*, 96–102.

Steptoe, A., Gibson, E. L., Hamer, M., & Wardle, J. (2007). Neuroendocrine and cardiovascular correlates of positive affect measured by ecological momentary assessment and by questionnaire. *Psychoneuroendocrinology, 32*, 56–64.

Steptoe, A., Wardle, J., & Marmot, M. (2005). Positive affect and health-related neuroendocrine, cardiovascular, and inflammatory processes. *Proceedings of the National Academy of Science U S A, 102*, 6508-6512.

Stone, A. A., Neale, J. M., & Shiffman, S. (1993). Daily assessments of stress and coping and their association with mood. *Annals of Behavioral Medicine, 15*, 8–16.

Talal, A. H., & Drossman, D. A. (1995). Psychosocial factors in inflammatory bowel disease. *Gastroenterology Clinics of North America, 24*, 699–716.

Underwood, B., Froming, W. J., & Moore, B. S. (2006). Mood and personality: A search for the causal relationship.*Journal of Personality, 48*, 15-23.

Whalen, C. K., Jamner, L. D., Henker, B., Delfino, R. J. (2002). Smoking and moods in adolescents with depressive and aggressive dispositions: evidence from surveys and electronic diaries. *Journal of the American Academy of Child & Adolescent Psychiatry, 41*, 660-670.

Wright, R. J., Rodriguez, M., & Cohen, S. (1998). Review of psychosocial stress and asthma: an integrated biopsychosocial approach. *Thorax, 53*, 1066–1074.

In: Personality Assessment: New Research
Editors: Lauren B. Palcroft and Melissa V. Lopez
ISBN: 978-1-60692-796-0

Chapter 5

WEIGHT? WAIT! IMPORTANCE WEIGHTING OF SATISFACTION SCORES IN QUALITY OF LIFE ASSESSMENT

Chia-huei Wu*
Department of Psychology
National Taiwan University, Taiwan

ABSTRACT

Importance weighting is a common practice in Quality of Life (QOL) research. The basic idea is that items for specific life domains contained in a QOL measurement have different importance for different individuals; therefore, in capturing participants' perceptions, feelings, or evaluations in these domains, information on domain importance should be incorporated into the scoring procedure and reflected in the final score. Accordingly, importance weighting is proposed to serve this purpose, and the common procedure is to weight the satisfaction score by the importance score for each domain. This idea is so common that many instruments adopted this weighting procedure in their scoring system without examining its necessity and appropriateness. To date, there is extensive evidence to draw the conclusion of the (in)appropriateness of using importance weighting of satisfaction scores. Hence, the purpose of this article is to provide a systematic review of the literature on the issue of importance weighting. In the following sections, I first introduce the notion of importance weighting. Then, the empirical utility of importance weighting is reviewed to see if importance weighting contributes to predicting criterion variables. In the third section, the literature on the appropriateness of importance weighting based on a psychological perspective is reviewed. Finally, a conclusion on importance weighting and the implications for QOL are provided.

---

* Send correspondence to:
Chia-huei Wu
4F, No.147, Sec. 1, Xinguang Rd.,
Wenshan District, Taipei City 116, Taiwan (R.O.C.)
TEL: 886-2-86614712
Email: b88207071@ntu.edu.tw

INTRODUCTION

Importance weighting is a common practice in Quality of Life (QOL) research. The basic idea is that items for specific life domains contained in a QOL measurement have different importance for different individuals; therefore, in capturing participants' perceptions, feelings, or evaluations in these domains, information on domain importance should be incorporated into the scoring procedure and reflected in the final score. Accordingly, importance weighting is proposed to serve this purpose, and the common procedure is to weight the satisfaction score by the importance score for each domain. Frisch, Cornell, Villanueva, and Retzlaff (1992) described this idea as follows:

> The inventory's (the Quality of Life Inventory) scoring scheme reflects the assumption that a person's overall life satisfaction is a composite of the satisfactions in particular areas of life weighted by their relative importance to the individual. Thus, the product of the satisfaction and importance ratings for each area of life are computed (p.93).

This idea is so common that many instruments, such as the Comprehensive Quality Of Life Scale (ComQol) (Cummins, 1997), the Quality of Life Index (QOL Index) (Ferrans & Powers, 1985), the Quality of Life Inventory (QOL Inventory) (Frisch, 1992), the Quality of Life Profile-Adolescent version (QOLPAV) (Raphael et al., 1996), and the Flanagan Quality of Life Scale (QOLS) as reviewed in Dijkers (2003), adopted this weighting procedure in their scoring system without examining its necessity and appropriateness.

The utility and appropriateness of importance weighting of satisfaction scores has been examined in the literature on job satisfaction from the 1960s to the 1990s (e.g., Caston & Briato, 1983; Ewen, 1967; McFarlin & Rice, 1992; Mikes & Hulin, 1968; Rice, Gentile, & McFarlin 1991; Waters & Roach, 1971; Waters, 1969; Waters & Roach, 1971). Recently, similar discussion and examinations also appeared in quality of life research (e.g., Hsieh, 2003, 2004; Russell, Hubley, Palepu, & Zumbo, 2006; Trauer & Mackinnon, 2001; Wu 2008a; Wu, Chen, & Tsai, 2009; Wu & Yao, 2006a, 2006b). To date, there is extensive evidence to draw the conclusion of the (in)appropriateness of using importance weighting of satisfaction scores. Hence, the purpose of this article is to provide a systematic review of the literature on the issue of importance weighting.

In the following sections, I first introduce the notion of importance weighting. Then, the empirical utility of importance weighting is reviewed to see if importance weighting contributes to predicting criterion variables. In the third section, the literature on the appropriateness of importance weighting based on a psychological perspective is reviewed. Finally, a conclusion on importance weighting and the implications for QOL are provided.

1. IMPORTANCE WEIGHTING IN QUALITY OF LIFE

In this section, the rationale for using importance weighting in measuring QOL is introduced first. Then, several weighting methods used in QOL research and the popularity of the importance weighting method (i.e., multiplying satisfaction scores by importance scores) are reviewed.

1.1. The Conceptual Basis of Importance Weighting

Quality of Life (QOL) is a broad term describing an individual's perception of their life. In the literature, there are many definitions and measurements of QOL. Although there is no consensus, many definitions of QOL explicitly or implicitly mention that an individual's quality of life is based on his/her perception or feelings on circumstances in important life domains. For example, Frisch (1992) mentioned that "*life satisfaction or quality of life refers to an individual's subjective evaluation of the degree to which his or her most important needs, goals, and wishes have been fulfilled (p.29)*". Similarly, the WHOQOL Group defined QOL as "*an individual's perception of their position in life, in the context of the culture and value systems in which they live, and in relation to their goals, expectations, standards and concerns*" (World Health Organization [WHO], 1993, 1995). In this definition, the importance of the life domain is mentioned implicitly with an individual's goals, expectations, standards, and concerns (Skevington, O'Connell, & the WHOQOL Group, 2004). According to this perspective, identification of important life domains for an individual is a crucial step in assessing one's QOL. For example, O'Boyle (1994) indicated,

> "In assessing QOL, a person should be given an opportunity to identify areas that are important to him or her, to indicate how well he or she is doing in each particular area, and to judge the relative importance of each area to his or her overall QOL (p.8)." Similarly, Dijkers (2003) also mentioned that "If one wants to measure QOL as experienced by the person, choice of domains for inclusion in a QOL instrument should ideally be based on individual (rather than subgroup or disease category) selection and prioritization, and QOL instruments may be differentiated based on the degree to which they provide for that (p.s5)."

In the literature, several individualized QOL assessments have been developed. However, these instruments vary in the degree to which a person is given a chance to nominate the life areas that are utilized to qualify his/her QOL (see, Dijkers, 2003, for a review). For example, the Individual Quality of Life Interview (IQOLI), which was developed to detect the constructs and construct systems of an individual (Dijkers, 2003), is a typical individualized QOL assessment. In IQOLI, an individual's QOL is computed from his/her constructs matrix through a series of statistical analyses, providing a QOL score with indigenous meaning for an individual. In addition, the Schedule for the Evaluation of Individual Quality of Life (SEIQoL) is a QOL instrument that allows a person to nominate the five most important life domains in assessing his/her overall QOL from a semi-structured interview, and then, the level of QOL is evaluated on the basis of these five domains (O'Boyle, 1994). Generally, a QOL instrument that allows a person to nominate the constructs or life areas for QOL evaluation, such as IQOLI and SEIQoL, can be treated as a paragon of individualized QOL assessment.

However, in order to extend the usability in comparing the effect of health cares or evaluating the effectiveness of health resources management, most QOL instruments were developed to assess QOL for different groups or populations, not just for a single person. If this kind of QOL measurement is administered, different persons' QOL can only be evaluated on the same life domains. As a result, the process of how to obtain individualized QOL scores for different persons from the same life domains became an important issue in this kind of QOL measurement. Conventionally, following the idea that important life domains have more influence on individuals' overall QOL than less important domains, the global QOL is treated as the sum of importance-weighted scores in various specific life areas (e.g., Cummins, 1997; Diener, 1984; Diener, Emmons, Larsen, & Griffin, 1985; Ferrans & Powers, 1985; Frisch, 1992; Hsieh, 2003, 2004; McGrath & Bedi, 2004; Oliver, Holloway, & Carson, 1995; Raphael et al., 1996). As a result, given a set of life domains in a QOL measurement, in order to gain the individualized QOL score, researchers contrived to incorporate the information of domain importance into the final QOL score. In other words, except for assessing individuals' satisfaction on various life domains, researchers focused their attention on the "weighting value" of each domain and proposed several methods to incorporate the weighting value into the final QOL scores.

1.2. Weighting Approaches in Quality of Life Research

Generally, weighting methods in QOL research can be divided into two main categories, (1) statistical approaches and (2) direct rating approaches. In statistical approaches, regression analysis (O'Boyle, 1994; Perloff & Persons, 1988; Rose, Scholler, Klapp, & Bernheirn, 1998), factor analysis (Olschewski & Schumacher, 1990), and principal component analysis (Ki & Chow, 1995) have been used to extract weighting value for each life area.

In regression analysis, a criterion variable (usually, a global measure of QOL) is regressed on domain-specific QOL scores. Then, the regression coefficients (Perloff & Persons, 1988) or standardized regression coefficients (Rose et al., 1998) of each predictor (domain score) are regarded as the weighting value. This weighting method provides the best prediction on the criterion variable with the weighted score (Perloff & Persons, 1988). However, Perloff and Persons (1988) indicated "*When theory does not provide the weights in an index, weights may be calculated by using a multiple regression. Such an empirically determined index depends on the research question (dependent variable), the population, and the sample used, so no single set of weights is appropriate for all studies (p.95),*" suggesting that weighting values extracted from regression analysis could not be generalized to other criterion variables and samples. In other words, if different global QOL measures were used as the criterion variable, weighting values would be changed. In addition, the weighting values are sample-dependent. This characteristic not only suggests that the weighting values could not be generalized to other samples, but also implies that all subjects share the same set of weighting values, suggesting that all subjects have the same importance perception on these life areas; however, this characteristic contradict the viewpoint of individual-perspective QOL. Moreover, Campbell, Converse, and Rogers (1976) compared the regression coefficients and mean of importance rating (Likert-type rating) of each life domain to see if there is a consistent importance rank among 12 life areas. Their results revealed that the correlation between regression coefficients and importance ratings is 0.41, and marked discrepancies on several life domains were found. This finding suggests that regression coefficients can not capture individuals' importance perceptions on life domains.

Regarding factor analysis, domain-specific QOL scores are submitted to a factor analysis; then, factor loadings are treated as the weighting value (e.g., Olschewski & Schumacher, 1990). According to Gorsuch (1983), "*Factor loading refers to a measure of the degree of generalizability found between each variable and each factor (p.3).*" Thus, on the theoretical basis of factor analysis, factor loading does not have the meaning of relative importance of each item. Kaplan (1998) has indicated that the factor analysis solution and the relative importance of dimensions are conceptually and empirically independent. Johnson (1998) also indicated, "*Factor analysis does not distinguish variables as to their relative importance with respect to one another. It simply identifies underlying variables that are measuring independent and/or uncorrelated characteristics of the population being sampled (p.180).*" In addition, all subjects in a sample share the same set of factor loadings, which has the same drawback encountered in regression analysis. Therefore, weighting domain-specific QOL scores by factor loadings also cannot incorporate individuals' importance perceptions on these life domains into the final QOL score.

Finally, considering that factor loadings vary according to different factor extracting methods, Ki and Chow (1995) suggested that factor loading is not an optimal weighting value in calculating QOL scores in a multidimensional measurement. Thus, they proposed to use principal component analysis to acquire the weighting values. In their statistical procedure, they conducted factor analysis first to extract the appropriate number of factors and to identify the domains of each factor. Then, in calculating QOL scores for each factor-scale, principal component analysis was conducted to obtain the first component function for each factor-scale. The coefficients of the first component function were treated as the weighting value of each domain and were used to compute the weighted scores (component scores). According to the objective and statistical procedure of principal component analysis, the first principal component accounts for the maximum variance in the data (Sharma, 1996). Therefore, weighted scores computed from component weighting could account for the maximum variance for each factor-scale and preserve the most information of each factor-scale. However, the weighting method derived from principal component analysis, as factor analysis, does not incorporate individuals' importance perceptions for each domain; the coefficients of the first component function do not represent the subjective importance perception. In addition, all subjects in a sample share the same set of coefficients as well, just like regression analysis and factor analysis.

To sum up, since the weighting values derived from regression analysis, factor analysis, and principal component analysis cannot capture individuals' importance perceptions on each life domain, it is not surprising that weighting methods derived from these statistical methods were not commonly used. However, it does not imply that these statistical weighting methods are valueless. In fact, if the purpose is not to figure out the importance value of each life domain for an individual, these statistical weighting methods could be used for their original purpose.

Contrary to the statistical weighting approach, the direct rating approach is a common method to gain the weighting values in QOL research. It allows a person to report his/her importance perceptions on each life domain. Several instruments have adopted this weighting method, such as the Comprehensive Quality Of Life Scale (ComQol, Cummins, 1997), the Quality of life Index (QOL Index, Ferrans & Powers, 1985), the Quality of Life Inventory (QOL Inventory, Frisch, 1992), the Quality of Life Profile-Adolescent version (QOLPAV, Raphael et al., 1996), and the Flanagan Quality of Life Scale (QOLS, reviewed in Dijkers, 2003), to name a few.

In these QOL instruments, QOL is measured as life satisfaction, and except for the section of satisfaction rating, they also contain a section of importance rating in which participants are asked to rate the importance of each domain. Then, the weighted scores computed by multiplying satisfaction score with importance score for each domain are regarded as the individualized QOL score. At first glance, the direct rating method appears straightforward for importance weighting, since different life domains may have differing importance to an individual. As a result, some life domains may be more important to his or her QOL, and therefore the corresponding domains should contribute more to the total QOL score (McGrath & Bedi, 2004). Accordingly, the direct rating method is the most popular method for importance weighting in QOL measurement. Hence, this article mainly focuses on the direct rating method in importance weighting. In the following paragraphs, the term "importance weighting" is only referring to the direct rating method. Its utility and appropriateness are reviewed and discussed in following sections.

2. Utility of Importance Weighting

The purpose of this section is to review studies in investigating the predictive utility of importance weighting to see if the weighted satisfaction score is superior to the unweighted satisfaction score in predicting criterion measures. There were three ways for examining the predictive utility of importance weighting. The first one is to simply compare the correlation between the weighted satisfaction score and the criterion measures to the correlation between the unweighted satisfaction score and the criterion measures using conventional correlation analysis (Ewen, 1967; Hsieh, 2003; Mikes & Hulin, 1968; Russell et al., 2006; Waters & Roach, 1971; Waters, 1969; Waters & Roach, 1971; Wu, 2008a; Wu & Yao, 2006a). The second one is to see if importance weighting has an additional contribution in predicting criterion measures using moderated regression analysis (Caston & Briato, 1983; McFarlin & Rice, 1992; Rice, Gentile, & McFarlin, 1991; Russell et al., 2006; Wu & Yao, 2006a, 2006b). The third one is to compare the correlation between a latent factor of weighted satisfaction score and the latent factor of criterion measures to the correlation between a latent factor of unweighted satisfaction score and the latent factor of criterion measures from a formative model using partial least squares (Staples & Higgins,1998; Wu, Chen & Tsai, 2009). In the following paragraphs, results obtained from these three methods are summarized respectively. Related empirical research on job satisfaction and self satisfaction are also contained in this section to provide a comprehensive review.

2.1. Results from Conventional Correlation Analysis

According to the existing literature, the utility of importance weighting have been discussed in job satisfaction research since the 1960s. Using conventional correlation analysis, many job satisfaction studies have indicated that the weighted satisfaction score did not have a higher correlation with criterion variables than the unweighted satisfaction score, such as employees' turnover (e.g., Mikes & Hulin, 1968; Waters & Roach, 1971) and global job satisfaction (e.g., Caston & Briato, 1983; Ewen, 1967; Waters, 1969).

Similar findings were also obtained in QOL research with various weighting algorithms (e.g., Hsieh, 2003; Russell et al., 2006; Wu, 2008a; Wu & Yao, 2006a). Russell et al. (2006) used the Injection Drug User Quality of Life Scale (IDUQOL) (Brogly, Mercier, Bruneau, Palepu, & Franco, 2003) to compare the effectiveness of importance weighting on satisfaction scores in predicting convergent, discriminant, and criterion measures. A total of 241 participants drawn from the Vancouver Injection Drug User Study provided their satisfaction and importance scores on 21 life domains and also completed measures of global life satisfaction, self-esteem, social desirability, and demographic information. They computed correlations between weighted/unweighted satisfaction scores and all other measures and used Steiger's (1980) Z test to examine the differences between correlations. Their findings showed that the total weighted and unweighted satisfaction scores had no significant difference in their correlations with other measures. In addition, when specific domains in the IDUQOL were selected and correlated with their corresponding criterion measures, weighted and unweighted satisfaction scores only had two different correlations among sixteen comparisons. Hence, they concluded that importance weighting did not have additional predictive effectiveness.

In a similar vein, Wu and Yao (2006a) examined whether the weighted satisfaction score is superior to the unweighted satisfaction score in predicting a global life satisfaction measure using weighting algorithms proposed in the ComQol (Cummins, 1997), the QOL Index (Ferrans & Powers, 1985), the QOL Inventory (Frisch, 1992), and the QOLPAV (Raphael et al., 1996). A total of 130 undergraduate students in Taiwan provided their satisfaction and importance ratings on 15 domains of the campus life. Unweighted satisfaction ratings and the four kinds of weighted scores computed by the four algorisms were correlated with global life satisfaction and the resulting correlations were statistically examined to see if there were significant differences between weighted and unweighted scores. Results showed that the four kinds of weighted scores did not have higher correlations with global life satisfaction than the unweighted satisfaction scores.

In addition to the existing weighting algorithms, Hsieh (2003) proposed seven algorithms with different assumptions on importance weights to explore possible effects of importance weights. He used both ratings and ranks of importance as weighting factors. The first three algorithms were proposed for satisfaction and importance rating scores. They were:

$$DI = \sum(S_i \times I_i) / \sum I_i, \quad (1)$$

$$DI_{sqrt} = \sum(S_i \times \sqrt{I_i}) / \sum\sqrt{I_i}, \quad (2)$$

and

$$DI^2 = \sum(S_i \times I_i^2) / \sum I_i^2 \quad (3)$$

where S_i is the satisfaction rating of domain i, and I_i is the value of the importance rating of domain i. The first algorithm assumes that importance ratings have a linear weighting effect. The second algorithm assumes that importance ratings have a non-linear weighting effect with weight increased at a decreasing rate. The third algorithm assumes that importance ratings have a non-linear weighting effect with weight increased at an increasing rate.

The other four algorithms were developed for importance ranks. They were:

$$DR = \sum(S_i \times \mathrm{R}_i) / \sum R_i \quad (4)$$

$$DR_{sqrt} = \sum(S_i \times \sqrt{R_i}) \,/\, \sum\sqrt{R_i} \tag{5}$$

$$DR^2 = \sum(S_i \times R_i^2) \,/\, \sum R_i^2 \tag{6}$$

and

$$DInr = \sum(S_i \times R_i) \,/\, \sum(I / R_i) \tag{7}$$

where S_i is the value of satisfaction rating of domain i; R_i is the importance ranks of domain i. The fourth algorithm assumes that weight increased as a simple linear function. The fifth one algorithm assumes that weight increased at a decreasing rate (or decreased at an increasing rate). The sixth algorithm assumes that weight increased at an increasing rate (or decreased at a decreasing rate). The last algorithm assumes that weight is proportionally inverse with respect to its rank.

In his study (Hsieh, 2003), 90 participants aged fifty and above in the greater Chicago area provided their satisfaction ratings, importance ratings, and importance ranks on eight life domains by telephone interviews. The seven kinds of weighted scores computed by the seven algorithms were compared to the unweighted satisfaction ratings in their correlations with three measures of global life satisfaction. His results revealed that only weighted scores (DR^2 and DInr) computed by the sixth and the seventh algorithm had slightly higher correlations (*rs* = 0.46) than the unweighted satisfaction ratings ($r = 0.39$) with the single-item measure of global life satisfaction. On the other two measures of global life satisfaction, all weighted scores did not have higher correlations than the unweighted satisfaction ratings. As a result, Hsieh (2003) concluded that "*the weighted average of domain satisfactions using domain ranking is a better indicator of global life satisfaction than the simple sum or average of domain satisfactions (p. 227).*"

However, Hsieh (2003) did not perform a statistical test to examine if the correlations of the two weighted scores (DR^2 and DInr) were significantly higher than the correlation of the unweighted satisfaction scores. Moreover, his conclusion on domain ranking was not supported in Wu's (2008a) study. Wu (2008a) applied the same four algorithms for importance ranks proposed by Hsieh (2003). A total of 167 undergraduate students in Taiwan provided their satisfaction ratings and importance ranks on 12 life domains and also completed three measurements for the global life (two of them were single-item measures). Correlation analysis and correlation-difference tests showed that the four weighted satisfaction scores were not superior to the unweighted satisfaction score in predicting all three global measures. Hence, Hsieh's (2003) conclusion should be taken with caution.

Although the correlation analysis is a common procedure in examining the weighting effect, many researchers have proposed that the correlational approach was not an appropriate method to test the effect of multiplicative score (e.g., Arnold & Evans, 1979; Caston & Briato, 1983; Evans, 1991; Glass, 1968; Schmidt, 1973). The reason is that correlation between a product variable (such as the weighted score) and a third variable was dependent on the scales of the two original variables (Arnold & Evans, 1979; Bohrnstedt & Goldberger, 1969; Evans, 1991; Schmidt, 1973). On the exact covariance of products of random variables, Bohrnstedt and Goldberger (1969) showed that the correlation between a product variable and a third variable based on an assumption of multivariate normality is (as cited in Arnold & Evans, 1979)

$$r_{z,xy} = \frac{\mathrm{cov}(z, xy)}{\sigma_z \sigma_{xy}} \tag{8}$$

where

$$\mathrm{cov}(z, xy) = \bar{x}\,\mathrm{cov}(y, z) + \bar{y}\,\mathrm{cov}(x, z) \tag{9}$$

$$\sigma_{xy}^2 = \bar{x}^2 \sigma_y^2 + \bar{y}^2 \sigma_x^2 + 2\bar{x}\bar{y}\,\mathrm{cov}(x, y) + \sigma_y^2 \sigma_x^2 + \mathrm{cov}^2(x, y) \tag{10}$$

$$\sigma_z^2 = \frac{\Sigma(z - \bar{z})}{n} \tag{11}$$

According to the preceding equations, the means and the variance of the two original variables (x and y) would influence the covariance and the variance of a product variable (xy), and then have substantial impact on the correlation involving the product variable. In other words, linear transformation of the two original variables alters their means and variances, and then results in fluctuation in the zero order correlation between the product variable (xy) and a third variable (z) (Arnold & Evans, 1979). In the context of importance weighting, this statistic property implies that the correlation coefficient between a weighted score and a global life satisfaction measure may be fluctuated by changing the zero-point on the interval scale of importance or satisfaction rating. As a result, correlation analysis cannot provide a reliable result for examining the effect of importance weighting. The appropriate method to examine the effect of a product variable (such as the weighted score) is moderated regression analysis (Arnold & Evans, 1979; Cohen, 1978; Evans, 1991). Findings of moderated regression analysis on importance weighting are reviewed in the next section.

2.2. Results from Moderated Regression Analysis

Given the inappropriateness of correlation analysis in examining the weighting effect, several studies have adopted moderated regression analysis to examine the effect of importance weighting (for job satisfaction research, Caston & Briato, 1983; Rice, Gentile, & McFarlin 1991, McFarlin & Rice, 1992; for life satisfaction research, Russell et al., 2006; Wu & Yao, 2006a, 2006b). In these studies, moderated regression analysis was used to regress global job satisfaction on domain importance, domain satisfaction, and their interaction (domain satisfaction × domain importance) to see if the interaction term has a significant effect in predicting the global job satisfaction. The idea that domain satisfaction has a stronger relation with the overall life satisfaction among people regarding the domain as higher importance than people regarding the domain as lower importance can be directly examined by moderated regression analysis. The hypothesized model is displayed in Figure 1.

If the domain importance has a moderating effect, that is, the interaction term created by multiplying domain satisfaction with domain importance is significant in predicting the overall life satisfaction, it can be concluded that weighting domain satisfaction with domain importance is desirable in accounting for the overall life satisfaction. On the contrary, if the interaction term is not significant, it can be suggested that the importance weighting is trivial in accounting for individuals' overall life satisfaction.

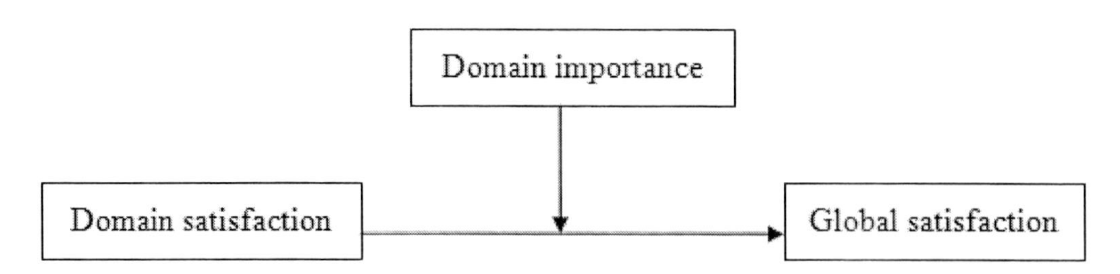

Figure 1. The hypothesized model for importance weighting of domain satisfaction.

Caston and Briato's (1983) study was the first study using moderated regression analysis to regress overall job satisfaction on domain satisfaction, domain importance, and their interaction (domain satisfaction × domain importance) among 13 domains to see if the interaction has a significant effect in predicting overall job satisfaction. Data representing the job satisfaction of 401 registered nurses in a large Western metropolitan area were analyzed. Rather than building models for each domain, the overall job satisfaction was regressed on all domains' satisfaction, importance, and their interactions at the same time. Their result showed that including all interaction terms can significantly account for additional variation of overall job satisfaction. However, if we take a closer look at the regression coefficients, there was only one out of 13 domains that had a significant interaction effect. Therefore, their finding implied that weighting domain satisfaction with domain importance might not authentically contribute to predicting overall job satisfaction.

Rice, Gentile, and McFarlin (1991) conducted moderated regression analyses for 12 domains to see if domain importance moderates the relationship between domain satisfaction and global satisfaction. Data from 97 employed college students from Buffalo, New York, were analyzed. In each model, global satisfaction was regressed on domain satisfaction, domain importance, and their interaction (domain satisfaction × domain importance). Among the 12 job domains, the interaction term was significant on one domain, demonstrating that domain importance does not generally influence the degree to which domain satisfaction contributes to overall job satisfaction.

In McFarlin and Rice's (1992) study, they used satisfaction and importance ratings of 8 job domains from two employee samples (366 workers in Albany, New York, and 675 employees of a large Midwestern bank in the U.S.A.) to build moderated regression models. By either regressing overall job satisfaction on all domains' satisfaction, importance, and their interactions at the same time or by regressing overall job satisfaction on an domains' satisfaction, importance, and their interaction for each domain, their results revealed that domain importance failed to moderate the relation between domain satisfaction and overall job satisfaction.

Regarding life satisfaction research, Russell et al. (2006) conducted regression analysis to analyze their data on the IDUQOL (Brogly et al., 2003). Among 21 regression models for each domain, only two models had significant interaction effects of domain satisfaction and importance in predicting global life satisfaction. Wu and Yao (2006a) also performed the same analysis on 15 life domains using data obtained from 130 undergraduate students in Taiwan. Their results showed that only one domain had a significant interaction effect of domain satisfaction and domain importance on global life satisfaction. This finding was also replicated in another study with a sample of 167 undergraduate students in Taiwan (Wu & Yao, 2006b). In this study, 12 life domains were selected and only one domain had a significant interaction effect of domain satisfaction and domain importance on global life satisfaction.

In summary, findings obtained from regression analysis revealed that domain importance did not moderate the relationship between domain satisfaction and global life satisfaction, suggesting that weighting domain satisfaction with domain importance did not contribute to predicting global life satisfaction.

2.3. Results from Partial Least Squares Analysis

Given the reviewed findings from correlation analysis and moderated regression analysis, it can be said that importance-weighted satisfaction scores, compared to unweighted satisfaction scores, did not have an additional contribution in predicting criterion variables. However, Hsieh (2004) did not think these findings were sufficient to justify the abandonment of incorporating importance weighting into QOL instruments. He thought that incorporating importance weighting into QOL instruments is appropriate, but the critical issue is how to weight. He proposed a formative model as the theoretical basis to compute the importance-weighted satisfaction score. In a formative model, the latent construct is a linear combination of its indicators; that is, manifest indicators are used to define latent variables. One can empirically defined the meaning of domain satisfaction from importance-weighted satisfaction scores.

The perspective of a formative model is related to the bottom-up theory of satisfaction judgment. The bottom-up theory regards evaluations in various life domains as contributing to the evaluation of life as a whole (Diener, 1984; Diener, Suh, Lucas, & Smith, 1999). Hence, from the bottom-up perspective, a formative model can be used as the measurement basis for domain-specific measures of satisfaction as suggested by Hsieh (2004).

To date, only two studies applied a formative model and used partial least squares (PLS) technique to address the issue of importance weighting. The first one was conducted by Staples and Higgins (1998). Using data obtained from 3,804 employees in a large Canadian company, they built a formative model for domain-specific measures of job satisfaction either by weighted or unweighted satisfaction scores to predict global job satisfaction and examined if weighted satisfaction scores have a stronger effect in predicting global job satisfaction. Their results showed that weighted scores are not superior to unweighted scores in predicting global job satisfaction.

Staples and Higgins' (1998) finding was also obtained in Wu, Chen and Tsai's (2009) study. Wu et al. adopted the same procedure to examine the utility of importance weighting in three datasets on life, self, and job satisfaction. In the life satisfaction dataset, 237 undergraduate students in Taiwan provided their responses. In the self satisfaction dataset, another 269 undergraduates in Taiwan provided their responses. Finally, in the job satisfaction dataset, 557 staff members in seven Taiwan provincial hospitals provided their responses. Measures of domain satisfaction, domain importance, and global satisfaction were collected in each dataset. Partial least squares analysis was also used in model estimation. Results of the three databases all revealed that unweighted satisfaction scores have a stronger predictive effect on global satisfaction measures than weighted satisfaction scores, indicating that importance weighting on satisfaction scores did not have an empirical benefit.

Given the results from the four databases, it can be seen that importance weighting did not have additional contributions in predicting global measures under the perspective of a formative model with the PLS technique.

2.4. Brief Summary

This section reviews results on the utility of importance weighting in predicting criterion measures, especially global satisfaction. Results obtained from correlation, regression, and partial least squares analysis all indicated that weighting satisfaction scores with importance rating scores did not have additional contribution in predicting global satisfaction. All these findings were reliable and cross-validated in various studies with different populations. Hence, it can be concluded that importance weighting did not have its expected utility in predicting criterion measures.

3. Appropriateness of Importance Weighting

In this section, I review studies examining the psychological foundation of importance weighting from Locke's range-of-affect hypothesis (Locke, 1969, 1976). In the following parts, Locke's range-of-affect hypothesis is first introduced; then, studies examining the range-of-affect hypothesis are reviewed. Finally, a brief summary is provided.

3.1. Locke's Range-of-Affect Hypothesis

In Locke's (1969, 1976) job satisfaction theory, he indicated that responses of an affective evaluation (e.g., satisfaction) reflect a dual value judgment: (1) the discrepancy between what the individual wants and what he/she perceives himself/herself as getting, and (2) the importance of what is wanted to the individual. He also proposed that the level of satisfaction was influenced by the interaction of have-want discrepancy and importance. The hypothesized model of range-of-affect hypothesis is displayed in Figure 2.

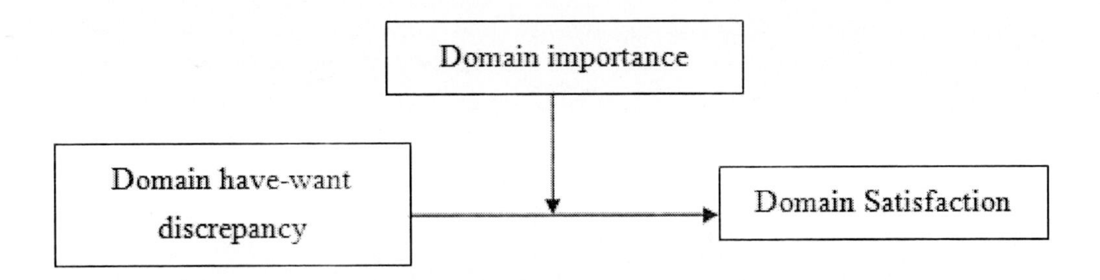

Figure 2. The hypothesized model of range-of-affect hypothesis.

In this framework, *the amount of the value wanted* (have-want discrepancy) by the person and *how much the person wants that amount* (importance) are distinguished, and both of them interactively determine the level of satisfaction. Specifically, Locke (1969, 1976) claimed that given the amount of discrepancy, domains with high personal importance could produce a wide affective reaction ranging from great satisfaction to great dissatisfaction, and domains with low personal importance, on the other hand, could only produce a restricted affective reaction to the neutral point of the satisfaction-dissatisfaction dimension. This statement was termed the *range-of-affect hypothesis* (Locke, 1969, 1976) to describe that given the amount of discrepancy, the range of satisfaction rating on a domain is determined by the domain importance. Figure 3 displays the hypothesized interaction plot in the range-of-affect hypothesis. Accordingly, the range-of-affect hypothesis asserted that domain satisfaction has incorporated the information of domain importance, which rendered weighting domain satisfaction with domain importance redundant.

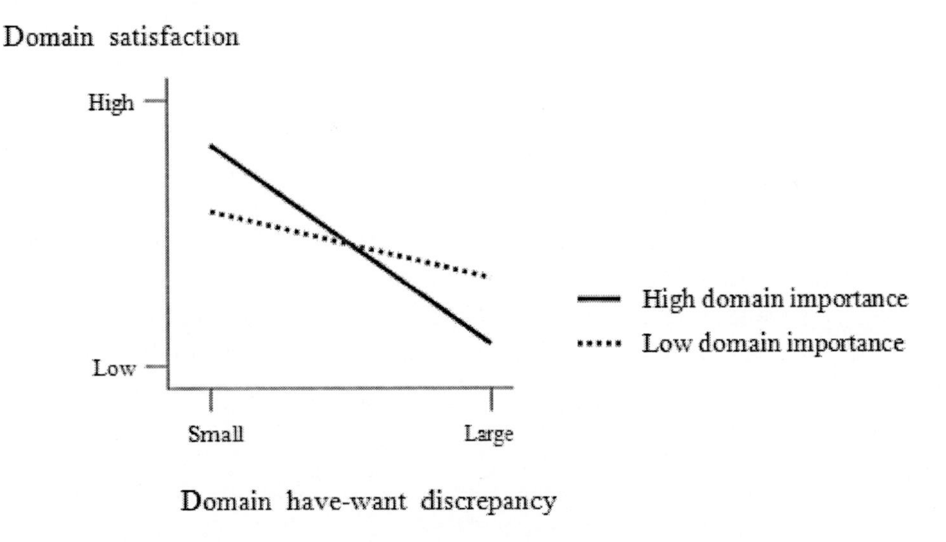

Figure 3. The hypothesized interaction plot in the range-of-affect hypothesis.

This range-of-affect hypothesis can be described either in an interpersonal (between subjects) or in an intrapersonal (within subjects) framework. In an interpersonal framework, the hypothesis describes that the relationship between domain have-want discrepancy and domain satisfaction is expected to be stronger among people attaching high importance to that domain than people attaching low importance to that domain. In an intrapersonal framework, the hypothesis is depicted that, for a person's response, the relationship between domain have-want discrepancy and domain satisfaction is expected to be stronger on the high-importance domain than the low-importance domain. Both of these interpretations have been supported in empirical studies with different research designs. These studies are reviewed in the following sections.

3.2. Studies on Range-of-Affect Hypothesis in an Interpersonal Framework

The range-of-affect hypothesis was usually examined by survey research in an interpersonal framework (for job satisfaction, McFarlin, Coster, Rice, & Cooper-Alison, 1995; McFarlin & Rice, 1992; Mobley & Locke, 1970; Rice et al., 1991a; for life satisfaction, Wu & Yao, 2006b; for self satisfaction, Wu & Yao, 2008). That is, the relationship between domain have-want discrepancy and domain satisfaction was expected to be stronger among people attaching high importance to the said domain than to people attaching low importance to that domain.

Regarding job satisfaction, Mobley and Locke (1970; Study 1) asked 72 undergraduate volunteers to rate their current conditions, expected conditions, satisfaction, and importance on 25 job domains and also rate their overall work satisfaction. Discrepancy score was indicated by the difference scores between ratings for current and expected conditions. They correlated the discrepancy scores with overall work and job satisfaction for domains rated as high, moderate, and low importance. As predicted by the range-of-affect hypothesis, the size of correlations between discrepancy scores and overall work and job satisfaction decreased as domain importance decreased. Using the same data, they also divided participants into four conditions according to their discrepancy and importance scores for each domain (high/low discrepancy × high/low importance). Then, for each domain, they compared the difference in domain satisfaction between high and low discrepancy groups under high and low importance conditions, respectively, and found that the difference in domain satisfaction was greater under high importance conditions than low importance conditions. In addition, Mobley and Locke (1970; Study 5) also showed that the variability of satisfaction ratings produced by a domain is proportional to the importance of that domain, supporting that domains with higher importance would have a wider range on dissatisfaction-satisfaction scale. Their findings suggested that satisfaction ratings already reflect a personal appraisal of the importance of the domain. Accordingly, Mobley and Locke (1970) suggested that multiplying satisfaction scores by importance scores is redundant.

Rice et al. (1991a) asked 97 working college students to provide data concerning 12 job domains. Overall job satisfaction and domain satisfaction on 12 job domains were measured by common satisfaction questions. In addition, domain have-want discrepancy was measured in a form of "facet amount[1]", which taps have-want discrepancy indirectly and is conceptually

[1] According to Locke and Latham (1990), have-want discrepancy can be measured by several alternative methods, including (a) direct reports of facet amount (e.g., "How much opportunity for promotion do you have on your job?"), (b) comparisons of current facet amount against some explicit standard of comparison (e.g., "Compared to what you currently have, do you want more, less, or the same opportunity for promotion on your job?"), or (c) difference scores calculated by subtracting a direct report of facet amount from a specified

equivalent to a measure of have-want discrepancy. Finally, participants also completed seven alternative measures for assessing the importance of 12 job domains, including four rating methods, two ranking methods, and a point-distribution method. A composite importance value of each domain was computed from these seven measures. On examining Locke's range-of-affect hypothesis (1969, 1976), moderated regression analyses were conducted for each domain to see if domain importance moderates the relationship between domain amount and domain satisfaction. In each model, domain satisfaction was regressed on domain amount, domain importance, and their interaction (domain amount × domain importance). Among the 12 job domains, the interaction term was significant on 9 domains, and the interaction plots of these domains, like Figure 3, revealed that the relationship between domain amount and domain satisfaction was generally stronger among people who regard the domain as higher in importance than people who regards the domain as lower in importance.

In McFarlin and Rice's (1992) study, domain satisfaction was regressed on domain have-want discrepancy, domain importance, and their interaction on 8 job domains within two employee samples. They found that 5 models had significant interaction effects for one sample and 6 models had significant interaction effects for the other sample. The interaction patterns they found were consistent with Figure 3, showing that the relationship between perceived have-want discrepancy scores and domain satisfaction is generally stronger for subjects rating the domain high, as opposed to low, in importance.

McFarlin et al. (1995) examined Locke's range-of-affect hypothesis in a sample of 122 employees of a large South African corporation. Have-want discrepancy, amount, importance, and satisfaction ratings of 12 job domains were used to test the hypothesis. In the regression models using domain have-want discrepancy, domain importance, and their interactions to predict domain satisfaction, 11 models had significant interaction effects. In the regression models using domain amount, domain importance, and their interactions to predict domain satisfaction, 7 models had significant interaction effects. The interaction pattern confirmed Locke's range-of-affect hypothesis. The slopes of the regression lines predicting domain satisfaction were always steeper for respondents reporting high domain importance than for respondents reporting low domain importance.

Regarding life satisfaction, Wu and Yao (2006b) conducted the same regression analysis to predict domain satisfaction by domain have-want discrepancy, domain importance, and their interactions on 12 life domains with a sample of 167 undergraduate students in Taiwan. Among the 12 domains, 8 domains had significant interaction effects of domain have-want discrepancy and domain importance. The interaction pattern also showed that the slope between domain satisfaction and domain have-want discrepancy was steeper for respondents reporting high domain importance than for respondents reporting low domain importance.

The same finding was also obtained in Wu and Yao's (2008) study, in which domain satisfaction was regressed by domain have-want discrepancy, domain importance, and their interactions on 7 self-concept domains. Among the 7 domains, 5 domains had significant interaction effects of domain have-want discrepancy and domain importance. The interaction pattern also confirmed the hypothesized interaction pattern in the range-of-affect hypothesis.

---

standard of comparison (e.g., current promotion opportunity minus wanted promotion opportunity) (as cited in Rice, Gentile, & McFarlin, 1991). Locke and Latham (1990) claimed that all three approaches are conceptually equivalent. All of them measure value fulfillment (the gap between have and want conditions), either directly or indirectly.

Hence, for survey research, the range-of-affect hypothesis was supported in job, life, and self satisfaction.

In addition to survey research, Rice, Markus, Moyer, and McFarlin (1991) conducted two 2 × 2 (domain importance × amount of discrepancy) factorial experiments to test the range-of-affect hypothesis to see if the high/low importance and high/low amount of discrepancy have a significant interaction effect on satisfaction rating. The four conditions of each experiment were created by four scenarios, in which high/low importance and high/low amount of discrepancy were manipulated. Participants were randomly assigned to one condition and asked to put themselves in the position of the person portrayed in the scenario. After reading the materials, participants were asked to rate the level of satisfaction in that situation from the point of view of the person portrayed in the scenario. Their results supported Locke's range-of-affect hypothesis (1969, 1976), revealing that in the high importance conditions, the slope of discrepancy amount and satisfaction was steeper than the slope in the low importance conditions.

There were also several studies that did not examine the range-of-affect hypothesis directly, but did find similar results depicted in the range-of-affect hypothesis (Friedlander, 1965; Trauer & Mackinnon, 2001; Welham, Haire, Mercer, & Stedman, 2001). For example, Friedlander (1965) and Trauer and Mackinnon (2001) indicated that domains of extreme satisfaction/dissatisfaction are more important than mild satisfaction/dissatisfaction domains, supporting that the responses of satisfaction have a wider range on dissatisfaction-satisfaction scale for the high-importance domain.

Moreover, in Welham et al.'s (2001) study, they asked participants to rate their real status and their ideal status on the same scale, in which four descriptions were ranged from worst (1) to best (4) condition. These two ratings were used to compute a have-want discrepancy score for that domain. In addition, participants were also asked to rate the importance and satisfaction of that domain. Then the correlations between real status and domain satisfaction of each domain were compared with those between the importance-weighted discrepancy and domain satisfaction of each domain. The results revealed that importance-weighted discrepancies were more strongly related to domain satisfaction than the real status alone, suggesting that weighting have-want discrepancy scores with domain importance could improve the prediction for domain satisfaction. However, they only used correlation analysis to test this effect, not moderated regression analysis. Because correlation between a product variable (such as the weighted score) and a third variable is dependent on the scales of the two original variables (Arnold & Evans, 1979; Bohrnstedt & Goldberger, 1969; Evans, 1991; Schmidt, 1973), changing the zero-point of the original scale would change the correlation value. As a result, correlation analysis may not provide a reliable result for examining the effect of importance weighting. Hence, Welham et al.'s (2001) finding needs further replication.

3.3. Studies on Range-of-Affect Hypothesis in an Intrapersonal Framework

As stated previously, the range-of-affect hypothesis can be described in an intrapersonal framework. The intrapersonal framework was more desirable than the interpersonal framework in discussing the issue of importance weighting on satisfaction scores because an individual's QOL score was usually computed from his/her scores of various life domains.

Specifically, a common procedure of importance weighting on satisfaction scores is to multiply importance and satisfaction scores for a domain for an individual. If there were 10 life domains, then an individual's QOL score was computed by multiplying importance and satisfaction scores of the 10 life domains and averaging or summing these 10 weighted scores. In this within-subject situation, it is worth investigating if the strength of satisfaction/dissatisfaction of a life domain was stronger on more important domains than on less important domains for an individual when the have-want discrepancy of each domain was controlled. If Locke's hypothesis is supported in a within-subject design study, it could reveal that the perception of importance has already been considered when an individual makes a satisfaction evaluation of a life domain. Thus, it could be that weighting the domain satisfaction score with domain importance is unnecessary for an individual.

In the existing literature, Locke (1969), Mobley and Locke (1970), Wu and Yao (2007) and Wu (2008a, 2008b) have examined the range-of-affect hypothesis in an intrapersonal framework. Locke (1969), Mobley and Locke (1970), Wu and Yao (2007) conducted within-subject experiments to examine the range-of-affect hypothesis, whereas Wu (2008a, 2008b) using hierarchical linear modeling (multilevel modeling) technique to analyze within-subject data from surveys.

First, Locke (1969) manipulated the level of importance of a reaction time task with payment (high importance) and non-payment (low importance) for each successful trial. As predicted, participants' satisfaction or dissatisfaction with their performance was more extreme in a payment condition than a non-payment condition. However, in the manipulation check, only 7 out of 21 participants reported that the payment condition was more important than the non-payment condition. Thus, the study was not able to confidently attribute the findings to the level of importance, because the importance manipulation was not successful.

In addition, Mobley and Locke (1970) conducted three within-subject experiments (Study 2 to Study 4) in their research. In Study 2 of Mobley and Locke's (1970) research, participants were asked to select the most important and least important domains out of 10 domains. Then, within these two domains, participants were asked to indicate (a) the alternative that best described what his/her job is or was like (real status) on a 7-point verbally anchored scale, (b) the alternative that best described what the job should be or should have been like (ideal status) on the same 7-point verbally anchored scale, and (c) the degree of satisfaction with each of the seven alternatives specified in the scale, that is, the anticipated satisfaction (measured on a 21-point bipolar scale) if they engage in each alternative. From these ratings, domain discrepancies of the two domains were indicated by the gap between the real alternative and the ideal alternative and were divided into five categories (0, -1, -2, -3, and -4; other discrepancy levels were ignored). In addition, the satisfaction score for the real alternative represented actual satisfaction. Further, for each discrepancy level, the mean of domain satisfaction score across participants was calculated separately for the most and least important domains. In this procedure, only participants with at least one of the five discrepancy categories for both domains could be included. Therefore, of 102 participants, the data of only 34 were used. Although the result of this study supported the range-of-affect hypothesis, revealing that the relation between domain discrepancy and domain satisfaction was stronger for the most important than for the least important domain, the method of analysis assumed that the same discrepancy unit obtained from different domains has the same meaning. In addition, the analysis method lost too much information. Therefore, this is not an ideal experiment to examine the hypothesis.

In Study 3 of Mobley and Locke's (1970) research, they manipulated the high-low importance by two forms of a question in which intrinsic interest was used to manipulate the level of importance, assuming that the question content involving intrinsic interest would be more important. Participants were asked to indicate (a) the alternative that best described what his/her job is or was like (possible real status) in the context of a 7-point verbally anchored scale (that is, 7 alternatives); (b) the alternative that best described what the job should be or should have been like (want status) on the same 7-point verbally anchored scale; and (c) the degree of satisfaction of each of the seven alternatives, that is, the anticipated satisfaction (measured on a 21-point bipolar scale) if they engage in each alternative. From these ratings, domain discrepancy was indicated by the gap between the possible real alternative and want alternative and was divided into five categories (0, -1, -2, -3, and -4; other discrepancy levels were ignored). In addition, the mean satisfaction score for the seven alternatives represented anticipated satisfaction, which was used as the dependent variable. Their results showed that the relation between domain discrepancy and domain satisfaction was stronger for the higher important form (intrinsic) than that for the lower important form (non-intrinsic) on three domains. However, as in Study 2 in their research, many participants' data were eliminated prior to analysis because their manipulation check reports did not correspond to the manipulation of question content involving intrinsic interest as more important. In addition, the limited range of discrepancy (0, -1, -2, -3, and -4) also eliminated many participants' data.

Finally, in Study 4 of Mobley and Locke's (1970) research, they manipulated the high-low importance by real situation, in which two quizzes were taken in class. One was the regular quiz (high importance condition), which was a real test for the class, and the other one was the research quiz (low importance condition), which was a research purpose test (grades would not be reported to the instructor). All participants took part in these two tests and were asked to indicate their acceptable lowest grade on the test and the anticipated satisfaction if they got different level of grades. The gap of these two grades was used to index the level of have-want discrepancy. Finally, after knowing their actual test score, they were asked to rate their actual satisfaction for each test. As in the previous study, Mobley and Locke (1970) compared the relation between discrepancy and actual satisfaction for the high importance condition (regular quiz) and the low importance condition (research quiz). The results revealed that the relation between discrepancy and actual satisfaction for the regular quiz was stronger than that for the research quiz. However, the result was only determined for participants with large discrepancy, not for the entire sample. Therefore, although Locke (1969) and Mobley and Locke's (1970) within-subject experiments supported the range-of-affect hypothesis, given the limitations of importance manipulation and data analysis, the conclusions should be viewed with caution.

Recently, Wu and Yao (2007) conducted within-subject experiments with a more desirable experimental design to avoid the complex experiment procedure and data analysis used in Mobley and Locke's (1970) study. They used four scenarios to test the range-of-affect hypothesis. In each scenario, two people were described as wanting the same circumstances with respect to an ideal object defined by two dimensions. For example, in the first scenario, both A and B wanted "a large house in a convenient location." The house was the ideal object defined by the dimensions of size and location. However, in the scenario, A and B were described as having different opinions about the two dimensions. For example, A regarded size to be of greater importance than location, and B regarded location to be of greater importance than size. After reading this information, participants were asked to rate A's and B's level of satisfaction with respect to several objects. The proposed objects were defined by different levels of the same two dimensions, such as a 30-ping (1 ping = 3.3 square meters) house located in the city center (indicating convenient location), a 50-ping house located in the city center, a 30-ping house located in the suburbs, and a 50-ping house located in the suburbs. According to the range-of-affect hypothesis, it was predicted that when participants used A's viewpoint, the satisfaction ratings would depend on the size of the house, and when participants used B's viewpoint, the satisfaction ratings would depend on the location of the house. Indeed, in the four scenarios, when participants regarded one dimension as more important than the other, they were sensitive to the have-and-want gap for that dimension; the degree of satisfaction was affected. This finding reveals that altering participants' importance perceptions can affect satisfaction evaluations.

In addition to experimental examination, Wu (2008b) examined the range-of-affect hypothesis in a within-subject context using survey data collected in Wu and Yao's (2006b) study. Hierarchical linear modeling with a random-coefficients regression model was applied. At the first level (within-individual level), the satisfaction scores for each item were regressed on the have-want discrepancy, importance, and the interaction between have-want discrepancy and importance (have-want discrepancy × importance) of the same domain. At the second level (between-individual level), the intercept, coefficients of have-want discrepancy, importance, and the interaction between have-want discrepancy and importance at the first level were regarded as varying randomly over all participants. The mathematical equations for i items and j individuals of the model were:

Level-1:

$$SAT_{ij}=\beta_{0j}+\beta_{1j}(DIS_{ij}-\overline{DIS}_j)+\beta_{2j}(IMP_{ij}-\overline{IMP}_j)+\beta_{3j}(DIS_{ij}-\overline{DIS}_j)\times(IMP_{ij}-\overline{IMP}_j)+r_{ij}$$

Level-2:

$$\beta_{0j}=\gamma_{00}+\mu_{0j},$$
$$\beta_{1j}=\gamma_{10}+\mu_{1j},$$
$$\beta_{2j}=\gamma_{20}+\mu_{2j},$$
$$\beta_{3j}=\gamma_{30}+\mu_{3j},$$

$$\text{where } r_{ij}\sim N(0,\sigma^2) \text{ and } \begin{pmatrix}\mu_{0j}\\ \mu_{1j}\\ \mu_{2j}\\ \mu_{3j}\end{pmatrix}\sim N\left(\begin{pmatrix}0\\0\\0\\0\end{pmatrix},\begin{pmatrix}\tau_{00}&\tau_{01}&\tau_{02}&\tau_{03}\\ \tau_{10}&\tau_{11}&\tau_{12}&\tau_{13}\\ \tau_{20}&\tau_{21}&\tau_{22}&\tau_{23}\\ \tau_{30}&\tau_{31}&\tau_{32}&\tau_{33}\end{pmatrix}\right).$$

In this model, SAT means domain satisfaction, DIS means domain have-want discrepancy, and IMP means domain importance for the three main variables. All three variables were centered with respect to the mean of each individual to gain a meaningful intercept and avoid multicollinearity from interaction terms. The main focus was to determine whether the interaction effect between domain have-want discrepancy and domain importance was significant in predicting satisfaction across domains at the within-individual level. If so, it can be inferred that the relationship between domain have-want discrepancy and domain satisfaction is stronger among high importance domains than low importance domains for individuals and the range-of-affect hypothesis will be supported. Results showed that the three coefficients associated with domain have-want discrepancy, domain importance, and the interaction between domain have-want discrepancy and domain importance at first level were all significant in predicting domain satisfaction. The significant interaction effect revealed that the relationship between domain have-want discrepancy and domain satisfaction is stronger for high importance domains than low importance domains for an individual, supporting the range-of-affect hypothesis in an intrapersonal framework.

The same two-level linear model was also applied in Wu's (2008a) study, in which importance ranks, rather than importance ratings, were used. Similarly, at the first level (within-individual level), the satisfaction score of each domain was regressed on the have-want discrepancy, importance, and the interaction between have-want discrepancy and importance (have-want discrepancy × importance) of the same domain. At the second level (between-individual level), the intercept, coefficients of have-want discrepancy, importance, and the interaction between have-want discrepancy and importance at the first level were regarded as varying randomly over all participants. The same result was obtained. That is, given an individual, the negative relationship between domain have-want discrepancy and domain satisfaction is stronger when domain importance is higher.

3.4. Brief Summary

In this section, Locke's range-of-affect hypothesis (Locke, 1969, 1976) and related empirical studies are reviewed. Studies examining the range-of-affect hypothesis either in an interpersonal framework or in an intrapersonal framework all supported the hypothesis, showing that given the amount of discrepancy, range of satisfaction rating on a domain is determined by the domain importance. Accordingly, it can be said that domain satisfaction has incorporated the information of domain importance, which renders weighting domain satisfaction with domain importance redundant.

4. Summary and Implications

4.1. Conclusion on Importance Weighting of Satisfaction Scores

Importance weighting is a common procedure in calculating QOL scores. The basic idea of the procedure is that given a set of life domains, each domain would be differentially important to an individual's life. Therefore, on assessing his/her QOL, not only the current satisfaction of the life domain should be evaluated, but the importance of that life domain should also be considered. Accordingly, a QOL score is empirically defined as the importance-weighted satisfaction score of each domain. This viewpoint implicitly implies that satisfaction ratings and importance ratings are independent and that importance weighting would contribute to incorporating the meaning of importance into the satisfaction scores. However, according to Locke's (1969, 1976) theory and many empirical studies reviewed here (Friedlander, 1965; Locke, 1969; McFarlin et al., 1995; McFarlin & Rice, 1992; Mobley & Locke, 1970; Rice et al., 1991a, 1991b; Trauer & Mackinnon, 2001; Welham et al., 2001; Wu, 2008a, 2008b; Wu & Yao, 2006b, 2007; Wu & Yao, 2008), the satisfaction rating of a domain has reflected the judgment of importance of that domain. That is, a higher importance domain would lead to a wider range of satisfaction/dissatisfaction of that domain than a less important domain. Accordingly, the reason for weighting domain satisfaction with domain importance is untenable.

In addition, studies examining the utility of importance weighting also indicated that weighting satisfaction scores with importance scores did not have additional contributions in predicting criterion measures (Caston & Briato, 1983; Ewen, 1967; Hsieh, 2003; McFarlin & Rice, 1992; Mikes & Hulin, 1968; Rice et al., 1991a; Russell et al., 2006; Staples & Higgins,1998; Waters & Roach, 1971; Waters, 1969; Waters & Roach, 1971; Wu, 2008a; Wu, Chen, & Tsai, 2009; Wu & Yao, 2006a, 2006b). Hence, it can be concluded that there is no solid basis to weight satisfaction scores with importance, and there is also no empirical contribution of importance weighting in predicting criterion measures.

4.2. The Role of Importance Rating in QOL Research

According to existing findings, it could be said that weighting domain satisfaction with domain importance is not appropriate. However, it doesn't imply that importance rating is not valuable in assessing individuals' QOL. In fact, information about domain importance is important for understanding an individual's QOL. According to Locke's range-of-affect hypothesis, satisfaction of a life domain was determined by the degree of have-want discrepancy and the importance of that domain, suggesting that the domain discrepancy and the domain importance were the two components that result in the observed degree of satisfaction. Accordingly, it could be said that a satisfaction-based QOL score is not sufficient to understand an individual's perception of that life domain, since a particular satisfaction level could result from a small have-want discrepancy with higher importance or a large have-want discrepancy with lower importance. Therefore, acquiring the information of domain discrepancy and domain importance could lead researchers to comprehensively evaluate and understand an individual's QOL.

In addition to understanding an individual's QOL, Skevington et al. (2004) indicated that information about domain importance is useful for instrument developers or researchers to evaluate if domains are relevant to the research sample and population for whom the scale is intended. Moreover, domain importance information is also useful to identify the value differences among different diseased, social, or cultural groups. For example, Saxena, Carlson, Billington, and Orley (2001), on behalf of the WHOQOL Group, investigated the value difference among age, gender, and center (cultural) groups by the importance rating of WHOQOL-BREF domains.

Regarding health care, information of domain importance can facilitate health services provider in designing appropriate health services for an individual or a group, thus enhancing the efficiency of health care. Oishi, Diener, Suh, and Lucas (1999) have indicated that intraindividual changes in satisfaction were strongly influenced by the degree of success in the domains that individuals value. This implies that understanding which life domain is more important and enhancing the performance of that domain is crucial for QOL promotion. In summary, arguing that weighting domain satisfaction with domain importance is unnecessary does not imply that the information of domain importance is not valuable in QOL assessment.

4.3. Implications on QOL Promotion

According to Locke's hypothesis, there are two components that influence the degree of satisfaction on a specific life domain. The first one is have-want discrepancy; the other one is the value (importance) of that domain. Accordingly, we could promote an individual QOL by a "have-want discrepancy" pathway and a "value perception" pathway.

The first pathway to promote life satisfaction is to reduce the have-want discrepancy in life domains, because have-want discrepancy is regarded as the root of satisfaction/dissatisfaction (e.g., Campbell, Converse, & Rogers, 1976; Calman, 1984; Diener et al., 1985; Locke, 1969, 1976; Michalos, 1985; Shin & Johnson, 1978) and many empirical studies have shown that the range of have-want discrepancies determines the level of satisfaction (e.g., Cohen, 2000; Schulz, 1995; Vermunt, Spaans, & Zorge, 1989; Welham et al., 2001; Wu & Yao, 2006a). In a recent study, Wu (2008c) further reported that satisfaction measurement involves an implicit have-want comparison. In his study, relationships between direct have-want discrepancy, amount, and satisfaction, which vary in their degree of explicitness, were examined. The have-want discrepancy measure explicitly asks respondents to rate the discrepancy between what they have and what they want (e.g., "What is the difference between your energy level and the level you would like to have?"). The amount measure requires respondents to think about the amount of discrepancy between what one has and what one wants, but does not explicitly ask about that (e.g., "Do you have enough energy for everyday life?"). Finally, the satisfaction measure is assumed to incorporate a component of the have-want comparison, but does not ask respondents to consider such a comparison in the question (e.g., "Are you satisfied with your energy?"). Results of correlation analysis showed that satisfaction has a closer relation with amount than have-want discrepancy. In addition, results of conventional mediation analysis and multilevel path analysis both showed that have-want discrepancy influences amount, which then influences satisfaction, suggesting that transformation of have-want status comparison into satisfaction evaluation occurs via an intermediate stage (amount) during which the have-want status comparison is made indirectly. This is evidence for the discrepant nature of satisfaction evaluation. As a result, it is a straightforward approach to enhance an individual's life satisfaction by reducing have-want discrepancy in life domains through promoting the present condition or demoting the ideal standard. In promoting the present condition, we can help an individual to attain his/her ideal status to make his/her present circumstance match their ideal conditions. In demoting the ideal standard, we can help an individual set reasonable goals.

In addition to reducing the gap between the present condition and the want condition, there is another pathway to enhance an individual's quality of life. It is to attune the importance perception of life domains according to the level of have–want discrepancy of each domain, which is termed the "value perception" pathway. That is, we can enhance an individual's life satisfaction by shifting their importance perceptions in life domains. This approach does not change their original ideal standards of each area, but adjusts the importance hierarchy of life areas. By this approach, an individual can experience higher QOL without changing their goals of each life domain. This proposition has been supported in various empirical studies. For example, several studies have found that people will change the importance of life domains or re-conceptualize the meaning of life according to their health status (e.g., Jansen, Stiggelbout, Nooij, Noordijk, & Kievit, 2000; Rapkin, 2000; Rapkin & Shwartz, 2004; Schwartz, Coulthard-Morris, Cole, & Vollmer, 1997). In addition, based on a self-regulation perspective, Wrosch and Scheier (2003) pointed out that quality of life was related to the process of giving up unattainable goals and finding new and meaningful goals to pursue. They argued that people who confront unattainable goals are better able to disengage from those goals and to re-engage in alternative, meaningful activities. Many empirical studies have found that people who can shift their importance perception of different life goals according to their situations have higher life satisfaction (e.g., Moskowitz, Folkman, Collette, & Vittinghoff, 1996; Rapkin, 2000; Tunali & Power, 1993; Wrosch & Heckhausen, 1999; Wrosch, Scheier, Miller, Schulz & Carver, 2003). Moreover, in self-concept research, it has been found that people tend to stress their self-concept with better performance (e.g., Crocker, Karpinski, Quinn, & Chase, 2003; Hardy & Moriarty, 2006), and people with a strong tendency to discount the importance of worse self-concepts have higher self-esteem (Pelham & Swann, 1989). As a result, it can be said that attuning importance perception of life domains can be an alternative way to enhance one's quality of life.

In a recent study, Wu (2009) investigated if the have-want discrepancy pathway and the value perception pathway both have their unique effect in promoting global life satisfaction. He used the dataset in Wu and Yao's (2006a) study, in which 332 undergraduate students provided their satisfaction, importance, and perceived have–want discrepancy ratings on 12 life domains and their global life satisfaction scores. In order to capture the effect of value perception pathway, he first constructed an index, termed shifting tendency, by correlating discrepancy scores with importance scores across 12 domains for each individual. Then, these Pearson correlation coefficients were transformed into Fisher's Z values. Higher values of this index indicated a stronger tendency of stressing life domains with lower discrepancy and discounting life domains with larger discrepancy. Wu (2009) first conducted a correlation analysis to show that (1) average discrepancy had positive relations with average domain satisfaction and global life satisfaction, (2) shifting tendency also had positive relation with average domain satisfaction and global life satisfaction and (3) shifting tendency did not have a significant relation with the average discrepancy. He then conducted hierarchical regression analysis to show that both average discrepancy and shifting tendency had a significant effect in predicting average domain satisfaction and global life satisfaction. This finding showed that the have-want discrepancy and the value perception pathways are two independent pathways for promoting individuals' quality of life.

The independent roles of the have-want discrepancy and the value perception pathways were also shown in another study (Wu, Tsai, & Chen, 2009). Wu et al.'s study was to explain how the positive views (perceived control, optimism, and self-enhancement) proposed by Cummins and Nistico (2002) maintain life satisfaction. Their study assumed that people with strong positive views would have (1) higher self-esteem, (2) a lower have-want discrepancy in life domains, and (3) a stronger shifting tendency across life domains, which then lead to a higher life satisfaction. A total of 272 undergraduates in the study completed questionnaires measuring sense of control, optimism, self-enhancement, self-esteem, have-want discrepancy, and importance of 15 life domains, as well as global life satisfaction. A structural equation model was built to examine the mediation effects of the three pathways on the relationship between positive views and global life satisfaction. Their results showed that the relationship between positive views and life satisfaction was completely mediated by self-esteem, have-want discrepancy, and shifting tendency, and that the three mediation paths were independent. This finding indicated that the three pathways of enhancing self-esteem, reducing have-want discrepancy, and changing importance perceptions had unique effects to explain how positive views maintain life satisfaction. This finding showed again that the have-want discrepancy and the value perception pathways are two independent pathways for promoting individuals' quality of life.

4.4. The Relationship between Domain and Global Satisfaction

The null contribution of importance weighting on domain satisfaction in predicting global satisfaction raised a question on the relationship between domain and global satisfaction. Based on the existing findings, at item level it was found that the relationship between domain satisfaction and global satisfaction is not moderated by the degree of domain importance (McFarlin & Rice, 1992; Rice et al., 1991a; Wu & Yao, 2006a, 2006b). Hence, it can be said that global satisfaction does not result from importance-weighted domain satisfaction. But, what is the relationship between domain and global satisfaction?

The relationship between domain and global satisfaction was usually discussed from the top-down and bottom-up theories. In brief, the top-down perspective regards evaluations in various life domains as resulting from evaluation of life as a whole (Diener, 1984, 1999; Lance, Mallard, & Michalos, 1995). Conversely, the bottom-up perspective regards evaluations in various life domains as contributing to the evaluation of life as a whole (Diener, 1984, 1999; Lance et al., 1995). The idea of importance weighting on domain satisfaction is in line with the bottom-up perspective but ignores the possibility of the reversed direction, as stated in the top-down theory. The existing literature indicates that top-down and bottom-up theories are not mutually exclusive.

For example, Headey, Veenhoveen, and Wearing (1991) test the two-way causation (top-down and bottom-up) between global and domain satisfaction using panel data. Their findings revealed that marriage satisfaction involved both top-down and bottom-up processes. Job, standard of living, and leisure only involved the top-down process, and friendship and health did not have a significant effect in either of the processes. Later, Lance et al. (1995) tested alternative theoretical models that specified bottom-up, top-down, and bidirectional relationships between overall life satisfaction and satisfaction with 11 life domains using several structural equation models. Their results showed that the bidirectional model was the best model, suggesting a non-recursive relationship between global measures and domain-specific measures. Recently, Wu and Yao (2007b) examined the relationship between global and domain measures of quality of life from a psychometric perspective by three different factor structure models. The best model they found was a three-factor model in which one factor (representing quality of life) influences both global and domain measures, another factor (representing global approach) only influences global measures, and yet another factor (representing domain approach) only influences domain measures. This model suggests that global measures and domain measures did assess the same construct on quality of life. However, the measurement approaches they adopted (global or domain approach) also have substantial impact on the meaning of the scores. Hence, given the existing findings, both top-down and bottom-up pathways may co-exist.

4.5. Importance Weighting on Health Status Scores

In this article, it has been shown that the importance weighting of satisfaction scores is not necessary and has no empirical predictive contribution. However, if QOL was measured as health status (i.e., participants' current health conditions), is it appropriate to weight status-based QOL with item importance? According to Locke's range-of-affect hypothesis, it is inappropriate because an individual's affective evaluation of his/her life is based on the discrepancy between have-want circumstances, not the have status only.

Empirically, several studies also reported that the importance-weighted health status score is not superior to the unweighted health status score. Mozes and Shabtai (1996) have showed that, compared with the unweighted status score, weighting domain status scores with importance scores did not lead to a beneficial effect with regard to (1) the ability to discriminate diseased and non-diseased patients and patients with five different levels of global assessment of QOL, (2) responsiveness of total score, and (3) predictiveness of one year mortality. In addition, McGrath and Bedi (2004) compared the performance of weighted and unweighted versions of an oral health-related quality of life measure regarding (1) the discrimination among different age groups (< 65 vs. 65 and older) and social class (higher and lower), (2) the association with self-report oral health, and (3) the predictive ability in identifying those in prosthetic need. They reported that the weighted score was not superior to the unweighted score in these aspects. Thus, findings of Mozes and Shabtai (1996) and McGrath and Bedi (2004) also raised the question of the value of importance weighting on health status scores. Although several studies suggested that importance weighting is a valuable procedure for QOL assessment (Byrne, Hailey, & Johnson, 1995; Laman & Lankhorst, 1994), they did not compare the performance of weighted and unweighted scores in their studies, and they did not provide cogent evidence with which to draw their conclusions.

Similar findings on weighting status scores with importance scores were also obtained in self-esteem research. Based on the notion proposed by James (1980) that a person's overall self-evaluation was based on the weighted average of specific self-concept, many studies strived to examine whether the importance of domain self-concept has an impact on the relationship between domain self-concept and global self-esteem. Driving from James' (1980) notion, Rosenberg (1965; Hoge & McCarthy, 1984; Marsh, 1986) proposed the interactive hypothesis that the size of contribution of certain domain self-concept to global self-esteem depends on the level of importance of that domain self-concept to an individual. This interactive hypothesis was similar to the importance-weighting on domain satisfaction discussed previously, but there is one difference; that is, the weighting procedure is applied to self-concept (participants' self-descriptions), not to self-satisfaction or self-discrepancy between actual and ideal self. Hence, the weighting issue in self-esteem research can also be regarded as weighting current condition (have) with importance values, just like weighting the current health status with importance values in QOL research.

Many empirical studies examining importance weighting on self-concept also obtained null findings. For example, Hoge and McCarthy (1984) asked participants to rate their self-concept on specific domains, the importance of each domain, and their global self-esteem. Further, they compared the performance of unweighted and importance-weighted specific self-concept scores in correlating global self-esteem and found that weighted domain self-concept scores did not have a higher correlation with global self-esteem than the unweighted scores. Later, Marsh (1986) used multiple regression models to examine the interactive hypothesis among domain self-concept, domain importance, and global self-esteem. In his study, 24 regression models were conducted to examine if the interaction term of domain self-concept and domain importance would have a significant effect in predicting global self-esteem. His results showed that only 7 models have significant interaction effects, suggesting that the interactive hypothesis was weakly supported. Further, Marsh (1993) conducted two studies to investigate how global self-esteem is related to domain self-concept using importance scores of specific domains as weighting values. His results showed that importance weighting on self-concept also did not account for more variance of global self-esteem. Recently, Lachowicz-Tabaczek (1998) and Hardy and Moriarty (2006) also conducted moderated regression analysis to examine if domain self-concept and domain importance have interaction effect in predicting global self-esteem. Their results also showed that domain importance did not moderate the relationship between domain self-concept and global self-esteem. Therefore, given the empirical findings reviewed here, importance weighting on the current status scores did not have additional predictive contribution.

CONCLUSION

In this review, the reason of using importance weighting on satisfaction scores has been introduced. The intuitive idea of importance weighting was not supported. Many studies showed that weighting satisfaction scores with importance values did not contribute to accounting for more variance of criterion variables. Moreover, Locke's range-of-affect hypothesis (Locke, 1969, 1976) further indicated that a satisfaction evaluation has already contained an importance judgment. His hypothesis has been supported in various studies in different contents, such as job, life and self satisfaction. Hence, it can be concluded that it is not necessary to statistically weight satisfaction scores with importance values.

In addition to the issue of importance weighting, this review also provided implications of QOL promotion from Locke's range-of-affect hypothesis (Locke, 1969, 1976). Two pathways, "have-want discrepancy" and "value perception" pathways, were proposed to promote an individual's QOL. Two studies (Wu, 2009; Wu, Tsai, & Chen, 2009) have already found that these two pathways have their unique effects in promoting QOL and also played independent roles in mediating the positive effect between positive views and global life satisfaction. Moreover, studies examining Locke's range-of-affect hypothesis also provide an implication on the relationship between domain and global satisfaction. Existing findings suggested that the relationship between domain and global satisfaction is not simply equal to the sum of importance-weighted domain satisfactions. Conversely, domain and global satisfaction can mutually influence each other. Finally, weighting the current status scores with importance values is also discussed based on Locke's range-of-affect hypothesis

(Locke, 1969, 1976). It is still suggested not to weighting status scores with importance values because of no theoretical basis and additional predictive contribution.

REFERENCES

Arnold, H. J., & Evans, M. G. (1979). Testing multiplicative models does not require ratio scales. *Organizational Behavior and Human Performance, 24*, 41-59.

Bohrnstedt, G., & Goldberger, A. (1969). On the exact covariance of products of random variables. *Journal of the American Statistical Association, 64*, 1439- 1442.

Brogly S, Mercier C, Bruneau J, Palepu A, Franco E. (2003). Towards more effective public health programming for injection drug users: Development and evaluation of the Injection Drug User Quality of Life Scale. *Substance Use & Misuse,* 38, 965–992.

Byrne, H. A., Hailey, B. J., & Johnson, J. T. (1995). The use of weighted scores with the Functional Assessment of Cancer Therapy (FACT) scales. *Journal of Psychosocial Oncology, 13*, 57-77.

Calman, K. C. (1984). Quality of life of cancer patients - A hypothesis. *Journal of Medical Ethics, 10*, 124-127

Campbell, A., Converse, P. E., & Rogers, W. L. (1976). *Quality of American life: Perceptions, evaluations and satisfaction*. New York: Russell Sage Foundation.

Caston, R. J., & Briato, R. (1983). On the use of facet importance as a weighting component of job satisfaction. *Educational and Psychological Measurement, 43,* 339-350.

Cohen, E. H. (2000). A facet theory approach to examining overall and life facet satisfaction relationships. *Social Indicators Research, 51*, 223-237

Cohen, J. (1978). Partialed products are interactions: Partialed powers are curve components. *Psychological Bulletin, 85,* 858-866.

Crocker, J., Karpinski, A., Quinn, D. M., & Chase, S. (2003). When grades determine self-worth: Consequences of contingent self-worth for male and female engineering and psychology majors. *Journal of Personality and Social Psychology, 85*, 507–516

Cummins, R. A. (1997). *Comprehensive Quality of Life Scale – Adult: Manual.* Australia: Deakin University.

Diener, E. (1984). Subjective well-being. *Psychological Bulletin, 95*, 542-575.

Diener, E., Emmons, R. A., Larsen, R. J., & Griffin, S. (1985). The Satisfaction with Life Scale. *Journal of Personality Assessment, 49*, 71-75.

Dijkers, M. P. (2003). Individualization in quality of life measurement: Instruments and approaches. *Archives of Physical Medicine and Rehabilitation, 84*, S3-14.

Evans, M. G. (1991). The problem of analyzing multiplicative composites: Interactions revisited. *American Psychologist, 46*, 6-15.

Ewen, R. B. (1967). Weighting components of job satisfaction. *Journal of Applied Psychology, 51*, 68-73.

Ferrans, C., & Powers, M. (1985). Quality of Life Index: Development and psychometric properties. *Advances in Nursing Science, 8*, 15-24.

Friedlander, F. (1965). Relationships between the importance and the satisfaction of various environmental factors. *Journal of Applied Psychology, 49*, 160-164.

Frisch, M. B. (1992). Use of the Quality of Life Inventory in problem assessment and treatment planning for cognitive therapy of depression. In A. Freeman & F. M. Dattlio (Eds.), *Comprehensive casebook of cognitive therapy* (pp. 27-52). New York: Plenum Press.

Frisch, M. B., Cornell, J., Villanueva, M., & Retzlaff, P. J. (1992). Clinical validation of the Quality of Life Inventory: A measure of life satisfaction for use in treatment planning and outcome assessment. *Psychological Assessment, 4*, 92-101.

Glass, G. V. (1968). Correlations with products of variables: Derivations and implications for methodology. *American Educational Research Journal, 5*, 721-728.

Gorsuch, R. L. (1983). *Factor analysis* (2nd ed.). Hillsdale, NJ: Lawrence Erlbaum.

Hardy, L., & Moriarty, T. (2006). Shaping self-concept: The elusive importance effect. *Journal of Personality, 74*, 377-402.

Headey, B., Veenhoveen, R. & Wearing, A. (1991). Top-down versus bottom-up theories of subjective well-being. *Social Indicator Research, 24*, 81–100.

Hoge, D. R., & McCarthy, J. D. (1984). Influence of individual and group identity salience in the global self-esteem of youth. *Journal of Personality and Social Psychology, 47*, 403–414.

Hsieh, C. M. (2003). Counting importance: The case of life satisfaction and relative domain importance. *Social Indicators Research, 61*, 227-240.

Hsieh, C. M. (2004). To weight or not to weight: The role of domain importance in quality of life measurement. *Social Indicators Research, 68*, 163-174.

Jansen, S. J., Stiggelbout, A. M., Nooij, M. A., Noordijk, E. M., & Kievit, J. (2000). Response shift in quality of life measurement in early-stage breast cancer patients undergoing radiotherapy. *Quality of Life Research, 9*, 603–615.

James, W. (1890). *The Principle of Psychology*. New York: Holt, Rinehart and Winston .

Johnson, D. E. (1998). *Applied multivariate methods for data analysis*. Pacific Grove, CA: Duxbury Press.

Kaplan, R. M. (1998). Profile versus utility based measures of outcome for clinical trials. In M. J. Staquet, R. D. Hays, & P. M. Fayers (Eds.), *Quality of life assessment in clinical trials: Methods and practice* (pp. 69-90). London: Oxford University Press.

Ki, F., & Chow, S. C. (1995). Statistical justification for the use of composite scores in quality of life assessment. *Drug Information Journal, 29*, 715-727.

Lachowicz-Tabaczek, K (1998). The relation between domain-specific self-perceptions and their importance to global self-esteem: On the sources of self-worth. Polish Psychological Bulletin, 29, 231-254.

Laman, H., & Lankhorst, G. J. (1994). Subjective weighting of disability: An approach to quality of life assessment in rehabilitation. *Disability & Rehabilitation, 16*, 198-204.

Lance, C. E., Mallard A. G. & Michalos, A.C. (1995). Tests of the causal directions of global-life facet satisfaction relationships. *Social Indicators Research, 34*, 69–92.

Locke, E. A. (1969). What is job satisfaction? *Organizational Behavior and Human Performance, 4*, 309-336.

Locke, E. A. (1976). The nature and causes of job satisfaction. In M. D. Dunnette (Ed.), *Handbook of industrial and organizational psychology*, pp. 1297-1343. Chicago: Rand McNally.

Locke, E. A., & Latham, G. P. (1990). *A theory of goal setting and task performance*. Englewood Cliffs, NJ: Prentice Hall.

Marsh, H. W. (1986). Global self-esteem: Its relation to specific facets of self-concept and their importance. *Journal of Personality and Social Psychology, 51,* 1224-1236.

Marsh, H. W. (1993). Relations between global and specific domains of self: The importance of individual importance, certainty, and ideals. *Journal of Personality and Social Psychology, 65*, 975-992.

McFarlin, D. B., Coster, E. A., Rice, R. W., & Coopper-Alison, T. (1995). Facet importance and job satisfaction: Another look at the range of affect hypothesis. *Basic and Applied Social Psychology, 16*, 489-502.

McFarlin, D. B., & Rice, R. W. (1992). The role of facet importance as a moderator in job satisfaction processes. *Journal of Organizational Behavior, 13*, 41-54.

McGrath, C., & Bedi, R. (2004). Why are we "weighting"? An assessment of a self-weighting approach to measuring oral health-related quality of life. *Community Dentistry and Oral Epidemiology, 32*, 19-24.

Michalos, A. C. (1985). Multiple discrepancies theories (MDT). *Social Indicators Research, 16*, 347-413

Mikes, P. S., & Hulin, C. L. (1968). Use of importance as weighting component of job satisfaction. *Journal of Applied Psychology, 52*, 394-398.

Moskowitz, J. T., Folkman, S., Collette, L., & Vittinghoff, E. (1996). Coping and mood during AIDS-related caregiving and bereavement. *Annuals of Behavioral Medicine, 18*, 49–57.

Mozes, B., & Shabtai, E. (1996). The contribution of personal rating to the clinimetric functioning of a generic quality of life instrument. *Journal of Clinical Epidemiology, 12*, 1419-1422.

O'Boyle, C. (1994). The Schedule for the Evaluation of Individual Quality of Life (SEIQoL). *International Journal of Mental Health, 23*, 3-23.

Oliver, N., Holloway, F., & Carson, J. (1995). Deconstructing quality of life. *Journal of Mental Health, 4*, 1-4.

Olschewski, M., & Schumacher, M. (1990). Statistical analysis of quality of life data in cancer clinical trials. *Statistics in Medicine, 9*, 749-763.

Perloff, J. M., & Persons, J. B. (1988). Biases resulting from the use of indexes: An application to attributional style and depression. *Psychological Bulletin, 103*, 95-104.

Pelham, B. W., & Swann, W. B. (1989). From self-conceptions to self-worth: On the sources and. structure of global self-esteem. *Journal of Personality and Social Psychology, 57*, 672-680

Raphael, D., Rukholm, E., Brown, I., Hill-Bailey, P., & Donato, E. (1996). The quality of life profile-Adolescent version: Background, description, and initial validation. *Journal of Adolescent Health, 19*, 366-375.

Rapkin, B. D. (2000). Personal goals and response shifts: Understanding the impact of illness and events on the quality of life of people living with AIDS. In C.E. Schwartz, & M.A.G. Sprangers (Eds.), *Adaptation to changing health: Response shift in quality of life research*. Washington D.C.: American Psychological Association.

Rapkin, B. D., & Shwartz C. E. (2004). Toward a theoretical model of quality of life appraisal: Implications of findings from studies of response shift. *Health and Quality of Life Outcomes, 2*, 14.

Rice, R. W., Gentile, D. A., & McFarlin, D. B. (1991a). Facet importance and job satisfaction. *Journal of Applied Psychology, 76*, 31-39.

Rice, R. W., Markus, K., Moyer, R. P., & McFarlin, D. B. (1991b). Facet importance and job satisfaction: Two experimental tests of Locke's range of affect hypothesis. *Journal of Applied Social Psychology, 21*, 1977-1987.

Rosenberg, M. (1965). *Society and the adolescent self-image*. Princeton, NJ: Princeton University Press.

Rose, M., Scholler, G., Klapp, B. P., & Bernheim, J. L. (1998). Weighting dimensions in generic QOL questionnaires by Anamnestic Comparative Self-Assessment: Different weights in different diseases. *Quality of Life Research, 7*, 655.

Russell, L., Hubley, A. M., Palepu, A., & Zumbo, B. D. (2006). Does weighting capture what's important? Revisiting weighted and unweighted scores with a quality of life measure. Social Indicators Research, 75, 141-167.

Saxena, S., Carlson, D., Billington, R., & Orley, J. on behalf of the WHOQOL Group (2001). The WHO quality of life assessment instrument (WHOQOL-Bref): The importance of its items for cross-cultural research. *Quality of Life Research, 10,* 711-721.

Schmidt, F. L. (1973). Implications of a measurement problem for expectancy theory research. *Organizational Behavior and Human Performance, 10*, 369-368.

Schulz, W. (1995). Multiple-discrepancies theory versus resource theory. *Social Indicators Research, 34*, 153-169

Schwartz, C. E., Coulthard-Morris, L., Cole, B., & Vollmer, T. (1997). The quality-of-life effects of Interferon-Beta-1b in multiple sclerosis: An Extended Q-TWiST analysis. *Archives of Neurology,* 54, 1475–1480.

Sharma, S. (1996). *Applied multivariate techniques*. New York: Wiley.

Shin, D. C., & Johnson, D. M. (1978). Avowed happiness as an overall assessment of the quality of life. *Social Indicators Research, 5*, 475-492

Skevington, S. M., O'connell, K., & the WHOQOL Group. (2004). Can we identify the poorest quality of life? Assessing the importance of quality of life using the WHOQOL-100. *Quality of Life Research, 13*, 23-34.

Staples, D. S., & Higgins, C. A. (1998). A study of the impact of factor importance weightings on job satisfaction measures. *Journal of Business and Psychology, 13*, 211-232.

Steiger, J. H. (1980). Tests for comparing elements of a correlation matrix. *Psychological Bulletin, 87*, 245–251.

Trauer, T., & Mackinnon, A. (2001). Why are we weighting? The role of importance ratings in quality of life measurement. *Quality of life Research, 10*, 579-585.

Tunali, B., & Power, T. G. (1993). Creating satisfaction: A psychological perspective on stress and coping in families of handicapped children. *Journal of child psychology and psychiatry, 34*, 945–957.

Vermunt, R., Spaans, E., & Zorge, F. (1989). Satisfaction, happiness and well-being of Dutch students. *Social Indicators Research, 21*, 1-33

Waters, L. K. (1969). The utility of importance weights in predicting overall job satisfaction and dissatisfaction. *Educational & Psychological Measurement, 29,* 519-522.

Waters, L. K., & Roach, D. (1971). Comparison of unweighted and importance- weighted job satisfaction measures for three samples of female office workers. *Psychological Reports, 28,* 779-782.

Welham, J., Haire, M., Mercer, D., & Stedman, T. (2001). A gap approach to exploring quality of life in mental health. *Quality of Life Research, 10*, 421-429.

World Health Organization (1993). *WHOQOL study protocol*. Geneva, Switzerland: WHO (MNH/PSF/93.9).

World Health Organization (1995). *Resources for new WHOQOL centers*. Geneva, Switzerland: WHO (MNH/PSF/95.3).

Wrosch, C., & Heckhausen, J. (1999). Control processes before and after passing a developmental deadline: Activation and deactivation of intimate relationship goals. *Journal of Personality and Social Psychology, 77*, 415-427.

Wrosch, C., & Scheier, M. F. (2003). Personality and quality of life: The importance of optimism and goal adjustment. *Quality of Life Research, 12*, 59-72.

Wrosch, C., Scheier, M. F., Miller, G. E., Schulz, R., & Carver, C. S. (2003). Adaptive self-regulation of unattainable goals: Goal disengagement, goal re-engagement, and subjective well-being. *Personality and Social Psychology Bulletin, 29*, 1494-1508.

Wu, C. H. (2008a). Can we weight satisfaction score with importance ranks across life domains? *Social Indicators Research, 86, 468-480.*

Wu, C. H. (2008b). Examining the appropriateness of importance weighting on satisfaction score from range-of-affect hypothesis: Hierarchical linear modeling for within-subject data. *Social Indicators Research, 86*, 101-111.

Wu, C. H. (2008c). The role of perceived discrepancy in satisfaction evaluation. *Social Indicators Research, 88*, 423-436.

Wu, C. H. (2009). Enhancing quality of life by shifting importance perception among life domains. *Journal of Happiness Studies, 10*, 37-47.

Wu, C. H., Chen, L. H., & Tsai, Y. M. (2009). Investigating importance weighting from a formative model with partial least squares analysis. *Social Indicators Research, 90*, 351-363.

Wu, C. H., Tsai, Y. M., & Chen, L. H. (2009). How do positive views maintain life satisfaction? *Social Indicators Research, 91, 269-281.*

Wu, C. H., & Yao, G. (2006a). Do we need to weight satisfaction scores with importance ratings in measuring quality of life? *Social Indicators Research, 78*, 305-326.

Wu, C. H., & Yao, G. (2006b). Do we need to weight item satisfaction by item importance? A perspective from Locke's range-of-affect hypothesis. *Social Indicators Research, 79*, 485-502.

Wu, C. H., & Yao, G. (2007a). Importance has been considered in satisfaction evaluation: An experimental examination of Locke's range-of-affect hypothesis. *Social Indicators Research, 81*, 521-541.

Wu, C. H., & Yao, G. (2007b). Examining the relationship between global and domain measures of quality of life by three factor structure models. *Social Indicators Research, 84*, 189-202.

Wu, C. H., & Yao, G. (2008). The role of domain importance on self satisfaction: A perspective from Locke's range-of-affect hypothesis. Manuscript submitted for publication.

In: Personality Assessment: New Research
Editors: Lauren B. Palcroft and Melissa V. Lopez
ISBN: 978-1-60692-796-0

Chapter 6

A PSYCHO-SOCIAL APPROACH TO MEANINGS AND FUNCTIONS OF TRAIT LABELS

***Astrid Mignon*[1*] *and Patrick Mollaret*[2]**
1) Université de Lille 3, France
E-mail address: astrid.mignon@univ-lille3.fr
Phone: 03 20 41 69 55.
2) Université de Reims, France

ABSTRACT

In daily life, adjectives as "sympathetic" "aggressive" are used to speak about people. But what do we mean when we say that Mary is sympathetic? What kind of knowledge do we communicate about Mary? This chapter aims at analyzing the different meanings of those adjectives within trait psychology and social psychology frameworks. In trait psychology, they are called "personality traits" and are defined as "generalized and personalized determining tendencies - consistent and stable modes of an individual's adjustment to his environment" (Allport & Odbert, 1936, p. 26). Sympathetic is considered as a descriptive psychological property of Mary. This definition is convenient in personality assessment tradition, because it enables the measure of individual differences based on correlational design. Nevertheless, this definition of traits is subordinate to the study of personality and individual differences and does not enable to analyse the meaning and the function of traits-labels. In social psychology, two complementary perspectives share the idea that trait labels are polysemous entities and that their meaning is directly linked to their social function. The perspective of the theory of traits as generalized affordances (Beauvois & Dubois, 2000) enables to distinguish evaluative knowledge- how others act toward targets who possess these traits (behavioral affordances)-, from descriptive knowledge- how targets who possess theses traits act (descriptive behavior)-, deemed to be of limited importance in trait common usage. Sympathetic is used to communicate the social value of Mary, her social affordance which guides my own behavior towards Mary (I invite Mary to my birthday) rather than her psychological property. The other perspective stipulates that traits refer to both the descriptive behaviors and the descriptive states (Mollaret & Mignon, 2007). Sympathetic

[*] Please address correspondence to: Astrid Mignon, U.F.R. de Psychologie, Université de Lille 3, B.P. 06149, 59653 Villeneuve d'Ascq Cedex, France

is also a descriptive knowledge of Mary's states Mary's state (e.g. Mary feels happy). This description implying a state verb directs a perception of Mary as acted by the situation (Brown and Fish, 1983). We will report new research, based on experimental design, showing that person perception depends on the function of personality traits which is determined by social practices. Implications of different meanings of traits, both for individual differences and also for other kind of judgments (e.g. judgment of responsibility) will be presented.

Keywords: affordance, evaluative practices, evaluative and descriptive knowledge, polysemy of trait labels, social desirability, social utility.

INTRODUCTION

This chapter is aimed at analysing the social and the psychological functions of the register of trait describing words. We will suggest different answers rooted in (1) trait psychology and (2) social psychology. Within trait psychology, psychological terms are used to describe personality and individual differences. Basically, trait psychology is a strategy of measurement of personality based on the correlational technique that is used to specify the main dimensions of personality and individual differences. Trait psychology actually fulfils many practical objectives. Both the foundations and the limitations of trait psychology are exposed in the first part of the contribution. The second part defends an alternative approach to the meaning of psychological terms that is based on psycho-social investigations. Here, psychological terms are no more envisaged as personality variables. Rather, their meanings and functions are determined in relation to a socially determined usage and not just in relation to the designation of differences between human beings. In particular, we will show how traits are used for evaluative purpose.

TRAIT PSYCHOLOGY: BASIS AND LIMITATIONS

Lexical Hypothesis and Factorial Approach

The trait psychology approach is based on the lexical hypothesis, well defined by Goldberg: « The variety of individual differences is nearly boundless, yet most of these differences are insignificant in people's daily interactions with others and have remained largely unnoticed. Sir Francis Galton may have been among the first scientists to recognize explicitly the fundamental lexical hypothesis-namely that the most important individual differences in human transactions will come to be encoded as single terms in some or all of the world's languages » (Goldberg, 1990, p. 1216). Within this framework, the natural language is seen as a valid source for personality assessment, and many lexical studies have been carried out to delimit the lexical field of personality terms. In their pioneering work, Allport & Odbert (1936) have establish a list from an unabridged English dictionary of 17 953 words (representing 4,5% of total words) considered to be labels for concepts referring to personality, that could be used to «distinguish the behavior of one human being from that of another » (Allport & Odbert, 1936, p. 24). Words were organized in four major categories.

The first category included personality traits (4504 words), which were defined as « broad patterns of determining tendencies that confer upon personality such consistency as it displays. (p.13) Generalized and personalized determining tendencies--consistent and stables modes of an individual's adjustment to his environment. Obvious examples are aggressive, introverted, sociable. (p. 26) ». The second category "states" included words that were defined by Allport and Odbert (1936) as « present activity, temporary states of mind and mood..... typical terms are abashed, gibbering, rejoicing, frantic. » (p. 26). Remaining terms were categorized either as social evaluation (e.g. irritating, excellent, insignificant) or as physical characteristics, metaphorical or terms of doubtful relevance to personality. Note that the two first categories will be of main interest in this chapter. The Allport and Odbert's (1936) taxonomy was certainly very exhaustive in the description of the structure of the overall psychological lexicon. Their proposition to delimit the field of personality terms to 4 504 adjectives is still accepted among personality researchers. However, because it is not practical to ask people to describe themselves on 4 504 terms, personality researchers have tried to reduce the initial list.

The factor analysis is one of the statistical techniques most commonly used in the study of personality. The factor analysis identifies groups of highly intercorrelated variables and determines the number of underlying factors measured by a set of traits. The redundant traits are removed, and the large number of traits can be reduced to few personality factors. For example, Raymond Cattell (1947, 1957) revised the list to 171 (less than 1 percent of the Allport and Odbert's initial list), conducted an oblique factor analysis on descriptions made by subjects who rated people they knew on the 171 traits, and finally reduced the trait list to 16 personality factors. Trait theorists assume that traits are continuous dimensions on which people vary. Tupes & Christal (1961) reported the results of re-analyses of Cattell's own correlation and data collected from ratings by others, varying in length of acquaintanceship. The factor analysis revealed "five relatively strong and recurrent factors and nothing more of any consequence" Tupes and Christal (1961, p.13-14). Norman (1963) has replicated this five factors structure. Since Norman's study, many researchers have conducted similar studies that support the five factors taxonomy (e.g. Goldberg, 1981; Goldberg, 1990; Goldberg & Saucier, 1995; McCrae & Costa, 1987). Many writers have adopted the names used by Norman (1963) to designate the five factors, which are extroversion, agreeableness, conscientiousness, emotional stability and culture. The five factor solution has given rise to two complementary research traditions: the "*Big Five*" a term coined by Goldberg (1981) which resumes lexical studies using self-report data, and the "*five-factor model*" (FFM) which refers to studies of traits using personality questionnaires deemed to measure the personality of individuals. Two complementary goals of research are attached to each tradition. The Big Five tradition aims at identifying the dimensions underlying adjectives that encode enduring individual differences in natural language (i.e. "personality traits"). Lexical studies are carried out to summarize the major dimensions of variation in raters' descriptions of the global traits of targets. It provides one tool for summarizing global individual differences in the population. Note that the empirical attempt to generalize the Big Five structure across languages and cultures (Saucier & Goldberg, 1996, 2006) is particularly important to prove that the factorial structure is not a linguistic epi-phenomenon (see the critical perspectives below). The second goal aims at assessing personality with the five dimensions (FFM tradition). The claim of five factor theorists is that behavior can be best predicted and explained by the measurement of five dominant personality factors. This goal begun with McCrae and Costa (1985a, b, 1987), who studied personality with questionnaire scales based on the 16 PF (Cattell, Eber, & Tatsuoka, 1970). In 1992, they included an extensive list of traits and showed that their questionnaire scales (NEO personality Inventory – Revised) was consistent with the Big Five. More recently, McCrae and Costa (1996, 1999, 2006) have made an ambitious theoretical proposition about the origin of the five factors. They have proposed the "Five-Factor theory" (FFT), a theoretical attempt to describe the nature, origins, and developmental course of personality traits. In their rephrasing about the origin of trait, McCrae and Costa (2006, p.233, our translation) wrote that "personality traits are endogenous basic tendencies". Here, the factors are not merely descriptive labels but psychological structures possess by all individuals; they are claimed to constitute "the universal raw material of personality" (McCrae & Costa, 1996, p. 66). The FFT posits the biological origin of the five factors. Although McCrae and Costa (2006) recognize that culture and environment may influence behaviors to a certain degree, the tenet of the FFT is that the structure of personality is independent of any external contingency. McCrae and Costa (2006) recognize themselves that the FFT is actually very polemical, and some authors consider that it lacks of empirical evidences (e.g. Cervone, 2006). However, this recent development of the factorial approach clearly indicates that eminent trait psychologists are confident in the factorial technique to reveal genuine individual tendencies of individuals.

Despite all theoretical dissentions, questionnaires aimed at assessing the five dimensions of personality (e.g. The NEO-PI-R) have been widely used as predictors of important life outcomes, including personality disorders, vocational interests, political orientation, marital adjustment, and job performance (McCrae & Costa, 2003). Although the rationale of personality inventories is simple enough, it is based on a postulate that deserves attention. The self-report version of the NEO-PI-R (the most commonly used) consists of 240 items (descriptions of behavior). Subjects have to estimate to what extent the 240 behavioral descriptions are applicable to themselves on a 5-points scale, ranging from "strongly disagree" to "strongly agree". Authors of the five-factor approach are thus confident in peoples hability to describe themselves on behavioral items. Nevertheless, many personality researchers have documented that self-report instruments designed to measure personality were vulnerable to response bias (Edwards, 1953; Hogan & Nicholson, 1988). Gosling, John, Craik and Robins (1998) have documented that self-reports tend to be positively distort (in a manner to give oneself a more positive image). In many situations (e.g. job selection) test takers may be motivated to respond to items in a manner that maximizes a desired outcome. The question of whether job applicants distort their responses to personality measures when responding for selection purposes is still a source of discussion among researcher. That said, the controversy only concerns the social conditions of the optimal application of personality testing, not the rightfullness of personalitity testing per se. In short, personality questionnaires are considered to be a valid source of knowledge if responders are "sincere" when describing themselves. However, responses to items may be influenced by other factors that are independent from the conscious intention of the respondant to fake (see Mollaret and Lefeuvre's work below).

Another postulate of trait psychology has to be specified. As Kenny (1991) put it "the most valued instrument used by psychologists is the human observer" (p. 156). Human observers are thus supposed to be a valid source of knowledge about personality, and the comparison between judgments by self and observers are envisaged as an indispensable tool for researchers in personality judgment. Specifically, self-ratings are envisaged as accurate criteria to compare observer ratings with. Many researches into personality judgments have investigated whether traits were observable attributes by measuring self-observers agreement on Big Five dimensions, and results tend to show that self-observers correlations are significant for conscientiousness and extraversion dimensions. Consequently, both extraversion and conscientiousness are actually envisaged as the most observable attributes of the Big Five. In sum, the postulate that observation may reflect social reality is central to the use of such judgments in personality research. One important consequence the realistic status assigned to observers judgment is that the agreement among judges in personality ratings (i.e. consensus among judges) may be due to an accurate perception of personality attributes. Indeed, consensus among judges is actually seen as an important criterion of the accuracy of personality judgment provided by observers (or judges) on targets. This point we be discussed in the next session of the chapter (see Mollaret, Méhault & Savarin, 2005; Mollaret & Nicol, 2008).

The conceptual coherence of the lexical approach to personality may be sum up as follows. Lexical units included in the natural language are envisaged as valid tools to investigate personality and individual differences, and the factorial technique enables personality researchers to reduce the huge personality lexicon to a more limited number of dimensions. Self and observers ratings on dimensions may reflect social reality, because people are supposed to envisage others and themselves as objects of knowledge. Traits are thus considered as accurate vectors of the *descriptive knowledge* of people (i.e. their psychological properties). In the second part of this chapter (social psychological approach), we will investigate whether the psychological lexicon really delivers descriptive knowledge and examine the possibility of an alternative knowledge of self and others include in the psychological lexicon: the evaluative knowledge.

The Lexical Hypothesis and the Factorial Approach in a Critical Perspective

Although actually dominant within personality researchers, the factorial approach based on the lexical hypothesis is problematic in some ways.

The Critic of Traits as Abstract Mental Concepts

In trait psychology, personality score should be useful as predictors of individual's behaviors. Based on a review of the personality literature, Mischel (1968) in his enormously influential book "Personality and Assessment" pointed out the lack of consistency of individuals' behaviors across situations (overall .30). He showed that studies aimed at describing personality tendencies with natural language failed to show the hypothetical coherence of behaviors and that the variability of behavior must be due to a situational demand and to error (see also Mischel & Peake, 1982). Mischel's radical departure from the traditional lexical approach has been widely criticized (see Epstein, 1979; Funder, 1999; Goldberg, 1990), and his main message is still controversial. In our view, the main point is that Mischel's conception of personality is undoubtly incompatible with the traditional factorial approach to personality. As Shweder (2006) noted, the most important lesson of "Personality and Assessment" is that abstract mental concepts like "personality traits" are not appropriate tools to understand the (hypothetical) coherence of human behavior.

D'Andrade (1965, 1974) and Shweder (1982) have demonstrated that the consistency of personality structure is an artefact of implicit meanings in the vocabulary. Psychological description reflects a meta-linguistic activity rather than a descriptive activity. Those researchers claimed that the personality structure is not derived from observations of co-occurrences among behaviors in the real world, but can be explained by the similarity of trait labels. This systematic distortion hypothesis has been supported by two kind of evidence. First, the structure of rated behavior matrices (correlation matrices computed from memory-based ratings of actual targets) were closely related to conceptual association matrices (similarity of meaning judgments among the same concepts used for ratings). Second, the conceptual association matrices do not always correspond to the structure of actual behaviors matrices. Since the personality assessment with questionnaire requires retrospective ratings, those findings are consistent with the argument that personality trait structure reflects the similarity between traits rather than reflecting actual behaviors. Shweder and d'Andrade (1980) claim that in self-ratings, people used a theory about "what is like what" (semantic similarities) rather than "what goes with what" (real co-occurrences in behaviors). Similarly, Beauvois (1984) argued that personality psychologists have made confusion between two radically different questions, namely (1) how to classify people? (real individual differences) and (2) how do people classify? (conceptual categories of individual differences). Shweder (1977) claims that personality traits cannot be discovered in behaviors. Rather, traits may be added to behaviors in order to create a conceptual coherence that distorts the social reality. The systematic distortion hypothesis is grounded from a radically different starting point than the lexical approach. Contrary to the realistic tenet of the lexical approach, traits are not seen as good tools for encoding behaviors. Instead, traits are conceptualized as tools that make a psychological sense of the social environment. Those conceptual associations are the so-called implicit personality theories that is shared beliefs by naïve psychologist about which traits tend to co-occur. At this stage, we retain from Shweder's and Mischel's conception that (1) traits are not the most appropriate tools to encode the objective reality and (2) the conceptual coherence of psychological descriptions by observers may reflect semantic similarities rather than the capture of objective reality (see also Beauvois, 1984).

More fundamentally, the definition of traits as designation of individual differences is in no way rooted in a theoretical consideration about the meaning of psychological terms. The lexical hypothesis is inextricably linked to the galtonian project to study the variability within and between groups of humans. Although convenient within such an empirical project, the lexical hypothesis originality formulated by Galton is based on the unverified postulate that the natural language mirrors the real differences between beings. Identifying the structure of psychological lexicon to the structure of real interindividual differences is, in fact, very problematic from an epistemological point of view. In order to study the meaning of psychological terms, language philosophers might propose to consider the psychological vocabulary independently of any empirical project. For example, wittgensteinian investigations about meaning (see Wittgenstein, 1953) invites researcher to investigate the meaning of words in close relation to their social context of utilisation. Meaning is therefore not like a "set in a stone". Rather, the meaning of any term is linked to social practices (what Wittengstein calls "forms of life"). If we take the wittgensteinian lesson seriously (and we think we should) we have to abandon the realistic postulate of the lexical hypothesis and move research towards the study of social practices leading to a particular utilization of trait-words (for a more detailed presentation, see Mollaret, 1998, in press). As we will further advocate, the conceptual similarities between traits may be explained by the social necessity to provide evaluatively coherent psychological portraits in the most evaluative social contexts rather than by the encoding of social reality.

Another Conception of Behavioral Coherence

Mischel's radical criticism of the traditional factorial approach has given rise to a new theoretical and methodological orientation to personality assessment, named "socio-cognitive" approach (see Cervone & Shoda, 1999). Here, the coherence of behaviors is not supposed to correspond to "personality traits" revealed via the factorial technique. In other words, personality is no more conceive as a general orientation revealed by five basic tendencies. Instead personality works as a "if...then" system defined at an individual level. For example, Smith might say to himself, (1) "if there's no music at the party, then I will keep on drinking alone at the bar" and (2) "if there is music at the party, then I will dance with Mary, Jane, Laura, Ursula and so on". Thus, Smith may exhibit two different kinds of behaviors (depending on a situational criterion) but both behaviors are coherent within his own "if...then" system. However, if one's adopt a lexical framework, Smith's behaviors may appear inconsistent. The first one could be labelled "introvert" while the second one could be labelled "extravert". The two behaviors appear to be inconsistent only if the researcher adopts the natural language to describe behaviors. The socio-cognitive approach initiated by Mischel clearly shows that the psychological lexicon may not be appropriate to describe people. Instead, it may be efficient to fulfil other social functions that we will describe further in this chapter.

The Factorial Technique does not Allow any Conclusion at the Individual Level

As the FFT orientation clearly indicates, the factorial technique is used by some trait psychologists to isolate basic individual tendencies. However, a dimension revealed by the factorial technique is not supposed to be present within individuals (see Borsboom, Mellengerg & Van Heerden, 2003). Statistically, factorial analysis requires variance and can be applied only if individuals are different in their response to an item. This criterion, although obvious to anyone with basic statistical notions, is very problematic. Lamiell (1987, 2003) clearly indicates that this "epistemological requirement of variance" completely undetermined the dominant interpretation of personality tests scores at the individual level. Lamiell's reasoning is quite simple. The factorial approach requires individual differences to be applied. A dimension revealed by the factorial technique exists if –and only if- individuals are different on that dimension. How could this dimension be present in all individuals if it can not be defined within individuals? In other words, how could variations between individuals determine intra-individual properties? As Lamiell (2006) put it, the interpretation of personality scores as individual tendencies reflects more a locutionary practice than a scientific inference. To make that point more explicit, there is no evidence that prove that two identical scores to a personality questionnaire are determined by a same causal force lodged in individuals. Individuals may obtain the same scores on a personality inventory but for different, perhaps qualitative, reasons. As Borsboom et al. (2003) suggest, it is much better to keep to a strictly interindividual interpretation of inventories (see also Caprara & Cervone, 2000). In a telling analogy, Cervone (2006) suggests comparing psychological statements with statements about the reliability of automobiles. Suppose that an insurer has carried out a test of the reliability of automobiles. To say that an auto is not reliable necessarily means that it is less reliable than other autos. This is the only use of the "reliability" trait, as a statement about the reliability of an auto does not help us to understand how it works. Reliable is in no way a causal force that can explain the tendency of any auto to work or not to work. If an auto breaks down, its driver has to ask a garage for assistance, not an auto insurer specializing in reliability scores. There is no point a mechanic knowing the auto's "reliability score". Factorial approach based on interindividual differences could be unproblematic if interpretation of personality scores were maintained at the interindividual level. Unfortunately, recent developments within trait psychology take the opposite direction and speculate on the biological basis of personality scores.

Conclusion

The notion that natural language provides a satisfactory basis for the study of psychology is unique in the history of science, according to Saucier and Goldberg (1996). Saucier and Goldberg (1996) justify this epistemological continuity between naive and scientific knowledge in the field of personality studies by stressing the fact that knowledge stemming from naive science cannot be dissociated from the phenomenon under scrutiny. If a linguistic community uses concepts to evoke social relations, states, beliefs or personality, these are assumed to correspond to a reality which needs to be studied in every aspect. However, this postulate is based on the faulty premise that individuals are intuitive scientist or intuitive statisticians inclined to construct a descriptive knowledge of their social environment. As we will now show, this description is too restrictive and in that the descriptive knowledge of others certainly not prevalent in real social interactions. Both common sense psychology and scientific psychology are embedded in social practices that are partly independent of a descriptive knowledge of people.

A Psycho-Social Approach to Trait Labels: Traits as Polysemous Entities

In this part, we will present two complementary perspectives on the social functions of traits, sharing the idea that the meaning of traits has to be analyzed independently of any empirical consideration about personality and individual differences. Effectively, the psycho-social orientation takes the radically different starting point and proposes to envisage the meaning of traits concomitantly to the social practices in which they are used. In the conception of traits as generalized affordances proposed by Beauvois and Dubois (2002), the function of traits is attached to evaluative social practice. Here, traits labels are used in daily life to communicate people's social value. The conception of traits as state and behavioral descriptions proposed by Mollaret and Mignon (2007) defend that two conceptions of human beings are convey by a trait label.

The Social Anchoring of the Use of Traits

From the Person to the Social Agent: The Role of Evaluative Practices

In an important meta-theoretical contribution, Beauvois (1976) has proposed to make a connection between the use of traits and evaluative practices observed in social organizations (e.g. school, work, family etc). Precisely, note that within this conception, "evaluative" refer to the social value produced by a social organization. According to Beauvois, as soon as an individual participates to a social organization, he becomes a *social agent* to whom behaviors' potential value is defined *by and in* this social organization. The behaviors' values are socially contingent in that they are defined within the organizational context. Since the general principle of membership turnover in social organizations (Etzioni, 1964), evaluation practices consist in distributing social reinforcements (gratifications, promotions…) to social agents. The exercise of power and evaluation practices, especially in our individualistic and liberal societies, implies the use of personology, i.e. the use of traits-labels. As Pansu (2006) noted "…the evaluative practices of persons whose position grants validity to their judgments and to the sanctions that follow from them (teachers, social workers, managers, recruiters, etc.) are more largely determined (than those of persons in other positions such as here students) by considerations of a personological nature, with trait-based explanations seeming to carry a great deal of weight in assessments of social agents." (p. 9). This claim has been well demonstrated within the norm of internality framework (e.g. Beauvois & Le Poultier, 1986; Pansu, 2006). Within social practices, the socially contingent value of behavior is being transferred on the psychological nature of the social agent who produced those behaviors. This is the naturalization process. Personology plays a key role in social evaluation practice, because it provides a systematic knowledge of naturalized social value manifested in social relations. One important point is that the trait-label communicates the person's value in a given social environment, i.e. the *evaluative knowledge* that serves to state the value of the social agent. This does not come to say that it communicates a *descriptive knowledge*, i.e. a statement about the properties of persons. Let's take an example to illustrate that point. If Ted -a school teacher- says to Paul -his colleague- that John -a pupil- is immature, he does not simply refer a descriptive category of behaviors. The psychological function of the trait label (immature) is principally not to inform Paul on the kind of *individual* John may be. First and foremost, immature is an evaluative label addressed to inform his colleague on the social value of this particular *pupil*. In other terms, immature directly communicates a social evaluation of this pupil and works like an evaluative criterion. Importantly, the evaluative criterion enables schoolteachers to know how they have to act themselves towards the pupil. The above example makes clear that the function of traits is embedded in the evaluative practice of social agents (i.e. pupils, schoolteachers, colleagues) and can not be reduced to descriptive categories of behaviors. In the next parts, we will point up the nature of the evaluative knowledge convey by trait labels and the analyzed the function of trait label within social perception framework.

The Two Dimensions of Social Value

Some cues converge to show that the psychological lexicon is structured by two orthogonal dimensions. In this paragraph, we will examine the rationale of this two-factor solution and subsequently present an evaluative conception of the two dimensions. In our framework, the two-factor structure appears to be more suitable than the five structure presented in the first session of the chapter. Two pieces of evidence may justify this theoretical decision. First, the two-factor structure appears to be the more universal across languages and cultures than the Big-Five (Saucier, Hampson & Goldberg, 2000). Effectively, the method used by McCrae and Costa (e.g. McCrae et al., 2004) to assess the universality of the five factor solution consists in translating items from English into other languages and then demonstrating that the translated items are organized along the same dimensions as the original English ones. A far more demanding test is to identify the most important personality concepts within each linguistic and cultural context, derive an indigenous factor structure from those variables, and then examine the extent to which this new structure corresponds to previously proposed models (see Saucier et al., 2000). If this method is used, then the two-factorial solution appears to be the most generalizable across languages and cultures. Second, the two factors structure is relatively impervious to variable-selection effects; it appears whether there is a restricted or inclusive selection of variables (Saucier, 1997). This latter point is theoretically important, because the selection criterion to include or exclude the lexical units from the factorial analysis is certainly arbitrary (see below). Consequently, the two factors solution is certainly the more robust one.

Such a factor structure has been supported by a variety of theoretical models. Bakan (1966), initially labelled the two factors Agency and Communion, but the two-factors solution may be aligned with some of the other sets of dual personological constructs reviewed by Digman (1997), Osgood, May and Miron (1975, valence and activity) or Hogan's (1983, getting ahead and getting along). The content of dimensions is similar in all these conceptions. The first factor (agency in Bakan's conception) contrasts terms like *dynamic, dominant* or *energetic,* with terms like *introvert, pessimistic or submissive* whereas the other factor (communion) contrasts terms like *warm, friendly* or *sociable* with terms like *quarrelsome, cold* or *aggressive*. Peeters (e.g. Peeters, 1992) has proposed an evaluative conception of the two-factorial solution where both dimensions refer to the individual adaptation to the social environment. The adaptive value of the dimensions is grounded from two perspectives. The first perspective is that of the self. Traits such as *dynamic* and *dominant* (versus their opposites) are expected to involve unconditionally positive (versus negative) adaptive consequences for the possessor of the traits. In Peeters' terms these traits define a power-related evaluative dimension referred to self-profitability (SP). The second general perspective is that of the other who has to deal with the possessor of the trait. It defines a likeability-related dimension marked by traits such as *warm* and *friendly* (versus their opposites) that are expected to involve unconditionally positive (versus negative) adaptive consequences for the other. This dimension has been referred to as "other-profitability" (OP). SP and OP are presumably universal dimensions akin to a wide variety of two-dimensional models of implicit personality theory (e.g., Rosenberg & Sedlak, 1972).

According to Beauvois (1995, 2003, 2005; see also Dubois & Beauvois, 2005), the two fundamental dimensions underlying trait structures communicate two dimensions of value: social desirability (D) which refers to affective valence or motivation and social utility (U) which corresponds to the fundamental principle of evaluation in a society. Precisely, social desirability is defined as "the known suitability of the event, object, or person to the motivations of the social collective's members [and to the extent to which they are liked or disliked by other people] and social utility, defined as the known suitability of the event, object, or person to the options that characterized the social functioning of the system to which the collective belongs" (Beauvois, 2003, p. 251). Social desirability corresponds to the the “valence” dimension in Osgood et al.’s affective meaning system and denotes the person‘s “likableness” in his/her relationships with others. This dimension is embedded in interpersonal relations. Social utility is linked to the functional requirements of an actual given social environment or organization, and indicates how well one meets those requirements. Consequently, social utility reflects the degree to which a social agent can succeed within his social environment. Note that social utility value has to be taken in a quasi-economic sense that is the person’s marketable value and not its functional connotations, that is the services that this person might perform for others. Empirical evidence of the rationality of the two dimensions has been brought in a series of studies conducted by Cambon (2006a; 2006b). Studies were designed to show that each dimension is associated with specific criteria which validate the Beauvois’ conception, in particular his conception of the second dimension as a quasi-economic value scale. It was attended that social desirability traits should be used to communicate the likeableness of people and should differentiate people we like to those we don’t like, people who have a lot of friends to those who have not a lot of friends. Social utility traits should be associated with financial value and economic status and should differentiate people who have a lot of money with those who have not a lot of money, those who have qualities that will help them to get on in life to those who lack such qualities. Cambon (2006a, study 1a and 1b) has examined effects of activation of social utility and social desirability on trait descriptions using criteria respectively financial value and repeated exposure as operationalizations. In study 1a, the degree of activation of social utility (within-subjects factor) consisted to associate, via an evaluative conditioning procedure, neutral faces targets to banknote differing in their intensity of value (low : 50, middle : 200, high : 500 francs[1]). In study 1b, the degree of activation of social desirability (within-subject factor) consisted to vary the number of exposure (0, 2, 7 or 12 times) of the same neutral faces targets. This operationalization is based on the famous mere exposure effect (Zajonc, 1968): more often a person is seen the more pleasing and likeable that person appears to be. In both studies, participants had to rate faces with traits coming from either social utility or social desirability. The two activations have had an impact on evaluative consistency[2]. Globally, the activation of utility social via financial value has an impact only on traits from social utility (the higher is the activation, the stronger is the evaluative consistency of ratings on social utility traits) and not on traits from social desirability. On the other hand, the activation of social desirability has an impact only on traits from social desirability (the higher is the activation, the stronger is the evaluative consistency of ratings on social desirability traits). Those empirical data support the definition of the two dimensions: an economic criterion is well linked to the social utility and an affective criterion is well linked to the social desirability. In another study, Cambon (2002; see also 2004) analysed the link between occupational activities and trait description. In our liberal societies, the economic capitalist functioning emphasizes the produce of wealth and exchange values (Adam Smith). Then, as suggested by Cambon (2002), occupational activities concerning

[1] Studies were produced before the introduction of euro in France and “franc” was the French money used in France at that time.

[2] The measure of the evaluative consistency was calculated by subtracting from negative trait of social utility (or social desirability) scores the positive trait of social utility (or social desirability) scores divided by the number of trait coming from of social utility (or social desirability). A high evaluative consistency indicates that participants had use the value of trait to describe the targets.

with production (production director, electronic engineer) are more socially valued because they aim to produce more capital gain, more economic value, compared to those concerning with services (sales director, sales engineer). In other words, production activities are judged to better meet the requirements of a given society than service activities. In his study, Cambon showed that persons with production occupations were described with trait labels of social utility whereas persons with service occupations that fulfil the personal needs of people in their social lives were described with trait labels of social desirability.

The evaluative conception of traits has the potential to initiate a new look on the social determinants of interjudge agreement (or consensus). The descriptive conception of social judgment that prevails in trait psychology drives to conceive consensus as an accuracy criterion of social perception. A number of studies carried out within trait psychology have suggested that consensus depends on a variety of factors, including the observability of the trait, the acquaintanceship between observers (or judges) and targets, the cross-situational consistency of targets' behaviour on traits, etc… In this framework, consensus is a measure of how well observers have use traits to categorize behaviours or other observable cues. The evaluative conception does not deny that observable cues are indeed important in trait judgment. However, it stipulates that traits are evaluative adjectives that communicate the social value of behaviors. Consequently, the more judgment has evaluative implications (e.g. job selection, evaluation of employees) the more trait-labels should be employed to categorize behaviors. Although behaviours are intrinsically ambiguous (see Kenny, 1991) the social value of behaviours may be spontaneously perceived in evaluative settings. Imagine that Mary is hesitant in her way of speaking. Mary's behaviour is descriptively ambiguous in that it may be associated to many different explanations or mental concepts. For example "Mary is hesitating because she is tired", "Mary does not want to appear as a pretentious person" are plausible explanations that are not evaluative diagnosis. On the contrary, trait-labels like self-effacing, timorous or fearful clearly communicate the negative social value of Mary (a negative social utility). Because the most commonly use of trait-labels is to communicate social value, they should be consensually employed to make evaluative judgment. Thus the evaluative conception, envisages interjudge agreement on traits as an indicator of the degree to which social perception is grounded in an evaluative context. This reasoning has been applied in an experiment carried out by Mollaret, Méhault and Savarin (2005). We used the social relation model proposed by Kenny and LaVoie (1984) to introduce two different contexts of zero-acquaintance judgments. Unacquainted subjects were put into small groups (4 individuals) and instructed to rate one another on social desirability and social utility traits. Half of the subjects were told that the purpose of the study was to try to understand how people make personality judgment about each other after a short interaction. The other half of the subjects were told that the purpose of the experiment was to simulate a recruitment task consisting in a collective interview. The experimenter then asked to subjects of both conditions to answer to a series of questions aimed at facilitating the interaction. Results show that consensus on trait-labels (measured by the proportion of target variance) was higher in the "recruitment" condition than in the "personality judgment" condition. Although this result confirms our hypothesis, it is insufficient alone to prove the situational interpretation of consensus attached to the evaluative approach. An alternative explanation may be that individual differences in behaviors were indeed more pronounced under the recruitment instruction. This interpretation is incompatible, however, with some other results we obtained within the evaluative conception framework that will be detailed below. Recently, Mollaret and Nicol (2008) have proposed an interesting complement to the Mollaret et al. (2005) study. Following the idea that traits were relevant tools to communicate the social value of social agents, we hypothesized that trait assignation would be facilitated under a recruitment task compared to a personality description task. Subjects were instructed to rate an unacquainted target (presented on a 90 seconds video clip) on social desirability and social utility under and to play the role of either a recruiter or a psychologist. Results show that the recruiter instruction leads to accentuate the evaluative consistency of ratings on dimensions, to make the judgment less equivocal (i.e. a diminishing of the proportion on non-responses on trait labels), to make trait assignation to the target quicker (i.e. a decreasing of the decision time to affect trait-labels to the target). In sum, both Mollaret and al.'s (2005) study and Mollaret and Nicol's (2008) study proceed to introduce the social context of judgment in order to manipulate the social function of trait-labels.

Implications of the evaluative conception of trait labels for self-description have been recently investigated by Mollaret and Lefeuvre (2008). As is evident from the above presentation of the lexical approach, responses to self-administrated questionnaires are typically interpreted as veridical indicators of the extent to which individuals possess certain personality attributes. Precisely, the self-description of personality is presumed to be valid as long as the respondent does not intentionally manage his impression or tries to fake good. In the evaluative conception, however, the self-description of oneself is not conceived as an attempt to describe behavioral tendencies. Rather, we propose to envisage self-description has a socially anchored situation in which respondent are inclined to rate their own social desirability and social utility. Nevertheless, the social necessity to judge oneself as socially desirable or useful may vary among contexts. Because traits from social utility are most prominent in organizational contexts, we reasoned that respondent should enhance their own social utility scores when personality inventories are applied for selection purposes (e.g. job selection). Importantly, we aimed at showing that the predicted self-enhancement on social utility does not correspond to a deliberate intention to fake. We tried to show that it should be conceived as an adaptive but not deliberate response to a social demand. Our experiment was composed of two phases. First, we asked subjects to rate the social desirability and the social utility of a reduce version of the NEO-PI-R questionnaire. For each of the 60 behavioral items, undergraduate students in psychology were instructed to respond to two questions, namely (1) how many friends may have an individual whose behavior is analogous to the description of the item; (2) how much money may earn an individual whose behavior is analogous to the description of the item. Results show that some items of the big-five were clearly saturated on the social utility dimension while others were saturated on the social desirability dimension. The first part of the experiment makes clear that the supposedly descriptive items of the NEO-PI-R do have evaluative implications. In the next phase, we asked to students from a management school to complete the reduce version of the NEO-PI-R under two different experimental conditions (between-subjects factors). In the first condition, the questionnaire was simply presented as a "personality test" (classic instruction), in the second condition, it was presented as a "personality test aimed at assessing the competence of managers". In both conditions, students were instructed to respond sincerely to all of the 120 items. Thus, contrary to most studies on response distortion, we did not induced subjects to deliberately fake their responses. Results showed that subjects of the second condition had significantly enhanced their responses more on traits of social utility than on traits of social desirability.

This experiment allow a conceptual clarification of the so called “response distortion” to personality questionnaires. Most authors committed in the study of impression management in personality questionnaires employ the expression “social desirability” when referring to the motivation to give oneself a positive image. This expression simply refers to a general strategy to distort response in a way that is more socially valorised but it does not permit any theoretical prediction on the nature of response modification. On the contrary, the desirability/utility distinction accredited within the evaluative makes clear the need to study response to personality questionnaire in connection with social contexts.

Traits as Generalized Affordances

The theory of traits as generalized affordances (Beauvois & Dubois, 2000) enables to distinguish evaluative knowledge -- how others act toward targets who possess these traits (behavioral affordances) --, from descriptive knowledge -- how targets who possess theses traits act (descriptive behavior) --, deemed to be of limited importance in trait usage. McArthur and Baron (1983) proposed an ecological theory of social perception, which is rooted in the Gibsonian theory of object perception. The main idea is that social perception serves an adaptive function either for the survival of the species or for the goal attainment of individuals. The general assumption “perceiving is for doing” focuses attention on the intrinsic connection between action and perception. The ecological conception suggests that the environment is perceived in terms of its functional properties rather than its descriptive qualities. These functional properties involve affordances, that is, opportunities to act on objects. The term *affordanc*e was defined by Gibson (1979, p. 127) as what the environment “offers the animal, what it provides or furnishes, either good or ill”. Gibson’s theory is influenced by Koffka's (1935) work on Gestalt psychology about *demand character*, where he states that “each thing says what it is … a fruit says ‘eat me’; water says ‘drink me”; thunder says ‘fear me”; and woman says ‘love me’” (p.7). The action relevant properties have to be understood in terms of values intrinsic to the agent, but affordances are not subjective values, they are “…not properties of the experiences of observer” Gibson (1979, p. 137). For example, the effectively of the “climbability” affordance of stairs is better specified as a ratio of rise height / leg length rather than some extrinsically quantified value (e.g. 18 inches, 2 feet) (Warren, 1995). An affordance is an emergent property picked up and revealed during during a course of action. The climbability of stairs is invariant but the perception of the “climbability » depends upon the action course in which the actor is engaged. Affordances are directly picked up without requiring the access to knowledge of descriptive properties.

Applying this gibsoninan perspective to social psychology, McArthur and Baron (1983) defend that “what we perceive in others are their affordances, which are defined as the opportunities for acting or being acted upon that a particular target provides” (Zebrowitz, 1990, p.49). According to those researchers, social perception can change according to the judge’s actual attunement (looking for a sexual partner, an assistant, or a travel companion) and is influenced by social context. They advanced that perception of affordance should be more accurate than general abstract qualities as trait perception because affordance provide information that are contextually circumscribed in which they are perceived (e.g. Zebrowitz & Collins, 1997). Within a gibsonian conception, the accuracy criteria of social judgment leads in the success of the interaction that immediately follow the detection of affordances. Thus, social perception can change according to the judge’s actual but attunement (looking for a sexual partner, an assistant, or a travel companion). While Zebrowitz and Collins (1997) advocated the affordance approach over descriptive traits, other theorists have argued that concepts of trait and affordance were intrinsically connected (Beauvois & Dubois, 2000).

Beauvois and Dubois (2000) conceptualize affordances as categorized into to trait labels. For example, imagine that Domitille is alone in a party and search for someone to speak to. Soon after, she catches sign of Jean who affords here that she could enter easily in conversation with him. She immediately decides to speak to him; the interaction is successful because Jean makes her feel comfortable, he makes jokes and so on. The interaction that Domitille had with Jean is a consequence of is own course of action. Consequently, Jean is perceived by Domitille in regards to what he permits her to realize in the context of her own course of action (here someone to speak to). At this stage, the detection of affordances is circumscribed to Domitille's actual attunement. But imagine that the day after the party, Domitille evokes Jean to her best friend Marie. What could she say about Jean? Certainly that he is really *warm* and *talkative*. And what Marie would retain about Jean? Certainly that he is someone with whom she could have a drink or someone with whom it is easy to speak to. In other words, the accurately detected affordances are transferred into a general knowledge under a trait label. Thus, trait labels are *generalized affordances*, generalizations of what Jean afforded to Domitille in a specific interaction. Traits became a general evaluative knowledge which is no more restrictive to the situation which specifics affordances were detected. Traits labels inform Marie about the nature of the relation between Domitille and Jean. Thus, traits serve to master social environment, to guide interactions and to take decisions about others (what I can do with a given person). As previously noted, the acquisition of the evaluative knowledge is generated via the evaluation practices and social relations. In our liberal societies, social values are more often referred to the human nature than to the social organization. Beauvois and Dubois (2000) conceive that the descriptive knowledge can also be provided by trait labels but emphasize that evaluative knowledge is dominant in everyday life because the use of trait does not take place in social vacuum. Traits generate knowledge that is action-oriented but not knowledge about the true nature, i.e. psychological causes of the behavior[3].

The contribution of the evaluative conception consisted also in concrete operationalization of the two knowledge contains in trait labels that enable to analyze the importance of affordances in social judgment. Two different categories of behaviors are attached to descriptive and evaluative knowledge, respectively. The descriptive knowledge consists to observe targets and to categorize their behaviors with the appropriate trait-label. The descriptive knowledge is therefore operationalized by the Targets' Behaviors (TBs). Importantly, most social cognition research is aimed at investigating how the descriptive knowledge works. For example, research into spontaneous trait inference (e.g. Todorov & Uleman, 2004) is designed to investigate how traits are inferred from targets' behavior; research on dispositional inference (e.g. Trope, 1986) is conducted to study how people draw inference on personality from the observation of targets' behaviors. In fact, the descriptive knowledge is based on the most common definition of trait labels as descriptive categories of behaviors. The evaluative knowledge refers to the detection of social affordances, i.e. the social behavior one can engage with a target. Consequently, the evaluative knowledge is

[3] While the conception of the "man as a scientist" prevails in the trait approach, the evaluative approach pertains to the conception of a "man as an evaluative animal" who evaluates the social usefulness of his environment in regard to his own actions (see Beauvois, 1990).

operationalized by Others' Behavior toward the target (OB). An OB may be seen as a semantic correspondent to a social affordance, because it designates the action that the judge envisages towards the target (e.g. "someone you can share your feelings with"). The Beauvois and Dubois' (1992) study clearly shows that OBs are equally good exemplars of traits than TBs. For example, "someone who always admits his own mistakes" (TB-descriptive knowledge) and "someone people go to for an objective opinion" (OB-evaluative knowledge) are equally representative of the trait "honest". Moreover, Beauvois and Dubois have shown that the decision times to associate behaviors to traits tend to be slightly weaker for OB compared to TB. Thus, the evaluative meaning of traits labels is at least equally accessible to the descriptive component. In a similar vein, Mignon and Mollaret (2002, preliminary study) have shown that when subjects were given a list of traits and instructed to link only one trait to its best OB or TB exemplar (between-subjects condition) the percentage of similar associations were obtained with a high degree of frequency in both conditions.

The differences between the descriptive and evaluative modes of social judgments have been established with a variety of person perception studies. Dubois and Tarquinio (1998) have demonstrated that there are social contexts in which trait labels spontaneously refer to evaluative categories of OBs. Specifically, they have shown that OBs were spontaneously provided when social workers had to describe a job applicant. More generally, a personnel selection task should trigger judgments that are more oriented toward an evaluative knowledge. The distinction between descriptive and evaluative knowledge allows us to regard the detection of individual differences as the product of evaluative knowledge about the usefulness of others in relation to one's own actions. Because OBs express the social relations that a judge is ready to engage with a target, they have more in common with selection (evaluative knowledge) than with observation (descriptive knowledge). Moreover, OBs should lead to evaluatively consistent description of targets (i.e. homogeneity of person perception across items on social desirability and social utility dimensions). Mignon and Mollaret (2002, see also Mollaret & Mignon, 2003) tested these hypotheses in a zero-acquaintance study. Subjects had to rate several targets on 12 OB scales, 12 TB scales or 12 trait label scales (between-subjects factor). Traits were representative of either social desirability or social utility. OB and TB were equally representative of trait label. Targets were shown in silent video clips, each lasting eight seconds. Subjects of the TB condition had to judge the targets according to the 12 behaviors they might have ("Is it someone who is affected by what goes on around him?"). Those in the OB condition had to do likewise, but according to the 12 behaviors they might adopt towards the target ("Is it someone you could share your feelings with?"). Those in the "trait" condition expressed these judgments directly using 12 trait labels ("Is he a sensitive person?"). Results showed individual differences were strongly accentuated in the OB compared to TB and trait label conditions (see Figure 1). The evaluative consistency of ratings was lower with TBs than with OBs and traits (see Figure 2). Our results confirm that the judgment of individual differences on traits is not simply a matter of observation of existing individual differences. Rather, judgment of individual differences is a consequence of the evaluative knowledge implying the selection of persons within social interactions. Results on evaluative consistency show that targets are roughly perceived as good or bad on social desirability and social utility dimensions.

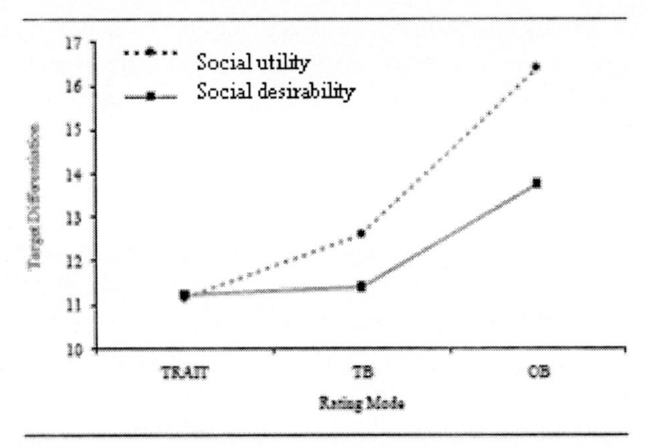

Note. Individual differences were computed by the sum of the absolute differences between each of the 12 ratings and the mean score on that dimension. A high score indicates that targets were judged very differently on a particular dimension, whereas a low score indicates that targets are judged similarly.

Figure 1. Target differentiation on social desirability and social utility for 3 rating modes.

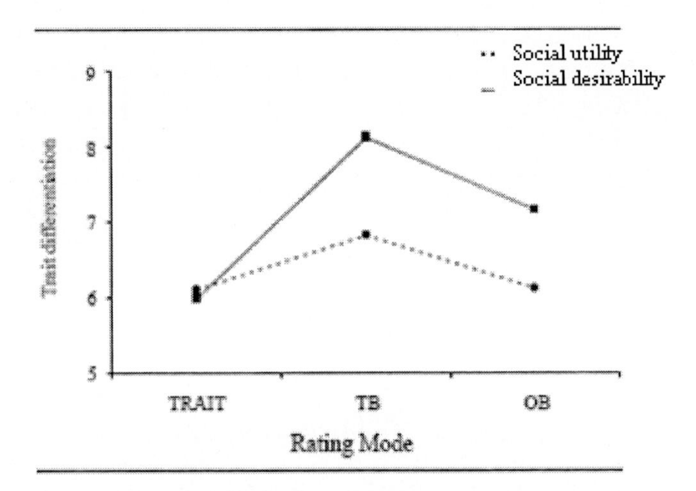

Note. Evaluative consistency was computed by the sum of the absolute deviations between each of a participant's six ratings of a dimension and the participant's mean score on that dimension. A high differentiation score indicates a lack of coherence of the items designed to tap a particular dimension.

Figure 2. Evaluative consistency of ratings on social desirability and social utility for 3 rating modes.

Traits as State Descriptions

As previously noted, the meaning of psychological vocabulary has to be analyzed regardless of any such empirical considerations. The evaluative aspect of the perception of individual differences is not supposed to cover the entire meaning of traits. There is at least one other possible meaning, associated with social practices that have nothing to do with selection. Personality theorists have consensually adopted the Allport and Odbert's distinction between trait (stable) and state (temporally) labels. A large number of personality assessment instruments have been constructed to measure trait or state but not both. However, this distinction could be more arbitrary than explicit and discrete as has been taken for granted for personality theorist. In an important work, Allen and Potkay (1981) has shown that the implicit postulates underlying the distinction were no more than researchers' beliefs which are easily contradicted by some analyzes. For example, one of these beliefs is that the distinction is really clear for laypersons. Greenberg, Saxe and Bar-Tal (1978) asked laypersons to judge 115 labels on their perceived stability, an important criterion that is used to distinguish trait from state. Their findings showed that 28 % of the 25 most stable labels were listed by Allport and Odbert as non traits and 36% of the least stable labels were categorized as traits by Allport and Odbert. Apart from the debate engaged by the Allen and Potkay's article (see also Allen & Potkay, 1983; Chaplin, John & Goldberg, 1988; Fridhandler, 1986; Zuckerman, 1983), the fact that categories are fuzzy for lay persons can be interpreted in two ways. The first one is to think that labels were badly categorized by Allport and Odbert. In other words, trait labels are not ambiguous but criteria used to categorized labels were not relevant and should be improved. The second one is to hypothesis that trait labels have different meanings: trait-labels are seen as both stable behavioral tendencies and transitory states. Some French researchers have considered this polysemic hypothesis of trait labels and showed that even the most prototypical trait label could denote both behavior and state occurrences. An objective distinction can be made between behaviors and states (Brown & Fish, 1983; Semin & Marsman, 1994). Descriptions of behaviors refer to a visible manifestations and are constructed with action verbs (e.g. to help, to hit, to run away) whereas descriptions of states refer to invisible manifestations and are constructed with state verbs (e.g. to feel, to want, to like, to detest). Let's take an example extracted from Mollaret (in press). "Aggressive" can be illustrated just as well by the description "to give a curt response to a checkout girl" (behavior) as by the description "to feel one's nerves getting the better of one" (state), and "lethargic" can be linked to "sluggish" (behavior) but also to "lacking energy" (state), while "dynamic" can correspond not only to "playing sport before going to work" (behavior) but also to "feeling full of energy" (state). It thus appears that traits labels may refer to two different categories of events (see also Mollaret, 1996)

Properties of Behavior and State Descriptions and Consequences for Social Judgment

The conception of traits as behavioural and state descriptions is based on Brown and Fish's (1983) work about the implicit causality of verbs. They have demonstrated that attribution of an event described by simple subject-verb-object (s-v-o) sentence lead to drastic differences in causal attribution whether the verb describes an action (e.g., Ted *helps* Paul) or a state (e.g., Ted *likes* Paul): action verbs elicit attribution to the actor (i.e., Ted), whereas state verbs elicit attribution to the stimulus (i.e., Paul). Action verbs activate an agent – patient schema associated with specific semantic roles: Ted is an agent which causes the action undergoed by the patient Paul. State verbs activate a stimulus-experiencer schema: Paul is a stimulus giving rise to the experience of liking living by the experiencer Ted. Using the Kelley's (1967) model, Brown and Fish (1983) showed that action and state verbs were associated with different patterns of causal attribution. In the Kelley's (1967) covariation model of causal attribution, lay persons are supposed to collect data about three causal information, conceived dichotomously as high or low, to attribute an event to some characteristic of the person (internal factors) or to the environment (external factors). The consensus concerns the extent to which other people behave or feel in the same way in a similar situation. If many people act or feel as the actor, the generalization across people is high, if few, then the consensus is low. The distinctiveness concerns generalization across stimuli. If the actor acts or feels the same with other stimuli, distinctiveness is low, if the actor does not act or feel the same with other stimuli, then generalization across stimuli is high. The consistency refers to the extent to which the person behaves or feels towards the stimulus every time/in any situations. Consistency is less important here and can be set aside. As predicted by Kelley (1967), McArthur (1972) showed that low consensus and low distinctiveness lead to an internal attribution, i.e. attribution to the actor implied in the event whereas high consensus and high distinctiveness lead to an external attribution, i.e. attribution to the stimulus implied in the event. As Brown and Fish (1983) showed, action verbs are associated with low consensus and low distinctiveness whereas state verbs are associated with high consensus and high distinctiveness. In other words, the sentence "Ted *helps* Paul" calls for an internal attribution to the actor (Ted is helpful) because the action verb "to help" maps the following pattern: few other persons help Paul and Ted is seen as the kind of person who helps many people. The sentence "Ted likes Paul" calls for an external attribution, i.e. a stimulus attribution (Paul is really gentle) because the state verb "to like" maps the following pattern: many other people like Paul, and Ted likes few people. As seen, Ted and Paul are not defined in grammatical terms as subject and object of a sentence but rather in terms of roles played in the interaction depicted by a sentence.

We designed two studies to show that action and state verbs in French language are associated with specific properties[4]. Our aim was to replicate Brown and Fish's (1983) effects of verbs on consensus and stimulus distinctiveness parameters within French language: low consensus and low distinctiveness in action verb condition and high consensus and high disctinctivess in state verb condition. We also wanted to examine the differences between action and state verbs on other attributional and causal parameters: controllability, internal and external caused, and trait ascription. In line with Brown and Fish's reasoning, we hypothesized that behavioral descriptions are seen as more controllable and internally causes than state descriptions. Participants had to judge a series of "Subject-Action verb-Object" or "Subject-state verb- object" descriptions (between-subjects factor). Based on a preliminary study, the two kinds of descriptive sentences were selected to be equally representative and good illustrations of a trait. For example, "David (subject) proposed (action verb) to Pierre (object) to share his spare-time » and "David (subject) felt (state verb) comfortable with Pierre (object) » were selected as equally good illustrations of "nice". Participants had to judge the degree to which the subject (i.e. David) was "nice" on a 7-points scale (1: "not at all nice" and 7: "extremely nice"). This measure ensures that action and state descriptions active in a similarly degree the use of a trait label to speak about person.

To measure consensus, participants were asked to estimate the percentage of people acting (or felling) as the subject (i.e. David). The consensus is high when the score is high. The stimulus distinctiveness was measured with a 7-points scale ranging from 1 (the event

[4] To avoid halo effect between measures, we decided to design two separate studies enrolling different samples. Some descriptions were used in the studies. Controllability and consensus were measured in study 1;

appears only with Pierre) to 7 (the event appears with everybody). The distinctiveness is low when score is high. The controllability was measured on a 7-points scale ranging from 1 (uncontrollable) to 7 (controllable). Perception of causality was measured by subtracting score on the internal cause scale (the role of the subject, i.e. David, is: 1 "absolutely not important" to 7 "absolutely important") from score on the external cause (the role of the object, i.e. Pierre, is: 1 "absolutely not important" to 7 "absolutely important"). The more the score is high, the more the event is seen as internally caused by the subject (David) rather than externally caused the object (Pierre).

Table 1. Properties of behavioral and state descriptions

		Nature of the description			
		state	**behavioral**	*F*	*p*
Study 1 (N=52; behavior condition: 26, state condition: 26)	Controllability	3,66	5,06	F(1,50)=63,598	<.000001
	Consensus	62	56,4	F(1,50) = 3,2	<.08
	Trait ascription	5,26	5,55	F(1,50) = 4,96	<.04
Study 2 (N=43; behavior condition : 21, state condition: 22)	Perception of causality	0,11	0,89	F(1,41) = 14,15	<.006
	Stimulus distinctiveness	3,51	4,22	F(1,41)=17,14	<.0002
	Trait ascription	4,91	5,17	F(1,41)=2,33	NS

Results (see Table 1), show that behavioral descriptions are seen as more controllable, less consensual, caused by the actor, more generalized to all stimulus than state descriptions. In both conditions, trait ascriptions scores indicate that behavioral and state descriptions are efficient for judging the application of trait label to the subject[5]. Trait labels can be depicted by two kinds of sentences referring to two kind of knowledge, each associated with specific properties. Behavioral descriptions reinforces a lay conception of person who controls his act, whose acts are voluntarily manifested, who is unique in his way of acting, who is at the origin of the behavior. In other words, humans are seen to be different from each others in their disposition to behave as agents and to behave consistently. State description gives rise to a lay conception of person acted by environmental stimuli. Here, human beings are seen to be equivalent in their capacity to feel states, everyone can experiment a variety of opposite states which are situationally determined, and uncontrollable.

distinctiveness and Locus of control were measured in study 2. Trait ascription was measured in the two studies.

5 In study 1, it seems that the trait ascription is influenced by the controllability and consensus measures because the trait ascription is higher in behavior condition than in state condition (p < .04) but no differences appears in study 2. Despite the difference between the two conditions in study 1, it should be noted that trait ascription in state condition is at a high level (5.26) above the scale mean (4) which means that state verb is efficient to give rise to the use of trait labels. This analysis is confirmed by findings of study 2, in which no differences appear between the two conditions.

Those findings lead us to assume that two conceptions of human beings are contained in a trait label: agent mode and experiencer mode. Our further aim was to show that the dominance of the agent mode or experience mode depends on the trait practice. Our claim is the use of trait labels as behavioral descriptions (agent mode) versus as state descriptions (experiencer mode) should have an impact on indicators such as individual differences, evaluative consistency among personality ratings and judgment of responsibility. We expected that compared to the use of traits as behavioural categories, the use of traits as state categories should attenuate individual differences, evaluative consistency and responsibility. As previously said, the conception of person in our liberal and individualistic societies is linked to values of autonomy, responsibility, which enhance the perception of person as an agent rather than as an experiencer. The perception of person as an agent enables evaluation social practices which are necessary in social organizations. For those reasons, we predicted that trait labels are used by default to define person as an agent, and pattern of results should be equal in the control condition and in the agent mode condition.

A research program initiated by Mollaret and Mignon aimed at testing this hypothesis. This research program is based on the independent experiences paradigm which included two phases of a same experience presented to experimental participants as two distinct studies[6]. This paradigm insures that effects of the practice of trait labels on social judgments are not conscientiously accessible to participants. In our research, the linguistic task takes place in the first phase. It is designed to manipulate the use of traits as either behavior or state categories. Effects of the linguistic task are examined in the second phase (the judgment phase). Usually, participants of the control condition are only enrolled in the second phase. Globally, the linguistic task leads participants to associate trait labels and behavioral or state descriptions (between-subjects factor). For example, in several of our studies, participants were asked to rate the extent to which three behavioural or state descriptions were prototypical of a series of traits, by answering on scales ranging from -3 (very unrepresentative of the trait) to +3 (very representative of the trait). The three descriptions consisted of a representative exemplar, an average exemplar, and an unrepresentative exemplar. In the agent mode condition, traits were exemplified by behaviors. For example, "aggressive" was exemplified by "somebody who answers unpleasantly" (representative), "somebody who criticizes anyone" (average), and "somebody who affirms that life is wonderful" (unrepresentative). In experiencer mode condition, traits were exemplified by state descriptions. For example, the label "aggressive" was exemplified by "somebody who feels he is losing his/her calm" (representative), "somebody who feels frustrated" (average), and "somebody who feels that life is worth living" (unrepresentative).

The effect of practice of traits has first been established by Mollaret (2003) on similarity judgments between traits. This study does not examine effects on person perception but semantically links between traits. Mollaret (2003) hypothesized that a practice of trait labels as state description (experiencer mode condition) would accentuate the similarity between traits with opposed valence compared to a practice of trait labels as behavioral description (agent mode condition) or to with no practice of trait labels (control condition). Effectively,

[6] To insure that participants really believe that they are enrolled in two different studies, each phase differs on different parameters: experimenter, location place, aim of the study.... We also checked the perceived link between the two phases by asking some questions to participants. Usually, participants were unaware of the manipulation and did not think that the first task (phase 1) has an impact on their response in the second task (phase 2).

an experiencer mode should give rise to a conception of a person that can *experience* opposite states which leads to attenuate the distinction between traits from opposite valence. Results support the hypothesis: similarity between traits of opposite valence was higher in state mode condition than in agent mode and the control conditions. Importantly, the observed effect is not restrictive to the trait labels that were directly practiced as state or behavioral descriptions in phase 1, but extend to traits that were not practiced during the practice phase. Thus, the use of trait labels activates a general mode of thought that is not reduced to the practiced exemplars. The absence of difference between agent mode and control conditions confirmed that the agent mode correspond the dominant way of thinking about people.

Mollaret and Mignon (2007) have applied the same paradigm to investigate consequences of trait practice on the perception of familiar persons. Participants had first to rate traits as behavioral descriptions (agent condition) or as state descriptions (experiencer condition). Then, they had to think about four familiar persons, located at the four poles of the two dimensions of social desirability ("a person they like", "a person they don't like") and social utility ("a person who has qualities to get on in life", "a person who lacks qualities to get on in life"). Control participants were directly enrolled in the second phase. Results show that, compared to agent mode and control conditions, state mode condition attenuated (1) the evaluative consistency of trait ratings within a dimension (2) the perceived differentiation between people. The linguistic context modifies some perceptions that one believes that they are the most stable, those of very familiar person. As predicted, pattern of results were similar in agent mode condition and in control condition, which supports that the function of general trait labels is to designate people as social agents, which enables to evaluate them.

A further step is gained by Mignon and Mollaret (2007). In this research, participants had to rate themselves after being induced by either agent mode or state mode. Results showed that self-descriptions were less evaluatively consistent after a state mode induction than after an agent mode induction or with no induction. One can imagine that what he says about himself may be determined by social context as for example recruitment and that he uses in conscientious manner a self-presentation strategy for example to describe himself. But, lay personologist would certainly think that his knowledge of himself is deep and stable, and that what he said about him is certainly not unconscientiously modulate by external factors as a simple linguistic context. More globally, this study showed that the introspection strategy is sensitive to external factors.

Taking together, those findings showed that the trait label is associated with two kind of knowledge: one enhances the perceptions of person as an agent and one enhances perceptions of person as experiencer. These two modes of perception exist in a trait label, but the agent mode is the dominant one. The activation of a specific mode modifies the use of trait labels in person perception and the nature of the knowledge. Implications of the action/state modes are not restrictive to personality judgments. Judgments of responsibility of criminal acts are also influenced by the linguistic context (Mignon & Mollaret, 2004). After completing a linguistic induction task, participants had to read two stories, one describing a target who robbed a radio in a car, the other one describing another target who was under arrest for sending drug in the street. Then, participants rated targets on several scales (e.g. responsibility, attribution). It appeared that targets were judged less responsible for the criminal act in the state mode condition than in the action mode condition or in the control condition. One more time, participants were unaware that the linguistic task has had an influence on their judgment.

CONCLUSION

The main message of this contribution rests on the theoretical proposition to link the definition of psychological vocabulary to social practices. When this is done, it appears that the so called "personality traits" are in fact polysemous adjectives attached to different social practices. By way of a conclusion, we will comment the psychological function of the individual difference model as it appears within the psycho-social approach to trait labels. The psycho-social approach predicts that the more people are involved in a social practice that calls for the selection of individuals, the more the model of individual differences will apply. Studies conducted so far show that the most evaluative side of person perception correspond to the use of traits as tools expressing others' behavior towards targets (OBs), while the least evaluative side corresponds to their use as tools describing states. Effectively, the Mignon and Mollaret's (2002) study reveals that targets are better differentiated when subjects are induced to use traits as evaluative categories of OB, and the Mollaret, Méhault and Savarin's (2005) study proves that an evaluative context of judgment (a recruitment task) leads to accentuate target variance (i.e. target differentiation across judges). Beyond the accuracy of the individual difference model, the psycho-social approach raises the question of its social function. In our view, the individual difference model should not be considered as an appropriate starting point for the scientific knowledge of individuals. Indeed, as shown by Lamiell (1987) or Cervone (2006), attempts to describe psychological properties within this model are far from satisfactory. We therefore propose that individual difference model better corresponds to the widespread social practice consisting in selecting individuals according to social objectives. The question arises of the nature of descriptive knowledge. In this contribution we have documented that trait-labels were exemplified by to kinds of description of people, namely (1) the description of behaviors and (2) the description of states. While the trait-behavior link has been abundantly documented, fewer studies have conducted to investigate the relation between trait-labels and state descriptions. Meanwhile, the extension of trait meaning to the designation of state is potentially fruitful. Following Brown and Fish (1983) we have shown that behavior and state descriptions were attached to radically different implicit causalities and we have documented that the practice of traits labels as state descriptions leads to attenuate evaluative judgments and perception of individual differences. As shown in the final part of this contribution, the definition of trait-labels as state description corresponds to an experiencer mode of social judgment that can be experimentally induced. Results show, however, that the experiencer mode of judgment is supplanted by the agent mode within our western societies. The dominance of the agent mode can be regarded as a consequence of an "individualistic" conception of human beings, in that each individual is regarded as an *independent system*, endowed with his or her own individuality. A potentially stimulating issue concerns the use of trait-labels within collectivist and *interdependent systems* (cf. Markus & Kitayama, 1991). Here, the experiencer mode of social perception could become dominant because of the great importance assign to social roles and social interactions in the constitution of "personality". We are thus confident in the psycho-social approach to personality judgment in clarifying some classic social issues.

References

Allen, B.P. & Potkay, C.R. (1981). On the arbitrary distinction between states and traits. *Journal of Personality and Social Psychology, 41,* 916–928.

Allen, B.P. & Potkay, C.R. (1983). Just as arbitrary as ever: comments on Zuckerman's rejoinder. *Journal of Personality and Social Psychology, 44,* 1087–1089.

Allport G.W. & Odbert, H.S. (1936). Trait names: a psycho-lexical study. *Psychological Monographs, 47,* (whole no. 211).

Bakan, D. (1966). *The duality of human existence: Isolation and communion in Western man.* Boston, MA: Beacon.

Beauvois, J.-L. (1976). Problématique des conduites sociales d'évaluation. *Connexions, 19,*7-30.

Beauvois, J.-L. (1984). *La psychologie quotidienne.* Paris. P.U.F

Beauvois, J.-L. (1987). The intuitive personologist and the individual differences model. *European journal of social psychology, 17*, 81-94.

Beauvois, J.-L. (1990). L'acceptabilité sociale et la connaissance évaluative. *Connexions, 56,* 7-16.

Beauvois, J.-L. (1995). La connaissance des utilités sociales. *Psychologie Française, 40*, 375-388.

Beauvois, J.-L. (2003). Judgment norms, social utility, and individualism. In N. Dubois (Ed.), *A sociocognitive approach to social norms* (pp.123-147). London: Routledge.

Beauvois, J.-L. (2005). *Les illusions libérales, individualisme et pouvoir social. Petit traité des grandes illusions.* Grenoble: Presses Universitaires de Grenoble.

Beauvois, J.-L. & Dubois, N. (1992). Traits as evaluative categories. *Cahiers de Psychologie Cognitive/European Bulletin of Cognitive Psychology, 12,* 253-270.

Beauvois, J.-L. & Dubois, N. (2000). Affordances in social judgment: experimental proof of why it is a mistake to ignore how others behave towards a target and look solely at how the target behaves. *Swiss Journal of Psychology*, *59,* 16-33.

Beauvois, J.-L. & Le Poultier, F. (1986). Norme d'internalité et pouvoir social en psychologie quotidienne. *Psychologie Française, 31,* 100-108.

Borsboom, D., Mellenbergh, G.J. & van Heerden, J. (2003). The theoretical status of latent variables. *Psychological Review, 110,* 203–219.

Brown, R. & Fish, D. (1983). The psychological causality implicit in language. *Cognition 14,* 237–273.

Cambon, L. (2002). Désirabilité et utilité sociale, deux composantes de la valeur. Une exemplification dans l'analyse des activités professionnelles [Desirability and social utility, two components of value. An exemplification in the analysis of occupational activities]. *L'Orientation Scolaire et Professionnelle, 31*, 75-96.

Cambon, L. (2004). La désirabilité sociale et l'utilité sociale des professions et des professionnels. In: J.L. Beauvois, R.V. Joule, J.M. Monteil (Eds.), *Perspectives cognitives et conduites sociales* (Vol.9). Rennes: Presses Universitaires de Rennes.

Cambon, L. (2006a). Social desirability and social utility: Two evaluative dimensions of personality traits. *Revue Internationale de Psychologie Sociale - International Review of Social Psychology, 19,* 125-151.

Cambon, L. (2006b). La fonction évaluative de la personnologie, vers la mise en évidence de deux dimensions de la valeur: la désirabilité sociale et l'utilité sociale. *Psychologie Française, 51,* 285-305.

Caprara, G.V. & Cervone, D. (2000). *Personality: Determinants, dynamics, and potentials.* New York: Cambridge University Press.

Cattell, R.B. (1947). Confirmation and clarification of primary personality factors. *Psychometrika,* 12, 1997-220.

Cattell, R. B. (1957). *Personality and motivation structure and measurement.* Yonker-on-Hudson, N.Y.: World Books.

Cattell, R. B., Eber, H. W. & Tatsuoka, M. M. (1970). Handbook for the Sixteen Personality Factor Questionnaire (16PF). Champaign, IL: IPAT.

Cervone, D. (2006). Systèmes de personnalité au niveau de l'individu : vers une évaluation de l'architecture socio-cognitive de la personnalité. *Psychologie Française, 51,* 357-376.

Cervone, D. & Shoda, Y. (Eds.) (1999). *The coherence of personality: Social-cognitive bases of consistency, variability, and organization.* New York: Guilford.

Chaplin, W. E, John, O. P. & Goldberg, L. R. (1988). Conceptions of states and traits: Dimensional attributes with ideals as prototypes. *Journal of Personality and Social Psychology, 54,* 541-557.

Costa, P.T. & McCrae, R.R. (1985). *The NEO Personality Inventory manual.* Odessa, FL: Psychological Assessment Resources.

Costa, P.T. & McCrae, R.R. (1992). NEO PI-R Professional Manual. Odessa, FL: Psychological Assessment Resources.

D'Andrade, R.G. (1965). Trait Psychology and Componential Analysis. *American Anthropologist, 67,* 215-228.

D'Andrade, R.G. (1974). Memory and the Assessment of Behavior. In T. Blalock (Ed.), *Measurement in the social sciences* (pp. 159-186). Chicago: Aldine-Atherton.

Digman, J.M. (1997). Higher order factors of the Big Five. *Journal of Personality and Social Psychology, 73,* 1246-1256.

Dubois, N. & Beauvois, J.-L. (2005). Normativeness and individualism. *European Journal of Social Psychology, 35,* 123-146.

Edwards, A. L. (1953). The relationship between the judged desirability of a trait and the probability that the trait will be endorsed. *Journal of Applied Psychology, 37,* 90–93.

Epstein, S. (1979). The stability of behavior: I. on predicting most of the people much of the time. *Journal of Personality and Social Psychology, 37,* 1097–126

Etzioni, A. (1964). *Modern Organizations,* Prentice – Hall, Englewood Cliffs.

Fridhandler, B.M. (1986). Conceptual note on state, trait, and the statetrait distinction. *Journal of Personality and Social Psychology, 50,* 169-174.

Funder, D.C. (1999). Personality Judgment: a Realistic Approach to Person Perception. New York: Academic Press.

Gibson, J.J. (1979). *The ecological Approach to Visual Perception.* Boston: Houghton-Mifflin.

Goldberg, L.R. (1981). Language and individual differences: The search for universals in personality lexicons. In L. W. Wheeler (Ed.), *Review of personality and social psychology* (Vol. 2, pp. 141-165). Beverly Hills, CA: Sage.

Goldberg, L.R. (1990). An alternative "Description of personality": the Big Five factor structure. *Journal of Personality and Social Psychology, 59,* 1216–1229.

Goldberg, L.R. & Saucier, G. (1995). So what do you propose we use instead? A reply to Block. *Psychological Bulletin, 117*, 221-225.

Gosling, S.D., Robins, R.W. & Craik, K.H. (1998). Do people know how they behave? Self-reported act frequencies compared with on-line codings by observers. *Journal of Personality and Social Psychology, 74,* 1337-1349.

Greenberg, M.S., Saxe, L. & BarTal, D. (1978). Perceived stability of trait labels. *Personality and Social Psychology Bulletin, 4, 59-62.*

Hogan, R. (1983). A socioanalytic theory of personality. In M. M. Page (Ed.), *Nebraska Symposium on Motivation* (pp. 336-355). Lincoln: University of Nebraska Press.

Hogan, R. & Nicholson, R.A. (1988). The meaning of personality test scores. *American Psychologist, 43, 621–626.*

Kelley, H.H. (1967). Attribution in social psychology. *Nebraska Symposium on Motivation, 15*, 192-238.

Kenny, D.A. (1991). A general model of consensus and accuracy in interpersonal perception. *Psychological Review, 98,* 155-163.

Koffka, K. (1935). *Principes of gestalt psychology.* New-York: Harcourt Brace.

Lamiell, J.T. (1987). *The Psychology of Personality: an Epistemological Inquiry.* New York: Columbia University Press.

Lamiell, J.T. (1988). Dialectical reasoning and the epistemology of impression formation. *Revue Internationale de Psychologie Sociale,1*, 12-26.

Lamiell, J.T. (2003). Beyond Individual and Group Differences: Human Individuality, Scientific Psychology, and William Stern's Critical Personalism. Thousand Oaks, CA: Sage.

Markus, H. & Kitayama, S. (1991). Culture and the self: implications for cognition, emotion, and motivation. Psychological Review, 98, 224–253.

McArthur, L.A. (1972). The how and what of why: Some determinants and consequences of causal attributions. *Journal of Personality and Social Psychology, 22*, 171-193.

McArthur, L.Z. & Baron, R.M. (1983). Toward an ecological theory of social perception. *Psychological Review, 90*, 215-238.

McCrae, R.R. & Costa, P.T. (1985a). Updating Norman's adequate taxonomy: Intelligence and personality dimensions in natural language and in questionnaires. *Journal of Personality and Social Psychology, 49, 710-721.*

McCrae, R.R. & Costa, P.T. (1985b). Openness to experience. In R. Hogan & W. H. Jones, *Perspectives in personality* (Vol. 1, pp. 145-172). Greenwich, CT: JAI Press.

McCrae, R.R. & Costa, P.T. (1987). Validation of the five-factor model of personality across instruments and observers. *Journal of Personality and Social Psychology, 52*, 81-90.

McCrae, R.R. & Costa, P.T., Jr. (1996). Toward a new generation of personality theories: Theoretical contexts for the Five-Factor Model. In J. S. Wiggins (Ed.), *The Five-Factor Model of personality: Theoretical perspectives* (pp. 51-87). New York: Guilford.

McCrae, R.R. & Costa, P.T., Jr. (1999). A Five-Factor Theory of personality. In L. A. Pervin & O. P. John (Eds.), *Handbook of personality: Theory and research* (2nd ed., pp. 139-153). New York: Guilford.

McCrae, R.R. & Costa, P.T., Jr. (2003). *Personality in adulthood: A Five-Factor Theory perspective* (2nd. Ed.). New York: Guilford.

McCrae, R.R. & Costa, P.T. (2006). Perspectives de la théorie des cinq facteurs (TCF): Traits et culture. *Psychologie Française, 51,* 227-244.

McCrae, R.R., Costa, P.T., Jr., Martin, T.A., Oryol, V.E., Rukavishnikov, A.A., Senin, I.G., et al., (2004). Consensual validation of personality traits across cultures. *Journal of Research in Personality, 38,* 179–201.

Mignon, A. & Mollaret, P. (2002). Applying the affordance conception of traits: a person perception study. *Personality and Social Psychology Bulletin, 28,* 1327–1334.

Mignon, A. & Mollaret, P. (2004). Utiliser les traits comme des états : conséquences sur le jugement de responsabilité. Communication orale au colloque de l'ADRIPS, Lausanne, septembre 2004.

Mignon, A. & Mollaret, P. (Juin 2007). Pratique des traits et jugement des personnes : nouvelles perspectives. *Trente années de psychologie sociale avec Jean-Léon Beauvois : bilan & perspectives. Paris, France.*

Mischel, W. (1968). *Personality and assessment.* New York: Wiley.

Mollaret, P. (1996). La polysémie des traits : une approche bi-factorielle des mots-traits et de la personnologie. Unpublished doctoral dissertation, Université Pierre Mendès France, Grenoble.

Mollaret, P. (1998). Redéfinir les traits. *L'Année Psychologique, 98,* 545-567.

Mollaret, P. (2003). Jugements de similitude entre traits : les effets de l'apprentissage d'une fonction du lexique. *Revue Internationale de Psychologie Sociale/International Review of Social Psychology, 16,* 131–149.

Mollaret, P. (in press). Using common psychological terms to describe other people: from lexical hypothesis to polysemous conception. Theory and Psychology.

Mollaret, P. & Lefeuvre, R. (2008). La connaissance de l'utilité sociale du NEO PI R dans les situations à fort enjeu social. Septième colloque international de psychologie sociale en langue française, Iasi, Roumanie.

Mollaret, P., Méhault, C. & Savarin, C. (2005). Juger la valeur sociale ou la personnalité ? Enjeux sociaux dans la perception des différences individuelles. *Revue Internationale de Psychologie Sociale, 18,* 55-76.

Mollaret, P. & Mignon, A. (2007). Polysemy of traits and judgment of familiar people. *European Journal of Social Psychology, 37,* 339-346.

Mollaret, P. & Nicol, D. (2008). Assigning trait adjectives in an evaluative context is quicker, easier and more consistent. *Psychological Reports, 102,* 797-804 .

Mischel, W. (1979). On the interface of cognition and personality: Beyond the person-situation debate. *American Psychologist,* **3***4*, 740-754.

Mischel, W. & Peake, P.K. (1982). In search of consistency: measure for measure. In *Consistency in Social Behavior: The Ontario Symposium,* ed. M.P. Zanna, E.T. Higgins, C.P. Herman, pp. 187–207. Hillsdale, NJ: Erlbaum

Norman, W.T. (1963). Toward an adequate taxonomy of personality attributes: replicated factor structure in peer nomination personality ratings. *Journal of abnormal and Social Psychology, Vol.66,6,*574-583.

Osgood, C.E., May, W. & Miron, M. (1975). *Cross-cultural universals of affective meaning.* Urbana: University of Illinois Press.

Pansu, P. (2006). The internality bias in social judgments : A sociocognitive approach. In: Columbus, A. (Ed.), Advances in Psychology Research (Vol. 40). Nova Science Publishers, New York, pp. 75–110.

Passini, E.T. & Norman, W.T. (1966). A universal conception of personality structure? *Journal of Personality and Social Psychology, 4,* 44--49.

Peeters, G. (1992). Evaluative meanings of adjectives in vitro and in context: Some theoretical implications and practical consequences of positive-negative asymmetry and behavioral-adaptive concepts of evaluation. *Psychologica Belgica, 32,* 211-231.

Rosenberg, S. & Sedlak, A. (1972). Structural representations of implicit personality theory. In L. Berkowitz (Ed.), *Advances in Experimental Social Psychology* (Vol. 6, pp. 235-297). New York: Academic Press.

Saucier, G. (1997). Effects of variable selection on the factor structure of person descriptors. *Journal of Personality and Social Psychology, 73*, 1296-1312.

Saucier, G. & Goldberg, L.R. (1996). The language of personality: Lexical perspectives on the five-factor model. In J. S. Wiggins (Ed.), *The five-factor model of personality: Theoretical perspectives.* (pp. 21-50): Guilford Press, New York, NY, US.

Saucier, G. & Goldberg, L.R. (2006). Personnalité, caractère et tempérament: la structure translinguistique des traits. *Psychologie Française, 51,* 265-384.

Saucier, G., Hampson, S.E. & Goldberg, L.R. (2000). Cross-language studies of lexical personality factors. In S. E. Hampson (Ed.), *Advances in personality psychology* (Vol. 1, pp. 1-36). East Sussex, England: Psychology Press.

Semin, G.R. & Marsman, G. (1994). Multiple inference inviting properties of interpersonal verbs: Event instigation, dispositional inference and implicit causality. *Journal of Personality and Social Psychology, 67,* 836-849.

Shweder, R.A. (1975). How relevant is an individual difference theory of personality? *Journal of Personality, 43,* 455–484.

Shweder, R.A. (1977). Likeness and likelihood in everyday thought: Magical thinking in judgments about personality. *Current Anthropology, 18,* 637-648.

Shweder, R.A. (1982). Fact and artifact in trait perception: The systematic distortion hypothesis. In B. A. Maher & W. B. Maher (Eds.), *Progress in experimentalpersonality Research* (Vol. 2, pp. 65-101). New York: Academic Press.

Shweder, R. (2006). Des personnes et des situations aux préférences et contraintes. *Psychologie Française, 51,* 327-336.

Shweder, R.A. & D'Andrade, R.G. (1980). The Systematic Distortion Hypothesis. In R.A. Shweder (Ed.), Fallible Judgment in Behavioral Research. Special Issue of New Directions for Methodology of Social and Behavior Sciences, No. 4. San Francisco : Jossey-Bass.

Todorov, A. & Uleman, J. S. (2004). The person reference process in spontaneous trait inferences. *Journal of Personality and Social Psychology, 87*, 482-493.

Trope, Y. (1986). Self-assessment and self-enhancement in achievement motivation. In R. M. Sorrentino & E.T. Higgins (Eds.), *Handbook of motivation and cognition: Foundations of social behavior* (Vol 1, pp. 350-378). New York: Guilford Press.

Tupes, E.C. & Christal, R.E. (1961). Recurrent personality face based on trait ratings. *USAF ASD Technical Report (No. 61-67).*

Warren W.H. (1995). Constructing an Econiche. In Flack J., Hancock P., Caird J., Vicente K. (Eds.) *Global Perspectives on the Ecology of Human-Machine Systems (volume 1)*, pp. 121-156. Hillsdale, New Jersey, Lawrence Erlbaum Associates.

Wittgenstein, L. (1953). *Philosophical Investigations*. Oxford: Blackwell.

Zajonc, R.B. (1968). Attitudinal effects of mere exposure. *Journal of Personality and Social Psychology Monograph*, 9, 1-27.

Zebrowitz, L.A. (1990). *Social perception*. Pacific Grove, CA: Brooks/Cole.

Zebrowitz, L.A. & Collins, M.A. (1997). Accurate social perception at zero acquaintance: the affordances of a Gibsonian approach. *Personality and Social Psychology Review, 1,* 204-223.

Zuckerman, M. (1983). The distinction between trait and state scales is not arbitrary: Comment on Allen & Potkay's "On the arbitrary distinction between trait and state." *Journal of Personality and Social Psychology*, 44, 1083-1086.

In: Personality Assessment: New Research
Editors: Lauren B. Palcroft and Melissa V. Lopez
ISBN: 978-1-60692-796-0

Chapter 7

COMPARING THE PSYCHOMETRIC PROPERTIES OF THE COMMON ITEMS IN THE SHORT AND ABBREVIATED VERSIONS OF THE JUNIOR EYSENCK PERSONALITY QUESTIONNAIRES: A MEAN AND COVARIANCE STRUCTURES ANALYSIS APPROACH

Rapson Gomez* [*1] ***and Andre Gomez*** [2]
[1]School of Psychology, University of Tasmania, Australia
John W. Fisher, School of Education, University of Ballarat, Victoria, Australia
[2]School of Psychology, Deakin University, Melbourne, Australia

ABSTRACT

This study used the mean and covariance structures analysis approach to examine if there is measurement and construct invariance across the common items of the abbreviated (JEPQRA) and short (JEPQRS) versions of the Junior Eysenck Personality Questionnaire Revised (JEPQR). Participants were adolescents, between 15 and 17 years of age. One group of 439 participants completed the JEPQRA, while another groups of 466 participants completed the JEPQRS. The findings showed equivalency for factor structure, loadings, variances, covariances, and mean scores. Most of the item intercepts and error variances were also invariant. The implications of these results for the development of shorter questionnaires from their longer counterparts are discussed in relation to the JEPQR, and for questionnaires in general.

Keywords: Junior Eysenck Personality Questionnaire Revised - Short, Junior Eysenck Personality Questionnaire Revised – Abbreviated, Invariance, Mean and Covariance Structures Analysis.

---

* Corresponding Author: Rapson Gomez, School of Psychology, University of Tasmania, Private Bag 30 Hobart, Tasmania, Australia 7001. Electronic mail may be sent to Rapson.Gomez@utas.edu.au

A tradition with personality measures is to develop shorter versions from their longer counterparts. Generally, the shorter versions have the same instructions for completion, response formats, and the items are worded as in the longer versions. One major personality measure that reflects this tradition is the Junior Eysenck Personality Questionnaire Revised (JEPQR; Corulla, 1990). The aim of the current study was to use the mean and covariance structures analysis approach to examine the comparability or invariance of the ratings for the 24 common items present in the 48-item short (JEPQRS; Corulla, 1990) and 24-item abbreviated (JEPQRA; Francis, 1996) versions of this questionnaire.

The JEPQR is a revision of the Junior Eysenck Personality Questionnaire (JEPQ) that was developed by Eysenck and Eysenck (1975) to measure the personality of children and adolescents. The original JEPQ is an 81-item self-rating questionnaire, with measures for the personality traits of extraversion, neuroticism and psychoticism, as conceptualized in Eysenck model of personality (1952). It also has a lie scale for measuring dissimulation. All 81-items are dichotomous, and are rated as either "yes" or "no". As the psychoticism scale in the original JEPQ showed weak psychometric properties, Corulla (1990) attempted to improve it. He added eight new items and called it the JEPQ Revised (or JEPQR). This revised version showed better psychometric properties for the psychoticism scale.

Based on the results of a principal component exploratory factor analysis (EFA) of the JEPQR, Corulla (1990) suggested a short 48-item version. The short version, or JEPQRS, has 12 items each for extraversion, neuroticism, psychoticism, and lie. All items have the same wordings as in the JEPQR. These items were selected on the basis of their higher factor loadings. For this questionnaire, Corulla found acceptable reliabilities (Cronbach's α values) for all but the lie factor (around .73 for extraversion, .72 for neuroticism, .71 for psychoticism, and .53 for lie). Also, there were high correlations between corresponding JEPQRS and JEPQR scales (.90 for extraversion, .93 for neuroticism, .92 for psychoticism, and .93 for lie among boys; and .87 for extraversion, .94 for neuroticism, .90 for psychoticism, and .94 for lie among girls). A more recent study of the JEPQRS by Scholte and De Bruyn (2001) supported its factor structure, and found reliability values for the factors that were similar to that reported by Corulla (1990). The study also found high correlations between corresponding JEPQRS and JEPQR scales (.83 for extraversion, .95 for neuroticism, .86 for psychoticism and .92 for lie).

To provide an even shorter version, Francis (1996) developed the JEPQRA. It has 24 items, with six items for each of the four factors (extraversion, neuroticism, psychoticism and lie). The JEPQRA was developed from ratings provided for the JEPQRS. Essentially, the six items were selected in terms of satisfactory item to the rest of the test correlations (or corrected item-total correlation). Except for lie, the other JEPQRA factors showed reasonable reliabilities (Cronbach's alpha values were .66 for extraversion, .70 for neuroticism, .61 for psychoticism, and .57 for lie). Also, there were high correlations between corresponding JEPQRS and JEPQRA scales (.91 for extraversion, .92 for neuroticism, .88 for psychoticism, and .89 for lie). Other studies have generally supported these findings (Maltby & Talley, 1998; Scholte & De Bruyn, 2001). For example, Scholte and De Bruyn (2001) found that principal component EFA supported the 4-factor structure. The reliabilities were somewhat similar to those reported by Francis (1996). Scholte and De Bruyn (2001) also reported high correlations between corresponding JEPQRA and JEPQRS scales (.88 for extraversion, .93 for neuroticism, .81 for psychoticism, and .89 for lie), and between corresponding JEPQRA and JEPQR scales (.76 for extraversion, .88 for neuroticism, .71 for psychoticism, and .83 for lie).

Overall, therefore, the results of past studies of the various versions of the JEPQ have generally provided support for their factor structures, and the reliabilities of the three personality scales (extraversion, neuroticism, and psychoticism) in them. Also, past studies have shown high correlations between corresponding factors across the different versions.

A notable feature in the development of the different versions of the JEPQ is that the shorter versions of the JEPQ have been developed using items with good psychometric properties from the longer versions. For both the JEPQRS and JEPQRA, the items included were those with relatively better psychometric properties in their longer counterparts. Implicit in this practice is the belief that the psychometric properties of the items selected from the longer versions for the shorter versions will be retained in the shorter versions. So far this assumption and therefore the psychometric properties of items in the shorter forms of the JEQP with the same items in the longer forms of the JEPQ have not been compared empirically.

One of the most powerful methods for evaluating equivalency or invariance in a measure is the mean and covariance structures analysis approach (Cheung & Rensvold, 2000; Little, 1997; Meredith, 1993; Steenkamp & Baumgartner, 1998, Vandenberg & Lance, 2000). With this approach we can examine configural invariance, metric invariance, scalar invariance, and error variances invariance for the measurement model. In terms of different versions of a questionnaire, the test for configural invariance will show if the different versions have the same overall factor structure or pattern of factor loadings, while the test for metric invariance will show if the strength of the relationships between like items and their underlying constructs are the same across the different versions. The test for scalar invariance will show if the same items across the different versions have the same intercept values, or expressed differently, whether like items across the different versions have the same item mean values corresponding to the zero value of the underlying constructs. Thus support for scalar invariance means that the measurement scales for like items have the same intervals and zero points. In contrast, lack of support for scalar invariance means that this is not the case. The test for invariance in error variances, which is generally considered a stronger test of measurement invariance, will show if like items in the different versions have the same amounts of measurement error. If there is support for both metric and error variances for like items then it is possible to infer that these items have comparable reliability values across the different versions of the questionnaire (Steenkamp & Baumgartner, 1998).

Assuming there is some or partial support for the measurement model, the mean and covariance structures analysis approach can tests for invariance at the construct level for factor variances, covariances, and latent mean scores. The advantage of examining invariance for latent scores via the mean and covariance structures analysis framework is that it will allow us to take into account a priori information about the degrees of non-invariance in the measurement model. For different versions of a questionnaire, invariance in factor variances would mean that the latent constructs in the different versions have the same variance, while invariance in factor covariances would mean that the intercorrelations between the different factors in the different versions are the same. Invariance in latent mean scores would imply that there is no difference for the mean scores of the latent constructs across the different versions.

The aim of the current study was to examine if there is measurement and construct invariance across the 24 items of the JEPQRA and the same items in the JEPQRS when all its 48 items are rated. For convenience and clarity, we will refer to the latter set of ratings as JEPQRS/A. This study used the mean and covariance structures analysis approach to examine invariance. In this study we tested invariance for both the measurement and construct models. For the measurement model, configural, metric, scalar, and error variances invariance were examined. For the construct model, invariance for latent variances, latent covariances, and latent mean scores were examined.

This study is useful for a number of reasons. Firstly, in relation to the JEPQR measures, a number of researchers have suggested that because of the high correlations between corresponding factors across the different versions, the shorter versions can be used when time pressure dictates it or when brief measures for extraversion, neuroticism or psychoticism are needed (Corulla, 1990; Francis, 1996; Maltby & Talley, 1998; Scholte & De Bruyn, 2001). This view implies close comparability for the psychometric properties of the items and scores derived from the different versions of the JEPQR, which as pointed out has yet to be comprehensively demonstrated. Given the recommendations made by these researchers, it is important to test if there is at least invariance for the items that are common in the different versions of the JEPQR. Support for invariance for these items can be taken as providing some support for the use of the shorter versions as proxies for the longer versions. In contrast, if this is not found, then the use of the shorter versions as proxies for the longer versions is questionable. Secondly, the findings in this study will have some general implications in relation to the development of shorter versions of questionnaires from their longer counterparts. It will throw some insights into the appropriateness of the usual approach of using items with good psychometric properties in a questionnaire to develop shorter versions of that questionnaire. Thirdly, as far as we are aware, no study has used the mean and covariance structures analysis for testing invariance across short versions of questionnaires developed from their longer counterparts. Thus this study can be seem as providing an illustration of the application of the mean and covariance structures analysis approach for testing invariance across different versions of a questionnaire.

METHOD

Participants

There were two samples in the study. Sample 1 completed the JEPQRA. This group comprised 438 adolescents (218 males and 220 females). Their ages ranged from 15 to 17 years, with a mean age of 16.25 years (*SD* = 0.79). Sample 2 completed the JEPQRS. This group comprised 446 adolescents (226 males and 220 females). Their ages also ranged from 15 to 17 years, with a mean of 16.20 years (*SD* = 1.00). The two groups did not differ in age, t (882) = 0.75, *ns*. The effect size for age difference between these groups was also low, with Cohen's d being .06. Participants were recruited from 18 secondary schools in Victoria, Australia. About 70% of adolescents who were contacted participated in this study. As no information is available on the adolescents who did not participate, it was not possible to ascertain if there were differences between those who participated and those who did not participate in this study.

The occupational status of the parents of participants, based on the Australian Standard Classification of Occupations (Australian Bureau of Statistics, 1996), were as follows for Sample 1: professional 18%, managerial 24%, clerical 20%, skilled trades 19%, unskilled trades 10%, allied trades 5%, pensioner and unemployed 4%. For sample 2, they were as follows: professional 19%, managerial 20%, clerical 22%, skilled trades 19%, unskilled trades 9%, allied trades 6%, pensioner and unemployed 5%. Based on a rating scale of "1 = professional" to "7 = pensioner and unemployed", the mode for parent occupational status was 4 for both samples, Thus both samples may be regarded as middle class.

Measures

This study used two measures, which were the Junior Eysenck Personality Questionnaire Revised Short (JEPQRS; Corulla, 1990), and the Junior Eysenck Personality Questionnaire Revised Abbreviated (JEPQRA; Francis, 1996). As noted in the introduction, the JEPQRS has 48 items, with 12 items each for the extraversion, neuroticism, psychoticism, and lie factors. The JEPQRA has 24 items, with six items each for the extraversion, neuroticism, psychoticism, and lie factors. The JEPQRA was developed from ratings provided for the JEPQRS. Essentially, the six items for each factor were selected in terms of satisfactory item to rest of test (construct) correlations. The psychometric properties of the JEPQRS and JEPQRA were described in detail in the introduction. For this study the Cronbach's α values were .75 for extraversion, .74 for neuroticism, .71 for psychoticism, and .59 for lie. For the JEPQRA, they were .68 for extraversion, .70 for neuroticism, .68 for psychoticism, and .56 for lie. Thus apart from the lie scales in the JEPQRS and the JEPQRA, the reliability values for the other scales in both versions were quite acceptable.

Procedure

Participants were contacted through their school. The plain language statement to potential participants and their parents indicated that the study was addressing aspects of adolescent behavior. Following ethics approval, and subsequent consent from both parents and their adolescents, participants were asked to complete either the JEPQRA or JEPQRS. As already noted, participants in Sample 1 completed the JEPQRA, while participants in Sample 2 completed the JEPQRS. The allocation of participants into the two samples was randomized. These questionnaires were completed in groups during class time, and they were collected immediately after they were completed in class.

Analytical Procedures

The measurement and construct invariance across the JEPQRA and the JEPQRS were tested using the sequence of analyses proposed by Cheung and Rensvold (2002). This sequence is shown in Table 1. As shown in the table, for the measurement model, the configural invariance model (M1) is the first to be examined. This is supported if this model shows good fit. When the configural invariance model is supported, the metric invariance model (M2) can be tested. This is examined by constraining the factor loadings of like items equal across the two versions of the questionnaire. Metric invariance is inferred if M2 does not differ from M1. Following this test, the scalar invariance (M2) can be examined. This is tested by constraining the intercept values (in addition to factor loadings) of like items equal across the different versions. Scalar invariance is inferred if M3 does not differ from M2. The test for invariance in error variances involves constraining the same error variances (in addition to the factor loadings) equal across the two versions (M4). Error variances invariance is supported if M4 does not differ from M2.

Following the tests for invariance for the measurement model, the invariance for the construct model is tested. As shown in Table 1, invariance for factor variances (M5) is examined by constraining the factor variances of the latent factors (in addition to item intercepts and factor loadings) equal across the versions of the questionnaire, and this is supported if M5 does not differ from M3. Invariance for factor covariances (M6) is examined by constraining the factor covariances of the latent factors (in addition to item intercepts and factor loadings) equal across the versions, and this is supported if M6 does not differ from M3. Invariance for latent means (M7) is examined by constraining the latent mean (in addition to factor variances, item intercepts, and factor loadings) equal across the different versions of the questionnaire, and this is supported if M7 does not differ from M5.

It is to be noted that the sequence of analyses described above tests if a given level of invariance is fully satisfied or not. When full invariance is not satisfied, partial invariance can be explored. When full metric invariance is not established, the researcher can determine the source of the non-invariance by freeing, progressively, the loadings in M1 for items across the questionnaires, until a final partial metric invariance model is obtained. This final partial metric invariance model will have only those like items with equal loadings constrained equal across the different questionnaire versions. The test for partial scalar invariance is conducted by equating the intercepts of only those like items with equal factor loadings. If invariance is not supported, the source of the non-invariance can be explored, as explained for testing partial metric invariance. When there is only partial metric invariance, then the test for error variances invariance will involve equating the errors for only those items with equal factor loadings. Again if this initial model is not supported, the source of the non-invariance can be explored using a similar strategy to that described for testing partial metric invariance. The final partial scalar invariance model can be revised appropriately to test for invariance in factor variances, covariances and latent mean scores.

All the CFA models in this study were tested using LISREL 8.54 (Joreskög, Sorböm, du Toit & du Toit, 1996). Given multivariate non-normality for the JEPQRA and JEPQRS/A (described in more detail in the results section), this study used maximum likelihood with robust estimation to ascertain statistical fit (Byrne, 1998). This procedure corrects for the lack of normality, resulting in a robust scaled chi-square statistic referred to as the Satorra-Bentler chi-square statistic (S-Bχ^2).

Table 1. Nested Models Tested for Measurement and Construct Invariance

Model Type/(Model Number)	Across Model Constraints	Models compared	Conceptual Meaning
Configural (M1)	Non	Overall fit	The same items are associated with the latent factors in both questionnaires
Metric (M2)	M1 with equality constrained on all factor loadings	M2 – M1	The strength of the association of the items with their latent constructs are the same across the questionnaires
Scalar (M3)	M2 with equality constrained on all intercepts	M3 – M2	The metric scale (mean and interval values) of like items are the same across the questionnaires
Error variances (M4)	M2 with equality constrained on all error variances	M4 – M2	Items have the same measurement error values across the questionnaires
Factor variances (M5)	M3 with equality constrained on all factor variances	M5 – M3	The amount of variability of the latent constructs are the same across the questionnaires
Factor covariances (M6)	M3 with equality constrained on all factor covariances	M6 – M3	The relationships among the latent constructs within the questionnaires are the same across the questionnaires
Latent means (M7)	M4 with equality constrained on all latent mean scores	M7 – M4	The mean level of corresponding latent scores of the constructs are the same across the questionnaires

As χ^2 values are inflated by large sample sizes, fit was examined using three practical fit indices. They were the root mean squared error of approximation (RMSEA; Steiger, 1990), the goodness-of-fit index (GFI), and the comparative fit index (CFI; Bentler, 1990). The RMSEA provides a measure of model fit relative to the population covariance matrix when the complexity of the model is also taken into account. For large sample size, RMSEA values less than .08 have been suggested as good fit (Browne & Cudeck, 1993). The GFI compares the hypothesized model with no model at all, while the CFI provide a measure of the fit of the hypothesized model relative to the independent model. For both the GFI and CFI, the values usually ranging from 0.00 to 1.00, and for both, values above .90 indicate good fit (Bentler, 1990). Of these practical indices, the RMSEA is particularly important in this study, given the complexity of the models evaluated. Cheng and Rensvold (2002) have shown that this index is not influenced by model complexity.

To determine differences between models, the difference in their S-Bχ^2 values was used. As this difference is not distributed as a chi-square, it is necessary to adjust for this difference. This was done using the correction formula proposed by Satorra and Bentler (1999). This formula is as follows:

$$\Delta\text{S-B}\chi^2 = (d_0 - d_1)\,(T_0 - T_1)/\,(d_0T_0/T_0^* - d_1T_1/T_1^*).$$

In the above formula, T_0^* and T_1^* are the S-Bχ^2 values for models M_0 (the more restrictive model) and M_1 (the less restrictive model), respectively, that are being compared. T_0 and T_1 are the minimum fit χ^2 values for M_1 and M_1, respectively, while d_0 and d_1 are the *df* values for M_1 and M_1, respectively. Given that $\chi 2$ values are overly sensitive to sample sizes and model fit for large numbers of constraints (Cheung & Rensvold, 2002; Little, 1997; Mash, Balla, & McDonald, 1988), as is the case in this study, the critical value was set at p = .001 level, rather than the usual p = .05 level.

RESULTS

Descriptive Scores and Multivariate Skewness and Kurtosis

Table 2 shows the mean and standard deviation values of the ratings of the 24 items of the JEPQRA and these same 24 items in the JEPQRS. The multivariate normality of the 24 items in both versions was examined using PRELIS 2.51 (Joreskög, & Sorböm. 1996). There was significant multivariate skewness (141.84, $z = 63.29$, $p < .001$) and kurtosis (703.77, $z = 14.89$, $p < .001$) for the JEPQRA. There was also significant multivariate skewness (98.64, $z = 44.67$, $p < .001$) and kurtosis (678.67, $z = 11.81$, $p < .001$) for the JEPQRS/A. Thus the assumption of multivariate normality for both versions for the 24 items was violated.

Table 2. Mean and Standard Deviation (SD) Scores, and Brief Descriptions of the JEPQRA and JEPQRS/A Items

Item number in				Mean (*SD*)			
Model	JEPQRA	JEPQRS	Brief item description	JEPQRA		JRPQRS/A	
1/E	1	1	Can you get a party going?	.69	(.47)	.74	(.44)
2/E	5	6	Are you rather lively?	.79	(.41)	.83	(.38)
3/E	13	26	Do you like going out a lot?	.81	(.39)	.84	(.37)
4/E	18	36	Find it hard to enjoy a lively party?	.89	(.31)	.83	(.37)
5/E	20	38	Rather be alone or with others?	.87	(.34)	.79	(.41)
5/E	22	44	Let yourself go at a party?	.89	(.32)	.83	(.38)
7/N	7	8	Do you often feel fed-up?	.71	(.45)	.74	(.44)
8/N	8	11	Easily hurt when people find fault?	.53	(.50)	.48	(.50)
9/N	9	12	Hard to sleep because of worry?	.49	(.50)	.43	(.50)
10/N	10	16	Sometimes feel life is not worth living?	.33	(.47)	.35	(.48)
11/N	15	29	Worry if you made a fool of self?	.50	(.50)	.52	(.50)
12/N	24	47	Are your feelings rather easily hurt?	.48	(.50)	.43	(.50)
13/P	2	2	Enjoy hurting people you like?	.05	(.22)	.09	(.28)
14/P	3	3	Important to have good manners?	.07	(.25)	.08	(.28)
15/P	6	7	Enjoy practical jokes that hurt people?	.29	(.46)	.36	(.48)
16/P	12	24	Get into a lot of fights?	.22	(.41)	.19	(.40)
17/P	21	41	More trouble at school than others?	.26	(.44)	.34	(.47)
18/P	23	45	Sometimes bully and tease others?	.14	(.34)	.22	(.41)
19/L	4	5	Always do as you are told at once?	.14	(.35)	.13	(.34)
20/L	11	19	Throw paper on floor if no basket?	.52	(.50)	.65	(.48)
21/L	14	28	Said anything bad about anyone?	.04	(.20)	.06	(.24)
22/L	16	31	Take anything that belonged to others?	.26	(.44)	.17	(.37)
23/L	17	35	Ever greedy?	.36	(.48)	.27	(.45)
24L	19	37	Always say sorry when rude?	.69	(.46)	.66	(.48)

CFA of the JEPQRA and JEPQRS/A

Initially, the fit of the JEPQRA and JEPQRS/A were examined using single group CFA. For both measures, the hypothesized models were the same. This was an oblique 4-factor model. The four latent factors were extraversion, neuroticism, psychoticism, and lie. Simple structure was maintained, with all the six extraversion items loading on only the extraversion latent factor, all the six neuroticism items loading on only the neuroticism latent factor, all the six psychoticism items loading on only the psychoticism latent factor, and all the six lie items loading on only the lie latent factor. Also the error variances of all 24 items were freely estimated, but not allowed to correlate with each other. In order to set the metrics of the four latent variables, one of their items was fixed to unity. The same items were fixed for the models involving the JEPQRA and JEPQRS/A. These were items 1, 7, 13, and 19 for extraversion, neuroticism, psychoticism, and lie, respectively, as shown in Table 2, column 1.

The fit indices of the CFA for the JEPQRA were S-Bχ^2 (df = 246) = 559.15, RMSEA = .054, GFI = .90, and CFI = .83, while these values for the JEPQRS/A were S-Bχ^2 (df = 246) = 555.00, RMSEA = .053, GFI = .90, and CFI = .86. Thus for both questionnaire versions, their RMSEA and GFI values showed good fit. As the CFI is known to be reduced when the model tested is complex (Cheung & Rensvold, 2002), as is the case here, the results involving the RMSEA and GFI values can be taken as providing adequate support for the models involving the JEPQRA and JEPQRS/A. Given this, the hypothesized models in these analyses were used for the tests involving invariance.

Invariance across the JEPQRA and JEPQRA

Table 3 shows the practical fit indices for the model used for testing configural invariance (M1). These values for the RMSEA and GFI were good, thereby supporting configural invariance. At the statistical level, there was no support for full metric invariance (M1 versus M2). Further analyses (as described previously) indicated that two items (number 12 & 17 in Table 2) were not invariant.

The ΔS-Bχ^2 was also significant between the partial metric invariant model (M2A) and the partial scalar invariant model (M3). Additional analyses for scalar invariance indicated that six items (numbers 4, 5, 6, 22, 23, and 24 in Table 2), in addition to the two items that were freely estimated in the CFA model were not invariant. The ΔS-Bχ^2 was significant between the partial metric invariant model (M2A) and the partial error variances invariant model (M4). There were differences in the error variances for seven items (numbers 4, 6, 9, 13, 18, 21, and 22 in table 2), in addition to two items that were freely estimated. There was no difference across the JEPQRA and JEPQRS/A for latent variances (M5 v versus M3A), covariances (M6 versus M3A), and latent mean scores (M7 versus M5).

In order to further examine the pattern of invariance and non-invariance across the JEPQRA and JEPQRS/A, a final invariance model was computed. In this model all invariant loadings, intercepts, error variances, factor variances and covariances, and latent mean scores were equated across the two questionnaires. The analysis for this model resulted in the following fit indices: S-Bχ^2 (df = 545) = 1254.81, RMSEA = .056, GF1 = .93, and CFI = .90. This model had good fit.

Table 3. Results of Test for Measurement and Construct Invariance Across the JEPQRA and JEPQRS/A

Model (M)	S-Bχ^2	*df*	RMSEA	GFI	CFI	M Compared	Δdf	ΔS-Bχ^2
M1 Configural invariance	1168.85	492	.053	.90	.85		-	-
M2 Full metric invariance (M1 with equality constrained on all factor loadings)	1219.20	512	.057	.90	.84	M2 - M1	20	50.12*
M2A Final partial metric invariance (M1 with equality constrained on all invariant factor loadings)	1208.23	510	.056	.90	.84	M2A - M1	18	39.50
M3 Partial scalar invariance (M2A with equality constrained on all intercepts for items with invariant factor loadings)	1313.05	528	.058	.90	.82	M3 - M2A	18	106.26*
M3A Final partial scalar invariance (M2A with equality constrained on all items with invariant intercepts and loadings)	1234.84	522	.056	.90	.84	M3A - M2A	12	27.72
M4 Partial error variances invariance (M2A with equality constrained on all error variances for items with invariant factor loadings)	1371.35	532	.057	.90	.83	M4 - M2A	22	138.25*
M4A Final partial error variances invariance (M2A with equality constrained on all items with invariant error variances and loadings)	1241.86	525	.056	.89	.84	M4A - M2A	15	34.05
M5 Full factor variances (M3A with equality constrained on all factor variances)	1239.56	526	.056	.90	.84	M5 - M3A	4	5.32
M6 Full factor covariances (M3A with equality constrained on all factor covariances)	1239.56	526	.055	.90	.84	M6 - M3A	6	4.00
M7 Overall equal latent means	1262.28	530	.056	.90	.83	M7 - M4	4	16.57

Note. *p<.001; S-Bχ^2= Satorra-Bentler chi-square; RMSEA= root mean square error of approximation; GFI = goodness of fit index; CFI= comparative fit index. The non-invariant loadings were for items 12 & 17. The non-invariant intercepts were for items 4, 5, 6, 22, 23 & 24 (items 12 & 17 were freely estimated due to inequality in factor loadings). The non-invariant error variances were for items 4, 6, 9, 13, 18, 21 & 22 (items 12 & 17 were freely estimated due to inequality in factor loadings). All item numbers refer to item model number, as indicated in Table 2.

Table 4 shows the parameter estimates for the final invariance model. As shown in the table, of the two items with non-invariant factor loadings, one was for a psychoticism item, with a higher level in the JEPQRA/S.

Table 4 . Parameter Estimates for the Final Invariance Model

Item number in			Factor loadings		Item intercepts		Error variances	
Model	JEPQRA	JEPQRS/A	JEPQRA	JEPQRS/A	JEPQRA	JEPQRS/A	JEPQRA	JEPQRS/A
1/E	1	1	1.00	1.00	-	-	0.16(.01)	0.16(.01)
13/P	2	2	1.00	1.00	-	-	0.04(.01)	0.07(.01)
14/P	3	3	0.91(.28)	0.91(.28)	0.02(.07)	0.02(.07)	0.06(.01)	0.06(.01)
19/L	4	5	1.00	1.00	-	-	0.11(.01)	0.11(.01)
2/E	5	6	0.99(.38)	0.99(.38)	0.11(.27)	0.11(.27)	0.11(.01)	0.11(.01)
15/P	6	7	2.45(.67)	2.45(.67)	0.17(.15)	0.17(.15)	0.15(.03)	0.15(.03)
7/N	7	8	1.00	1.00	-	-	0.18(.01)	0.18(.01)
8/N	8	11	2.56(.53)	2.56(.53)	- 1.36(.49)	-1.36(.49)	0.13(.01)	0.13(.01)
9/N	9	12	1.58(.34)	1.58(.34)	- 0.70(.31)	-0.70(.31)	0.23(.01)	0.18(.01)
10/N	10	16	1.05(.46)	1.05(.46)	- 0.42(.37)	-0.42(.37)	0.21(.04)	0.21(.04)
20/L	11	19	2.32(.94)	2.32(.94)	0.28(.25)	0.28(.25)	0.19(.01)	0.19(.01)
16/P	12	24	2.03(.55)	2.03(.55)	0.07(.11)	0.07(.11)	0.12(.01)	0.12(.01)
3/E	13	26	0.93(.29)	0.93(.29)	0.16(.21)	0.16(.21)	0.10(.01)	0.10(.01)
21/L	14	28	0.44(.33)	0.44(.33)	- 0.01(.08)	-0.01(.08)	0.04(.01)	0.06(.01)
11/N	15	29	1.72(.39)	1.72(.39)	- 0.74(.35)	-0.74(.35)	0.20(.01)	0.20(.01)
22/L	16	31	1.42(.63)	1.42(.63)	0.07(.22)	-0.02(.14)	0.17(.01)	0.12(.01)
23/L	17	35	1.54(.71)	1.54(.71)	0.15(.26)	0.06(.15)	0.19(.01)	0.19(.01)
4/E	18	36	0.73(.34)	0.73(.34)	0.38(.25)	0.26(.15)	0.07(.01)	0.12(.01)
24L	19	37	1.99(.83)	1.99(.83)	0.42(.27)	0.39(.19)	0.18(.01)	0.18(.01)
5/E	20	38	0.90(.38)	0.90(.38)	0.22(.29)	0.13(.27)	0.10(.01)	0.10(.01)
17/P	21	41	1.35(.72)	2.50(.59)	0.18(.17)	0.16(.12)	0.17(.02)	0.15(.02)
6/E	22	44	0.96(.29)	0.96(.29)	0.21(.23)	0.13(.23)	0.06(.01)	0.10(.01)
18/P	23	45	1.74(.48)	1.74(.48)	0.06(.09)	0.06(.09)	0.09(.01)	0.13(.01)
12/N	24	47	2.97(.66)	2.68(.57)	- 1.70(.63)	-1.51(.50)	0.10(.02)	0.11(.02)

Note. The items are arranged as presented in the JEPQRA. The numbers in bold are non-invariant parameters. Numbers in brackets are standard error values.

The other item was a neuroticism item, and here the loading on the JEPQRA was higher. In relation to the intercepts, both the items that were freely estimated because of non-invariance in factor loadings showed negligible differences. There were three extraversion items, and three lie items with non-invariant intercepts. For all these six non-invariant intercepts, the values were higher for the JEPQRA. In terms of non-invariant error variances, both the items that were freely estimated because of non-invariance in factor loadings again showed negligible differences. There were two extraversion items with invariant error variances, both being higher for the JEPQRS/A. There was also one neuroticism item, with this being higher for the JEPQRA. There were two psychoticism items, with both being higher for the JEPQRS/A. There were two lie items, with one being higher for the JEPQRA and the other being higher for the JEPQRS/A.

Discussion

The study used the mean and covariance structures analysis approach to examine if there is measurement and construct invariance for the 24 items of the JEPQRA and the same 24 items in the JEPQRS, when all its 48 items are rated (i.e., JEPQRS/A). For the measurement model, there was support for configural invariance. However there were some differences for metric, error variances, and scalar invariance. This finding for configural invariance indicates that the items that are associated with the different latent factors in JEPQRS will also be associated with the same latent factors in the JEPQRA. In relation to metric invariance, this study found invariance for all but two items. This can be taken as providing fairly good support for metric invariance for these items. This means that the strength of the relationships between most of the items and their underlying constructs in the JEPQRA will be what they would be in the JEPQRS.

The test for scalar or intercept invariance showed non-invariance in 6 items. Three were extraversion items, and three were lie items. As the test for scalar invariance show whether like items across the different versions have the same item mean values corresponding to the zero value of the underlying construct, the findings here indicate that 18 out of the 24 items in the JEPQRS have the same metric scales or intervals and zero points when these items are presented as part of the JEPQRA. In contrast, six items, three items being extraversion and other three items being lie items, do not have the same metric scales across these versions. For these six items, the values were higher for the JEPQRA than the JEPQRS. This means that respondents will provide higher ratings for some of the extraversion and lie items when they are rated as part of the JEPQRA, compared to when they are rated as part of the JEPQRS.

The test for error variances invariance showed non-invariance for 7 items. Among these were two extraversion, one neuroticism, two psychoticism, and two lie items. The non-invariant error variances involving the extraversion and psychoticism were higher for the JEPQRS. For neuroticism, it was higher for the JEPQRA. For lie items, one value was higher for the JEPQRA, while the other value was higher for the JEPQRS. These findings indicate that the reliability values of some of the items in the JEPQRA will differ from what their values would be in the JEPQRS. Although some items may increase in reliability in the

JEPQRA, there would be more items that will decrease in reliability when they are presented in the JEPQRA.

In relation to the construct model, the findings in this study indicated invariance across the JEPQRA and JEPQRS/A for all the corresponding latent variances, covariances, and latent mean scores. Taken together, these findings indicate that the variances, intercorrelations, and mean scores of all the four latent constructs in the JEPQRA would be the same as in the JEPQRS, when these constructs for the latter measure are derived from only the 24 items that comprise the JEPQRA.

Taken together, the findings in this study for the measurement and construct models indicate that when the JEPQRS is completed, collation of only the 24 items that are present in the JEPQRA to form the four latent constructs will produce constructs that have the same factor structure, factor loadings, standard deviations, intercorrelations, and mean scores as in the JEPQRA. In addition, for most items, the intercepts and error variances will be the same. Although there were some non-invariant intercepts and error variances, this may be not problematic. This is because for most personality scales, the scores that are used to examine substantive issues are the latent scores, which were found here to be invariant in their variances, covariances and latent mean scores. At a more general level, some researchers have suggested that for the measurement model, invariance is only needed at the configural and metric levels, and that there is need for only partial invariance for these measurement models (Byrne, 1998; Raju, Laffittee, & Byrne, 2002). These were found in this study. Thus it can be argued that the findings here can be taken as providing sufficient support for the equivalency in the psychometric properties of the common items across the JEPQRA and JEPQRS. If this view is accepted, it then follows that when the JEPQRS is completed, the twenty-four items that are present in the JEPQRA can be used to derive a measure that will be comparable to the JEPQRA.

The findings in this study have some general implications in relation to the development of shorter versions of questionnaires from their longer counterparts. Like the JEPQ, in most instances, the shorter versions of questionnaires have been developed using items with good psychometric properties in the longer versions. This practice takes for granted that items with good psychometric properties can be selected from the longer versions to from the corresponding shorter versions. The results of this study showed that there was fairly good support for invariance across the common items in the JEPQRS and JEPQRA. If this finding can be generalized, it would mean that the assumption that we can use items with good psychometric properties from the longer versions for the shorter versions is reasonable.

In concluding, although this study suggested that it is appropriate to develop shorter versions of the JEPQR from their longer counterparts, the findings and inferences made in this study need to be viewed with some limitations in mind. Firstly, it is possible that the findings here may be specific to the common items in the JEPQRA and JEPQRS, and not to the common items in the JEPQRA and JEPQR, or the JEPQRS and JEPQR, or to short and long versions of other questionnaires. Secondly, because only one pair of questionnaire was examined, it can be argued that it is premature to generalize the results in this study to other longer and short versions of questionnaires. Thirdly, it is possible that the findings may be relevant to only the samples examined in this study. Fourthly, it is important to note that the current study focused on the quantitative differences and not the qualitative differences in psychometric properties of long and short questionnaires. Clearly more studies are needed in this area. Future studies may wish to examine the invariance across the common items of different versions of many different types of questionnaires in many different samples. It would be valuable if these studies adopt the mean and covariance structures analysis approach proposed here, as this would have the potential to provide more useful findings.

REFERENCES

Australian Bureau of Statistics (1996). *Estimated Resident Population by Sex and Age (Catalogue No. 3201.2).* Canberra, Australia: Author.

Bentler, P. M. (1990). Comparative fit indexes in structural models. *Psychological Bulletin, 107,* 238-246.

Byrne, B. M. (1998). *Structural equation modelling with LISREL, PRELIS, and SIMPLIS: basic concepts, applications, and programming.* New Jersey: Lawrence Erlbaum Associates, Inc, Publishers.

Browne, M. W. & Cudeck, R. (1993). Alternative ways of assessing model filt. In K. A. Bollen & J. S. Long (Eds.), *Testing structural equations, models* (pp. 136-162). Newbury Park, CA: Sage.

Cheung, G. W. & Rensvold, R. B. (2002). Evaluating goodness-of-fit indices for testing measurement invariance. *Structural Equation Modeling, 9,* 233-255.

Corulla, W. J. (1990). A revised version of the psychoticism scale for children. *Personality and Individual Differences,* 11, 65-76.

Eysenck, H. J. (1952). *The scientific study of personality.* London: Routledge & Kegan Paul.

Eysenck, H. J. & Eysenck, S. B. G. (1975). *Manual of the Eysenck Personality Questionnaire (adult and junior).* London: Hodder & Stoughton.

Eysenck, H. J. & Eysenck, S. B. G. (1991). *Manual of the Eysenck Personality Scales.* London: Hodder & Stoughton.

Francis, L. J. (1996). The development of an abbreviated form of the Revised Junior Eysenck Personality Questionnaire (JEPQR-A) among 13-15 year olds. *Personality and Individual Differences, 21,* 835-844.

Joreskög, K. G. & Sorböm, D. (1996). *LISREL 8: User's reference guide.* Chicago, IL: Scientific Software.

Joreskög, K. G., Sorböm, D., du Toit, A., & du Toit, M. (1996). *LISREL 8: New statistical features.* Lincolnwood, IL: Scientific Software International, Inc.

Little, T. D. (1997). Mean and covariance structures (MACS) analyses of cross-cultural data: Practical and theoretical issues. *Multivariate Behavioral Research, 32,* 53-76.

Maltby, J. & Talley, M. (1998). The psychometric properties of an abbreviated form of the Revised Junior Eysenck Personality Questionnaire (JEPQR-A) among 12-1 5 –year old U.S. young persons. *Personality and Individual Differences, 24,* 891-893.

Mash, H. W., Balla, J. R. & McDonald, R. P. (1988). Goodness-of-fit indices in confirmatory factor analysis: The effect of sample size. *Psychological Bulletin, 103,* 391-410.

Meredith, W. (1993). Measurement invariance, factor analysis and factorial invariance. *Psychometrika,* 58,525-543.

Raju, N. S., Laffitte, L. J. & Byrne, B. M. (2002). Measurement equivalency: A comparison of methods based on confirmatory factor analysis and item response theory. *Journal of Applied Psychology, 87,* 517-529.

Satorra, A. & Bentler, P. M. (1999). *A scaled difference chi-square test statistic for moment structure analysis*. (UCLA Statistics Series 260). Los Angeles: University of California, Department of Psychology.

Scholte, R. H. J. & DeBruyn, E, E. J. (2001). The Revised Junior Eysenck Personality Questionnaire (JEPQR-R): Dutch replications of the full-length, short, and abbreviated forms. *Personality and Individual Differences, 31,* 615-625.

Steenkamp, J. E. M. & Baumgartner, H. (1998). Assessing measurement invariance in cross-national consumer research. *Journal of Consumer Research, 25,* 78-90.

Steiger, J. H. (1990). Structural model evaluation and modification. *Multivariate Behavioral Research, 25*, 173-180.

Vandenberg, R. J. & Lance, C. E. (2000). A review and synthesis of the measurement invariance literature: Suggestions, practices, and recommendations for organizational research. *Organizational Research Methods, 3,* 4-69.

In: Personality Assessment: New Research
Editor: Lauren B. Palcroft & Melissa V. Lopez
ISBN 978-1-60692-796-0

Chapter 8

SUCCESSFUL PSYCHOPATHY: UNRESOLVED ISSUES AND FUTURE DIRECTIONS

Kristin Landfield, Meredith Jones and Scott Lilienfeld
Department of Psychology, Emory University, Atlanta, Georgia, USA

In 1982, at age 16, Barry Minkow started ZZZZ Best (pronounced “Zee Best”) carpet cleaning company in his parents' garage. Minkow soon franchised ZZZZ Best into a chain, and by age 20, he was the boy wonder of Wall Street and CEO of a $300 million company. Then Los Angeles mayor Tom Bradley declared the day ZZZZ Best went public “Barry Minkow Day.” Minkow was a media darling and appeared on the Oprah Winfrey show as a model young entrepreneur. A whiz at generating capital, he borrowed money from a usurious lender and obtained $2000 from his grandmother. He gradually convinced more and more investors to buy into ZZZZ Best, offering promises of large dividends. Eventually, Minkow branched into an insurance restoration business that claimed to restore buildings from fire and water damage in excess of $50 million (Akst, 1990).

Minkow’s company, however, wasn’t quite what it appeared to be. In fact, it never operated as a profitable business. Indeed, the insurance restoration business performed no restorations and was little more than a paper trail. By age 22, Barry had been convicted of 57 counts of fraud and sentenced to serve 25 years in federal prison. He had forged $13,000 worth of money orders from a liquor store. He also stole and sold his grandmother's jewelry, staged break-ins at ZZZZ Best’s offices, and amassed illegal credit card charges. Moneys from the companies investors were being used to launder narcotics….the list goes on.

According to his biographer Daniel Akst (1990), Minkow used quick-talking and confidence tricks to dupe thousands of people. Barry was charming and engaging, spontaneous and fearless, and ambitious and egotistical. According to Akst (1990), “Barry amazed everybody right up until the end. Some of his lieutenants have felt remorse, or shame, or the need to rationalize. Barry’s personality, by contrast, appears seamlessly, coherently false, free of guilt or worry over what he has done. Even at the end, his insincerity was utter” (p. 266). At his sentencing, Judge Dickran Tevrizian told, Minkow, "You're dangerous because you have this gift of gab, this ability to communicate," adding, "You don't have a conscience." Remarkably, after serving a number of years in prison, Minkow emerged several years ago as a successful evangelical minister.

In many respects, Barry Minkow embodies many or most of the features of the still controversial construct of successful psychopathy. Psychopathy, traditionally regarded as a largely or entirely unsuccessful disorder, is increasingly coming to be recognized as a condition sometimes associated with successful, perhaps even above average, functioning (Lilienfeld, 1994; Lykken, 1995). Indeed, over the past decade, research on successful psychopathy has increased markedly in quality and quantity. Nevertheless, this intriguing body of literature raises at least as many questions as answers.

Psychopathy: What it is, and What it isn't

As traditionally conceptualized, psychopathy comprises a constellation of interpersonal, affective, and behavioral traits, including glib charm, shallow affect, deceit, lack of insight, and poor impulse control. Most psychopaths display a peculiar mix of being superficially likeable and engaging yet interpersonally destructive.

The Cleckley Criteria

In his classic book, "The Mask of Sanity," Hervey Cleckley (1941) delineated 16 criteria to describe individuals who were psychopathic:

1. Superficial charm and good intelligence
2. Absence of delusions and other signs of irrational thinking
3. Absence of nervousness or psychoneurotic manifestations
4. Unreliability
5. Untruthfulness and insincerity
6. Lack of remorse and shame
7. Inadequately motivated antisocial behavior
8. Poor judgment and failure to learn by experience
9. Pathologic egocentricity and incapacity for love
10. General poverty in major affective reactions
11. Specific loss of insight
12. Unresponsiveness in general interpersonal relations
13. Fantastic and uninviting behavior with drink and sometimes without
14. Suicide threats rarely carried out
15. Sex life impersonal, trivial, and poorly integrated
16. Failure to follow any life plan

Cleckley's landmark descriptions depicted someone to similar to Minkow, and included the terms, "intelligent," "confident," "likeable," "charming," "poised," and "witty" (1941, pp. 339-340, 349). Moreover, although many of Cleckley's case histories described markedly unsuccessful individuals, including career criminals, they also included people with relatively mild manifestations of these traits ("partial psychopaths") who were at least somewhat successful, including businessmen and psychiatrists.

Misconceptions about Psychopathy

Despite much research on the symptoms and clinical presentation of psychopathy, many common misconceptions persist. One frequent misconception is that psychopathy is synonymous with psychosis, or that all psychopaths are psychotic. Psychosis refers to a loss of touch with reality, often characterized by disorganized thoughts, hallucinations, delusions, and extreme paranoia. When Cleckley (1941) described psychopathy, he noted that psychopaths are not insane in the sense of having lost touch with reality (i.e., they are not psychotic). Instead, following Pritchard (1836), he described them as "morally insane," suggesting that they have a deficit in conscience. David Koresh, infamous for leading the Branch Davidian religious sect in the tragic 1993 Waco, Texas siege, is often portrayed by the media as a psychopath (Lacayo, 1993). Koresh, however, was almost surely psychotic, and under the delusion that he was a prophet. An additional common misconception is that all psychopaths engage in violent behavior. Although psychopaths display many personality traits and characteristics commonly associated with an increased risk of violence (e.g., poor impulse control, disregard for the well-being of others, lack of remorse or shame), violent behavior in and of itself is not a symptom of psychopathy (Freedman, 2001). Indeed, some authors have suggested that psychopathic personality characteristics may be expressed in a variety of phenotypes, perhaps ranging from extreme violence to some highly socially adaptive expressions (Lilienfeld, 1994).

Antisocial Personality Disorder and How it Differs from Psychopathy

The Diagnostic and Statistical Manual of Mental Disorders IV-Text Revision (DSM-IV-TR, American Psychiatric Association, 2000) implies that psychopathy and the diagnosis of Antisocial Personality Disorder (ASPD) are largely or entirely synonymous. ASPD is an umbrella diagnosis denoting a persistent pattern of a broad range of antisocial and criminal infractions. Thus, its diagnosis relies heavily on behavioral indicators, whereas psychopathy presumably is a more specific disorder that emphasizes core personality traits, such as guiltlessness and lovelessness (Lykken, 1995; McCord & McCord, 1964). As a consequence, the DSM category of ASPD may lump together a heterogeneous group of individuals who are etiologically and phenotypically dissimilar (Cunningham & Reidy, 1998; Rogers & Dion, 1991). Indeed, research demonstrates that psychopathy is not equivalent to ASPD (Skeem, Poythress, Edens, Lilienfeld, & Cale, 2003). Lilienfeld (1994) noted that 50%-80% of incarcerated offenders meet diagnostic criteria for ASPD (Hart & Hare, 1997), but only 15-30% of incarcerated offenders in North America meet criteria for psychopathy (Hart & Hare, 1997).

Research on Incarcerated Populations

Because psychopaths are found readily in prisons, most research on psychopathy has relied on incarcerated samples. Although the high levels of psychopathic traits in prisons are expedient for research purposes, exclusive reliance on criminal samples raises a number of potential problems. First, incarcerated samples tend to be composed individuals who, by virtue of their criminal behavior, are largely or entirely unsuccessful. Thus, prison samples are not conducive to studying successful psychopathy. Limiting the study of psychopathy to offenders may underestimate the high levels of psychopathic traits in the general population by overlooking psychopaths who function effectively, or at least under the radar of the penal system. Surprisingly little is known about the existence of such individuals, their presentation, and what distinguishes successful psychopaths from incarcerated ones. Without research on noncriminal populations, it will be difficult or impossible to understand the construct successful psychopathy.

What is "Successful" Psychopathy?

Cleckley (1941) used the term "incomplete manifestations" of psychopathy to describe individuals who, on the surface appear to be thriving members of the community, but who are defective in their emotional and interpersonal capacities. More recently, Widom (1977) extended Cleckley's discourse by describing many noncriminal psychopaths as inherently "successful," and Ray and Ray (1982) conjectured that a "healthy dose" of certain psychopathic traits (e.g., low anxiety) may be beneficial in certain settings. Still other authors have used such terms as "subclinical," (Babiak & Hare, 2006; Lynam, 1999) or "ambulatory," (Ray & Ray, 1982) "adaptive," (Sutker & Allain, 1983), "aberrant self promoters," (Gustafson, 1996), and "social" psychopathy (Smith, 1985) to describe a putative subset of individuals who share many or all psychopathic personality features, but who manage to avoid criminal behavior or escape detection.

Psychopathic "Niches"

Despite the obvious negative aspects of the disorder, psychopaths' superficial charm, persuasiveness, fearlessness, and social dominance may proffer advantages in some social domains or occupations, such as business, politics, and entertainment (see below) (Hall & Benning, 2006; Lykken, 1995; Ray & Ray, 1982). Hall and Benning (2006), among others, have posited that psychopathic individuals' interpersonal manipulativeness and charisma may render them especially likely to success in certain "niches." Babiak and Hare (2006), for example, have described business psychopaths as "snakes in suits" who quickly rise to power in corporations and then exploit others mercilessly. Nevertheless, there is little or no research to bear out these intriguing speculations.

Definitional Issues

Another factor hampering progress in studying successful psychopathy is ambiguity surrounding definition of the construct itself (Hall & Benning, 2006). Some questions that require clarification are:

(1) Can a successful psychopath also have a criminal history, or is a criminal record a rule-out criterion? Although conceptualizations and operationalizations of successful psychopathy vary, successful psychopaths are sometimes viewed as individuals who have not engaged in antisocial behavior.
(2) Does the category of "successful psychopathy" include individuals who commit criminal behavior but evade apprehension? Lilienfeld (1994) and Hall and Benning (2006) suggested that non-incarcerated psychopaths may benefit from protective factors, such as intelligence and adequate planning ability, that allow them to avoid imprisonment.
(3) Are individuals who embody most or all of the personality features of psychopaths but refrain from antisocial behavior psychopathic?
(4) Does "successful psychopathy" require that individuals with psychopathic tendencies engage in enviable, prosocial, or even heroic behaviors, such as leadership?

In Hume's (1777) terminology, these questions are analytical rather than synthetic in nature. They require agreement in definition and do not lend themselves to empirical resolution, but they highlight several obstacles to validating the construct. For the construct to be clarified, there first needs to be broad agreement on the object of study.

Clinical Lore of the Successful Psychopath

Successful psychopaths have become an entrenched component of clinical lore and the popular media. Hall and Benning (2006) pointed to movies, television shows, historical figures, and more contemporary newsworthy individuals as potential examples of successful psychopaths. They cited Gordon Gekko from *Wall Street;* Alan Shore from *Boston Legal;* President Lyndon Baines Johnson; and Andrew Fastow and Kenneth Lay, both former Enron executives, as fictional and factual people with prominent psychopathic features. Similarly, Lykken (1995) described Winston Churchill, former Prime Minister of Great Britain, and test pilot Chuck Yeager (who broke the sound barrier) as possessing many attributes of psychopathy. These individuals avoided serious antisocial behavior, but nevertheless displayed many of the interpersonal and affective characteristics of psychopathy, including social poise, charisma, fearlessness, and risk-taking Lykken (1995) described them as individuals who had the genetic "talent" for psychopathy, but who were socialized to avoid serious antisocial behavior.

The "Dark Triad" of Personality

Central aspects of psychopathy overlap with such other well-known clinical constructs as narcissism and Machiavellianism. Understanding successful psychopathy requires necessitates an understanding of how, if at all, successful psychopathy differs from these constructs. For instance, Machiavellianism is a constellation of traits comprising interpersonal manipulation, self-interested strategies, and self-aggrandizing deception (Christie & Geis, 1970; McHoskey, Worzel & Szyarto, 1998). Narcissism is characterized by grandiosity, perceived entitlement, attention-seeking, excessive egocentrism, and interpersonal exploitation (Exline, Baumeister, Bushman, Campbell, & Finkel, 2004; Raskin & Hall, 1979).

The intersection of psychopathy with narcissism and Machiavellianism has come to be known as the "Dark Triad" of personality (Jakobowitz & Egan, 2006; McHoskey, 1995; Paulhus & Williams, 2002), reflecting the high degree of intercorrelation among the three constructs (Hare, 1991; Skinner, 1988; Smith & Griffith, 1978). Successful psychopathy might be the expression of the overlapping conceptual space, in which the affective deficits of psychopathy intersect with Machiavellian and narcissistic proclivities. Nevertheless, some important aspects of successful psychopathy, such as superficial agreeableness, are probably not fully accounted for by this hypothesis. Perhaps the less adaptive expressions of psychopathy are buffered by narcissistic impression-management as narcissistic individuals may be concerned with obtaining respect from others (see also Lykken, 1995). Such concern with one's reputation could direct otherwise antisocial impulses toward more socially desirable expressions. Nevertheless, the intriguing possibility that narcissism tempers the full expression of psychopathy has yet to be studied systematically.

Hero Hypothesis and Successful Psychopathy

Lykken (1995) argued that the primary deficit in psychopathic individuals is a lack of fear. He noted anecdotally that heroes are often individuals who overcome fear in dangerous situations and that some heroes may share the trait of fearlessness with classic psychopaths (Lykken, 1982). Lykken further suggested that early parenting practices can channel the expression of fearlessness into either antisocial (e.g., criminal) or prosocial (e.g.,heroic) outlets. For example, some individuals who engage in treacherous combat respond to potentially traumatic situations by an inability to act in the moment or by developing severe psychological responses to war-time stress. In contrast, other soldiers can face dangerous and potentially deadly situations with skill and equanimity. Although systematic studies of such individuals are lacking, a subset of them may possess the lack of fear characteristic of psychopaths. As Lykken (1982), proposed, the psychopath and hero may be "twigs from the same branch."

The early NASA astronauts may have been similarly marked by fearlessness (Lykken, 1995). They dared to fly faster, higher, and in ways that had never been tried before. Tom Wolfe's (1979) brilliant history of the early U.S. space program, *The Right Stuff*, provides many examples of fearlessness among NASA test pilots. In one case, Wolfe described a test pilot who lost control of his plane and was plummeting to his death; instead of panicking, he calmly radioed the controller that he did not know what he did wrong and listed off the procedures he used to attempt to recover control of his plane. Many of the pillots were able to face unknown and dangerous situations with calm and restraint.

Still, these examples are only conjectural, as virtually no research systematically examines the relation between psychopathy and heroism. In the only published research effort to examine this possibility, Patrick, Edens, Lilienfeld, Poythress, and Benning (2006) found that the "fearless dominance" factor of the Psychopathic Personality Inventory (see "Psychopathic Personality Inventory" section below) was positively correlated with a construct they termed "everyday heroism," which comprises heroic behaviors that many or most people have had they opportunity to display in daily life (e.g., stopping to assist a stranded motorist, breaking up a fight among strangers). Nevertheless, further investigation of the "psychopath-hero" hypothesis is clearly warranted.

Assessment of Successful Psychopathy

Although psychopathy has traditionally been measured among incarcerated populations, more recent innovations have allowed for the assessment of psychopathy among noninstitutionalized populations. Such measures have facilitated research on successful psychopathy.

The Self-Report Psychopathy Scale

The Self-Report Psychopathy Scale-Revised (SRP-III; Hare, 1985; Paulhus, Hemphill, & Hare, in press) was derived from the Psychopathy Checklist (PCL; Hare, 1980), now the PCL-Revised (Hare, 1991/2003), which is the most widely used psychopathy measure in forensic settings. Items on the SRP-III were selected on the basis of distinguishing high and low scorers on the PCL. Like the PCL-R, the SRP-III comprises items assessing both core psychopathic personality features and antisocial behaviors. It correlates positively with other self-report measures of psychopathy, social deviance, and delinquency (Derefinko & Lynam, 2006; Paulhus & Williams, 2002).

Psychopathic Personality Inventory

The Psychopathic Personality Inventory (PPI; Lilienfeld & Andrews, 1996), now the PPI-Revised (PPI-R; Lilienfeld & Widows, 2006), has emerged as a promising self-report measure of psychopathic traits in nonclinical populations. Research using relatively well-adjusted individuals (e.g., college students at top-tier universities) has found convergent validity between the PPI and measures of theoretically related constructs. For example, PPI total scores are positively related to observers' ratings of Cleckley's (1941) criteria for psychopathy and self-report and interview measures of ASPD and narcissism. Further, the PPI shows discriminant validity from self-reported fears and anxiety (Lilienfeld & Andrews, 1996). Using the PPI, research among nonclinical populations has identified a factor structure that may be similar to that found in incarcerated populations, as well as parallel behavioral and personality correlates, such as positive associations with measures of narcissistic and borderline personality features and negative associations with measures of anxiety disorder symptoms (Benning, Patrick, Hicks, Blonigen, & Krueger, 2003; Edens, 2004; Salekin, Trobst, & Krioukova, 2001).

Levenson Primary and Secondary Psychopathy Scales

Levenson's Primary and Secondary Psychopathy Scales (Levenson, Kiehl, & Fitzpatrick, 1995) are also aimed at identifying psychopathic characteristics in nonincarcerated populations. These scales are associated with measures of such theoretically related constructs as disinhibition, boredom-proneness, antisocial behavior (Levenson et al., 1995; McHoskey, Worzel, & Szyarto, 1998) and narcissism (Skeem et al., 2003). Such findings indicate that the Levenson Psychopathy Scales are valid for assessing at least certain aspects of psychopathy. Nevertheless, the Primary Scale appears to be more strongly associated with the more antisocial aspects of psychopathy than with its core interpersonal and affective features (Lilienfeld & Fowler, 2006) and may not be ideal for detecting the personality features of psychopathy in high functioning populations. Falkenbach, Poythress, Falki, and Manchak (2007) found that the PPI showed more robust convergent validity with ostensibly related criterion variables (e.g., aggression) and more robust divergent validity with ostensibly unrelated criterion variables (e.g., anxiety) than did the Levenson scales. Thus, they concluded that the PPI may outperform the Levenson Scales in detecting psychopathy in nonclinical samples.

Assessment Using the Five Factor Model of Personality

Miller, Lynam, Widiger and colleagues (e.g., Lynam, 2002; Miller et al, 2005; Derefinko & Lynam, 2006; Widiger & Lynam, 1998) argued that psychopathy can be assessed and described using the Five Factor Model (FFM), a broadband model of personality that comprises five dimensions: Neuroticism, Extraversion, Openness, Agreeableness, and Conscientiousness. One benefit to this approach is that psychopathy and other extreme variants of personality can presumably be assessed on the same scale and using the same descriptive terminology as both normal-range personality traits and other personality disorders. Although this approach may be useful for detecting personality features of psychopathy in noninstitutional populations, no studies using this approach have yet to investigate successful psychopathy *per se*.

Detecting the Successful Psychopath: Modern Research Efforts

Although researchers have made preliminary efforts at studying psychopathy in successful or nonincarcerated populations, the lion's share of writing on the topic has lacked systematic research to buttress its claims. Nevertheless, there have been several notable exceptions.

Detecting Successful Psychopaths using Extant Personality Measures

Widom (1977, 1978) attempted to solicit a sample of non-institutionalized psychopaths by recruiting them from advertisements in underground Boston newspapers. She included several of the Cleckley criteria for psychopathy in the description: "Wanted: charming, aggressive, carefree people who are impulsively irresponsible but are good at handling people and at looking after number one" (p. 675). Individuals who responded to the advertisement were screened to ensure they met Cleckley's description of psychopathy. Widom reported that these individuals shared many of the same psychometric and familial characteristics as "unsuccessful" psychopaths. For example, they scored similarly to incarcerated psychopaths on a number of personality inventories, including the California Psychological Inventory (CPI; Gough, 1960) and Minnesota Multiphasic Personality Inventory (MMPI; McKinley & Hathaway, 1944), and they exhibited elevated rates of parental alcoholism. Nevertheless, most of this sample also met criteria for sociopathy (Robins, 1966), which are similar to the criteria for ASPD. Despite Widom's pioneering attempt at studying this elusive population, it is difficult to draw conclusions about "successful" psychopathy from her findings. In particular, it is unclear whether her methods and recruitment differentially selected psychopathic individuals *per se*, or whether they recruited individuals with externalizing psychopathology more generally.

Ray and Ray (1982) administered several personality and attitudes measures, including the Psychopathic deviate (Pd) scale from the MMPI, to randomly selected individuals drawn from electoral records in Australia. Ray and Ray found that Pd scores were positively related to Machiavellianism, self-reported interpersonal skill, and associated with a tendency to self-disclose socially undesireable information. They concluded that "as long as psychopaths keep out of trouble, they may have advantages over others" (p. 135). Nevertheless, their findings are also difficult to interpret for similar reasons as Widom's (1977, 1978) study. The MMPI Pd scale correlates only weakly with core personality features of psychopathy (Harpur, Hare, & Hakstian, 1989; Lilienfeld, 1994, 1999) and does not exclude nonpsychopathic individuals with high levels of antisocial behavior.

Sutker and Allain (1983) examined "adaptive" psychopathy in medical students selected on the basis of elevated scores on the MMPI Pd and Ma (Hypomania) scales. Their "adaptive" psychopaths shared many personality correlates of criminal psychopathy, such as elevated sensation seeking. Nevertheless, their use of the MMPI Pd and Ma scales was problematic for this avenue of study, as these scales do not adequately distinguish Cleckley psychopathy from ASPD (Lilienfeld, 1999).

Gustafson and Ritzer (1995) dubbed subclinical psychopaths as "aberrant self-promoters," (ASPs) thus describing a group of individuals characterized by both narcissistic personality and antisocial features. They used a series of statistical methods to identify a putatively distinct group of ASPs who show similar PCL-R scores as psychopathic prisoners. In samples of undergraduates, Gustafson and Ritzer (1995) administered 179 self-report personality items, drawn from various personality scales (e.g., the Self-Report Psychopathy Scale, the Narcissistic Personality Inventory) designed to assess such variables as psychopathy, self-esteem, narcissism, antisocial behavior, impulsivity, and other related constructs. Using cluster analyses, individuals' scores were grouped by similarity to one another on each variable. Next, factor analyses were conducted on the items to yield higher-order factors composed of covarying items. Finally, Gustafson and Ritzer (1995) conducted a Q factor analysis, in which homogeneous clusters of individuals were identified. A pattern emerged that was consistent with the conceptualization of ASP. From these overlapping findings, the researchers concluded that ASPs are a distinct subset of high-functioning individuals who share many features with criminal psychopaths.

Although these important studies provide a preliminary basis for understanding successful psychopathy, they are limited by a lack of specificity in their measures and inconsistency in operationalizations of this construct. Further research on successful psychopathy will be facilitated by the adoption of measures more specific to psychopathy (e.g., PCL-R, PPI) and by clearer operationalizations of this construct.

Psychopathy as a Dimensional Disorder

There has been recent success in assessing psychopathy along a dimension in noncriminal populations such as college students (e.g., Belmore & Quinsey, 1994; Benning, Patrick, Hicks, Blonigen, & Krueger, 2003; Edens, Marcus, Lilienfeld, Poythress, 2006). Benning et al. (2003) performed a factor analysis on the PPI scales in a noncriminal (student) sample. They found two independent factors of psychopathy, which each bore differential correlates (but see Neumann, Malterer, & Newman, 2008, for conflicting findings on the PPI's factor structure). The first factor ("fearless dominance") was related to high dominance, low anxiety, and venturesomeness. In many respects, this factor appears analogous to the construct of successful psychopathy. The second factor ("impulsive antisociality") was related to substance abuse, low socioeconomic status and verbal ability, and poor behavioral constraint.

Patrick (2006) argued that prevailing conceptualizations and measures of psychopathy do not capture adequately the adaptive aspects of psychopathy described in Cleckley's (1941) case studies. He classified Cleckley's 16 criteria into three higher-order categories: positive adjustment, chronic behavioral deviance, and interpersonal-affective traits. Prior nomenclatures typically highlight interpersonal-affective and behavioral deviance aspects of psychopathy but fail to give due weight to its potentially advantageous characteristics. In adding the positive adjustment category, Patrick highlighted the paradoxical nature of the syndrome, in that traits signaling positive adjustment (e.g., charm, stress immunity) co-exist with notably maladaptive features (e.g., inadequately motivated antisocial behavior). Understanding successful psychopathy will require identifying conditions under which positive adjustment eclipses maladaptive behavior, how positive adjustment and antisocial behavior relate to the interpersonal and emotional features of psychopathy (are they two distinct consequences of emotional deficits?), and whether other variables alter the relations among these three categories.

Successful Psychopathy: Evidence from Psychophysiology and Neurobiology

More recently, promising findings have emerged from psychophysiological and neuroimaging research. Such work identifying potential differences in physiological patterns and neural substrates between criminal and noncriminal psychopaths.

Ishikawa, Raine, Lencz, Bihrle, and Lacasse (2001) recruited participants from five temporary agencies in southern California. By obtaining state court records and confidential self-report, they identified 16 individuals who scored high in psychopathy who had criminal histories ("unsuccessful psychopaths") and 13 who scored high in psychopathy who did not have criminal histories ("successful psychopaths"). In addition, they recruited 23 subjects who were low in psychopathy and had no criminal history. Based on PCL-R scores, they found that, "successful" psychopaths were less impulsive and demonstrated better executive function on the Wisconsin Card Sorting Test (WCST; Heaton, Chelune, Talley, Kay & Curtis, 1993) than "unsuccessful" psychopaths. Successful psychopaths also exhibited higher levels of autonomic stress reactivity compared with controls, whereas unsuccessful psychopaths exhibited reduced autonomic stress reactivity. Elevated levels may reflect better attentional processing or higher levels of anxiety, both of which could assist successful psychopaths in evading detection or in diminishing their risk for antisocial behavior (Raine, Venables, & Williams, 1995).

Benning, Patrick, and Iacono (2005) found that participants with high scores on the PPI fearless dominance factor (as opposed to the impulsive antisociality factor) showed a diminished electrodermal response to aversive pictures compared with those who were low in fearless dominance. People high on this interpersonal-affective dimension may lack the social apprehension and fear that inhibit most people low on this dimension from engaging in antisocial behaviors (Benning, Patrick, Blonigen, Hicks, & Iacono, 2005).

Again recruiting from temporary agencies, Raine, Lencz, Birhl, LaCasse, and Colletti (2000) screened people using clinical interviews to ascertain the extent to which they demonstrated psychopathic characteristics. Using structural magnetic resonance imaging (MRI), they found a 22.3 percent less prefrontal gray matter among unsuccessful psychopaths compared with controls and successful psychopaths (Yang, Raine, Lencz, Bihrle, LaCasse, & Colletti, 2005). Because prefrontal gray matter is pivotal for decision-making and impulse control, these deficits may explain the differential expressions of psychopathic characteristics in successful as opposed to unsuccessful psychopath.

More speculatively, Raine, Ishikawa, Arce, Lencz, Knuth, and Bihrle (2004) that the hippocampus also plays a key role in fear conditioning in specific situations, and argued that structural differences between successful and unsuccessful psychopaths in the hippocampus may account for passive avoidance deficits (failure to inhibit behavior that leads to aversive consequences) among criminal psychopaths. Fewer than half of the controls and noncriminal psychopaths had an asymmetrical hippocampus, whereas 94% of the unsuccessful psychopaths exhibited asymmetry such that the right side was larger than the left. Consequently, psychopaths with impaired hippocampal function may have trouble modifying their behavior in the face of aversive consequences (Raine et al., 2004). Nevertheless, because Raine et al.'s (2004) findings regarding hippocampal asymmetry have not yet been independently replicated, this possibility remains conjectural.

Although these studies demonstrated structural and functional differences between incarcerated and nonincarcerated psychopaths, they do not answer whether such noncriminal psychopaths are genuinely "successful" and opposed to merely less unsuccessful than most incarcerated psychopaths. Indeed, temporary agencies are likely to employ individuals who have repeatedly been unsuccessful at other professions. Further structural brain imaging research among more successful populations of individuals with high levels of psychopathic traits is therefore warranted.

FUTURE DIRECTIONS IN UNDERSTANDING THE SUCCESSFUL PSYCHOPATH

The results of these studies offer promising and exciting new directions for understanding successful psychopathy. Patrick's (2006) "dual-process" model of psychopathy conceptualizes psychopathy as a two-fold disorder, comprising some attenuated emotional reactivity on the one hand, and deficits in inhibitory control, on the other (Fowles & Dindo, 2006; Patrick & Bernat, in press). According to this model, emotional reactivity and inhibitory control contribute differentially to the phenotypic expression of psychopathic personality. The model offers one explanation for potential subtypes of psychopathy, including successful psychopathy, as the relative strength of each of these processes in psychopathic individuals may influence the degree to which they can inhibit antisocial behavior. Successful psychopaths may be marked by lower emotional reactivity than unsuccessful psychopaths, which could help them to abstain from the socially deviant aspects of psychopathy.

Despite promising progress in the validation of the successful psychopathy construct, myriad questions remain. Various research strategies may further this area of study. First, studies should be conducted using large sample sizes. Although it may be difficult to recruit a large number of individuals who satisfy operationalizations of successful psychopathy, doing so will be necessary to ascertain the characteristics of individuals who comprise this category. Sampling from the political world and from business organizations in which many of the traits of a successful psychopath may be valued may yield samples that better differentiate successful from unsuccessful psychopathy. In these professions, certain attributes of successful psychopathy may facilitate professional development and occupational success.

An understanding of the etiology of successful psychopathy should also be a focus of future research It is unclear whether successful psychopaths are born with the "genetic talent" for psychopathy but have been effectively socialized (Lykken, 1995), or whether successful psychopathy is a largely learned and adaptive lifestyle. One set of technique to shed light on this question are behavior-genetic methods, which systematically examines genetic and environmental influences on the etiology and clinical presentation of disorders. For example, studies of monozygotic (genetically identical) twins who are discordant in "clinical" psychopathy (as operationalized by high scores on the PCL-R or other well validated psychopathy instruments) may be helpful in examining this question, as discordant co-twins may exhibit some of the personality features of successful psychopathy. Moreover, this approach may allow investigators to identity protective factors (e.g., peer influences, parenting practices) that account for the differences in behavioral expression within twin pairs.

Indeed, a particularly critical consideration in future research on successful psychopathy is the investigation of buffering variables that may attenuate the expression of the behavioral deviance often associated with psychopathy. Hall and Benning (2006) noted that intelligence, socio-economic status, planning abilty, and autonomic hyperreactivity are among the variables with theoretical and practical importance for regulating psychopathic impulses. They also urged further investigation of putative protective factors (e.g., parental characteristics, social functioning) that may enhance socialization, thus limiting the perpetration of antisocial behavior among psychopathic individuals. Indeed, it is not clear whether successful psychopaths merely have a less extreme form of the same basic disorder as their criminal counterparts, although recent research (Raine et al., 2004) indicates that structural brain differences may differentiate criminal from noncriminal psychopaths. A better understanding of the etiology and developmental trajectory of psychopathy may point us toward decisive environmental influences that mitigate against the expression of antisocial behavior in predisposed individuals.

Note

It is not clear that criminal versus noncriminal psychopaths comprise two separate groups that are etiologically and catergorically distinct. For ease of discussion, however, we use this distinction to highlight the differences between successful versus unsuccessful psychopathy.

References

Akst, D. (1990). Wonder Boy: Barry Minkow, the Kid Who Swindled Wall Street. New York, NY: Scribner's.

American Psychiatric Association, (2000). Diagnostic and Statistical Manual of Mental Disorders, fourth edition, Text Revision (DSM-IV-TR). American Psychiatric Association, Washington DC, USA, 2000.

Babiak, P. & Hare, R. D. (2006). Snakes in Suits: When Psychopaths Go To Work. New York: Regan Books.

Belmore, M. F. & Quinsey, V. L. (1994). Correlates of psychopathy in a noninstitutional sample. *Journal of Interpersonal Violence, 9*(3), 339-349.

Benning, S. D., Patrick, C. J., Blonigen, D. M., Hicks, B. M., & Iacono, W. G. (2005). Estimating facets of psychopathy from normal personality traits: A step toward community epidemiological investigations. *Assessment, 12*(1), 3-18.

Benning, S. D., Patrick, C. J., Hicks, B. M., Blonigen, D. M., & Krueger, R. F. (2003). Factor structure of the Psychopathic Personality Inventory: Validity and implications for clinical assessment. *Psychological Assessment, 15*(3), 340-350. Benning, S. D., Patrick, C. J., & Iacono, W. G. (2005). Psychopathy, startle blink modulation, and electrodermal reactivity in twin men. *Psychophysiology, 42*(6), 753-762.

Christie, R. & Geis, F. (1970). *Studies in Machiavellianism*. New York: Academic Press.

Cleckley, H. (1941). *The Mask of Sanity*. St. Louis, MO: Mosby.

Cunningham, M.D., & Reidy, T.J. (1998). Antisocial personality disorder and psychopathy: diagnostic dilemmas in classifying patterns of antisocial behavior in sentencing evaluations. *Behavioral Sciences & the Law, 16*, 333-51.

Derefinko, K. & Lynam, D.R. (2006). Convergence and divergence among self-report psychopathy measures: A personality-based approach. *Journal of Personality Disorders, 20*, 261-280.

Edens, J. F. (2004). Effect of response distortion on the assessment of divergent facets of psychopathy. *Assessment, 11*(1), 109-112.

Edens, J. F., Marcus, D. K., Lilienfeld, S. O., & Poythress, N. G. (2006). Psychopathic, not psychopath: Taxometric evidence for the dimensional structure of psychopathy. *Journal of Abnormal Psychology, 115*(1), 131-144.

Exline, J. J., Baumeister, R. F., Bushman, B. J., Campbell, W. K., & Finkel, E. J. (2004). Too proud to let go: Narcissistic entitlement as a barrier to forgiveness. *Journal of Personality and Social Psychology, 87*, 894–912.

Falkenbach, D., Poythress, N., Falki, M., & Manchak, S. (2007). Reliability and validity of two self-report measures of psychopathy. *Assessment, 14*(4), 341-350.

Fowles, D. C. & Dindo, L. (2006). A dual-deficit model of psychopathy. In C. J. Patrick (Ed.), *Handbook of psychopathy*. New York: Guilford Press.

Freedman, D. (2001). False prediction of future dangerousness: Error rates and Psychopathy Checklist-Revised. *Journal of the American Academy of Psychiatry and Law, 29*, 89-95.

Gustafson, S. B. (1996). Aberrant self-promotion: The dark side of normal. In D. J. Cooke, A. E. Forth, J. P. Newman, & R. D. Hare (Eds.), *Issues in criminological and legal psychology: No. 24, International perspective on psychopathy* (pp. 61-62). Leicester, UK: British Psychological Society.

Gustafson, S. B. & Ritzer, D. R. (1995). The dark side of normal: A psychopathy-linked pattern called Aberrant Self-Promotion. *European Journal of Personality, 9*, 147-183.

Hall, J. R. & Benning, S. D. (2006). The "successful" psychopath: Adaptive and subclinical manifestations of psychopathy in the general population. In C. J. Patrick (Ed.), Handbook of psychopathy. New York: Guilford Press.

Hare, R. D. (1985). A comparison of procedures for the assessment of psychopathy. *Journal of Consulting and Clinical Psychology, 53*, 7-16.

Hare, R.D. (1991). The Hare Psychopathy Checklist-Revised PCL-R. , Multi-Health Systems, Toronto, Ontario.

Hare, R. D. (1993). Without Conscience: The Disturbing World of the Psychopaths Among Us. New York: Simon & Schuster (Pocket Books).

Harkness, A. R. & Lilienfield, S. O. (1997). Individual differences science for treatment planning: Personality traits. *Psychological Assessment, 9*: 349–360.

Harpur, T. J., Hakstian, A. R. & Hare, R. D. (1988). Factor structure of the Psychopathy Checklist. *Journal of Consulting and Clinical Psychology, 56*, 741-747.

Hart, S. D. & Hare, R. D. (1997). The association between psychopathy and narcissism: Theoretical views and empirical evidence. In E. Ronningstam (Ed.), *Disorders of narcissism: Theoretical, empirical, and clinical implications* (pp.415-436). Washington: American Psychiatric Press.

Heaton, Chelune, Talley, Kay & Curtis, 1993

Hemphill, J. F., Hare, R. D. & Wong, S. (1998). Psychopathy and recidivism: a review. *Legal and Criminological Psychology, 3*, 139–170.

Hume, David. (1777). *An Enquiry concerning Human Understanding*, Nidditch, P. N. (Ed.), 3rd. ed., Oxford: Clarendon Press, 1975.

Ishikawa, S. S., Raine, A., Lencz, T., Bihrle, S., & Lacasse, L. (2001). Autonomic reactivity and executive functions in successful and unsuccessful criminal psychopaths from the community. *Journal of Abnormal Psychology, 110*, 423-432.

Jakobwitz, S. & Egan, V. (2006). The dark triad and normal personality traits. *Personality and Individual Differences*, 40, 331-339.

Lacayo, R. (1993, May). In the grip of a psychopath. *Time Magazine*, 141(18), 12.

Levenson, M. R., Kiehl, K. A. & Fitzpatrick, C. M. (1995). Assessing psychopathic attributes in a noninstitutionalized population. *Journal of Personality and Social Psychology, 68*(1), 151-158.

Levy,F., Hay, D.A. & Bennett, K.S.(2006). A genetic study of ADHD:A current review and future prospects. *International Journal of Disability, Development and Education*. 53:5-20.

Lilienfeld, S. O. (1994). Conceptual problems in the assessment of psychopathy. Clinical *Psychology Review*, 14, 17-38.

Lilienfeld, S. O. (1998). Methodological advances and developments in the assessment of psychopathy. *Behaviour Research and Therapy, 36*, 99-125.

Lilienfeld, S. O. (1999). The relation of the MMPI-2 Pd Harris-Lingoes subscales to psychopathy, psychopathy facets, and antisocial behavior: Implications for clinical practice. *Journal of Clinical Psychology, 55*, 241-255.

Lilienfeld, S.O. & Fowler, K. A. (2006) The self-report assessment of psychopathy: Problems, pitfalls, and promises. In C. J. Patrick (Ed.), *Handbook of psychopathy* (pp. 107-132). New York: Guilford.

Lilienfeld, S.O. & Widows, M.R. (2006). *Psychopathic Personality Inventory Revised: Professional Manual.* Lutz, FL: Psychological Assessment Resources, Inc.

Lykken, D. T. (1957). A study of anxiety in the sociopathic personality. *Journal of Abnormal and Social Psychology, 55*, 6-10.

Lykken, D. T. (1982). Research with twins: The concept of emergenesis. *Psvchophvsiology, 9,* 361 -373.

Lykken, D. T. (1995). *Antisocial Personalities*. Hillsdale, NJ: Erlbaum.

Lynam, D. R. (2002). Psychopathy from the perspective of the 5-factor model of personality. In P. T. Costa & T. A. Widiger (Eds.), *Personality disorders and the five-factor model of personality, 2nd Edition* (pp. 325-348). Washington: American Psychological Association.

Lynam, D. R., Whiteside, S. & Jones, S. (1999). Self-reported psychopathy: A validation study. *Journal of Personality Assessment, 73*(1), 110-132.

McCord, W. & McCord, J. (1964). *The psychopath: An essay on the criminal mind.* Princeton, NJ: Van Nostrand.

McHoskey, J. (1995). Narcissism and Machiavellianism. *Psychological Reports, 77*, 757–759.

McHoskey, J. W., Worzel, W. & Szyarto, C. (1998). Machiavellianism and psychopathy. *Journal of Personality and Social Psychology, 74*(1), 192-210.

McKinley, J. C. & Hathaway, S. R. (1944) The MMPI: V. Hysteria, hypomania and psychopathic deviate. *Journal of Applied Psychology, 28*, 153–174.

Miller, J.D., Bagby, R.M., Pilkonis, P.A., Reynolds, S.K., & Lynam, D.R. (2005). A simplified technique for scoring the DSM-IV personality disorders with the Five-Factor Model. *Assessment, 12*, 404-15.

Patrick, C. J. (2006). Back to the future: Cleckley as a guide to the next generation of psychopathy research. In C. J. Patrick (Ed.), *Handbook of psychopathy*. New York: Guilford Press.

Patrick, C. J. & Bernat, E. M. Neurobiology of Psychopathy: A Two-Process Theory.

Patrick, C. J., Edens, J. F., Poythress, N. G., Lilienfeld, S. O., & Benning, S. D. (2006). Construct validity of the Psychopathic Personality Inventory two-factor model with offenders. *Psychological Assessment, 18*, 204-208.

Paulhus, D. L., & Williams, K. M. (2002). The dark triad of personality: narcissism, Machiavellianism and psychopathy. *Journal of Research in Personality, 36*, 556–563.

Pritchard, J. C. (1836). *Treatise on insanity*. London: Sherwood Gilbert and Piper.

Ray, J.J. & Ray. J.A.B. (1982). Some apparent advantages of subclinical psychopathy. *Journal of Social Psychology*, 1(17), 135-142.

Raine, A., Ishikawa, S. S., Arce, E., Lencz, T., Knuth, K. H., Bihrle, S., LaCasse, L., & Colletti, P. (2004). Hippocampal structural asymmetry in unsuccessful psychopaths. *Biological Psychiatry, 55*(2), 185-191.

Raine, A, Lencz, T, Bihrle, S, LaCasse, L, & Colletti, P (2000): Reduced prefrontal gray matter volume and reduced autonomic activity in antisocial personality disorder. *Archives of General Psychiatry 57*:119 –127.

Raine, A., Venables, P. H. & Williams, M. (1995). High autonomic arousal and electrodermal orienting at age 15 years as protective factors against criminal behavior at age 29 years. American Journal of Psychiatry, 152, 1595-1600 (findings alsoreported and discussed in Science, 1995,270,1123-1125).

Raskin, R. & Hall, C. S. (1979). A narcissistic personality inventory. *Psychological Reports, 45*, 590.

Robins, L.N. (1966). *Deviant children grown up*. Baltimore: Williams and Wilkins.

Rogers, R. & Dion, K. L. (1991). Rethinking the DSM III-R diagnosis of antisocial personality disorder. *Bulletin of the American Academy of Psychiatry and Law, 19*, 21-31.

Salekin, R. T., Trobst, K. K. & Krioukova, M. (2001). Construct validity of psychopathy in a community sample: A nomological net approach. *Journal of Personality Disorders, 15*(5), 425-441.

Skeem, J. L., Poythress, N., Edens, J. F., Lilienfeld, S. O., & Cale, E. M. (2003). Psychopathic personality or personalities? Exploring potential variants of psychopathy and their implications for risk assessment. *Aggression and Violent Behavior*, 8, 513-546.

Skinner, N. F. (1988). Personality correlates of Machiavellianism: VI. Machiavellianism and the psychopath. *Social Behavior and Personality*, 16, 33–37.

Smith, R. J. (1985). The concept and measurement of social psychopathy. *Journal of Research in Personality, 19*, 219-231.

Smith, R. J. & Griffith, J. E. (1978). Psychopathy, the Machiavellian, and anomie. *Psychological Reports,* 42, 258

Sutker, P. B. & Allain, A. N. (1983). Behavior and personality as-sessment in men labeled adaptive socipaths. *Journal iof Behavioral Assessment*, *5*,65–79.

Widiger, T. A. & Lynam, D. R. (1998). Psychopathy and the five-factor model of personality. In T. Millon & E. Simonsen (Eds.), *Psy-chopiathy: Antisocial, criminal, and violent behavior* (pp. 171–187). New York: Guilford.

Widom, C. S. (1977). A methodology for studying non- institutionalized psychopaths. Journal of *Consulting and Clinical Psychology*, 45, 674-683.

Wolfe T. (1979) *The Right Stuff.* New York: Bantam Books.

Yang, Y., Raine, A., Lencz, T., Bihrle, S., LaCasse, L., & Colletti, P. (2005). Volume reduction in prefrontal gray matter in unsuccessful criminal psychopaths. *Biological Psychiatry, 57*(10), 1103-1108.

In: Personality Assessment: New Research
Editor: Lauren B. Palcroft & Melissa V. Lopez
ISBN 978-1-60692-796-0

Chapter 9

SCORE RELIABILITY IN PERSONALITY RESEARCH

Matt Vassar, Denna L. Wheeler and Jody A. Worley

INTRODUCTION

Score reliability is a central feature of measurement. Both researchers and practitioners are under ethical obligation to ensure that any assessment devise utilized have strong psychometric qualities. This is true when the instrument is needed to conduct research or used to derive therapeutic goals. However, a simple knowledge of the reliability coefficient is not sufficient. A true understanding of reliability theory is necessary to fulfill this obligation. Helms, Henze, Sass, and Mifsud (2006) rightly note the reliability data are often treated as "mystical forces that supercede validity rather than as data that should be analyzed and interpreted in a manner analogous to validity data" (p. 631). Hence, the primary ambition of this chapter is to inform the reader of reliability theories and estimation procedures, including the assumptions underlying such estimates, and provide researchers and practitioners with accessible information for the interpretation and reporting of reliability data. Before this goal may be pursued, however, it is necessary to briefly mention the theoretical nature of personality measurement.

Personality measurement is a reflection of personality theory. Specifically, there are two major theoretical models of personality measurement. One is appropriate for the types of psychometric analyses discussed in this chapter; the other is not. Researchers must examine the theoretical basis for personality measurement and not blindly follow a given set of procedures. The two models have been given various names. Hershberger (1999) used the terms *taxonomic* and *dimensional* to describe these models of personality. Speaking in broader terms, but reflecting the same theoretical foundation, Bollen and Lennox (1991) used the terms *causal indicators* and *effect indicators*, and more recently, Edwards and Bagozzi (2000) used the terms *formative* and *reflective* constructs.

The fundamental difference between the two models is found in the question: *Does a response reflect the construct or define the construct?* The taxonomic (a.k.a. formative) model posits that a person possesses a particular trait when he/she endorses one or more indicators of the trait. The dichotomously scored MMPI is an example of this theoretical model. For example, the following brief stems from the MMPI Somatization scale, *No ear ringing, Bothered by acid stomach, Skin doesn't break out,* all measure some form of physical complaint but are not necessarily related to each other. One would not expect substantial inter-item correlations on a formative scale. A taxonomic scale is simply a composite of individual items with higher levels of endorsement reflecting a higher trait level. Traditional psychometric analysis including coefficient alpha estimation is not appropriate for taxonomic measures and should not be interpreted.

By contrast, the dimensional (a.k.a. reflective) model posits that a person's level on a trait is reflected in his/her response to items. The items reflect more or less extreme positions on the trait but all items reflect a single trait and, therefore, significant inter-item correlations are expected. Classical test theory (CTT), reliability analysis, and factor analysis all assume the use of reflective measurement and treat measures as functions of latent variables and error. The measurement issues discussed in this chapter assume the use of a dimensional measure of personality.

In any testing, measurement or assessment context there is a desire to have consistency and accuracy among test scores. A frequently used method for evaluating a measurement device is the degree of reliability among the scores obtained. The term, reliability, is used in different ways to refer either to the stability of scores over time, the equivalence of scores across alternative measures or forms of a measurement instrument, or the internal consistency of scores produced by the items included on a particular instrument administered in a single setting. The higher the degree of reliability among scores, the more confident we can be that similar scores would be obtained if the same instrument or inventory was administered to the same individuals in the future, all else being equal. In addition to thinking about reliability as the consistency of scores within or between measures, or across time, reliability can also be interpreted as the extent to which the scores reflect measurement error.

The differences observed between scores produced from a particular measurement scale that are attributable to anything other than real differences in aspects of the trait being measured are termed *measurement error*. Measurement error may originate from a variety of sources in the process of measurement. Some of the sources may be systematic and occur with repeated administrations of the scale. Other sources of error may be random or unsystematic and therefore occur in unpredictable ways across repeated measurements. For example, measurement error results when the obtained scores are related to an associated attribute. That is, the observed scores include measurement error if the scores are related to something other than the trait being measured. Measurement error may also result from temporary conditions in the setting or environment in which the scores were acquired. Likewise, if scores are influenced by the process of administering the instrument, such as how the instructions were explained or the time allowed for completion, measurement error is observed in the reduction of the observed reliability of scores.

Types of Score Reliability

Different definitions and conceptions of error have led to different approaches to the estimation of reliability. The different estimates of reliability vary depending on the specific sources of error being addressed. For this reason, it is misleading to refer to the reliability of an instrument. Reliability is a characteristic of the scores obtained from the use of an instrument; reliability is not a property of the instrument itself. Thompson and Vacha-Haase (2000) and many others have demonstrated the variable nature of reliability, and how particular sample or scale characteristics may lead to fluctuation in reliability coefficients across administrations of the same measure. Thus, reliability is not an immutable scale property but rather a fluctuating characteristic of its test scores. Throughout the chapter, the reader will note the term *score reliability* to reflect this distinction. When reliability is reported for a set of scores it is important to note the type of reliability being reported. The most common approaches to reliability are presented below in the three broad categories mentioned previously: stability, equivalence, and internal consistency.

If a single test or instrument is sufficient to assess the property of interest, but the test user is interested in the consistency in responses over time, the common approach to evaluating stability is the *test-retest method*. In this situation, a likely source of measurement error is the systematic variation in examinee responses around the true score. The test administrator can estimate the influence of this variation on test score reliability by administering the test to an individual or group of respondents, wait an acceptable period of time, re-administer the test to the same individual or group, and then calculate the correlation coefficient between the two sets of scores. Some authors refer to the derived correlation coefficient obtained from this test-retest method as the "coefficient of stability," (Crocker & Algina, 1986, p. 133; Pedhazur & Schmelkin, 1991, p. 88).

An underlying assumption associated with the use of the test-retest method is that the theoretical true score is constant and any imperfection in the obtained correlation between the two sets of scores is attributable to random measurement errors that have occurred. The interpretation of the stability coefficient as an estimate of score reliability raises some interesting questions about this underlying assumption. For example, if a low coefficient is obtained, does it indicate that the test provides an unstable estimate of the property or trait assessed, or does it imply that the trait itself is unstable? An alternative consideration is that perhaps there are carry-over effects such that responding to a set of items from one set of items from the first administration influences the responses on the second administration. In any event, information on the stability of scores is crucial in the context of many practical assessment situations.

One way to avoid some of the problems in the test-retest method is to estimate reliability by correlating scores from two similar forms of the same measure. The *alternate* or *parallel forms* method requires administering both forms of the instrument to the same group of respondents. As in the test-retest method, the forms should be administered within a very short amount of time. The estimate of reliability is obtained by computing the correlation coefficient between the two sets of scores. This correlation coefficient is referred to as a "coefficient of equivalence," (Crocker & Algina, 1986, p. 132; Pedhazur & Schmelkin, 1991, p. 89). Test administrators can have greater confidence that the different forms may be used interchangeably when there is a higher numerical value for the coefficient of equivalence. One limitation associated with the alternate forms method is the challenge of constructing parallel forms and determining the level of invariance or measurement equivalence across forms.

When the items or subparts of an instrument measure the same phenomenon, and the scores across the items are consistent, the items are considered homogeneous. *Internal consistency* describes estimates of reliability based on the average correlation among the items within a test instrument. There are several techniques for estimating internal consistency reliability. The most common estimation techniques for internal consistency include split-half methods and coefficient alpha (commonly referred to as Cronbach's alpha). Hogan, Benjamin and Brezinzki (2000) examined the frequency of use of various types of reliability coefficients and found that one or more estimates of internal consistency reliability (split-half, coefficient alpha, KR-20, or an unspecified technique referred to only as internal consistency) accounted for 77.5% of the 801 cases they found of reported reliability estimates in professional journals from 1991 to 1995. One specific technique for estimating internal consistency, coefficient alpha, was the most frequently reported estimate of reliability overall (66.5%), including estimates of stability and equivalence.

Having introduced in broad, conceptual terms the basic forms of reliability that may be considered when using a measurement scale, we now focus attention on specific techniques for reliability estimation. The methods for estimating reliability depend on a combination of theoretical orientation and psychometric assumptions. The following section presents a variety of ways to approach reliability estimation, the assumptions associated with each estimate, as well as issues related to computation and interpretation. Specifically, we detail two coefficients of internal consistency (coefficient alpha and Tarkkonen's rho) as well as approaches using generalizability theory and item response theory. Many other means of estimating reliability coefficients have also been proposed including omega, theta (see Ferketich, 1990, for computational details of omega and theta), maximal reliability (Li, Rosenthal, & Rubin, 1996), and stratified alpha (Cronbach, Shonenman, & McKie ,1965), to name a few. The premise of this chapter is not to provide procedural detail for estimation of each coefficient but rather to alert researchers to issues for consideration when confronted with reliability data.

Estimation Methods for Score Reliability

Generally, reliability can be understood within either of two psychometric theories, random sampling theory or item response theory (Marcoulides, 1999). Within random sampling theory, there are two approaches to reliability estimation, classical test theory and generalizability theory. By far, the most common approach to reliability estimation in applied research is classical test theory which shall be discussed first.

The essence of the classical test theory (CTT) or classical true score theory is that any observed score is composed of two elements, a true score and random error (Crocker & Algina, 1986). The measurement error component is assumed to be uncorrelated with the true score as well as other error components. This assumption leads to the definition of reliability as the correlation between two perfectly parallel forms of a test, that is, tests that have equivalent true scores and error variances. This correlation would reflect the proportion of variance in the observed scores associated with the true score.

Coefficient Alpha

Coefficient alpha is the most widely used estimate of internal consistency reliability (Henson, 2001). This is likely due to ease of calculation and interpretation and the fact that it is supported by popular software packages such as SAS and SPSS. Alpha, however, is based on very strict statistical assumptions and can severely underestimate reliability when these assumptions are violated. Coefficient alpha provides a reasonable estimate of internal consistency only when the scale items are essentially tau-equivalent (Graham, 2006; Miller, 1995). The assumption of tau-equivalence or true-score equivalence requires that items are equivalent measures of the construct. Mathematically this means that inter-item variance and covariances are equivalent. In a factor analytic context this is equivalent to saying that all items have equivalent factor loadings on a single factor (Miller, 1995). Alpha underestimates reliability if the assumption of tau-equivalence is not met. Graham (2006) empirically demonstrates the effects of model violation on reliability estimates using structural equation modeling procedures. When reliability for data that violated tau-equivalence was analyzed under both tau-equivalent and congeneric conditions (i.e. items that measure the same latent trait but with possibly differing degrees of precision and varying amounts of error), the coefficient alpha estimate of reliability was dramatically lower under tau-equivalence than the estimate based on the better fitting congeneric model. Specifically, the estimates for two data sets that differed only in the severity of tau-equivalent model violation, were .76 and .56, the latter representing lesser model violation and the former representing more severe model violation. The reliability estimates for the respective congeneric models were .97 and .99 respectively. It is rare in published studies to find researchers evaluating instruments for tau-equivalence (either informally through visual inspection of item characteristics or more formally through factor analytic procedures) prior to the use of alpha as an estimate of internal consistency, yet it seems plausible to argue the congeneric model would better fit many constructs related to personality research than the essentially tau-equivalent model. In light of both theoretical and empirical evidence of coefficient alpha's underestimation of reliability when tau-equivalence is violated it is recommended that authors interpret alpha cautiously.

Generalizability Theory

As previously mentioned, the error component in Classical Test Theory is assumed to be a single random variable. Generalizability Theory or "G" theory is an extension of Classical Test Theory (CTT) that provides a mechanism to partition the error variance into components and evaluate multiple sources of error simultaneously. G-theory is based on the same statistical assumptions of CTT, including random sampling of subjects, uncorrelated measurement errors, and tau-equivalence, but G-theory extends CTT in several ways. First, traditional CTT reliability analysis is capable of assessing only one type of measurement error at a time while G-theory allows for the simultaneous evaluation of multiple sources of error and their interaction effects (Marcoulides, 1999). Classical test theory provides for several types of reliability estimates (i.e. internal consistency, stability, inter-rater). Each estimate provides information on a particular type of error variance. Since these error estimates are distinct and cumulative (Thompson, 2003) it is difficult to determine a true estimate of reliability in the presence of multiple sources of error. Using ANOVA techniques, G-theory partitions error variance across items (internal consistency), occasions (stability), and/or judges (inter-rater).

Additionally, G-theory allows for the computation of an appropriate reliability coefficient depending on the type of decision to be made (Thompson, 2003). CTT produces reliability coefficients that are appropriate only for relative decisions. Relative decisions refer to the ordering of persons on a construct. G-theory, in addition to producing a coefficient appropriate for relative decisions, can produce a coefficient appropriate for absolute decisions. Absolute decisions refer to a criterion based evaluation of performance. These types of decisions are particularly important to clinicians who may make diagnostic judgments using personality inventory test scores.

The generalizability or "G" coefficient reflects the proportion of observed score variance that is universe-score variance (i.e. true-score variance). In other words, the proportion of variance that is generalizable to some defined universe. The variance components are calculated using ANOVA techniques and proportions of variance and G-coefficients are calculated based on ratios of variance components. Shavelson and Webb (1991) provide a thorough, yet accessible explanation of study designs and computation of variance components.

Scale dimensionality is another issue to evaluate prior to reliability analysis. Both congeneric and tau-equivalent models assume unidimensionality. "Indeed, the most striking problem of Cronbach's alpha is its built-in assumption of one-dimensionality" (Vehkalahti, Puntanen, & Tarkkonen, 2006, p.16). The most common measures of personality (e.g. MMPI, NEO, CPI, etc.) are multidimensional. Coefficient alpha and generalizability theory are only appropriate for unidimensional scales. Reliability estimates for multidimensional scales that may not adhere to the strict requirements of tau-equivalence may be more accurately represented by Tarkkonen's Rho (Vehkalahti, Puntanen, & Tarkkonen, 2006).

Tarkkonen's rho

Tarkkonen and Vehkalahti (2005) propose an alternative to Cronbach's alpha for analyzing score reliability. The strict psychometric assumptions (i.e. equivalent inter-item variance and covariance and unidimensionality) required to meaningfully interpret alpha are often not tenable and may seldom be presented in personality research. Tarkkonen's rho, like alpha, is based on classical true score theory and makes the same assumptions regarding measurement error. That is, measurement error is random and uncorrelated with true scores. The major difference between alpha and rho is that alpha requires unidimensionality and tau-equivalence for accurate estimation of reliability, whereas rho is a multivariate extension of CTT and imposes no measurement model assumptions for estimation. The computation of rho is similar to that of alpha or generalizability coefficients in that "[t]he variances of the measurement scales are decomposed . . . and Tarkkonen's rho is obtained, according to the definition of reliability, by dividing the . . . variance generated by the true scores by the total variation" (Vehkalahti , Puntanen, & Tarkkonen, 2006, p. 10).

Some knowledge of matrix arithmetic is required as rho must be calculated using matrix operations since it is not available in popular statistical software packages. The authors of the current chapter replicated an example presented by Tarkkonen and Vehkalahti (2005) to assess the practicality of utilizing rho for reliability analysis as part of an applied research study. The computations were completed with relative ease using SPSS matrix syntax and the results replicated those published by Tarkkonen and Vehkalahti (2005).

The analyses proceed as a two-tiered process. First the measurement model is evaluated for structural validity. Following an exploratory or confirmatory factor analysis of the instrument, a coefficient is produced for each factor, ρ_f, that represents the reliability of the factor image. The required matrices for reliability computations include the inter-item correlation matrix and the pattern matrix produced from item level factor analysis. The formula for the reliability coefficient(s) is: $\rho_f = diag[(B'B)^2] \times [diag(B'\Sigma B)]^{-1}$ where B represents the factor pattern matrix and Σ represents the inter-item correlation matrix (Tarkkonen & Vehkalahti, 2005).

The second phase of analysis is an evaluation of the measurement scales. The goal is to create scales with the highest predictive validity and the first step is to establish item weights. Scale weights can be computed using traditional multiple linear regression. A criterion is selected and the items are used as predictors. The regression coefficients serve as item weights in reliability analysis and the reliability coefficient is calculated as follows: $\rho = \frac{a'BB'a}{a'\Sigma a}$, where a represents the vector of regression coefficients. Finally, scales are created using the factor scores as weights. The reliabilities of the factor scores are assessed with the following formula: $\rho_s = diag[(B'\Sigma^{-1}B)^2] \times [diag(B'\Sigma^{-1}B)]^{-1}$. Tarkkonen and Vehkalahti (2005) provide the following recommendation regarding weighted scales utilizing linear regression and factor scores: "If any criteria are available, the weights for the items can be estimated by the regression method. Otherwise, it is a good practice to compute the factor scores and weight them according to the theory." (Tarkkonen & Vehkalahti, 2005, p.188).

To give the reader a sense of the contrast between coefficient alpha and Tarkkonen's rho, the current authors computed coefficient alpha for two scales using the inter-item correlation matrix provided by Tarkkonen and Vehkalahti (2005) as an empirical example of the computation and interpretation of rho. The coefficient alpha internal consistency reliability estimates were .78 and .79 for verbal ability and deductive ability scales respectively. The rho estimates for the factor images were .92 and .86 and the rho estimates for the factor scores were .99 and .85. The differences among the reliability estimates might generate very different interpretations regarding the quality of measurement and results produced from subsequent analyses.

There are numerous studies that explore the affects of various measurement design elements on coefficient alpha. (Barnette, 2000; Chang ,1994; Cook et al., 2001;

Greer et al., 2006; Jacoby & Matell, 1971; Onwuegbuzie & Daniel, 2002). These include item variance, item distribution, scale length, sample size, and response format. Similar studies do not exist for generalizability theory or Tarkkonen's rho. A summary of the finding from the studies of coefficient alpha are presented. The absence of similar findings for generalizability theory and rho should not imply that these reliability techniques are immune to influence from measurement design but simply that a body of literature does not yet exist exploring these issues.

Coefficient alpha is a function of inter-time covariance. The size and direction of inter-item correlations will directly influence alpha. It is no surprise then that when item skew was evaluated for effect on reliability estimates, Greer, et al. (2006) found that increasing levels of skew decreased inter-item correlations which led to decreased estimates of alpha. Interestingly, skew had less affect on alpha when using Likert-type scales with more than five response options. This led Greer et al. (2006) to recommend "using more rather than fewer levels" (p. 1358) and to transform or rank skewed items prior to analysis.

Because coefficient alpha is influenced by item variance it is often suggested that a larger number of response options on Likert-type scales will increase item variance and thus improve internal consistency estimates. A number of researchers have empirically tested this hypothesis with consistently surprising results (Chang, 1994; Cook, et al., 2001; Jacoby & Matell, 1971; Weems & Onwuegbuzie, 2001). Chang (1994) reported that a four-point Likert scale produced higher reliability estimates than a six-point scale. Jacoby and Matell (1971) also examined the effect of various rating formats on internal consistency estimates and found no statistically significant difference in results among formats that ranged from 2 to 19 response options. The most ambitious study (Cook et al., 2001) to test this hypothesis used a large, diverse sample (n = 4407) to evaluate the reliability estimates for persons using an unnumbered graphic slider with theoretically unlimited response options compared to a 9 point Likert scale. Once again no significant difference in alpha estimates was found although the estimates from the 9-point scale were slightly higher than those for the graphic slider. The only exception was a study by Weems and Onwuegbuzie (2001) who found that an increase in the number of response categories increased alpha. The greatest gains were achieved when moving from an odd number of response categories to the next higher even number of categories leading Weems and Onwuegbuzie (2001) to conclude that the use of midpoint categories may reduce internal consistency estimates. Unfortunately, these results were based on analyses that eliminated persons who provided middle category responses. This produced a substantial increase in alpha, .70 to .94 but recall that alpha is a function of inter-item correlation. When middle category responses are removed from a data set, bivariate correlation is increased (Shavelson, 1996). The reported increase in alpha may be a statistical artifact resulting from the method of analysis.

These results may be a result of test-taker behavior rather than a result of statistical or psychometric factors (Chang, 1994; Weems & Onwuegbuzie, 2001). It seems that more response categories as well as odd numbered categories give increased opportunity for response set or response bias. Onwuegbuzie and Daniel (2002) suggest that persons who select the midpoint option have similar personal characteristics including negative self-perceptions about their level of creativity, low levels of self-oriented perfectionism, and low levels of hope. Personality researchers should be aware that using a mid-level category may be associated with one or more response bias issues identified in these studies.

In addition to the number of response options, researchers have studied the effects of item stems (i.e. directly worded and negatively worded items) and the direction of response options (i.e. Strongly Agree to Strongly Disagree vs. Strongly Disagree to Strongly Agree). Scales that include negatively worded items consistently produce lower internal consistency estimates of reliability (Barnette, 2000; Weems & Onwuegbuzie, 2001). Specifically, Barnette (2000) found that the alpha estimate for directly worded stems across all response options was .831, while the corresponding alpha for mixed item stems was .697. The ordering of the response options did not appear to significantly affect alpha estimates although the highest coefficient alpha estimates were achieved with all directly worded item stems combined with mixed response options (i.e. some of the response options ranged from SA to SD while others ranged from SD to SA).

Research on test-retest reliability estimates is mixed. Jacoby and Matell (1971) found no difference in test-retest reliability based on number of response options while Chang (1994) reported that test-retest reliability was improved when scales used different numbers of response options. These seemingly conflicting results should be interpreted with caution as the studies used different research methodology and analysis techniques.

Sample characteristics may also affect alpha estimates. When a sample is too homogeneous coefficient alpha may be low as a result of the reduction in item variance. Roberts and Onwuegbuzie (2003) proposed two indices to evaluate sample homogeneity, a *relative mean item variance index* and a *relative squared standard error of estimate index.* The *relative mean item variance index* is simply the ratio of two variance components. The numerator consists of the difference in the mean item variance for the current sample and the mean item variance for a comparison sample and the denominator is the mean item variance for the comparison sample. The closer the numerator is to zero the more similar the current sample is to the comparison group. Likewise, the *relative squared standard error of estimate index* is the quotient of the difference in current sample and comparison group squared standard errors of estimate, and the squared standard error of the comparison group. Researchers working with clinical samples (e.g. clinically depressed adults, bi-polar adults, etc) may find reduced reliability estimates related to sample homogeneity. These findings should be interpreted and the relative mean item variance index and the relative squared standard error of estimate index provide a quantitative way to interpret reduced internal consistency estimates when using homogenous samples.

Item Response Theory

Item Response Theory (IRT) offers an alternative to the CTT model of measurement. A thorough discussion of IRT is beyond the scope of this chapter (see Bond & Fox, 2007; Embretson & Reise, 2000; or Yu, Jannasch-Pennell, & DiGangi, 2008 for accessible introductions to IRT fundamentals). The goal here is to provide the reader with a conceptual understanding of the information provided by an IRT approach to personality measurement particularly as it relates to reliability or consistency of measurement.

In CTT reliability and standard error of measurement are functions of the test scores for a particular sample (Thompson, 2003). They do not reflect a universal characteristic of a test. IRT, however, offers the ability to estimate parameters that are neither sample nor item dependent. In classical test theory, an individual item is judged based on the strength of its correlation with the test. Item-test correlation provides the researcher with information on how well the item distribution and the test distribution correspond but provides no information on the quality of the item. In IRT, item quality is judged by the item information curve. Item information curves reflect the discrimination ability that an item provides at various levels of a latent trait (Reise, 1999). This is especially beneficial in test construction as the researcher can select items that provide maximum information at various trait levels. Item information curves can be summed to produce a test information curve that "indicates exactly where on the trait continuum the test provides maximal information" (Reise, 1999, p. 228).

The test information curve or test information function replaces the CTT concept of reliabiltity as a single index of internal consistency. The test information function provides information on the precision of the test at various trait levels. The standard error of measurement is calculated as the reciprocal of the square root of the information function and, therefore, also varies at different trait levels. CTT uses a single estimate for the standard error of measurement and assumes SEM to be constant for a given sample.

Although IRT is a powerful measurement tool, there are major obstacles to its widespread use for constructing and evaluating personality measures. IRT requires special software for analysis making technical components of analysis a challenge particularly for applied researchers. In addition, empirical studies have demonstrated that IRT and CTT often select the same items, have a strong correlation between total scores, and report high correlations between difficulty and discrimination parameters (Embretson & Reise, 2000). In light of this evidence most researchers would choose to use the more accessible CTT methods of analysis.

Standards for Interpreting Reliability Coefficients

In addition to careful selection of the reliability estimation method based on the measurement model and other considerations, another recurrent matter among researchers and practitioners involves minimally accepted standards, or benchmarks, for reliability estimates. It is quite common in social science disciplines for researchers to conclude that a reliability estimate of .70 is acceptable. The majority of these researchers cite one of Jum Nunnally's psychometric theory textbook editions to justify the use of a particular test if its score reliability falls at or above this target. As we will discover shortly, Nunnally's recommendations changed with subsequent editions of his text and are much more elaborate than a simple .70 benchmark.

A number of authors posit that benchmarks for reliability coefficients rest upon the intended outcome decision. Linn and Gronlund (2000) provide a heuristic based on reliability demands and the nature of a decision. They argue that high reliability is demanded when the decision is: (1) important; (2) final; (3) irreversible; (4) unconfirmable; (5) concerns individuals; or (6) has lasting consequences. On the other hand, low reliability is tolerable when the decision: (1) is of minor importance, (2) is made in early stages of decision making, (3) is reversible, (4) is confirmable by other data, (5) concerns groups, (6) has temporary effects. Linn and Gronlund, however, offer now specific numeric criteria for interpreting a high reliability coefficient from a low one. Murphy and Davidshofer (1988) suggest that high levels of reliability are necessary when tests are used to make final decisions about people or if individuals are to be sorted into a large number of groups based on relatively small individual differences. Lower levels of reliability may be acceptable if test scores are used for preliminary rather than final decisions or if tests are used to sort people into a small number of categories based upon gross individual differences.

Another issue for consideration, forwarded by Cronbach and Gleser (1965), is called the bandwidth-fidelity dilemma. The term bandwidth, from communication theory, refers to the amount of information that can be included in a message. Fidelity reflects the accuracy with which this information may be conveyed. Within the context of measurement, a decision must be made between measuring a narrowly-defined construct with a high degree of accuracy or a broader attribute with less accuracy. Of course, as previously discussed, a number of other issues affect the magnitude of the reliability coefficient. Each should be taken into consideration when developing or selecting a particular instrument.

The guidelines for the interpretation of reliability information are not straightforward. Nonetheless, a number of authors have proposed guidelines to facilitate interpretation of reliability coefficients (see Table 1). Going back some 80 years, Helmstadter (1964) reminds us of T. L. Kelly's (1927) classical guide for the interpretation of reliability coefficients for achievement tests. If tests are to be used to evaluate a level of group accomplishment, Kelly suggested a coefficient of .50. A coefficient of .90 was recommended in cases where differences in level of group accomplishment in two or more performances were to be evaluated. A reliability estimate of .94 was suggested if assessing level of individual accomplishment and a coefficient of .98 was recommended to evaluate differences in level of individual accomplishment on two or more performances. Helmstadter correctly notes that such stringent requirements are seldom adhered to today.

Nunnally's psychometric theory textbooks have become the prevailing source for reliability benchmark information. His recommendations have been summarized in Table 1. The reader will notice one important distinction between Nunnally's first (1967) and second editions (1978). For early stages of research, Nunnally (1967) recommended reliability coefficients of .50 to .60, adding that estimates above .80 may not be practical in terms of time or efficiency. In Nunnally's (1978) second edition, this coefficient was elevated to .70 for early stages of research. This modification was not amended in the latest edition (Nunnally & Bernstein, 1994) of the text. Henson (2001) correctly notes that researchers may take advantage of this change, citing Nunnally's first edition if low reliability coefficients are found (.50 - .60) or referencing his second edition if the loftier .70 criterion is reached.

Perhaps even more commonplace is the incorrect citation of Nunnally's .70 value as a rule of thumb for acceptable levels of score reliability. To illustrate this point, Lance, Butts, and Michels (2006) conducted a search of the Social Science Index for the Nunnally (1978) text between 2000 and 2004 across 11 journals. Of the 90 citations found, 44% referenced the .70 cutoff criterion in various ways. Through their thoughtful analysis of Nunnally's second edition, the authors correctly conclude that, "Nunnally's 'Standards of Reliability' section did not proclaim .70 as a universal standard of reliability", and "did not indicate that .70 reliability was adequate for research…or practice…" (p. 206). It is no wonder that Lance and colleagues refer to this as one urban myth common to research!

Each of Nunnally's editions provides a range of guidelines dependent on the intended use of the test. A coefficient of .80 or greater is suggested in an applied setting when cut-scores are being used (such as the decision to place a child in special education). Estimates in the .90 to .95 range are recommended in the settings where important decisions are based, at least in part, on test scores.

As can be seen from Table 1, recommendations vary from author to author. The lowest "useful" estimate recommended was 0.20, which the authors claim have clinical, though not psychometric, utility (Rust & Golombok, 1989). With the exception of Remmers and Gage (1955)'s .50 recommendation, (suggested almost 15 years before Nunnally's book was published) most authors appear to recommend a coefficient of .70 for basic research purposes.

Higher estimates are often recommended depending on the nature of the decision to be made from test scores. In contrast, we agree with Murphy and Davidshofer (1988) that an estimate of .70 should be considered a low estimate.

Table 1. Reliability recommendations by previous authors

Author	Recommendation
Aiken (1997)	.70 may be sufficient if differentiating between groups of people; at least .85 if differentiating between or within individuals
Domino & Domino (2006)	at least .80 to be considered reliable, although .80 may be too harsh a criterion for shorter scales
Groth-Marnat (1997)	.70 acceptable for research purposes; .90 if test is used to make clinical decisions
Guilford (1936; 1954)	No hard-and-fast rules can be stated for how high reliability coefficients should be
Hogan (2003)	depends on the use of the test; if used for research concerning group averages, a lesser degree of reliability may be acceptable; cites Nunnally and Bernstein (1994), Kaplan and Saccuzzo (2001), and Murphy and Davidshofer (1998) as benchmarks but makes no specific recommendation; cautions that one should be wary regarding the acceptance of lower reliability coefficients for shorter tests.
Kaplan & Saccuzzo (1982; 1993; 2005)	.70 to .80 may be good enough for most purposes in basic research; coefficients above .90 may be a waste of time and effort in refining research instruments (citing Nunnally, 1978); reliability extremely important in clinical settings, such that a coefficient of .90 may not be high enough; .95 or greater if test is used to make a decision affects a person's future.
Kline (1979)	around .70 (citing Guilford, 1956)
Kline (1993)	reliabilities should be ideally high, around .90 especially for ability tests; should never be below .70 (citing Guilford, 1956, and Nunnally, 1978)
Leary (1995)	.70 or greater considered adequate reliability
Lichtenberg & Goodyear (1999)	.85 or above when test scores are used to make decisions about individuals.
Loewenthal (1996)	typical estimates range from 0.70 - 0.95

Table 1. (Continued)

Author	Recommendation
McCall (1939)	.70 is sufficiently reliable for most purposes; .90 if test scores are used to make important judgements about individuals.
Mehrens & Lehmann (1984)	depends of the use of the test scores; no benchmark provided.
Murphy & Davidshofer (1988)	.60 is unacceptably low; .70 regarded as low; .80 or more considered moderate to high; .90 is considered high
Noll (1957); Noll, Scannell, & Craig (1979)	around .75 if test scores are used to study groups; .95 or higher for individual differentiation.
Nunnally (1967)	.50-.60 will suffice for early stages of research on predictor tests or hypothesized measures of a construct; for basic research coefficients above .80 are often wasteful; .80 is suggested for applied research when, for example, cut scores are involved; .90 suggested in applied settings when important decisions are made with .95 the desirable standard.
Nunnally (1978); Nunnally & Bernstein (1994)	.70 will suffice for early stages of research on predictor tests or hypothesized measures of a construct; for basic research, coefficients above .80 are often wasteful; .80 suggested for applied research when cut scores are involved; .90 suggested in applied settings when important decisions are made with .95 being the desirable standard.
Remmers & Gage (1955)	For research purposes, psychologists may find test useful if their reliability coefficients are as low as .50.
Rust & Golombok (1989)	Score reliability of personality measures of greater than 0.70 is expected; low reliabilities of 0.2 and lower are not unusual on projective tests and maybe useful in clinical settings to provide a diagnostic framework.
Schultz & Whitney (2005)	.70 or higher
Thorndike (1997); Thorndike & Hagen (1977)	offers no specific benchmark

Table 1. (Continued)

Author	Recommendation
Tyler & Walsh (1979)	not too much to expect that a reliability coefficient should be about .90, though for some purposes measures with lower score reliability may be used.
Whitla (1968)	.80s and .90s are sufficient for most purposes that involve using scores as information about individuals; .70s and low .80s are adequate for most purposes that involve using summaries of scores as information about groups.
Wilson (2005)	offers no specific benchmark

In order to further precision in measurement and reduce measurement error, we recommend reliability coefficients of .80 or greater for purposes of research. We reiterate Murphy and Davidshofer's naming convention for reliability coefficients: unacceptably low estimates would be in the .60 range, low estimates would be in the .70 range, .80 moderate to high, .90 would be considered high. Adhering to a standardized naming convention is important, particularly since there is so much confusion and ambiguity regarding the interpretation of reliability coefficients (Helms, Henze, Sass, & Mifsud, 2006).

Additional Considerations for Reporting and Interpreting Reliability Data

Given that reliability is not an inherent property of a measurement device, it is crucial that researchers calculate and report reliability coefficients from their own data. A number of suggestions are recommended here for purposes of proper interpretation and usage of reliability information. We borrow liberally from the works of Helms, Henze, Sass, and Mifsud (2006) and Onwuegbuzie and Daniel (2002), both of which provided detailed and excellent recommendations for reporting reliability information. Readers are directed to these useful guides for enhanced understanding of these issues.

Reliability coefficients are merely estimates of a theoretical reliability parameter. These estimates, like other statistics, are subject to sampling variability. Due to this variability, the reliability coefficient alone does not provide information regarding the proximity of the estimate from the true parameter. In situations in which assumptions are violated, such as essential tau-equivalence, the reliability coefficient may be an over-estimate or an under-estimate of the actual reliability parameter. To help remedy the discrepancy between the reliability estimate and the theoretical reliability, confidence intervals should be calculated and reported about the sample-specific reliability estimate. Confidence intervals provide the reader with a range of values in which the theoretical estimate is assumed to fall. A number of methods have been suggested for calculating confidence intervals for reliability estimates. Such detail is beyond the scope of this chapter, but interested readers may consult Onwuegbuzie and Daniel (2000) or Fan and Thompson (2001) for details.

Even in the best of examples, researchers may report reliability estimates using actual data; however, sub-group reliabilities are seldom, if ever, presented. Onwuegbuzie and Daniel (2000) determined that it is possible to obtain a high reliability estimate for the total sample if the reliability coefficient for one sub-group is low while high for the other group. Furthermore, using data from sub-groups with different reliability estimates can inflate Type I and Type II errors as well as attenuate effect sizes (Onwuegbuzie & Daniel, 2002). Therefore, it is recommended that researchers not only report reliability estimates for the overall sample but also should augment this information with reliability information from any sub-groups of interest. Confidence intervals may also be calculated for reliability estimates for sub-groups.

Low reliability estimates, in most cases, are problematic since measurement error accounts for a large percentage of the observed score variance. However, low reliability estimates may also be obtained in situations where data were collected from homogeneous samples. Heterogeneous, diverse samples have been found to yield higher estimates of score reliability than homogeneous samples. It is therefore recommended that researchers perform additional analyses if low reliability estimates are obtained. Roberts and Onwuegbuzie (2003) have provided two useful indices for detecting sample homogeneity when reliability estimates are low. These indices, *the mean item variance index* and the *relative squared standard error of estimate index*, have been detailed elsewhere in this chapter (see the section entitled Coefficient Alpha for explanations of these indices). We recommend examining and reporting these indices when observed reliability coefficients are unacceptably low.

Other recommendations for the reporting of reliability data have also been forwarded, including the use of tables (see Feldt & Ankenmann, 1999 for power table) to estimate the sample size needed to achieve a particular level of reliability, the reporting of relevant sample demographics (such as gender, mean age, and ethnicity) and sample scale responses (means and standard deviations) for comparison between current data and the normative sample(s), and issues regarding item deletion based on data analysis. These issues are each relevant, and the reader may wish to explore these issues in greater detail. Given that the reporting, analysis, and interpretation of reliability information could be never-ending, we focused attention on those issues we feel make the most practical contribution above and beyond the tradition of only reporting of the reliability coefficient.

CONCLUSION

The reader has been presented with the two broad psychometric theories for conceptualizing the reliability coefficient as well as estimation procedures for the calculation of reliability estimates within these theories. It is hoped that individuals will utilize this information carefully when conducting research or selecting an assessment device. If traditional methods for the estimation of reliability are used (e.g., coefficient alpha), we have provided useful information that will enhance the interpretation of these coefficients.

REFERENCES

Aiken, L. R. (1997). Questionnaires and inventories: Surveying opinions and assessing personality. New York: John Wiley & Sons.

Barnette, J. J. (2000). Effects of stem and Likert response option reversals on survey internal consistency: If you feel the need, there is a better alternative to using those negatively worded stems. Educational and Psychological Measurement, 60, 361-370.

Bollen, K. & Lennox, R. (1991). Conventional wisdom on measurement: A structural equation perspective. *Psychological Bulletin, 110,* 305-314.

Chang, L. (1994). A psychometric evaluation of 4-point and 6-point Likert-type scales in relation to reliability and validity. Applied Psychological Measurement, 18, 205-215.

Cook, C., Heath, F., Thompson, R. L., & Thompson, B. (2001). Score reliability in web-or internet based surveys: Unnumbered graphic rating scales versus Likert-type scales. Educational and Psychological Measurement, 61, 697-706.

Crocker, L. & Algina, J. (1986). Introduction to classical and modern test theory. Belmont, CA: Wadsworth.

Cronbach, L. J., Schönemann, P. & McKie, D. (1965). Alpha coefficients for stratifiedparallel tests. Educational and Psychological Measurement, 25, 291-312.

Domino, G. & Domino, M. L. (2006). Psychological testing: An introduction (2nd Edition). New York: Cambridge University Press.

Edwards, J. R. & Bagozzi, R. P. (2000). On the nature and direction of relationships between constructs and measures. Psychological Methods. 5, 155-174.

Embretson, S. E. & Reise, S. P. (2000). Item response theory for psychologists. Mahwah, NJ: Lawrence Erlbaum.

Ferketich, S. (1990). Internal consistency estimates of reliability. Research in Nursing & Health, 13, 437-440.

Graham, J.M. (2006). Congeneric and (essentially) tau-equivalent estimates of score reliability. *Educational and Psychological Measurement, 66,* 930-934.

Greer, T., Dunlap, W. P., Hunter, S. T., & Berman, M. E. (2006). Skew and internal consistency. *Journal of Applied Psychology, 91,* 1351-1358.Groth-Marnat, G. (1997). *Handbook of psychological assessment (3rd Edition).* New York: John Wiley & Sons.

Guilford, J. P. (1936). *Psychometric methods (1st Edition).* New York: McGraw-Hill.

Guilford, J. P. (1954). *Psychometric methods (2nd Edition).* New York: McGraw-Hill.

Helmstadter, G. C. (1964). *Principles of psychological measurement.* New York: Appleton-Century-Crofts.

Henson, R. K. (2001). Understanding internal consistency reliability estimates: A conceptual primer on coefficient alpha. *Measurement and Evaluation in Counseling and Development, 34,* 177-189.

Hershberger, S.L. (1999). Introduction to personality measurement. In Embretson, S.E., & Hershberger, S.L. (Eds.), *The new rules of measurement: What every psychologist and educator should know* (pp. 153-158). Mahwah, NJ: Lawrence Erlbaum.

Hogan, T. P. (2003). *Psychological testing: A practical introduction.* New York: John Wiley & Sons.

Hogan, T. P., Benjamin, A. & Brezinzki, K. L. (2000). Reliability methods: A note on the frequency of use of various types. *Educational and Psychological Measurement, 60,* 523-531.

Jacoby, J. & Matell, M. S. (1971). Three-point Likert scales are good enough. *Journal of Marketing Research, 8,* 495-500.

Kaplan, R. M., & Saccuzzo, D. P. (1982). *Psychological testing: Principles, applications, and issues.* Belmont, CA: Brooks/Cole.

Kaplan, R. M., & Saccuzzo, D. P. (1993). *Psychological testing: Principles, applications, and issues* (3rd Edition). Pacific Grove, CA: Brooks/Cole.

Kaplan, R. M. & Saccuzzo, D. P. (2005). *Psychological testing: Principles, applications, and issues* (6th Edition). Belmont, CA: Thomson Wadworth

Kline, P. (1979). *Psychometrics and psychology.* London: Academic Press.

Kline, P. (1993). *The handbook of psychological testing.* London: Routledge.

Leary, M. R. (1995). *Introduction to behavioral research methods* (2nd Edition). Pacific Grove, CA: Brooks/Cole.

Li, H., Rosenthal, R. & Rubin, D. B. (1996). Reliability of measurement in psychology: From Spearman-Brown to maximal reliability. *Psychological Methods, 1,* 98-107.

Lichtenberg, J. W. & Goodyear, R. K. (1999). *Scientist-practitioner perspectives on test interpretation.* Boston, MA: Allyn & Bacon.

Linn, R. L. & Gronlund, N. E. (2000). *Measurement and assessment in teaching (8th Edition).* Upper Saddle River, NJ: Prentice Hall.

Loewenthal, K.M. (1996). *An introduction to psychological tests and scales.* London: UCL Press.

Lucke, J. F. (2005). The α and the ω of congeneric test theory: An extension of reliability and internal consistency to heterogeneous tests. *Applied Psychological Measurement, 29,* 65-81.

Marcoulides, G. A. (1999). Generalizability theory: Picking up where the Rasch IRT model leaves off? In Embretson, S.E., & Hershberger, S.L. (Eds.), *The new rules of measurement: What every psychologist and educator should know* (pp. 129-152). Mahwah, NJ: Lawrence Erlbaum.

Mc Call, W. A. (1939). *Measurement.* New York: The MacMillan Company.

Mehrens, W. A. & Lehmann, I. J. (1984). *Measurement and evaluation in education and psychology* (3rd Edition). New York: Holt, Rinehart, & Winston.

Murphy, K. R. & Davidshofer, C. O. (1988). *Psychological testing: Principles and applications.* Englewood Cliffs, NJ: Prentice Hall.

Noll, V. H. (1957). *Introduction to educational measurement.* Cambridge, MA: The Riverside Press.

Noll, V. H., Scannell, D. P. & Craig, R. C. (1979). *Introduction to educational measurement* (4th Edition). Boston, MA: Houghton Mifflin.

Nunnally, J. C. (1967). *Psychometric theory.* New York: McGraw-Hill.

Nunnally, J. C. (1978). *Psychometric theory (2nd Edition).* New York: McGraw-Hill.

Nunnally, J. C. & Bernstein. I. H. (1994). *Psychometric theory (3rd Edition).* New York : McGraw-Hill.

Onwuegbuzie, A. J. & Daniel, L. G. (2002). A framework for reporting and interpreting internal consistency reliability estimates. *Measurement and Evaluation in Counseling and Development, 35,* 89-103.

Pedhazur, E. J. & Schmelkin, L. P. (1991). *Measurement, design, and analysis: An integrated approach.* Hillsdale, NJ: Lawrence Erlbaum.

Reise, S. P. (1999). Personality measurement issues viewed through the eyes of IRT. In Embretson, S.E., & Hershberger, S.L. (Eds.), *The new rules of measurement: What every psychologist and educator should know* (pp. 219-241). Mahwah, NJ: Lawrence Erlbaum.

Remmers, H. H. & Gage, N. L. (1955). *Educational measurement and evaluation (revised edition).* New York: Harper & Brothers.

Roberts, J. K. & Onwuegbuzie, A. J. (2003). Alternative approaches for interpreting alpha with homogenous subsamples. *Research in the Schools, 10,* 63-69.

Rust, J. & Golombok. S. (1989). *Modern psychometrics (2nd Edition).* London: Routledge.

Shultz, K. S. & Whitney, D. J. (2005). *Measurement theory in action: Case studies and exercises.* Thousand Oaks, CA: Sage Publications.

Shavelson, R. J. & Webb, N. M. (1991). *Generalizability theory: A primer.* Newbury Park, CA: Sage.

Tarkkonen, L. & Vehkalahti, K. (2005). Measurement errors in multivariate measurement scales. *Journal of Multivariate Analysis, 96,* 172-189.

Thompson, B. (1994). Guidelines for authors. *Educational and Psychological Measurement, 54,* 837-847.

Thompson, B. (Ed.) (2003). *Score reliability: Contemporary thinking on reliability issues.* Thousand Oaks, CA: Sage.

Thompson, B. & Vacha-Haase, T. (2000). Psychometrics is datametrics: The test is not reliable. *Educational and Psychological Measurement, 60*, 174-195.

Thorndike, R. L., & Hagen, (1977). *Measurement and evaluation in psychology and education* (4th Edition). New York: John Wiley & Sons.

Thorndike, R. M. (1997). *Measurement and evaluation in psychology and education (6th Edition).* Upper Saddle River, NJ: Prentice Hall.

Tyler, L. E. & Walsh, W. B. (1979). *Tests and measurements (3rd Edition).* Englewood Cliffs, NJ: Prentice Hall.

Vehkalahti, K., Puntanen, S. & Tarkkonen, L. (2006). Estimation of reliability: A better alternative for Chronbach's alpha. Reports on Mathematics 430, Department of Mathematics and Statistics, University of Helsinki, Helsinki, Finland, {http://mathstat.helsinki.fi/reports/Preprint430.pdf}

Waller, N. G. (1999). Searching for structure in the MMPI. In Embretson, S.E., & Hershberger, S.L. (Eds.), *The new rules of measurement: What every psychologist and educator should know* (pp. 185-217). Mahwah, NJ: Lawrence Erlbaum.

Weems, G. H. & Onwuegbuzie, A. J. (2001). The impact of midpoint responses and reverse coding on survey data. *Measurement and Evaluation in Counseling and Development, 34,* 166-176.

Whitla, D. K. (1968). *Handbook of measurement and assessment in behavioral sciences.* Reading, MA: Addison-Wesley.

Wilson, M. (2005). *Constructing measures: An item response modeling approach.* Mahwah, NJ: Lawrence Erlbaum.

Yu, C.H., Jannasch-Pennell, A., & DiGangi, (2008). A non-technical approach for illustrating item response theory, *Journal of Applied Testing Technology, 9,* {http://www.testpublishers.org/jattmain.htm}.

In: Personality Assessment: New Research
Editor: Lauren B. Palcroft & Melissa V. Lopez
ISBN 978-1-60692-796-0

Chapter 10

RESTYLING PERSONALITY ASSESSMENTS

Willem K.B. Hofstee
The Heymans Institute, University of Groningen
Grote Kruisstraat 1-2
9712 TS Groningen, Netherlands
tel. +31 50 3636366
w.k.b.hofstee@rug.nl

ABSTRACT

Personality is a matter of assessment, not an objective natural science; at least for the near future, that alternative is not in sight. Consequently, students of personality might as well try to optimize their assessment methods as such. One obstacle to optimal personality assessment is reliance on self-report, and the subjective definition of personality that it implies. To enhance the reliability and validity of assessments, knowledgeable others should be enlisted to report on the characteristic behavior of the target person. This intersubjective approach to personality appears to have consequences for the content of personality questionnaires: A shift from experiential to behavioral item content is appropriate. Another obstacle to faithful assessment is the reliance on relative scales in reporting about personality. The implied model, based on classical applied statistics, ignores the bipolar nature (e.g., introverted vs. extraverted) of personality assessments; its range of application is limited to approaches in which individuals are compared with one another. I explore the consequences of an alternative psychometric-statistical model based on proportional scores on a bipolar scale. Its side-effect is to challenge current ideas about personality structure.

Keywords: personality assessment, self-report, other-report, intersubjectivity, item content, biproportional scale, personality structure.

Introduction

Systematic personality assessment is a four-party game: A diagnostician D asks questions to judges or assessors J about the target person P, and reports to an audience A. The script may be condensed in a number of ways, of which self-report is the most popular one. Accumulations of roles, however, cannot mask the fact that personality data consist of judgments rather than objective measurements, and deserve specific methodological reflection. I focus on the two central phases in the assessment process: first, the communication between D and J, in which personality assessments of P are gathered; second, on the phase in which D processes the data in order to report to A about P. With respect to both phases, my aim is to contribute to faithful communication, in the interest of A. My primary concern are cases where P and A are the same individual, rather than settings where P has mere object status; still, that makes it all the more important to distinguish between A and P.

Two central recommendations result from the analysis. With respect to the data gathering phase, the emphasis should be on third persons J rather than self-report; the instruments – questionnaires in a wide sense – should be geared to that application. With respect to the reporting phase, faithful communication is served by using an absolute scale, specifically, a bipolar proportional (biproportional, for short) format, rather than customary relative scales. Between the lines of the analysis, a pragmatic conception of personality diagnosis emerges which aims at making the individual wiser, even if sadder, about the social effects of his or her characteristic behaviors.

Personality Assessors: Others Versus Self

For practical purposes, personality is judgmental rather than natural. No one can claim to have measured anybody's personality in a legitimate sense of the word: In between the person and the score, there is a human assessor, whether that be the individual himself or herself, a third person, or the diagnostician himself or herself. Even behavior observation (e.g., Borkenau, Riemann, & Spinath, 2000), if it is to be relevant, is inescapably subjective to some extent.

One reaction to this state of affairs is to ignore and deny it, and to act as if we were walking on firm natural ground, to the bewilderment of bystanders who see us drowning in the quicksand of opinions, for lack of proper precautions. Another way of reacting is to acknowledge the precariousness of our database as a temporary affair, awaiting solid stepping-stones in the swamp. The most likely candidate for a reductionist solution to the predicament of personality is the genome. Behavior-genetic researchers have rendered an invaluable service to personality by showing that there must be something solid out there. However, one may envisage the condition under which we should be ready to substitute any objective indicator for fallible assessments of personality: The correspondence between the two should be close enough to perfect after correction for the unreliability of the assessments, so that it is just noise we are discarding. By any reasonable standard, the fulfillment of that condition is not in sight (Hofstee, 2003).

In the meantime, which may take a long while or even forever, we might as well get serious about assessing personality, rather than hesitating forever between objective measurement, which is unattainable so far, and subjective judgment, which does not provide solid ground. The obvious way out is to turn intersubjective. The basic question in personality is about someone's characteristic behavior. For the time being, the only legitimate answer is in a relative consensus of assessors who know that person well enough. Our scientific job is to capture that consensus. Trying to do so is difficult enough. We might as well take pride in it, rather than neglecting our assignment. We are by no means alone in this: Sociologists, lawyers, linguists and many others are called upon to make sense out of human judgment.

A judgmental definition of personality does not mean that personality does not exist. That would be the case in a subjective conception: If personality would be in the eye of the individual beholder, we would have as many personalities as there are relevant beholders including ourselves, and therefore, no personality. However, personality does exist in the relative consensus of the beholders, as a person main effect apart from any perceiver main effects and person-perceiver interaction.

Self-Report

An intersubjective definition of personality is not a plea to do away with self-report, but to reflect on its proper place. First, to the extent that self-reports agree with assessments by others, they add to the reliability of assessments. Thus in the general case, the person himself or herself may profitably be enlisted as a member among others on the board of assessors. Some would predict that the self-reporter would in fact play a leading role, precisely: that self-report would show a higher correspondence with the board average than a single other-report would, the reason being that self is better informed. Others would argue that people do not tend to focus on their own behavior but on the environment; this fundamental attribution error would cause them to be outliers amidst the others. Which of the two will appear to be the case is of course an empirical matter.

Second, one may wish to use self-report as a surrogate for personality assessment. As long as we realize that it is not the real thing, that strategy may be rational from a cost-benefit point of view: On the one hand, self-report is less representative than an average over judges, in which idiosyncrasies are cancelled out; on the other, it is cheaper, and the contribution of any additional assessor is subject to the law of diminishing returns as specified by the Spearman-Brown formula. However, with electronically administered questionnaires both the initial and additional costs are reduced to a fraction of what they were in the times when self-report took over personality assessment (see, Vazire, 2006).

Third, to the extent that subjective personality deviates systematically from the consensus of others, such deviations may be found clinically relevant. A person who regards himself or herself as a savior of the human kind may be judged intolerant (if nothing else) by others. In clinical diagnosis and treatment, discrepancies are potentially much more relevant than would appear from the virtual absence of self-other comparisons in practice. At the very least, a client could benefit from a systematic confrontation between the two perspectives; the exclusive self-report approach, which implicitly grants sovereignty to the individual's subjective definition of his or her personality, is hardly productive in this respect. Instead of self-report, a diagnostician might be even more interested in the extent to which the individual is able to predict the consensus of others, turning a personality questionnaire into a measure of psychological intelligence (see, Hofstee, 2001).

Finally, a self-report questionnaire may be conceived as a projective test: The responses are not to be taken at face value, but require psychodynamic interpretation by experts. The classical example consists of items like "I never lie", originally intended as indicative of dishonesty (rather than honesty), but later interpreted as a sign of rigidity. There is no problem in principle with dynamic interpretation, as self-perceptions are subject to bias by any reasonable standard. A practical problem, however, is how these interpretations may be validated. The obvious criterion is again in the consensus of others who know the target individual well enough: The implied expert prediction is that a person who finds himself or herself utterly honest, would be found rigid by significant others. If that prediction would fail, the expert might realize that these others' judgments are more relevant to the client than expert dynamic interpretation – barring cases in which the social future of the client revolves around dynamic experts rather than lay significant others. For the general case, the moral seems to be that the expert does better asking significant others directly than taking a speculative detour via the target person.

In summary, the relative consensus of others provides the point of reference in personality assessment. All nuances and seeming exceptions reaffirm rather than weaken this point. A personality diagnostician *D*'s task is to solicit the assessments of a sufficient number of significant others using an appropriate questionnaire phrased in the third person singular.

Personality Language

The judgmental status of personality implies an emphasis on ordinary language in describing individual differences. Personality consists of things people say about each other's characteristic behaviors, rather than, for example, a set of natural elements as in chemistry. The dominance of the lexical paradigm (see, e.g., De Raad, 2000) reflects that judgmental emphasis.

The lexical paradigm has many problems, and much of the history of personality consists of attempts to face them. A comprehensive inventory of personality talk would consist of not only trait adjectives, but also of nouns, verbs, sentences, paragraphs, up to biographies and novels. Moreover, each of these subsets is fuzzy. Furthermore, ordinary language is subject to culture and history. Still, it is probably fair to say that the lexical approach has yielded a workable and robust core definition of personality. At the very least, there is no viable alternative. In earlier days, myriads of theoretical concepts have been put forward, referring to all sorts of underlying mechanisms. However, one should acknowledge that these concepts and mechanisms had metaphorical, not causal status. It is one thing to be inspired by an analogy between, for example, a particular physiological mechanism and a way of behaving, but quite another to empirically demonstrate a one-to-one correspondence between the two. Most would-be technical terms in personality have the same as-if status as everyday trait words like hard and soft: There is no corresponding state of nature that causes the trait.

Expert diagnosticians might object that they need technical terms in their communication with other professionals, making assessments in terms of everyday language irrelevant. The proper question, however, is whether such lay judgments can be translated into technical terms, and the answer is affirmative. By way of a demonstration experiment (Hofstee, 1999),

I asked clinicians to score their favorite personality disorder – to wit, its prototype, not a particular client – on an everyday-language personality questionnaire. The instrument was the Five-Factor Personality Inventory (FFPI, Hendriks, Hofstee, & De Raad, 1999), which does not contain any pathological items or technical terms. The prototypical disorder profiles, averaged over some 5 experts each, appeared to be clearly distinguishable; for example, the histrionic and avoidant personality disorders were 6 standard deviations apart on the extraversion factor, and the same distance was found between dependent and antisocial on agreeableness. The only two profiles that were close together were narcissistic and antisocial, even though their difference on the conscientiousness factor was still 1.4 standard deviations. The demonstration is not to suggest that actual clients should be expected to have such extreme scores, but it does prove that naïve assessments are easily associated with technical terms. Even intra-professional communication should be expected to profit from the prototyping procedure: Even though there was considerable consensus among the experts, idiosyncratic profilings were also observed; for an extreme example, the between-experts standard deviation ran up to 1.8 with respect to the agreeableness of the dependent disorder.

Third-Person Questionnaires

The language of personality questionnaires betrays their near-exclusive reliance on self-report, the only clear exception being the FFPI (Hendriks, Hofstee, & De Raad, 1999) which was phrased in the third person singular right from the start. Shifting the emphasis to an intersubjective definition of personality appears to bring about more than just a straightforward grammatical transposition: The questionnaire concept undergoes subtle semantic and pragmatic changes as well. The transition is best envisaged by following our (Mosterman & Hofstee, 2006) attempts to transpose certain items from established personality questionnaires.

Take the MMPI-type item "Somebody is trying to poison me". Evidently, the third-person equivalent is not "Somebody is trying to poison him/her", the answer to which would be relevant in a court rather than a clinic, but a transposition preceded by "He/she feels/thinks/finds/fears that ...". Advocates of a subjective definition of personality might even hold that the item cannot be transposed at all, as others cannot look inside the person. However, in an intersubjective context the item may still be found personality-relevant in at least two ways. First, the person may have shared such feelings with the significant others in question, enabling them to give an informed answer to the item. In that case, the item is paradoxically relevant in that it reflects a measure of trust in that audience (even if not in humans in general). More precisely, it is the correspondence between self and others – or lack of it – that makes the item valuable. Second, an affirmative answer may indeed represent a mere guess by someone trying to take the point of view of the person; in that case, it is relevant as a way of saying that the target person is paranoid. In any event, the intersubjective program does not dictate the discarding of experiential items. However, what one might find is that such items place the responsibility for someone's personality on his or her significant others, by requiring them to take that person's own perspective; in the long run, the individual may be better served by the reverse process, which is taking the others' point of view.

The relational nature of typical third-person items, in their turn, is illustrated by attempts to transpose them to the first person singular. Take "he/she overestimates himself/herself". In the first person, the answer would be paradoxical: If I agree that I overestimate myself, I am no longer overestimating myself; if I disagree, one might take that as just another proof of the proposition. The only way to meaningfully answer the item is to take a third person's perspective. It would thus seem correct to say that the intersubjective conception of personality defines it by its social effects. However, the pragmatic implications of the approach are rather the reverse: In the rebound, a reporting to the individual on his or her effective personality fosters that person's awareness of it, in the best psychological tradition of promoting the person's autonomy through enlightment.

Reporting Assesments: Absolute versus Relative Scales

After having collected judgments by knowledgeable assessors, the diagnostician's task is to process the data and communicate the outcome to the audience. Traditionally, assessments are handled by interval scaling and corresponding correlational analysis. The implication is that we are exclusively interested in comparative assessment. Our methodology is directed to questions such as who is more extraverted, John or Mary; our exclusive application perspective seems to be the choosing between individuals, as in personnel selection. Apparently, we do not even allow ourselves to ask whether Mary is at all extraverted, or an extravert. For, at an early stage in our scientific development we have decided that means are meaningless, that raw scores can be transformed at will, and that our scales do not contain any natural reference point. Therefore, to ask whether Mary is extraverted rather than introverted all by herself, is asking a silly question, the kind of thing that should be left to unenlightened laypersons. In other words, we have ruled out absolute judgment, in the sense of pitting an individual against some standard instead of comparing individuals amongst each other.

One may object that students of personality have given much attention to another alternative to interindividual comparison, namely, intra-individual comparison, or a person-centered approach as opposed to the dominant variable-centered approach. However, even in such ipsative conceptions of personality, scores have routinely been standardized per variable, thus column-wise, before taking the row-wise perspective. This interval-scaling reflex has peculiar consequences. For an elementary illustration, take the following set of raw assessment scores on a bipolar proportional scale running from –1 to +1:

	Extr	Neur
A	+.50	+.20
B	+.30	–.05
C	+.00	–.05

Person A shows a clear preponderance of extraverted over introverted behavior, and is slightly on the neurotic side; person B is more mildly but also more exclusively extraverted, and C does not have much personality at all in these respects. After column-wise standardization, however, these scores are as follows:

Extr		Neur
A	1.14	1.41
B	.16	–.71
C	–1.30	–.71

Whereas the assessors judged that extraversion was more applicable to persons A and B than neuroticism, these persons are now depicted primarily in terms of neuroticism. In the standardization process, person C has suddenly become clearly introverted. It is as if you are being told that you actually like cod-liver oil because the average person despises it even more than you do. Not even small children buy that, only psychologists do. The assessors in the example might well shake their heads in disbelief over the way their judgments are twisted around. Surely, one may come up with sophisticated rationalizations for contaminating the intra-individual perspective with interindividual standardization. But the suspicion lingers that it arose from a statistical reflex, rather than from methodological reflection.

The moral of the story so far is not that absolute scaling is needed for intra-individual comparison. The point is that comparison, whether row-wise or column-wise, ipsative or normative, is not the only legitimate perspective on personality. The other perspective consists of assessment in absolute terms, or comparing the person with a standard if one wishes. There are many situations in life where absolute judgment is in place. If the question is whether a client is resilient enough to profit from a particular treatment, or whether a student is clever enough for a particular kind of school, or whether an applicant has a positive expected value for the organization, the proper answer is not in comparing individuals. If, in an individual setting, the question is whether the individual is talented enough to pursue an artistic career, the answer is not in exploring his or her potential in other fields. Absolute judgment is appropriate in many basic and applied problems involving thresholds, and our addiction to interval scaling is no valid excuse for shunning these problems.

Next, those of us who have paid attention to absolute scales will be inclined to think of them in terms of all-positive quantities or counts (see, most notably, Cohen et al., 1999). However, the domain of personality, or qualities in general, is best represented in a bipolar fashion. I have therefore proposed the bipolar proportion or percentage scale to represent assessments (Hofstee, 2002). An attractive interpretation of scale points is in terms of balance: For example, a score of $p = +.50$ may be viewed as a $.75 - .25$ (or $½[p + 1] - ½[1 - p]$) surplus of positive over negative instances of a trait. Thus the recommended scoring of the familiar 5-point Likert scale is [–1, -.5, 0, +.5, 1].

The argument in favor of absolute scales is best appreciated referring to cases in which they make a difference, that is, when variables have a clearly skewed distribution (e.g., conscientiousness). Take Mary, whose score on a biproportional conscientiousness scale is +.2, whereas the average in the relevant population is +.6; the question is whether Mary should be reported to be conscientious or sloppy. An appropriate way of viewing such a diagnosis is in terms of prediction: On the basis of her past characteristic behavior, as assessed by knowledgeable others in relevant situations, should we predict that she will behave conscientiously in a future sample of such situations? Ideally, the assessors have given the diagnostician a probability estimate, more precisely, a balance of probabilities: Their informed guess is that Mary will behave conscientiously in 60% of the relevant situations, and unconscientiously in 40%, the balance being +.2. Thus, in the absence of other relevant information, the diagnostician should predict that Mary will behave conscientiously in the next situation, even though that prediction is very uncertain (note that the prediction is not that Mary will behave somewhat conscientiously, whatever that may mean). Does the fact that the population balance is 80% − 20% = +.6, so that Mary is a lot less conscientious than average, change that prediction? At the very least, it does not detract from her positive score; on the contrary, any bayesian would consider the population mean as relevant prior information, and regress her score towards the mean so that it would be increased instead of decreased. So, relative scaling only serves to obfuscate the meaning of the assessment.

The Likeness Coefficient

Accepting an absolute scale for non-comparative purposes leads to alternative measures of association. For, if one would compute Pearson correlations between absolute scores, the scale would retroactively be turned into an interval scale. The problem is illustrated by the following example:

	Assessors		
	1	2	3
A	.9	.8	-.8
B	.8	.9	-.9

Between assessors *1* and *2*, the Pearson correlation is −1, whereas their absolute agreement on the [−1 ...+1] scale is high by any reasonable standard; between assessors *1* and *3*, the correlation is +1, but their agreement is highly negative in absolute terms. So a coefficient of association is needed that reflects the absolute character of the scale. We (Hofstee, 2002; Hofstee & Ten Berge, 2004a,b) have proposed using the simplest index of all for biproportional scales, namely, the cross-product average or Likeness coefficient $L = \Sigma XY/N$. In the example above:

	Likenesses		
	L_{12}	L_{13}	L_{23}
A	+.72	-.72	-.64
B	+.72	-.72	-.81
Mean	+.72	-.72	-.725

Note that *L* is defined in the individual case: Each person has his or her own set of Likeness coefficients. Together, these intra-individual coefficients would express the intra-individual trait structure if *1, 2,* and *3* were traits instead of assessors. Note also that the Likeness coefficient at the aggregate level is the mean of the individual coefficients, in other words, the interindividual trait structure is the mean of the intra-individual structures. Thus a long-lasting controversy between the person-oriented and variable-oriented approaches in personality has dissolved: They have become each other's counterpoint in a harmonious melody.

Perhaps the trumpets of this methodological victory should be muted somewhat because of a complication: The *L*-coefficient is sensitive to the size of the scores. Pairs of identical scores give a perfect *L* only if both scores are extreme, that is, ± 1. On the one hand, this property expresses a fact of life: For example, one would hardly say that two persons are alike *qua* extraversion if both their scores on that trait were close to the scale midpoint; one would look for another trait. On the other hand, the likeness interpretation does not correspond with more familiar conceptions of association, such as covariation and identity. There exists a radical solution to this complication, namely, dichotomizing the scores to [+1, -1]. That turns the *L*-coefficient, as well as Zegers and Ten Berge's (1985) Identity coefficient and Tucker's (1951) *phi* into an agreement coefficient proposed by Holley and Guilford (1964), among others, which equals $2p - 1$, with p the proportion of agreements. One might call this dichotomizing the typological solution. It has some primitive appeal to it, although it runs counter to our collective taste for nuances, and to the investments that we have made in developing continuous models.

Personality Structure

Finally, the toolbox consisting of biproportional scales and Likeness coefficients enables an alternative approach to summarizing assessment data over judges and over items. The obvious method is raw-scores principal component analysis. Principal components are optimally weighted averages of scores. Setting the sum of the absolute weights w to 1 (i.e., $\Sigma|w| = 1$), the principal-component scores are on the same biproportional scale as the original scores.

In an illustrative study (Hofstee & Ten Berge, 2004a), we extracted five such principal components. The scores on each of these raw-score components were almost perfectly (R>.98) predictable from the scores that were found in a classical, standardized big-five solution. Still, the raw-scores solution looks radically different. Table 1, containing the component scores of the first 12 persons, gives an impression.

Table 1: Bipolar Proportional Scores on 5 Principal Components

1	2	3	4	5
0.14	-0.09	-0.05	0.02	0.03
0.22	0.07	0.04	0.10	0.07
0.30	-0.03	0.01	0.04	-0.03
0.23	-0.11	0.06	0.06	0.04
0.41	-0.07	-0.08	0.02	-0.05
0.14	0.22	0.04	0.18	0.04
0.22	0.07	-0.02	0.03	-0.02
0.27	-0.19	-0.04	0.04	0.16
0.23	0.00	-0.13	0.02	0.13
0.30	0.01	0.10	-0.01	0.03
0.34	0.23	-0.06	-0.04	-0.01
0.39	-0.02	0.01	-0.07	0.17

Scores in the range of −.25 to .25 may be called neutral. So, half of these persons, 35% in the total sample, have no personality at all, in an absolute as opposed to comparative sense. The nonneutral scores are concentrated on the first principal component, which represents socially desirable or moral behavior. In the total sample, 95% of the persons had positive scores on this component; of these, 63% were nonneutral. The taxonomy of personality that arises from these findings is mainly that by far the most people are faintly to mildly OK; a few are not.

Rammstedt and others (2004) reported on a typological study that also found three kinds of persons: desirable, undesirable, and neutral. The main difference is in the distribution over types. Rammstedt and others used standardized scores, which leads to a more even distribution. The skewed distribution resulting from our approach is more realistic.

Our approach provides a convenient, person-oriented procedure for deciding on the number of principal components. This is because the size of the components is also reflected in the component scores, instead of only in the loadings as in standard principal component analysis. Table 2, in which the component scores have been standardized column-wise to simulate the standard solution, illustrates the point.

Table 2: Standard Scores

1	2	3	4	5
-1.45	-0.78	-0.61	-0.19	-0.23
-0.53	0.50	0.76	**1.05**	0.32
0.39	-0.30	0.31	0.12	**-1.05**
-0.41	-0.94	**1.07**	0.43	-0.09
1.66	-0.62	**-1.07**	-0.19	**-1.32**
-1.45	**1.69**	0.76	**2.30**	-0.09
-0.53	0.50	-0.15	-0.04	-0.91
0.05	**-1.57**	-0.46	0.11	**1.55**
-0.41	-0.06	**-1.83**	-0.19	**1.14**
0.39	0.02	**1.68**	-0.66	-0.23
0.86	**1.77**	-0.76	**-1.13**	-0.77
1.43	-0.22	0.31	**-1.60**	**1.68**

The standardized scoring gives the familiar picture of highly differentiated scores per component; moreover, since the components are orthogonal, every person is likely to receive a characteristic score on at least one component (only one person does not have much of a personality). For the same reason, however, these standardized scores are unfit for a decision on the number of principal components. Using the absolute scores, one can apply familiar criteria, for example, whether any persons have a nonneutral score on a particular component, or whether any persons have their highest score on a particular component. With the 133 persons in our study, the results were as follows:

Component	1	2	3	4	5
Nonneutral score on component	81	4	3	0	0
Highest score on component	113	12	5	1	2

According to these figures, three principal components are worth considering. Still, the pile-up on the first factor is in contrast with the differentiation provided by the familiar taxonomy of five big orthogonal components. This is where the abridged-circumplex model (Hofstee, De Raad, & Goldberg) comes to rescue. It takes secondary loadings into account. I apply this model to the principal-component scores, instead of the loadings. In Table 3, a person who has his or her highest score on the first principal component, but a secondary score on the third component, is placed in the **1+** column, **3+** row (if both scores are positive). With 3 components and 6 poles, one may form 30 types. Unsurprisingly, the first principal component dominates the structure, so that most types are empty or nearly empty (containing fewer than 5% of the persons in the sample). What remains is the magical number of 5 types scoring primarily (see, column) on the **1+** pole, see, Table 3.

Table 3: Person Types in Terms of Primary (Column) and Secondary (Row) Scores on Principal Components

	1+	1-	2+	2-	3+	3-
1+	25	×	2	3	-	-
1-	×	-	2	-	-	1
2+	21	1	-	×	-	-
2-	18	-	×	-	1	1
3+	8	1	-	-	-	×
3-	9	-	1	-	×	-

Together, these types covering over 60% of the sample may give an acceptable taxonomy of normal personality, if one realizes that many of the remaining persons in the sample had neutral scores on all type vectors. Deviant types show low frequencies. For example, the sample contains one person whose highest score is on **1–** (Takes advantage of others, Abuses people's confidence, Insults/hurts people, etc.) and whose secondary score is on **2+** (Takes charge, wants to pull the strings, Makes his/her own rules, etc.), suggesting a narcissistic personality disorder, and one person who combines abusive (**1–**) with neurotic (**3+**, Needlessly worries a lot, Is afraid that he/she will do the wrong thing, Worries himself/herself to death) behavior, suggesting a borderline type.

In a clinical sample, deviant types might be expected to show higher frequencies. Hofstee, Barelds, and Ten Berge (2006) applied the toolbox consisting of biproportional scaling, raw-scores principal component analysis using *L*-coefficients, and abridged-circumplex typing to self-report questionnaire data of psychiatric patients. Although a number of clinical types could be identified, among which a nervous, an obsessive-compulsive, and a shy type, the results were sobering in a number of ways. First, a depressive syndrome, which could be clearly identified on the basis of the questionnaire items, contained no individuals. Even though there can be no doubt that some patients were relatively depressive, their personalities appeared not to be dominated by that syndrome in an absolute sense. Second, two prominent types were best characterized as resilient, respectively, indignant, neither of which can be called pathological. Third, a sizeable proportion of these individuals could not be classified at all, meaning that they had no salient personality in an absolute sense. That does not mean that they were normal statistically: The average normal person is characterized by a deviation from the scale midpoint in a socially desirable direction. It does mean that these patients should not be predicted to behave abnormally in relevant situations – if their self-reports were representative in that respect. That is quite different from diagnosing almost every individual in any population as relatively disturbed in one way or another, as in relative statistics.

CONCLUSION

On reflection, there is much continuity between the standard view in personality structure and the present model based on absolute scores. On the one hand, over the past years I (see, e.g., Hofstee, 2003) have drawn attention to the large first principal component, or p-factor, even in standard analysis, arising from the fact that the correlations between variables scored in socially desirable direction are overwhelmingly positive. On the other hand, the even larger first principal component of absolute scores does not preclude further differentiation. What happens is that the orthogonal big-five structure folds into an oblique one of lower dimensionality.

The habit of standardizing scores rests on two considerations. One is that raw scores on tests containing different numbers of items would be incomparable. Patricia Cohen and others (1999) have shown that the Percentage of Maximum Possible (POMP) scale provides a superior solution to that problem even in the area of aptitude and achievement. Our biproportional scale may be viewed as a bipolar version of the POMP scale. The other reason for using standard scores was their relation to the normal distribution. However, that statistical model is massively and systematically violated in personality assessments, where almost all distributions are skewed in socially desirable direction.

For comparative purposes, it does not matter what scale one uses. That implies that standard scores have no specific merit even in that situation. For absolute purposes involving some kind of threshold, standard scores are unfit. A logical conclusion is that biproportional or bipercentage scores are superior, since threshold decisions occur much more frequently than classical applied statistics would lead us to believe. In fact, there are reasons to suspect that the study of personality has allowed itself to be led astray by statistical conventions.

Finally, and returning to the first part of this Chapter, biproportional scores are indispensable in reporting assessments by significant others to the person in question. The pragmatic structure of that communication is such that a diagnostician tells the individual that people find him or her to be *X*, with *X* a summary label for that person's characteristic behaviors. On using relative scales, all *X* would be transformed in socially undesirable direction, as the population mean is invariably above the scale midpoint, by a substantial margin. Not only would relative reporting be biased; it would moreover have a destructive effect on the person's relations with significant others.

REFERENCES

Borkenau, P., Riemann, R. & Spinath, F.M.(2000). Behaviour genetics of personality: The case of observational studies. In: Hampson, S.E. (Ed.), *Advances in personality psychology, Vol. 1.* (pp.107-137). New York, NY: Psychology Press.

Cohen, P., Cohen, J., Aiken, L.S., & West, S.G. (1999). The problem of units and the circumstance for POMP. *Multivariate Behavioral Research, 34,* 315-346.

De Raad, B. (2000). *The big five personality factors: The psycholexical approach to personality.* Seattle: Hogrefe.

Hendriks, A. A. J, Hofstee, W.K.B., & De Raad, B. (1999). The five-factor personality inventory. *Personality and Individual Differences, 27,* 307-325.

Hofstee, W.K.B. (1999). Profielen van persoonlijkheidsstoornissen [Profiles of personality disorders]. *De Psycholoog, 34,* 381-384.

Hofstee, W.K.B. (2001). Intelligence and personality: Do they mix? In: J.M. Collis & S. Messick (Eds.), *Intelligence and personality: Bridging the gap in theory and measurement,* pp. 43-60. Mahwah, NJ: Erlbaum.

Hofstee, W.K.B. (2002). Types *and* variables: Towards a congenial procedure for handling personality data. *European Journal of Personality, 16,* 89-96.

Hofstee, W.K.B. (2003). Structures of personality traits. In: I.B. Weiner (Ed.), *Handbook of psychology:* Th. Millon & M.J. Lerner (Volume Eds.), *Volume 5: Personality and social psychology* (pp. 231-254). Hoboken, NJ: Wiley.

Hofstee, W.K.B., De Raad, B., & Goldberg, L.R. (1992). Integration of the big five and circumplex approaches to trait structure. *Journal of Personality and Social Psychology, 63,* 146-163.

Hofstee, W.K.B. & Ten Berge, J.M.F. (2004a). Personality in proportion: A bipolar proportional scale for personality assessments, and its consequences for trait structure. *Journal of Personality Assessment, 83,* 120-127.

Hofstee, W.K.B. & Ten Berge, J.M.F. (2004b). Representing assessments: Reply to McGrath and Ozer. *Journal of Personality Assessment,* 83, 136-140.

Holley, J.W. & Guilford, J.P. (1964). A note on the G-index of agreement. *Educational and Psychological Measurement, 24,* 749-753.

Mosterman, R.M., & Hofstee, W.K.B. (2006). Beoordeling van persoonlijkheid: zelfbeoordeling, derdenbeoordeling en expertbeoordeling [Assessment of personality: self-assessment, other-assessment, and expert assessment] www.psychologenpraktijkelf.nl.

Rammstedt, B., Riemann, R., Angleitner, A., & Borkenau, P. (2004). Resilients, overcontrollers, and undercontrollers: The replicability of the three personality prototypes across informants. *European Journal of Personality, 18,* 1-14.

Tucker, L.R. (1951). *A method for synthesis of factor analytic studies* (Personnel Research Section Report No. 984). Washington, DC: Department of the Army.

Vazire, S. (2006). Informant reports: A cheap, fast, and easy method for personality assessment. *Journal of Research in personality, 40,* 472-481.

Zegers, F.E. & Ten Berge, J.M.F. (1985). A family of association coefficients for metric scales. *Psychometrika,* 50, 17-24.

In: Personality Assessment: New Research
Editor: Lauren B. Palcroft & Melissa V. Lopez
ISBN 978-1-60692-796-0

Chapter 11

THEORY AND PRACTICE IN THE USE AND INTERPRETATION OF LIKERT-TYPE SCALES WITHIN A CROSS-CULTURAL CONTEXT

Boaz Shulruf*
University of Auckland, New Zealand

ABSTRACT

This Chapter introduces theoretical and empirical comprehensive models that combine three well-established theories and relate to the underlying cultural contexts of individuals completing Likert-type questionnaires. The theoretical model incorporates the stages of responding to Likert-type questionnaires, the effects of response sets and cross cultural effects measured by collectivist and individualist attributes. This theoretical model, named the ImpExp, is empirically tested by measuring the effects of a range of response biases (social desirability, extreme/mid point response set, 'don't know' response, acquiescence, and context) and collectivist and individualist attributes. This results in a second model, the Collectivist-Individualist Model of Response Bias (CIMReB), which suggests an explanation for the way in which collectivist and individualist attributes affect how people respond to Likert-type questionnaires. The CIMReB relates to the five stages of the cognitive process of responding to questions and partially supports the ImpExp model.

These two models together provide a comprehensive framework for the design and implementation of psychological scales within cross cultural contexts. The main findings indicate that collectivist and individualist attributes interact with other response sets and mostly affect the magnitude of the answers (i.e. the extent to which extreme responses are used). The actual content of the answers is affected to a lesser extent. Some examples are

* For correspondence please contact:
Dr. Boaz Shulruf
Faculty of Education
The University of Auckland,
Private Bag 92019
Auckland, New Zealand
Tel: +64 9 3737599 ext 89463
b.shulruf@auckland.ac.nz

provided to demonstrate the usefulness of the models in interpreting answers to Likert-type questionnaires within cross cultural and cross national environment. The Chapter concludes with some practical recommendations relating to the design and analysis of such questionnaires.

Keywords: individualism, collectivism, Likert-type questionnaires, responses sets, response bias.

Answering a questionnaire is not a simple singular task, but rather a series of processes involving judgments based on several cognitive decisions made by the respondent. Tourangeau and Rasinski (1988) suggested that answering questions about attitudes involves at least four stages: interpretation and determination of the relevant attitude; retrieval of relevant beliefs and feelings; applying those beliefs and feelings to the appropriate judgement; and using that judgement to select the appropriate response (see also Sudman, Bradburn, & Schwarz, 1996 who listed similar stages). In a more recent review, Schwarz and Oyserman (2001) suggested a slightly modified model. They posited five stages in the responding process. The first three stages are similar to those proposed by Tourangeau and Rasinski, but Schwarz and Oyserman defined a fourth stage as 'mapping the answer onto the response format', and a fifth stage that involves editing the answer for social desirability.

These models, however, have been developed on different questionnaire formats: Schwarz and Oyserman (2001) developed their model based on questions about behaviour, while Tourangeau and Rasinski (1988) developed their model based on questions about attitudes. Questionnaire settings may also lead to different emphases being placed on the various stages. For example, answering a pen and paper questionnaire is different from answering a computer or web questionnaire (Buchanan et al., 2005), and interviewing is different from filling out questionnaires (Schwarz & Oyserman, 2001). Although these issues raise the need for a generic model that can relate appropriately to a range of formats and settings, in this Chapter various models are combined into a single comprehensive model that relates to the underlying cultural contexts of the individuals completing the questionnaire. Notably this model is the first to incorporate three well-established theories. These are:

a) stages of responding to Likert-type questionnaires (Schwarz & Oyserman, 2001; Sudman & Bradburn, 1974; Sudman, Bradburn, & Schwarz, 1996; Tourangeau, 2003; Tourangeau & Rasinski, 1988);
b) response sets (Bradburn, Sudman, Blair, & Stocking, 1978; Cronbach, 1946; Knowles & Nathan, 1997; Krosnick & Schuman, 1988; McClendon, 1991; Moorman & Podsakoff, 1992; Paulhus, 1991; Schwarz, Hippler, Deutsch, & Strack, 1985; Sudman & Bradburn, 1974; Swearingen, 1998; Tourangeau, 1991; van Herk, Poortinga, & Verhallen, 2004); and
c) cross cultural effects measured by collectivist and individualist attributes (Harzing, 2006; Hui & Triandis, 1989; Kim, Triandis, Kagitcibasi, Choi, & Yoon, 1994; Smith, 2004; Triandis, 1995; Uskul & Oyserman, 2005).

This theoretical model, named the ImpExp model, claims that there are two main stages invoked in respondents responding to questionnaires. The first is the Impression stage, which relates to multi-source information retrieval to form an "impression". Such resources include the actual questions, the context of the questionnaire (namely who asks the questions, or where the questionnaire is carried out) (Bless, Igou, Schwartz, & Waenke, 2000; Tourangeau, 1991; Tourangeau & Rasinski, 1988), and the respondents' history or previous experience, knowledge, values and beliefs. (Schwarz & Oyserman, 2001; Tourangeau & Smith, 1996). However, not all of this information is retrieved at the same time. For example, cognitive retrieval normally follows content and contextual retrieval, as the latter stimulates the first (Schwarz & Oyserman, 2001; Sudman, Bradburn, & Schwarz, 1996; Tourangeau & Rasinski, 1988).

Once information has been retrieved, the second stage of question-response - the Expression stage - is activated. This stage relates to information expressed by the respondent and consists of two sub-stages: a decision-making stage, and an 'answer-editing-tuning' stage that determines the contents of the actual answers (Schwarz & Oyserman, 2001; Sudman, Bradburn, & Schwarz, 1996; Tourangeau & Rasinski, 1988).

Thus, when responding to attitude items the respondent passes through three Impression and two Expression stages: (1) understanding and interpreting the content of the question; (2) retrieving environmental and contextual information; (3) retrieving relevant information and related behaviour, events, constructs, beliefs and feelings; (4) comprehending and judging all the available data (content and context) and decision-making; and (5) selecting the answer from within the available range of answers, and making additional adjustment given the circumstances retrieved in stages (2) and (3).

An important addition is that the ImpExp model also distinguishes between two types of response bias: the Impression-Response-Bias and the Expression-Response-Bias. The Impression-Response-Bias relates to the cognitive process of question response - namely: the retrieval of environmental and contextual information; the retrieval of relevant information and related behaviour, events, constructs, beliefs and feelings; the comprehension/ judgement of the entire available data (content and context); and the decision-making. Thus, this type of response bias includes context, self-deception enhancement and impression management. It is clear that the common feature of these response biases relates to the content of the questions and affects the respondents in terms of how and what to answer.

The second type of response bias - the Expression-Response-Bias - relates to the last stage of question response, namely: aligning the interpreted response to the available range of answers and adjusting for the social norms or circumstances, previously retrieved in the second and third stages. This type of response bias includes the 'Extreme Response Set' and the 'Neutral Response Set'. The common feature of these response biases is that they affect the answer *after* the decision has been made. That is rather than affecting the meaning (direction) of answers this response bias only affects the magnitude given to answers.

Any person completing a questionnaire is embedded in a cultural context - an additional dimension added to the ImpExp model; that is, it takes into account whether the person is more attuned to a collectivist or individualist disposition. Accumulating evidence suggests that cultural attributes, such as collectivism and individualism, can affect responses made on questionnaires (Brew, Hesketh, & Taylor, 2001; Matsuda, Harsel, Furusawa, Kim, & Quarles, 2001; Schwarz & Oyserman, 2001; Stening & Everett, 1984; Tourangeau & Rasinski, 1988; Triandis, 1996). The ImpExp model combines response biases with the effects of collectivism and individualism and, in doing so, provides a comprehensive framework that could assist in identifying response biases *and* help to control for a range of cultures.

Underpinning the ImpExp model are two conceptual frameworks. The first presents the theoretical argument that various response sets may interfere with the "truthfulness" of participant's attitudes while the second – which includes the dimensions of collectivism and individualism in the five stages - argues that these dimensions affect the intensity of the response sets at each stage.

The Collectivist-Individualist Impression-Expression (ImpExp) Model of Responding to Questionnaires

The ImpExp model combines the two dimensions of Impression and Expression with collectivism and individualism (see Figure 1), each stage being affected by different features of the questionnaire. The first stage, understanding and interpreting the content of the question, is affected by the 'Don't Know' response set. The second stage, retrieving environmental and contextual information, is affected by context (e.g. question and item order) and possibly by some element of collectivism-individualism. (Collectivists, for example, may be more attentive to social contexts than individualists and therefore allow contextual issues to influence their answers more.) The third stage, retrieving relevant information and related behaviour, events, constructs beliefs and feelings, is affected by egoistic and moralistic perceptions related to social desirability, and possibly influenced by collectivist and individualist attributes (Paulhus & John, 1998). Hence, it is expected that answers provided by collectivists would be more susceptible to social desirability effects than answers provided by individualists. The fourth stage, comprehending and judging the entire available data (content and context) and decision-making, is affected by collectivism-individualism and the effects of impression management and self-deception enhancement, the basic behaviours related to social desirability. The fifth and final stage, interpreting the answer within the available range of answers, is affected by the extreme/neutral response set and acquiescence, which are mediated by individualism.

An interesting feature that evolves from this model is the dynamics of the data flux. In the first four stages information is received by the respondent and a decision is made. The decision is based on the content of the question, the context and the socio-cultural attributes of the respondent. While the first four stages deal with the content of the answer, the final fifth stage is different. Here, only the magnitude (use of extreme/neutral anchors) of the answer is determined; the previously determined content remains intact.

Thus, two identical questions, asked within different contexts, and/or answered by people with different values and beliefs, will be dealt with differently by respondents. An important contribution to understanding the process of responding to questionnaires is made by the ImpExp model in its inclusion of collectivism and individualism and the suggestion that individualism and collectivism affect the decisions made by respondents when answering questionnaires. This is important as it means that being high on individualism and low on collectivism (and vice versa) may result in different answers from respective respondents. The model suggests that individualism and collectivism have fundamental effects on respondents' answers, predominantly by affecting the type of information which is retrieved (internal and external). Although related to internal information retrieval, social desirability is also directly involved in the decision-making stage implying that cultural attributes filter the information before individual psychological attributes take effect. This is an interesting distinction and worthy of further empirical investigation.

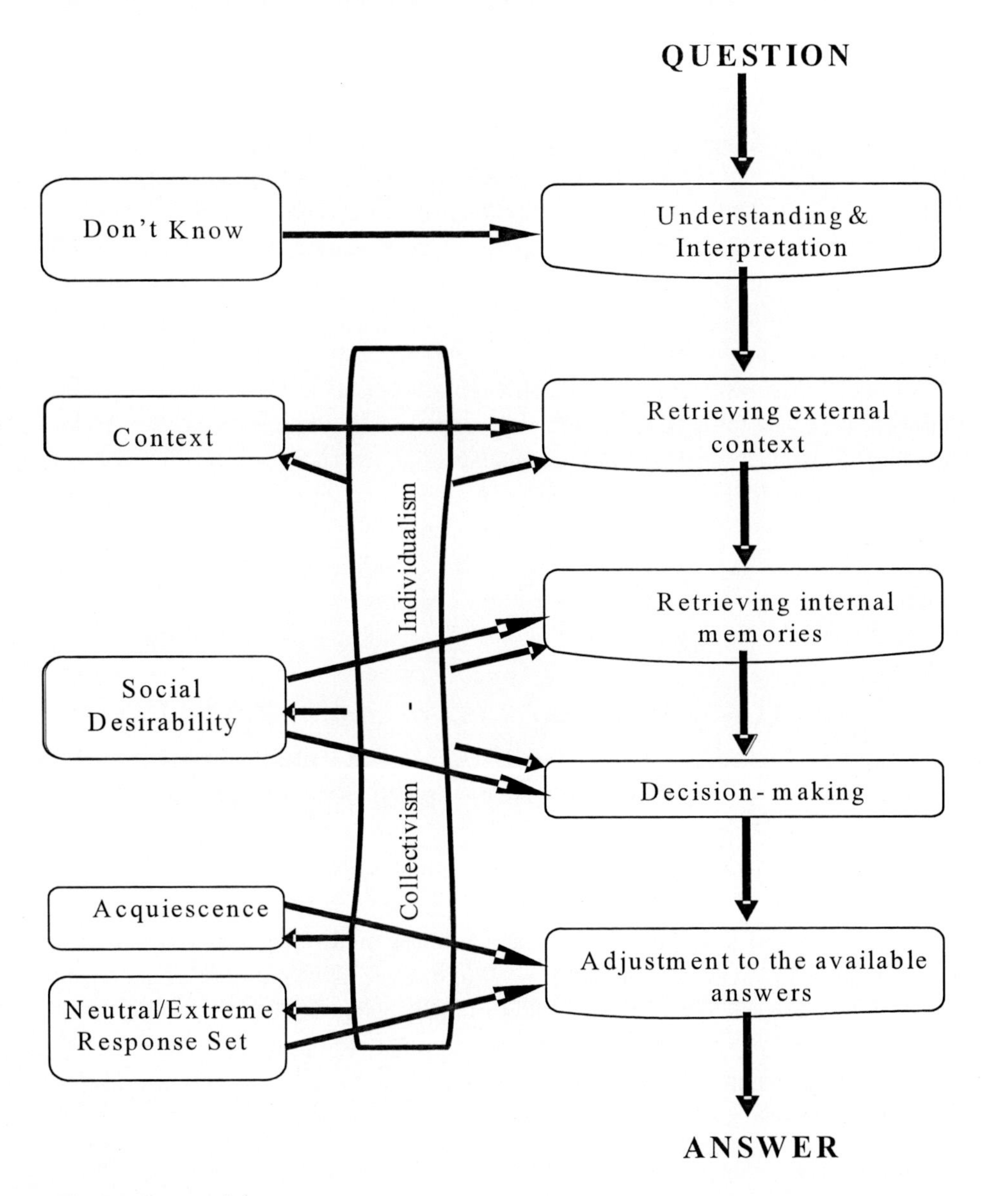

Figure 1 The ImpExp model.

The ImpExp model suggests that aggregating responses to multiple-response attitudinal questionnaires may reduce possible effects of social desirability, individualism and collectivism, and context on answers, particularly since the ImpExp model argues that individualism and collectivism affect the magnitude of the answers more than their content (i.e. decision making). Further, it supports avoidance of mid-point or neutral anchors on questionnaires, particularly when respondents are low on individualism. Finally, applying these suggestions will allow multiple-response questionnaires to be employed across a wider range of social and cultural environments while minimising risks of social and cultural related biases.

Since the ImpExp model is new, it is impossible to present empirical studies which have used this model. However, by using cluster analysis Shulruf et al (Shulruf et al., in review) show that collectivism and individualism intertwine with each other. For example, Shulruf at al suggest that European cultures are more individualist than non-European; and that Chinese are more collectivist than non-Chinese cultures, in line with previous studies (Oyserman, Coon, & Kemmelmeier, 2002; Triandis, 1995). However, recent findings, which used the AICS for measuring collectivism and individualism across five countries, also show that on the frequency scale of collectivism and individualism Chinese tend to use low frequency answers whereas Europeans tend to use high frequency answers on both collectivism and individualism (Shulruf et al., in review). Conceptualising these findings within the context of the ImpExp model may provide better understanding of this phenomenon. According to the ImpExp model it is reasonable to argue that the differences in the answers given by Chinese and Europeans relate to the Expression phase of responding to questions, namely to the stage where they adjust their answers to fit the available options on the scale.

Although this model is based on empirical data gathered from a large number of studies, it is still not sufficient. Hence the next two sections in this Chapter summarise the empirical findings of studies specifically designed to identify the effects of collectivism and individualism on responses to Likert-type questionnaires.

From Theory to Practice: Measuring the Effect of Collectivist and Individualist Attributes on Likert-Type Questionnaires (Study 1)

In this part of the Chapter empirical evidence in support for the theoretical ImpExp model is provided. Since it was impossible to find any previous study that measured the interactions between collectivism and individualism and a range of response sets measured on a scale other then the collectivism- individualism, Shulruf et al (2006) undertook such a study. This study aimed to empirically test the ImpExp model by measuring the effects of a range of response biases (social desirability, extreme/mid point response set, 'don't know' response, acquiescence, and context) and collectivist and individualist attributes (Shulruf, Hattie, & Dixon, 2007).

Method

A set of scales was set up to measure the effects of individualism and collectivism on responses to Likert-type questionnaires. The measure for collectivism and individualism used in this study was the AICS which has been found to be highly reliable (alpha > .70 for both collectivism and individualism) and valid across a range of populations (Shulruf et al., in review; Shulruf, Hattie, & Dixon, 2007). The measures of response sets included five measures each at a different section of the questionnaire. The first section measured two dimensions of social desirability via the short version of BIDR-6 (Pauls & Stemmler, 2003):

Self Deception Enhancement (SDE) and Impression Management (IM). The remaining response sets were based on a measure of thoughts and beliefs about family, as this topic was deemed relevant to all respondents. Items were adapted from the Family Assessment Measure (Skinner, Steinhauer, & Sitarenios, 2000) and the Family Adaptability and Cohesion Evaluation Scales (FACES III) (Olson, 1986). It is important to note that there is a debate in the literature over whether the attribute of familism relates to the collectivism-individualism domains (Oyserman, Coon, & Kemmelmeier, 2002); however, Shulruf et al. (2007) and Oyserman et al., (2002) suggested that familism does not relate to either individualism or collectivism per se; rather, family values relate to both individualists and collectivists equally.

The Extreme Response Set was calculated by measuring the proportion of items the respondent answered marking '1' and '6' — the most extreme options (Greenleaf, 1992). The Acquiescent Response Set was calculated by measuring the proportion of the positive responses to five pairs of items, in which one item in each pair was phrased positively (e.g. "Children should be expected to spend time with their family every weekend") and the second item (which appeared on another page) was phrased negatively (e.g. Children should **not** be expected to spend time with their family every weekend"). If no acquiescence bias is evident the respondents should give 50% negative answers and 50% positive answers. Indication of acquiescence is when more than 50% of the answers are positive. Conversely, if less than 50% of the answers are positive, this would indicate a tendency to answer negatively (Baumgartner & Steenkamp, 2001; Knowles & Condon, 1999). Neutral answers were measured by the proportion of '4's that were marked ('Neither agree nor disagree'). Finally, the Don't Know Set was measured by the proportion of '7's (Don't Know) that were marked (Coombs & Coombs, 1976; Francis & Busch, 1975).

The effect of context was measured by the difference in the answers given to two items that were placed following a priming item: children's rights ("q 52" – "Children's rights are the most important in families"). On another page, a further two items that were similar, but not identical, were placed following an item priming youth delinquency ("q71" - "Youth delinquency could be reduced if parents were stricter"). In this way, two opposite contexts were primed before similar questions were asked, thus allowing any consistent difference in the consecutive answers to be regarded as context effect (Bless, Igou, Schwartz, & Waenke, 2000; Tourangeau & Rasinski, 1988).

Results

The sample for this study comprised a group of undergraduate students enrolled in Foundation Studies at a tertiary institution in New Zealand. Of the 350 students invited to participate 261 (75%) completed the questionnaire. With questionnaires from international students excluded (n = 11) due to low-level language skills, the final sample comprised 250 students. Of these 250 participants, a quarter were males; about a third (32%) identified themselves as belonging to Pacific nations, 17% as Maori (indigenous New Zealanders), 15% as European New Zealanders, 22% as Asians, and 10% reported other ethnicities. The age distribution was wide: 66% were between 15-25 years of age, 22% were between 26-35 years, 10% between 36-45 years and 3% were aged 46 or older.

The analyses commenced by estimating correlations between collectivism, individualism and the response styles (Table 1). Individualism was found to be more highly correlated with the Extreme Response Set and with the two dimensions of social desirability: Self Deception Enhancement (SDE) and Impression Management (IM). Collectivism, on the other hand, was more highly correlated with the Extreme Response Set and with Acquiescence. However, although Acquiescence was positively correlated with collectivism, the correlation was low. Furthermore, correlations between context, Don't Know (DK), and the neutral response style and collectivism and individualism were low ($r<.12$) and not significant.

The ImpExp model (Shulruf, Hattie, & Dixon, 2008) suggests that in the process of responding to questions, the effects of social desirability and context precede the effect of the extreme/midpoint response set. Hence, a structural model (Figure 2), based on the ImpExp model, was then designed and tested. The structural model, which appears to have good fit (RMSEA = .058, CFI =.774; chi-square = 902.690, df= 520), provides greater insight into the interactions between collectivism, individualism and the response sets than was possible from the set of correlations presented in Table 1.

It appears that individualism is positively associated with context, SDE and IM, whereas collectivism is negatively associated with context and SDE, but unrelated to IM. Furthermore, context is negatively associated with midpoint responses and positively associated with extreme responses; SDE is positively associated with extreme responses. Therefore, it seems that the effects of collectivism and individualism on extreme and neutral response sets are mediated by context and SDE respectively.

Table 1. Correlations between response sets and Collectivism and Individualism

	Collectivism	Individualism
Self Deception Enhancement	-.01	.28**
Impression Management	.12	.16**
Context	-.11	.01
Extreme Response Set	.20**	.25**
Neutral Response Set	-.03	-.04
Don't Know	.04	-.05
Acquiescent Response Set	.14*	.12

* $p<.05$
** $p<.01$

Discussion

The main objective of this study was to identify the extent to which individualist-collectivist orientations influence responses to self-reported, Likert-type questionnaires, measured by a range of response sets such as: social desirability (Self Deception Enhancement, Impression Management), Extreme Response Set, Neutral Response Set,

'Don't Know' Response Set, tendency for acquiescence, and contextual effects (i.e. question order). The findings of the current study suggest that collectivist and individualist attributes may directly affect the content of answers (through interaction with social desirability and context-related response sets), and indirectly affect the magnitude of the answers (through the interaction of the tendency to provide more extreme responses - individualists- or more neutral responses - collectivists). No effects of collectivism and individualism were found on the 'Don't Know' response style and tendency for acquiescence.

The empirical model labelled the *Collectivist-Individualist Model of Response Bias* (CIMReB) (Figure 2), suggests a comprehensive explanation of the way in which collectivist and individualist attributes affect the way people respond to Likert-type questionnaires. The CIMReB relates to the five stages of the cognitive process of responding to questions (Shulruf, Hattie, & Dixon, 2008) and partially supports the ImpExp model.

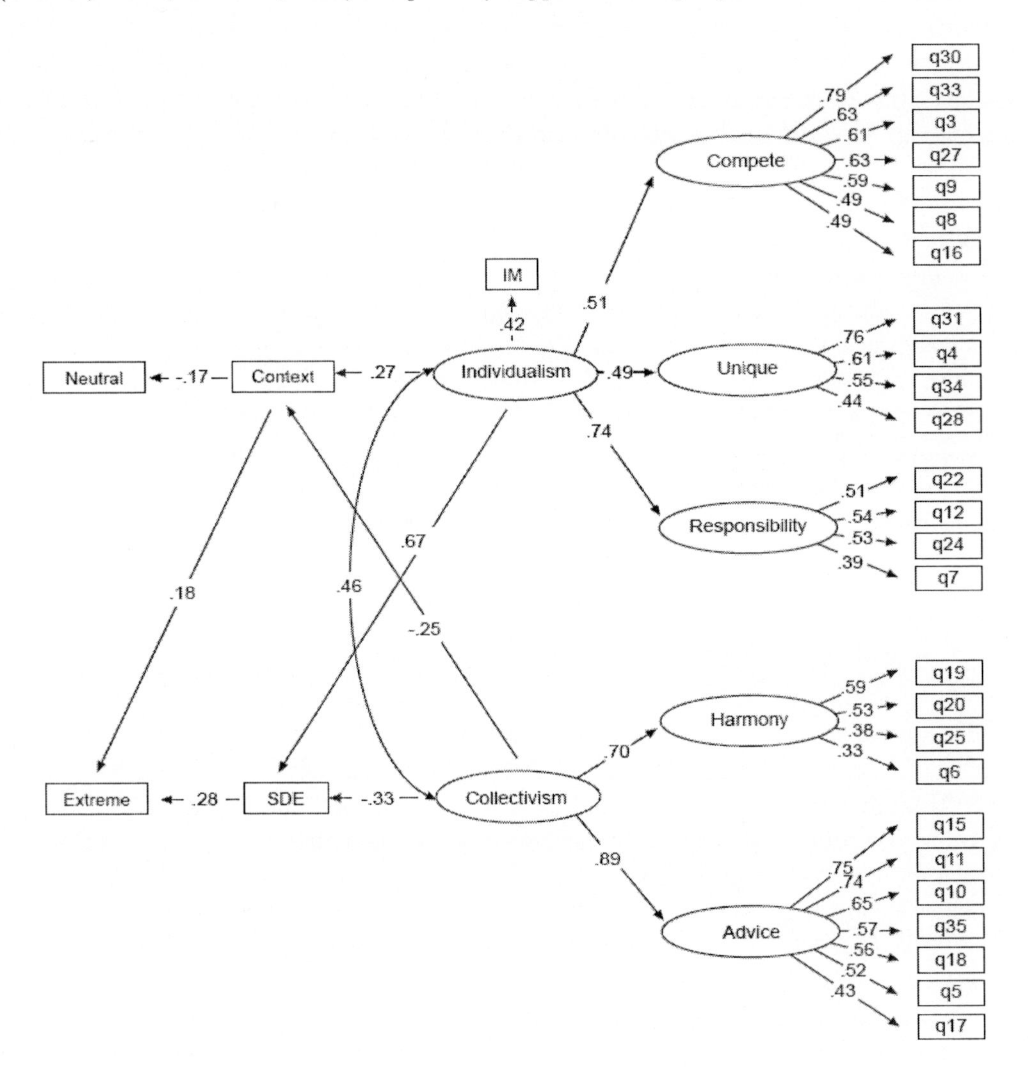

Figure 2 The CIMReB model.

The Collectivist-Individualist Model of Response Bias suggests that individualism and collectivism have direct effect on the Impression-Response-Bias and indirect effect (through context and Self Deception Enhancement) on the Expression-Response-Bias. This suggests that individualist and collectivist attributes affect the *decision* made by the respondent, namely the content of the answers. This is an important finding as it means that being high on individualism and low on collectivism (and vice versa) may lead to different questionnaire answers (via the content or the actual decision making). The indirect effect of individualism/collectivism on the magnitude of the answers (tendency to give extreme/midpoint responses), however, is smaller.

It is noteworthy that the extreme and neutral response sets, which are Expression Response Biases, do not stand alone. These response biases are affected by collectivist and individualist attributes, as well as via SDE and the questionnaire's context. This is an important finding since it suggests that measuring extreme or neutral responses alone, without controlling for Impression Response Biases and without considering the respondents' cultural attributes (i.e. collectivism and individualism), would provide an incomplete explanation of the findings. In some cases this might be misleading and may provide wrong interpretations of the answers supplied. It is therefore suggested that any further research on Expression Response Biases also considers attributes of Impression Response Biases, as well as attributes of collectivism and individualism.

Impression Management was found to be positively correlated with individualism, but did not affect any of the Expression Response Biases. Being high on IM means that respondents tend to present themselves as a 'nice person', a 'good citizen' or even 'saint-like' (Paulhus & John, 1998; Pauls & Stemmler, 2003). As found in the current study, individualists who are more competitive and feel more responsible to themselves and to their environment are also more likely to exaggerate their 'saint-like' behaviour. Furthermore, individualists, who normally emphasise their uniqueness, are likely to be scored high on IM, distinguishing themselves from others by claiming higher moralistic behaviours. Unlike individualists, collectivists tend to be neutral towards IM since they would either like to be seen as a positive member of the group, or wish to avoid expressions implying they differ from (i.e. are better than) others (Andersen, Reznik, & Chen, 1997; Oyserman, Coon, & Kemmelmeier, 2002).

The focus on ego enhancement and the desire to 'stand out from the crowd' within the SDE response set (Paulhus, 1991; Paulhus & John, 1998; Pauls & Stemmler, 2003) may explain the positive correlation between SDE and individualism, which is described as prioritizing the self and explicitly enhancing one's own self-esteem (Triandis, 1996), as well as being competitive and having distinctive personal attitudes and opinions (Markus & Kitayama, 1991; Oyserman, Coon, & Kemmelmeier, 2002; Triandis, 1989). All such attributes are linked by the notion of positive distinction of the self from others.

The negative relationship between SDE and collectivism may be explained by the reverse attributes of the collectivist. Collectivists tend to identify themselves as members of the group they belong to (Markus & Kitayama, 1991; Triandis, 1996), meaning that they undermine their ego in relation to others. Consequently, it is expected that collectivism would be negatively correlated with ego enhancement, which is a core component of SDE, as indicated by the results.

Contrary to what previous studies suggested (Gudykunst, Matsumoto, Ting-Toomey, & Nishida, 1996; Morling & Fiske, 1999; Triandis, 1989; Triandis, Bontempo, Villareal, Asai,

& Lucca, 1988), individualism is positively - and collectivism is negatively - correlated with context. The context, as measured in this study, comprised the priming of two notions: children's rights and youth delinquency. Each notion was preceded by very similar questions, each phrased slightly differently. These contexts relate to two different social norms that are likely to contradict each other. The negative correlation found between collectivism and context can be explained by the tendency of collectivists (unlike individualists) to remember their own observed behaviour and avoid visible discrepancy; in this case, maintaining consistency within similar questions (Ji, Schwarz, & Nisbett, 2000). Moreover, individualists, who emphasise personal responsibility and freedom of choice (Waterman, 1984), may be more attentive to the notion of children's rights than collectivists, who tend to believe in a tighter social structure. Thus, collectivists may be more consistent with their answers across different contexts than individualists, as the CIMReB suggests.

The positive relations between SDE and the Extreme Response Set were expected since, by definition, both attributes share a significant portion of exaggeration. Furthermore, those who score high on SDE tend to exaggerate their self-perception on personality dimensions such as intelligence and creativity (Paulhus & John, 1998). Therefore, it was expected that they would be more decisive as they believe that they 'know the right answer'.

In terms of Expression-Response-Bias, it was confirmed that collectivists apply more neutral responses and less extreme responses than individualists (Chun, Campbell, & Yoo, 1974; Lee & Green, 1991; Stening & Everett, 1984). The effects of collectivism and individualism on extreme and neutral response styles are indirect, namely mediated by SDE and context, and might explain the mixed evidence found in other studies.

Although previous studies indicate that acquiescence was correlated with collectivism (Bond & Smith, 1996; Grimm & Church, 1999), it was not found in the current study. The reason for this may relate to the differences between the methods employed in previous studies and the current study. Previous studies compared people from different cultures, ethnic groups or nations, assuming they were individualists (US) or collectivists (Asians). In the current study participants were defined as collectivists or individualists solely by their scores on the AICS, regardless of their ethnicity or nationality. Therefore, it is suggested that acquiescence may be more related to specific cultures' ways of expression, rather than to individualism and collectivism, which can vary within cultures, as the recent literature suggests (Heine, Lehman, Peng, & Greenholtz, 2002; Shulruf et al., in review; Voronov & Singer, 2002).

The CIMReB suggests mediating effects of SDE and context on the relationships between individualism and collectivism, and extreme and neutral response styles. However, further research on the linkages between response styles, response biases and the process by which people answer questions is needed. Better understanding of these linkages might clarify the way response styles affect peoples' answers, which may then lead to an increase in the accuracy and validity of Likert-type questionnaires.

Attributes of individualism and collectivism affect the way people respond to questionnaires. The current study indicates that this effect is moderated by SDE and context, and is exhibited by the extent to which people apply extreme or neutral responses. In practice, this outcome suggests that aggregating responses of multiple-response attitudinal questionnaires may reduce possible effects of individualism, collectivism, SDE and context on the answers. Furthermore, it supports avoidance of mid-point or neutral anchors on these questionnaires. Finally, applying these recommendations will allow the employment of multiple-response questionnaires in multicultural environments, while minimising risks of cross-culturally related biases.

The next section expands the empirical evidence to a range of nations and cultures to enhance the robustness of the theoretical and empirical models discussed above.

From Theory to Practice: Cross-National or Cross-Cultural Effects (Study 2)

So far, two models have been introduced: the theoretical ImpExp model of responding to Likert-type questionnaires, and the empirical CIMReB model which partially supports the ImpExp model. Important questions to ask now are: How does it work in practice? and How important is it to consider the effects of response sets and collectivism and individualism when interpreting results of attitudinal questionnaires within cross-cultural contexts? This section addresses these particular questions and demonstrates the differences in answers to a questionnaire on concepts of competition across different cultures.

Method

The participants in this study comprised 293 undergraduate students from a university in Hong Kong (n=172) and a polytechnic in New Zealand (n=121). The participants answered two questionnaires: the first was the AICS (Shulruf, Hattie, & Dixon, 2007) which measured their collectivist and individualist behaviours; the second was the Hong Kong Competitiveness Questionnaire (HKCQ), which was developed to measure three concepts of competitiveness, as well as provide reasons for being competitive (Shulruf, Watkins, & Hattie, in progress).

Results

Since the questionnaires were applied in two different countries, New Zealand and China, and in two different languages, English and Chinese, there was a need to measure possible biases relating to the countries and languages. A comparison of the scores distribution of the AICS and the HKCQ revealed that, in comparison to New Zealanders, Chinese consistently use the lower range of the scale (Figure 3), which suggests the need for score standardisation (Fischer, 2004). Hence, all of the AICS and HKCQ raw scores were modified to z-scores within each country. This means that measures of collectivism and individualism are relative to within-country means. This standardisation is justifiable since people tend to compare themselves to others they know, i.e. the people around them (Heine, Lehman, Peng, & Greenholtz, 2002).

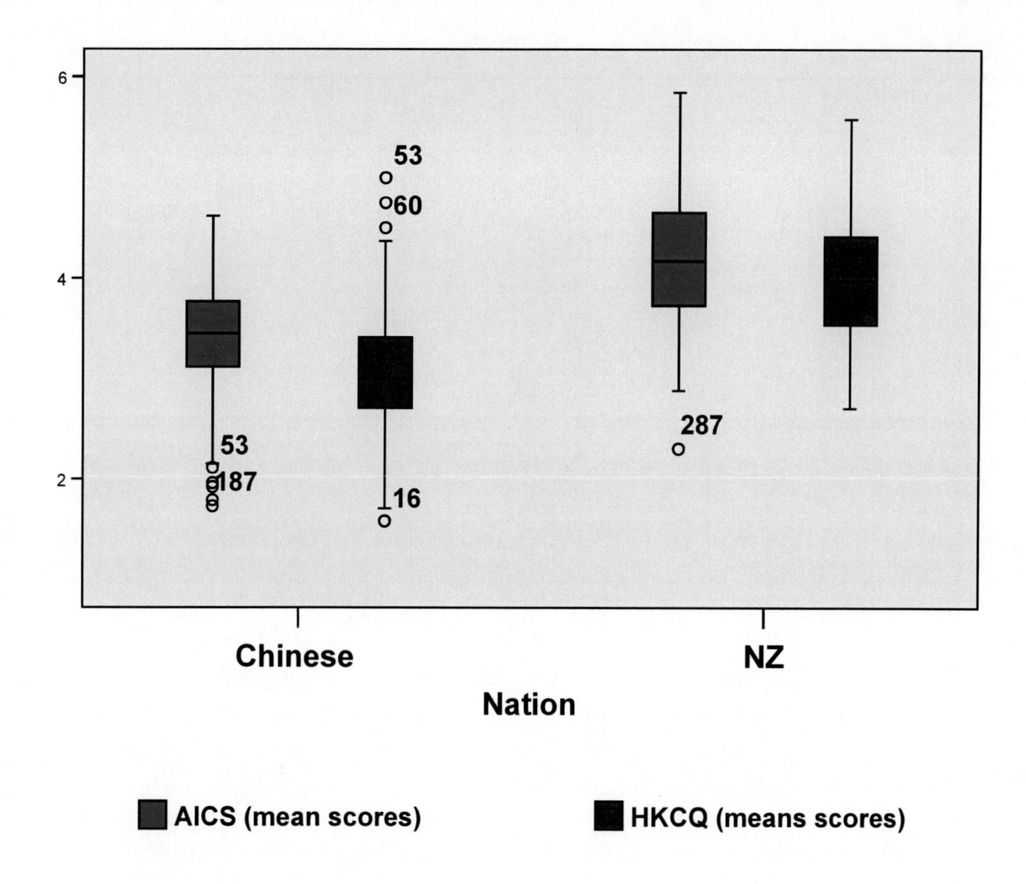

Figure 3. Scores distribution (AICS & HKCQ) by country.

Following standardisation, K-mean cluster analysis was carried out using the within-country standardised AICS scores to identify the collectivists and individualists within the groups. This cluster analysis revealed that there were four groups: HC-LI (high on collectivism and low on individualism); HI-LC (high on individualism and low on collectivism); HI-HC (high on both collectivism and individualism); and LI-LC (low on both collectivism and individualism).

Within the response sets mentioned earlier in this Chapter, only the Extreme Response Set could be measured. The Extreme Response Set was measured by the proportion of extreme responses (i.e. '1' Strongly disagree; and '6' Strongly agree) given by the respondents. The results (Figure 4) indicate that, even after standardising the scores for collectivism and individualism within nations, collectivism and individualism do affect the tendency to give extreme answers - and in an unexpected way. Within the Chinese respondents no significant differences were found across the collectivist-individualist clusters. Within the New Zealanders, however, the results were different: the LH-LI group used less extreme responses than any of the other groups across the two countries; and the HC-HI group used more extreme responses than any of the other groups, but this was significant only in comparison to the New Zealanders' LC-LI group, and most of the Chinese groups, except the LC-LI group.

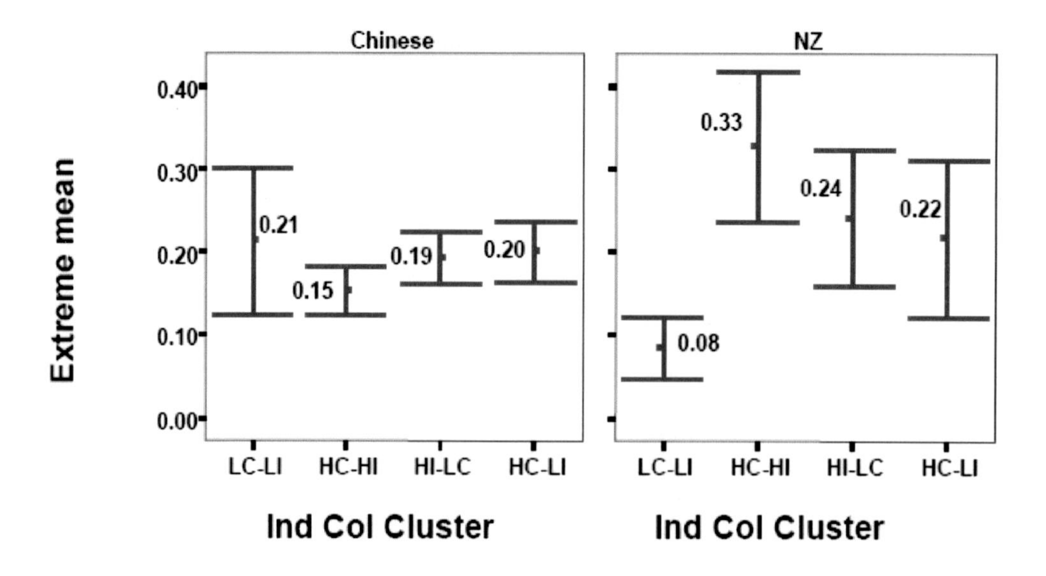

Figure 4. Extreme Response Set, by nation and by collectivism and individualism.

The next analysis that took place aimed to identify whether Chinese and New Zealanders conceive competition in a similar way. To measure this, three linear regressions models were established where each included one of the following dependent variables: 'competition is a game'; 'competition is about winning'; and 'competition is a social tool'. Each of these models included the independent variables: nationality, collectivism, individualism, and gender. The results (regression coefficients and 95%CI) are presented in Figure 5 and Table 2. The results indicate that these three concepts are weaker among Chinese in comparison to New Zealanders.

Nonetheless, it is also clear that individualism, and to lesser extent collectivism, affects the way people conceive competition. Notably, individualism positively correlates with the concepts of 'competition as social tool' and 'completion is a game', yet it is negatively correlated with the concept that 'competition is about winning'. A further interesting finding derived from this dataset was that the correlation between individualism (standardised within country) and extreme responses (proportion of '1's and '6's marked on a 1-6 scale) was small, but statistically significant (r=.13 p=.03).

It appears that using the aggregated scores for the three concepts of competition decrease the effect of nation, collectivism and individualism on the regressions (see the standardised coefficients), although the directions of the effects did not change. The importance of this finding is twofold. First, it suggests that using aggregated data for attitudinal scales may reduce cross-cultural biases. Second, it provides further support to both the empirical (CIMReB) and the theoretical (ImpExp) models by indicating that collectivism and individualism affect the magnitude of answers to Likert-type attitudinal questionnaires. Furthermore, in this particular study effects of context or social desirability were not measured, so it was impossible to estimate the effect of the interaction between collectivism and individualism with social desirability and context on the concepts of competition.

Table 2. Effects of individualism and collectivism on perception of competition

			Unstand. Coeff.	Std. Error	Stand.Coeff.	t	Sig.	95%CI for B	
								Lower Bound	Upper Bound
			B		Beta				
Compete is a game	Raw data	(Constant)	4.25	0.08		51.80	0.000	4.09	4.41
		Nation1.0	-1.79	0.12	-0.75	-14.57	0.000	-2.03	-1.54
		Z.Individualism	0.35	0.10	0.16	3.65	0.000	0.16	0.54
		Z.Collectivism	0.08	0.09	0.04	0.90	0.369	-0.10	0.26
		Male1.0	0.24	0.12	0.11	2.02	0.044	0.01	0.48
		R Square	0.72						
Compete is a game	Aggregated data	(Constant)	0.73	0.03		27.47	0.000	0.68	0.78
		Nation1.0	-0.49	0.04	-0.68	-12.22	0.000	-0.56	-0.41
		Z.Individualism	0.11	0.03	0.17	3.45	0.001	0.05	0.17
		Z.Collectivism	0.00	0.03	0.01	0.14	0.888	-0.05	0.06
		Male1.0	0.05	0.04	0.08	1.37	0.171	-0.02	0.13
		R Square	0.66						
Compete is about winning	Raw data	(Constant)	3.84	0.11		34.34	0.000	3.62	4.06
		Nation1.0	-1.60	0.17	-0.58	-9.62	0.000	-1.92	-1.27
		Z.Individualism	-0.23	0.13	-0.10	-1.78	0.075	-0.49	0.02
		Z.Collectivism	0.09	0.12	0.04	0.75	0.456	-0.15	0.33
		Male1.0	0.15	0.16	0.06	0.95	0.342	-0.16	0.47
		R Square	0.56						
Compete is about winning	Aggregated data	(Constant)	0.63	0.03		18.58	0.000	0.56	0.70
		Nation1.0	-0.42	0.05	-0.52	-8.25	0.000	-0.51	-0.32
		Z.Individualism	-0.07	0.04	-0.09	-1.67	0.097	-0.14	0.01
		Z.Collectivism	0.03	0.04	0.05	0.90	0.370	-0.04	0.11
		Male1.0	0.04	0.05	0.05	0.73	0.467	-0.06	0.13

		R Square	0.51						
Compete is a social tool	Raw data	(Constant)	4.60	0.07		62.59	0.000	4.45	4.74
		Nation1.0	-1.04	0.11	-0.55	-9.54	0.000	-1.26	-0.83
		Z.Individualism	0.40	0.09	0.24	4.68	0.000	0.23	0.57
		Z.Collectivism	0.17	0.08	0.11	2.15	0.033	0.01	0.33
		Male1.0	0.01	0.11	0.01	0.09	0.930	-0.20	0.22
		R Square	0.62						
Compete is a social tool	Aggregated data	(Constant)	0.84	0.03		32.08	0.000	0.79	0.90
		Nation1.0	-0.21	0.04	-0.35	-5.27	0.000	-0.28	-0.13
		Z.Individualism	0.13	0.03	0.24	4.14	0.000	0.07	0.19
		Z.Collectivism	0.03	0.03	0.06	1.06	0.289	-0.03	0.09
		Male1.0	-0.02	0.04	-0.03	-0.49	0.622	-0.09	0.06
		R Square	0.50						

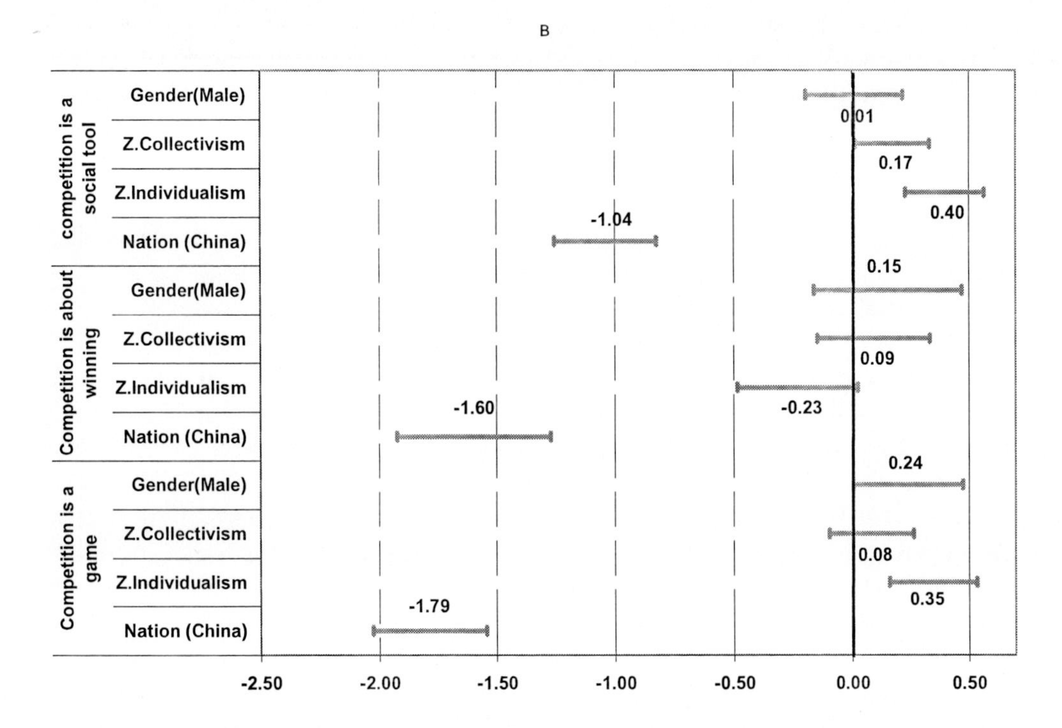

Figure 5. Linear regression coefficients of three concepts of competition.

These results indicate that individualism - and to lesser extent collectivism - may confound results of attitudinal scales within cross-cultural contexts. A major question remains: How to deal with these confounders? As suggested earlier in this Chapter, a possible solution is aggregating the results of Likert-type questionnaires. To test the effectiveness of this method, three more linear regressions models were established that used the same independent variables indicated above (Figure 5). The dependent variables, however, were the aggregated scores of each of the three concepts of competition (game, winning, social tool) where all the 'disagree' scores were re-scored as 0, and all the 'agree' scores were re-scored as 1.

General Discussion and Conclusions

This Chapter has discussed issues relating to the effect of collectivism and individualism on responses to Likert-type attitudinal questionnaires. It began by introducing the ImpExp theoretical model that conceptualises the stages of responding to questions with a range of response sets and collectivism and individualism (Shulruf, Hattie, & Dixon, 2008). Since the ImpExp model is too complex to be empirically tested in a single study the introduction of the CIMReB was an ambitious attempt to test the ImpExp model; it was partially successful, particularly in terms of the interactions between collectivism and individualism with social desirability, context effects and extreme response bias. However, within this particular study it was impossible to measure how these effects related to the specific stages of responding to questions (Schwarz & Oyserman, 2001; Sudman, Bradburn, & Schwarz, 1996; Tourangeau & Rasinski, 1988).

In order to take this knowledge to the next level and try to identify whether collectivist and individualist attributes affect responses to Likert-type questionnaires involved applying the models to a different data set. The data set from a study measuring the concepts of competition in New Zealand and China was used for this purpose (Shulruf, Watkins, & Hattie, in progress). The results (shown in Figure 5 and Table 2) clearly indicate that individualism - and to lesser extent collectivism - has a small but distinct effect on concepts of competition, even when the measures of collectivism and individualism are standardised within each country.

Since concepts of competition relate to the meaning of competition rather than to the individuals' level of competitiveness, it is suggested that cultural orientations such collectivism and individualism, regardless nationality and language, do affect answers given on Likert-type questionnaires. These findings support a large body of literature (for example see, Arce-Ferrer, 2006; Gudykunst, Matsumoto, Ting-Toomey, & Nishida, 1996; Harzing, 2006; Middleton & Jones, 2000; Smith, 2004; Uskul & Oyserman, 2005; Wong, Rindfleisch, & Burroughs, 2003). It is noteworthy that the Likert scale used in the Shulruf et al (in progress) study ranged from '1' 'Strongly disagree' to '6' 'Strongly agree'. Hence the impact on the content of the answers is likely to affect answers that are close to the middle of the scale (i.e. 3 'Slightly disagree' or 4 'Slightly agree'), which is in line with both ImpExp and CIMReB models. Moreover, it also appears that the correlation between individualism and extreme responses, although small, was statistically significant (r=.13 p=.03) which provides further support for these models, suggesting that individualism and collectivism affect the magnitude of the answers (Shulruf, 2007; Shulruf, Hattie, & Dixon, 2006; Shulruf, Hattie, & Dixon, 2008).

Although aggregating answers on the concepts of competition into 'Agree' and 'Disagree' reduced the effects of collectivism and individualism on the answers (Table 2) it had only limited effect on the actual results. Bearing in mind that collectivism and individualism may also affect the content of answers it is suggested that, when answers to attitudinal questionnaires converge towards the middle point or the neutral anchor, it is important to control the results for measures of collectivism and individualism in order to remove cultural-related biases that may affect the actual answers. However, when the answers diverge from the midpoint the effects of collectivism and individualism are unlikely to affect the content of the answers, just their magnitude. Hence, in these cases there is no need to control for collectivism and individualism and aggregating the anchors to 'Agree' and the 'Disagree' would suffice.

In conclusion, this Chapter theoretically conceptualises the process of responding to Likert-type questionnaires where response sets and cultural effects are considered (the ImpExp model). This theoretical model was followed by the introduction of an empirical model (CIMReB) where both models are in line with each other. The Chapter was concludes with some practical examples demonstrating how these models could be applied when using Likert-type questionnaires. Although the research in this area is relatively developed, very few studies have integrated this knowledge to offer practical yet robust solutions for researchers who apply attitudinal questionnaires within culturally diverse populations.

REFERENCES

Andersen, S. M., Reznik, I., & Chen, S. (1997). The self in relation to others: Cognitive and motivational underpinnings. In J. G. Snodgrass & R. L. Thompson (Eds.), *The self across psychology* (pp. 233-275). New York: Academy of Sciences.

Arce-Ferrer, A. J. (2006). An Investigation Into the Factors Influencing Extreme-Response Style *Educational and Psychological Measurement, 66*(3), 374-392.

Baumgartner, H. & Steenkamp, J.-B. E. (2001). Response styles in marketing research: A cross-national investigation. *Journal of Marketing Research, 38*(2), 143-156.

Bless, H., Igou, E. R., Schwartz, N., & Waenke, M. (2000). Reducing context effects by adding context information: The direction and size of context effects in political judgment. *Personality and Social Psychology Bulletin, 26*(9), 1036-1045.

Bond, R. & Smith, P. B. (1996). Culture and conformity: A meta-analysis of studies using Asch's (1952b, 1956) line judgment task. *Psychological Bulletin, 119*(1), 111-137.

Bradburn, N. M., Sudman, S., Blair, E., & Stocking, C. (1978). Question threat and response bias. *Public Opinion Quarterly, 42*(2), 221-234.

Brew, F. P., Hesketh, B. & Taylor, A. (2001). Individualist-collectivist differences in adolescent decision making and decision styles with Chinese and Anglos. *International Journal of Intercultural Relations, 25*(1), 1-19.

Buchanan, T., Ali, T., Heffernan, T. M., Ling, J., Parrott, A. C., Rodgers, J., et al. (2005). Nonequivalence of on-line and paper-and-pencil psychological tests: The case of the prospective memory questionnaire. *Behavior Research Methods, 37*(1), 148-154.

Chun, K.T., Campbell, J. B. & Yoo, J. H. (1974). Extreme response style in cross-cultural research: A reminder. *Journal of Cross-Cultural Psychology, 5*(4), 465-480.

Coombs, C. H. & Coombs, L. C. (1976). "Don't know": Item ambiguity or response uncertainty? *Public Opinion Quarterly, 40*, 497-514.

Cronbach, L. J. (1946). Response sets and test validity. *Educational and Psychological Measurement, 6*, 475-494.

Fischer, R. (2004). Standardization to Account for Cross-cultural Response Bias a Classification of Score Adjustment Procedures and Review of Research in JCCP. *Journal of Cross-Cultural Psychology, 35*(3), 263-282.

Francis, J. D. & Busch, L. (1975). What we now know about "I Don't Knows" (in Current Research). *The Public Opinion Quarterly, 39*(2), 207-218.

Greenleaf, E. A. (1992). Measuring extreme response style. *Public Opinion Quarterly, 56*(3), 328-351.

Grimm, S. D. & Church, A. (1999). A cross-cultural study of response biases in personality measures. *Journal of Research in Personality, 33*(4), 415-441.

Gudykunst, W. B., Matsumoto, Y., Ting-Toomey, S., & Nishida, T. (1996). The influence of cultural individualism-collectivism, self construals, and individual values on communication styles across cultures. *Human Communication Research, 22*(4), 510-543.

Harzing, A.W. (2006). Response Styles in Cross-national Survey Research: A 26-country Study. *International Journal of Cross Cultural Management, 6*(2), 243-266.

Heine, S. J., Lehman, D. R., Peng, K., & Greenholtz, J. (2002). What's wrong with cross-cultural comparisons of subjective Likert scales?: The reference-group effect. *Journal of Personality and Social Psychology, 82*(6), 903-918.

Hui, C. & Triandis, H. (1989). Effects of culture and response format on extreme response style. *Journal of Cross-Cultural Psychology, 20*(3), 296-309.

Ji, L.J., Schwarz, N. & Nisbett, R. E. (2000). Culture, autobiographical memory, and behavioral frequency reports: Measurement issues in cross-cultural studies. *Personality and Social Psychology Bulletin, 26*(5), 585-593.

Kim, U., Triandis, H., Kagitcibasi, C., Choi, S.-C., & Yoon, G. (Eds.). (1994). *Individualism and collectivism: Theory, method, and applications*. Thousand Oaks, CA: Sage.

Knowles, E. S. & Condon, C. A. (1999). Why people say "yes": A dual-process theory of acquiescence. *Journal of Personality and Social Psychology, 77*(2), 379-386.

Knowles, E. S. & Nathan, K. T. (1997). Acquiescent responding in self-reports: Cognitive style or social concern? *Journal of Research in Personality, 31*(2), 293-301.

Krosnick, J. A. & Schuman, H. (1988). Attitude intensity, importance, and certainty and susceptibility to response effects. *Journal of Personality and Social Psychology, 54*(6), 940-952.

Lee, C. & Green, R. T. (1991). Cross cultural examination of Fishbein behavioral intentions model. *Journal of International Business Studies, 22*, 289-305.

Markus, H. R. & Kitayama, S. (1991). Culture and the self: Implications for cognition, emotion, and motivation. *Psychological Review, 98*(2), 224-253.

Matsuda, Y., Harsel, S., Furusawa, S., Kim, H.-S., & Quarles, J. (2001). Democratic values and mutual perceptions of human rights in four Pacific Rim nations. *International Journal of Intercultural Relations, 25*(4), 405-421.

McClendon, M. J. (1991). Acquiescence and recency response-order effects in interview surveys. *Sociological Methods and Research, 20*, 60-103.

Middleton, K. L. & Jones, J. L. (2000). Socially desirable response sets: The impact of country culture. *Psychology and Marketing, 17*(2), 149-163.

Moorman, R. H. & Podsakoff, P. M. (1992). A meta-analytic review and empirical test of the potential confounding effects of social desirability response sets in organizational behaviour research. *Journal of Occupational and Organizational Psychology, 65*(2), 131-149.

Morling, B. & Fiske, S. T. (1999). Defining and measuring harmony control. *Journal of Research in Personality, 33*(4), 379-414.

Olson, D. H. (1986). Circumplex Model VII: Validation studies and FACES III. *Family Process, 25*(3), 337-351.

Oyserman, D., Coon, H. M. & Kemmelmeier, M. (2002). Rethinking individualism and collectivism: Evaluation of theoretical assumptions and meta-analyses. *Psychological Bulletin, 128*(1), 3-72.

Paulhus, D. L. (1991). Measurement and control of response bias. In J. P. Robinson, P. R. Shaver, L. S. Wrightsman & F. M. Andrews (Eds.), *Measures of personality and social psychological attitudes* (Vol. 1, pp. 17-59). San Diego: Academic Press.

Paulhus, D. L. & John, O. P. (1998). Egoistic and moralistic biases in self-perception: The interplay of self-deceptive styles with basic traits and motives. *Journal of Personality, 66*(6), 1025-1060.

Pauls, C. A. & Stemmler, G. (2003). Substance and bias in social desirability responding. *Personality and Individual Differences, 35*(2), 263-275.

Schwarz, N., Hippler, H.J., Deutsch, B., & Strack, F. (1985). Response scales: Effects of category range on reported behavior and comparative judgments. *Public Opinion Quarterly, 49*(3), 388-395.

Schwarz, N. & Oyserman, D. (2001). Asking questions about behavior: Cognition, communication, and questionnaire construction. *American Journal of Evaluation, 22*(2), 127-160.

Shulruf, B. (2007). *Collectivism and Individualism: Questioning the answers, invited presentation for the symposia "Personal conceptions of competence: Perspectives, development and intercultural questions".* Paper presented at the The 10th European Congress of Psychology, Prague.

Shulruf, B., Alesi, M., Ciochină, L., Faria, L., Hattie, J., Hong, F., et al. (in review). Measuring Collectivism and Individualism in the Third Millennium. *Asian Journal of Social Psychology.*

Shulruf, B., Hattie, J. & Dixon, R. (2006). *The influence of individualist and collectivist attributes on responses to Likert-type scales.* Paper presented at the 26th International Association of Applied Psychology, 17-21 July Athens.

Shulruf, B., Hattie, J., & Dixon, R. (2007). Development of a New Measurement Tool for Individualism and Collectivism. *Journal of Psychoeducational Assessment, 25* (4), 385-401.

Shulruf, B., Hattie, J., & Dixon, R. (2008). Factors affecting responses to Likert type questionnaires: Introduction of the ImpExp, a new comprehensive model. *Social Psychology of Education: An International Journal, 11*(1), 59-78.

Shulruf, B., Watkins, D. & Hattie, J. (in progress). Interactions between collectivist and individualist attributes and concepts of competition.

Skinner, H., Steinhauer, P., & Sitarenios, G. (2000). Family Assessment Measure (FAM) and process model of family functioning. *Journal of Family Therapy, 22*(2), 190-210.

Smith, P. B. (2004). Acquiescent Response Bias as an Aspect of Cultural Communication Style. *Journal of Cross-Cultural Psychology, 35*(1), 50-61.

Stening, B. & Everett, J. (1984). Response styles in a cross-cultural managerial study. *Journal of Social Psychology, 122*(2), 151-156.

Sudman, S. & Bradburn, N. M. (1974). *Response effects in surveys.* Chicago: Aldine Publishing Company.

Sudman, S., Bradburn, N. M. & Schwarz, N. (1996). *Thinking about answers: The application of cognitive processes to survey methodology.* San Francisco: Jossey-Bass.

Swearingen, D. L. (1998). *Response sets, item format, and thinking style: Implications for questionnaire design.* U Denver, US, 1.

Tourangeau, R. (1991). Context effects on responses to attitude questions: Attitudes as memory structure. In N. Schwarz & S. Sudman (Eds.), *Context effects in social and psychological research* (pp. 35-47). New York: Springer-Verlag.

Tourangeau, R. (2003). Cognitive aspects of survey measurement and mismeasurement. *International Journal of Public Opinion Research, 15*(1), 3-7.

Tourangeau, R. & Rasinski, K. A. (1988). Cognitive processes underlying context effects in attitude measurement. *Psychological Bulletin, 103*(3), 299-314.

Tourangeau, R. & Smith, T. W. (1996). Asking sensitive questions: The impact of data collection mode, question format, and question context. *Public Opinion Quarterly, 60*(2), 275-304.

Triandis, H. (1989). The self and social behavior in differing cultural contexts. *Psychological Review, 96*(3), 506-520.

Triandis, H. (1995). *Individualism and collectivism.* Boulder, CO: Westview Press.

Triandis, H. (1996). The psychological measurement of cultural syndromes. *American Psychologist, 51*(4), 407-415.

Triandis, H., Bontempo, R., Villareal, M. J., Asai, M., & Lucca, N. (1988). Individualism and collectivism: Cross-cultural perspectives on self in group relationships. *Journal of Personality and Social Psychology, 54*(2), 323-338.

Uskul, A. K. & Oyserman, D. (2005). Question Comprehension and Response: Implications of Individualism and Collectivism. In B. Mannix, M. Neale & Y. Chen (Eds.), *Research on Managing Groups and Teams: National Culture & Groups*. Oxford: Elsevier Science.

van Herk, H., Poortinga, Y. H. & Verhallen, T. M. (2004). Response styles in rating scales: Evidence of method bias in data from six EU countries. *Journal of Cross-Cultural Psychology, 35*(3), 346-360.

Voronov, M. & Singer, J. A. (2002). The myth of individualism-collectivism: A critical review. *Journal of Social Psychology, 142*(4), 461-480.

Waterman, A. S. (1984). *The psychology of individualism*. New York: Praeger.

Wong, N., Rindfleisch, A. & Burroughs, J. (2003). Do Reverse-Worded Items Confound Measures in Cross-Cultural Consumer Research? The Case of the Material Values Scale. *Journal of Consumer Research, 30*, 72-91.

In: Personality Assessment: New Research
Editor: Lauren B. Palcroft & Melissa V. Lopez
ISBN 978-1-60692-796-0

Chapter 12

CONSTRUCT AND RESPONSE BIAS CORRELATES IN SUMMATED SCALE DEFINITIONS OF PERSONALITY TRAITS

John T. Kulas[1] and Alicia A. Stachowski[2]
1) Saint Cloud State University, Saint Cloud, Minnesota, USA
2) George Mason University, Fairfax, Virginia, USA

ABSTRACT

Graphic rating scales are frequently used in the collection of self-report data. Although the specification of these response scales is common, they have been identified as being particularly susceptible to several response biases – most notably acquiescence, central tendency, and extremity. The possibility that these response styles may be more or less prominent in individuals of different *trait* standing has been acknowledged, but has resulted in conflicting conclusions and recommendations. The current chapter posits that response biases are particularly problematic in the assessment of personality, because they may be characterized as sources of true construct variance (i.e., extreme option endorsement or avoidance, central tendency, and yeah/nay-saying are facet dimensions of some FFM constructs). Unfortunately, the source of true construct variance is scattered across different traits. This is problematic for establishing trait orthogonality – if "other" construct variance is introduced into FFM measurement because of response bias, scale correlations would be expected not solely because of construct association, but also because of measurement method/response bias shared across trait specifications. We used a large archival dataset to estimate relationships between FFM trait (and subfacet) standing and response styles along a 5-point graphic rating scale (ranging from response options of Very Inaccurate to Very Accurate). In addition to identifying personological content associated with acquiescence and extremity, implications of this investigation: 1) point toward some of the observed FFM trait correlations potentially being attributable to response style confounds, and 2) suggest adjective checklists or forced-choice formats may be preferable to graphic rating scale specification in personality assessment.

Introduction

Fundamentally the concern and focus of the current chapter is in the source(s) of variance in personality trait definitions. We speculate that some measured trait variance (and estimated associations between traits) with assessments that offer graphic rating response scales reflects characteristics of the *response scale* that are differently attended to by different individuals. With operative preferences (generally called response biases), measured trait variance does not exactly parallel true trait variance. This is particularly irksome if the source of unwanted variance is unknown systematic error (biased assessment) versus random error (lack of reliable measurement). Recommendations abound regarding reliability of assessment, but are less pointed regarding "what to do" with response bias in assessment. The current chapter presents some evidence suggesting that certain people use response scales differently than others in personality assessment. Knowledge of why (or what type of person) systematically varies is important because it addresses the "unknown" aspect of unknown systematic variance.

We focus the current investigation on three commonly investigated response biases in personality assessment. *Acquiescence* refers to a "tendency to answer affirmatively to a question no matter what its content" (Knowles & Nathan, 1997, p. 293). This effect (as investigated in the current chapter), however, applies more broadly to both those who tend to agree, as well as those who have a general proclivity toward disagreement. Operationally, acquiescence can therefore come in the form of "yea-sayers", who have a tendency to agree with statements, or "nay-sayers", who have a tendency to disagree with statements (Couch & Keniston, 1960). *Extremity* is characterized by the tendency to endorse the most extreme response categories regardless of content (Greenleaf, 1992). Finally, *central tendency* refers to, "the tendency to use the middle category regardless of content" (Baumgartner & Steenkamp, 2001, p. 143). Consistent across these three definitions is the "regardless of item content" component and specific applicability to odd-numbered graphic rating scales.

Measuring Personality

Personality traits are identified a number of different ways. The most popular assessments of the five factor model (FFM) of normal personality, the NEO-FFI or NEO-PI-R (Costa & McCrae, 1985), specify graphic response scales that range from agreement to disagreement. Trait definitions are identified through a simple summation algorithm across keyed items. However, a number of other methods of assessment exist. For example, assessments sometimes offer a forced choice-type response format. The Minnesota Multiphasic Personality Inventory (MMPI; revised MMPI-2) utilizes a true-false format. The Eysenck Personality Questionnaire (Eysenck, Eysenck, & Barrett, 1985) uses a yes/no format. Some instruments specify adjective checklists. The Personality Adjective Check List (Strack, 1987) is an example, comprised of 105-items intended to tap personality traits reflective of DSM-III-R classifications. The current chapter is focused on personality measures that specify a valenced continuum (i.e., so called graphic rating or Likert-type response scales). Personality here is assessed by presenting item prompts and a *rating scale* typically asking respondents for graded evaluations of accuracy or agreement with the construct indicator. For instance, the NEO scales specify an agreement continuum, while Goldberg's (1992; 1999) FFM measures provide either five- or nine-point accuracy-oriented graphic rating scales.

Respondent orientations toward these types of assessments are typically viewed through the lens of a cognitive processing model. Such models of self-report response commonly specify at least four processes: comprehension, retrieval, judgment, and response (e.g., Tourangeau, Rips, & Rasinski, 2000). During the comprehension step, a person attends to the meaning of the item prompt, identifying what piece of information is being requested (Lehnert, 1978). The second step, retrieval, involves recalling information identified in step one from long-term memory. This step, in and of itself, is a complex process encompassing a sequence of generating retrieval cues, recalling individual memories, and compiling information. The judgment step involves evaluating the completeness and usefulness of the memories, drawing inferences based on their accessibility, and integrating the information retrieved from memory in order to provide a response. Providing a response that maps onto the categories offered via the response options comprises the final step (Tourangeau et al., 2000).

In this final step, they suggest that some people "work hard to choose the best possible answer; others may be content to pick the first acceptable answer they consider" (p. 14). We focus our investigation on this final step as well. It seems plausible, based on the above model of survey response, that people may not only vary in their interpretation of the survey items (in this case evaluations of personality traits), but in their interpretation and use of the response options. Here, while acknowledging that interpretation and use of response options can be primed from the content of a survey (e.g., Schuman & Presser, 1981), our focus remains on the investigation of relatively stable tendencies toward differential use of the proffered options.

Response Bias in Personality Assessment

A *response bias* is a "systematic tendency to respond to a range of questionnaire items on some basis other than the specific item content" (Paulhus, 1991, p. 17). The bias may arise from either the testing situation itself (e.g., ambiguously-worded items), or from a more stable tendency to respond to surveys in a given manner (a "style"). A *response set* is a form of response bias whereby a situational demand (e.g., time pressure) temporarily causes an individual to respond a certain way (e.g., tendency toward extreme ratings). Cronbach (1946) defines a response set as, "a habit or temporary disposition that causes a person to respond to test items differently than he would if the same content were presented in a different form" (p. 46). Response *style*, however, is characterized by a consistent bias across both time and situations (Cronbach, 1946; Jackson & Messick, 1958).

Of the many forms of bias described in the literature, acquiescence "bias" has probably received the most interest as it relates to personality assessment (see Baumgartner & Steenkamp, 2001 for a summary of different forms of response biases). Acquiescence has been treated both as a pervasive response style, reflecting stable personological differences, as well as a transient response set, primed by some element of the assessment context. Central tendency and extremity, although attended to in the literature (and by personality measurement specialists), have not received as much attention regarding potential pervasive respondent characteristics. We believe these three different response tendencies are particularly susceptible to personality correlates, therefore rendering them of interest from a "contributor to variance in trait definitions" perspective. The brief literature review to follow highlights some of the potential individual differences that have been previously associated with these three response tendencies.

Acquiescence

Krosnick (1999) reviewed the literature on causes of acquiescent responding and described three common explanations: (1) personality, (2), social status, and (3) abilities and motivation to "optimize". Bentler, Jackson, and Messick (1971) differentiated between two forms of acquiescence: (1) agreement acquiescence, which is a tendency to agree or give positive ratings to all items, and (2) acceptance acquiescence, which is a tendency to endorse all items as true of oneself. Paulhus (1991) describes several measures of acquiescence including related measures of socially desirable responding. Knowles and Nathan (1997) found that acquiescence was positively correlated with simplicity (avoiding contemplative thoughts) and organization, and negatively related to intolerance. Acquiescent responding was not, however, related to social concerns such as self-deception or impression management. Thus, they suggest acquiescent responders tended to be cognitively simple, rigid in their mental organization, and somewhat intolerant of alternatives. Krenz and Sax (1987) attributed acquiescence to uncertainty. Stricker (1974) noted weak but consistent associations between acquiescence and conformity and independence.

Extreme Response Style

Research on correlates of extreme response option endorsement (i.e., the "outermost" valenced category) has largely centered around variables related to anxiety. Berg and Collier (1953), for instance, found a positive relationship between anxiety and endorsement of the extreme response category. Lewis and Taylor (1955) came to a similar conclusion using a sample of 129 high and 151 low-anxiety participants (selected from an initial sample of 2,000 undergraduate students). Likewse, Hernández, Drasgow, and González-Romá (2004) suggested that apprehensive, insecure, or worrying people were more likely to select extreme response options, as opposed to a more central option. The relationship between anxiety and extreme response category attraction may be more complex than this, however. Crandall (1965) uncovered an interaction between anxiety and gender in extreme category use such that women scoring high on a measure of anxiety were more prone to using the extreme response categories than were high anxiety men. Extreme response styles may also be negatively related to intellectual ability (Meisenberg, Lawless, Lambert, & Newton, 2006). Meisenberg and Williams (2008) found it to be negatively related to education. Moreover, extreme response style may be related to being "rigid" in thoughts and/or personality, or an intolerance for ambiguity. Schutz and Foster (1963) found an "inflexibility" factor associated with extreme responses. Brengelmann, in a group of studies (1958, 1959, 1960a, 1960b) also concluded that extreme responding was associated with "rigid" personality.

Central Tendency

Research on use of the middle response category, in general, has focused on the content of items, and why such content would lead to a middle category endorsement. Shaw and Wright (1967) originally posited three respondent intentions with middle category endorsements of attitude objects. Individuals may select this category 1) when they have no attitude regarding the object, 2) when they are "balanced" in terms of evaluation of the attitude object, or 3) when they have not clearly defined their attitude toward an object (often referred to as ambivalence – the inability to decide whether to agree or disagree). Kulas, Stachowski, and Haynes (2008) noted increased use of the middle category when a "not applicable" response option was not made available. Hernández et al. (2004) suggest that there may be specific personality correlates of middle response category use (more reserved people more likely to use a middle category, as opposed to people classified as outgoing). These authors conclude that outgoing people are more likely to share opinions, behaviors, and feelings. On the contrary, maturity does appear to be related to central tendency bias, perhaps because people become more sensitive to their own feelings as they age (less mature people tend to select this category with greater frequency; Hernández et al., 2004). Table 1 summarizes past research documenting individual difference correlates of the three response biases of focus.

Table 1. Content Associations

Source	***Association with Extreme Response Style***
Berg & Collier, 1953	Anxiety
Brengelmann, 1958, 1959, 1960a, 1960b	Rigidity/Tolerance for Ambiguity
Crandall, 1965	Anxiety & Gender
Kerrick, 1954	Anxiety & IQ
Lewis & Taylor, 1955	Anxiety
Meisenberg &Williams, 2008	Age, Education, & Income
Meisenberg, Lawless, Lambert, & Newton, 2006	IQ
Schutz & Foster, 1963	Inflexibility
Source	***Association with Acquiescence***
Couch & Keniston, 1960	Conformity & Impulsiveness
Knowles & Nathan, 1997	Mental Organization, Simplicity, & Intolerance
Krendz & Saks, 1987	Uncertainty
McGee, 1962	Stimulus Acceptance, Inhibition, & Conformity
Meisenberg, Lawless, Lambert, & Newton, 2006	IQ
Messick & Frederikson, 1958	Verbal Ability
Peabody, 1966	Uncertainty
Weaver, 2005	Neuroticism
Source	***Association with Midpoint Response Style***
Bishop, 1987	Ambivalence
DuBois & Burns, 1975	Ambiguity/Lack of Applicability

Table 1. (Continued)

Source	*Association with Midpoint Response Style*
Hernández, Drasgow, and González-Romá, 2004	Reservedness & Sensitivity
Madden & Klopfer, 1978	Ambivalence
Kulas, Stachowski, & Haynes, 2008	Uncertainty/Lack of Applicability
Mann, Phillips, & Thompson, 1979	Ambiguity
Presser & Schuman, 1980	Intensity
Ryan, 1980	Ambiguity

Summary and Research Agenda

The current chapter examines relationships between FFM traits and response scale option endorsement, demonstrating that *response styles* are at least partially associated with indicators used to identify FFM trait standing. Through investigating an archival IPIP dataset, over 6 million individual item responses were investigated for response style associations with measured traits. Specifically, we apply an item bias methodology across categories of response style in an attempt to uncover content associations with individuals identified as being prone or averse to response styles of acquiescence, central tendency, and extremity (after conditioning these individuals' item response on trait definitions).

Methods

Participants

A total of 21,588 individuals completed a 300-item web-based personality assessment between August, 1999 and March, 2000. Of those, 7,859 (36.4%) were male and 13,729 (63.6%) were female. The mean age was 26.24 years (*SD* = 10.79).

Materials

The International Personality Item Pool (IPIP) is an internet-housed item bank that at the time of investigation consisted of 2,036 indicators of 280 personality "scales". The items and scales of the IPIP are available to all (they are free of copyright restrictions) at http://ipip.ori.org/. For the current investigation, respondents provided internet-based responses to only 300 pre-identified items (see, for descriptions of this instrument, Goldberg, 1999; Johnson, 2005). These 300 items represent an IPIP version of Costa and McCrae's NEO-PI-R (1992). The response format consisted of a five-point graphic rating scale: 1 (Very Inaccurate), 2 (Moderately Inaccurate), 3 (Neither Accurate nor Inaccurate), 4 (Moderately Accurate), and 5 (Very Accurate). Within the FFM framework, 146 of the 300 items are scored positively (i.e., oriented toward the scale's keyed direction), while 154 are reverse scored.

Procedure

The 300-item IPIP was reduced to a balanced 174-item measure, and the 126 remaining items were used to identify individuals who could be viewed as expressing response styles. The general procedures followed a method of identifying individuals who could be classified as prone to tendencies of acquiescence, central tendency, or extremity. These individuals were contrasted to individuals who could be classified as *not* being prone to these response sets (or, in the case of acquiescence, prone to nay-saying). Individuals were therefore categorized as yea- or nay-sayers, middle category endorsers or avoiders, and extreme category endorsers or avoiders. Analyses of differential item functioning (DIF) were then performed across identified groups, looking for item content that might speak to response-set content (i.e., what makes an acquiescent person acquiesce, etc.). It should be noted that this technique is only helpful to the extent that the assessment is comprised of elements associated with the characteristics associated with group differentiation.

Operationalizations of Groups

In order to achieve balanced scales within both FFM and facet dimensions, six items per facet dimension were retained for FFM construct identification. Items were retained randomly within facet dimensions by placing item numbers in valence- and facet-identified piles and selecting either two or three item numbers per pile[1]. This resulted in a 174 balanced-item FFM measure.

The 126 items that were excluded from the 174-item FFM measure were retained to identify yeah- and nay-saying, extreme endorsing and avoiding, and middle category prone and averse groups. For the yea- and nay-sayers, response category endorsements across all 126 items *regardless of scoring valence* were tallied and grouped into positive ("moderately accurate" and "very accurate") and negative ("moderately inaccurate" and "very inaccurate") response tendencies. Acquiescence was estimated through counting the total number of positive responses (regardless of item direction), while trait scores were estimated through reverse-scoring negatively valenced item responses, and then summing individual item responses[2]. Extreme and middle category endorsers were identified through a tally of "very accurate" and "very inaccurate" or "neither accurate nor inaccurate" responses. Using the above grouping methods, 4,590 individuals were uniquely identified as yea-sayer or nay-sayer, middle category user or avoider, or extreme category endorser or avoider. Nine hundred and twenty-seven individuals were included in two of the six possible groupings, and sixty-eight individuals were included in all three investigations.

---

[1] The Excitement-Seeking and Cheerfulness facets of the Extraversion dimension and Morality of the Agreeableness dimension precluded the inclusion of 6 balanced items per facet – these three facets, therefore, were defined by 2 positive and 2 negatively-framed items (and the Extraversion and Agreeableness scales were therefore identified by 32 and 34 items, respectively).

[2] In order to limit the impact of artifactual variance, all investigated items were excluded from scale definitions following the recommendation of Kulas, Merriam, & Onama (2008).

Differential Item Functioning (DIF) Analyses

Zumbo's (1999) extension of the binary logistic regression approach to the multi-category logistic regression application was used for DIF identification. The ordinal logistic regression approach is appealing (relative to, for instance, the generalized Mantel-Haenszel statistic) because it not only identifies the presence or absence of DIF, but also estimates the effect size of DIF through computation of R^2 indices. The R^2 indices provide estimates of the percent of variance in trait scores attributable to group membership, above and beyond the percent of variance accounted for by trait standing. The analysis proceeds through a hierarchical framework, first regressing the item response on trait standing, then on category membership, then on a multiplicative trait x category term. The analysis therefore proceeds through three stages, the first stage essentially serving a covariate function (implementing a conditioning variable), with the next two phases indicating the presence or absence of uniform and non-uniform DIF, respectively. The researcher must choose which items to investigate, testing for DIF in one item at a time. The presence of DIF is evaluated against a chi-square difference statistic, with either 1 (Stage 2 minus Stage 1 [uniform DIF]) or 2 (Stage 3 minus Stage 1 [uniform and non-uniform DIF]) degrees of freedom. Effect size indices are calculated similarly (R^2 differences).

Zumbo's (1999) ordinal logistic regression model is expressed as:

$$logit\left[P(Y \leq j)\right] = \alpha_j + b_{1tot} + b_{2group} + b_{3(tot*group)}$$

where logit odds are calculated for selection of a response at point "j" or less in comparison to odds associated with selecting a higher response (in this current investigation, there are 5 "j" categories). The logit is the natural logarithm of the simultaneous ratio of 4 (j-1) probabilities. The analysis conducts separate intercepts (α's) for each of the j-1 cumulative probabilities. The procedure therefore calculates j-1 logistic curves (similar to boundary response functions used in graded response IRT or Rasch models [cf., Andrich, 1978; Samejima, 1969]). Similar to the Samejima (1969) assumption of a common a-parameter across boundary response functions (ogives), the ordinal logistic regression model assumes equal slopes of the cumulative logistic curves (ogives). For the current study, DIF was investigated through individually examining each of the 174 FFM measure items across yeah- and nay-saying, middle category endorsing or avoiding, and extreme category user or avoider groups.

ANALYSES

Figure 1 demonstrates a slight overall preference for endorsement of the "accurate" response options across 6,476,400 individual item responses (300 items x 21,588 respondents). On average, respondents endorse

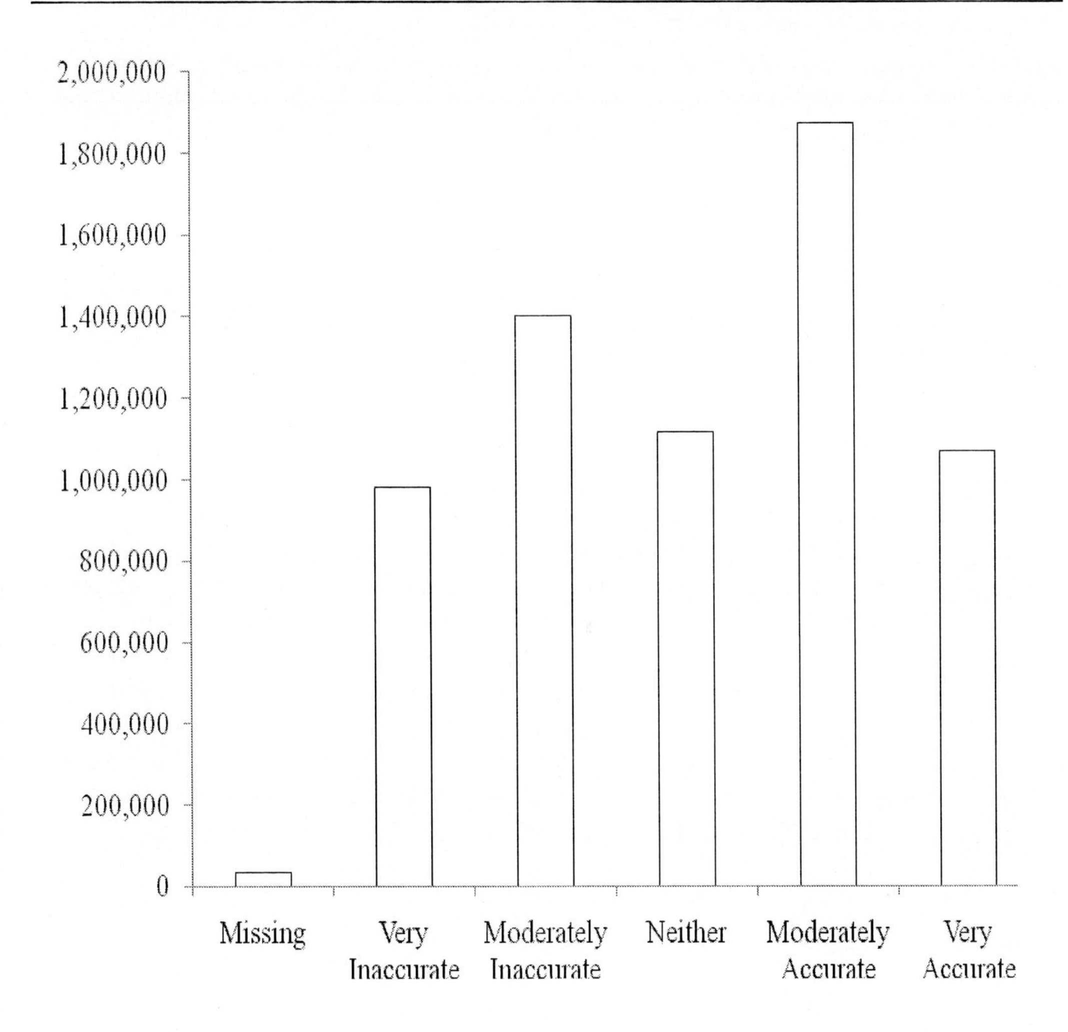

Figure 1. Absolute number of empirical category endorsements ($k = 300$, $n = 21{,}588$).

either "moderately accurate" or "very accurate" on 25.9 more items than they choose to endorse "inaccurate" or "very inaccurate" across all 300 items ($t = 126.5$; $p < .05$). This effect is most prominent in the "moderate" response option (as would be expected from visual inspection of Figure 1). A fairly even split of individuals was noted on extreme categories (41% chose "very inaccurate" more often than "very accurate", 57% chose "very accurate" more often than "very inaccurate"), whereas the moderate options exhibited a large preference differential (85% of respondents chose "moderately accurate" more often than "moderately inaccurate" across the 300 items, while only 13% of respondents chose "moderately inaccurate" more often than "moderately accurate"). Endorsement of the middle response option was slightly more common than endorsement of either extreme, but less frequent than a "moderate" valenced endorsement.

Regardless of the overall trait levels of the sample considered, with relatively balanced scales (and equal pole-leaning item *difficulties*), the numbers of positively and negatively valenced responses would be expected to be roughly equal (with roughly equal numbers of positively- and negatively-valenced item prompts) if yeah- and nay-saying tendencies were not present. The absolute endorsements in Figure 1 hint at *acquiescence* as the most prominent response bias in operation (with extreme and middle category endorsement relatively less prevalent). Table 2 presents descriptive scale information for each of the "trait" definitions retained in the 174-item "IPIP-NEO" measure.

Table 2. 174-item Internal Consistency Estimates (FFM-Level)

FFM Construct	# items	α	*Mean* (*SD*) of corrected item-total *r*'s
Neuroticism	36	.92	.48 (.13)
Conscientiousness	36	.92	.46 (.10)
Agreeableness	34	.86	.37 (.10)
Openness to Experience	36	.87	.38 (.08)
Extraversion	32	.90	.43 (.18)

As a fairly crude check on the consistency of the 174-item factor structure across the 3 investigations, a repeated-measures ANOVA was conducted, treating item R^2 values as individual data points and acquiescence, central tendency, and extremity groups as IV's ($F_{(2,346)} = 223.19$; $p < .01$). The extremity groups exhibited the highest average scale associations ($R^2 = 30.3$) with central tendency ($R^2 = 24.6$) and acquiescent samples ($R^2 = 20.4$) demonstrating lower mean scale-item associations. Correlations of item-scale associations showed that although overall item levels of scale variance explained differed across the three samples, the *pattern* of item-scale associations tended to be similar ($r_{central/extreme} = .97$; $r_{central/acq} = .87$; $r_{extreme/acq} = .85$).

Acquiescence

Total sample respondents ranged from one individual who chose 106 more positive than negative endorsements to one individual who chose 124 more negative than positive endorsements (the average effect across the 21,588 respondents was 12 more positive than negative endorsements [*SD* = 32.9]). The top and bottom 5% of positive (n = 1,093 yeah-sayers) versus negative (n = 1,182 nay-sayers) endorsers were retained for all DIF analyses. Retained yeah-sayers averaged 45.5 more positive than negative responses across the 126 items (*SD* = 8.0). Retained nay-sayers averaged 18.8 more negative than positive responses (*SD* = 6.7).

Central Tendency

Using the same basic approach as with acquiescence, individual responses were tallied for middle category endorsements. The top 5% (roughly) middle category endorsers (44 to 91 middle category endorsements; n = 1,168) and avoiders (0 to 2 endorsements; n = 949) were retained for DIF analyses.

Extremity

Extreme category endorsers (n = 1,170) ranged in frequency of choosing the "very accurate" or "very inaccurate" response options (the 5% split resulted in a range of 75 to 126 extreme category endorsements across the 126 items). Extreme category avoiders (n = 1,086) used either extreme option zero to ten times.

DIF Analyses

The average DIF effect across items was most prominent across acquiescence (R^2 = 5.8; *SD* = 5.7) and extremity samples (R^2 = 6.0; *SD* = 5.3), with the central tendency groups exhibiting very little DIF variance across the 174 indicators (R^2 = 3.4; *SD* = 2.7). Using a $\Delta\chi^2$ critical value to identify meaningful DIF is not entirely informative, as the χ^2 statistic is biased toward rejection with large sample sizes. Table 3 presents the largest DIF effect sizes.

Table 3. DIF Items (Central Tendency, Extremity, and Acquiescence)

Effect	Effect Size (R^2)	Item	FFM Dimension (scoring)	Facet
Acquiescence	32.78	Enjoy being reckless.	Extraversion (+)	Excitement-Seeking
	30.39	Do crazy things.	Conscientiousness (-)	Cautiousness
	24.10	Enjoy wild flights of fantasy.	Openness to Experience (+)	Imagination
	23.84	Make rash decisions.	Conscientiousness (-)	Cautiousness
	19.83	Love excitement.	Extraversion (+)	Excitement-Seeking
Extremity	29.01	Take no time for others.	Agreeableness (-)	Altruism
	27.34	Often make last-minute plans.	Conscientiousness (-)	Cautiousness
	23.42	Seek quiet.	Extraversion (-)	Gregariousness
	22.84	Obstruct others' plans.	Agreeableness (-)	Morality
	21.79	Can handle complex problems.	Neuroticism (-)	Vulnerability
	21.35	Am able to stand up for myself.	Neuroticism (-)	Self-Consciousness
Central Tendency	18.36	Obstruct others' plans.	Agreeableness (-)	Morality
	12.35	Can handle complex problems.	Neuroticism (-)	Vulnerability
	10.21	Seek quiet.	Extraversion (-)	Gregariousness
	10.18	Readily overcome setbacks.	Neuroticism (-)	Vulnerability

(ΔR^2) deemed non-trivial – the convention used here was to report the highest magnitude DIF items within an effect size range of roughly 10% (acquiescence and extremity) or those items exhibiting an ΔR^2 greater than 10%[3] (central tendency). The table reports response style associations with trait variance – after accounting for (i.e., conditioning on) item variance. Three of the most extreme items reported as exhibiting DIF across middle category endorsers and avoiders were also found to exhibit DIF across extreme and non-extreme endorsement groups, while the reported yea- and nay-saying indicators were associated only with the acquiescence analyses.

CONCLUSION

Generally, while the process of responding to an item would appear to be time and labor-intensive (Tourangeau et al., 2000), the typical response to a questionnaire item takes less than five seconds (Bassili & Fletcher, 1991). This prompts one to question whether respondents are fully attending to item prompt content or rather relying on response-scale preferences. The DIF results suggest that individuals identified as engaging in response styles introduce non-specified variance into trait definitions. Unfortunately, with the current assessment, the indicators of these sources of variance were not constrained within one FFM dimension, but scattered across all five. Yea- and nay-sayers, for example, introduce a seemingly inhibition-oriented confound, with indicators crossing Extraversion, Conscientiousness, and Openness to Experience scales. Our findings with acquiescence are therefore most similar to the conclusions of Couch and Keniston (1960), who cited *impulsiveness* as a key contributor to acquiescence.

The acquiescence response style also exhibited the strongest DIF-based content associations. For the presented items, between roughly 20 and 33% of item variance (see Table 3) was associated with yea- or nay-saying status, above and beyond the item's association with its corresponding scale/intended trait of measurement. The similarities among these items channel the somewhat dated perspective that there is an uninhibited, rash, thrill-seeking, or careless aspect to individuals susceptible to this form of response bias. The item similarities for extremity and central tendency biases were less clear. The central tendency investigations resulted in less group differentiation; in fact, no effect size greater than 20%. The extremity analyses point toward an individualism component (crossing Agreeableness, Conscientiousness, Extraversion, and Neuroticism constructs; most similar to the findings of Brengelmann, 1958, 1959, 1960[a], and 1960[b], and Schutz & Foster, 1963), although the extremity-oriented item similarities are less consistent than those associated with acquiescence.

The strong associations (noted by DIF effect sizes) suggest an individual difference component to acquiescence and extreme category use. The results of the central tendency analyses suggest that this bias may be best classified as a response *set,* brought upon by item characteristics such as clarity or ambiguity, moreso than respondent characteristics. This conclusion is consistent with the majority of research looking into middle category

[3] Full tables of χ^2 and R^2 values for each of the 174 investigated items are available from the first author upon request.

endorsement and suggests a simple remedy to this response bias: generate clear, unambiguous indicators. The recommendations for "dealing with" extremity and acquiescence are trickier.

One common recommendation for addressing response bias is to construct balanced scales (i.e., specify an equal number of positively- and negatively-framed item prompts). The addition of negatively-framed items, however, often reveals a method effect/factor (see, for example, Knight, Chisholm, Marsh, & Godfrey, 1988) and may adversely affect construct validity (see, for example, Quilty, Oakman, & Risko, 2006). A different option is consistent with the premise that it is the response scale *options* that are attended to differently. This position – balancing the direction of the *response options* rather than the item stems - is advocated by Barnette (2000). Although this procedure has not been specifically applied to response bias investigations, it may prove a viable alternative to balanced item specification (which does not seem to limit acquiescence; i.e., Figure 1).

One of the particularly problematic issues raised in this investigation of response biases is the proper identification of trait scores with operative response biases – *some* individuals have unwanted construct variance contributing to their personality scale scores. This means that yea-sayers, for example, would be expected to exhibit different scale scores and cross-trait associations than would nay-sayers (because of shared item content across FFM scales that is tapping into yea-/nay-saying), even if the yea- and nay-sayers were, for example, equally Extraverted. Fundamentally, this highlights issues about the adequacy of the FFM as an exhaustive taxonomy of inter- and intra-individual differences. Clearly there are inter-individual differences that are not explicitly captured by the FFM framework (at least as specified by our 174-item IPIP instrument and group operationalizations). These inter-individual differences, however, contribute only modest amounts of inter-individual differentiation compared to the specified FFM dimensions. The FFM is clearly a well-researched and widely-accepted framework of personality – our point is that researchers need to be careful in how the FFM is measured. The specification of graphic rating scales may not be ideal, as they introduce response-style confounds into FFM trait specification.

With the method implemented in the current chapter, the identification of content associations is limited by the items (randomly) chosen for inclusion or exclusion in the scale definition. Of the 300 possible content items, only 174 were investigated. The problem of "content of the assessment" as potential limiters of response-style variance, however, is not limited to our method. Any investigation is limited in the choice of (potential) correlates administered. It is simply not possible to exhaustively test all possible associations with individual differences in response style. We are also capitalizing on the strength or weakness of item-scale association and operationalization of "response style" groups. The procedure we used ignores important differences between individuals within a group (e.g., "chronic" and relatively more moderate yea-sayers were all grouped into one "yea-sayer" group). If these response styles are personological manifestations, they are perhaps better represented by dimensional/scaled measurement.

The take-home message is that there are meaningful personological confounds within both the acquiescence and extremity response styles – it would seem as though an alternative measurement approach is warranted for personality assessment specialists concerned with these response styles (for instance, if the population is deemed susceptible to these response sets [for example, cognitively challenged populations, e.g., Sigelman, Budd, Spanhel, & Schoenrock, 1981]) Both Jackson (1967) and Krosnick (1999) recommend the use of forced choice or multiple choice response formats because of the inextractable acquiescence effect.

Using a different methodology, we concur that acquiescence (and extremity) have individual difference correlates that confound trait specifications with summated graphic rating scales. Our recommendations follow those of Jackson (1967), Krosnick (1999), and Barnette (2000) – there are many assessment alternatives to the popular Likert-type rating scale. When elements of the rating scale are correlated with the object of measurement, it is time to find a new rating scale.

REFERENCES

Andrich, D. (1978). A rating formulation for ordered response categories. *Psychometrika, 43,* 561-573.

Barnette, J. J. (2000). Effects of stem and likert response option reversals on survey internal consistency: If you feel the need, there is a better alternative to using those negatively worded stems. *Educational and Psychological Measurement, 60,* 361-370.

Bassili, J. N., & Fletcher, J. F. (1991). Response-time measurement in survey research: A method for CATI and a new look at nonattitudes. *Public Opinion Quarterly, 55,* 331-346.

Baumgartner, H., & Steenkamp, J. E. M. (2001). Response styles in marketing research: A cross-national investigation. *Journal of Marketing Research, 38,* 143-156.

Bentler, P. M., Jackson, D. N., & Messick, S. (1971). Identification of content and style: A two-dimensional interpretation of acquiescence. *Psychological Bulletin, 76,* 186-204.

Berg, I. A., & Collier, J. S. (1953). Personality and group differences in extreme response sets. *Educational and Psychological Measurement, 13,* 164-169.

Bishop, G. F. (1987). Experiments with the middle response alternative in survey questions. *Public Opinion Quarterly, 51,* 220-232.

Brengelmann, J. C. (1958). The effects of exposure time in immediate recall on abnormal and questionnaire criteria of personality. *Journal of Mental Science, 104,* 665-680.

Brengelmann, J. C. (1959). Abnormal and personality correlates of certainty. *Journal of Mental Science, 105,* 142-162.

Brengelmann, J. C. (1960a). Extreme response set, drive level, and abnormality in questionnaire rigidity. *Journal of Mental Science, 106,* 171-186.

Brengelmann, J. C. (1960b). A note on questionnaire rigidity and extreme response set. *Journal of Mental Science, 106,* 187-192.

Costa, P.T., & McCrae, R.R. (1985). The NEO Personality Inventory manual. Odessa, FL: Psychological Assessment Resources.

Costa, P. T., Jr. & McCrae, R. R. (1992). *Revised NEO Personality Inventory (NEO PI-R™) and NEO Five-Factor Inventory (NEO-FFI) Professional Manual.* Odessa, FL: Psychological Assessment Resources.

Couch, A. & Keniston, K. (1960). Yea-sayers and nay-sayers: Agreeing response set as a personality variable. *Journal of Abnormal and Social Psychology, 60,* 151-174.

Crandall, J. E. (1965). Some relationships among sex, anxiety, and conservatism of judgment. *Journal of Personality, 33,* 99-107.

Cronbach, L. (1946). Response sets and test validity. *Educational and Psychological Measurement, 6,* 475-494.

DuBois, B., & Burns, J. A. (1975). An analysis of the meaning of the question mark response category in attitude scales. *Educational and Psychological Measurement, 35,* 869-884.

Eysenck, S. B., Eysenck, H. J., & Barrett, P. (1985) *Personality and Individual Differences, 6,* 21-29.

Goldberg, L. R. (1992). The development of markers for the big-five factor structure. *Psychological Assessment, 4,* 26-42.

Goldberg, L. R. (1999). A broad-bandwidth, public-domain, personality inventory measuring the lower-level facets of several five-factor models. In I. Mervielde, I. Deary, F. De Fruyt, & F. Ostendorf (Eds.), *Personality psychology in Europe, Vol. 7* (pp. 7-28). Tilburg, The Netherlands: Tilburg University Press.

Greenleaf, E. A. (1992). Improving rating scale measures by detecting and correcting bias components in some response styles. *Journal of Marketing Research, 29,* 176-188.

Hernández, A., Drasgow, F., & González-Romá, V. (2004). Investigating the functioning of a middle category by means of a mixed-measurement model. *Journal of Applied Psychology, 89,* 687-699.

Jackson, D. N. (1967). Acquiescence response styles: Problems of identification and control. In I. A. Berg (Ed.), *Response Set in Personality Measurement*, Aldine, Chicago.

Jackson, D. N. & Messick, S. (1958). Content and style in personality assessment. *Psychological Bulletin, 55,* 243-252.

Johnson, J. A. (2005). Ascertaining the validity of individual protocols from Web-based personality inventories. *Journal of Research in Personality, 39*, 103-129.

Kerrick, J. S. (1954). The effects of intelligence and manifest anxiety on attitude change through communications. Unpublished doctoral dissertation, University of Illinois.

Knight, R. G., Chisholm, B. J., Marsh, N. V., & Godfrey, H. P. (1988). Some normative, reliability, and factor analytic data for the revised UCLA Loneliness Scale. *Journal of Clinical Psychology, 44,* 203-206.

Knowles, E. S. & Nathan, K. (1997). Acquiescent responding in self-reports: Social concern or cognitive style? *Journal of Research in Personality, 31,* 293-301.

Krenz, C. & Sax, G. (1987). Acquiescence as a function of test type and subject uncertainty.

Krosnick, J. A. (1999). Survey research. *Annual Review of Psychology, 50,* 537-567.

Kulas, J. T., Merriam, J. & Onama, Y. (2008). Item-Trait Association, Scale Multidimensionality, and Differential Item Functioning Identification in Personality Assessment. *Journal of Research in Personality, 42,* 1102-1108.

Kulas, J. T., Stachowski, A. A. & Haynes, B. A. (2008). Middle response functioning in Likert responses to personality items. *Journal of Business and Psychology, 22,* 251-260.

Lehnert, W. (1978). *The process of question answering: A computer simulation of cognition.* Hillsdale, NJ: Erlbaum.

Lewis, N. A., & Taylor, J. A. (1955). Anxiety and extreme response preferences. *Educational and Psychological Measurement, 15,* 111-116.

Madden, T. M., & Klopfer, F. J. (1978). The "cannot decide" option in Thurstone-type attitude scales. *Educational and Psychological Measurement, 38,* 259-264.

Mann, I. T., Phillips, J. L., & Thompson, E. G. (1979). An examination of methodological issues relevant to the use and interpretation of the semantic differential. *Applied Psychological Measurement, 3,* 213-229.

McGee, R. K. (1962). The relationship between response style and personality variables: I. The measurements of response acquiescence. *The Journal of Abnormal and Social Psychology, 64,* 229-233.

Meisenberg, G., Lawless, E., Lambert, E., & Newton, A. (2006). The social ecology of intelligence on a Carribean island. *Mankind Quarterly, 46,* 395-433.

Meisenberg, G., & Williams, A. (2008). Are acquiescent and extreme response styles related to low intelligence and education? *Personality and Individual Differences, 44,* 1539-1550.

Messick, S., & Frederikson, N. (1958). Ability, acquiescence, and "authoritarianism". *Psychological Reports, 4,* 687-697.

Paulhus, D. L. (1991). Measurement and control of response bias. In J. P. Robinson, P. R. Shaver, & L. W. Wrightsman (Eds.), *Measures of Personality and Social Psychological Attitudes* (pp. 17-59). San Diego, CA: Academic Press.

Peabody, D. (1966). Authoritarianism scales and response bias. *Psychological Bulletin, 65,* 11-23.

Presser, S., & Schuman, H. (1980). The measurement of a middle position in attitude surveys. *Public Opinion Quarterly, 44,* 70-85.

Ryan, M. (1980). The Likert scale's midpoint in communications research. *Journalism Quarterly, 57,* 305-313.

Samejima, F. (1969). Estimation of latent ability using a response pattern of graded scores. *Psychometrika Monograph, 17.*

Schuman, H. & Presser, S. (1981). Questions and answers in attitude surveys. New York: Academic Press.

Schutz, R. E., & Foster, R. J. (1963). A factor analytic study of acquiescent and extreme response set. *Educational and Psychological Measurement, 23,* 435-447.

Shaw, M. E., & Wright, J. M. (1967). Scales for the measurement of attitudes. New York: McGraw-Hill.

Sigelman, C. K., Budd, E. C., Spanhel, C. L., & Schoenrock, C. J. (1981). When in doubt, say yes: Acquiescence in interviews with mentally retarded persons. *Mental Retardation, 19,* 53-58.

Strack, S. (1987). Development and validation of an Adjective Check List to assess the Millon Personality Types in a normal population. *Journal of Personality Assessment*, 51, 572-587.

Stricker, L. J. (1974). Response styles and 16 PF higher order factors. *Educational and Psychological Measurement, 34,* 295-313.

Tourangeau, R., Rips, L. J. & Rasinski, K. (2000). *The psychology of survey response.* Cambridge: Cambridge University Press.

Quilty, L. C., Oakman, J. M. & Risko, E. (2006). Correlates of the Rosenberg self-esteem scale method effects. *Structural Equation Modeling, 13,* 99-117.

Weaver, J. B. III. (2005). Mapping the links between personality and communicator style. *Individual Differences Research, 3,* 59-70.

Zumbo, B. D. (1999). *A Handbook on the Theory and Methods of Differential Item Functioning (DIF): Logistic Regression Modeling as a Unitary Framework for Binary and Likert-type (Ordinal) Item Scores.* Ottawa, ON: Directorate of Human Resources Research and Evaluation, Department of National Defense.

In: Personality Assessment: New Research
Editor: Lauren B. Palcroft & Melissa V. Lopez

ISBN 978-1-60692-796-0

Chapter 13

ACADEMIC AND EVERYDAY PROCRASTINATION AND THEIR RELATION TO THE FIVE-FACTOR MODEL

Gidi Rubenstein

ABSTRACT

Procrastination is a complex psychological behavior that affects everyone to some degree or another. This study examined academic procrastination (AP) and procrastination in everyday life (EP) and their relations to the Five-Factor Model (FFM) of personality among 267 male and female Israeli students, who filled in a demographic questionnaire, the shortened version of Costa and McCrae's (1992) NEO-FFI, Milgram, Srolof, and Rosenbaum's (1988) everyday life procrastination scale, and Toubiana and Milgram's (1992) academic procrastination scale. The two types of procrastination were strongly and positively associated with one another, AP was positively related to neuroticism (N) and extraversion (E) and negatively related to conscientiousness (C); and EP was also positively related to N but not to E and negatively related to C. Stepwise regression analyses indicated that when EP is the dependent variable, only AP, A, and E are included in the regression equation, whereas when AP is the independent variable, EP and all the FFM variables are included in the equation. Men scored significantly higher than women on AP but not on EP. In light of these findings, we discuss a personality typology of procrastinators, based on the FFM.

PROCRASTINATION IN EVERYDAY LIFE

Procrastination is a complex psychological behavior that affects everyone to some degree or another (Lay, 1986). Avoidance of taking action, unfulfilled promises to complete tasks, and using excuses to rationalize procrastination and to avoid guilt are some of the dimensions often mentioned by researchers in the field (e.g., Ellis & Knaus, 1977). Procrastination influences everyone and has a destructive potential (Rothblum et al., 1986). It also causes enormous economic losses in commercial companies (O'Donoghe & Rabin, 1999). Americans spend huge amounts of money on paying fines as a result of postponing tax payments (Loewenstein, 1992). Procrastination may cause significant health damages as well.

White, Wearing, and Hill (1994) showed that postponed decisions about cancer treatment may cause unnecessary health deterioration. Procrastination also results in postponing dental treatment, diet, physical activity and smoking cessation (Bogg & Roberts, 2004), to mention just a few health damages.

Academic Procrastination

Academic studies are one of the fields, in which procrastination is most outstanding. Ellis and Knaus (1977) estimated that 95% of the students demonstrate procrastination to one degree or another. Why is this behavior so frequently observed among students? Academic studies play a major role in current Western society. Parents usually put heavy pressure on their children's academic achievements as of early childhood. This parental pressure does not decrease over the years, but frequently increases. This achievement-seeking socialization causes individuals to consider academic success as top priority. This process may result in maladaptive perfectionism, which causes reversed outcome (Struthers et al., 2000).

Academic studies are also one's first opportunity for autonomic life, which involves time management for the sake of meeting academic tasks, scheduled in terms of months. This kind of schedule puts limits, on one hand, and yet leaves enough leeway for time regulation, on the other hand – a combination which may create fertile situational ground for procrastination (Ferrari & Beck, 1998). Support for this dynamics can be found in the increase of procrastination during studies, which hurts academic performance in research fields involving a high degree of free choice with respect to choosing topics or duration of work. Seminar papers, Master theses, and doctoral dissertations would be milestones in this process. However, no intelligence differences were found between procrastinators and non-procrastinators (Van Eerde, 2003). While procrastinators may have some success in the early stages of their studies, things tend to get worse as time goes by and the academic tasks become more complicated. The procrastinating students become aware to the fact that they may be unable to accomplish complicated tasks under time pressure, and their frustration increases (Milgram et al., 1998). Rothblum et al. (1986) have found that academic procrastination is positively related to generalized anxiety as well as to more specific forms of anxiety, such as test and social anxiety.

Procrastination and Personality

Rothblum et al. (1986) argue that procrastination involves more than just time management problems or mal cognitive skills, but rather, that it is based in one's personality. Procrastinators' self-esteem is rather low and it appears that they postpone their tasks, believing that they lack the ability to successfully carry them out (Ferrai & Emmons, 1995). Knaus adds that procrastination is often an attempt to protect self-esteem by individuals, who experience fear of failure, whereas Ruthblum et al. (1986) argue that procrastinators experience fear of success.

Is procrastination just a behavior or is it a personality trait? To be defined as a trait, a phenomenon has to be consistent across different situations and over time. Elliot (2002) found procrastination level to be quite consistent over a 10-year period of time. Twin studies show high correlation among identical twins with respect to procrastination level, thus suggesting a genetic basis (Arvey et al., 2003). Older studies, however, show low correlation between everyday and academic procrastination (e.g., Ellis & Knaus, 1977), suggesting that these are two situation-dependent behaviors rather than a consistent personality trait. This low correlation could, however, be explained by the unique character of student life, which is full of remote destination dates, thus offering multiple opportunities for procrastinate behavior (Ferrari & Beck, 1998).

Procrastination, Achievement Motivation and Gender Differences

According to McClelland et al.'s (1953) research, achievement-motivated people have certain characteristics in common, including the capacity to set high ("stretching") personal but obtainable goals; the concern for personal achievement rather than the rewards of success; and the desire for job-relevant feedback rather than for attitudinal feedback. These individuals are also motivated by a combination of ambition for success, which increases one's coping behavior, and fear of failure, which restrain this behavior. Ferrari and Emmons (1995) showed that fear of failure plays a major role in the development of procrastinate behavior. Achievement motivation of women was considered to be lower than that of men over many years. More specifically, fear of failure, which inhibits achieving behavior, was found to be higher among women. However, while McClelland et al. (1953) assumed consistent differences with respect to achievement motivation and fear of failure through actual study and career achievements, this approach has changed in light of the diminishing gender differences in various fields. Studies have shown that achievement motivation of women is similar to that of men, although it may be differently expressed. For instance, excellence in house holding was important for women in the past, and their achievement motivation would have taken the form of traditional conservative values. The same seemed to be true with respect to fear of failure. Both men and women were motivated by fear of failure in fields which were important to them, while nowadays members of both genders attribute the same importance to more similar fields of life (Hyde, 1991).

The Five Factor Model (FFM) of Personality

The FFM focuses upon those behaviors that the individuals express while dealing with people, changing circumstances and their environment. The two remaining behavioral dimensions relate to work and depression situations. The five personality tests measure intensity of behaviors in these five areas. Agreeableness (A) refers to how we react to opinions of others, Openness to Experience (O) refers to ease with change and new thoughts and ideas, Extraversion (E) refers to the preference of gathering over solitude, Conscientiousness (C) refers to achievement of goals, perseverance and planning (mainly at work), and Neuroticism (N) refers to the degree of one's nervousness, emotional instability and vulnerability to negative emotionality (Costa & McCrae, 1992). A most recent study

(Rubinstein, in press a) indicates a statistically significant and strong negative correlation between N and E, a low negative correlation between N and C, and a low positive correlation between A and O. Schouwenburg and Lay (1995) found that procrastination was largely associated with lack of conscientiousness, a finding which is in accord with responsibility, achievement motivation and target-oriented behavior as elements of conscientiousness (Howard & Howard, 1998); tentativeness and impulsiveness, as facets of neuroticism; and lack of extraversion (essentially in terms of inactivity), a finding which is supported by the description of procrastination as characterized by seclusion, shyness, and total reluctance to receive help from others (Anderson, 2003). Howard and Howard (1998) described an open individual as having many fields of interest and enjoying new and unknown situations, while Ellis & Knaus (1977) showed that procrastinators would do their best to avoid new and unfamiliar tasks and situations. While agreeableness consists of complaisance, sympathy and trust of others (Costa, 1991), rebelliousness, fanatical protection of one's autonomy and reluctance to follow instructions of others are major motives in the development of procrastinate behavior (Burka & Yuen, 1983).

HYPOTHESES

Based on the above reviewed literature, we predict:

1. Positive correlation between everyday and academic procrastination (Ellis & Knaus, 1977).
2. Negative correlation between extraversion and the two kinds of procrastination (Anderson, 2003; Schouwenburg & Lay,1995).
3. Negative correlation between conscientiousness and the two kinds of procrastination (Howard & Howard, 1998; Schouwenburg & Lay,1995).
4. Positive correlation between neuroticism and the two kind of procrastination (Milgram et al., 1992; Schouwenburg & Lay, 1995).
5. Negative correlation between openness to experience and the two kinds of procrastination (Ellis & Knaus, 1977; Howard & Howard, 1998).
6. Negative correlation between agreeableness and the two kinds of procrastination (Burka & Yuen, 1983; Costa, 1991).
7. No significant gender procrastination differences.

METHOD

Participants

Two hundred and sixty seven Israeli students (124 women and 143 men, mean age = 24.04 years) volunteered to participate. Most of them were undergraduate students (89.9%), with only 8.6% graduate and 1.5% post-graduate students. All of them mastered the Hebrew language. The vast majority of the students were single (89.9%) and the others were married. The students were selected from different academic departments to avoid bias, which might have been caused by field of study (35.2% studied social sciences, 24.8% studied humanities, 19.5% studied exact and life sciences, 12.7% studied law, and 7.9% studies medicine). They were recruited from two universities and two colleges.

Materials

Demographic Questionnaire

The first page of the research form included items on age, gender, family status, studies (degree and department) and academic institution (university vs. college).

NEO-FFI

An authorized shortened Hebrew translation of Costa and Mccrae's (1992) the NEO-FFI was used in the present study. It consists of 60 items, 12 for each FFM variable. For each item, participants express agreement or disagreement on a five-point Likert type scale, ranging from "completely disagree" (1) to "fully agree" (5). Half of the items in each sub-scale are worded positively, and the other half negatively, to avoid response set bias. The items of the different sub-scales are mixed, so that every fifth item represents one of the FFM. Cronbach's alphas for the present study are 0.77 for Neuroticism (N), 0.70 for Extraversion (E), 0.69 for Openness to Experience (O), 0.71 for Agreeableness (A), and 0.83 for Conscientiousness (C).

Everyday Procrastination Scale (EPS)

To measure procrastination in everyday life we used Milgram, Srolof, & Rosenbaum's (1988) scale, which consists of 20 tasks, referring to work, studies, personal life and social life. Participants are asked to rate their procrastination with respect to each task on a four-point Likert type scale, ranging from "right away" (1) to "at the last minute or later" (4). Cronbach's alpha of this scale in the present study is 0.89.

Academic Procrastination Scale (APS)

To measure procrastination in academic studies we used Toubiana and Milgram's (1992) scale, which consists of 10 items indicating postponement of learning tasks and four items indicating immediate performance of such tasks. Participants are asked to rate their responses on a five-point Likert type scale, ranging from full disagreement (1) to full agreement (5). Cronbach's alpha of this scale in the present study is 0.91.

Procedure

Two investigators administered the research forms during classes in different courses in two universities and two colleges, after being granted permission of the instructors (who were also present in class while the questionnaire was administered). Participants were asked not to write their names on the forms in order to fully protect their anonymity. The investigators read the instructions to the participants prior to administration of the questionnaires, which lasted 20 minutes, and were available to them for clarification questions. The investigators collected the forms after all the participants in a specific class completed them.

RESULTS

Pearson and Partial Correlations

In order to examine the associations predicted in the hypotheses we first computed Pearson correlation coefficients among the FFM variables and the two kinds of procrastinations (see Table 1). The strongest correlation was found between EP and AP. E, on the other hand, correlated significantly, however rather weakly, with AP but not with EP. A significant negative but rather weak correlation is evident between A and EP, a finding which is in accord with our prediction, but no significant correlation exists between A and AP. The lack of associations between O and both kinds of procrastination is also not supportive of our prediction.

Table 1. Intercorrelations Between the FFM, Academic Procrastination (AP) and Everyday Procrastination (EP)

	EP	E	C	A	O
AP	.55**	.11*	-.44**	-.01	0.10
N		-.21**	.25*	-.18**	.15**
E			.15**	0.05	0.08
C				-.13	-.10
AP					0.05

*p<.05
**p<.01

However, both N and C significantly and strongly correlated with both kinds of procrastination. This correlation may be partly the result of the negative correlation between N and C, which was found both in this study and in four other Israeli studies (Rubinstein, 2005; Rubinstein, in press a, in press b, in press c). The negative correlations between C and both AP and EP are stronger than the positive correlations, which were found between N and both kinds of procrastination. Given the negative correlation between N and C and the strong positive correlation between both kinds of procrastination, we also computed partial correlations between these four variables. The correlation between C and AP, controlling for N, indeed decreases from r = -.44, p<.01 to r = -.39, p<.01, and the correlation between C and EP, controlling for N, decreases from r = -.32, p<.01 to r = -.28, p<.01. When the two kinds of procrastination are controlled for each other as well, the partial correlation between C and AP (controlling for both N and EP) decreases to r = -.30, p<.01, while the correlation between C and EP (controlling for both N and AP) completely disappears, r = -.09, p = *ns*.

The correlation between N and AP, when C is controlled for, also decreases from r = .30, p<.01 to r = .21, p<.01, while the correlation between N and EP, controlling for C decreases from $r = .22, p<.01$ to $r = .15, p<.05$. When the two kinds of procrastination are controlled for each other as well, the partial correlation between N and AP (controlling for both C and EP) decreases to $r = .16, p<.05$, while the partial correlation between N and EP (controlling for both C and AP) completely disappears as well, $r = .06$, $p = ns$.

Regression Analyses

Given the differences between the simple and partial correlations reported above, we also run stepwise regression analyses in order to examine the relative contributions of each FFM variable, which account for the variance in both kinds of procrastination. In the first analysis the FFM variables, as well as the AP, were the independent variables, and the EP was the dependent variable (see Table 2). AP was included in the regression equation at the first step, A was included at the second step, and E at the third step, while O, C, and N were not included in the equation. The first model, in which only AP is included, accounts for 30.7% of the EP variance; the second model, which includes both AP and A, accounts for additional 3.2% of the variance; while the third model, which includes AP, A, and E, adds only 1.4% to this variance. The regression equation, which included AP, A, and E, is significant, $F(3, 263) = 47.80, p<.01$, the multiple regression coefficient being .59.

Table 2. Summary of Stepwise Regression Analysis for Variables Predicting Everyday Procrastination (N = 267)

	Variable	B	SE B	β	t	R^2
Step 1						0.31
	AP	0.42	0.04	0.55	10.83**	
Step 2						0.34
	AP	0.42	0.04	0.55	11.04**	
	AP	-.02	0.06	-.18	3.58**	
Step 3						0.35
	AP	0.43	0.04	0.57	11.34**	
	AP	.18	0.06	-.16	3.18**	
	E	-.15	0.06	-.12	2.39*	

*$p<.05$
**$p<.01$

In the second analysis AP was the dependent variable, while EP and the FFM were the independent variables. This analysis comprised of six steps. All the independent variables were included in the regression equation through these steps, as can be seen in Table 3, and have significant effects on AP in the following descending order: EP, C, E, N, A, and O. The six independent variables account for 46.9% of the variance in AP, 30.7% of which are being explained by EP alone. This regression equation is significant, $F(6, 260) = 38.20, p<.01$, the multiple regression coefficient being .47.

Table 3. Summary of Stepwise Regression Analysis for Variables Predicting Academic Procrastination (N = 267)

	Variable	B	SE B	*β*	t	R^2
Step 1						0.31
	EP	0.73	0.07	0.55	.55**	
Step 2						0.38
	EP	0.60	0.07	0.46	.46**	
	C	-.43	0.08	-.29	-.29**	
Step 3						0.42
	EP	0.62	0.07	0.47	.47**	
	C	-.47	0.07	-.32	-.32**	
	E	-.31	0.08	-.20	-.20**	
Step 4						0.45
	EP	0.58	0.06	0.44	.44**	
	C	-.42	0.07	-.29	-.29**	
	E	-.31	0.08	-.20	-.20**	
	N	-.21	0.06	0.17	-.17	
Step 5						0.46
	EP	0.60	0.06	0.46	.46**	
	C	-.41	0.07	-.28	-.28**	
	E	-.34	0.07	0.22	.22**	
	N	0.24	0.06	0.20	.20**	
	A	0.16	0.07	0.11	.11*	
Step 6						0.47
	EP	0.60	0.06	0.46	.46**	
	C	-.40	0.07	-.27	-.27**	
	E	-.34	0.07	0.22	.22**	
	N	0.26	0.06	0.22	.22**	
	A	0.16	0.07	0.11	.11*	
	O	0.15	0.07	0.10	.10*	

* $p<.05$

** $p<.01$

As we can see, while only AP, A, and E are included in the first regression equation, where EP is the dependent variable, EP and all the FFM variables are included in the second regression equation, where AP is the dependent variable. This would indicate a lower covariance between AP and the FFM variables, which is also evident from the changes in β values in both analyses. As can be seen from Tables 2 and 3, when EP is the dependent variable, β values increase with each further step, whereas when AP is the dependent variable, they decrease with each step.

Gender Differences

Finally, to test our last hypothesis, which predicted no procrastination gender differences, we carried out two ANCOVAs, in which one kind of procrastination was the dependent variable, gender was the independent variable, and the other kind of procrastination, the FFM variables, and Age were the covariates. Unlike our prediction, men ($M = 2.97$, $SD = .77$) were more academically procrastinate than women ($M = 2.77$, $SD = .65$), $F(1, 258) = 6.92$, $p<.05$ - with significant effects of EP, $F(1, 258) = 82.86$, $p<.001$, N, $F(1, 258) = 23.28$, $p<.001$, E, $F(1, 258) = 25.08$, $p<.001$, A, $F(1, 258) = 8.79$, $p<.005$, and C, $F(1, 258) = 34.83$, $p<.001$. However, the EP difference between men ($M = 2.34$, $SD = .60$) and women ($M = 2.18$, $SD = .50$), $F(1, 258) = 2.65$, was non-significant - with significant effects of Age, $F(1, 258) = 4.19$, $p<.05$, AP, $F(1, 258) = 69.18$, $p<.001$, A, $F(1, 258) = 6.85$, $p<.05$, and C, $F(1, 258) = 4.99$, $p<.05$.

DISCUSSION

Everyday and Academic Procrastination

The purpose of this study was to examine the association between the FFM and both everyday and academic procrastination. Unlike previous studies (Ellis & Knaus, 1977), we used Milgram, Srolof, and Rosenbaum's (1988) newer EP scale, which covers a wide variety of life situations with a potential for procrastinate behavior. We found a strong positive correlation between the two kinds of procrastination, as hypothesized, as well as higher level of AP ($M = 2.88$, $SD = 0{,}73$) than EP ($M = 2.26$, $SD = 0.55$). This higher AP may be explained to Ferrari and Beck's (1988) claim about student life, which provide multiple opportunities for procrastinate behavior. Different procrastination levels in different situations are also demonstrated by DeRoma et al. (2003), who found that different teaching methods yield different procrastination levels. For instance, high test frequency compelled students to make a change and be less procrastinating, a finding which implies that procrastination is situation-dependent. The wide variety of situations covered by the EP measure used in this study may, therefore, explain the higher correlation between EP and AP.

Procrastination and the FFM

The positive correlation between AP and E, as weak as it is, as well as the inclusion of E in the regression equations of both kinds of procrastinations, are in agreement with Reiser's (1984) claim that undertaking too many tasks are an essential characteristic of both procrastinators and extraverts. Moreover, E is one of just two of the FFM variables, included in the EP equation, which suggests a unique association between E and procrastination.

The negative correlations between C and both kinds of procrastination may suggest that these two variables are, to a certain degree, opposites of one another. A C item like "I know how to plan my work, so that it will be carried out on time" illustrates how high C scorers demonstrate a non-procrastinate behavior. However, the perfectionist part of C (e.g., "I aspire to excellence in everything that I do") might also be maladaptive and therefore positively related to procrastination (Struthers et al., 2000). C is included in the second of the six AP regression equation steps, whereas it is not included at all in the EP equation, which also supports seeing procrastination as situation-dependent.

The positive correlations between N and the two kinds of procrastination supports Brown's (1991) claim that procrastination is ego-dystonic, suggesting that this behavior is not the result of intentional carelessness or simple indifference. Both Pearson correlation coefficients and the regression analyses suggest that N is more strongly related to AP than to EP. It is not included at all in the EP equation, while it enters in the fourth step of the AP equation, which may suggest deeper emotional conflicts with respect to AP because of the great pressure associated with academic achievements in Western culture (Struthers et al., 2000) and the increasing evidence about the association between perfectionism and various mental disorders (Flett & Hewitt, 2002).

A correlated only with EP and entered to the EP equation in the second step but only in the fifth step to the AP equation. While procrastination in everyday life may involve passive-aggressive behavior which hurts inter-personal relationships, AP is directed mainly against one's self. This passive-aggressive aspect of procrastination in everyday life is supported by Mulry et al.'s (1994) therapeutic approach, in which individuals, who are asked to postpone tasks, carry them out immediately as an expression of rebelliousness.

Finally, O has not correlated with either type of procrastination, which may be the result of the low reliability of this FFM scale. Its entering to the AP equation in the last step may indeed weakly support the contrast between focusing required by academic tasks and the multiple stimulations, needed by high O scorers. However, such speculation should be referred to with reservation.

Gender Differences

The slightly higher, though statistically significant, AP level of men vs. women – along with the non-significant EP gender difference – supports Hyde's (1991) claim, suggesting that members of both genders attribute the same importance to more similar fields of life. However, when it comes to AP, men may still be more achievement socialized (Mclleland, 1953), taking the paradoxical form of procrastination as an expression of maladaptive perfectionism with reversed outcome (Struthers et al., 2000).

Future Research

Given the associations found in this study between the FFM and the two kinds of procrastination, further studies might aim at a personality typology of procrastinators defined by some of the FFM variables. One type of procrastinators may have performance anxiety, which may be the result of maladaptive perfectionism, defined by high levels of both N and C. A combination of high E and low C may, on the other hand, define a seeking-sensation type of procrastinator. Ego-syntonic vs. ego-dystonic procrastinators can be defined by their N scores. Therapeutic attempts to actively involve procrastinate students in the learning process by transferring responsibility for success from the instructor to the student (Cross &

Steadman, 1996) have had only partial positive outcome (Young et al., 2000). A personality typology of procrastinators may enhance the development of specific therapeutic strategies for specific types of procrastinators.

REFERENCES

Anderson, C. J. (2003). The psychology of doing nothing: Forms of decision avoidance result from reason and emotion. *Psychological Bulletin, 129*, 139-167.

Arvey, R. D., Rotundo, M., Johnson, W., & McGue, M. (2003). *The determinants of leadership: The role of genetics and personality.* Paper presented at the 18th Annual Conference of the Society for Industrial and Organizational Psychology, Orlando.

Bogg, T., & Roberts, B. W. (2004). Conscientiousness and health-related behaviors: A meta-analysis of the leading behavioral contributors to mortality. *Psychologica Bulletin, 130*, 887-919.

Brown, R. T. (1991). Helping students confront and deal with stress and procrastination. *Journal of College Student Psychotherapy, 6*, 87-102.

Burka, J. B. & Yuen, L. M. (1983). *Procrastination: Why you do it, what to do about it.* Reading, MA: Addison-Wesley.

Byrne, D. (1974). *An introduction to personality: research theory and application.* NJ: Prentice-Hall.

Costa, P. T., Jr., & McCrae, R. R. (1992). *Neo PI-R: Professional manual.* Odessa. FL: Psychological Assessment Resources.

Costa, P. T. (1991). Clinical use of the Five-Factor Model: An introduction. *Journal of Personality Assessment, 57*, 393-398.

Cross, P. K., & Steadman, M. H. (1996). *Classroom research: Implementing the scholarship of teaching and learning*. SF: Jossey-Bass.

DeRoma, V. M., Young, A., Mabrouk, S. T., & Brannan K. P. (2003). Procrastination and student performance on immediate and delayed quizzes. *Education, 124,* 40-48.

Elliot, R. (2002). *A ten-year study of procrastination stability*. Unpublished Master Thesis, University of Louisana, Monroe.

Ellis, A. & Knaus, W. J. (1977). *Overcoming procrastination*. NY: New American Library.

Ferrari J. R., Harriott, J. S, Evans, L., Lecik-Michna, D. M., & Wenger J. M. (1998). Exploring the Time Preferences by Procrastinators: Night or Day, Which is the One? *European Journal of Personality, 11*, 187–196.

Ferrari, J. R. & Beck, B. L. (1998). Affective responses before and after fraudulent excuses by academic procrastinators. *Education, 118*, 529–538.

Ferrari, J. R. & Emmons, R. A. (1995) Methods of procrastination and their relation to self-control and self-reinforcement: An exploratory study. *Journal of Social Behavior and Personality, 10*, 135–142.

Flett, G. L. & Hewitt, P. L. (2002). Perfectionism and maladjustment: An overview of theoretical, definitional, and treatment issues. In G. L. Flett and P. L. Hewitt (Eds.), *Perctionism: Theory, research, and treatment* (pp. 5-32). Washington, DC: American Psychological Association.

Gray, J. A. (1987). Perspectives on anxiety and impulsivity: A commentary. *Journal of Research in Personality, 21*, 493-509.

Howard, P.J. & Howard, J.M. (1998). *An introduction to the five-factor model for personality for human resource professionals*. Austin, TX: Leornian.

Hyde J.S. (1991). *Half the human experience*. Lexington, MA: DC Heath & Company.

Knaus, W. J. (2000). Procrastination, blame, and change. *Journal of Social Behavior and Personality, 15*, 153-166.

Lay, C. H. (1986). At last, my research article on procrastination. *Journal of Research in Personality, 20*, 474-495.

Loewenstein, G. (1992). The fall and rise of psychological explanations in the economics of intertemporal choice. In G. Loewenstein & J. Elster (Eds*.), Choice over time* (pp. 30-34). NY: Russell Sage Foundation.

McClelland D. C., Atkinson J. W., Clark R. A. & Lowel E. G. (1953). *The achievement motive*. NY: Appleton Century Crofts.

Milgram, N.A., Mey-Tal G., Levison Y. (1998). Procrastination, generalized or specific, in college students and their parents. *Personality and individual differences, 25*, 297-316.

Milgram, N. A., Sroloff, B., & Rosenbaum, M. (1988). The procrastination of everyday life. *Journal of Research in Personality, 22*, 197-212.

Milgram, N.A, Gehrman, T & Keinan G. (1992). Procrastination and emotional upset: A typological model. *Personality and Individual Differences, 13*, 1307-1313.

Mulry, G., Fleming, R., & Gottschalk, A. C. (1994). Psychological reactance and brief treatment of academic procrastination. *Journal of College Student Psychotherapy, 9*, 41-56.

O'Donoghue, T & Rabin, M. (1999) "Doing it now or later": American economic of instruction course. *Educational Communication, and Technology Journal. 32*, 41-49.

Reiser, R A. (1984). Reducing student procrastination in a personalized system of instruction course. *Educational Communication and Technology*, *32*, 41-49.

Rothblum E. D., Solomon L. J., & Murakami, J. (1986). Affective, cognitive and behavioral differences between low and high procrastinators. *Journal of Counseling Psychology, 33*, 388-394.

Rubinstein, G. (2005). The Big Five among male and female students of different faculties. *Personality and Individual Differences, 38,* 1495-1503.

Rubinstein, G. (in press a). The Big Five and self-esteem among overweight dieting and non-dieting women. *Eating Behaviors*.

Rubinstein, G. (in press b). Two behavioral indicators of dependency and the five- factor model of personality. *Psychology and Psychotherapy: Theory, Research and Practice*.

Rubinstein, G. (in press c). The Five Factor Model (FFM) among Four Groups of Male and Female Professionals. *Journal of Research in Personality*.

Schouwenburg, H. C. & Lay C. H. (1995). Trait procrastination and the big-five factors of personality, *Personality and Individual Differences, 18,* 481-490.

Struthers C. W., Perry R. P., & Menec, V. H. (2000). An examination of the relationship among academic stress, coping, motivation, and performance in college. *Research in Higher Education, 41*, 581-594.

Toubiana, Y. & Milgram, N.A., (1992). *School anxiety and procrastination in children and their parents*. Unpublished report, Tel-Aviv University.

Van Eerde, W. (2003). A meta-analytically derived nomological network of procrastination. *Personality and Individual Differences, 35*, 1401-1418.

West, R. J., Blander, J., & French, D. (1993). Mild social deviance, Type-A behavior pattern and decision-making style as predictors of self-reported driving style and traffic accident risk. *British Journal of Psychology, 84*, 207-219.

White, V. M., Wearing, A. J., & Hill, D. J. (1994). Is the conflict model of decision making applicable to the decision to be screened for cervical cancer? A field study. *Journal of Behavioral Decision Making, 7*, 57–72.

Young, M. R., Barab, S. A., & Garrett, S. (2000). Agent as detector: An ecological perspective on learning by perceiving-acting systems. In D. H. Jonassen and M. Land (Eds.), *Theoretical Foundations of Learning Environments* (pp. 147-171). London: Lawrence Erlbaum.

In: Personality Assessment: New Research
Editor: Lauren B. Palcroft and Melissa V. Lopez

ISBN: 978-1-60692-796-0

Chapter 14

PERSONALITY AND ATTITUDE TOWARD DREAMS

Barbara Szmigielska and Małgorzata Hołda
Jagiellonian University, Kraków, Poland

ABSTRACT

Dream research focuses mainly on the formal characteristics of dreams (e.g., mood, realism, coloring, dream recall frequency) and dream content but little research has been conducted to date on the functional aspects of dreams. Dreams have always been the focus of human enquiry and have always played a significant part in human life. Every society has developed its own theories of dreams. Therefore, the functional aspects of dreams such as affective response to dreams and dreaming (liking/disliking, fear, curiosity etc.), subjectively perceived role of dreams, private concepts of dreams and dreaming, or different kinds of behavior influenced by dreams (trying to interpret one's own dreams, believing they have special meaning, behaving according to the clues offered by the dream, sharing dreams with other people, etc.) all seem to be equally important in the investigation of dreams. In studies on the functional aspects of dreams, the term *attitude toward dreams* is commonly used. No clear definition of attitude toward dreams has been provided, however. Furthermore, different studies take different components of attitude into account — some measure only the affective response to dreams, others also consider beliefs about dreams or the influence of dreams on waking life. Because of this ambiguity, the present authors propose their own definition of attitude toward dreams based on the classical, three-component definition of attitude. Some of the previous research has shown that attitude toward dreams correlates substantially with personality traits, particularly with the openness to experience factor of the Five Factor model of personality. Some results also suggest a relationship between attitude toward dreams and neuroticism. The present study was designed to explore the relationship between attitude toward dreams and the Big Five personality factors. The sample consisted of 108 participants aged 19-33, 62 women and 46 men. Attitude toward dreams was measured with a 56-item self-report scale (Attitude toward Dreams Scale – ADS) specifically developed for the present study and psychometrically verified. Participants also completed the Polish version of the NEO-PI-R.

Introduction

Most dream research focuses on dream content and the formal characteristics of dreams (e.g., mood, realism, coloring, dream recall frequency). The functional aspects of dreams deserve equal attention, however, although research to date has failed to provide an unequivocal answer to the question of what functions dreams actually serve. There are very many competing ideas and researchers representing various disciplines are still disputing not only the nature of dreams but also their functions.

Dream research is replete with methodological stumbling blocks. The functions of dreams cannot be studied directly because the researcher only has access to dream reports, not dreams per se. The dreamer can only report the dream when in a waking state. If we want to test the hypothesis that dreams can help to solve the dreamer's personal problems, the dreams must first be remembered and then recalled (Schredl, 2003). Therefore dream researchers always enquire about experiences to which the dreamer only has access retrospectively. The dreamer's report is affected not only by the dream experience itself but also by his or her ability to remember dreams as well as by his or her beliefs and ideas about dreams and attitudes toward dream content or ability to recall dreams, none of which are construed at the exact time of the dream experience (Antrobus, 2000; Beaulieu-Prévost & Zadra, 2005b). It is also possible that it is not the dream itself but thinking about the dream that affects the dreamer's later waking life and behavior (Schredl, 2003).

Dream researchers should therefore study the subjectively perceived functions of dreams and related concepts. It is important to investigate such functional aspects as the dreamer's emotional attitude toward his or her dreams, dream perception, the role of dreams for the individual or his or her private dream theories.

Existing Research on Attitude Toward Dreams

Dreams have always been an object of attention and have always played an important role in people's lives. Practically every culture has developed theories in this area of human experience and even today there are many popular dream theories (Hall, 1997; Szmigielska & Hołda, 2007; Robbins & Tanck, 1991). In many communities, both tribal and western, it is common practice to share one's dreams (Domhoff, 1999; Holda, 2006; Tedlock, 1991; Wax, 2004). Many therapeutic schools use working with dreams on the assumption that dreams are psychologically significant and clinically valuable phenomena (Clark, 1994; Crook Lyon & Hill, 2004; Dombeck, 1991; Natterson, 1993; Pesant & Zadra, 2004; Wilmer, 1982). Dreams can also have a major effect on waking life as demonstrated, for example, by nightmare (Belicki, 1992; Levin, 1994) and anthropological research (Stewart, 2004; Tedlock, 1991, 2004). Many people are convinced that dreams can suggest solutions to everyday problems or inspire creative activity (Knudson, 2001; Schredl & Erlacher, 2007). It has also been reported that people quite often have dreams which they believe have changed their lives (Dement & Vaughan, 1999; Hartmann, 2008; Knudson, Adame & Finocan, 2006; Schredl & Erlacher, 2007).

There has been little research on the functional aspects of dreams, especially work on the subjective perception of dreams and their functions in the lives of individuals. Some of the research which has been done focuses solely on isolated functional aspects such as dream sharing (Dombeck, 1991; Siuta & Szmigielska, 2005), the effect on waking mood and well-being (Belicki, 1992; Levin, 1994), working with dreams in psychotherapy (Clark, 1994; Livingston, 2001; Pesant & Zadra, 2004; Schredl, Bohusch, Kahl, Mader & Somesan, 2000) or private beliefs about dreams (Hall, 1997; Robbins & Tanck, 1991; Szmigielska & Hołda, 2007).

Other researchers have attempted a broader approach to the functional aspects of dreams by referring to the attitude toward dreams concept. Most of this work has been done in two contexts. First are studies of the frequency of dream recall. In this approach the determinants and correlates of dream recall are the focus of attention. Dream recall has been found to correlate with attitude toward dreams (Robbins & Tanck, 1988; Schredl, Nürnberg & Weiler, 1996; Schredl, Brenner & Faul, 2002; Schredl, Ciric, Götz & Wittman, 2003; Schredl, Wittman, Ciric and Götz, 2003; Tonay, 1993). The second group of studies is concerned with psychotherapy that involves working with dreams or the effectiveness of training in dream interpretation skills. In this approach, the focus is, among other things, on the determinants' underlying motivation to engage in such therapy or training (both the patient's and the therapist's). It has frequently been demonstrated that one of the motivating factors is the attitude of the patient and the therapist toward dreams (Clark, 1994; Crook & Hill, 2003; Crook Lyon & Hill, 2004; Hill, Diemer & Heaton, 1997; Hill et al., 2006).

No research has been conducted to date, however, in which attitude toward dreams is the main focus of attention. Neither has a precise definition of attitude toward dreams been offered in the literature. Assumedly people who engage in various behaviors such as writing down their dreams, keeping dream diaries, trying to analyse or interpret their dreams have more positive attitudes toward dreams (Wolcott & Strapp, 2002). No precise definition of attitude toward dreams has been formulated, however. Neither has researchers reached consensus as to what elements should be included in this category and how to measure it.

Most investigators treat attitude toward dreams unidimensionally (Beaulieu-Prévost & Zadra, 2007; Hill et al., 1997; Cernovsky, 1984). For example, Hill et al. (1997) developed the Attitude Toward Dreams questionnaire (ATD). This questionnaire has 11 items concerning motivation to remember dreams, paying attention to them, sharing dreams and giving them meaning, and beliefs concerning the meaning of dreams in human life. Factor analysis yielded a one-factor structure of attitude toward dreams thus conceptualized. The questionnaire was eventually modified (Hill et al., 2001). Attitude Toward Dreams – Revised (ATD-R) has 9 items. Factor analysis once again confirmed the one-factor structure of the measured variable. There is also a Chinese version of the ATD-R (Tien, Lin & Chen, 2006) with similar psychometric parameters.

Schredl et al. (1996) proposed a different approach to attitude toward dreams. In their questionnaire measuring attitude toward dreams, they included four groups of items measuring various aspects of dream recall as well as positive, neutral or negative attitude toward dreams. This questionnaire was also modified in subsequent studies (Schredl, Ciric et al., 2003). The new version contains two groups of items relating to dream recall and general attitude toward dreams. Factor analysis yielded a two-factor structure: dream recall and negative attitude toward dreams. However, the authors themselves admit that the questionnaire only measures selected aspects of attitude toward dreams (Schredl, Ciric et al., 2003).

Efforts have also been made to measure attitude toward dreams using items from other instruments. Cernovsky (1987) in his study used one MMPI item to measure attitude toward dreams ("A person should try to understand his/her dreams and be guided by or take warning from them"). Beaulieu-Prévost and Zadra (2005a), in turn, adopted three items from the McGill Sleep and Dream Questionnaire, originally a 72-item instrument measuring various aspects of sleep and dreaming including dream recall frequency, nightmare frequency and content, conscious dreams, recurrent dreams, and attitude toward dreams.

Definition of the Attitude Toward Dreams

As we can see from the foregoing review, there are many ambiguities in research on the attitudes toward dreams. The concept of attitude toward dreams is present in the literature but when it comes to actual research, various aspects of this phenomenon are studied and the attitude itself is not defined unequivocally. Consensus is lacking as to its criteria and components as well as assessment instruments ensuring comparable results.

Therefore, the authors propose their own definition of attitude toward dreams in the present study. This definition follows the classical, three-component definition of attitude (Ajzen, 1988; McGuire, 1985) to enable as broad an approach to the functional aspects of dreams as possible: attitude toward dreams is a relatively stable, individual emotional stance toward dreams, a set of beliefs and concepts about dreams and a set of behaviors relating to dreams. The authors also assume, following the example of other researchers, that attitude toward dreams is a general construct (Schredl, Ciric et al., 2003; Schredl, Wittmann et al., 2003) and that it is relatively stable (Rochlen, Ligiero, Hill & Heaton, 1999; Schredl et al., 2002).

Due to the specific character of the dream phenomenon it was therefore assumed that attitude toward dreams is a unipolar attitude ranging from lack of involvement to involvement (treating the attitude as a unipolar dimension was postulated by, e.g., Bohner and Wänke, 2002). A review of the existing research suggests that interest in dreams and many dream-related behaviors (dream sharing, interpreting, effect on behavior) are associated with both positive and negative emotions. One of the most frequent reasons why people share their dreams is dream content which can be pleasant (funny, peculiar) or unpleasant (e.g., anxiety-provoking). It has frequently been found that people share their dreams in order to reduce the anxiety evoked by a nightmare (Hołda, 2006; Szmigielska, 1996, 1999; Szmigielska & Hołda, 2007). It has also been found that negative dream-related emotions have a more powerful effect on waking mood than positive emotions (Schredl & Doll, 1998). Individuals who often have nightmares pay more attention to their dreams than individuals who seldom have nightmares and they also view them as more important for their daily functioning; they more often declare that their dreams are meaningful for them and affect their wellbeing and mood (Belicki, 1992; Berquier & Ashton, 1992; Levin, 1994). It therefore seems that both positive and negative emotions should be located at one end of the attitude toward dreams continuum and that intensity rather than valence should be the focus of attention. In other words, attitude intensity rather than positive and negative attitude extremes are the issue.

An additional argument in favor of such a conceptualization of attitude toward dreams is that no statements concerning negative behaviors directed "against" one's dreams can be found in any of the available scales measuring the different aspects of the attitude under discussion (Cernovsky, 1984; Hill et al., 1997; Hill et al., 2001; Schredl et al., 1996; Schredl et al., 2002; Schredl, Ciric et al., 2003). Neither have such statements been found in analyses of free utterances concerning dreams gathered by means of interviews (Szmigielska & Hołda, 2007) or in our review of the research literature on dreams or other sources (popular literature, self-help books, internet forums and blogs etc.). In other words, it seems that all we can refer to is the presence or absence of certain behaviors, not "positive" or "negative" behaviors. We have therefore decided not to present attitudes toward dreams on a "positive-negative" attitude continuum but to present them instead on a continuum ranging from "lack of involvement" to "involvement".

Attitude toward dreams according to our definition contains three components: an emotional one, a cognitive one and a behavioral one. Each of these components can be described on the "lack of involvement – involvement" continuum.

The emotional component of attitude toward dreams involves emotional stance toward dreams, the emotions which dreams evoke in the individual and the effect dreams have on the individual's waking mood. Lack of involvement is signified by indifference toward dreams, disinterest and lack of any effect of dreams on mood upon awakening and/or later in the day. Involvement is signified by arousal of intense (positive or negative) emotions by dreams. We are not talking about emotions aroused whilst dreaming but about the emotional attitude toward one's own dreams and emotions which are triggered on awakening, during the waking hours, due to the dream when the individual likes to dream, is interested in or even fascinated with his/her dreams, or when the dreams evoke anxiety. As we mentioned before, both positive and negative emotions can emerge at this attitudinal pole.

The cognitive component of attitude toward dreams refers to the private concept of dreams and dreaming, attaching meaning to dreams and perceiving them as valuable phenomenon. Lack of involvement refers to the situation when person does not have a private concept of dreams or explains them only in terms of biology or physiology. Involvement is related to having a private theory of dreams, attaching meaning (symbolic, metaphysical, prophetical or any other) to dreams and believing that dreams are valuable for some reason (they are a source of self-knowledge or a channel of communication with "another world" etc.).

Table 1. The components of attitude toward dreams

	Lack of involvement	Involvement
Emotional component	- Indifference toward dreams - Disinterest in dreams - Dreams do not affect mood upon awakening or during the day	- Dreams evoke intense (positive or negative) emotions - Considerable interest in dreams (fascination) - Dreams have considerable effect on mood upon awakening and/or during the day
Cognitive component	- No dream theory - Purely "biological" explanations	- Private dream theory - Attaching meaning to dreams

Table 1. (Continued)

	Lack of involvement	Involvement
Behavioral component	- Not sharing dreams - Not recording dreams - Not interpreting dreams - Not thinking about dreams - Ignoring dream "cues"	- Sharing dreams - Recording dreams - Interpreting dreams - Thinking about dreams - Behaving according to dream "cues"

The behavioral component of attitude toward dreams involves all dream-related behaviors such as sharing, writing down or interpreting dreams, thinking about them as well as their effect on waking behavior. Lack of involvement is signified by lack of dream sharing, not writing them down, not interpreting them or thinking about them, or ignoring cues provided by dreams. Involvement refers to reporting one's dreams, talking about them to other people, recording them, trying to interpret them or thinking about them and behaving according to the cues the individual thinks they provide. Table 1 gives a brief summary of the different components of attitude toward dreams.

ATTITUDE TOWARD DREAMS AND PERSONALITY

One of the purposes of the quoted research on dream recall frequency was to identify the relations between dream recall and the dreamer's personality (Blagrove & Akehurst, 2000; Cernovsky, 1984; Levin, Fireman & Rackley, 2003; Schredl, 2002a; Schredl, Jochum & Souguenet, 1997; Tonay, 1993; Watson, 2003). In these studies it was assumed, after Schonbar (1965), that dream recall frequency is part of a broader life-style and is related to creativity, fantasy proneness and openness. More thorough analysis revealed, however, that personality traits are related not to dream recall per se but to attitude toward dreams. Personality was much more strongly correlated with attitude toward dreams than with dream recall frequency (Schredl et al., 1996; Schredl, Ciric et al., 2003). Schonbar's (1965) hypothesis therefore needs to be modified: attitude toward dreams rather than dream recall itself is part of the broader life-style (Beaulieu-Prévost & Zadra, 2005a; Schredl, Ciric et al., 2003), all the more so that attitude is a more general construct, comparable with personality traits (Schredl, Wittmann et al., 2003).

It has been demonstrated that people who are interested in their dreams, attribute great significance to them, think and talk about them score higher on Openness to experience on the NEO-PI-R (Schredl, Ciric et al., 2003; Schredl , Wittman et al., 2003; Siuta & Szmigielska, 2005). Openness to experience also correlates positively with declared frequency of dreams believed by reporters to inspire their creativity (Schredl & Erlacher, 2007).

It has also been found that individuals who score high on neuroticism dream more frequently and the accompanying emotions are usually negative (Lang & O'Connor, 1984; Zubala, 2005). These individuals share their dreams more frequently (Siuta & Szmigielska, 2005) and attribute symbolic meaning to them, they are also more likely to declare that their dreams affect their morning mood and overall waking state (Lang & O'Connor, 1984).

The purpose of the present study was to determine the relation between attitude toward dreams and individual traits according to the Five-Factor Theory of Personality. The following hypotheses were formulated:

1 attitude toward dreams and openness to experiences are related;
2 attitude toward dreams and neuroticism are related.

Additionally, the following research question was formulated: is attitude toward dreams related to the remaining five-factor personality traits, that is extraversion, agreeableness and conscientiousness?

METHOD

Participants and Procedure

The study was run on 108 participants, 62 women and 46 men, aged from 19 to 33 years (mean age 22.4 years). Most of the participants were students studying various courses (law – 28.7%, liberal arts – 25.9%, biological sciences – 11.1%; technological sciences – 10.2%; languages – 4.6%). The remaining, non-student participants (12.1%) had secondary or higher education. The students were credited for their participation.

Instruments

Attitude toward dreams was assessed with an instrument developed by one of the present authors, the Attitude toward Dreams Scale (ADS).1 This scale has 56 items covering the three definitional attitude components: emotion, cognition and behavior. Each item is rated on a five-point Likert scale.

The ADS was submitted to factor analysis and three subscales were extracted. The first subscale, generalized attitude (GA), has 30 items pertaining to interest in dreams ("Dreams fascinate me", "I read about dreams a lot", "I am interested in dreams" etc.) and dream-related behavior ("I try to interpret my dreams", "I wonder what a dream could mean", "I share my dreams" etc.) as well as items indicating lack of involvement with dream life ("Dreams are just a physiological phenomenon", "I don't care about dreams", "Dreams do not mean anything", "It's not worth dealing with dreams", "I am indifferent as far as dreams are concerned" etc.). The second subscale, metaphysical attitude (MA), has 15 items pertaining to metaphysical dream beliefs and concepts ("I believe that my dreams are prophetic", "Dreams enable astral journeys" etc.), attributing importance to dreams ("I never ignore my dreams", "Dreams always try to convey a message to us" etc.), negative emotions evoked by dreams ("Dreams sometimes give me forebodings", "I am afraid that some of my dreams may come true" etc.) and taking guidance from dream cues ("I warn people if I dream that something

---

[1] The ADS was constructed by Małgorzata Hołda. The standardization study (N=243) revealed satisfactory psychometric parameters: internal consistency α=0.96, $r_{test\text{-}retest}$=0.91 (p<0.001). This scale only has experimental status at present but it is going to be published shortly.

bad has happened to them" etc.). The third subscale, psychological attitude (PA), has 11 items pertaining to psychological dream concepts ("Dreams make us aware of our feelings, needs and strivings", "Dreams help us to get rid of the tension we experience when we are awake", "Dreams reflect our waking emotions", "In our dreams we see the objects of our desire" etc.).

Each subscale is scored separately (GA: 30-150 points; MA: 15-75 points; and PA: 11-55 points) and a global score is also calculated (ADS: 56-280 points). The subscales have the following reliabilities: GA α=0.95, MA α=0.90, PA α=0.89. Correlations between the subscales range from r=0.40 to r=0.59 (p<0.001). The scale can be used with adolescents and adults.

Personality traits were assessed with the Polish adaptation of the NEO-PI-R (Siuta, 2006).

Results

All the NEO-PI-R subscale scores were normally distributed in the studied sample. Comparison with the NEO-PI-R normalization sample (N=279), however, revealed slightly higher openness to experience in both women and men (p<0.001) and slightly lower agreeableness in men (p<0.05). Men and women also differed on most scales as can be seen in Table 2.

Table 2. Means and standard deviations for the NEO-PI-R

NEO-PI-R	Women (N=62) M	SD	Men (N=46) M	SD	t
Neuroticism	103,8	24,3	89,6	25,8	2,93**
Extraversion	115,8	23,3	106,1	21,8	2,20*
Openness to experience	130,2	18,9	122,0	22,8	2,02*
Agreeableness	111,8	16,6	100,2	23,8	2,98**
Conscientiousness	115,8	21,9	112,0	26,8	0,81

*p<0,05 **p<0,01

The mean ADS scores for women and men did not differ from the means for the standardization sample (N=243). Men and women differed, however, on their global scores and scores for two subscales (Table 3).

Table 3. Means and standard deviations for the ADS

ADS	Women (N=62) M	SD	Men (N=46) M	SD	*t*
Global score	190,2	28,8	169,9	36,6	3,23**
GA	112,6	18,9	100,4	25,2	2,85**
MA	38,2	9,9	32,4	10,5	2,96**
PA	39,5	6,5	38,0	7,3	1,13

**p<0,01

The correlations between attitude toward dreams and personality traits are presented in Table 4. Attitude toward dreams correlated significantly with openness to experience and neuroticism. The remaining correlation coefficients were not significant.

Table 4. Correlations between NEO-PI-R and ADS

NEO-PI-R	Total sample (N=108)	Women (N=62)	Men (N=46)
Neuroticism	0,28**	0,30*	0,14
Extraversion	0,12	0,15	-0,04
Openness to experience	0,45***	0,20	0,62***
Agreeableness	0,18	0,07	0,13
Conscientiousness	-0,09	-0,20	-0,06

*p<0,05 **p<0,01 ***p<0,001

Attitude toward dreams in men and women correlates with different personality traits, neuroticism in women and openness to experience in men (Fig. 1).

Table 5. Correlations between NEO-PI-R (facets of neuroticism) and ADS

Facets of neuroticism	Total sample (N=108)	Women (N=62)	Men (N=46)
Anxiety	0,26**	0,29*	0,13
Angry hostility	0,07	0,05	0,04
Depression	0,25**	0,19	0,22
Self-consciousness	0,30**	0,22	0,28
Impulsiveness	0,22*	0,31*	0,07
Vulnerability	0,20*	0,30*	-0,10

*p<0,05 **p<0,01 ***p<0,001

Correlation coefficients between attitude toward dreams and all the NEO-PI-R facets were also calculated. Significant correlations only emerged for the facets of neuroticism and openness to experience. Similar, significant correlations were found between attitude toward dreams and all the facets of neuroticism except *angry hostility*. Men and women differed however, just as they did for the global score. Significant correlations in women were found for *anxiety*, *impulsiveness* and *vulnerability*. In men, none of the correlation coefficients between attitude toward dreams and the facets of neuroticism were significant. The details are presented in Table 5.

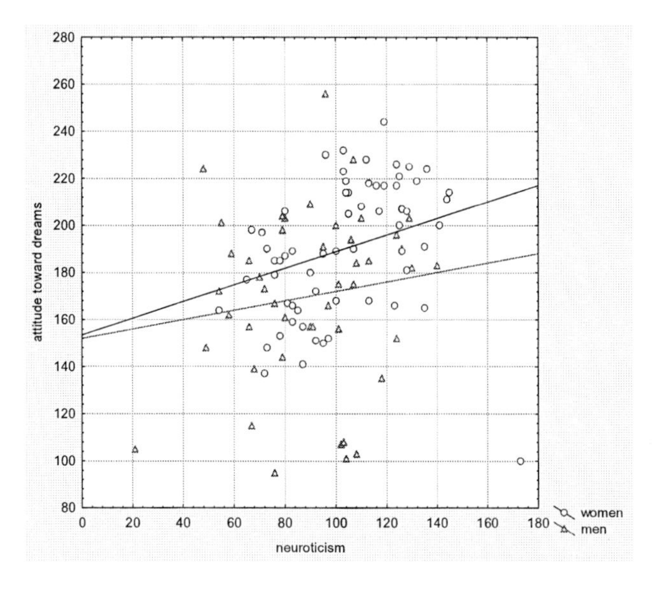

Figure 1. Continued on next page.

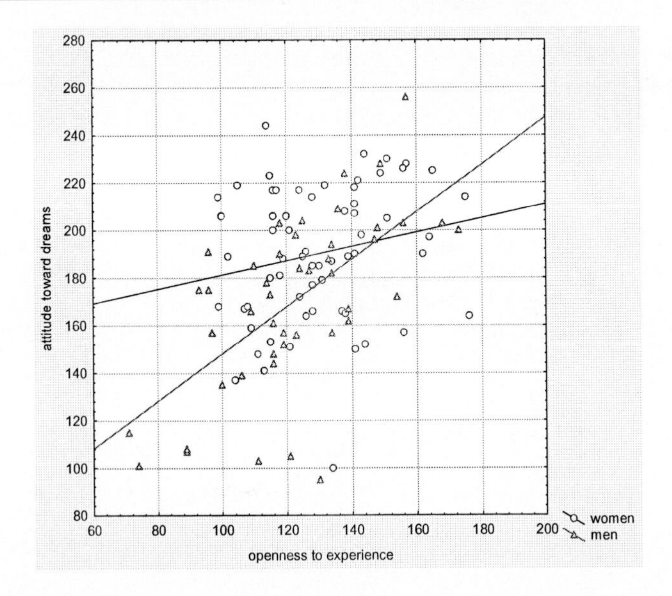

Figure 1. Correlation between attitude toward dreams on the one hand and neuroticism and openness to experience on the other in men and women

As far as openness to experience is concerned, the following facets correlated with attitude toward dreams: *fantasy*, *aesthetics*, *feelings* and *ideas*, both in the whole sample and in men. Only the correlation with *aesthetics* was significant in women, however. The details are presented in Table 6.

Table 6. Correlations between NEO-PI-R (facets of openness to experience) and ADS

Facets of openness to experience	Total sample (N=108)	Women (N=62)	Men (N=46)
Fantasy	0,36***	0,18	0,47**
Aesthetics	0,49***	0,28*	0,60***
Feelings	0,46***	0,18	0,61***
Actions	0,08	0,00	0,07
Ideas	0,23*	0,10	0,42**
Values	0,14	0,00	0,25

*p<0,05 **p<0,01 ***p<0,001

Correlations between the different ADS subscales and personality traits were also calculated. Neuroticism correlated with all the ADS subscales whereas openness to experience only correlated with GA (generalized attitude) and PA (psychological attitude). The results are presented in Table 7.

Table 7. Correlations between ADS subscales and NEO-PI-R (N=108)

	ADS	GA	MA	PA
Neuroticism	0,28**	0,20*	0,36***	0,24*
Extraversion	0,12	0,10	0,05	0,18
Openness to experience	0,45***	0,47***	0,19	0,34***
Agreeableness	0,18	0,15	0,16	0,17
Conscientiousness	-0,09	-0,17	-0,01	0,04

*p<0,05 **p<0,01 ***p<0,001

Once again, men and women had different correlation patterns. In women, neuroticism was strongly correlated with MA (metaphysical attitude) and openness to experience correlated weakly albeit significantly with GA (generalized attitude).

Weak but significant correlations were also found between PA (psychological attitude) and extraversion and between GA (generalized attitude) and conscientiousness. The results are shown in Table 8.

Table 8. Correlations between ADS subscales and NEO-PI-R for women (N=62)

	ADS	GA	MA	PA
Neuroticism	0,30*	0,16	0,51***	0,06
Extraversion	0,15	0,18	-0,07	0,26*
Openness to experience	0,20	0,26*	0,01	0,11
Agreeableness	0,07	0,14	-0,18	0,16
Conscientiousness	-0,20	-0,25*	-0,16	0,14

*p<0,05 **p<0,01 ***p<0,001

The correlations between personality traits and the ADS subscales for men are shown in Table 9.

Table 9. Correlations between ADS subscales and NEO-PI-R for men (N=46)

	ADS	GA	MA	PA
Neuroticism	0,14	0,14	0,05	0,40**
Extraversion	-0,04	-0,10	0,09	0,04
Openness to experience	0,62***	0,61***	0,29	0,54***
Agreeableness	0,13	0,04	0,31*	0,15
Conscientiousness	-0,06	-0,14	0,11	-0,09

*p<0,05 **p<0,01 ***p<0,001

As we can see in Table 9, in men neuroticism correlated with PA (psychological attitude) and openness to experience correlated strongly with GA (generalized attitude) and PA (psychological attitude). Agreeableness correlated with MA (metaphysical attitude).

CONCLUSION

The findings of this study have confirmed the hypotheses. Attitude toward dreams correlated positively with openness to experience and neuroticism, thus corroborating earlier findings (Beaulieu-Prévost & Zadra, 2005a; Lang & O'Connor, 1984; Schredl et al., 1996; Schredl, Ciric et al., 2003; Schredl, Wittman et al., 2003; Siuta & Szmigielska, 2005).

The correlations are strong for openness to experience, especially in the male sample. Attitude toward dreams correlated with the following facets of openness to experience: fantasy, aesthetics, feelings and ideas. The relation between attitude toward dreams and openness is further confirmed by the fact that the participants had higher openness scores than the general population. This may suggest greater involvement with, and interest in, dream life in individuals with high levels of openness to experience. It is also possible that such individuals are more interested in psychological research in general, not only in dream life.

As far as neuroticism is concerned, the correlations are slightly weaker albeit significant and their pattern is consistent. Nearly all the facets of neuroticism (anxiety, depression, self-consciousness, impulsiveness and vulnerability) correlate with attitude toward dreams. Only angry hostility showed no relation to this attitude. Individuals who score high on neuroticism are more likely to have dreams whose emotional tone is negative (Lang & O'Connor, 1984; Zubala, 2005). Emotional tone can also have a significant effect on mood upon awakening and when not asleep. This has been demonstrated by powerful correlations between sleep-related emotions and emotions experienced during the waking hours (Yu, 2007). It has also been reported that individuals who often have nightmares pay more attention to their dream life than individuals who seldom have nightmares and more frequently declare that their dreams are important for them; their dreams are also more likely to affect their well-being and mood during the day (Belicki, 1992; Berquier & Ashton, 1992; Levin, 1994). Perhaps the negative emotional tone of their dreams is what causes people with high levels of neuroticism to pay more attention to their dreams and to be more involved with their dream life and hence to have a more involved attitude (and higher ADS scores). This is consistent with other already quoted findings showing that these people share their dreams more frequently (Siuta & Szmigielska, 2005) and invest them with symbolic meaning and are also more likely to declare that their dreams affect their waking mood and general daytime wellbeing (Lang & O'Connor, 1984).

When the results were submitted to more detailed analysis, differences between women and men emerged. In women, attitude toward dreams correlated significantly with neuroticism and three of its facets, anxiety, impulsiveness and vulnerability. As far as openness to experience is concerned, only aesthetics correlated significantly with ADS. In men, neither neuroticism nor any of its facets correlated with attitude toward dreams whereas significant correlations emerged for openness to experience and four of its facets, fantasy, aesthetics, feelings and ideas. These differences may be due to differences between men and women as to the motives for involvement with one's dream life. Perhaps involvement in women is more emotionally motivated than in men in whom the motivation may be more cognitive. Consequently, women may tend to focus on the emotions accompanying their dreams (and their effect on their waking state) and hence to pay more attention to their dreams and orient their everyday lives accordingly. Men, meanwhile, may respond to dreams less emotionally but show greater interest in them and hence their involvement may be of a more cognitive persuasion.

Analysis of the relation between personality traits and the various ADS subscales lends support to this suggestion. Neuroticism correlated with all the ADS subscales but most strongly with MA (metaphysical attitude). Items in this subscale refer to metaphysical dream beliefs and concepts, attributing importance to dreams, negative emotions invoked by dreams, and adherence to dream cues. Openness to experience, meanwhile, only correlated with GA (generalized attitude) and PA (psychological attitude) subscales. Hence, neuroticism was more strongly correlated with the emotional aspects of attitude toward dreams, the effect of dreams on mood and behavior and related beliefs about dreams (e.g. about the prophetic nature of dreams). Openness to experience correlated more strongly with overall interest in dream life as a phenomenon and more rational theories of dreams.

These patterns are even more evident when we consider gender. In women, neuroticism only correlated with MA (metaphysical) subscale and openness to experience only correlated with GA (generalized) subscale. In men, neuroticism correlated with PA (psychological) subscale whereas openness to experience correlated with GA and PA subscales (generalized and psychological). Moreover, women scored higher than men on GA and MA whereas the PA subscale did not differentiate between men and women.

The results suggest that women and men have different patterns of motivation to engage in their dream life. It is possible, however, that the more powerful connection between attitude toward dreams and neuroticism in women and between attitude toward dreams and openness to experience in men is related to dream recall frequency. Women are known to have better dream recall than men (Garfield, 1988; Schredl & Doll, 1998; Schredl & Piel,

2003, Schredl et al., 1996; Schredl, Sahin & Schäfer, 1998); very few researchers have failed to replicate this pattern (Stepansky et al., 1998; Watson, 2003). This may be why dreams trigger more intense emotions in women; men, on the other hand, frequently cannot recall their dreams and are interested in them for purely cognitive reasons.

It has repeatedly been demonstrated that women are more interested in their dream life and pay more attention to it. Their attitude toward dreams is also more positive (Domino, 1982; Robbins & Tanck, 1988; Schredl et al., 1996; Schredl, Ciric et al., 2003; Schredl, Wittmann et al., 2003). The present study corroborates these findings. Women scored significantly higher on the ADS than men. It has also been demonstrated that attitude toward dreams is related to dream recall frequency (Robbins & Tanck, 1988; Schredl et al., 1996; Schredl et al., 2002; Schredl, Ciric et al., 2003; Schredl, Wittmann et al., 2003; Tonay, 1993). The direction of this relationship is not clear, however. It is hard to say whether women's greater involvement with dream life has a positive effect on their dream recall frequency. We know that dream recall frequency improves considerably when we draw participants' attention to their dreams, encourage them to remember them or simply have them participate in dream studies (Cohen, 1969; Halliday, 1992; Schredl, 2002b). On the other hand it is equally possible that people who recall their dreams well become more interested in them because they want to make their experience meaningful (Schredl, Ciric et al., 2003). Clearly, more work needs to be done on the relationship between attitude toward dreams and personality and researchers also need to consider the role of dream recall frequency in this relationship.

In the present study we also wanted to know whether there is any relationship between attitude toward dreams and the remaining five-factor personality traits, that is, extraversion, agreeableness and conscientiousness. No such relationship emerged at the level of global NEO-PI-R and ADS scores. Isolated relationships were found, however, between the ADS subscales and these traits. In women, extraversion correlated positively with PA (psychological attitude) and conscientiousness correlated negatively with GA (generalized attitude). In men, agreeableness correlated positively with MA (metaphysical attitude). It is hard to interpret these relationships, however, and further research and analysis is needed.

The present study showed that it is worth defining and assessing attitude toward dreams more broadly than has traditionally been the practice. A more multidimensional approach opens up new gateways to the comprehensive and precise study of human attitudes toward dreams and their possible determinants.

References

Ajzen, I. (1988). *Attitudes, personality and behavior*. Chicago: Dorsey.

Antrobus, J.S. (2000). Dreams: Theories and research. In A.E. Kazdin (red.), *Encyclopedia of psychology, Vol. 3*. Washington: APA; New York: Oxford University Press.

Beaulieu-Prévost, D., & Zadra, A. (2005a). Dream recall frequency and attitude towards dreams: A reinterpretation of the relation. *Personality and Individual Differences, 38*, 919-927.

Beaulieu-Prévost, D., & Zadra, A. (2005b). How dream recall frequency shapes people's beliefs about the content of dreams. *North American Journal of Psychology, 7*, 253-264.

Beaulieu-Prévost, D., & Zadra, A. (2007). Absorption, psychological boundaries and attitude towards dreams as correlates of dream recall: two decades of research seen through a meta-analysis. *Journal of Sleep Research, 16*, 51-59.

Belicki, K. (1992). Nightmare frequency versus nightmare distress: Relations to psychopathology and cognitive style. *Journal of Abnormal Psychology, 101*, 592-597.

Berquier, A., & Ashton, R. (1992). Characteristics of the frequent nightmare sufferer. *Journal of Abnormal Psychology, 101*, 246-250.

Blagrove, M., & Akehurst, L. (2000). Personality and dream recall frequency: Further negative findings. *Dreaming, 10*, 139-148.

Bohner, G., & Wänke, M. (2002). *Attitudes and Attitude Change*. Hove: Psychology Press.

Cernovsky, Z.Z. (1984). Dream recall and attitude toward dreams. *Perceptual and Motor Skills, 58*, 911–914.

Cernovsky, Z.Z. (1987). Attitude towards dreams and MMPI measures of psychopathology in male chronic alcoholics. Journal of Human Behavior, 24, 30-32.

Clark, A. J. (1994). Working with dreams in group counseling: Advantages and challenges. *Journal of Counseling & Development, 73*, 141-144.

Cohen, D.B. (1969). Frequency of dream recall estimated by three methods and related to defense preference and anxiety. *Journal of Consulting and Clinical Psychology, 33*, 661-667.

Crook, R.E., & Hill, C.E. (2003). Working with dreams in psychotherapy: The therapists' perspective. *Dreaming, 13*, 83-93.

Crook Lyon, R. E., & Hill, C. E. (2004). Client reactions to working with dreams in psychotherapy. *Dreaming, 14*, 207-219.

Dement, W.C., & Vaughan, C. (1999). *The promise of sleep*. New York: Delacorte Press.

Dombeck, M. (1991). *Dreams and professional personhood: The contexts of dream telling and dream interpretation among American psychotherapists.* New York: State University of New York Press.

Domhoff, G.W. (1999). *The "purpose" of dreams*. Retrived November, 6, 2008 fromhttp://dreamresearch.net/Library/purpose.html

Domino, G. (1982). Attitudes toward dreams, sex differences and creativity. *Journal of Creative Behavior*, *16*, 112-122.

Garfield, P. (1988). *Women's bodies, women's dreams*. Nowy Jork: Ballantine Books.

Hall, D.H. (1997). *Beliefs about dreams and their relationship to gender and personality* [abstract]. Dissertation Abstracts International: Section B: The Sciences and Engineering, 57(7-B), s. 4766.

Halliday, G. (1992). Effect of encouragement on dream recall. *Dreaming, 2*, 39-44.

Hartmann, E. (2008). The Central Image makes "big" dreams big: The Central Image as the emotional heart of the dream. *Dreaming, 18*, 44-57.

Hill, C.E., Crook-Lyon, R.E., Hess, S.A., Goates-Jones, M., Roffman, M., Stahl, J., Sim, W., & Johnson, M. (2006). Prediction of session process and outcome in the Hill dream model: Contributions of client characteristics and the process of the three stages. *Dreaming, 16*, 159-185.

Hill, C.E., Diemer, R.A., & Heaton, K.J. (1997). Dream interpretation sessions: Who volunteers, who benefits, and what volunteer clients view as most and least helpful. *Journal of Counseling Psychology, 44*, 53-62.

Hill, C.E., Kelley, F.A., Davis, T.L., Crook, R.E., Maldonado, L.E., Turkson, M.A., Wonnell, T.L., Suthakaran, V., Zack, J.S., Rochlen, A.B., Kolchakian, M.R., & Codrington, J.N. (2001). Predictors of outcome of dream interpretation sessions: Volunteer client characteristics, dream characteristics, and type of interpretation. *Dreaming, 11*, 53-72.

Hołda, M. (2006). Opowiadanie snów jako zjawisko społeczne [Sharing dreams as a social phenomenon]. *ALBO albo. Problemy psychologii i kultury, 4*, 38-48.

Knudson, R.M. (2001). Significant dreams: Bizarre or beautiful? *Dreaming, 11*, 167-177.

Knudson, R.M., Adame, A.L., & Finocan, G.M. (2006). Significant dreams: Repositioning the self narrative. *Dreaming, 16,* 215-222.

Lang, R.J., & O'Connor, K.P. (1984). Personality, dream content and dream coping style. *Personality and Individual Differences*, *5*, 211-219.

Levin, R. (1994). Sleep and dreaming characteristics of frequent nightmare subjects in auniversity population. *Dreaming*, *4*, 127-137.

Levin, R., Fireman, G., & Rackley, C. (2003). Personality and dream recall frequency: Still further negative findings. *Dreaming, 13*, 155-162.

Livingston, M.S. (2001). Self psychology, dreams and group psychotherapy: Working in the playspace. *Group, 25*, 15-26.

Natterson, J.M. (1993). Dreams: The gateway to consciousness. In G.M.V. Delaney (red.), *New directions in dream interpretation* (pp. 41-75). New York: State University of New York Press.

Pesant, N., & Zadra, A. (2004). Working with dreams in therapy: What do we know and what should we do? *Clinical Psychology Review, 24*, 489-512.

Robbins, P.R., & Tanck, R.H. (1988). Interest in dreams and dream recall. *Perceptual and Motor Skills*, *66*, 291-294.

Robbins, P.R., & Tanck, R.H. (1991). Theories of dreams held by American college students. *Journal of Social Psychology, 131*, 143-145.

Rochlen, A.B., Ligiero, D.P., Hill, C.E., & Heaton, K.J. (1999). Effects of training in dream recall and dream interpretation skills on dream recall, attitudes, and dream interpretation outcome. *Journal of Counseling Psychology, 46*, 27-34.

Schonbar, R.A. (1965). Differential dream recall frequency as a component of „life style". *Journal of Consulting Psychology, 29*, 468-474.

Schredl, M. (2002a). Dream recall frequency and openness to experience: A negative finding.*Personality and Individual Differences, 33*, 1285-1289.

Schredl, M. (2002b). Questionnaires and diaries as research instruments in dream research: Methodological issues. *Dreaming, 12*, 17-26.

Schredl, M. (2003). Dream research: Integration of physiological and psychological models. In E.F., Pace-Schott, M. Solms, M. Blagrove, & S. Harnad (red.), *Sleep and dreaming. Scientific advances and reconsiderations* (pp. 213-215). New York: Cambridge University Press.

Schredl, M., Bohusch, C., Kahl, J., Mader, A., & Somesan, A. (2000). The use of dreams inpsychotherapy. A survey of psychotherapists in private practice. *The Journal of Psychotherapy Practice and Research, 9*, 81-87.

Schredl, M., Brenner, C., & Faul, C. (2002). Positive attitude towards dreams: Reliability and stability of a ten-item scale. *North American Journal of Psychology, 4*, 343-346.

Schredl, M., Ciric, P., Götz, S., & Wittman, L. (2003). Dream recall frequency, attitude toward dreams and openess to experience. *Dreaming, 13*, 145-153.

Schredl, M., & Doll, E. (1998). Emotions in Diary Dreams. *Consciousness and Cognition, 7*, 634-646.

Schredl, M., & Erlacher, D. (2007). Self-reported effects of dreams on waking-life creativity: An empirical study. *The Journal of Psychology, 141*, 35-46.

Schredl, M., Jochum, S., & Souguenet, S. (1997). Dream recall, visual memory, and absorption in imaginings. *Personality and Individual Differences, 22*, 291-292.

Schredl, M., Nürnberg, C., & Weiler, S. (1996). Dream recall, attitude toward dreams, and personality. *Personality and Individual Differences, 20*, 613-618.

Schredl, M., & Piel, E. (2003). Gender differences in dream recall: data from four representative German samples. *Personality and Individual Differences, 35*, 1185-1189.

Schredl, M., Sahin, V., & Schäfer, G. (1998). Gender differences in dreams: do they reflect gender differences in waking life? *Personality and Individual Differences, 25*, 433-442.

Schredl, M., Wittmann, L., Ciric, P., & Götz, S. (2003b). Factors of home dream recall: a structural equation model. *Journal of Sleep Research, 12*, 133-141.

Siuta, J. (2006). *Inwent*arz Osobowości NEO-PI-R Paula T. Costy Jr i Roberta R. McCrae. *Adaptacja polska. Podręcznik [The NEO-PI-R Personality Inventory by Paul T. Costa Jr and Robert R. McCrae. Polish adaptation. Manual]*. Warszawa: Pracownia Testów Psychologicznych PTP.

Siuta, J., & Szmigielska, B. (2005). *Osobowościowe uwarunkowania opowiadania marzeń sennych [The personality determinants of dream reporting]*. XXXII Zjazd Polskiego Towarzystwa Psychologicznego, Kraków.

Stepansky, R., Holzinger, B., Schmeiser-Rieder, A., Saletu, B., Kunze, M., & Zeitlhofer, J.(1998). Austrian dream behavior: Results of a representative survey. *Dreaming, 8*, 23-30.

Stewart, C. (2004). Introduction: dreaming as an object of anthropological analysis. *Dreaming, 14*, 75-82.

Szmigielska, B. (1996). *Marzenia senne w życiu młodzieży [Dreams in adolescents' life]*. V Ogólnopolska Konferencja Psychologów Rozwojowych, Łódź.

Szmigielska, B. (1999). *Children's and adolescent's reports on their dreams*. IX European Conference on Developmental Psychology, Greece.

Szmigielska, B., & Hołda, M. (2007). Students' views on the role of dreams in human life. *Dreaming, 17*, 152-158.

Tedlock, B. (1991). The new anthropology of dreaming. *Dreaming, 1*, 161-178.

Tedlock, B. (2004). The poetics and spirituality of dreaming: A Native American enactive theory. *Dreaming, 14*, 183-189.

Tien, H.-L.S., Lin, C.-H., & Chen, S.-C. (2006). Dream interpretation sessions for college students in Taiwan: Who benefits and what volunteer clients view as most and least helpful. *Dreaming, 16*, 246-257.

Tonay, V.K. (1993). Personality correlates of dream recall: Who remembers?. *Dreaming, 3*, 1-8.

Watson, D. (2003). To dream, perchance to remember: Individual differences in dream recall. *Personality and Individual Differences, 34*, 1271-1286.

Wax, M.L. (2004). Dream sharing as social practice. *Dreaming, 14*, 83–93.

Wilmer, H.A. (1982). Dream seminar for chronic schizophrenic patients. *Journal for the Study of Interpersonal Processes, 45*, 351-360.

Wolcott, S., & Strapp, C.M. (2002). Dream recall frequency and dream detail as mediated by personality, behavior, and attitude. *Dreaming, 12*, 27-44.

Yu, C.K-C. (2007). Emotions before, during, and after dreaming sleep. *Dreaming, 17*, 73-86.

Zubala, A. (2005). Wpływ neurotyzmu oraz stylów przywiązania na ilość i jakość marzeń sennych [The impact of neuroticism and attachment styles on the quantity and the quality of dreams]. *Sen, 5*, 39-47.

In: Personality Assessment: New Research
Editor: Lauren B. Palcroft and Melissa V. Lopez
ISBN: 978-1-60692-796-0

Chapter 15

SOCIAL DOMINANCE ORIENTATION, AMBIVALENT SEXISM, AND ABORTION: EXPLAINING PRO-CHOICE AND PRO-LIFE ATTITUDES

***Danny Osborne*[1] *and Paul G. Davies*[2]**
[1]University of California, Los Angeles, California, USA
[2]University of British Columbia, Okanagan, British Columbia

ABSTRACT

Abortion continues to be one of the most hotly debated issues in American politics. Despite its prominence in the public discourse, little social psychological work has been done to understand the ideological bases of individuals' attitudes toward abortion. The current chapter seeks to address this oversight by using social dominance theory (Sidanius and Pratto, 1999) and the theory of ambivalent sexism (Glick and Fiske, 1996) to explain attitudes toward abortion. Specifically, we argue that individuals with a preference for group-based hierarchy – a variable referred to as social dominance orientation (SDO) – use beliefs about gender roles in order to justify their attitudes toward abortion. We tested this hypothesis by having 242 participants complete the SDO scale (Pratto, Sidanius, Stallworth, and Malle, 1994) and the Ambivalent Sexism Inventory (ASI; Glick and Fiske, 1996) – a measure that divides gender role attitudes into two components: 1) hostile sexism (HS) and 2) benevolent sexism (BS). After controlling for religiosity and previous abortion experience, multiple regression analyses indicated that SDO was significantly associated with attitudes toward both elective abortion (e.g., the woman wants an abortion, regardless of the reason) and traumatic abortion (e.g., the woman is pregnant as a result of rape or incest). The relationships between SDO and attitudes toward the two types of abortion were, however, mediated by the ASI. Specifically, HS and BS mediated the relationship between SDO and opposition to elective abortion, while only BS mediated the relationship between SDO and opposition to traumatic abortion. The implications of these findings are discussed within the context of intergroup relations.

INTRODUCTION

"The states are not free, under the guise of protecting maternal health or potential life, to *intimidate* women into continuing pregnancies."

– Supreme Court Justice Harry Blackmun (emphasis added).

The debate over abortion, as indicated in the above quote, has often been characterized as an unequal balance of power between men and women. In particular, feminist scholars and others concerned with women's rights have asserted that abortion is largely focused around males' domination of females and the attempted regulation of women's bodies (e.g., see Fried, 1988; Roberts, 1998). Unfortunately, while such an assertion lends itself to empirical validation, little theoretical work within psychology has attempted to explain attitudes toward abortion in terms of dominant/subordinate gender relations.

Social dominance theory, a framework that combines psychological, group, and societal level variables into a single explanation of intergroup relations, provides an opportunity to assess the issue of abortion from such a standpoint. Sidanius and Pratto (1999) argue that, whenever there is an economic surplus within a given social system, group-based hierarchies will invariably arise. They further posit that individuals within these societies will differ in the degree to which they support the resulting group-based inequalities. Specifically, individuals who are high on social dominance orientation (SDO) are more likely to favor dominant/subordinate relationships between groups, while those who are low on SDO are more likely to favor egalitarian relationships between groups. In support of this proposition, SDO has been shown to be positively correlated with various forms of anti-black prejudice (e.g., biological racism and symbolic racism; van Hiel and Mervielde, 2005), as well as being a marker of generalized prejudice (Duckitt, Wagner, Plessis, and Birum, 2002). Thus, SDO appears to be a strong predictor of attitudes toward social inequality in a variety of settings.

Important to the discussion on SDO is the ideologies that help justify one's attitudes toward social inequality. Specifically, social dominance theory suggests that individuals adopt legitimizing myths (i.e., belief systems) to provide moral and/or intellectual justification for group-based inequality (Sidanius and Pratto, 1999). For example, an individual may adopt negative stereotypes of outgroup members in order to justify the unequal distribution of resources between the dominants and subordinates of a given society (see Jost and Banaji, 1994). In fact, Pratto, Sidanius, Stallworth, and Malle (1994) have shown that SDO positively correlates with support for the Protestant work ethic and anti-Black prejudices, along with many other ideologies that can be used to justify group-based inequality. Thus, legitimizing myths provide an important mechanism through which individuals are able to justify their attitudes toward social inequality.

Given the importance of legitimizing myths to social dominance theory, gender role attitudes should be associated with justifying individuals attitudes toward social policies that affect women (see Sidanius and Pratto, 1999; also see Jost and Kay, 2005). More pertinent to the discussion on the relationship between SDO and attitudes toward abortion, gender role attitudes should be used to justify one's stance on the abortion issue. Consistent with this proposition, research has demonstrated that there is a relationship between gender role attitudes and attitudes toward abortion. In particular, individuals who hold traditional gender role attitudes show less support for abortion than individuals who hold less traditional gender role attitudes (Strickler and Danigelis, 2002). This effect has been demonstrated in a variety of contexts including the United States (Wang, 2004), Slovenia (Wall et al., 1999), and Greece (Bahr and Marcos, 2003). Further substantiating this claim, attitudes toward premarital sex, a variable closely associated with traditional gender role attitudes, is also associated with attitudes toward abortion; the less tolerant individuals are of premarital sex, the less supportive they are towards abortion (Jelen, Damore, and Lamatsch, 2002). Thus, beliefs about gender roles have a substantial impact on one's attitudes toward abortion.

Despite the seemingly clear relationship between gender role attitudes and one's attitudes toward abortion, recent theoretical and empirical developments find that gender role attitudes are not unidimensional. Rather, Glick and Fiske's (1996, 2001) theory of ambivalent sexism argues that traditional gender role attitudes can be separated into hostile and benevolent subcomponents. The hostile subcomponent, referred to as hostile sexism (HS), is characterized by an outwardly negative and punitive orientation toward women who violate traditional gender roles. Conversely, the benevolent subcomponent, referred to as benevolent sexism (BS), is characterized by a subjectively positive orientation toward women who conform to traditional gender roles. Together, HS and BS work to maintain traditional gender relations within contemporary society.

Considerable work has been done to illustrate the punitive aspects of HS. Research has found that individuals who score high on HS have less favorable attitudes toward gender non-conforming women (i.e., a career woman) than do individuals who score low on HS (Glick, Diebold, Bailey-Werner, and Zhu, 1997). Similarly, women who are perceived as being sexually promiscuous are met with greater hostility than women who are seen as not being sexually promiscuous (Sibley and Wilson, 2004). Not surprisingly, the higher individuals score on HS, the more tolerant they are of spousal abuse (Glick, Sakalli-Ugurlu, Ferreira, and Auguiar de Souza, 2002), as well as sexual harassment in the workplace (Russell and Trigg, 2004). Thus, the punitive nature of HS extends to a variety of situations where women are perceived to have violated traditional gender roles.

While HS involves punishing women who violate traditional gender roles, the idealization of women found in BS is partly contingent upon a woman's sexual purity. Research indicates that individuals who score high on BS have less favorable attitudes toward women who engage in premarital sex than do individuals who score low on BS (Sakalli-Ugurlu and Glick, 2003). Additionally, the higher individuals score on BS, the more likely they are to blame a victim of acquaintance rape (Abrams, Viki, Masser, and Bohner, 2003; Viki and Abrams, 2002). Likewise, when compared with individuals who score low on BS, individuals who score high on BS recommend shorter prison sentences for rapists (Viki, Abrams, and Masser, 2004). Thus, in the eyes of the benevolent sexist, a woman is expected to protect her sexual purity under all circumstances.

Current Investigation

The current chapter investigated the relationship between SDO and attitudes toward abortion by administering a series of surveys to internet users recruited from various websites (e.g., Craigslist.com, Myspace.com, Facebook.com, and online political discussion boards). Since previous theoretical and empirical work has shown that SDO is a general orientation toward social inequality (e.g., Duckitt et al., 2002; Pratto et al., 1994; Sidanius and Pratto, 1999), it was predicted that individuals who score high on SDO would be less supportive of both elective abortion (e.g., the woman wants an abortion, regardless of the reason) and traumatic abortion (e.g., the woman is pregnant as a result of rape or incest). For these individuals, a woman's ability to choose to have an abortion is a step towards social equality and should thus be met with opposition.

As suggested by social dominance theory (Sidanius and Pratto, 1999), attitudes toward specific policies are believed to be justified by legitimizing myths relevant to the given social group. These legitimizing myths are, in turn, related to one's general attitudes toward social inequality (i.e., SDO). Therefore, the relationship between SDO and attitudes toward abortion should be mediated by legitimizing myths that justify one's stance on the abortion issue. That is, gender role attitudes were predicted to provide the justification for holding attitudes in support of – or in opposition to – abortion. Specifically, individuals who score high on HS and BS should be more likely than individuals who score low on HS and BS to oppose elective abortion. Elective abortion, for the hostile sexist, is a case in which a woman made a choice to engage in sexual relations and should thus "pay the consequences" of her actions (i.e., carry the pregnancy to term).

Moreover, to the extent that abortion is associated with the women's rights movement, hostile sexists should see elective abortion as a challenge to male authority. Conversely, the benevolent sexist places an emphasis on sexual purity (e.g., see Sakalli-Ugurlu and Glick, 2003) and should see elective abortion as a violation of this principle. Thus, HS and BS are expected to be related to opposition to elective abortion, but for slightly different reasons.

The case of traumatic abortion is considerably more complex. Abortion for traumatic reasons represents a scenario in which a woman had either no choice in becoming pregnant (e.g., cases of rape or incest), or is confronted with trying circumstances surrounding her pregnancy (e.g., carrying the pregnancy to term would compromise the mother's life). It is difficult to conceive of how individuals who score high on HS could feel punitive toward women in these circumstances. That is, individuals who score high on HS should *not* see traumatic abortion as a case in which a woman's sexual promiscuity has "caught up with her." Thus, HS should be unrelated to attitudes toward traumatic abortion.

Individuals who score high on BS should see the case of traumatic abortion in a different light. Recall that BS is related to victim blaming in cases of rape (Abrams et al., 2003; Viki and Abrams, 2002). As such, in comparison with individuals who score low on BS, individuals who score high on BS should be less sympathetic to a woman who was raped and is considering having an abortion. Additionally, traditional gender-roles place an emphasis on having women make sacrifices for their family. This suggests that individuals who score high on BS would expect a woman to place the needs of her family in front of her own when contemplating an abortion under traumatic circumstances. Thus, it was predicted that individuals who score high on BS would be opposed to traumatic abortion.

METHOD

Participants

Participants were 242 internet users (163 women and 39 men; 40 participants did not indicate their sex) whose ages ranged from 17 to 78 (M = 34.4, SD = 13.4). Of the participants who indicated their racial identity, 151 were White, 12 were Asian Americans, 10 were Latino/as, 6 were African Americans, 6 were Middle Eastern Americans, 1 was Native American, and 14 were classified as other (42 participants did not indicate their ethnicity).

Materials

Two versions of a 58-item survey that assessed one's preference for social inequality (i.e., SDO; Pratto et al., 1994), ambivalent attitudes toward women (i.e., ASI; Glick and Fiske, 1996), attitudes toward abortion, and demographic information were developed for the current study. One version of the survey started with the SDO scale, followed by the ASI. The other version of the survey started with the ASI, followed by the SDO scale. Both versions of the survey concluded with the attitudes toward abortion and demographic information questionnaires.

The two versions of the survey were created in order to control for the possibility that participants' responses on the SDO scale influenced how they responded to the ASI (or vice versa). Preliminary data analyses indicated that the separate survey forms did not affect scores on the SDO or ASI. Therefore, survey order is not included a factor in the remainder of the analyses.

Social Dominance Orientation. Pratto and colleagues' (1994) 16-item social dominance orientation (SDO) scale was used in the current study. The SDO scale consists of a series of statements concerning attitudes toward group inequality. An example item is: "No one group should dominate in society" (reverse-scored). Items from the SDO scale were evaluated on a 7-point Likert scale with anchors at 1 (I feel very negative about this statement) and 7 (I feel very positive about this statement; α = .93). Higher scores indicate greater preference for group inequality.

Ambivalent Sexism. Glick and Fiske's (1996) 22-item ambivalent sexism inventory (ASI) was used in the current study. The ASI consists of 11 items that assess benevolent sexism (BS) and 11 items that assess hostile sexism (HS). An example BS item is: "Every man ought to have a woman whom he adores." An example HS item is: "Feminists are making entirely reasonable demands of men" (reverse-scored). Items from each subscale were rated on a 6-point Likert scale with anchors at 0 (disagree strongly) and 5 (agree strongly; α's = .82 and .90 for BS and HS, respectively). Higher scores indicate greater degrees of sexism on the respective scale.

Attitudes Toward Abortion. An 8-item survey assessing participants' attitudes toward abortion was used in the current study. Seven of these items came from the General Social Survey. These items consist of scenarios in which a woman is seeking an abortion for elective purposes (e.g., the woman doesn't want the child) or traumatic purposes (e.g., the pregnancy is a result of rape; see Bahr and Marcos, 2003). An example elective abortion item is: "The woman is not married and does not want the child." An example traumatic abortion item is: "The woman's health is seriously endangered by the pregnancy." Each item was rated on a 7-point Likert scale with anchors at 1 (strongly oppose) and 7 (strongly support; α's = .95 and .84 for elective and traumatic abortion, respectively). Higher scores indicate greater degrees of support for the given abortion issue. The last item on this survey read: "Have you ever been in a relationship in which you or your partner had an abortion?" (yes/no).

Demographic Information. A 12-item demographic questionnaire was developed for the current study. Eight of these items assessed the participants' age (fill in the blank), gender (male or female), sexual orientation (Gay/Lesbian, Straight, or Bisexual), highest level of education (Some high school, High school graduate, Some college, College graduate, Graduate/professional school), race/ethnicity (Asian, Black, Mexican/Latino/a, White, or other), zip code (fill in the blank), religious affiliation (Buddhist, Catholic, Jewish, Muslim, Protestant, other, or none), and, if applicable, type of Protestant (Born-again, Fundamentalist, Evangelical, or other).

The remaining 4 items assessed the religiosity of the participant. Three of these items were rated on a 7-point Likert scale with anchors at 1 (strongly disagree) and 7 (strongly agree). An example item from this subset is: "Religion has no place in my life" (reverse-scored). The fourth item assessed the frequency of attendance to religious services (reverse-scored) using a 7-point Likert scale with anchors at 1 (more than twice a week) and 7 (never; α for the 4-item religiosity scale = .92). Higher scores indicate greater degrees of religious commitment.

Procedure

Internet users were recruited to participate in the current study through popular online websites (e.g., Craigslist.com, Myspace.com, Facebook.com, and online political discussion boards). This was done by posting an advertisement introducing the principle investigator on the aforementioned websites, followed by a quick overview of the study (i.e., a survey on internet users' attitudes about important social issues). The advertisement concluded with a link that sent participants directly to our study hosted on Surveymonkey.com. Participants who followed this link read a screen that provided information regarding their rights as a participant. If the participants chose to continue with the study, they were randomly assigned to complete one of the two versions of the survey.

Results

Given our hypothesis that BS and HS mediate the relationship between SDO and attitudes toward abortion, we conducted two separate two-stage multiple regression analyses on attitudes toward elective and traumatic abortion. The first stage of analyses was conducted in order to assess the direct relationship BS and HS have with attitudes toward elective and traumatic abortion while controlling for religiosity and abortion experience (i.e., whether or not the participant has had an abortion). Thus, for the first stage of analyses, religiosity and abortion experience were entered into the first block, SDO scores were entered into the second block, and BS and HS scores were entered into the third block of our regression model. Participants' attitudes toward 1) elective abortion and 2) traumatic abortion were then separately regressed onto this model.

The second stage of analyses was conducted in order to determine the relationship between SDO and 1) BS and 2) HS. This was achieved by entering religiosity and abortion experience in the first block and SDO into the second block of our regression model. Participants' 1) BS and 2) HS scores were then separately regressed onto this model.

The standardized beta weights (after controlling for religiosity and abortion experience) for both of the 2-stage multiple regression analyses are combined and presented in Figure 1. As can be seen, SDO was negatively associated with support for elective and traumatic abortion. In other words, the higher one's level of SDO, the less likely he or she was to support elective (β = -0.16, p = 0.01) and traumatic (β = -0.16, p = 0.02) abortion. There was also a strong positive relationship between SDO and both forms of sexism. Specifically, the higher one's level of SDO, the higher his or her level of BS (β = 0.36, p < 0.01) and HS (β = 0.51, p < 0.01).

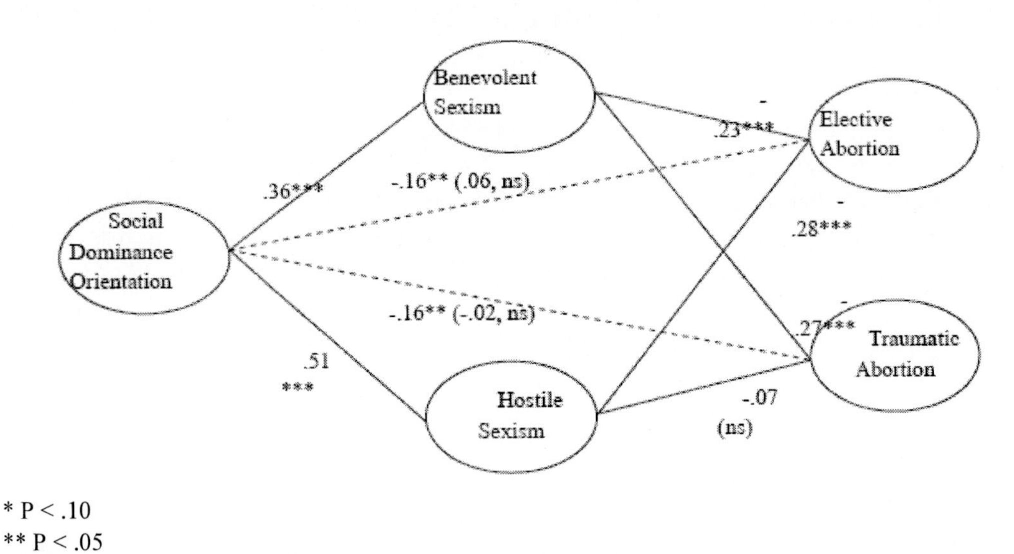

* P < .10
** P < .05
*** p < .01

Figure 1. Multiple regression analyses for attitudes toward abortion while controlling for religiosity and previous abortion experience. Values represent standardized beta weights.

Figure 1 also displays the relationships between the two types of sexism and attitudes toward abortion. These relationships indicated that the higher one's level of BS, the less likely he or she was to support elective (β = -0.23, p < 0.01) and traumatic (β = -0.27, p < 0.01) abortion. HS, however, was only related to attitudes toward elective abortion. Specifically, the higher one's level of HS, the less likely he or she was to support elective abortion (β = -0.28, p < 0.01).

One should note that, when considering the influence of BS and HS, the relationship between SDO and attitudes toward elective abortion drops from β = -0.16 (p = 0.01) to β = 0.06 (*ns*). Likewise, when considering the influence of BS and HS, the relationship between SDO and attitudes toward traumatic abortion drops from β = -0.16 (p = 0.02) to β = -0.02

(*ns*). Sobel tests confirmed that BS and HS mediated the relationship between SDO and attitudes toward elective abortion (z = -2.72, $p < 0.01$, and z = -3.27, $p < 0.01$, respectively), while only BS mediated the relationship between SDO and attitudes toward traumatic abortion (z = -2.97, $p < 0.01$; Sobel test for HS as a mediator, z = -.90, *ns*; see Baron and Kenny, 1986).

Discussion

The current chapter investigated the relationship between attitudes toward group-based inequality, gender role attitudes, and attitudes toward abortion. As predicted, SDO was significantly associated with attitudes toward elective and traumatic abortion. Specifically, individuals who scored high on SDO were more likely than individuals who scored low on SDO to oppose both elective and traumatic abortion. This finding is not surprising given the demonstrated relationship between SDO and attitudes toward African Americans (van Hiel and Mervielde, 2005; Pratto et al., 1994) and women (Sidanius and Pratto, 1999). Indeed, SDO appears to be best conceived as a general attitudinal orientation toward a variety of social groups (see Duckitt et al., 2002; Pratto et al., 1994; Sidanius and Pratto, 1999).

We also found strong support for our hypothesis regarding the relationship between gender role attitudes and attitudes toward abortion. Previous research has shown that individuals with traditional gender role attitudes are more likely to oppose abortion than individuals with less traditional gender role attitudes (Jelen et al., 2002; Strickler and Danigelis, 2002; Wang, 2004); a finding that has been replicated across cultures (Bahr and Marcos, 2003; Wall et al., 1999). Our data are consistent with these findings, as we have shown that higher levels of BS and HS are associated with lower levels of support for abortion.

Where our results differ from previous research is in our conceptualization of gender role attitudes and how they relate to attitudes toward abortion. Given the recent theoretical work uncovering the pernicious role benevolent attitudes play in intergroup relations (e.g., see Jackman, 1994), as well as the insights gained from Glick and Fiske's (1996, 2001) work on ambivalent sexism, we predicted that both hostile and benevolent attitudes toward women would be associated with lower levels of support for elective abortion. We found strong support for this prediction. Individuals who scored high on BS were more likely than individuals who scored low on BS to oppose elective abortion. Likewise, individuals who scored high on HS were more likely than individuals who scored low on HS to oppose elective abortion.

The importance of our – and other theorists' – distinction between BS and HS is clearly demonstrated when looking at attitudes toward traumatic abortion. Despite the fact that both BS and HS predicted attitudes toward elective abortion, only BS predicted attitudes toward traumatic abortion. This suggests that individuals who score high on BS feel that a woman should always avoid having an abortion, regardless of the circumstances. A possible explanation for these surprising, yet predicted, results can be found when assessing the content of BS. Glick and Fiske (1996, 2001) conceptualize BS as a subjective idealization of women who, among other things, remain chaste. Abortion appears to be seen as a violation of this chastity for individuals who score high on BS. Likewise, part of the content of BS idealizes traditional motherhood. It is possible that individuals who score high on BS feel that women should make communal sacrifices for their family, regardless of the circumstances (e.g., situations where the woman's health is endangered by the pregnancy). While these explanations are based on sound theory, they remain open questions. Future research would be well-advised to address these possibilities.

The findings of the current investigation also add to the growing body of literature showing that benevolent and hostile attitudes toward women, though closely associated, remain orthogonal concepts. In a study on attitudes toward rape victims, Viki and colleagues (2004) found that individuals who scored high on BS, but not HS, were more likely than individuals who scored low on BS to blame the victim of an acquaintance rape. A similar study found that HS, but not BS, was associated with a propensity to commit a rape; males who scored high on HS were more likely to identify with the perpetrator of an acquaintance rape than males who scored low on HS (Abrams et al., 2003). This suggests that, in accordance with our findings, BS and HS are distinct concepts. Uncovering the mechanisms responsible for the differential ways BS and HS affect attitudes toward women appears to be a fruitful area of investigation for future research.

The finding that BS and HS had different effects on attitudes toward traumatic abortion is also consistent with social dominance theory's conceptualization of legitimizing ideologies. According to social dominance theory, legitimizing ideologies are used to provide support – either moral or intellectual – for one's attitudes toward specific issues (Sidanius and Pratto, 1999). Given the empirical demonstration that attitudes toward elective and traumatic abortion are conceptually distinct (Bahr and Marcos, 2003), it is reasonable to expect that they would require separate justifications. The results produced in the current study support this intuition.

LIMITATIONS

Though the current study offers the scientific community important insights into the dynamics behind individuals' attitudes toward abortion, no study is without its limitations. In the current study, we relied solely on correlational analyses to support our conclusions. As such, the direction of causality implied in our model should not be taken for granted. It is possible that one's attitudes toward abortion simultaneously influence his or her attitudes toward group-based inequality and gender role attitudes. Alternatively, one's gender role attitudes may influence his or her attitudes toward group-based inequality, which in turn influences the person's stance on the abortion issue. Finally, it is possible that all of the variables addressed in the current study have a reciprocal relationship with each other.

Despite these various possibilities, we have considerable theoretical rationale for our model. As noted previously, SDO is conceptualized as a general attitudinal orientation towards a variety of social groups (Sidanius and Pratto, 1999). Conversely, ambivalent attitudes toward women, as measured by the ASI, are directed specifically toward women. Given our theoretical orientation, it would be unlikely for attitudes toward a specific group to influence one's general orientation toward a variety of mutually-exclusive social groups (e.g., Arabs, African Americans, etc.). It is more plausible – and consistent with social dominance theory – for attitudes to begin with a vague notion (e.g., a general orientation toward social inequality) and move toward more specific attitude objects (e.g., specific social policies). Nevertheless, until experimental research is conducted to explore the causal relationships between SDO, gender role attitudes, and attitudes toward abortion, the direction of causality posited in the current study will remain an open issue.

In addition to the question regarding the direction of causality, one might question the representativeness of our sample. The current study was based on internet users' attitudes toward abortion. We find this, however, to be a particular strength of our study. Research within social psychology has primarily relied on college students as participants, a population that has yet to develop stable attitudes toward social and political issues (see Sears, 1986). Given the political nature of the current study, venturing outside of the standard population used in social psychological studies provides a more realistic test of our hypotheses. Moreover, internet samples have been shown to mirror the general population more closely than samples comprised of college students (Gosling, Vazire, Srivastava, and John, 2004). This suggests that studies using internet samples may be *more* representative of the target population than studies relying exclusively on college students. The fact that our sample consisted entirely of internet users should be seen as a strength – not a weakness – of the current investigation.

Conclusion

The intensity of the partisan debates over the topic of abortion during 2005 (e.g., the Senate hearings over the confirmation of Samuel Alito to the Supreme Court, as well as an abortion ban that was proposed in South Dakota) suggests that the factors influencing one's attitudes toward abortion is a much needed topic of investigation. The information presented in the current chapter satisfies this need by uncovering some of the psychological dynamics behind this divisive issue. Specifically, we have shown that individuals' attitudes toward social inequality influence their stance on abortion. We have also shown that benevolent and hostile attitudes toward women play unique roles in legitimize this relationship. Such findings are consistent with both social dominance theory (Sidanius and Pratto, 1999) and the theory of ambivalent sexism (Glick and Fiske, 1996, 2001), illustrating the multi-faceted nature of this topic. While we may have provided the reader with more questions than answers, we feel that the information presented in the current chapter has brought us closer to understanding the complexity behind individuals' attitudes toward abortion. It is only through the implementation of systematic explorations that we can begin to understand the factors that make abortion such a divisive issue within the American electorate.

References

Abrams, D., Viki, G. T., Masser, B., and Bohner, G. (2003). Perceptions of stranger and acquaintance rape: The role of benevolent and hostile sexism in victim blame and rape proclivity. *Journal of Personality and Social Psychology, 84,* 111-125.

Bahr, S. J., and Marcos, A. C. (2003). Cross-cultural attitudes toward abortion: Greeks versus Americans. *Journal of Family Issues, 24,* 402-424.

Baron, R. M., and Kenny, D. A. (1986). The moderator-mediator variable distinction in social psychological research: Conceptual, strategic, and statistical considerations. *Journal of Personality and Social Psychology, 6,* 1173-1182.

Duckitt, J., Wagner, C., Plessis, I., and Birum, I. (2002). The psychological bases of ideology and prejudice: Testing a dual process model. *Journal of Personality and Social Psychology, 83,* 75-93.

Fried, A. (1988). Abortion politics as symbolic politics: An investigation into belief systems. *Social Science Quarterly, 72,* 137-154.

Glick, P., Diebold, J., Bailey-Werner, B., and Zhu, L. (1997). The two faces of Adam: Ambivalent sexism and polarized attitudes toward women. *Personality and Social Psychology Bulletin, 23,* 1323-1334.

Glick, P., and Fiske, S. T. (1996). The ambivalent sexism inventory: Differentiating hostile and benevolent sexism. *Journal of Personality and Social Psychology, 70,* 491-512.

Glick, P., and Fiske, S. T. (2001). An ambivalent alliance: Hostile and benevolent sexism as complementary justifications for gender inequality. *American Psychologist, 56,* 109-118.

Glick, P., Sakalli-Ugurlu, N., Ferreira, M. C., and Auguiar de Souza, M. (2002). Ambivalent sexism and attitudes toward wife abuse in Turkey and Brazil. *Psychology of Women Quarterly, 26,* 292-297.

Gosling, S. D., Vazire, S., Srivastava, S., and John, O. P. (2004). Should we trust web-based studies? A comparative analysis of six preconceptions about internet questionnaires. *American Psychologist, 59,* 93-104.

Jackman, M. R. (1994). *The velvet glove: Paternalism and conflict in gender, class, and race relations.* Berkeley: University of California Press.

Jelen, T. G., Damore, D. F., and Lamatsch, T. (2002). Gender, Employment status, and abortion: A longitudinal analysis. *Sex Roles, 47,* 321-330.

Jost, J. T., and Banaji, M. (1994). The role of stereotyping in system justification and the production of false consciousness. *British Journal of Social Psychology, 22,* 1-27.

Jost, J. T., and Kay, A. C. (2005). Exposure to benevolent sexism and complementary gender stereotypes: Consequences for specific and diffuse forms of system justification. *Journal of Personality and Social Psychology, 88,* 498-509.

Pratto, F., Sidanius, J., Stallworth, L. M., and Malle, B. F. (1994). Social dominance orientation: A personality variable predicting social and political attitudes. *Journal of Personality and Social Psychology, 67,* 741-763.

Roberts, D. E. (1998). The future of reproductive choice for poor women and women of color. In R. Weitz (Ed.), *The politics of women's bodies: Sexuality, appearance, and behavior* (270-277). New York: Oxford University Press.

Russell, B. L., and Trigg, K. Y. (2004). Tolerance of sexual harassment: An examination of gender differences, ambivalent sexism, social dominance, and gender roles. *Sex Roles, 50,* 565-573.

Sakalli-Ugurlu, N., and Glick, P. (2003). Ambivalent sexism and attitudes toward women who engage in premarital sex in Turkey. *The Journal of Sex Research, 40,* 296-302.

Sears, D. O. (1986). College sophomores in the laboratory: Influences of a narrow data base on social psychology's view of human nature. *Journal of Personality and Social Psychology, 51,* 515-530.

Sibley, C. G., and Wilson, M. S. (2004). Differentiating hostile and benevolent sexist attitudes toward positive and negative sexual female subtypes. *Sex Roles, 51,* 687-696.

Sidanius, J., and Pratto, F. (1999). *Social dominance: An intergroup theory of social hierarchy and oppression.* New York: Cambridge University Press.

Strickler, J., and Danigelis, N. L. (2002). Changing frameworks in attitudes toward abortion. *Sociological Forum, 17,* 187-201.

van Hiel, A., and Mervielde, I. (2005). Authoritarianism and social dominance orientation: Relationships with various forms of racism. *Journal of Applied Social Psychology, 35,* 2323-2344.

Viki, G. T., and Abrams, D. (2002). But she was unfaithful: Benevolent sexism and reactions to rape victims who violate traditional gender role expectations. *Sex Roles, 47,* 289-293.

Viki, G. T., Abrams, D., and Masser, B. (2004). Evaluating stranger and acquaintance rape: The role of benevolent sexism in perpetrator blame and recommended sentence length. *Law and Human Behavior, 28,* 295-303.

Wall, S. N., Frieze, I. H., Ferligoj, A., Jarosova, E., Paulknerova, D., Horvat, J., et al. (1999). Gender role and religion as predictors of attitude toward abortion in Croatia, Slovenia, the Czech Republic, and the United States. *Journal of Cross-Cultural Psychology, 30,* 443-465.

Wang, G. (2004). Social and cultural determinants of attitudes toward abortion: A test of Reiss' hypotheses. *The Social Science Journal, 41,* 93-105.

In: Personality Assessment: New Research
Editor: Lauren B. Palcroft and Melissa V. Lopez

ISBN: 978-1-60692-796-0

Chapter 16

FACTOR STRUCTURE, SEX EFFECTS AND DIFFERENTIAL ITEM FUNCTIONING OF THE JUNIOR EYSENCK PERSONALITY QUESTIONNAIRE REVISED - ABBREVIATED: A MULTIPLE-INDICATORS MULTIPLE-CAUSES APPROACH

***Rapson Gomez**[1] *and Andre Gomez*[2]**

[1]School of Psychology, University of Tasmania, Australia
[2]School of Psychology, Deakin University, Australia

ABSTRACT

The Junior Eysenck Personality Questionnaire Revised-Abbreviated (JEPQR-A) provides scales for measuring extraversion, neuroticism, psychoticism, and lie. This study used the multiple-indicators multiple-causes model procedure, with robust estimation, to examine simultaneously the factor structure of the JEPQR-A, the differential item functioning (DIF) of the JEPQR-A items as a function of sex, and the effects of sex on the JEPQR-A factors, controlling for DIF. Male (*N* =218) and female (*N* = 220) adolescent participants, between 15 and 17 years of age completed the JEPQR-A. The results provided support for the 4-factor structure of the JEPQR-A. Although an extraversion item and a psychoticism item showed DIF, their magnitudes were small. Controlling for DIF, females scored higher than males for the extraversion and neuroticism factors, while males scored higher for the psychoticism factor.

Keywords: JEPQR, MIMIC, Gender, Factor Structure, Differential Item Functioning,

* Corresponding Author: Rapson Gomez, School of Psychology, University of Tasmania, Private Bag 30 Hobart, Tasmania, Australia 7001. Electronic mail may be sent to Rapson.Gomez@utas.edu.au.

Several self-rating questionnaires for children and adolescents have been used for measuring Eysenck's (1952) personality traits of extraversion, neuroticism and psychoticism. These questionnaires include a lie scale for measuring dissimulation. The initial questionnaire was the 81-item Junior Eysenck Personality Questionnaire (JEPQ; Eysenck & Eysenck, 1975). In order to improve the psychometric properties of this questionnaire, Corulla (1990) developed an 89-item revision, called the Junior Eysenck Personality Questionnaire Revised (JEPQR), and a shorter 48-item version, called the .Junior Eysenck Personality Questionnaire Revised – Short Form (JEPQR-S), respectively. More recently, Francis (1996) developed a 24-item abbreviated version, called the Junior Eysenck Personality Questionnaire Revised–Abbreviated (JEPQR-A). This study used the multiple-indicators multiple-causes procedure, with robust estimation, to examine the differential item functioning (DIF) of the JEPQR-A items as a function of sex, and the effects of sex on the JEPQR-A factors, controlling for DIF.

The JEPQR-A was developed from the JEPQR-S (Francis, 1996). Each scale has six items. The items were selected in terms of satisfactory item to total scale score correlations. The four factors of the JEPQR-A showed reasonable reliabilities (Cronbach's α was .66 for extraversion, .70 for neuroticism, .61 for psychoticism, and .57 for lie). Also, there were high correlations between corresponding JEPQR-S and JEPQR-A scales. Subsequent studies of the JEPQR-A have supported the findings for reliabilities and relationships between factors (Maltby & Talley, 1998; Scholte & De Bruyn, 2001). For example, Scholte and De Bruyn found that principal component analysis supported the 4-factor structure, with separate factors for extraversion, neuroticism, psychoticism, and lie. The reliabilities were similar to those reported by Francis (1996). Given such properties, the JEPQR-A has been proposed as a useful research instrument when brief measures for extraversion, neuroticism or psychoticism are needed (Francis, 1996; Maltby & Talley, 1998; Scholte & De Bruyn, 2001).

Overall, the JEPQR-A appears to have reasonable psychometric properties. However there are a number of limitations in existing data on its psychometrics. All existing factor analyses of the JEPQR-A have been based on exploratory procedures involving mainly principal component analysis (PCA). Traditional exploratory procedures, including PCA, are limiting. Such procedures are not theory driven and they use raw scores that are not free of error variances. In addition, PCA produces meaningful results for only continuous data that have multivariate normal distribution (Bock, Gibbons, & Muraki, 1988). Since the items in the JEPQR-A are dichotomous, the item ratings would lack multivariate normality. Thus the use of PCA can be seen as inappropriate for testing the factor structure of the JEPQR-A.

In contrast to PCA, structural equation modeling (SEM) procedures are theory driven and use item scores that are free of error variances. With SEM it is also possible to use robust procedures that can correct for multivariate non-normality of a data set (Curran, West, & Finch, 1996). Flora and Curran (2004) have recommended the use of robust weight least squares (WLS) estimation, especially for small to medium size samples, with non-normal data set, which characterize ordinal, including dichotomous, response format items.

The multiple-indicators multiple-causes (MIMIC) model is a special form of SEM that can be used to test the factor structure of a questionnaire and the effects of one or more exogenous predictors (or covariates) on the latent factors (Joreskog & Goldberger, 1975). A significant direct effect indicates that the latent factor score will vary with different levels of the predictor. The basic MIMIC model can be extended to include direct paths between an exogenous predictor and the endogenous item indicators. When an exogenous variable is a grouping variable, such as sex (male vs female), then the inclusion of direct paths from this predictor grouping variable will enable the evaluation of the effect of the grouping variable on the latent factor, and the effect of the grouping variable on the indicators. In a MIMIC model with direct and indirect effects, the direct paths represent differences in responses to the item indicators that can be attributed to the predictor, after controlling for the relevant latent factor. Thus this model can test for differential item function (DIF). If an item shows DIF across two groups, it means that individuals in the two groups will endorse different ratings for the same level of the underlying trait that the item is measuring. An item is considered to have no DIF if there is no group difference in an item, over and above the difference in the latent factor (Millsap & Everson, 1993). When direct effects are non-significant it means that the items concerned have no DIF. In contrast, when direct effects are significant it means that the items concerned have DIF.

Forrest, Lewis, and Shevlin (2000) used the basic MIMIC procedure to examine the factor structure of the adult version of the Eysenck Personality Questionnaire Revised-Abbreviated (EPQR-A; Francis, Brown, & Philipchalk, 1992), and the effects of sex on the EPQR-A latent factors. Their findings indicated that sex contributed significantly to the predictions of the latent factors for neuroticism, psychoticism and lie, but not extraversion. More specifically, females scored higher than males for neuroticism and lie, while males scored higher than females for psychoticism. As this study did not parameterize direct effects between sex and the EPQR-A items, it cannot be assured that their findings were not confounded by DIF in the EPQR-A items.

As the JEPQR-A has been offered as a useful research instrument when brief measures for extraversion, neuroticism or psychoticism are needed (Francis, 1996; Maltby & Talley, 1998; Scholte & De Bruyn, 2001), it is useful to know if ratings on this measure for the items are influenced by sex differences. To date, there has been no such study. Existing data for the JEPQR-A scales, based on *t*-test, have generally supported higher psychoticism and lower neuroticism scores for males (Francis, 1996; Maltby & Telley, 1998; Scholte & De Bruyn, 2001). The findings for the extraversion and lie scores have been less consistent. For lie, Scholte and De Bruyn (2001) found higher scores for females, while Francis (1996) and Maltby and Telley (1998) found no difference. While the study by Francis (1996) found higher extraversion scores for females, the studies by Maltby and Telley (1998) and Scholte and De Bruyn (2001) found no sex difference. All these findings, however, need to be viewed with some caution because in a *t*-test, the DIF that may be present in the items are not taken into consideration when computing group difference. Thus findings many be confounded by DIF in items.

The aim of the current study was to use the MIMIC procedure, involving robust WLS estimation, to test the factor structure of the JEPQR-A, the DIF for the JEPQR-A items as a function of sex, and the effects of sex on the JEPQR-A latent factors after taking into account DIF. Although the multiple group CFA procedure can also be used (Vanderberg & Lance, 2000), this method is thought to provide questionable results for small sample sizes (Muthen, 1989), as is the case in the current study, with 218 males and 220 females. Another reason for using the MIMIC procedure is that it allowed for controlling the possible confounding effects of age on the latent factors. This is important as existing data shown that JEPQR-A ratings are influenced by age (Francis, 1996). Modeling for such covariates is difficult and complex with the traditional multiple-group CFA procedures.

Figure 1 shows the MIMIC path model tested in this study. As shown, part of the model involved the loadings of relevant JEPRQ-A items on their respective latent factors.

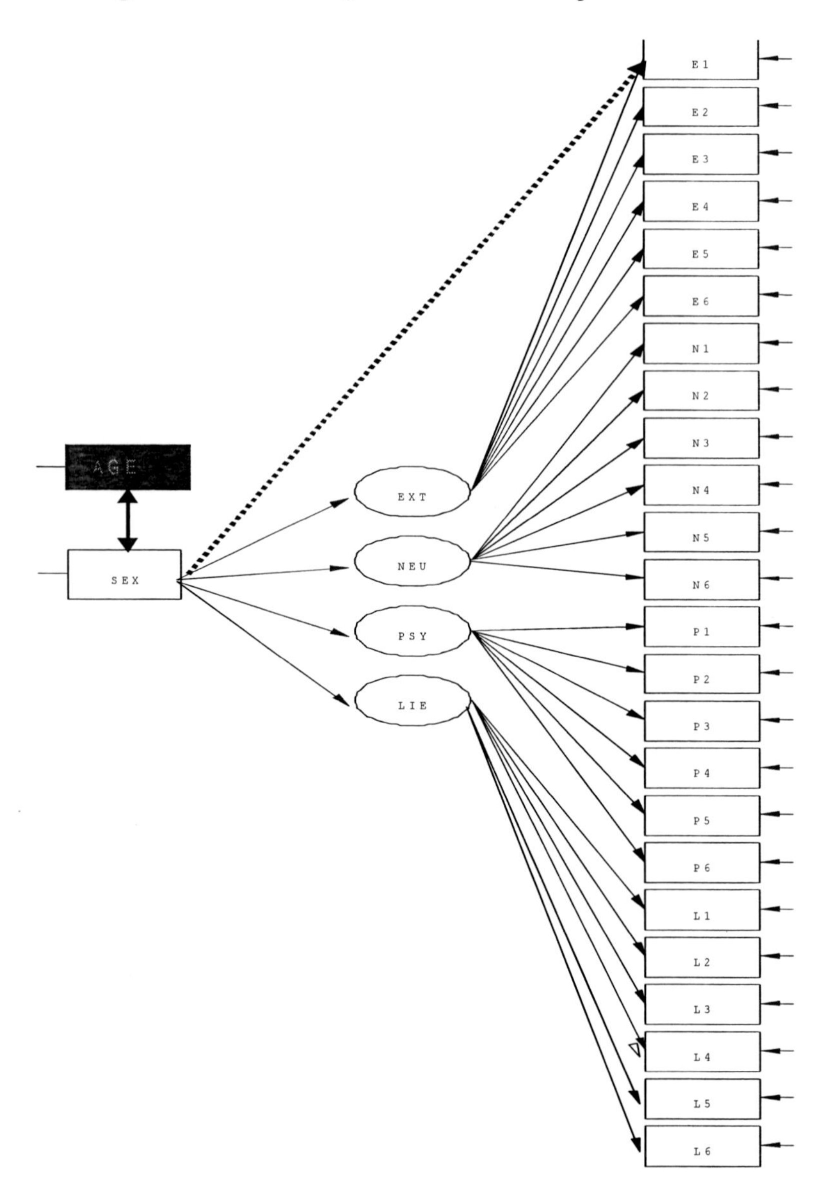

Note. EXT = extraversion, NEU = neuroticism, PSY = psychoticism, LIE = lie.

The dash line represents a differential item functioning path. In the actual model, there were differential item functioning paths from sex to all the JEPQR-A, except those fixed for reference purpose (i.e., E6, N5, P1, L5).

Figure 1. MIMIC path diagram of model used in the study (for clarity the correlations between the latent factors are not shown in the figure).

This is essentially a confirmatory factor analysis (CFA) model of the JEPQR-A. In addition, the latent factors were regressed on sex and age (as shown by the arrow pointing from sex and age to the latent factors). Age, retained as a continuous variable, was included as a covariate to control for any confounding relationship with the JEPQR-A factors. To test DIF, all the JEPQR-A items (except the items fixed for identification purpose) were regressed on sex (as shown by the arrow pointing from sex to the items). Significant direct effects between sex and the items will indicate items that have DIF as a function of sex. For this study, males were coded 1, and females were coded 0. Thus positive significant associations between sex and the JEPQR-A factors or items will indicate higher scores for males, while negative significant associations between sex and the JEPQR-A factors or items will indicate lower scores for males. Here the unstandardised direct effect of sex on the latent factors can be viewed as the mean difference in the latent factors scores between males and females, based on the metrics of the marker indicators of the factors.

Based on existing data, it was predicted that all items would have significant loadings on their respective latent factors. In the absence of existing data, no prediction was made for DIF. Also as existing data on sex differences for the JEPQR-A scales could have been confounded by DIF, no predictions were made for the effects of sex on the four JEPQR-A factors. We suspected however that males will have higher scores for psychoticism and lower scores for neuroticism.

METHOD

Participants

The participants comprised 438 adolescents (218 males and 220 females). They were all between 15 and 17 years of age, with a mean age of 16.25 years (*SD* = 0.79). Participants were recruited from 9 secondary schools in Victoria, Australia. Altogether, about 70% of adolescents who were contacted participated in this study.

Measures

The study used the JEPQR-A (Francis, 1996), described in the introduction. The Cronbach's α values in this study were .68 for extraversion, .70 for neuroticism, .68 for psychoticism, and .56 for the lie scales.

Procedure

Following consent from directors of education, school principals, teachers, parents and participants, research assistants distributed the set of questionnaires to be completed by participants in their classrooms. The set of questionnaires comprised a cover letter, the JEPQR-A (and other questionnaires covering stress and anxiety that are not analyzed in this study). The cover page of each questionnaire set contained the plain language statement about the study. This indicated that the study was addressing aspects of stress and personality, and that participation was voluntary. Those who agreed to participate completed the questionnaires in class, and returned them to sealed boxes before they left. The order of the questionnaires was randomized across participants. Opportunities for debriefing were available to all participants.

DATA ANALYSIS

The MIMIC analysis was conducted using M*plus* software (Muthen & Muthen, 2006). As noted previously, robust WLS was used for the analysis. In order to compute the direct paths from the exogenous variable to the set of items of a factor in a MIMIC model, it is necessary for at least one path from the exogenous variable to the relevant set of items to be set to zero, as this can provide a reference variable against which the effects of the other paths can be computed. Without this, the model is not identified. In this study, it was necessary to fix at least one path each from sex to the extraversion, neuroticism, psychoticism and lie items to zero (anchor items). To select appropriate anchor items, all direct paths in the MIMIC model were fixed to zero. The modification indices (MI) of these paths were examined. The MI of a path provides an indication of how much the fit of the model will improve if the path is freely estimated. Thus low MI values will suggest little improvement. Given this, for each factor the item with the lowest MI was selected to be used as the anchor item for that factor in the final MIMIC model.

Statistical fit was ascertained using the robust WLS fit function χ^2. This index shows the closeness of fit between the unrestricted sample covariance matrix and the restricted (model) covariance matrix. As χ^2 values are inflated by large sample sizes, model fit are also evaluated by approximate fit indices, such as root mean squared error of approximation (RMSEA; Steiger, 1990) and the comparative fit index (CFI; Bentler, 1990). The RMSEA provides a measure of model fit relative to the population covariance matrix when the complexity of the model is also taken into account, while the CFI provides a measure of the fit of the hypothesized model relative to the independent model. The guidelines suggested by Hu and Bentler (1999) are that RMSEA values $< .06$ is taken as good fit, .07 to .08 as moderate fit, .08 to .10 as marginal fit, and $> .10$ as poor fit. For CFI, values above .95 are taken as good fit, and values between .90 and .95 are taken as acceptable fit. Although recent studies have raised some concerns about these guidelines (e.g., Marsh, Hau, & Wen, 2004; Yuan, 2005; see also Barrett, 2007), the same studies and others have supported their use for model evaluation, but cautioned against interpreting these guidelines as golden rules (e.g., Bentler, 2007; Mulaik, 2007; Steiger, 2007). Although the Hu and Bentler guidelines may be too stringent (Marsh et al., 2004), they were used in the current study to evaluate model fit so as to avoid the possibility of Type 1 error. Thus model fit was evaluated in terms of the WLS χ^2, RMSEA and CFI values.

RESULTS

Descriptive Scores and Multivariate Skewness and Kurtosis

Table 1 shows the mean and standard deviation values of the ratings of the 24 items of the JEPQR-A. There was significant multivariate skewness (141.84, $z = 63.29$, $p < .001$) and kurtosis (703.77, $z = 14.89$, $p < .001$). Thus, as expected, the assumption of multivariate normality was violated.

Table 1. Mean and Standard Deviation (SD) Scores, and Brief Descriptions of the JEPQR-A Items

Item # in Model	Item # in Questionnaire	Brief item description	Mean (SD)
E1	1	Can you get a party going?	.69 (.47)
E2	5	Are you rather lively?	.79 (.41)
E3	13	Do you like going out a lot?	.81 (.39)
E4	18	Find it hard to enjoy a lively party?	.89 (.31)
E5	20	Rather be alone or with others?	.87 (.34)
E6	22	Let yourself go at a party?	.89 (.32)
N1	7	Do you often feel fed-up?	.71 (.45)
N2	8	Easily hurt when people find fault?	.53 (.50)
N3	9	Hard to sleep because of worry?	.49 (.50)
N4	10	Sometimes feel life is not worth living?	.33 (.47)
N5	15	Worry if you made a fool of self?	.50 (.50)
N6	24	Are your feelings rather easily hurt?	.48 (.50)
P1	2	Enjoy hurting people you like?	.05 (.22)
P2	3	Important to have good manners?	.07 (.25)
P3	6	Enjoy practical jokes that hurt people?	.29 (.46)
P4	21	More trouble at school than others?	.26 (.44)
P5	23	Sometimes bully and tease others?	.14 (.34)
P6	12	Get into a lot of fights?	.22 (.41)
L1	4	Always do as you are told at once?	.14 (.35)
L2	11	Throw paper on floor if no basket?	.52 (.50)
L3	14	Said anything bad about anyone?	.04 (.20)
L4	16	Take anything that belonged to others?	.26 (.44)
L5	17	Ever greedy?	.36 (.48)
L6	19	Always say sorry when rude?	.69 (.46)

Evaluation of Fit of the Hypothesized Model

The SEM analysis for the final MIMIC model resulted in the following fit indices: χ^2 (df = 266) = 623.92, $p < .001$, RMSEA = .055, CFI = .90. Although the χ^2 was significant, thereby indicating no statistical support for the model, in terms of the guidelines for approximate fit indices, proposed by Hu and Bentler (1999), the RMSEA value indicates good fit, while the CFI value indicates acceptable fit for the model. Given that the χ^2 values are inflated by relatively large sample sizes, the findings for the approximate fit indices in the study can be taken as providing sufficient support for the MIMIC model.

FACTOR STRUCTURE OF THE JEPQR-A

Table 2 shows the factor loadings on the JEPQR-A items. All but three items loaded at or above .45 on their respective factors. The exceptions were the neuroticism item "hard to sleep because of worry" (item N3), and the lie items "take anything that belonged to others" (item L4) and "ever greedy" (item L5). However items loaded significantly on respective factors.

Table 2. MIMIC Model: Standardised Factor Loadings and Regression Coefficients for Direct Effects between Sex and the JEPQR-A Items

Item: Model # /Brief description	Loading	*b*	Standard Error	*β*
Extraversion items				
E1. Can you get a party going?	0.69***			
E2. Are you rather lively?	0.72***	0.00	0.33	0.00
E3. Do you like going out a lot?	0.83***	0.41	0.33	0.12
E4. Find it hard to enjoy a lively party?	0.75***	1.18**	0.39	0.35
E5. Rather be alone or with others?	0.84***	0.68	0.42	0.20
E6. Let yourself go at a party?	0.90***	0.67	0.37	0.20
Neuroticism items				
N1. Do you often feel fed-up?	0.62***	0.68	0.50	0.20
N2. Easily hurt when people find fault?	0.85***	0.24	0.61	0.07
N3. Hard to sleep because of worry?	0.33***	-0.48	0.38	-0.14
N4. Sometimes feel life not worth living?	0.51***	0.23	0.47	0.07
N5. Worry if you made a fool of self?	0.52***	-	-	-
N6. Are your feelings rather easily hurt?	0.81***	-0.59	0.53	-0.18
Psychoticism items				
P1. Enjoy hurting people you like?	0.76***	0.05	0.61	0.01
P2. Important to have good manners?	0.47***	1.30*	0.56	0.39
P3. Enjoy practical jokes that hurt people?	0.47***	0.45	0.38	0.14
P4. More trouble at school than others?	0.87***	-0.60	0.59	-0.26
P5. Sometimes bully and tease others?	-	-	-	-
P6. Get into more fights than others?	0.81***	-1.02	0.57	-0.31
Lie items				
L1. Always do as you are told at once?	0.53***	0.08	0.57	0.02
L2. Throw paper on floor if no basket?	0.57***	0.74	0.58	0.22
L3. Said anything bad about anyone?	0.45**	0.39	0.71	0.12
L4. Take anything that belonged to others?	0.42***	0.17	0.41	0.05
L5. Ever greedy?	0.31**	-	-	-
L6. Always say sorry when rude?	0.60***	-0.67	0.60	-0.20

Note. Items E1, N1, P1 and L1 were the reference items for the relevant latent factors. For direct effects, the reference items were E1, N5, P5 and L5.

b and β are unstandardised and standardised coefficients.

p < .05, **p < .01, ***p < .001.

EVALUATION OF DIRECT SEX EFFECT ON THE JEPQR-A ITEMS

Table 2 also shows the direct effects of sex on the JEPQR-A items. These effects were not significant for all the neuroticism and lie items. For extraversion, there was one item that showed DIF (item E3 – “find it hard to enjoy a lively party”). There was also one psychoticism item that showed DIF (item P2 - “important to have good manners”). The DIF for both items were positive. As males were coded 1 and females were coded 0, the findings for items E3 and P2 indicate higher scores for males. Based on the unstandardised coefficients (see Table 2), males scored 1.18 units more than females for E3. For P2, males scored 1.30 units more than females. Table 2 shows that the standardized coefficients for all items ranged from .00 to .35. As standardized coefficients can be viewed as equivalent to Cohen’s *d*, the magnitude of these effects (includes those for sex on E3 and P2) can be considered low, based on Cohen’s (1992) guidelines, i.e., small = .20, medium = .50, and large = .80.

EVALUATION OF SEX AND AGE EFFECTS ON THE JEPQR-A FACTORS

Table 3 shows the regression coefficients of the four JEPQR-A factors on sex and age. In relation to age, there were significant associations with neuroticism, psychoticism and lie factors, thereby supporting the inclusion of age as a covariate in the MIMIC model. Table 3 shows that sex contributed significantly to the predictions of the factors for extraversion, neuroticism and psychoticism, but not lie. The lack of significant effect for sex on lie means no sex difference for lie.

Table 3. MIMIC Model: Regression Coefficients between Sex and Age with the JEPQR-A Factors

Predictors	Unstandardised	Standard Error	Standardised
Extraversion			
Sex	-0.78**	0.30	-0.34
Age	0.10	0.06	0.12
Neuroticism			
Sex	-1.44**	0.51	-0.69
Age	0.21***	0.06	0.26
Psychoticism			
Sex	1.16*	0.52	0.46
Age	-0.23**	0.07	-0.24
Lie			
Sex	-0.94	0.53	-0.53
Age	0.20**	0.07	0.29

$^*p < .05$, $^{**}p < .01$, $^{***}p < .001$.

The unstandardised coefficients for the paths involving extraversion, neuroticism and psychoticism were -0.78, -1.44 and 1.16, respectively. Given that males were coded 1 and females were coded 0, it follows that males scored 0.78 units lower than females for extraversion, 1.44 units lower than females for neuroticism, and 1.16 units higher than females for psychoticism, after taking into account DIF in the items. The standardized coefficients for extraversion, neuroticism and psychoticism were -0.34, -0.69 and .46, respectively (see Table 3). Thus the magnitude of these effects can be considered low, based on Cohen's (1992) guidelines.

DISCUSSION

The findings here showed that with the exception of the neuroticism item for "hard to sleep because of worry", and the lie items for "take anything that belonged to others" and "ever greedy", all other items loaded at or above .45 on their respective factors. Nevertheless all items loaded significantly on their respective factors. These findings are consistent with existing data for the JEPQR-A (Francis, 1996; Maltby & Talley, 1998; Scholte & De Bruyn, 2001), and they indicate that the JEPQR-A items are reasonably good indicators of their respective latent factors. It is to be noted, however, that the findings here extend existing data in important ways as, unlike previous studies, the current study used SEM with robust WLS estimation procedure.

The results of the DIF analyses showed no DIF for all the neuroticism and lie items, five out of the six extraversion items, and five out of the six psychoticism items. The extraversion item that showed DIF was "find it hard to enjoy a lively party", while the psychoticism item with DIF was "important to have good manners". For both items, the findings showed that the same level of the relevant traits would lead males to endorse higher item ratings. As "important to have good manners" was reversed scored, the DIF in this item indicates that for the same level of the psychoticism trait, males will endorse lower ratings. It is to be noted, however, that the effect sizes of all items for the DIF analysis were of low magnitude. These findings can be interpreted to mean that the JEPQR-A is generally well suited for use by both males and females, and scores from these groups could be directly compared.

The findings in the study also showed that after taking into account DIF in the items, females had higher scores than males for the extraversion and neuroticism factors, while males had higher scores than females for the psychoticism factor. These differences were however of low magnitude. The study also found no sex difference for lie. The findings here are supportive of existing data for the JEPQR-A scales that show higher psychoticism and lower neuroticism scores for males (Francis, 1996; Maltby & Telley, 1998; Scholte & De Bruyn, 2001), higher extraversion among females (Francis, 1996), and no sex difference for lie (Francis, 1996; Maltby & Telley, 1998). However, unlike previous studies, the current study provided a clearer test of the effects of sex, as it controlled for DIF in the JEPQR-A items and the confounding effects of age on the JEPQR-A latent factors.

Although this study suggests that sex differences exist for the extraversion, neuroticism, and psychoticism JEPQR-A factors, these findings need to be viewed with some caution. This is because Shevlin, Bailey, and Adamson (2002) have shown that sex differences for adults on the EPQR-A factors can be better accounted for by sex role differences than sex as such. Thus it may be that male adolescents are not less extraverted or less neurotic than adolescent females, but they can relate less to the extraversion and neuroticism items of the JEPQR-A because these items are less congruent to their sex-role. Similarly, it is possible that the males in this study scored higher for psychoticism because these items are more congruent to their sex-role. If so, then it is possible that this study's findings may be related to sex-role rather than sex differences. Unfortunately, as the study did not include a sex-role measure, this possibility could not be evaluated. Future studies may wish to examine this possibility. Given the advantages of the MIMIC procedure, it will be useful if future studies use this procedure.

REFERENCES

Barrett, P. (2007). Structural equation modeling: Adjusting model fit. *Personality and Individual Differences, 42*, 815-824.

Bentler, P. M. (1990). Comparative fit indexes in structural models. *Psychological Bulletin, 107,* 238-246.

Bock, R. D., Gibbons, R. & Muraki, E. (1988). Full-information item factor analysis. *Applied Psychological Measurement, 12*, 261-280.

Cohen, J. (1992). A power primer. *Psychological Bulletin, 112*, 155-159.

Corulla, W. J. (1990). A revised version of the psychoticism scale for children. *Personality and Individual Differences, 11*, 65-76.

Curran, P. J., West, S. G. & Finch, J. F. (1996). The robustness of test statistics to normality and specification error in confirmatory factor analysis. *Psychological Methods, 1*, 16-29.

Eysenck, H. J. (1952). *The scientific study of personality.* London: Routledge & Kegan Paul.

Eysenck, H. J. & Eysenck, S. B. G. (1975). *Manual of the Eysenck Personality Questionnaire (adult and junior).* London: Hodder & Stoughton.

Flora, D. B. & Curran, P. J. (2004). An empirical evaluation of alternative methods of estimation for confirmatory factor analysis with ordinal data. *Psychological Methods, 9*, 466-491.

Forrest, S., Lewis, C. A. & Shevlin, M. (2000). Examining the factor structure and gender bias of the Eysenck Personality Questionnaire Revised-Abbreviated. *Personality and Individual Differences, 29,* 579-588.

Francis, L. J. (1996). The development of an abbreviated form of the Revised Junior Eysenck Personality Questionnaire (JEPQR-A) among 13-15 year olds. *Personality and Individual Differences, 21,* 835-844.

Francis, L. J., Brown, L. B. & Philipchalk, R. (1992). The development of an abbreviated form of the Revised Eysenck Personality Questionnaire (EPQR-A): Its use among students in England, Canada, the USA and Australia. *Personality and Individual Differences, 13,* 443-449.

Hu, L. T. & Bentler, P. M. (1999). Cut-off criteria for fit indices in covariance structure analysis: conventional criteria versus alternatives. *Structural Equation Modeling, 6*, 1-55.

Joreskog , K. G. & Goldberger, A. S. (1975). Estimation of a model with multiple indicators and multiple causes of a single latent variable. *Journal of American Statistical Association, 70*, 631-639.

Maltby, J. & Talley, M. (1998). The psychometric properties of an abbreviated form of the Revised Junior Eysenck Personality Questionnaire (JEPQR-A) among 12-15 –year old U.S. young persons. *Personality and Individual Differences, 24*, 891-893.

Marsh, H.W., Hau, K. T. & Wen, Z. (2004). In search of golden rules: Comment on hypothesis-testing approaches to setting cutoff values for fit indexes and dangers in overgeneralizing Hu and Bentler's (1999) findings. *Structural Equation Modeling, 11*, 320-341.

Millsap, R. E. & Everson, H. T. (1993). Methodology review: statistical approaches for assessing measurement bias. *Applied Psychological Measurement, 17*, 297-334.

Mulaik, S. (2007). There is a place for approximate fit in structural equation modeling. *Personality and Individual Differences, 42*, 883-895.

Muthen, B. O. (1989). Latent variable modeling in heterogeneous population. *Psychometrika, 54*, 557-585.

Muthen, L. K. & Muthen, B. O. (2006). *Mplus user's guide* (4th ed.). Los Angeles, CA: Muthen & Muthen.

Scholte, R. H. J. & De Bruyn, E. E. J. (2001). The Revised Junior Eysenck Personality Questionnaire (JEPQR-R): Dutch replications of the full-length, short, and abbreviated forms. *Personality and Individual Differences, 31,* 615-625.

Steiger, J. H. (1990). Structural model evaluation and modification. *Multivariate Behavioral Research, 25*, 173-180.

Steiger, J. H. (2007). Understanding the limitations of global fit assessment in structural equation modeling. *Personality and Individual Differences, 42*, 893-898.

Shevlin, M., Bailey, F. & Adamson, G. (2002). Examining the factor structure and sources of differential functioning of the Eysenck Personality Questionnaire Revised – Abbreviated. *Personality and Individual Differences, 32,* 479-487.

Vandenberg, R. J. & Lance, C. E. (2000). A review and synthesis of the measurement invariance literature: Suggestions, practices, and recommendations for organizational research. *Organizational Research Methods, 3,* 4-69.

Yuan, K. H. (2005) Fit indices versus test statistics. *Multivariate Behavioral Research, 40*, 115-148.

In: Personality Assessment: New Research
Editor: Lauren B. Palcroft and Melissa V. Lopez
ISBN: 978-1-60692-796-0

SHORT COMMUNICATIONS

In: Personality Assessment: New Research
Editor: Lauren B. Palcroft and Melissa V. Lopez
ISBN: 978-1-60692-796-0

Short Communication A

ONLINE COLLABORATIVE LEARNING: THE CHALLENGE OF CHANGE

Baruch Offir[1*], Ingrid Barth[2] and Orit Zeichner[3]
Distance Learning Laboratory
School of Education
Bar-Ilan University
Ramat-Gan 52900, Israel
Tel No: + 972-3-5318046
Fax No: +972-3-5353319
offirb@mail.biu.ac.il
1) Prof. Baruch Offir (corresponding author)
Offir-e@inter.net.il; Offirb@mail.biu.ac.il
2) Dr. Ingrid Barth - ingbarth@zahav.net.il
3) Dr. Orit Zeichner - zeichno@mail.biu.ac.il

ABSTRACT

Desktop videoconferencing and project-based online collaborative learning can create new directions in higher education. However, the transition from the "safe space" of a conventional classroom course to a new learning environment often represents a major change for both faculty and students. Faculty need to know what kind of support can help students cope with the challenges of an unfamiliar learning environment in order to make this transition less difficult. In this paper we describe how we create conditions

* Prof.. Baruch Offir (corresponding author)
Head, Distance Learning Laboratory .
School of Education
Bar-Ilan University
Ramat-Gan 52900
Israel
Tel: +972-3-5318447
Fax: +972-3-5353319
Offir-e@inter.net.il
Offirb@mail.biu.ac.il

for an effective online collaborative learning environment within the framework of a course module. During the course, the students acquire judgment and decision making abilities for integrating technological systems into their field of expertise. We discuss the difficulties of evaluating outcomes in learning environments that are essentially different from conventional university courses. We conclude by sharing the lessons learned and identify critical factors that helped our students move from the familiar “chalk and talk” model to the relatively uncharted territory of project-based online collaborative learning and show that provision of “safe places” represents one of the most important contributions of online collaborative learning environments.

Keywords: videoconferencing, online collaborative learning, project-based learning, distance education.

Introduction

Changes related to teaching practices seem to evolve at a much slower pace than the technological innovations that have rapidly changed the landscape of tertiary level education. Levine and Sun (2002) and Twigg (2003) have indicated that faculty members often duplicate their conventional courses online, instead of utilizing the full potential of new media. Reeves, Herrington and Oliver (2004) and Jonassen, Peck and Wilson (1999), described highly innovative ways of using technology in educational contexts. These "blue-prints for change" represent a significant change in attitudes and beliefs of both faculty and students.

Literature Review

Herrington, Oliver and Reeves (2003) describe the “vision” of online collaborative learning as learners working together to solve complex problems and complete authentic tasks. Although this vision seems clear, many questions remain unanswered. These questions include: what makes a problem “complex”, how to create authentic tasks within the framework of an academic course, and why students would want to register for courses with innovative designs when traditional teacher-dominated lectures require much less time and effort. These questions require more coherent answers, especially for faculty who have minimal prior experience with designing and teaching in online collaborative learning environments. Furthermore, Reeves, Herrington and Oliver (2004) recently observed that “traditional” research methods have proved an insufficient basis for advancing the design and implementation of innovative collaborative learning environments. This position is reinforced by Anderson (2005), who suggests that a natural science research paradigm of blind control group studies and laboratory conditions is not attuned to the complex context of real educational settings.

New technology-based learning environments create new directions but also create fears of getting lost in unfamiliar and uncharted territory among both faculty and students. A learning space should therefore have sufficient support features that, as Palmer (1998) describes, "help students deal with the dangers of an educational expedition: places to rest, places to find nourishment, even places to seek shelter when one feels overexposed" (p. 75).

Desktop videoconferencing offers several learning advantages. However, this medium also represents what Anderson (2002) terms a relatively "lean" environment characterized by reduced paralinguistic cues. Firsthand experience with videoconferencing teaches students how reduced paralinguistic cues affect nonverbal messages. Students also learn how to use specific types of teacher-student interactions in videoconferencing to compensate for the reduction in non-verbal messages (Barth, 2005).

Working with desktop videoconferencing in a project-based real-world context gives students a clear understanding of (1) when and under what circumstances this medium should be used together with face-to-face communication rather than as a stand-alone distance learning option and (2) how this medium can be used to give different sectors of the community on-going access to specific areas of expertise (Offir, Barth, Lev, & Shteinbok 2003).

During the 1990's, we examined person-related variables that need to be factored into the design of effective learning environments. These variables include students' attitudes and self-image (Offir & Katz, 1992), as well as other psychological factors (Offir & Cohen-Fridel, 1998; Offir, Bezalel & Barth, 2007) that affect learning in a technology-based learning environment. Our research on the relationship between students' beliefs and misconceptions about their effectiveness as learners, affective-motivational feedback interventions and student dropout rates in a videoconference-based learning environment (Zeichner, 2007) indicated non-cognitive factors that need to be considered by faculty who teach in new learning environments.

This holistic multivariate approach relates to decisions that determine when and under what conditions technology-mediated communication should be integrated with face-to-face communication to improve the quality of educational opportunities and attain a range of different instructional goals. Conclusions from these studies form the empirical foundation for the learning environment described in this paper.

Utilization of desktop videoconferencing to form university-community partnerships can provide students with an opportunity to engage in project-based learning in an authentic context and enables higher education to contribute towards meeting the special needs of different sectors of the community. However, the transition from the "safe space" of the conventional classroom to the relatively "risky place" of a new learning environment represents a major challenge for most faculty and students. Additional exploratory and descriptive studies are therefore required to help faculty understand the types of issues that may arise when they move from merely replicating their conventional courses to exploring new directions in online learning contexts.

Faculty require clear and coherent guidelines that indicate "what works and why" in a higher education context in order to make the transition from teacher-dominated knowledge transmission to innovative learning environments. The central purpose of this paper is to describe "lessons learned" from four years of experience with a learning environment that integrates videoconferencing, project-based and online collaborative learning to create university-community partnerships.

Goals of the Course Module

The course module is based on the assumption that effective use of videoconferencing represents a potentially powerful means for achieving educational goals such as increasing equality and "narrowing the gaps" in society. However, full utilization of this potential will only occur if students who will work with these technologies in the future understand how videoconferencing can be used effectively to supplement school resources and serve the needs of different sectors of the community.

One goal of this module is to demonstrate the flexibility and cost-effectiveness that characterize desktop videoconferencing. These advantages essentially expand the concept of community to include specific populations with special needs who are no longer concentrated in one specific geographic locality. In this module, "hands on" use of desktop videoconferencing helps students learn how to use videoconferencing to disseminate expertise that benefits specific sectors of the community in geographically and socio-economically peripheral areas.

Another goal of this unit is to clarify the contribution of online collaborative learning. Although videoconferencing can play a key role in developing solutions for university-community partnerships, successful implementation of these solutions clearly requires much more than effective utilization of videoconferencing.

Our experience with this module indicates that one of the central contributions of project-based learning is the creation of conditions in which no individual student has the multi-faceted knowledge and range of skills required to design and implement an effective solution on his/her own. Unless students work together to supplement each others' strengths and off-set their weaknesses, they will not be able to cope effectively with the challenges and demands of project-based learning in university-community partnerships. The complexity of the problem being addressed in each of the four strands outlined above combines with the community context to create the necessary conditions for effective online collaborative learning.

Description of the Module

This module consists of four semester courses offered as an elective unit for students who are studying for a post-graduate degree in educational technology. Admission is open to students with a strong background and working knowledge in specific areas of education such as Special Education, Early Childhood, Educational Counseling, Educational Management and Curriculum Design. The first two semesters of this unit take place in a conventional classroom, and focus on theories, models and research findings students need to know in order to manage effective videoconference-based projects. Successful completion of the first two semesters is a necessary condition for admission to the second two semesters.

During the last two semesters the students move out of the classroom and into the community. The learning process in the second half of the unit is thus driven by real-world problems and special requirements of a specific target population. During the last two semesters, online collaborative learning replaces weekly classroom meetings, and students meet as a whole group only during the first orientation session. For the remainder of the year, the students in each of the four strands work in small groups and consult with the lecturer via email either directly or through their group coordinator. During the last two meetings of the year, all groups present a portfolio of work for peer review.

METHOD

A "distance learning" course is given at Bar-Ilan University for masters' and doctoral students. Towards the end of the first half of the unit, the students are introduced to the four strands of the project as well as to what the previous cohort of students accomplished with these populations. After selecting which of the four strands they would like to work with, the students who work with the same population form collaborative working groups. Each group of students appoints a coordinator who regularly consults with the faculty member responsible for this module. During the second half of the unit, students use the above studies as part of the knowledge-base that forms the design of their videoconference sessions and use the theories, models and research instruments acquired during the first two semesters in order to plan, teach and evaluate a series of videoconference-based sessions designed for their specific sector of the community.

The students' assignments include a “progress report” or reflective component that requires the students to identify factors that helped or hindered completion of the assignment. The progress report for the first assignment focuses on identification of group dynamics such as conflict resolution mechanisms that helped or hampered successful completion of the needs-assessment and goal-definition processes.

The second assignment consists of documenting their decision-making process during the design of the videoconference sessions. The students focus mainly on identifying the constraints and “trade-offs” they factored into the design process. The self-assessment component of the second component is designed to ensure that the students engage in productive reflection that crystallizes into a concrete set of “lessons learned” which contributes to improved performance in the third assignment.

Data collection before and after the videoconference transmissions represents the third assignment in this module. The students use both qualitative and quantitative data collection methods to assess the impact of the videoconference-based solutions they develop for addressing specific problems of the target population they are working with. The progress report component of this assignment requires the students to identify what they would do differently to make their videoconference-based solutions more effective in the future. Documentation of post-transmission conclusions enables the next cohort to benefit from the students' accumulated experience and to continue the university-community project more effectively, instead of having to "re-invent the wheel".

A case study design was adopted. According to Cresswell (2003), a case study design enables the researcher to explore a program, an event, an activity, a process or one or more individuals in-depth.

All post-graduate students who enrolled for this four-semester module participated in this study (*N*=57). Gender distribution consisted of approximately 70% female and 30% male students, whose ages ranged from 22 to 31. All participants had at least two years of previous teaching experience and were specializing in different areas of education.

Three forms of assessment were used in an attempt to triangulate evidence of learning: instructor assessment of assignments, peer assessment of project portfolios as well as self-assessment regarding the learning process and completion of assignments. Instructor assessment was given according to clearly-defined criteria that were explained at the beginning of the academic year. Completed assignments submitted by students in the previous cohort were also used to demonstrate implementation of instructor assessment criteria.

The peer assessment took place at the end of the academic year when groups of students from each strand presented their project portfolios. In-depth non-structured interviews were conducted with the students towards the end of fourth semester.

RESULTS

During the interviews, the students were asked about the teaching methods which they prefer in the learning process. Most of the interviewed students (22 out of 30) indicated the benefit of the teacher's presence during the learning process (Table 1).

Table 1. Students' attitudes towards the essential role of the teachers in the learning process, as expressed in the interview (*n*=30)

Question in the interview	Statements expressed by the interviewees	Number of students interviewed
What teaching method do you prefer in the learning process?	Comments mentioned in the interview which support the teacher's importance	22
	The teacher's presence affords confidence The teacher can identify my problems and difficulties by looking at me The teacher causes me to be in a framework Positive comments (feedback) and a pleasant learning atmosphere can be created only in the presence of a teacher	
	Comments mentioned in the interview which do not support the teacher's importance	8
	I do not need a good word from the teacher A clear explanation of the material is more important to me than how the material is transmitted Working with the computer also created interest for me	

Table 2 presents a summary of the advantages versus the disadvantages of collaborative distance learning compared to the teacher's roles as expressed in the interview. The advantages cited most often were that distance learning affords independence and convenience and that the method is immediate and available.

Table 2. Summary of the advantages versus the disadvantages of distance learning compared to the teacher's role as expressed in the interview (n=30)

The question	Advantages	Disadvantages
In your experience, what are the advantages and disadvantages of the distance learning method?	• Affords independence and convenience – 9 • A quiet working environment – 3 • Small learning groups and personal attention is felt – 3 • Creates interest and concentration – 4 • The method is immediate and available – 6	• Absence of feedbacks – 1 • Self-discipline – 1 • There is absence of company and there is a feeling of being "alone" - 3
In your experience, what are the advantages and disadvantages of the traditional method?	• Learning in a classroom comprises a framework for me – 7 • The explanations and the learning are all tangible and this makes it easier for me – 3 • The presence of the teacher in the classroom affords me confidence – 5 • The teacher can discern my difficulties at an early stage – 5 • I am awarded personal attention and feedbacks – 4	• The learning groups are very large and this hampers the amount of material learned – 2 • Less personal attention – 1 • There is a great chance that students with difficulties will hinder a large group of students – 3

The students also claimed that one of the main roles of the teachers in the learning process is the fact that they afford feedback (Table 3).

Table 3. Summary of the interviews on the teacher's role in the learning process (n=30)

Which of the teacher's behaviors evoke your motivation to learn?	• The motivation to learn comes from me and the teacher has no influence on me – 7 • Personal attention – 6 • Affording feedback – 12 • Creating interest – 5

Almost all students viewed the central contribution of university-community partnerships as increasing the level of sensitivity to the special needs of community sectors and a sense of satisfaction from having attempted to address these needs. However, the majority of students did not identify the contribution of partnerships in cognitive terms.

Perceptions regarding contributions of online collaborative learning were also reported in affective terms. This was reflected in the students' reports of accomplishment from meeting the challenge of "being thrown into the water" and coping with complex and unfamiliar situations. Most students reported that group problem solving increased their confidence in their ability to (1) cope with the challenges of the course module and (2) stay "on track" instead of being thrown "off-balance" when confronted with unexpected difficulties.

Many students related to the positive contributions of a number of specific design features. These features included course assignments that provided them with a sense of structure that helped them navigate their way through what they initially perceived as unfamiliar and extremely demanding territory. Other features perceived as contributing significantly to the students' learning included clearly defined goals, detailed task analysis, examples of previously completed assignments, explicit criteria for assignment assessment and timely instructor feedback.

Discussion

Although some attempts have recently been made to develop an instrument for conducting self and peer evaluations of the teamwork aspect of a collaborative learning assignment, for example Ellis and Hafner (2005), this represents only one of the components of the learning environment described in this paper. The difficulties of reconciling cognitive and affective domains in these partnerships have already been described by Krajewski-Jaime, Wiencek, Clifford, and Edgren (2003).

For students who are accustomed to the "chalk and talk" that characterizes the traditional university lecture, online collaborative learning that centers on university-community partnerships requires a much greater investment of time and effort. Standard student evaluation questionnaires for online courses that closely resemble conventional courses would thus not have reflected the students' perceptions of the relative contributions of the project-based online collaborative learning aspects of the module.

These questions become even more relevant when evaluation focuses on only one of a range of interacting components that comprise a complex and unfamiliar environment, such as project-based online collaborative learning.

As can be seen from the results, the interview data reflected a positive overall picture even though they do not provide concrete evidence of the relative advantages of this learning environment. This may be partially explained by the students' perceptions that this module was much more demanding than a conventional academic context. For students who are accustomed to the teacher-dominated knowledge-transmission model that characterizes the traditional university lecture, online collaborative learning that centers around university-community partnerships demands a much greater investment in terms of time and effort. Any attempt to obtain reliable and valid student evaluations of new learning environments will thus have to find effective ways to address this issue.

Specific student difficulties also related to the nature of group problem solving in the context of university-community partnerships. Successful completion of this module requires much more than mastery of subject content: A range of abilities, interpersonal skills and facilitating attitudes are also required, which not all students have in place. As several students pointed out, these abilities include the ability to listen to the voices of the population they are working with as well as the ability to decipher unspoken norms and codes of the target group and establish the credibility necessary to engage the target population in joint processes of needs-assessment and goal-definition.

In addition to these interpersonal skills and abilities, authentic problem-solving in a real-world context also requires a flexible mind-set and tolerance of ambiguity that enables students to take risks and attempt alternative solutions without any guarantees of successful outcomes. These demands partially explain why almost all the students reported that they initially felt overwhelmed by what they perceived as an extremely complex task that "stretched" them beyond the limits of their ability.

However, as mentioned before, these conditions also created a genuine need for collaborative learning. Despite the above-mentioned difficulties, almost all students indicated their willingness to participate in another course based on university-community partnerships and online collaborative learning. This would suggest that effective online collaborative learning played a key role in ensuring that all students who enrolled for this module succeeded in completing all the course requirements and attaining the goals of this module.

LIMITATIONS OF THE STUDY

Key questions remain unanswered regarding the difficulty of assessing student outcomes and collecting sufficient evidence of learning in innovative learning environments. According to a number of researchers, comparison studies also do not represent an appropriate methodology for exploring the relative advantages of online learning environments. Russell (1999), as well as Bernard, Lou, Abrami, Borokhovski, Wallet, Wade and Fiset (2003), for example, have shown that most media comparisons of student outcomes in conventional and distance learning environments are flawed and do not produce evidence of significant differences between outcomes across learning environments.

Student outcomes in project-based online collaborative learning environments are clearly difficult to quantify and almost impossible to compare with outcomes in a conventional lecture-based course. Content analysis of online collaborative learning protocols offers valuable insights. However, these analyses are extremely time-consuming and several methodological issues that characterize content analysis have been discussed in depth by Rourke, Anderson, Garrison, and Archer (2001).

As Dugery and Knowles (2003) suggest, a longitudinal approach to data collection should be adopted in these partnerships. For example, students may be able to evaluate the relative contribution of specific learning to their professional development only after they finish their studies and enter the workplace.

New learning environments require new methods for evaluating the full impact of these new directions. Additional guidelines as well as data collection methods are thus required to help faculty understand what works and why with regard to project-based online collaborative learning environments in higher education contexts.

CONCLUSION

Unless there is a genuine need for group members to work together, effective collaborative learning will not take place. University-community partnerships thus represent a positive way to create authentic real-world conditions for student collaboration in an academic context. Conversely, collaborative learning represents an essential condition, not just an optional "add-on" for effective university-community partnerships.

Based on our experience with the module described in this paper, we argue that provision of these "safe places" represents one of the most important contributions of online collaborative learning environments. Other features perceived as contributing significantly to the students' learning included clearly defined goals, detailed task analysis, examples of previously completed assignments, explicit criteria for assignment assessment and timely instructor feedback.

REFERENCES

Anderson, T. (2002). An updated and theoretical rationale for interaction. Itforum Paper #63, Retrieved February 14, 2003, from http://it.coe.uga.edu/itforum.

Anderson, T. (2005). Design-based research and its application to a call center innovation in distance education. *Canadian Journal of Learning and Technology, 31*(2).

Barth, I. (2005). *The influence of conventional and distance learning environments on university lecturers' interactions to support cognitive and metacognitive aspects of students' learning.* Unpublished dissertation, Bar-Ilan University, Israel.

Bernard, R. M., Abrami, P. C., Lou, Y., Borokhovski, E., Wade, A., Wozney, L., Wallet, P. A., & Cresswell, J. W. (2003). *Research design: Qualitative, quantitative and mixed methods approaches.* Thousand Oaks: Sage Publications.

Dugery, J. & Knowles, J. (2003). *University and community research partnerships: A new approach.* Charlottesville, VA: The Pew Partnership, University of Richmond.

Ellis, T. J. & Hafner, W. (2005). Project-based, asynchronous collaborative learning. *System Sciences.* Proceedings of the 37th Annual Hawaii International Conference.

Herrington, J., Oliver, R., & Reeves, T. C. (2003). Patterns of engagement in authentic online learning environments. *Australian Journal of Educational Technology,* 19(1), 59-71.

Jonassen, D. H., Peck, K. L. & Wilson, B. G. (1999). *Learning with technology: A constructivist perspective.* Upper Saddle River, NJ: Prentice-Hall Inc.

Krajewski-Jamie, E. R., Wiencek, P., Clifford, D., & Edgren, J. (2003). Reconciling the cognitive and affective dimensions of community engagement: A scholar's dilemma. *Metropolitan University: An International Forum, 14*(4), 102-115.

Levine, A. & Sun, J. C. (2002). *Barriers to distance education.* American Council on Education. Washington, D.C. Retrieved on March 20, 2004, from www.acenet.edu/bookstore.

Offir, B., & Cohen-Fridel, S. (1998). *Psychological factors in conducting interactive Distance Learning systems.* Edited by Austrian Computer Society, 779-787.

Offir, B. & Katz, Y. J. (1992). Computer-related attitudes and self-image as a function of learners' age. In R. M. Aiken (Ed.), *Information Processing 92: Education and Society (Volume 2*. (pp. 80-84). Amsterdam: Elsevier Science Publishers.

Offir, B., Barth, I., Lev, Y., & Shteinbok, A. (2003). Teacher-student interactions and learning outcomes in a distance learning environment. *The Internet and Higher Education*, 6(1), 65-75.

Offir, B., Bezalel, R. & Barth, I. (2007a). Introverts, Extroverts, and Achievement in Distance Learning Environment. *The American Journal of Distance Education,* 21(1), 3-20.

Palmer, P. J. (1998). *The courage to teach*. NY: John Wiley & Sons.

Reeves, T. C., Herrington, J., & Oliver, R. (2004). A development research agenda for online collaborative learning. *Educational Technology Research & Development*, 52(4), 53-65.

Rourke, L., Anderson, T., Garrison, D. R., & Archer, W. (2001). Methodological issues in the content analysis of computer conference transcripts. *International Journal of Artificial Intelligence in Education,* 12. Retrieved December 2, 2003, from http://chl.leeds.ac.uk

Russell, T. L. (1999). *The no significant difference phenomenon*. Raleigh: North Carolina State University.

Twigg, C. A. (2003). Quality, cost and access: The case for redesign. In M. S. Pittinsky (Ed.), The wired tower: Perspectives on the impact of the internet on higher education (pp. 111-143). Upper Saddle River, NJ: Prentice-Hall.

Zeichner, O. (2007). *The impact of different types of feedback and personality factors on students' achievement, satisfaction and perseverance in a distance learning environment.* Unpublished doctoral dissertation, Bar-Ilan University, Ramat Gan, Israel.

In: Personality Assessment: New Research
Editor: Lauren B. Palcroft and Melissa V. Lopez
ISBN: 978-1-60692-796-0

Short Communication B

THE INFLUENCE OF PERSONALITY AND SYMPTOMS SEVERITY ON FUNCTIONING IN PATIENTS WITH SCHIZOPHRENIA

Ana Fresan[a*], María García-Anaya [a], Rogelio Apiquian[b] and Humberto Nicolini [b]

a) Clinical Research Division, National Institute of Psychiatry Ramón de la Fuente, Mexico City, Mexico

b) Carracci Medical Group, Mexico City, Mexico

ABSTRACT

Introduction

Patients with schizophrenia exhibit a broad range of cognitive, emotional and behavioral symptoms that affect their psychosocial functioning. Research findings that link symptom dimensions to functioning in schizophrenia are inconsistent. This suggests that other variables may contribute to patients' functioning. It has been documented that personality differences are detectable among patients with schizophrenia and are stable after illness onset. Thus, personality seems to be a particularly promising form of individual difference that may be related to functioning in schizophrenia.

Objective

To determine the influence of personality features and symptom severity in the level of functioning of patients with schizophrenia.

---

* Correspondence
Ana Fresán, PsyD, PhD
Clinical Research Division. National Institute of Psychiatry Ramón de la Fuente.
Calz. México-Xochimilco No 101. Tlalpan, Mexico City, 14370, MEXICO.
Tel: (5255) 56 55 28 11 ext 204
Fax: (5255) 55 13 37 22
E-mail: fresan@imp.edu.mx

Method

One-hundred patients with schizophrenia were recruited. Diagnoses were based on the SCID-I. Symptom severity was assessed with the Scales for the Assessment of Positive and Negative Symptoms (SAPS and SANS) while personality was assessed using the Temperament and Character Inventory (TCI). The Global Assessment of Functioning (GAF) was employed to estimate global psychosocial functioning. Sample was divided in groups, based in a cutoff point of 60 of the GAF score, forming groups of high and low functioning.

Results

More than half of the patients were classified in the low functioning group (61%). Significant differences were found between groups in terms of symptom severity and temperament and character dimensions. The temperament dimension "Persistence" and the character dimension "Self-directedness" were significant predictors of low functioning as well as the negative symptom "Apathy."

Conclusions

Motivation and goal directed behaviors are important factors that promote an adequate functioning in patients with schizophrenia. Patients with a combination of low "Persistence" and low "Self-directedness" might be an especially vulnerable group for which efforts should be made to provide supportive and reinforcing treatment interventions.

Keywords: Temperament, Character, Personality, Functioning, Schizophrenia.

INTRODUCTION

Patients with schizophrenia exhibit a broad range of cognitive, emotional and behavioral symptoms which have been extensively studied. However, schizophrenia implies severe psychosocial limitations which are also recognized as core features of the disorder [1].

For many years, functional impairment in schizophrenia has been related to psychotic symptom severity [2]. Several studies indicate that negative symptoms are strongly associated to various functioning deficits and are strong predictors of long-term poor outcome [1, 3-7]. Nevertheless, the predictive ability of negative symptoms for functional impairment in patients with schizophrenia is not consistent, as their presence and severity vary during illness evolution and functional impairment may persist despite the absence of severe negative symptoms. Furthermore, it has been described that both positive and negative symptoms account less than 25% of the variance in social performance [8]. This suggests that other variables may contribute to patients' functioning impairment.

Personality seems to be a particularly promising form of individual difference that may be related to functioning in schizophrenia. It has been linked to how patients with schizophrenia express the illness [9, 10] and can affect the expression of some symptoms of the disease [11]. In this way, several studies showed that specific personality traits are related to higher levels of impairment and are also differentially associated with symptom dimensions [9, 12].

There are different theoretical approaches to personality, one of which is the psychobiological model of personality developed by Cloninger and colleagues [13-15]. This model takes into account the respective contribution of biologically-based mechanisms which are related to temperament and the environmentally-shaped processes related to character [15]. The four temperament dimensions of the model are considered to be stable throughout life, while character dimensions mature in response to social learning and life experiences.

Besides the comprehensive description of individual differences in feelings, thoughts and behaviours, the psychobiological model of personality offers and interesting theoretical background for the study of patients with schizophrenia. Research has indicated that stable personality differences are detectable among patients [16-18] and these differences may contribute to explain the heterogeneity observed in patients with schizophrenia in terms of symptom expression and severity, and level of functioning [12, 18, 19]. Eklund et al. [19] found that patients with schizophrenia with poor functioning exhibit higher scores on the temperament dimension harm avoidance, lower scores on persistence and, in terms of character dimensions, lower scores on self-directedness. Although this study offers valuable knowledge of the association between personality and functioning, it excludes the probable role of positive and negative symptoms in patients' functional impairment at the time of the assessment, which may provide more information about the heterogeneity found among patients with schizophrenia.

Thus, this study aims to determine the influence of personality features and symptom severity in the level of functioning of patients with schizophrenia. Specifically, we attempted (a) to compare positive and negative symptom severity between high and low functioning patients, (b) to compare temperament and character dimensions between groups; and (c) to determine which symptoms and personality dimensions are risk factors for functional impairment in patients with schizophrenia. We hypothesized that low-functioning patients will show more prominent positive and negative symptomatology and a different personality structure when compared to the high-functioning patients. Also, we predicted that the temperament dimension persistence and the character dimension self-directedness, as well as negative symptomatology will be risk factors for functional impairment in patients with schizophrenia.

METHOD

Subjects

One-hundred patients with diagnosis of schizophrenia as per DSM-IV criteria [20] were consecutively recruited from the outpatient admission wards at the National Institute of Psychiatry in Mexico City. All participants gave written informed consent after receiving a comprehensive explanation of the nature of the study. The Ethics Review Board of the NIP approved the study.

Assessment Procedures

Diagnoses were based on the Structured Clinical Interview for DSM-IV Axis I Disorders (SCID) [21]. Psychotic symptom severity was assessed with the Scale for the Assessment of

Negative Symptoms (SANS) [22] and the Scale for the Assessment of Positive Symptoms (SAPS) [23].The SANS scale has 25 items grouped in 5 categories: 1) affective flattening, 2) alogia, 3) avolition/apathy, 4) anhedonia, and 5) attention. The SAPS scale comprises 30 items designed to assess 4 categories: 1) hallucinations, 2) delusions, 3) bizarre behavior, and 4) positive formal thought disorder. Both scales have a scoring range from 0 to 5, where "0" denotes the absence of the symptom, and "5" the most severe form of the symptom [24].

Functioning was assessed with the Global Assessment of Functioning (GAF) scale which is considered the standard method for representing a clinician's overall judgment about a patient's current psychological, social and occupational functioning. As such, it is probably the single most widely used method for assessing impairment among patients with psychiatric disorders [25, 26]. The GAF's rating is made on a scale from 1 to 100 [20], where ratings between 1 to 10 indicate severe impairment and ratings over 81 indicating superior functioning. Sample was divided in high and low functioning groups, based in a cutoff point of 60 of the GAF score.

Personality was assessed using the Temperament and Character Inventory (TCI) [27, 28], a 240-question self-report instrument, which has been validated in Mexican population [29]. The first temperament dimension, *Novelty Seeking* (NS), is defined as a tendency of the subject to respond impulsively to novelty, to exhibit a quick loss of temper and an active avoidance to frustration. The second temperament dimension, *Harm Avoidance* (HA) is viewed as a bias in the inhibition of behaviors, such as pessimistic worry, passive dependent behaviors and rapid fatigability. *Reward Dependence* (RD), the third temperament dimension, is defined as a bias toward the maintenance of ongoing behaviors and the subject manifest social attachment and dependence on approval of others. The last temperament dimension, *Persistence* (PE), is viewed as a tendency to perseverance despite frustration and fatigue.

The character dimension, *Self-directedness* (SD), refers to the ability of an individual to control, regulate and adapt behavior to fit the situation in accordance to personal goals. The second character dimension, *Cooperativeness* (CO), account for individual differences in the acceptance of other people and measures features related to agreeability vs. self-centered aggression and hostility. *Self-transcendence* (ST) is viewed as the identification with everything conceived as essential and consequential parts of a unified whole. It refers to spiritual maturity, transpersonal identification and self-forgetfulness [15, 27, 28].

Demographic data and the information concerning the SANS and SAPS scales and the OAS were obtained by a personal interview with the patient and his/her relatives.

Statistical Analyses

Demographic and clinical characteristics description was done with frequencies and percentages for categorical variables and with means and standard deviations (S.D.) for continuous variables. Independent sample t-Tests were used to examine differences in positive and negative symptom severity, as well as for temperament and character dimensions between high and low functioning groups. A logistic regression analysis was performed with the backward-conditional stepwise selection method for the calculation of the likelihood of low functioning in patients with schizophrenia. The logistic regression model included TCI dimensions and positive and negative symptom categories as explanatory variables and functioning as the outcome. The significance level for tests was established at $p \leq 0.05$ (2-tailed).

RESULTS

a) Demographic and Clinical Data

A total of 56% (n=56) of the patients recruited were male and 44% (n=44) were women with a mean age of 31.6 ± 7.3 years (18 – 57 years) and an educational level of 9.7 ± 3.4 years (1 – 19 years). Most of the patients were single (91%, n=91) and unemployed (66%, n=66).

Diagnoses of the sample were paranoid schizophrenia (79%, n=79), undifferentiated schizophrenia (15%, n=15), and disorganized schizophrenia (6%, n=6). Age of illness onset was 19.9 ± 5.0 years (11 – 35 years) with a mean duration of untreated psychosis (DUP) of 158.8 ± 230.5 weeks (1 – 1352 weeks). A total of 75% (n=75) of the patients had been hospitalized at any time during their illness evolution with a mean of 4.0 ± 3.8 hospitalizations (1 – 20 hospitalizations).

Mean functioning score on the GAF scale was of 49.0 ± 17.5 (10 – 90 score range). According to the cutoff point of 60 in the GAF scale, 61% (n=61) of the total sample of patients were classified as having low-functioning and 39% (n=39) with high-functioning.

Patients in the low-functioning group were more frequently unemployed and tend to be single when compared to the high-functioning group. There were no significant differences between groups on other demographic features and both groups were comparable in terms of illness features (Table 1).

Table 1. Demographic and clinical data between low and high functioning groups

	Low-Functioning Patients (n=61)		High-Functioning Patients (n=39)		Statistics
	n	%	n	%	
Gender					
Male	31	50.8	25	64.1	x^2= 1.7, df 1,
Female	30	49.2	14	35.9	p=0.19
Laboral Status					
Employed	12	19.7	22	56.4	x^2= 14.3, df 1,
Unemployed	49	80.3	17	43.6	p<0.001
Marital Status					
Single	58	95.1	33	84.6	x^2= 3.1, df 1,
Married	3	4.9	6	15.4	p=0.07
Schizophrenia					
Paranoid	46	75.4	33	84.6	x^2=4.0, df 2,
Undifferentiated	9	14.8	6	15.4	p=0.12
Disorganized	6	9.8	0		

Table 1. (Continued)

	Low-Functioning Patients (n=61)		High-Functioning Patients (n=39)		Statistics
	n	%	n	%	
Previous Hospitalization					
Yes	49	80.3	26	66.7	x^2= 2.3, df 1,
No	12	19.7	13	33.3	p=0.12
	Mean	**SD**	**Mean**	**SD**	
Age (years)	31.9	8.0	31.1	6.1	t=-0.5, df 98, p=0.59
Educational level (years)	9.3	3.8	10.2	2.8	t=1.2, df 98, p=0.21
Age of illness onset (years)	19.9	5.1	20.1	4.8	t=0.1, df 98, p=0.84
DUP (weeks)	141.0	200.9	186.7	270.9	t=0.9, df 98, p=0.33
Number of Hospitalizations	4.4	4.1	3.4	3.1	t=-1.0, df 73, p=0.30

b) Symptom Severity Differences between Low and High Functioning Groups

Significant differences emerged between low and high functioning groups in terms of positive and negative symptom severity assessed by the SANS and SAPS scales. Patients with low functioning exhibited more prominent symptomatology when compared to the high-functioning group (Table 2).

Table 2. Symptom severity differences between low and high functioning groups

	Low-Functioning Patients (n=61)		High-Functioning Patients (n=39)		Statistic
	Mean	**SD**	**Mean**	**SD**	
SANS Scale					
Affective flattening	2.9	1.2	1.7	1.1	t=-4.9, df 98, p<0.001
Alogia	2.3	1.3	1.2	1.2	t=-4.2, df 98, p<0.001
Avolition/apathy	3.2	1.1	1.5	1.3	t=-6.8, df 98, p<0.001
Anhedonia	3.4	1.1	2.1	1.4	t=-4.8, df 98, p<0.001
Attention	2.2	1.3	1.2	1.3	t=-3.4, df 98, p=0.001
Total SANS score	14.1	5.0	7.8	5.5	t=-5.8, df 98, p<0.001

Table 2. (Continued)

	Low-Functioning Patients (n=61)		High-Functioning Patients (n=39)		Statistic
	Mean	SD	Mean	SD	
SAPS Scale					
Hallucinations	1.8	1.6	0.9	1.3	t=-2.9, df 98, p=0.004
Delusions	2.2	1.5	1.2	1.2	t=-3.2, df 98, p=0.002
Bizarre behavior	0.9	1.2	0.3	0.8	t=-2.8, df 98, p=0.005
Formal thought disorder	1.9	1.2	1.0	1.0	t=-4.0, df 98, p<0.001
Total SAPS score	7.0	4.6	3.6	3.4	t=-3.9, df 98, p<0.001

c) Comparison between Low and High Functioning Groups on theTCI Dimensions

The mean scores of the four temperament dimensions and the three character dimensions of low functioning and high functioning groups are shown in Table 3. As can be seen, the temperament dimension NS was significantly higher in the low functioning group while the PE dimension was significantly lower in this group. Also, significant differences emerged in the character dimensions between groups. Low-functioning patients exhibited lower scores on the three character dimensions. The mean HA and RD scores were not different between groups.

Table 3. Mean scores on TCI dimensions in patients with schizophrenia with low-functioning and high-functioning

TCI Dimension	Low-Functioning Patients (n=61)		High-Functioning Patients (n=39)		Statistic
	Mean	SD	Mean	SD	
Temperament					
Novelty Seeking	23.5	5.8	20.5	6.6	t=-2.3, df 98, p=0.01
Harm Avoidance	18.8	6.9	17.8	5.0	t=-0.7, df 98, p=0.45
Reward Dependence	12.0	3.4	13.1	3.1	t=1.4, df 98, p=0.14
Persistence	3.6	1.5	4.2	1.6	t=1.9, df 98, p=0.05
Character					
Self-directedness	21.6	7.0	26.4	6.8	t=3.4, df 98, p=0.001
Cooperativeness	25.4	7.3	29.3	6.5	t=2.7, df 98, p=0.007
Self-transcendence	15.9	6.4	19.1	5.3	t=2.6, df 98, p=0.009

d) Symptoms and Personality Dimensions as Predictors of Low Functioning in Patients with Schizophrenia

Positive and negative symptoms as well as temperament and character dimensions were included in a logistic regression model with the backward-conditional selection method. The final model explained 52% of the variance in the GAF categorization and was capable of correctly classifying 81.0% of the cases, being generally more exact on predicting patients with low functioning (86.9%) than patients with high functioning (71.8%). The procedure only included three predictors of low-functioning in patients with schizophrenia: a) negative symptom "apathy", where patients with moderate to severe apathy have a risk 3.0 higher of having low-functioning when compared to patients without this symptom (β=1.1, S.D.β=0.23, CI95%=1.9–4.9, $p<0.001$), b) patients with low persistence (PE) have 62% more risk of having low-functioning when compared to patients with higher scores on this dimension (β=-0.46, S.D.β=0.20, CI95%=0.42–0.94, p=0.02) and c) patients with low self-directedness (SD) have 91% more risk for having low-functioning when compared to those with high SD (β=-0.09, S.D.β=0.04, CI95%=0.83–0.99, p=0.03).

DISCUSSION

The aim of the present study was to determine the influence of personality features and symptom severity in the level of functioning of patients with schizophrenia. We hypothesized that low-functioning patients will show more prominent positive and negative symptomatology and a different personality structure when compared to the high-functioning patients. Also, we predicted that the temperament dimension persistence and the character dimension self-directedness, as well as negative symptomatology will be risk factors for functional impairment in patients with schizophrenia. In addition, as the Global Assessment of Functioning (GAF) is one of the scales most often used in routine clinical practice, this study offers a good opportunity to identify the possible existence of differences in its scoring according to patients' personality features.

Most of the patients included in our study were classified in the low-functioning group, with scores ranging from moderate to pervasive impairment. For patients with schizophrenia, this result may be considered as expected, as patients with psychoses are generally rated as having greater level of impairment [30-33].

Our findings confirm, as other authors have shown [31, 34, 35], that global functioning in patients with schizophrenia, as assessed by the GAF, is not influenced by some specific demographic features such as age or sex. Nevertheless, clinicians also take into consideration social functioning variables when rating the GAF. In the present study patients with low psychosocial functioning were less likely to be married and more frequently unemployed. These findings are congruent with descriptions of associations of some social functioning variables such as the extent of social networks and employment status with clinicians' ratings of global impairment by the use of the GAF [32-34, 36].

Nevertheless, it has been frequently reported that clinicians' ratings of patients' functioning is based mainly on the presence and severity of psychiatric symptoms [25, 31, 32, 34, 35, 37, 38], and our study is not the exception. Patients with low functioning exhibit more prominent positive and negative symptoms when compared to patients with high functioning. Until now, the specific role of psychotic symptoms on global functioning in patients with schizophrenia is not clear. In general, negative symptoms have been strongly related to measures of psychosocial functioning and are stronger predictors of functional impairment than positive symptomatology [39-41].

Specific demographic variables and psychiatric symptoms alone do not fully describe functional impairment in patients with schizophrenia. The comparison of the TCI scores reveal different personality profiles in low and high functioning groups, depending mainly on divergent levels of novelty seeking and persistence for the temperament dimensions, and for all character dimensions.

Novelty seeking has been considered as a stable personality dimension that is not influenced by psychopathological states [28]. Patients with higher scores in novelty seek may show extroverted, impulsive or extravagant behaviours that can be poorly timed and socially clumsy. These behaviours may reduce the ability of patients to meet defined roles in society and cause difficulties in social and occupational functioning. Low persistence, on the other hand, corresponds to inactive, indolent and unstable individuals who tend to give up easily and may be reflected as specific impairments in social conduct and aspects of decision making [42] in the context of global functioning in patients with schizophrenia.

Behaviours secondary to temperament features may be modified and conditioned by character, as a result of environmental contingencies and changes in the significance and salience of perceived stimuli to which the person responds. Individuals with low scores on character dimensions may have difficulties with self-acceptance, are intolerant and revengeful toward others and may feel self-conscious and unfulfilled [15]. Identification with others, a sense of purpose and a meaningful goal-directed behaviour are important factors that promote personal satisfaction and an adequate functioning in every person.

The regression analysis shows that low persistence, low self-directedness and apathy are the best predictors of functional impairment in patients with schizophrenia. This result shows an interesting association between these variables. Patients with apathy exhibit lack of motivation and goal directed behaviours [43], while low persistence and low self-directedness refers to persons who are less intrinsically motivated [44] with lack of self-determination and unable to control and adapt behaviours in accord to personal goals and values. Therefore, it seems that severity of apathy in our patients is just the reflection of these personality features that are related to functional impairment. This assumption supports the results of other studies that suggest that symptom dimensions of schizophrenia can be conceptualized partly as manifestations of personality [9, 18].

Individual differences in functioning that we observed in our patients appeared to result from a complex interaction of several personality dimensions, namely persistence and self-directedness. Although these variables cannot explain the whole construct of functioning in patients with schizophrenia, our analysis correctly predicted a large proportion of the low functioning and the high functioning patients suggesting that person centered variables such as personality features, account for some of the differences seen in patients with schizophrenia, including global functioning. It is important to consider that patients with schizophrenia can exhibit several personality features of more than one personality disorder, the use of the psychobiological model of personality may increase our understanding of the basis of the functional impairment observed in patients with schizophrenia from a multidimensional theoretical perspective, which may in turn be more useful than current categorical criteria of personality disorders.

In this way, for persons with schizophrenia, a combination of low persistence and low self-directedness may be of particular relevance as lack of motivation and goal directed behaviours can have a negative direct impact on illness adjustment and coping, limiting patients' ability to engage in reciprocal interactions with others. This will increase the risk of developing social withdrawal which may lead to social disabilities that affect patients' global functioning. Thus, these patients might be an especially vulnerable group for which efforts should be made to provide supportive and reinforcing treatment interventions that give patients' the opportunity to improve their psychosocial functioning.

Lastly, it should be noted that generalization of our findings is limited mainly by the use of the GAF as the only assessment of functioning. Although the GAF can be considered a useful measure of global functioning suitable for the assessment of patients with schizophrenia, future studies including separate clinical and sociofunctional assessments as well as longitudinal studies may be useful. On the other hand, a number of questions can be raised when evaluating personality in patients with schizophrenia. Although the validity of personality questionnaires is not well established in psychotic patients, it has been found that the psychobiological model of personality is suitable in Mexican patients with schizophrenia [45].

We can conclude that the assessment of personality in patients with schizophrenia is an important area of study in order to gain more knowledge about the disorder in terms of the individual differences observed among patients. Self-reported measurements of personality may have practical implications for the treatment and rehabilitation of patients with schizophrenia and its assessment should be included in routine clinical practice.

References

[1] Lenior, M., Dingemans, M., Linszen, D., De Haan, L., and Schene, A. (2001). Social functioning and the course of early-onset schizophrenia: Five-year follow-up of a psychosocial intervention. *Br J Psychiatry*; 179:53-58.

[2] Curson, D.A., Duke, P., Harvey, C.A., Pantelis, C., and Barnes, T.R.E. (1999). Four behavioural syndromes of schizophrenia: a replication in a second inner-London epidemiological sample. *Schizophr Res.* 37:165-176.

[3] Breier, A., Schreiber, J., Dyer, J., Pickar, D. (1991). National Institute of Mental Health longitudinal study of chronic schizophrenia: Prognosis and predictors of outcome. *Arch Gen Psychiatry*; 48:239-246.

[4] Herbener, E., Harrow, M. (2004). Are negative symptoms associated with functioning deficits in both schizophrenia and nonschizophrenia patients? A 10-year longitudinal analysis. *Schizophr Bull*;30:813-825.

[5] Ho, B., Nopoulos, P., Flaum, M., Arndt, S., Andreasen, N. (1998). Two-year outcome in first-episode schizophrenia: Predictive value of symptoms for quality of life. *Am J Psychiatry*; 155:1196-1201.

[6] Matousek, N., Edwards, J., Jackson, H. (1992). Social skills training and negative symptoms. *Behav Modif*; 16:39-63.

[7] McGlashan, T., Fenton, W.(1992) The positive-negative distinction in schizophrenia: Review of natural history validators. *Arch Gen Psychiatry*; 49:63-72.

[8] Lysaker, P.H. and Bell, D.B. (1995). Prominent negative symptoms and work impairment in schizophrenia. *Acta Psychiatr Scand.* 91:205-208.

[9] Lysaker, P., Bell, M., Kaplan, E., Greig, T., and Bryson, G. (1999). Personality and psychopathology in schizophrenia: The association between personality traits and symptoms. *Psychiatry*; 62:36-48.

[10] Russel, D., Booth, B., Reed, D., and Lauglin, P. (1997). Personality, social networks and perceived social support among alcoholixs. A structural equation analysis. *J Pers.* 63:649-69.

[11] Shea, M., Stout, R., Yen, S., Pagano, M., Skodol, A., Morey, L., Gunderson, J., McGlashan, T., Grilo, C., Sanislow, C., Bender, D., and Zanarini, M. (2004). Associations in the course of personality disorders and Axis I disorders over time. *J Abnorm Psychol.* 113:499-508.

[12] Lysaker, P., Wilt, M., Plascak-Hallberg, C., Brenner, C., and Clements C. (2003). Personality dimensions in schizophrenia: Association with symptoms and coping. *JJ Nerv Ment Dis.* 191:80-866.

[13] Cloninger, C. (1987). A systematic method for clinical description and classification of personality variants. A proposal. *Arch Gen Psychiatry*; 44:573-88.

[14] Cloninger, C. (1998). The genetics and psychobiology of the seven-factor model of personality, in Biology of personality disorders. Edited by Silk K. *American Psychiatric Press*, pp 63-92.

[15] Cloninger, C., Svrakic, D. and Przybeck, T. (1993). A psychobiological model of temperament and character. *Arch Gen Psychiatry*; 50:975-90.

[16] Donat, D., Geczy, B., Helmrich, J., and Lemay, M. (1992). Empirically derived personality subtypes in public psychiatric patients: Effects on self-reported symptoms, coping inclinations and evaluations of expressed emotion in care givers. *J Pers Assess*. 58:36-50.

[17] Gurrera, R., Nestor, P. and O'Donell, B. (2002). Personality traits in schizophrenia. Comparison with a community sample. *J Nerv Ment Dis.* 188:31-35.

[18] Guillem, F., Bicu, M., Semkovska, M., and Debruille, J. (2002). The dimensional symptom structure of schizophrenia and its association with temperament and character. *Schizophr Res.* 56:137-147.

[19] Eklund, M., Hansson, L. and Bengtsson-Tops, A. (2004). The influence of temperament and character on functioning and aspects of psychological health among people with schizophrenia. *Eur Psychiatry*; 19:34-41.

[20] American Psychiatric Association: Diagnostic and Statistical Manual of Mental Disorders, Fourth Edition. Washington, DC, American Psychiatric Association, 1994.

[21] First, M., Spitzer, R., Gibbon, M., and Williams, J. Structured Clinical Interview for DSM-IV Axis I Disorders (SCID-I), Clinician Version. Washington, D.C., American Psychiatric Press, 1996.

[22] Andreasen, N. The Scale for the Assessment of Negative Symptoms (SANS). Iowa City, University of Iowa, 1983.

[23] Andreasen, N. The Scale for the Assessment of Positive Symptoms (SAPS). Iowa City, University of Iowa, 1984.

[24] Andreasen, N. (1990). Methods for assessing positive and negative symptoms, in Modern Problems of Pharmacopsychiatry: Positive and Negative Symptoms and Syndromes. Edited by Andreasen NC Basel, *Karger*, pp 73-88.

[25] Endicott, J., Spitzer, R., Fleiss, J., and Cohen, J. (1976). The global assessment scale. A procedure for measuring overall severity of psychiatric disturbance. Arch Gen Psychiatry; 33:766-771.

[26] Piersma, H. and Boes, J. (1997). The GAF and psychiatric outcome: a descriptive report. *Community Ment Health J.* 33:35-41.

[27] Cloninger, C., Przybeck, T. and Svrakic, D. (1991). The Tridimensional Personality Questionnaire: U.S. normative data. *Psychol Rep.* 69(3 Pt 1):1047-57.

[28] Cloninger, C., Przybeck, T., Svrakic, D., and Wetzel, R. The Temperament and Character Inventory (TCI): a guide to its development and use, in Center for Psychobiology of Personality. St. Louis, MO, Washington University, 1994.

[29] Sánchez de Carmona, M., Paéz, F., López, J., and Nicolini, H. (1996). Traducción y confiabilidad del inventario de temperamento y carácter (ITC). *Salud Mental* 19(Supl 3):5-9.

[30] Alaja, R., Tienari, P., Seppa, K., Tuomisto, M., Leppavuori, A., Huyse, F., Herzog, T., Malt, U., Lobo, A. (1999). Patterns of comorbidity in relation to functioning (GAF) among general hospital psychiatric referrals. European Consultation-Liaison Workgroup. *Acta Psychiatr Scand*; 99:135-140.

[31] Moos, R., McCoy, L. and Moos, B. (2000). Global Assessment of Functioning (GAF) ratings: determinants and role as predictors of one-year treatment outcomes. *J Clin Psychol.* 56:449-461.

[32] Moos, R., Nichol, A. and Moos, B. (2002). Global Assessment of Functioning ratings and the allocation and outcomes of mental health services. *Psychiatr Serv.* 53:730-737.

[33] Phelan, M., Wykes, T. and Goldman, H. (1994). Global function scales. *Soc Psychiatry Psychiatr Epidemiol.* 29:205-211.

[34] Gaite, L., Vázquez-Barquero, J., Herrán, A., Thornicroft, G., Becker, T., Sierra-Biddle, D., Ruggeri, M., Schene, A., Knapp, M., Vázquez-Bourgon, J., and Group (2005). E: Main determinants of Global Assessment of Functioning score in schizophrenia: a European multicenter study. *Compr Psychiatry*, 46:440-446.

[35] Roy-Byrne, P., Dagadakis, C., Unutzer, J., and Ries, R. (1996). Evidence for limited validity of the revised global assessment of functioning scale. *Psychiatr Serv.* 47:864-866.

[36] Jones, S., Thornicroft, G., Coffey, M., and Dunn, G. (1995). A brief mental health outcome scale-reliability and validity of the Global Assessment of Functioning (GAF). *Br J Psychiatry*; 166:654-659.

[37] Faravelli, C., Servi, P., Arends, J., and Strik, W. (1996). Number of symptoms, quantification, and qualification of depression. *Compr Psychiatry*; 37:307-315.

[38] Skodol, A., Link, B., Shrout, P., and Horwath, E. (1988). The revision of axis V in DSM-III-R: should symptoms have been included? *Am J Psychiatry*, 145:825-829.

[39] Addington, J., Young, J., Addington, D. (2003). Social outcome in early psychosis. *Psychol Med*; 33:1119-1124.

[40] Puig, O., Penadés, R., Gastó, C., Catalán, R., Torres, A., Salamero, M. (2008). Verbal memory, negative symptomatology and prediction of psychosocial functioning in schizophrenia. *Psychiatry Res*; 28:11-17.

[41] Suslow, T., Schonauer, K., Ohrmann, P., Eikelmann, B., Reker, T. (2000). Prediction of work performance by clinical symptoms and cognitive skills in schizophrenic outpatients. *J Nerv Ment Dis*; 188:116-118.

[42] Barrash, J., Tranel, D. and Anderson, S. (2000). Acquired personality disturbances associated with bilateral damage to the ventromedial prefrontal region. Dev Neuropsychol. 18:355-38.

[43] Marin R. (1991). Apathy: a neuropsychiatric syndrome. *J Neuropsychiatry Clin Neurosci.*; 3:243-254.
[44] Gusnard, D., Ollinger, J., Shulman, G., Cloninger, C., Price, J., Van Essen, D., and Raichle, M. (2003). Persistence and brain circuitry. *Proc Natl Acad Sci U S A*; 100:3479-3484.
[45] Fresan, A., Apiquian, R., Nicolini, H., and Cervantes, J. (2007). Temperament and character in violent schizophrenic patients. *Schizophr Res.*; 94:74-80.

In: Personality Assessment: New Research
Editor: Lauren B. Palcroft and Melissa V. Lopez
ISBN: 978-1-60692-796-0

Short Communication C

Circumventing Self-Reflection When Measuring Emotions: The Implicit Positive and Negative Affect Test (IPANAT)

Markus Quirin, Miguel Kazén and Julius Kuhl
University of Osnabrueck, Institute of Psychology
Seminarstraße 20
49074 Osnabrück, Germany
Markus Quirin (mquirin@uos.de)
Miguel Kazén (mikazen@uos.de)
Julius Kuhl (j.kuhl@gmx.net)

Abstract

This paper presents a recently developed method for the indirect assessment of emotional traits and states, the Implicit Positive and Negative Affect Test (IPANAT). In the IPANAT individuals make judgments about the degree to which artificial words sound like mood adjectives (e.g., happy or helpless). It is proposed that cognitive representations of emotions as being dominant in individuals with high sensitivity to these emotions instantaneously bring the judgments into their line. Recent findings are summarized that speak for appropriate reliability and validity of the IPANAT. As a paper-pencil test, the IPANAT is easy in application and takes no longer than 2 minutes. These properties may render this measure attractive for both basic and applied psychology.

Keywords: implicit affect, mood, emotion, positive affect, negative affect, implicit measure, indirect assessment, judgment, affect infusion, diagnostics.

Introduction

To obtain information about an individual's emotional state, previous research has drawn mainly on explicit mood ratings, asking individuals about their mental states directly. One reason for extended use of self-reports of affect is that, like those of attitudes and personality, they usually show good reliability. Nonetheless, their validity has been criticized for at least two reasons.

The first major criticism about self-report measures in general is that people have only limited introspection about their mental representations and processes (Kihlstrom, 2000; LeDoux, 1996; Nisbett & Wilson, 1977). Even if some affective processes may be accessible to conscious awareness in principle, individuals with poor emotional intelligence have nonetheless difficulties recognizing or communicating them (Barrett, 2004; Hofmann, Gschwendner, & Schmitt, 2005; Taylor, 2000). The second major criticism of self-report measures refers to their susceptibility towards a number of psychological response tendencies and mechanisms that can bias the affect measure with or without the individual's awareness, for example, social desirability (Edwards, 1957), self-presentation (Goffman, 1956; Schlenker, 1980; Tedeschi, 1981), self-deception (Paulhus, 1984), or repression (Byrne, 1961). Individuals also tend to respond in a direction suggested by the researcher ("demand characteristics"), which is decisive to assess the validity of psychological studies (Polivy & Doyle, 1980; Rosenthal & Rosnow, 1969).

To circumvent the problems that plagued explicit measures in general, researchers have developed a series of implicit measures in a variety of research areas. These measures are non-reactive, that is, participants are either not aware of which exact psychological process or representation is being measured, or if they are, they are unable to deliberately influence the measurement (Fazio & Olson, 2003). While several methods have been developed over the past twenty years to assess implicit attitudes (Cunningham, Preacher, & Banaji, 2001; Fazio & Olson, 2003), implicit self-esteem (Koole& DeHart, in press), and implicit motives (e.g., Kuhl, Scheffer, & Eichstaedt, 2003; Schultheiss & Brunstein, 2001), valid and easy-to-apply tests to assess implicit affect are rather scarce or inexistent. Because of the above-mentioned limitations of explicit mood measures, this state of affairs is in stark contrast to the need for implicit affect measures in basic psychological research as well as in applied areas. To fill this gap, the Implicit Positive And Negative Affect Test (IPANAT) was developed, which measures the general dimensions of implicit positive and negative affect. The present work presents an overview of our recent and present research on implicit affect.

Implicit Affect

Several authors have proposed the notion of *implicit affect* or emotion (e.g., Kihlstrom, 2000; Kuhl, 2001; Lane, 2008; Öhman, Flykt, & Lundqvist, 2000; Winkielman & Berridge, 2004; Zajonc, 2000; but see early work of Zajonc, 1984). As demonstrated by a large number of studies, affective processes can remain completely unconscious but nonetheless influence human judgment, behavior, and physiology. In this vein, some authors use the term "implicit affect" exclusively to refer to such unconscious emotional states (Winkielman & Berridge, 2004), that is, those that occur without attention. In the present work, implicit affect is defined as the automatic activation of mental representations of affective experiences that can be consciously processed but need not be. This definition allows for the case that measures from indirect affect tests (i.e. implicit affect scores) can be consistent with measures from direct (self-report) affect tests (i.e. explicit affect scores). For example, consistency or inconsistency between implicit and explicit affect measures may depend on diverse situational factors such as the momentary capacity to attend to one's emotions, or peoples' ability to access emotional or self-relevant information in general (Lane, 2008; Quirin, Koole, & Kuhl, 2008; see Hofmann, Gschwendner, & Schmitt, 2005, for the case of implicit attitudes).

Methods that aim at indirectly measuring affect or affective processes reach from reaction time methods (e.g., Egloff & Schmukle, 2002; MacLeod, Mathews, & Tata, 1986; Williams, Mathews, & MacLeod, 1996), observational-categorizational methods (Ekman & Friesen, 1978), up to physiological measures (cf. Birbaumer & Öhman, 1994; Lang, 1995)[1]. These measures can barely be directly compared with the IPANAT because they assess specific types of affect rather than general dimensions of positive vs. negative affect. Moreover, whereas each of these methods has its specific merits and drawbacks (see Quirin, Kazén, & Kuhl, 2009), most of them share the problem of being relatively time consuming and not easy to use, both in their application and data analysis. These limitations in practicality are especially important to most psychologists interested in investigating implicit positive and negative affect.

The Implicit Positive and Negative Affect Test

The IPANAT (for an evaluation of the method, see Quirin, Kazén, & Kuhl, 2009; see Kuhl, 2005, for use in applied contexts) assesses *implicit positive affect* and *implicit negative affect*. To circumvent explicit judgments about one's personal affective states, the IPANAT relies on ratings about artificial words (FILNU, BELNI, etc.). Specifically, participants are asked to rate the extent to which each of a series of artificial words, which are putatively taken from an artificial language, expresses several kinds of mood states, such as happy or helpless. For example, consider the item "SUKOV – happy". How much does "SUKOV" sound like "happy"? Previous research has demonstrated that judgments about even unrelated, neutral objects (such as artificial words) are typically biased into the direction of the mood state of the judge (e.g., Forgas, 1995). Accordingly, if a person is in a positive mood, the judge is inclined to confirm a stronger fit between SUKOV and happy as when being in a neutral mood. Now consider the pair "SUKOV – helpless": Analogously, if a person is in a negative mood, he or she tends to confirm a stronger fit between SUKOV and helpless. Because the ratings are also biased by other factors such as subjective associations with the artificial word, we use average ratings of several artificial words combined with valence-congruent mood words (happy, cheerful, active, vs. helpless, tense, inhibited) to reduce error variance and strengthen the signal coming from a person's "true" affect. We have found that this test also comprises strong trait variance. As such, each individual has a certain tendency

---

[1] Indeed, in a broader sense, spontaneous facial expressions and physiological arousal may also be interpreted as implicit affect. However, we usually use the term implicit affect to refer to the activation of mental representations of affective experiences.

to affectively bias his ratings in the positive or negative range even in the relative absence of emotional situations.

To the extent that both emotional states and cognitive judgment are typically represented in a common neural network (Golomb, Lawrence, & Sejnowski, 1991; Zebrowitz, Fellous, Mignault, & Andreoletti, 2003; for early work on semantic networks related to affect, see Bower, 1981), its emotional and cognitive components cannot be easily separated. This integration (or "confounding") of cognition and emotion within parallel networks yields the rationale for our implicit affect measure. As a result of the common representation of affective and cognitive components, it can be expected that being in a positive or negative affective state may bias the perception of affectively neutral artificial words into the respective direction. Therefore, we assume that, in the IPANAT, affective states prime subjective judgments on the extent to which artificial words sound like emotional words. This model is compatible with the notions of affective priming (Murphy & Zajonc, 1993; see also Fazio & Olson, 2003) and affect infusion (Forgas, 1995).

The IPANAT is proposed to measure affect indirectly. In that respect, it has similarities with traditional projective or implicit tests (e.g., the Thematic Apperception Test) because in both tests the individual is not aware of the construct being measured and responds spontaneously to the stimuli presented (cf. McClelland, 1985). In contrast to traditional projective tests, however, the IPANAT capitalizes on standardized ratings rather than relying on the person's free interpretations of a stimulus configuration. We believe that this feature increases the reliability of the test as compared to traditional projective tests.

Empirical Research with the IPANAT

As reported by Quirin, Kazén, & Kuhl (2009, Study 1), factor analyses of the IPANAT revealed a clear pattern of two orthogonal dimensions with one dimension comprising only positive affect scores and the other comprising only negative affect scores. The two implicit affect scales showed to have adequate reliability and validity. Cronbach's Alphas and two-weeks test-retest correlations were above .80. Additionally, test-retest correlation over a period of one year was above .60, suggesting moderate stability of the scores. The latter finding suggests that the test is affected by trait variance, i.e., individual differences in the sensitivity to positive and negative affect ("affectivity"). This is corroborated by findings of implicit PA and NA being moderately correlated with affect-related personality measures such as extraversion and neuroticism, respectively, suggesting construct validity of the scales as trait measures of affectivity (Study 2). Although this is the case, the scales have also revealed to be sensitive to mood induction, which suggests that the test not only measures affective traits but affective states as well (Study 4). That is, in the relative absence of situationally aroused emotions, the IPANAT measures an affective trait, whereas changes in the IPANAT as a reaction to manipulated mood indicate an affective state. Notably, it was found in yet another study (Study 5) that the consistency between implicit and explicit affective states was high (r's > .55) when participants were instructed to report their (explicit) mood states intuitively and spontaneously. By contrast, there was no consistency between implicit and explicit affective states when participants were instructed to extantly reflect on their affect states before providing their ratings. These findings suggest validity of the

IPANAT because they are compatible with attitude research (see Wilson, Lindsey, & Schooler, 2000). The present findings suggest that relying on one's gut feelings rather than conscious reflections lead to more appropriate judgments about one's emotional states.

In a recent study, Quirin, Kazén, Rohrmann, and Kuhl (2009) used the IPANAT to predict cortisol regulation. As argued by the authors, implicit rather than explicit affectivity should be a predictor of physiological processes because both variables refer to spontaneous reactions rather than those resulting from deliberate reflection (cf. McClelland, Koestner, & Weinberger, 1989). Specifically, implicit negative affectivity (high sensitivity to threat stimuli) was expected to predict cortisol reactions to an acute negative affect induction, which consisted of a repeated auditory noise startle occurring at unpredictable intervals. On the other hand, because increased cortisol levels are typically associated with depression (reduced positive affect) rather than with anxiety (increased negative affect), low levels of implicit positivity were expected to predict high spontaneous cortisol levels across the day (e.g., Halbreich, 1985, for the relationship between depression and circadian cortisol). The two hypotheses were confirmed (see Quirin et al., 2009). Notably, explicit affectivity as measured with the PANAS was unrelated to cortisol regulation, supporting our general hypothesis of a closer association between indirectly than directly measured affectivity and bodily processes.

This general hypothesis was also confirmed by a study in which IPANAT negative affectivity but not explicit negative affectivity ("behavioral inhibition") predicted relative right frontal cortex activity under resting conditions as indicated by reduced alpha frequency in the electroencephalogram (Quirin, 2008). Both the above cortisol and electroencephalographic findings suggest that the inconsistent results reported in the literature on the relationship between personality variables related to affect and physiological processes, as exemplified by the cases of cortisol regulation and frontal cortex asymmetry, may occur because self-report but not non-reactive affectivity measures of affectivity are commonly used to predict spontaneous physiological or behavioral reactions. Thus, researchers may want to consider including indirect affectivity tests in studies aiming to predict the relationship between personality and physiological parameters.

Apart from physiological research, the IPANAT has also been used to investigate transient (state) social psychological phenomena such as defense mechanisms in the context of terror management theory (Pyszczynski, Greenberg, & Solomon, 1999). According to terror management theory, the activation of cognitions associated with an individual's death typically leads to a strengthening of the identification with one's own cultural worldview as part of a defensive coping process. Although it sounds plausible that the threat of mortality should engender negative affect that in turn leads to defensive coping, previous research has not reliably found self-reported negative affect in response to mortality salience manipulations, suggesting that the mere potential to experience threat rather than experienced threat itself instigates cultural worldview defense (Greenberg, Martens, Jonas, Eisenstadt, Pyszczynski, & Solomon, 2003).

Recently, we conducted two studies investigating the possibility that implicit rather than explicit NA may be elicited in response to mortality salience (death cognitions) exploring their potential mediating role for CWD responses (Quirin, Luckey, & Kuhl, 2008). In a first study, we found that German soldiers showed increases in implicit but not in explicit NA as a reaction to a mortality salience induction (writing down personal feelings as a reaction to photographs of terror acts) as compared to a control group. Additionally, we found that soldiers in the mortality salience but not in the control group denied the relevance of the study, which suggests repressive coping in this group. Consequently, the IPANAT seems capable of uncovering unconscious anxiety reactions elicited by mortality threat. In a second study with psychology students, we induced mortality salience by presenting a dramatic and tragic movie scene in which a boxer died after a championship fight, with his young son standing aside. We found that increases in implicit but not explicit NA predicted increased cultural worldview defense, as indicated by ratings on how close one feels to one's nation. These data suggest that the IPANAT is a useful tool to investigate repressed or denied negative affect in the context of cultural worldview defense and, potentially, in other research contexts as well.

Summary

Implicit affect refers to the automatic activation of mental representations of affective experiences and can be measured with indirect tests such as the IPANAT. The IPANAT includes two general scales measuring implicit PA and NA, both of which show adequate psychometric properties (reliability and validity) and revealed to be suitable for the measurement of automatic affective traits and states. Our recent studies suggest that the IPANAT is a useful tool for investigating affective processes in physiological and in social psychology research, both in correlational and experimental designs. Since accessibility vs. repression of affective reactions is an important issue in clinical and particularly psychosomatic research (Lane, 2008), the IPANAT may also be relevant for carrying out research in these psychological fields.

References

Barrett, L. F., (2004). Feelings or words? Understanding the content in self-report ratings of experienced emotion. *Journal of Personality and Social Psychology, 87*, 266-281.

Birbaumer, N., & Öhman, A. (Eds.). (1994). *The structure of emotion*. Toronto: Hogrefe.

Bower, G. H. (1981). Mood and memory. *American Psychologist, 36*, 129-148.

Byrne, D. (1961). The repression-sensitization scale: Rationale, reliability, and validity. *Journal of Personality, 29*, 334-349.

Cunningham, W. A., Preacher, K. J., & Banaji, M. R. (2001). Implicit attitude measures: Consistency, stability, and convergent validity. *Psychological Science, 121*, 163-170.

Edwards, A. L. (1957). The social desirability variable in personality assessment and research. New York: Dryden.

Ekman, P., & Friesen, W. V. (1978). *Facial action coding system: A technique for the measurement of facial movement*. Palo Alto, CA: Consulting Psychologists Press.

Fazio, R. H., & Olson, M. A. (2003). Implicit measures in social cognition research: Their meaning and uses. *Annual Review of Psychology, 54*, 297-327.

Forgas, J. P. (1995). Mood and judgment: The affect infusion model (AIM). *Psychological Bulletin, 117*, 39-66.

Goffman, E. (1956). *The presentation of self in everyday life*. Edinburgh: University of Edinburgh.

Golomb, B. A., Lawrence, D. T., & Sejnowski, T. J. (1991). Sexnet: A neural network identifies sex from human faces. In R. P. Lippman, J. Moody, & D. S. Touretzky (Eds.), *Advances in neural information processing systems.* (Vol. 3, pp. 572–577). San Mateo, CA: Kaufmann.

Greenberg, J., Martens, A., Jonas, E., Eisenstadt, D., Pyszczynski, T., & Solomon, S. (2003). Psychological defense in anticipation of anxiety: Eliminating the potential for anxiety eliminates the effect of mortality salience on worldview defense. *Psychological Science, 14*, 516-519.

Halbreich, U. A., G. M.; Shindledecker, R.; Zumoff, B.; Nathan, S. (1985). Cortisol secretion in endogenous depression. I. Basal plasma levels. *Archives of General Psychiatry, 42*, 904-908.

Hofmann, W., Gschwendner, T., & Schmitt, M. (2005). On implicit-explicit consistency: The moderating role of individual differences in awareness and adjustment. *European Journal of Personality, 19*, 25-49.

Kihlstrom, J. F., Mulvaney, S., Tobias, B. A., & Tobis, I. P. (2000). The emotional unconscious. In E. Eich & J. F. Kihlstrom (Eds.), *Cognition and emotion.* (pp. 30-86): Oxford University Press.

Koole, S. L., & DeHart, T. (in press). Self-affection without self-reflection: Origins, models, and consequences of implicit self-esteem. In C. Sedikides & S. Spencer (Eds.), *The Self in Social Psychology*. New York: Psychology Press.

Kuhl, J. (1994). Action and state orientation: Psychometric properties of the action control scales (ACS-90). In J. Kuhl & J. Beckmann (Eds.), Volition and personality: Action versus state orientation (pp. 47-59). Göttingen, Germany: Hogrefe.

Kuhl, J. (2001). Motivation und Persönlichkeit: Interaktionen psychischer Systeme [Motivation and personality: Interactions of mental systems]. Göttingen, Germany: Hogrefe.

Kuhl, J. (2005). TOP Manual. Osnabrück: Universität Osnabrück & IMPART GmbH.

Kuhl, J., Scheffer, D., & Eichstaedt, J. (2003). Der Operante Motiv-Test (OMT): Ein neuer Ansatz zur Messung impliziter Motive. In F. Rheinberg & J. Stiensmeier-Pelster (Eds.), Diagnostik von Motivation und Selbstkonzept (pp. 129-149). Göttingen: Hogrefe.

Lane, R. D. (2008). Neural substrates of implicit and explicit emotional processes: A unifying framework for psychosomatic medicine. *Psychosomatic Medicine, 70*, 214-231.

Lang, P.J. (1995). The emotion probe: Studies of motivation and attention. American Psychologist, 50, 372-385.

LeDoux, J. E. (1996). *The emotional brain: The mysterious underpinnings of emotional life.*: Simon & Schuster.

MacLeod, C., Mathews, A., & Tata, P. (1986). Attentional bias in emotional disorders. *Journal of Abnormal Psychology, 95*, 15-20.

McClelland, D. C., Koestner, R., & Weinberger, J. (1989). How do self-attributed and implicit motives differ? *Psychological Review, 96*, 690-702.

Murphy, S. T., & Zajonc, R. B. (1993). Affect, cognition, and awareness: Affective priming with optimal and suboptimal stimulus exposures. *Journal of Personality and Social Psychology, 64*, 723-739.

Nisbett, R. E., & Wilson, T. D. (1977). Telling more than we can know: Verbal reports on mental processes. *Psychological Review, 84*, 231-259.

Öhman, A., Flykt, A., & Lundqvist, D. (2000). Unconscious emotion: Evolutionary perspectives, psychophysiological data and neuropsychological mechanisms. In R. D. Lane & L. Nadel (Eds.), *Cognitive neuroscience of emotion.* (pp. 296-327): Oxford University Press.

Paulhus, D. L. (1984). Two-component models of socially desirable responding. *Journal of Personality and Social Psychology, 46*, 598-609.

Polivy, J., & Doyle, C. (1980). Laboratory induction of mood states through the reading of self-referent mood statements: Affective changes or demand characteristics? *Journal of Abnormal Psychology, 89*, 286-290.

Pyszczynski, T., Greenberg, J., & Solomon, S. (1999). A dual-process model of defense against conscious and unconscious death-related thoughts: An extension of terror management theory. *Psychological Review, 106*, 835-845.

Quirin, M. (2008). *The IPANAT: An implicit measure for the assessment of state and trait variation in approach-avoidance motivation.* Paper presented at the 28th International Congress of Psychology, Berlin.

Quirin, M., Kazén, M., & Kuhl, J. (2009). *When Nonsense Sounds Happy or Helpless: The Implicit Positive And Negative Affect Test (IPANAT).* Submitted for publication.

Quirin, M., Kazén, M., Rohrmann, S., & Kuhl, J. (2009). Implicit Affectivity Predicts Circadian and Reactive Cortisol: Using the Implicit Positive and Negative Affect Test. *Journal of Personality,* in press.

Quirin, M., Koole, S. L., & Kuhl, J. (2009). *Intuiting the Self: Development and Validation of the Experiential Self-Access Questionnaire.* Manuscript in preparation. University of Osnabrueck.

Quirin, M., Luckey, U., & Kuhl, J. (2008). *The Implicit Positive and Negative Affect Test: Investigating the Role of Implicit Emotion in Terror Management.* Paper presented at the 8th annual conference of the Society for Personality and Social Psychology, Albuquerque.

Rosenthal, R., & Rosnow, R. L. (Eds.). (1969). *Artifact in behavioral research.* New York: Academic Press.

Schlenker, B. R. (1980). *Impression management: The self-concept, social identity, and interpersonal relations.* Monterey, California: Brooks and Cole.

Schmukle, S. C., Egloff, B., & Burns, L. R. (2002). The relationship between positive and negative affect in the Positive and Negative Affect Schedule. *Journal of Research in Personality, 36*, 463-475.

Schultheiss, O. C., & Brunstein, J. C. (2001). Assessment of implicit motives with a research version of the TAT: Picture profiles, gender differences, and relations to other personality measures. *Journal of Personality Assessment, 77*, 71-86.

Taylor, G. J. (2000). Recent developments in alexithymia theory and research. *Canadian Journal of Psychiatry, 45*, 134-142.

Tedeschi, J. T. (Ed.). (1981). *Impression management. Theory and pychological research.* New York: Academic Press.

Williams, J. M. G., Mathews, A., & MacLeod, C. (1996). The emotional Stroop task and psychopathology. *Psychological Bulletin, 120*, 3-24.

Wilson, T. D., Lindsey, S., & Schooler, T. Y. (2000). A model of dual attitudes. *Psychological Review, 107*, 101-126.

Winkielman, P., & Berridge, K. C. (2004). Unconscious Emotion. *Current Directions in Psychological Science, 13*, 120-123.

Zajonc, R. B. (1984). On the primacy of affect. *American Psychologist ,39,* 117-123.

Zajonc, R.B. (2000). Feeling and thinking: Closing the debate over the independence of affect. In J.P. Forgas (Ed.), *Feeling and thinking: The role of affect in social cognition* (pp. 31–58). New York: Cambridge University Press.

Zebrowitz, L. A., Fellous, J.M., Mignault, A., & Andreoletti, C. (2003). Trait impressions as overgeneralized responses to adaptively significant facial qualities: Evidence from connectionist modeling. *Personality and Social Psychology Review, 7,* 194-215.

In: Personality Assessment: New Research
Editor: Lauren B. Palcroft and Melissa V. Lopez
ISBN: 978-1-60692-796-0

Short Communication D

STRUCTURED MMPI-2 CLIENT FEEDBACK IN THE IDENTIFICATION OF POTENTIAL SUPPLEMENTAL TARGETS OF CHANGE

Alan R. King*[*] *and Joseph C. Miller
University of North Dakota,
Grand Forks, North Dakota, USA

ABSTRACT

Contemporary structured psychotherapies are often designed for manualized, short-term (usually 12-16 sessions) delivery with observable and focused targets of therapeutic change. The time-limited nature of many contemporary psychotherapies limits therapists to a focus on a small number of treatment targets and objectives. The role of traditional psychometric testing in structured therapies has been difficult to discern from the literature. Reliance on broad trait based symptom inventories has been largely replaced by functional applied behavior analysis with an emphasis on observables. An additional shortcoming of traditional psychometric evaluation has been the absence of a systematic approach to identifying treatment targets from findings and providing clients digestible feedback about their results. The present article explores some of these theoretical and pragmatic limitations in the use of broad symptom inventories such as the Minnesota Multiphasic Personality Inventory (MMPI-2) in the course of assessment for short-term structured interventions. A method described previously in the literature (McCray & King, 2003) for providing systematic test feedback and identifying supplemental treatment goals was modified in this chapter for use with the MMPI-2. While unreasonable to expect full remission of broader maladaptive response tendencies through short term interventions, the recognition and partial attenuation of disruptive behavioral, attitudinal and emotional reactions to stressors could prove exceedingly helpful in a subset of clinical cases. Randomized controlled trials of structured therapies with and without reliance on traditional testing would provide a new and interesting line

[*] Correspondence should be sent to Alan R. King, Psychology Department, University of North Dakota, P.O. Box 8380, Grand Forks, ND 58202-8380 (alan_king@und.nodak.edu).

of research with potential promise for enhancing the efficacy and effectiveness of treatment.

Keywords: Minnesota Multiphasic Personality Inventory (MMPI-2), structured psychometric feedback, structured psychotherapies.

Structured MMPI-2 Client Feedback in the Identification of Potential Supplemental Targets of Change

A review of the contemporary psychotherapy literature reveals a decided trend toward the development of structured, often manualized, short-term therapies that can be applied in a systematic manner across a range of problem areas. This movement has been accelerated by cognitive-behavioral therapy (CBT) which has served as a vehicle for successful intervention for problems as diverse as depression (Butler, Chapman, & Forman, 2006), alcoholism (Anton, et al., 2006; Marlatt & Gordon, 1985), drug abuse (McKee, et al., 2007), obsessive-compulsive disorder (Watson & Rees, 2008), generalized anxiety disorder (Stanley, et al., 2003), post-traumatic stress disorder (DeRosa, et al., 2003; Smith, et al., 2007), schizophrenia (Turkington, Dudley, Warman, & Beck, 2004), chronic fatigue syndrome (Malouff, et al., 2008), and many others. A further expansion of the CBT treatment domain has accompanied the development of interventions which target the more generalized response tendencies manifested in personality disorders (Dialectical Behavior Therapy: Linehan, 1993; Beck, et al., 1990). Even psychoanalytically oriented therapists have embraced a structured and brief dynamic psychotherapy (Abbass, Sheldon, & Gyra, 2008; Levison & Strupp, 1999; Luborsky, 1984) approach for treatment of both Axis I and II conditions. While optimism for the modification of generalized response tendencies through short-term interventions grows, the role of traditional personality testing in these systematic intervention efforts remains largely undelineated in the treatment literature.

CBT, DBT, IPT, STDT and other structured short-term protocols identify a range of assessment instruments that are recommended for use in the diagnostic phase of treatment. The purpose of psychometric testing, when it occurs, is often to consider exclusion criteria. identify comorbid conditions that warrant separate attention, or to establish a baseline of severity that can be used in outcome measurements. The value of elevations on specific personality or other symptom scales in the treatment plan is seldom addressed in available literature. In fact, the incorporation of personality attributes into the short-term treatment process may more likely be discouraged. Markowitz (1998) warned IPT therapists not to confuse trait and state mood symptoms since IPT "eschews claims to character change" given "limitations of any brief therapy to alter long-established" personality qualities (see also Stuart & Robertson, 2003). A failure to consider more generalized response tendencies as supplemental targets of change may prove,however, to be unnecessarily limiting given the potential role of personality and other attributes in the genesis and maintenance of many presenting problems. Disillusionment with the value of trait-like measures in short-term treatment is a curious development given the historic value of psychological testing in the case formulation and treatment process (Derkeson & Stoore, 1999; Wedding & Faust, 1989; Leli & Filskov, 1984; Einhorn & Hogarth, 1978).

Are there theoretical or pragmatic reasons to exclude problem attributes identified from major psychometric inventories in short-term treatment planning? The potential nexus between both specific and generalized response tendencies and the etiology of psychiatric conditions seems evident enough. Perhaps the real limiting factor has been the lack of clarity in the literature regarding what clinicians should do with testing results once they are generated. A systematic approach could extend the value of traditional psychological testing into the short-term treatment domain.

SELECTION OF TARGETS FOR CHANGE INCONTEMPORARY PSYCHOTHERAPY

Structured short-term therapies attempt to target a small number of prominent cognitive, emotional and/or behavioral responses for progressive change. The usual course of the short-term therapies involve initial sessions dedicated to assessment and diagnostics with an emphasis on observable targets that can monitored over time. This chapter suggests that the customary assessments and treatment planning sessions be conducted as usual with the inclusion, when deemed appropriate by the practitioner, of a broad inventory such as the MMPI-2 (Butcher, et al., 2006; Graham, 2000, 2006), Millon Clinical Multiaxial Inventory (MCMI-III: Millon, Millon, & Davis, 1994), NEO-PI (Costa & McCrae, 1992), Personality Assessment Inventory (PAI: Morey, 1991), Coolidge Axis II Inventory (CATI: Coolidge & Merwin, 1992), or other instrument. Specialty scales also have been derived from the MMPI-2 for measure of personality disorders (Colligan, Morey, & Offord, 1994). These psychometric findings would then be used to guide the possible selection of a small number of response tendencies that would be selected largely *by the client* and incorporated into the case formulation and treatment plan. The inclusion of each supplemental target would have to be justified by evidence that the attribute appeared to either contribute directly to the presenting problem(s) or magnify Axis IV stressor(s) that indirectly detracted from treatment success.

MMPI-2 Test Feedback

The case formulation process in short-term therapies involves symptom identification often associated with a formal diagnosis along with the generation of a small number of hypotheses regarding the role of cognitive, behavioral, and/or emotional responses that serve to maintain the condition. Structured therapies rely on didactic and and homework assignments to assure that the client understands the principles of the therapy, accepts personal responsibility for change, and develops realistic expectations for the treatment outcome.

A psychometric inventory would be used to provide a broader assessment of current symptoms and functioning. The MMPI-2 would seem to be ideally suited for this purpose because of the extensive, unparalleled, scale by scale concurrent validation that has accumulated in the empirical literature. In fact, textbooks (Graham, 2006; Greene, 2000) offer specific descriptive phrases, provided by therapists and collateral sources, that have been associated with particular scale elevations over the years. The test validation process required these extensive linkages with observed behavioral, attitudinal, and emotional response tendencies to derive meaning from the results. These clinical correlates are well known within the professional community, and even first year clinical and counseling psychology graduate student spend extensive time learning to interpret MMPI-2 scale elevations and profiles. In fact, there are so many potential indicators that one can only imagine that variability of test feedback provided to clients by therapists nationwide. It also seems likely that clients would have a great deal of difficulty remembering clearly the nature of the feedback after it is given. An experienced practitioner need only ask a few clients about prior testing results to understand the futility of the feedback exercise when offered orally and unsystematically with no focused intent.

McCray & King (2003) described a systematic approach to providing test feedback from the MCMI-III within the context of a structured short-term therapy (IPT). The present chapter modifies their procedure for incorporation of MMPI-2 feedback into any treatment modality.

Practitioners should begin by first reviewing all assessment information to assure that the client does not meet any important exclusion criteria for participation (e.g., psychosis, active suicidality, etc.) in the selected treatment. The therapist would have to make a determination as to whether or not the MMPI-2 protocol was interpretable and valid using standard criteria. The feedback session could begin with a general discussion about the MMPI-2 and the use of such inventories in mental health assessment and treatment. Clients should be informed that the MMPI-2 identifies general behavioral, attitudinal, and emotional response tendencies that are correlated with scores on each of 10 major clinical dimensions or scales. The fallibility of psychological tests in general should be conceded to extend the client ample liberty to reject particular correlates that might be found to be inaccurate or unacceptable in some way. Clients should be reminded that many of the upcoming descriptive phrases will not accurately depict their tendencies since they were derived from large research samples that may not always generalize well to the individual. The purpose of the testing is to provide the client an opportunity to review research findings associated with selected profile elevations on the MMPI-2. The client will be extended the discretion to determine which of the attributes are accurate and which fail to reflect personal tendencies. The client and therapist can then discuss the possibility of trying to change attributes that seem to be associated with a significant level of emotional distress or impairment in interpersonal functioning.

Table 1 presents profile panels which detail the psychological attributes that are associated with elevations (with the exclusion of *Mf* Scale 5 which is more limited in meaningful correlates) on each of the MMMPI-2 clinical and validity scales. The wording of these attributes was copied, modified or derived from Graham's (2006) summary of research (pp. 66-90) for the ten clinical scales. Descriptive phrases were reworded to diminish the sense of afront that can accompany some attributes (i.e., to minimize stigma).

Table 1. Clinical attributes copied, modified or derived from MMPI-2 research as potential supplemental target for inclusion in structured short-term therapies

Profile 1	Profile 2
• Thinks a great deal about bodily concerns and physical symptoms • Finds that physical symptoms tend to increase with daily stress • Feels need to alert others to physical limitations to assure their proper recognition • Cares about others but finds it necessary to focus on the needs of self rather than others • Hates to complain but finds it necessary to get adequate help with concerns and problems • Is often disappointed and angered by others, particularly doctors • Feels cautious to avoid alienating doctors because of the need for numerous medications • Does not find talk about psychological issues to be helpful in dealing with personal problems • Often feels pessimistic, defeatist, unhappy and resigned	• Thinks about past events which bring guilt and shame • Thinks about past events which bring sadness and hopelessness • Tries not to think about future goals and ambitions • Finds that thoughts about personal issues often interfere with concentration on other things • Finds it hard to eat and sleep properly • Feels need to alert others to personal insecurities and inadequacies to assure proper recognition • Sometimes feels helpless and resigned that problems will not go away • Often feels that others do not care about him or her • Wishes feelings did not get hurt so easily by the comments and actions of others • Finds it hard to develop and maintain a wide range of interests • Finds it hard to make even minor decisions • Feels a need to seek reassurance from others for every major decision

An attempt was also made to word the descriptive phrases as specific cognitive, attitudinal, emotional, and/or behavioral response tendencies that could be subject to some change over time by motivated clients. Individual therapists may choose to alter the suggested wording to highlight or redefine target thoughts, feelings and behaviors in a preferred manner. The practitioner would assume responsibility to assure that the wording of the attributes corresponded with available validity data. Other legitimate MMPI-2 validity sources, including unitary peer-reviewed articles, could support additional descriptors or alternative wording.

Profile 3	Profile 4
• Feels troubled by physical symptoms that seem to come and go mysteriously • Often finds it hard to meet responsibilities because of physical and medical limitations • Expects a level of attention, affection and appreciation from others that is often missing • Feels often ignored, angry and resentful • Regrets that most relationships tend to be intense and short-lived • Resents that past behavior was often described by family members and others as childish • Prefers to cope with life challenges with a focus on feelings rather than logic • Often disappointed that others do not recognize personal virtues, motivations and achievements • Sometimes feels accused unfairly of trying to control or manipulate the emotions of others • Often finds that good nature is unappreciated and taken advantage of by others • Feels pressure to always look the best and make a good impression on others	• Encounters stress because of the urge to put authority figures in their place • Regrets hassles associated with past legal violations • Feels tired of accusations that he or she has lied to others • Feels tired of being accused to cheating on partner(s) • Thinks a lot about how family members are really to blame for present difficulties • Feels pressure to take whatever rewards are • present right now without waiting for the future • Feels tired of criticism that he or she never learns from experience • Resents accusation of under-achievement since he or she is smarter than most and never really tried • Resents being accused of caring more about self than others • Often feels accused unfairly of trying to con or take advantage of others • Sometimes feels that relationships are not worth it because of all of the turmoil • Resents criticism that jokes and comments are disrespectful and/or unfunny • Often annoyed by challenges to pursue • Uninteresting and unrealistic long-term goals • Feel need to immediately take action when offended or goal pursuits are obstructed • Believes it is necessary to make it clear that no one tells him or her what to do • Often annoyed when others try to put a guilt trip on him or her • Finds that most shortcomings and problems occur from people misinterpreting his or her actions • Desires even more exciting and pleasurable adventures and pursuits • Feels contempt for weak people who complain that everything is wrong or risky • Resents past troubles from alcohol/drug use or sexual behavior

Profile 6	**Profile 7**
• Resents past mistreatment by others and thinks a lot about ways to even the score • Often feels mistreated and picked on by others resents people who without hesitation express their opinions • Feels pressure to argue with others when they are dead wrong about things • Often feels annoyed when others fail to live up to high standards of conduct • Find it annoying when people bring their emotions into intellectual debate • Feel need to stay alert to threat and the manipulations of others • Find it annoying when people think they are funny by offering comments about others • Often feels contempt for others, especially those who try to read his or her mind and know what they are thinking	• Feels unable to meet many responsibilties because of many personal problems • Worries excessively about social acceptance and the opinions of others • Believes that he or she copes more poorly with stress than others • Finds it difficult to make even minor decisions tries as much as possible to precisely meet all rules and standards • Feels that there just is not time to seek or enjoy pleasurable pursuits • Finds that day-to-day stressors are so great that big problems cannot even be considered • Feels more distant toward others than they say they feel toward him or her • Feels largely maladjusted compared to others who are mostly worry free • Wishes feelings did not get hurt so easily by the comments and actions of others

This level of therapist discretion in the language used to provide test feedback would be no different than that presently applied in the field. The feedback of each practitioner, however, would subsequently be consistent from client to client given reliance on the specific wording selected for each profile panel. It is recommended that the therapist select the top one, two or three panels for the clinical scale dimensions where $T > 60$. Three additional panels were included at the end of Table 1 for validity scale attributes derived from interpretable profiles (L > 55; F = 50-65; K < 40) based on the earlier summaries (pp. 24-32) of Graham (2000). In all cases, professional judgment needs to be applied to assure that clients are sufficiently stable and prepared to consider meaningfully the attributes listed in the panel(s). The client is asked to read and circle each response tendency in the profile panel(s) that accurately represents a personal attribute. The therapist and client then revisit the circled items together to determine if any warrant further consideration as a possible target for change. If so, discussion might ensue about how the attribute might be measured and self-monitored over the course of treatment. Some simple and direct cognitive-behavioral suggestions might be offered as a mechanism for change in these areas that are peripheral to the presenting problem. This discussion should provide a more meaningful, detailed and consistent test feedback process along with the possible selection of additional targets for change that are hypothetically linked to the presenting problem(s) are Axis IV stressors.

Profile 8	Profile 9
• Feels socially alienated and avoids social contact • Prefers to lead a very private, even secretive, lifestyle • Allows self to dwell on thoughts of hopelessness and despair • Gives up easily when confronted by problems questions normalacy regarding many facets of functioning • Feels the ability to pursue only general, not specific, goals • Does not know how to approach problem solving in a systematic way • Acknowledges withdrawal into fantasy when stressed or feeling rejected • Wishes feelings did not get hurt so easily by the comments and actions of others • Finds it hard to eat and sleep properly	• Feels pressure to act rather than think • Has trouble inhibiting immediate responses to stressors • Commits to an unrealistic number of obligations and activities • Does not use time and efforts wisely • Does not see projects and commitments through to completion • Resists following a routine schedule despite requests from others • Often feels bored even during activities that others would find exciting • Regrets how easily he or she gets frustrated • Desires even more exciting and pleasurable adventures and pursuits • Finds risk-taking fun but sometimes regrettably costly • Regrets past trouble associated with sexual indiscretion(s) • Finds it annoying when others are pessimistic and defeatist • Feels strong desire to pursue big rather than small goals and ambitions • Regrets past trouble associated with legal violations • Often feels accused unfairly of trying to control or manipulate others

Scenarios Examples

How specifically might MMPI-2 test feedback advance the effectiveness of IPT for depression, DBT for self-harm behavior, or CBT for the treatment of bulimia nervosa? An inventory like the MMPI-2 may be useful in alerting therapists to potential comorbid psychiatric conditions that warrant simultaneous attention. A major symptom inventory may similarly identify whether or not potential clients meet exclusion criteria or bring other contraindications for the treatment under consideration. A comprehensive approach to intake assessment may also serve to reassure clients and oversight bodies that due diligence has been applied to the evaluation. The present chapter posits, however, that some additional specific advantages might be derived for treatment options such as the ones considered above. Consider the example of a 24-year-old single woman seeking CBT for bulimia nervosa.

Profile L	**Profile F**
• experiences stress when rules and social norms are not followed precisely • feels pressured and obligated to uphold and advance a high code of moral conduct • often feels troubled by the low virtues and morals shown by others • feels compelled to inform others of personal • achievements to assure recognition	• Often thinks of self as a failure • Often thinks about the future in pessimistic terms • Often assumes that negative first impression • Will be left on others • Believes he or she has few or no friends • Feels frustrated easily and finds it hard not to just give up • Often feels unfairly treated by others in life • Often feels unloved by family • Wishes feelings did not get hurt so easily by the comments and actions of others

Profile K
• Believes that bad things will happen if the wishes of authority figures are violated • Often thinks about inability to overcome daily problems in living • Finds it hard to react immediately and effectively to challenges • Often thinks critically and judgmentally about self and others • Gives up quickly when trying to meet challenges

Graham, 2000, 2006.

A *D* scale (2) elevation found in the course of IPT treatment of depression might enhance therapist focus on cognitive-emotional ("often feels that others do not care about him or her; wishes feelings did not get hurt so easily by the comments and actions of others") and behavioral ("feels need to alert others to personal insecurities and inadequacies to assure proper recognition; avoids conflict with others even when it seems necessary to protect personal interests; feels a need to seek reassurance from others for every major decision") response tendencies that interfere with the effective resolution of identified interpersonal disputes targetted in IPT.

A *Hy* scale (3) elevation found in the course of DBT treatment of self-harm behavior might identify a number of interpersonal stressors and cognitive-emotional reactions associated with maladaptive coping. These could include a high need for reassurance and attention ("expects a level of attention, affection and appreciation from others that is often missing; feels often ignored, angry and resentful"), excessive concern about the opinions of others ("feels pressure to always look the best and make a good impression on others"), feeling unappreciated for prior actions ("often disappointed that others do not recognize personal virtues, motivations and achievements; often finds that good nature is unappreciated and taken advantage of by others"), and a tendency to emote rather than think under stress ("prefers to cope with life challenges with a focus on feelings rather than logic").

A *Pt* scale (7) elevation found in the course of CBT treatment of bulimia nervosa might enhance recognition and motivation on the part of the client to diminish excessive "worries about social acceptance and the opinions of others" and try to ease up on excessive efforts "to precisely meet all rules and standards". The therapist may help the client challenge her distorted self-perception that she is "largely maladjusted compared to others who are mostly worry free". The purpose of the test feedback would be to identify more pervasive attributes that support and maintain the behaviors targeted for treatment. The rigor applied to self-monitoring and on-going assessment of these cognitions would be left to the discretion of the therapist.

References

Abbass, A., Sheldon, A., & Gyra, J. (2008). Intensive short-term dynamic psychotherapy for DSM-IV personality disorders: A randomized controlled trial. *Journal of Nervous and Mental Disease, 196(3)*, 211-216.

Anton, R.F., O'Malley, S.S., Ciraulo, D.A., Cisler, R.A., Couper, D., Donavan, D.M., Gastfriend, D.R., Hosking, J.D., Johnson, B.A., LoCastro, J.S., Longabaugh, R., Mason, B.J., Mattson, M.E., Miller, W.R., Pettinati, H.M., Randall, C.L., Swift, R., Weiss, R.D., Williams, L.D., & Zweben, A. (2006). Combined pharmacotherapies and behavioral interventions for alcohol dependence. The COMBINE study: a randomized controlled trial. *Journal of the American Medical Association, 295*:2003-2017.

Beck, A.T., & Freeman, A. (1990). *Cognitive therapy of personality disorders.* New York, N.Y.: Guilford Press.

Butcher, J.N., Dahlstrom, W.G., Graham, J.R., Tellegen, A., & Kaemmer, B. (1989). *Minnesota Multiphasic Personality Inventory-2 (MMPI-2): Manual for administration and scoring.* Minneapolis: University of Minnesota Press.

Butler, A.C., Chapman, J.E., & Forman, E.M. (2006). The empirical status of cognitive-behavioral therapy: A review of meta-analyses. *Clinical Psychology Review, 26(1)*, 17-31.

Coolidge, F.L. & Merwin, M.M. (1992). Reliability and validity of the Coolidge Axis II Inventory: A new inventory for the assessment of personality disorders. *Journal of Personality Assessment, 59(2)*, 223-238.

Colligan, R.C., Morey, L.C., & Offord, K.P. (1994). The MMPI/MMPI-2 personality disorder scales: Contemporary norms for adults and adolescents. *Journal of Clinical Psychology, 50(2)*, 168-200.

Costa, P., & McCrae, R. (1992). Normal personality assessment in clinical practice: The NEO Personality Inventory. *Psychological Assessment, 4(1)*, 5-13.

Derkeson, J., & Stoore, H. (1999). Psychodiagnostics and indications for treatment in cases of personality disorders: Some pitfalls. In Derkeson & C. Maffei (Eds.). *Treatment of Personality Disorders* (pp. 155-166). New York: Kluwer Academic/Plenum Publishers.

DeRosa,R., Pelcovitz, D., Kaplan, S. (2003). *Group treatment for adolescents with complex PTSD Manual.* North Shore University Hospital, Adolescent Trauma Treatment Development Center, National Child Traumatic Stress Network.

Einhorn, H.J., & Hogarth, R.M. (1978). Confidence in judgement: Persistence of the illusion of validity. *Psychological Review, 85(5)*, 395-416.

Graham, J.R. (2000). *MMPI-2: Assessing personality and psychopathology* (3rd Ed.). Oxford University Press, New York, N.Y.

Graham, J.R. (2006). *MMPI-2: Assessing personality and psychopathology* (4th Ed.). Oxford University Press, New York, N.Y.

Greene, R.L. (2000). *MMPI-2: An interpretive manual (2nd Ed.).* Needham Heights, MA: Allyn & Bacon.

Lili, D.A., & Filskov, S.B. (1984). Clinical detection of intellectual deterioration associated with brain damage. *Journal of Clinical Psychology, 40(6)*, 1435-1441.

Levison, H., & Strupp, H.H. (1999). Recommendations for the future of training in brief dynamic psychotherapy. *Journal of Clinical Psychology, 55*, 385-391.

Linehan, M. (1993). *Cognitive-behavioral treatment of borderline personality disorder.* New York, N.Y.: Guilford Press.

Luborsky, L. (1984). *Principles of psychoanalytic psychotherapy: A manual for supportive-expressive treatment.* NY: Basic Books.

Markowitz. J.C. (1998). *Interpersonal Psychotherapy* (Ed.). Washington, D.C.: American Psychiatric Press.

Malouff, J.M., Thorsteinsson, E.B., Rooke, S.E., Bhullar, N., & Schutte, N.S. (2008). Efficacy of cognitive-behavioral therapy for chronic fatigue syndrome: A meta-analysis. *Clinical Psychology Review, 28(5)*, 736-745.

Marlatt, G.A., & Gordon, J.R. (1985). *Relapse prevention maintenance strategies in the treatment of addictive behaviors (Eds).* New York: Guilford Press.

McCray, J.A., & King, A.R. (2003). Personality disorder attributes as supplemental goals for change in interpersonal psychotherapy. *Journal of Contemporary Psychotherapy, 33(2), 79-92.*

McKee, S.A., Carroll, K.M., Sinha, R., Robinson, J.E., Nich, C., Cavallo, D., & O'Malley, S. (2007). Enhancing brief cognitive-behavioral therapy with motivational enhancement techniques in cocaine users. *Drug and Alcohol Dependence, 91(1)*, 97-101.

Millon, T., Millon, C., & Davis, R. D. (1994). *Millon Clinical Multiaxial Inventory -III.* Minneapolis: National Computer Systems.

Morey, L. C. (1991). *Personality Assessment Inventory: Professional Manual.* Odessa, FL: Psychological Assessment Resources, Inc.

Smith, P., Yule, W., Perrin, S., Tranah, T., Dalgleish, T., & Clark, D.M. (2007). Cognitive-behavioral therapy for PTSD in children and adolescents: A preliminary randomized controlled trial. *Journal of American Academy of Child & Adolescent Psychiatry, 46(8)*, 1051-1061.

Stanley, M.A., Beck, G.J., Novy, D.M., Averill, P.M., Swann, A.C., Diefenbach, G.J., & Hopko, D.R. (2003). Cognitive-behavioral treatment of late-life generalized anxiety disorder. *Journal of Consulting and Clinical Psychology, 71(2)*, 309-319.

Stuart, S. & Robertson, M. (2003). *Interpersonal psychotherapy: A clinician's guide*. Hodder Arnold.

Turkington, D., Dudley, R., Warman, D.M., & Beck, A.T. (2004). *Journal of Psychiatric Practice, 10(1)*, 5-16.

Watson, H.J., & Rees, C.S. (2008). Meta-analysis of randomized, controlled treatment trials for pediatric obsessive-compulsive disorder. *Journal of Child Psychology and Psychiatry, 49(5)*, 489-498.

Wedding, D. & Faust, D. (1989). Clinical judgement and decision making in neuropsychology. *Archives of Clinical Neuropsychology, 4(3)*, 233-265.

In: Personality Assessment: New Research
Editor: Lauren B. Palcroft and Melissa V. Lopez
ISBN: 978-1-60692-796-0

Short Communication E

BEYOND THE TRAITS OF THE FIVE FACTOR MODEL: USING DEVIANT PERSONALITY TRAITS TO PREDICT DEVIANT BEHAVIOR IN ORGANIZATIONS

James M. LeBreton[1] and Jane Wu[2]
Purdue University
1) Department of Psychological Sciences
703 Third Street
Purdue University
West Lafayette, IN 47907 USA
765-496-9377
lebreton@psych.purdue.edu
2) Department of Psychological Sciences
703 Third Street
Purdue University
West Lafayette, IN 47907 USA
319-400-1963
jwu@psych.purdue.edu

Although the five factor model (FFM) has served as an important catalyst for personality-related organizational research, we agree with the suggestions of previous researchers that personality research should expand beyond this basic framework (Block, 1995; Lee & Ashton, 2004). This is especially true for researchers seeking to understand and predict counterproductive or deviant behaviors. The basic thesis of this commentary is that optimal, dispositionally-based prediction of counterproductive organizational criteria will be achieved when researchers begin assessing counterproductive personality traits. In short, we believe prediction may be enhanced by increasing the nomological convergence between our predictor and criterion spaces.

Although a number of aberrant personality traits may be relevant to predicting counterproductive and deviant behaviors, we briefly introduce three of the most promising traits labeled by some as the "Dark Triad" (Paulhus & Williams, 2002): Machiavellianism, narcissism, and psychopathy. Below we 1) define each of these traits, 2) describe how they are related to (but not redundant with) the global traits comprising the FFM, and 3) illustrate how these constructs may be mapped into the nomological space of organizational criteria (especially counterproductive and deviant work behaviors).

Machiavellianism

Individuals scoring high on measures of Machiavellianism (or high Machs) are characterized as manipulative, ambitious, dominant, distrusting, lacking empathy, and having a cynical view of humanity (Christie & Geis, 1970; McHoskey, Worzel, & Szyarto, 1998; Wilson, Near, & Miller, 1998). Such individuals focus their attention on self-centered motives, are willing to manipulate others for personal gain (Leone & Corte, 1994), and experience little empathy towards others (Abramson, 1973). As such, high Machs tend to have a deviant view of morality and perceive others as instruments to help them achieve their own personal goals and desires (Christie & Geis, 1970). Particularly troubling to organizational researchers is the fact that high Machs are often not perceived by others as intentionally engaging in manipulative or deceptive behaviors (Nelson & Gilbertson, 1991). Collectively, the organizational Machiavellian is the master manipulator. He or she perceives and interacts with others through a prism of control. Coworkers, subordinates, bosses, and customers are viewed as pawns on the Machiavellian's personal chess board.

Narcissism

Narcissism is characterized by self-aggrandizement, exhibitionism, and a sense of entitlement (Emmons, 1989; Morf & Rhodewalt, 2001; Raskin & Terry, 1988). Individuals high in narcissism tend to overestimate their abilities and underestimate the abilities of others (Campbell, Goodie, & Foster, 2004). Stated differently, they tend to take too much credit for their work/contributions while failing to award credit to others. This tendency may be partially due to the penchant for the narcissistic individual to more make extreme internal, global, and stable attributions for personal success compared to the average person (Rhodewalt & Morf, 1995). The narcissist values others only to the extent that they can reaffirm their inflated self-perceptions. Thus, narcissistic individuals are concerned not with maintaining interpersonal relationships per se, but with self-aggrandizement and the domination of others (Emmons, 1989). By extension, those high in narcissism often do not trust or care about others and may feel disdain towards others. Thus, it is not surprising that individuals high in narcissism struggle to maintain successful, long-term relationships. Collectively, the organizational narcissist is someone with an aggrandized self-perception. He or she has little use for others who do not reinforce this inflated self-perception leading the narcissist to perceive and interact with others through a prism of dominance, entitlement, and exploitation (Raskin & Terry, 1988).

PSYCHOPATHY

Psychopathy is a multifaceted construct consisting of at least three related facets (LeBreton, Binning, & Adorno, 2006). The first facet is associated with an *arrogant and deceitful interpersonal style*. Individuals scoring high on this facet tend to possess narcissistic qualities such as a grandiose sense of self and egocentricism. Such individuals are masters of deception, manipulation, self-promotion, insincerity, and lying (Cleckley, 1976; Hare, 1999; Lynam, 2002). They believe that rules do not apply to them, that they are deserving of special treatment, and often tend to be hypercritical of those that they believe may be a potential threat (Hare, 1991; LeBreton et al., 2006).

The second facet of psychopathy is associated with *deficient and dysfunctional emotional experiences*. Simply stated, individuals scoring high on this facet are emotionally impaired—they have muted and shallow affective experiences and are incapable of experiencing emotions such as shame, guilt, and remorse; most importantly, they lack the capacity for empathy (Cleckley, 1976; Hare, 1999). In addition, these individuals often have difficulty experiencing fear or anxiety (Cleckley, 1976; Hare, 1999). These elevated fear thresholds increase the likelihood of engaging in what most of us would see as risky or dangerous behavior.

The third facet of psychopathy is associated with *impulsive and irresponsible lifestyles*. Individuals scoring high on this facet tend to be unreliable, reckless, impulsive, and at times even parasitic (Hare, 1999). They fail to honor their commitments/obligations and are more likely to have volatile relationships with others (LeBreton et al., 2006). In addition, these individuals have a difficult time articulating and following through on long-term goals and plans. When these three facets intersect we encounter the full-blown psychopath.

Considered the most dangerous of the Dark Triad, psychopaths share characteristics similar to individuals high in narcissism and Machiavellianism but also demonstrate behaviors associated with being irresponsible, aggressive, and hostile. Indeed, all three traits comprising the Dark Triad are related to one another but all have unique patterns of divergent and convergent correlations with other personality traits and criteria (Paulhus & Williams, 2002). Collectively, the organizational psychopath represents the worst form of predator (Babiak & Hare, 2006). He or she does not experience the emotions which serve as checks-and-balances on the desires to engage in impulsive, dangerous, irresponsible, and aggressive behavior—desires that are normal and which we each experience at one time or another. Lacking the necessarily inhibitory filters, the organizational psychopath combines the worst features of the Machiavellian (i.e., master manipulator) and the worst features of the narcissist (i.e., entitlement and lack of empathy) with a generalized tendency towards aggression and deviant behavior.

RELATIONSHIP BETWEEN THE DARK TRIAD AND THE FIVE FACTOR MODEL

Extant research has documented that the traits of the Dark Triad are correlated with, but not redundant with the global traits of the FFM (Lynam, 2002). For example, Vernon, Villani, Vickers, and Harris (2008) reported that only 18% to 39% of the variance in the Dark Triad can be explained through the global traits of the FFM. Similarly, McClure and LeBreton (2008) found that global traits of extraversion, agreeableness, and conscientiousness explained only 30% of the variance in psychopathy scores and the addition of 16 theoretically relevant FFM facets only increased the variance explained to 63% (thus, over 1/3 of the variance in psychopathy scores remained unexplained by the FFM and its facets). In short, there is growing evidence that while the Dark Triad is correlated with elements of the FFM, it also has unique aspects which are not recoverable using the FFM or its facets. This is good news for organizational psychologists because it suggests the Dark Triad may be able to account for variance that is currently unaccounted for using the global FFM.

Integrating the Dark Triad into Industrial and Organizational Psychology

Although the traits of the FFM enjoy wide popularity in industrial and organizational psychology, the same can not be said of the traits comprising the Dark Triad. We conducted a search using PSYCINFO where we cross-referenced the terms Machiavellian/ Machiavellianism, narcissist/narcissism, and psychopath/psychopathy with the *Journal of Applied Psychology* and *Personnel Psychology*. We found only six papers for Machiavellianism, one for narcissism, and nine for psychopathy (three of which were book reviews). This is unfortunate because we believe these traits may make a value-added contribution to research being conducted by organizational psychologists.

Research conducted primarily by social and personality psychologists has explored the contribution that the Dark Triad traits make to the prediction of general deviance—their results have been promising. This research has linked the Dark Triad to behaviors such as theft, property and information misuse, as well as inappropriate verbal and physical behaviors towards others. For example, when encountering ambiguous situations, individuals high in narcissism have been found to react aggressively and such individuals are also more likely to respond aggressively when being given negative performance feedback (Barry, Chaplin, Grafeman, 2006). Others have found that Machiavellianism is associated with a willingness to be dishonest with high Machs being perceived as more convincing liars compared to low Machs (Geis & Moon, 1981).

Psychopathy has been linked to a variety of deviant behaviors in college student samples including cheating on exams, bullying, drug use, major and minor crime, and anti-authority misbehavior (Gustafson & Ritzer, 1995; Nathanson, Paulhus, & Williams, 2006; Williams & Paulhus, 2004). Higher levels of psychopathy have also been linked to a greater tendency to renege on bargains and a greater likelihood to sacrifice the concerns of others for their own self-interests (Russell, 1996). Furthermore, individuals high in psychopathy are manipulative and callous towards others, yet these are his/her least recognizable traits (Mahafeey & Marcus, 2006). As such, psychopaths may not be as readily perceived as engaging in inappropriate verbal or physical behaviors towards others—at least not initially. Boddy (2006) proposed that due to the difficulty others have in discerning these characteristics, psychopaths are able to successfully operate within organizations.

Within organizational psychology, researchers have reported that leaders scoring high on narcissism tend to be resistant to others' suggestions and blame others for their personal failure while claiming credit for the successes of others (Hogan, Raskin, & Fazzini, 1990). In addition narcissistic managers tend to be abusive and over-involved (Hogan, Curphy, & Hogan, 1994). Narcissism has also been found to be positively related with both self- and other-ratings of leadership (Judge, LePine, & Rich, 2006). This suggests coworkers may be confusing entitlement and aggrandizement with self-confidence. In general, Machiavellians, narcissists, and psychopaths are believed to share the common characteristic of manipulativeness or duplicity (Paulhus & Williams, 2002). This trait combined with a general disregard for the feelings of others makes individuals with Dark Triad traits particularly well-equipped to ascend the organizational ranks.

We believe a more comprehensive and systematic exploration of the Dark Triad is warranted in industrial and organizational psychology, especially when it comes to predicting job performance. The consensus among organizational researchers is that job performance may be decomposed into at least three key components: core task behavior, organizational citizenship behavior (OCB), and counterproductive work behavior (CWB; Rotundo & Sackett, 2002). We believe the latter two components may be especially well-suited to prediction using the Dark Triad. Indeed, we now know that organizations are not immune to acts of aggression, substance abuse, bullying and harassment, lying, cheating, and other forms of antisocial misbehavior (Bennett & Robinson, 2000; Gruys & Sackett, 2003). We advance that if one wishes to predict aberrant behavior in organizations (e.g., CWB), then expanding our portfolio of personality constructs to include aberrant traits is advised. Conversely, one may conceptualize withholding OCBs as a form of antisocial misbehavior; and thus, the Dark Triad may be equally useful for predicting low levels of OCB. That is, the Dark Triad is hypothesized to be useful for predicting the presence of extreme antisocial behavior (i.e., high CWB) and the absence of extreme prosocial behavior (i.e., low OCB). Given that the Dark Triad is not redundant with the global traits of the FFM, it seems reasonable to induce that the Dark Triad may very well predict such prosocial and antisocial behaviors, above and beyond the FFM. Indeed, there is some limited evidence to support such a proposition.

Penny and Spector (2002) found that narcissism was linked to counterproductive behavior (r = .27). Similarly, Judge et al. (2006) found that narcissism was negatively correlated with contextual performance (a proxy for OCB) and positively correlated with workplace deviance. In addition, Judge et al. found that narcissism was predictive of these criteria (as measured by supervisors) above and beyond the FFM. This implies that narcissism is capturing aspects of CWB and OCB not explainable using the traditional FFM. Finally, Zolynsky and LeBreton (2008) recently collected data assessing the traits of the FFM, the Dark Triad, and CWBs in a sample of 193 undergraduate students working part-time in a large metropolitan city. Using hierarchical regression they tested the incremental validity of the Dark Triad above and beyond the FFM. In step 1 they regressed the total CWB score onto the traits of the FFM ($R^2 = .29, p < .001$). In step 2 they added the Dark Triad and found these traits significantly incremented prediction above and beyond the FFM ($\Delta R^2 = .09, p < .001$).

Conclusion

Our goal in writing this commentary was to emphasize the importance of moving beyond the global traits of the FFM. We believe that one promising avenue for future research involves aberrant personality traits. Present research linking these personality traits to work-related behaviors has demonstrated:

1. The Dark Triad represents a set of aberrant personality traits that, while correlated with the global traits of the Five Factor Model, are not redundant with those traits.
2. The Dark Triad has been linked to a variety of different indicators associated with deviant and counterproductive behavior, and
3. The Dark Triad explains incremental (i.e., unique) variance in counterproductive behavior not explainable by the global traits of the Five Factor Model.

As a constellation of traits, the Dark Triad is hypothesized to predict a host of interpersonal problems and deviant behavior. As such, future organizational research employing these traits appears promising. Areas to explore might include how the Dark Triad is related to a) group and team effectiveness and performance, b) interpersonal negotiations and problem-solving, c) reactions to performance feedback, d) leadership effectiveness, derailment, and abusive supervision, e) perceptions of justice and fairness, f) mentor-mentee relationships, and g) emotional regulation and performance.

References

Abramson, E. E. (1973). The counselor as a Machiavellian. *Journal of Clinical Psychology, 29*, 348-349.

Babiak, P., & Hare, R. D. (2006). *Snakes in Suits.* New York: HarperCollins.

Barry, C. T., Chaplin, W. F., & Grafeman, S. J. (2006). Aggression following performance feedback: The influences of narcissism, feedback valence, and comparative standard. *Personality and Individual Differences, 41*, 177-187.

Bennett, R. J., & Robinson, S. L. (2000). Development of a measure of workplace deviance. *Journal of Applied Psychology, 85*, 349-360.

Block, J. (1995). A contrarian view of the five-factor approach to personality description. *Psychological Bulletin, 117*, 187-215.

Boddy, C. R. (2006). The dark side of management decisions: Organisational psychopaths. *Management Decision, 44*, 1461-1475.

Campbell, W. K., Goodie, A. S., & Foster, J. D. (2004). Narcissism, confidence, and risk attitude. *Journal of Behavioral Decision Making, 17*, 297-311.

Christie, R., & Geis, F. L. (1970). *Studies in Machiavellianism.* New York: Academic Press.

Cleckley, H. (1976). *The mask of sanity* (5th ed.).St. Louis MO: Mosby.

Emmons, R. A. (1989). Exploring the relations between motives and traits: The case of narcissism. In D. M. Buss & N. Cantor (Eds.), *Personality psychology: Recent trends and emerging directions* (pp. 32-44). New York: Springer-Verlag.

Geis, F. L., & Moon, H. (1981). Machiavellianism and deception. *Journal of Personality and Social Psychology, 41*, 766-775.

Gruys, M. L., & Sackett, P. R. (2003). Investigating the dimensionality of counterproductive work behavior. *International Journal of Selection and Assessment, 11*, 30-42.

Gustafson, S. B., & Ritzer, D. R. (1995). The dark side of normal: A psychopathy-linked pattern called aberrant self-promotion. *European Journal of Personality, 9*, 147-183.

Hare, R. D. (1991). *The Hare Psychopathy Checklist—Revised.* Toronto: Multi-Health Systems.

Hare, R. D. (1999), *Without Conscience: The Disturbing Word of the Psychopaths among Us*, Guilford Press, New York, NY.

Hogan, R., Curphy, G. J., & Hogan, J. (1994). What do we know about leadership: Effectiveness and personality. *American Psychologist, 49*, 493-504.

Hogan, R., Raskin, R., & Fazzini, D. (1990). The dark side of charisma. In. K. E. Clark & M. B. Clark (Eds.), *Measures of leadership* (pp. 343-354). West Orange, NJ: Leadership Library of America.

Judge, T. A., LePine, J. A., & Rich, B. L. (2006). Loving yourself abundantly: Relationship of the narcissistic personality to self- and other perceptions of workplace deviance, leadership, and task and contextual performance. *Journal of Applied Psychology, 91*, 762-776.

LeBreton, J. M., Binning, J. F., & Adorno, A. J. (2006). Subclinical psychopaths. In D. L. Segal and J.C. Thomas (Eds.), *Comprehensive Handbook of Personality and Psychopathology: Vol. 1. Personality and Everyday Functioning (pp. 388-411).* Wiley, New York.

Lee, K., & Ashton, M. C. (2004). Psychometric properties of the HEXACO Personality Inventory. *Multivariate Behavioral* Research, *39*, 329–358.

Leone, C. & Corte, V. (1994). Concern for self-presentation and self-congruence: Self-monitoring, Machiavellianism, and social conflicts. *Social Behavior and Personality: An International Journal, 22*, 305-312.

Lynam, D. R. (2002). Psychopathy from the perspective of the five-factor model. In P. T. Costa Jr., & T. A. Widiger (Eds.), Personality disorders and the five-factor model of personality (2nd ed.) (pp. 325-348). Washington, DC: American Psychological Association.

Mahaffey, K. J., & Marcus, D. K. (2006). Interpersonal perception of psychopathy: A social relations analysis. *Journal of Social and Clinical Psychology, 25*, 53-74.

McClure, T. & LeBreton, J. M. (2008). *Using the abridged big five circumplex (AB5C) model to predict psychopathy*. Unpublished manuscript, Wayne State University, Detroit, MI.

McHoskey, J. W., Worzel, W., & Szyarto, C. (1998). Machiavellianism and psychopathy. *Journal of Personality and Social Psychology, 74*, 192-210.

Morf, C. C., & Rhodewalt, F. (2001). Unraveling the paradoxes of narcissism: A dynamic self-regulatory processing model. *Psychological Inquiry, 12*, 177-196.

Nathanson, C., Paulhus, D. L., & Williams, K. M. (2006). Predictors of a behavioral measure of scholastic cheating: Personality and competence but not demographics. *Contemporary Educational Psychology, 31*, 97-122.

Nelson, G., & Gilbertson, D. (1991). Machiavellianism revisited. *Journal of Business Ethics, 10*, 633-639.

Paulhus, D. L., & Williams, K. M. (2002). The Dark Triad of personality: Narcissism, Machiavellianism and psychopathy. *Journal of Research in Personality, 36*, 556-563.

Penney, L. M., & Spector, P. E. (2002). Narcissism and counterproductive work behavior: Do bigger egos mean bigger problems? *International Journal of Selection and Assessment, 10*, 126–134.

Raskin, R., & Terry, H. (1988). A principal-components analysis of the Narcissistic Personality Inventory and further evidence of is construct validity. *Journal of Personality and Social Psychology, 54*, 890-902.

Rhodewalt, F., & Morf, C. C. (1995). Self and interpersonal correlates of the Narcissistic Personality Inventory: A review and new findings. *Journal of Research in Personality, 29*, 1-23.

Rotundo, M., & Sackett, P. R., (2002). The relative importance of task, citizenship, and counterproductive performance to global ratings of job performance: A policy capturing approach. *Journal of Applied Psychology, 87*, 66-80.

Russell, D. P. (1996). *Aberrant self-promotion versus Machiavellianism: A differentiation of constructs.* Unpublished master's thesis, Virginia Polytechnic and State University, Blacksburg, VA.

Vernon, P. A., Villani, V. C., Vickers, L. C., & Harris, J. A. (2008). A behavioral genetic investigation of the Dark Triad and the Big 5. *Personality and Individual Differences, 44*, 445-452.

Williams, K. M., & Paulhus, D. L. (2004). The factor structure of the Self-Report Psychopathy scale (SRP-II) in non-forensic samples. *Personality and Individual Differences, 37*, 765-778.

Wilson, D. S., Near, D., & Miller, R. R. (1998). Individual differences in Machiavellianism as a mix of cooperative and exploitative strategies. *Evolution and Human Behavior, 19*, 203-212.

Zolynsky, D., & LeBreton, J. M. (2008). *Contributions of the 'Dark Triad' and Big Five personality traits in determining counterproductive behaviors and attitudes*. Unpublished manuscript, Wayne State University, Detroit, MI.

In: Personality Assessment: New Research
Editor: Lauren B. Palcroft and Melissa V. Lopez

ISBN: 978-1-60692-796-0

Short Communication F

On the Test-Retest Reliability of the Autobiographical Memory Test

Filip Raes[1*], J. Mark G. Williams[2] and Dirk Hermans[1]
[1] Department of Psychology, University of Leuven, Belgium
[2] Department of Psychiatry, University of Oxford, UK

Abstract

The Autobiographical Memory Test (AMT; Williams & Broadbent, 1986) is frequently used by researchers to assess specificity of memory retrieval. This test asks respondents to describe a specific autobiographical memory in response to cue words. In contrast to the AMT's frequent use, however, little is known about its reliability. The present paper examined the test-retest reliability of the AMT. In five studies, undergraduates completed the Autobiographical Memory Test (AMT; Williams & Broadbent, 1986) twice, with mean time interval between test an retest varying over studies from 1 to 5 months. Each time, an alternate AMT was used at retesting. In a sixth study, depressed patients completed the AMT twice: once at admission to a hospital, and again 3 months later. Results document relatively satifactory test-retest reliability of the AMT in assessing people's level of memory specificity.

Keywords: Autobiographical memory; Autobiographical memory test; Test-retest reliability.

* Correspondence concerning this article should be addressed to Filip Raes, Department of Psychology, University of Leuven, Tiensestraat 102, B-3000 Leuven, Belgium. Electronic mail may be sent to filip.raes@psy.kuleuven.be.

On the Test-Retest Reliability of the Autobiographical Memory Test

The past two decades, experimental and clinical researchers in the field of cognitive psychology have been using the Autobiographical Memory Test (AMT; Williams & Broadbent) as the standard procedure for investigating specificity in the retrieval of autobiographical memories (AMs). Although different versions of this experimental task are currently in use (e.g., different numbers of cue words, different time limit for response to each cue), the general procedure is the following. For each of a set of cue words, respondents have to retrieve a specific event from the past that the cue word reminds them of. The important outcome variable is the extent to which responses given meet criteria for specificity, that is, the memory refers to one particular occasion or event that happened on a particular day ("The moment I opened the door and saw my father, whom I hadn't seen for ages" would be an example of a specific memory to the cue word surprised). The reason for the interest in this aspect of autobiographical memory is that there is a growing body of evidence suggesting that some clinical, especially depressed, groups respond with memories that fail to specify a particular occasion, and that this impairment predicts persistence of affective disturbance, reduces the specificity of the imagined future, and impairs problem solving (Williams, 2004). This reduced specificity of AMs, or "overgeneral memory" as it is often referred to, is now a well-documented information processing bias in memory recall in depression.

It is a bit surprising, then, that in contrast to the AMT's frequent use and the number of related publications, and in contrast to the possible future clinical utility of this laboratory task for the cognitive assessment of vulnerability to depression (see Frick, 2000), relatively few concerns have been raised about its psychometric properties. Although good inter-rater reliability is reported (e.g., Swales, Williams, and Woods, 2001, report kappa's of .92 and .85 for a clinical and a control group, respectively), little or nothing is known about the AMT's reliability in terms of its stability over time. In the present paper, we report data from five studies documenting relatively satifactory test-retest reliability of the AMT.

Method

Participants

Participants in Study 1 to 5 were all first-year psychology students at the University of Leuven (Belgium) and participated in return for course credit. In Study 6, participants were patients meeting DSM-IV criteria for Major Depressive Disorder (APA, 1995), and were recruited from three Belgian hospitals: Sint-Pieter Hospital of the University Hospitals (Leuven), Psychiatric Hospital Sint-Norbertus (Duffel), and University Centre Sint-Jozef (Kortenberg).

Materials

Autobiographical Memory Test (AMT; Williams & Broadbent, 1986)

The AMT was used in two formats: a written and an oral format. Participants were asked to write down a specific memory (written AMT) or to describe a specific memory (oral AMT) for each of 10 cue words. Different cues were used in the oral and written version and were embedded in the frame sentence "Can you write down/describe one specific moment or event that the word X reminds you of?". In the written AMT, participants were given a booklet with 13 pages, measuring 13.5 × 21 cm, printed on one side. On the first page, participants wrote down their name. On each of the subsequent pages, a cue word was printed and centred above. The first two cues were practice items: grass and bread. The next ten pages had the test words in the following fixed order: confidence [trust], scared, pleasurable, angry, courage, sad, calm [at ease, comfortable], bold, surprised, and stupid, with positive and negative cues alternating[1]. Instructions were read aloud to the participants. They were given 60 s to write down a memory in response to each cue word. First, the two practice words were administered to familiarize participants with the procedure. Then, the ten test words were done. When the 60 s time limit for a cue word was reached, participants were instructed to turn to the next page, and to start working on the following cue word. In the oral AMT, following the instructions and two practice words (bike and lens), participants were again asked to recall a specific memory to each of ten words. The words were read aloud by the experimenter and presented in a fixed order, with positive and negative cues alternating: friendly, angry, energetic, alone, calm, boredom, social, guilty, honest, and cowardly[2]. Again, participants were given 60 s time to retrieve and to orally describe a specific memory for each cue. For both AMT formats, the response to each cue was coded as either a specific memory or a non specific memory. The dependent variable was the number of specific responses.

Procedure

The written AMT was administered in group setting at Time 1 (test). At Time 2 the oral AMT was individually administered for retest[3]. In Studies 1 to 3, participants for the retest were selected on the basis of their specificity score on the written AMT[4]. In Study 4,

[1] The Dutch words were vertrouwen, bang, prettig, boos, moed, droevig, gerust, brutaal, verrast, and lomp. The Dutch practice items were gras and brood.

[2] The Dutch words were vriendelijk, kwaad, energiek, alleen, kalm, verveling, sociaal, schuldig, eerlijk, and laf. The Dutch practice items were fiets and lens.

[3] In Studies 1 to 3 the 10-item oral AMT was administered as described in the Materials section. In Study 4, an 18-item oral AMT was used at retest and cues where now preceded by the frame sentence "Can you think of one specific event or moment from your past when you felt X?" The cues in this 18-item AMT were lonely, successful, inferior, calm, scared, courageous, sad, honest, foolish [stupid], happy, jealous, relaxed, hurt, quiet [calm], guilty, proud, angry, and relieved (practice items: tense and enthusiastic). In Dutch these words were eenzaam, succesvol, minderwaardig, kalm, bang, moedig, verdrietig, eerlijk, dom, blij, jaloers, ontspannen, gekwetst, rustig, schuldig, trots, kwaad, en opgelucht (practice items: gespannen and enthousiast). So for this 18-item AMT, one cue was the same as in the oral AMT, namely scared.

[4] In each of these three studies a group of high-specific and a group of low-specific participants were selected. These are individuals who retrieved respectively ten specific or only six or less specific memories to the ten items of the written AMT. This was done to experimentally investigate differences in affective impact of an emotional event in function of high vs. low memory specificity (see Raes et al., 2003a, 2003b). Note that this selection of

participants were randomly selected for the retest. In Study 5 the written AMT was administered in group setting at Time 1 (test) and again at Time 2 (retest) with 10 different cues at Time 2[5]. In Study 6 the same oral AMT was individually administered at test and retest[6].

RESULTS AND DISCUSSION

Sample characteristics and results for the five studies are listed in Table 1. In all five studies, participants' specificity scores at test and retest were significantly correlated (range .53 to .68). Spearman rank correlation coefficients were calculated instead of Pearson correlations because AMT scores were not normally distributed at either Time 1 or Time 2.

These test-rest coefficients are in the range of 'marginal' to 'acceptable', following the reliability standards suggested by Barker, Pistrang and Elliott (1994). However, note that what we did in the first five studies could actually be regarded as a combination of investigating test-rest reliability and parallel or alternate forms reliability (a different form with other cues was used on the second occasion), which is a highly stringent test of reliability. Also, the two tests in these first five studies were administered under quite different conditions, which inevitably leads to some degree of unreliability on retesting (Kline, 1979, p. 4). Recall that for studies 1 to 4, at Time 1 the AMT is administered in group setting (large classroom environment with over 150 students), whereas at Time 2 the AMT is individually face-to-face administered in the experimenter's room. Moreover, at both occasions for studies 1 to 4, there is another important procedural difference between the two forms. At Time 1 participants have to write down their responses, whereas at Time 2 they are requested to verbally express their memories. Also, at this stage, the AMT procedure is not yet designed to be used to make predictions on an individual basis, which requires higher standards for reliability than in the case of basic research on groups.

---

somewhat 'extreme groups' may have led to some overestimation of test-retest coefficients. However, when we compare the observed correlations in Study 4 an 5, were no such extreme groups were used, with the correlations in Studies 1 to 3, we can conclude that the overestimation is only moderate.

[5] The cues for the written AMT at retest were the same as those used for the oral AMT that is described in the Materials section.

[6] The cues for the 18-item oral AMT were happy, sad, safe, angry, interested, clumsy, successful, emotionally hurt, surprised, lonely, relaxed, guilty, proud, scared, pleasurable, cowardly, carefree, and lazy (practice items: to enjoy, friendly, and naughty). The Dutch words were, respectively: gelukkig, verdrietig, veilig, kwaad, belangstellend, onhandig, succesvol, emotioneel gekwetst, verrast, eenzaam, ontspannen, schuldig, trots, bang, prettig, laf, zorgeloos, and lui (practice items: genieten, vriendelijk, and stout).

Table 1. Sample sizes at test and retest, age information (retest), mean interval in months between test and retest, and test-retest coefficients (Spearman rank correlation coefficient; r_s) for the six studies

	N (test)	*N* (retest)	f/m	M_{age}	(*SD*)	interval	r_s
Study 1 (de Decker, 2001)	158	47	39/8	18.26	(0.57)	2 months	r_s (47) = .62***
Study 2 (Raes et al., 2003a)	294	43	43/0	18.44	(0.63)	1 month	r_s (43) = .53***
Study 3 (Raes et al., 2003b)	407	72	72/0	18.08	(0.50)	1 month	r_s (72) = .68***
Study 4 (Raes et al., 2003c)	407	23	19/4	18.57	(0.66)	5 months	r_s (23) = .63***
Study 5	405	253	216/37	18.63	(1.73)	5 months	r_s (253) = .53***
Study 6	28	24	16/8	40.25	(12.41)	3 months	r_s (24) = .62***

Note. f/m = female/male ratio
****p* < .001, two tailed.

However, we do acknowledge that if we want to use the AMT procedure in the future as an individual measure (e.g., in the case of decision making as opposed to its application in basic research on groups, see for example Barker et al., 1994, p. 71; Nunnally, 1967, p. 226), higher reliability coefficients will be required. To obtain such a higher reliability standard for the AMT, increasing standardization and increasing the number of items are two options (Nunnally, 1967, p. 226). In this future case of using the AMT as an individual measure for assessment and decision making, we would recommend using the individual and oral administered AMT, rather than the in group administrable written AMT: Study 5, where the written group administrable AMT was used at both test and retest, yielded the lowest, yet still significant, stability coefficient. Most likely this can be explained by this particular modality of administration allowing less control over, for example, participants' correct understanding of the instructions. However, for group research purposes this written administration of the AMT might offer us a fast way of assessing AM specificity in a group setting, given the large correlations with the standard oral AMT. This individually administered AMT, as compared to a group administrable version, is obviously far more time consuming.

It would be useful if other researchers, when they report on research where the AMT is used, also report reliability data when available. This in order to further document the psychometric characteristics of this now frequently used instrument.

Despite these limitations and cautions, we suggest that the reported coefficients for the AMT cue-word procedure are relatively satisfactory and suggest that individuals' ability to retrieve specific AMs is stable over time. The results of these studies are consistent with previous findings that specificity of autobiographical memory retrieval represents a stable cognitive style (cf. Brittlebank, Scott, Williams, & Ferrier, 1993).

REFERENCES

American Psychiatric Association (1995). Diagnostic and statistical manual of mental disorders (4th Ed). Washington, DC: Author.

Barker, C., Pistrang, N., & Elliott, R. (1994). Research methods in clinical and counselling psychology. Chichester, UK: Wiley.

Brittlebank, A. D., Scott, J., Williams, J. M. G., & Ferrier, I. N. (1993). Autobiographical memory in depression: State or trait marker? *British Journal of Psychiatry*, 162, 118-121.

de Decker, A. (2001). The specificity of autobiographical memory retrieval style in adolescents with a history of trauma. Unpublished doctoral dissertation, University of Leuven, Belgium.

Frick, P. J. (2000). Laboratory and performance-basd measures of childhood disorders: Introduction to the special section. *Journal of Clinical Child Psychology*, 29, 475-478.

Kline, P. (1979). *Psychometrics and psychology*. London: Academic Press.

Nunnally, J. C. (1967). *Psychometric theory*. New York: McGraw-Hill.

Raes, F., Hermans, D., de Decker, A., Eelen, P., & Williams, J. M. G. (2003a). Autobiographical memory specificity and affect regulation: An experimental approach. *Emotion*, 3, 201-206.Raes, F., Hermans, D., Williams, J. M. G., & Eelen, P. (2003b). Reduced autobiographical memory specificity as a cognitive avoidance coping mechanism in affect regulation. Manuscript submitted for publication.

Raes, F., Hermans, D., Williams, J. M. G., & Eelen, P. (2003c). [Manipulation of autobiographical memory specificity]. Unpublished raw data.

Swales, M. A., Williams, J. M. G., & Wood, P. (2001). Specificity of autobiographical memory and mood disturbance in adolescents. *Cognition and Emotion*, 15, 321-331.

Williams, J. M. G., 2004. Experimental cognitive psychology and clinical practice: Autobiographical memory as a paradigm case. In J. Yiend (Ed.), *Cognition, Emotion and Psychopathology* (pp. 251-269). Cambridge, UK: Cambridge University Press.

Williams, J. M. G., & Broadbent, K. (1986). Autobiographical memory in suicide attempters. *Journal of Abnormal Psychology*, 95, 144-149.

INDEX

A

B

C

D

E

F

G

H

I

J

K

L

M

N

O

P

Q

R

S

U

V

W

Y